Harvard Studies in Medieval Latin

4

SOLOMON AND MARCOLF

VERNACULAR TRADITIONS

SOLOMON AND MARCOLF

VERNACULAR TRADITIONS

Edited by Jan M. Ziolkowski,

with the assistance of Edward Sanger and
Michael B. Sullivan

Department of the Classics, Harvard University
Distributed by Harvard University Press
Cambridge, Massachusetts, and London
2022

PRINTED IN THE UNITED STATES OF AMERICA

Library of Congress Cataloging-in-Publication Data

Names: Ziolkowski, Jan M., 1956- editor.
Title: Solomon and Marcolf : vernacular traditions / edited by Jan M.
  Ziolkowski ; with the assistance of Edward Sanger and Michael B. Sullivan.
Other titles: Salemon et Marcoul.
Description: Cambridge, Massachusetts : Department of the Classics, Harvard
  University, 2022. | Series: Harvard studies in medieval Latin ; 4 |
  Includes bibliographical references and index. | Summary: "The Latin
  prose Solomon and Marcolf, enigmatic in origins, has been a puzzle from
  long before the sixteenth-century French author François Rabelais
  through the twentieth-century Russian critic Bakhtin to today. Though
  often called a dialogue, the second of its two parts comprises a
  rudimentary novel with twenty episodes. In 2009 the "original" received
  at last an edition and translation with commentary as Harvard Studies in
  Medieval Latin 1. Solomon and Marcolf: Vernacular Traditions, volume 4
  in the series, displays the mysteries of the tradition. Solomon relates
  to the biblical king, but did Marcolf originate in Germanic or Eastern
  regions? Here lovers of literature and folklore may explore, in English
  for the first time, relevant texts, from the twelfth through the early
  eighteenth century. These astonishingly varied and fascinating pieces,
  from Iceland in the North and West through Russia in the East and Italy
  in the South, have been translated from medieval and early modern
  French, Russian, German, Icelandic, Danish, and Italian. The book opens
  with snapshots of two nineteenth-century polymaths, the Englishman John
  M. Kemble and Russian Aleksandr Veselovskii, whose hypotheses can now be
  evaluated. An appendix documents awareness of Solomon and Marcolf in
  late medieval and early modern times"-- Provided by publisher.
Identifiers: LCCN 2021041730 | ISBN 9780674271876 (cloth) | ISBN
  9780674271883 (paperback)
Subjects: LCSH: Salomon et Marcolphus--Adaptations. | Salomon et
  Marcolphus--Influence. | Salomon et Marcolphus--Translations into
  English. | Solomon, King of Israel--In literature.
Classification: LCC PA8420.S14 S65 2022 | DDC 873/.03--dc23/eng/20211028
LC record available at https://lccn.loc.gov/2021041730

To the Faculty and Students,
Past, Present, and Future
of the Committee on Degrees in Folklore & Mythology
and
of the Standing Committee on Medieval Studies
at Harvard University:
May They Flourish for Decades to Come

Contents

Contents

Illustrations

The illustrations in chapters 6 and 7 come from the following two manuscripts:

E = Frankfurt, Universitätsbibliothek Frankfurt am Main, MS germ. qu. 13 (paper, 1479), fols. 2r–88v (*Salman and Morolf*), 88v–128v (*The Book of Markolf*).

S = Stuttgart, Württembergische Landesbibliothek, Cod. HB XIII 2 (paper, 1467–69), fols. 300r–339r (*The Book of Markolf*).

1   Chapter 1. Bust of John Mitchell Kemble. Sculpted by Thomas Woolner in 1865. Property of Trinity College, Cambridge.

2   Chapter 1. Portrait of John Mitchell Kemble. Reproduced in Johnson, *William Bodham Donne*, 27.

3   Chapter 1. Portrait of John Mitchell Kemble as a young man. Reproduced in Brookfield, *The Cambridge "Apostles,"* illustration facing p. 160.

4   Chapter 1. Portrait of Aleksandr Veselovskii. Reproduced in Veselovskii, *Poetika*, image facing p. viii.

5   Chapter 6. Marcolf, disguised as a minstrel. S 333^r.

6   Chapter 6. Solomon and Salome play backgammon. E 1^v.

7   Chapter 6. Salome frees King Fore. E 16^v.

8   Chapter 6. Salome and Morolf play chess. S 309^v.

9   Chapter 6. Marcolf tonsures King Fore and lays a chaplain next to Salome in bed. S 315^v.

10 Chapter 6. Salman blows his horn. S 324^v.

11 Chapter 6. Morolf, disguised as a sickly old man, rides his donkey to his boat. E 71^v.

12 Chapter 6. Morolf and the mermaid. E 82^v.

Illustrations

Acknowledgments

Acknowledgments should go first to the contributors for their steadfast patience, to say nothing of the two colleagues from Dumbarton Oaks who flanked me in the editorial task of nurturing this Marcolfian monster to maturity. In the initial phase of the project I assembled a team and mobilized it efficiently, but later I was overwhelmed and allowed the whole endeavor to slip into a prolonged hibernation.

After my Rip Van Winkle-like emergence from administration-induced lethargy, the entire gang would have been entitled to turn crotchety. Instead, they responded graciously. If truth be told, the volume improved substantially through the delay, since the protraction enabled revision and rethinking with the advantage of clinical distance. Still, I wish to express apologies and appreciation to everyone who became inveigled into the enterprise more than ten years ago and has had to wait for definitive progress until today. A stalwart who warrants particular recognition for bearing with me all along is Ivy Livingston. She has handled the layout and much more for this volume, just as she did for its precursor. Thank you, one and all, for your indulgence.

To stretch the retrospection to a total of four decades, my appointment at Harvard University began in 1981–82. Upon arrival I was an unseasoned but spirited and hard-working twenty-four year-old. At the outset my assistant professorship was split between Classics and Comparative Literature, but soon I acquired other affiliations. One brought me onto the Standing Committee on Medieval Studies, another onto the Committee on Degrees in Folklore & Mythology. Both memberships facilitated engagement with faculty and students who had vast amounts to teach, about intellectual life and the humanities, as well as about humanity and humaneness, and of course about their specializations. Such words and phrases can sound like platitudes, but for me they have been realities informing not merely mind but also heart.

Two late colleagues played instrumental roles in enabling me to participate, Albert Lord (1912–91) as founder and exponent of "Folk & Myth" and Eckehard Simon (1939–2020) as an ever-encouraging medievalist. Those who would have any familiarity with the creation and perpetuation of the weekly Seminar on Medieval Literature or of any other work that they, I, or anyone else carried out during that period have mostly vanished too. The topics related to the Middle Ages, but they have morphed into what we label "ancient history." I cherish my recollections of such bygone happinesses and many others tied to them, and I nurture the wistful hope that Harvard may continue backing the accumulation of such knowledge and making of discoveries in these wonderful fields.

This book has been pieced together with the generosity and kindness of many helpers. These altruistic souls include comrade philologists from California to Scandinavia and even two long-dead translators, alongside faculty, former graduate students, and erstwhile undergraduates from Cambridge, Massachusetts. Thanks go to Peter Machinist for his helpful counsel on Shamir and *shamir*.

To pivot from reminiscing about specific people to thanking larger institutions, it pleases me to credit two German libraries for supplying digitizations of illustrations from two manuscripts and permission to reproduce them, Frankfurt am Main, Universitätsbibliothek (for Cod. HB XIII 2), and Stuttgart, Württembergische Landesbibliothek (for MS germ. qu. 13). Nicolas Bell, Librarian of Trinity College, Cambridge, arranged kindly for the photograph of the bust of John Mitchell Kemble, formerly in the college library, now in the quarters of Professor Emeritus Simon Keynes.

The chief components of this unusual compendium will merit close and critical scrutiny from experts in, to identify some of the languages and literatures, Old French, early Modern English, Old Russian, Middle High German, early Modern High German, Old Icelandic, Modern Danish, and Modern Italian. In days of yore, my own employer maintained capacity in areas of these types and advanced understanding of them. That era was precious, far finer and more fragile than we sometimes realized.

Jan M. Ziolkowski
Washington, DC
June 30, 2020

Abbreviations

References to the Latin *Dialogue of Solomon and Marcolf* printed in Ziolkowski, *Solomon and Marcolf*, 51–101, use the abbreviation "*S&M*" followed by a section number: thus "*S&M* 2.16" refers the reader to part 2, chapter 16 of the dialogue. References to other parts of the same volume use the abbreviation "*S&M* Z" followed by a page number: thus "*S&M* Z 313–14" refers the reader to pages 313–14.

S&M and *S&M* Z = Ziolkowski, Jan M. *Solomon and Marcolf.* Harvard Studies in Medieval Latin 1. Cambridge, MA: Harvard University Press, 2008.

STC = Pollard, Alfred W., and G. R. Redgrave, eds. *A Short-Title Catalogue of Books Printed in England, Scotland & Ireland and of English Books Printed Abroad, 1475–1640.* London: The Bibliographical Society, 1950.

STC2 = Pollard, Alfred W., and G. R. Redgrave. *A Short-Title Catalogue of Books Printed in England, Scotland & Ireland and of English Books Printed Abroad, 1475–1640.* 2nd ed. 3 vols. London: The Bibliographical Society, 1986–91.

Introduction
by Jan M. Ziolkowski

IN 2008 A BOOK OF MINE inaugurated what was then a brand new series, published under the aegis of the Department of the Classics, called Harvard Studies in Medieval Latin (for short, HSML). Along with various other trimmings, *Solomon and Marcolf* (henceforth, *S&M* Z) furnishes an edition and translation, with copious commentary and extended study, of a fascinating literary portmanteau that has most frequently borne the title *Dialogue of Solomon and Marcolf* (in Latin, *Dialogus Salomonis et Marcolfi*). This anonymous prose fiction pits the wise king familiar from Holy Writ against a wily peasant plucked from popular culture.

The trickster figure pervades folklore worldwide, but possibly nowhere more than in Europe during the Middle Ages. For example, Reynard the Fox registered such success that his name supplanted the prior noun for fox in French: as if Bugs usurped the niche for bunny in English, *renard* ousted the onetime *goupil*. Not within the animal kingdom but among *Homo sapiens*, Marcolf belongs to a category of lower-class protagonists who enjoyed especial popularity in medieval Germany. The best-known of the motley crew is probably Till Eulenspiegel, leading man of a German chapbook from 1515, a legendary village prankster whose moniker has now and then been anglicized (by translating its two elements word for word) as Owlglass. These antiheroes stand out for their ambivalent relationship with power, authority, and sagacity. The ugly and impudent rogue Marcolf, with bowels as big and boisterous as his brains, is cut from the same coarse cloth.

The coupling of Solomon and Marcolf has had notable visibility since the last four decades of the twentieth century, thanks to its salience in a classic of literary and cultural studies by Mikhail Mikhailovich Bakhtin (1895–1975). The Russian critic wrote *Rabelais and His World* decades earlier, but the vagaries of Soviet censorship prevented it from being printed in his mother tongue until 1965, after which it was rendered into English in 1968. The sixteenth-century French author François Rabelais (ca. 1494–ca. 1553) refers to Solomon and

Marcolf,[1] and partly on that basis the twentieth-century formalist makes much of the *Dialogue of Solomon and Marcolf.* In Bakhtin, the interaction between the two extremes embodied in Solomon and Marcolf becomes the centerpiece of millennia-old rituals. In these ceremonies, folk laughter is induced through parody of liturgy and other verbal forms of official conduct. Associated with the licentious spectacle of carnival and other celebrations, the mockery of common people by their peers allows the appropriation into comic literature of folk traditions, grotesque realism, and lowly abuse. A kind of mineshaft within medieval society allows rapid transit up from this low starting point, so that jesters and jokers may penetrate into high literature and royal courts: it turns out that nowhere is truly foolproof.

All told, *S&M* Z totals more than 450 pages. None of them will be replicated even partially here: a desire in this book has been to eschew resolutely any repetition and instead to assemble as much as possible of the wildly and wonderfully eccentric lore relating to Solomon ad Marcolf that had no place in a volume centered upon information germane to the Latin. That said, a thumbnail sketch of the *Dialogue of Solomon and Marcolf* may make sense as a reminder of the point of departure for this altogether fresh compendium, entitled *Solomon and Marcolf: Vernacular Traditions* (from now on, *SMVT*). The Latin text has the structure of a diptych. The first panel, apart from the briefest of prologues and epilogues, comprises 142 exchanges that set down in writing the thrust and parry between Solomon and Marcolf. Whereas Solomon's sources in the *Dialogue of Solomon and Marcolf* are preponderantly biblical, Marcolf often taps into vernacular proverbs. Speaking turds to power, he engages in pyrotechnic scatology. By the end, the unblushingly bawdy buffoon has given the ponderously pedantic potentate a bad beating.

When all is said and done, the tit for tat of this discourse builds on the reputation for wisdom of the sage and sovereign from the Hebrew Bible, demonstrated partly in a plethora of platitudes, sometimes drawn from the Book of Proverbs, and partly in the riddling contest that took place when the Queen of Sheba visited Jerusalem (3 Kings [1 Kings] 10:1–13). As the biblical tradition became distended and distorted with the passage of time, Solomon came to be matched with other contenders, such as a Chaldean pagan named Saturn in Old English literature and Old Testament notables such as Hiram, Abdimus, and Abdemon of Tyre in texts by Flavius Josephus, Guido of Bazoches, and William of Tyre, among others. Gradually an equivalence was drawn between some of these other personages and Marcolf.

---

[1] See appendix 1, item G43.

In contrast to the dialogue of the initial section, the second panel with which the colloquy is hinged lays out the comedy of a picaresque or anecdotal proto-novel. Continually abandoning blunt billingsgate and ribald repartee to devolve into crude practical jokes, these twenty chapters of narrative relate one encounter after another in which the grotesque rustic fool gets the better of the grand biblical ruler. Just when a reader thinks that the humiliation can grow no worse, it does—and then some. The penultimate chapter has the boor bare his buttocks and moon the monarch, while the ultimate one depicts Marcolf's ruse for escaping being hanged and for attaining his freedom. Overarching these episodes is the theme that nature prevails over nurture.

The halves of the *Dialogue of Solomon and Marcolf* may well have arisen separately in Flanders or the Netherlands, northern or northeastern France, or Germany, though all notions about localization are guesswork. The two pieces are sometimes hypothesized to have been welded into one whole long before the late twelfth or very early thirteenth century. The thinking has gone that they emanated from ecclesiastic, perhaps specifically monastic, milieus or at least that they circulated in them. Even before their presumptive composition around 1200, both the dialogic and narrative portions probably shuttled back and forth between oral and written transmission, in Latin as well as in vernacular languages. For now inexplicable reasons, approximately two centuries would have elapsed before 1410, when they were recorded in the earliest surviving manuscript. Were copies made but lost? Were variants learned by rote and carried predominantly by oral transmission? Or were other factors involved that we cannot even surmise, bound as we are by our own textuality?

As an extra, *S&M* Z provides a modern English version made from a Welsh text that was itself translated from the Latin in the closing quarter of the sixteenth century. It also has an appendix with thirty-four sources, analogues, and testimonia that compiles snippets from various other vernaculars such as Old English, Old High German, Old Occitan, Old French, Middle High German, and Middle English. For all that, the lens in *S&M* Z remains fixed upon the principal text in the learned language, explaining its constitution and decoding its import.

The Latin-oriented microscopy in *S&M* Z has a minimalist pendant here in appendix 2, which offers addenda and corrigenda to the edition, translation, and commentary in the earlier book. In contradistinction to the view through a jeweler's loupe, the present contribution to HSML has been designed to realize a telescopic panorama. Correspondingly, this volume shifts the purview from the microcosm of a single text to the macrocosm of heterogeneous facts surrounding it. The materials that have been rendered into English in this sequel are intended to facilitate the task of readers who have secured a grounding in the Latin and wish to gaze out from that stable footing to the vast galaxy of literature in other languages that swirls around it. Rather than replicating anything, the translations assembled here complement the earlier volume. Etymologically, the verb and noun *complement* fuse a prefix for "around" with a verbal element meaning "filling."

Those interested will find between these covers, in toto or at least in large measure, the English of substantial texts originally in Old French, Old Russian, Middle High German, Old Icelandic, early Modern Danish, and early Modern Italian. Put together with what the earlier tome delivered, the substance amassed sprawls across an immense geographical and chronological sweep. In time, these pieces cover at a minimum a half millennium from the twelfth through the early eighteenth century—from the so-called Twelfth-Century Renaissance through the thick of the Napoleonic era and Romanticism. In space, they sprawl longitudinally from the mid-Atlantic of Iceland in the West through Russia in the East, latitudinally from Iceland in the North through Italy in the South. But even these ranges of dates and places put the case conservatively. What holds all of these works together is that they have at their nub the hero or antihero Marcolf.

The so-called Solomon and Marcolf complex deserves to be enlarged by being referenced in the plural. Paired, *S&M* Z and *SMVT* will bolster appreciation of the extraordinary range that the complex achieved across and even beyond Europe, from the early Middle Ages all the way into the twentieth century. Ideally, the set would serve as launchpads for more profound probing and understanding of the relations among the wonderfully disparate stuff in the tradition. Although knowledge of the Latin *Dialogue of Solomon and Marcolf* has stayed reasonably strong, the hegemony of English has diminished familiarity with Solomon and Marcolf materials in most vernaculars.

In contrast, the Middle English version has exercised all the pull of a powerful magnet. The sole extant copy survives from a single printing made in 1492 at Gerard Leeu's workshop in Antwerp. It was reprinted first in 1892, a second time in 1995, and a third in 2012.[2] The math is simple: three times as many reprintings have been produced as there are exemplars of the original. The same imbalance can be detected in publications on a poem relating to Marcolf by the English priest and poet John Audelay (died ca. 1426).[3] Translations of the *Dialogue of Solomon and Marcolf* were made into German, Swedish, Dutch, Czech, and Polish, beyond the Welsh already noted. Yet over the past half century the

---

[2] In 1892 by E. Gordon Duff, in 1995 by Donald Beecher, and in 2012 by Nancy Mason Bradbury and Scott Bradbury, who printed the English facing the Latin text printed in 1488 on Leeu's press.

[3] Since the turn of the century, Susanna Fein has published an edition; Richard Firth Green, two articles; Derek Pearsall, one; and James Simpson, one.

only vernacular versions that have piqued as much curiosity as the English one have been in Italian dialects. The awareness of the tradition in Italy owes to the abiding influence of the author Giulio Cesare Croce (1550–1609), whose radical recasting of the material bought it a new life. More remote descendants are traceable in other modern European languages as well.

Alongside the facsimiles and editions of the Latin and English, a spate of articles has poured forth over the past two decades to survey the impact of the Solomon and Marcolf tradition on Middle English and early Modern English. This outpouring has been valuable, except that it has been accompanied and counterbalanced by nothing but a meager trickle of attention to Solomon and Marcolf texts in other languages. Scholarship is not a zero-sum game, but whatever the explanation may be, concentration upon the reflexes of Marcolf in late medieval and early modern England has coincided with the dominance of English as a global language to the detriment of other vernaculars.

The disproportion means that all other ramifications of what might be styled the Solomon and Marcolf heritage risk going underappreciated. Owing to the circumstances, the full scope of the weird and wonderful phenomena relating to this legacy may likelier be overlooked and forgotten now than at any time since before the nineteenth century, when the inquisitive and talented minds of John M. Kemble (1807–57) and Aleksandr Veselovskii (1838–1906) identified and scrutinized chief segments in the widely distributed traditions of Solomon and Marcolf. Both individuals substantially advanced research into the provenance and proliferation of the material.

In chapter 1 of *SMVT*, both the Englander and the Russian receive treatment in short sketches that examine their lives with a view to contextualizing their inquiries into Solomon and Marcolf. Kemble, inspired by Jacob of the Brothers Grimm, directed his efforts above all to Western Europe. His biases generally favored a Teutonic (or Germanic) birthplace for the corpus. Veselovskii arrived at the markedly different stance that like many other tales, those of Solomon and Marcolf had their inception in India and migrated westward. This presumption led him to pay close heed to authentication he could unearth in Slavic languages. Without ignoring the possibility of Talmudic sources, he looked especially to apocrypha or more properly pseudepigrapha. The first term denotes biblical writings not accepted within the canon of Scripture, the second specifically Jewish writings falsely ascribed to biblical patriarchs and prophets. Whereas Kemble's stature has held steady, the Russian's has plummeted unjustly ever deeper into the Lethe of scholarly oblivion.

Disseminated over a wide spatial span, legends that put on stage Solomon and Marcolf are attested from the early Middle Ages into the Romantic era of the early nineteenth century. Theories, both old and new, have sought to locate the wellspring of the dynamic duo in Jewish-oriental sources or in the eastern Mediterranean. The Pseudo-Gelasian Decree, a text from the seventh century but pretending to be from the very late fifth, makes reference to apocryphal literature that somehow showcased Solomon.[4]

The two most prolific branches of Marcolfian lore are on the one hand the Latin, with descendants in most Western European languages, and on the other the Germanic-Slavic. *SMVT* also contains offshoots in French (see chapter 2, chapter 3, and, for original-language texts, appendix 3). These pieces of writing from the twelfth and thirteenth centuries, lacking narrative frames, are restricted to dialogues between Solomon and Marcolf which in content have scant direct relation to the *Dialogue of Solomon and Marcolf*, beyond sharing some proverbs—but they do correspond in their conception roughly to the first half of the Latin work. In many of them, all of Marcolf's responses to Solomon concentrate upon the behavior of whores or prostitutes. The striking emphasis on sexuality and occasionally also on scatology displaces altogether the transgressive social views that stand out in many other types of Solomon and Marcolf material.

The poems from France betray tell-tale symptoms of their Frenchness in their intense misogyny and especially in their obsession with loose women. Perhaps significantly, the only two exceptions to this rule come in works that are flagged as having originated outside France. Thus one redaction is ascribed to a count of Brittany (see chapter 2, version D), while another 230 lines of poetry survive in a single manuscript roll of English production and provenance (see chapter 3). Maybe revealingly, the latter bit of verse—the only French-language composition in the Solomon and Marcolf corpus not from the Continent—sheds the theme of sexual promiscuity instead to deal systematically with the estates of medieval society. It proceeds from the highest tier in the hierarchy, Christian and king, to the lowest, woman. In other words, it reverts thematically to concerns about the social order that are central within the Marcolfian mindset in most other countries. A final item bears on the distinctive Gallicism of Marcolf's misogynistic insistence on whorishness in these texts: a translation of one version into English, brought out about 1527, is transcribed here (see chapter 4). Significantly, the printer was French-born and not a native Englander.

The Judgments of Solomon (*Sudy Solomona*), a piece of Old Russian prose translated in chapter 5, opens a window that looks out toward at least a few of the fascinating horizons from which the Solomon and Marcolf complexes may have emerged. The Slavic tale is transmitted within a Christian exegetic work whose

---

[4]   *S&M Z* 313–14.

very title signals its likely indebtedness to biblical traditions mediated through Byzantine Greek sources, with plausible and even likely Jewish influence.[5] One oddity of the text is a section describing interactions between Solomon and a personage called Kitovras, apparently the Russification of the Greek word for centaur. Intriguingly, the creature put in tandem with Solomon is once again portrayed as uniting human and animal traits, as may be implied by the etymology that could lie behind the name of Marcolf (*mark-wulf*) and with the many theriomorphic qualities of the peasant hero in the *Dialogue of Solomon and Marcolf*. At the same time, it also embraces vocabulary that points to exposure to the Talmud and Hebrew.

The two-part Latin text as found in *S&M* Z, combining a first half of dialogue with a second of narrative, was not adapted into other tongues until the very late fifteenth and sixteenth centuries. The English from 1492 has been mentioned already, as has the Welsh from the concluding quarter of the sixteenth century. Chapter 7 here in *SMVT* offers the English of *The Book of Markolf*. Although this Middle High German poem markets itself as a translation, it is a free adaptation. Its basic outline incorporates two episodes not previously attested in the original *Dialogue of Solomon and Marcolf* but widely familiar in folk literature, one being "The Old Woman as Trouble Maker" and the other "The Youth in the Beehive."[6] The title *Salomon and Markolf* has been commonly assigned to it, with *Spruchgedicht* (or "proverb poem") routinely appended by scholars to differentiate it from fifteenth- and sixteenth-century German prose adaptations of the Latin *Dialogue of Solomon and Marcolf*. These other texts are conventionally known as *Salomon and Markolf*, with the qualifier *Volksbuch* (loosely equivalent to the English "chapbook").

The shortest selection in this volume, offered in chapter 8, takes us to the heart of the puzzles and provocations that the Solomon and Marcolf complexes present. A single leaf written in Old Icelandic from 1400, but probably composed decades earlier in the fourteenth century, presents a fragment of a narrative that juxtaposes Salomon and Melkólfr. The reader is told about the wisdom of both the king of Jerusalem and the farm boy with whom he engages. Salomon poses Melkólfr a riddle much like one in the *Dialogue of Solomon and Marcolf* (2.1), but it is impossible to pin down how much the similarities and dissimilarities owe to the vagaries of oral transmission and how much to lost Eastern sources.

Chapter 9 presents *A Merry Conversation between King Salomon and Marcolfus* (*En Lystig Samtale imellem Kong Salomon og Marcolfus*), a translation of an 1805 Danish edition that is indebted to earlier German and Danish versions, which

5   Nissan 2014, 122–30.
6   See *S&M* Z 355–57.

themselves owe ultimately to the Latin. This selection typifies chapbooks that flourished in Germany from the mid-sixteenth century and that made the rounds in many regions of Europe even into the nineteenth. Put together, they are a monument to the permanency and pervasiveness of the *Dialogue of Solomon and Marcolf* in Latin as well as in the vernaculars into which it was translated.

Though less directly, the same text in the learned language was also the primary source for *The Sharpest Strategems of Bertoldo* (*Le sottilissime astutie di Bertoldo*, 1606) and *The Amusing and Ridiculous Simplemindedness of Bertoldino, Son of the Late and Cunning Bertoldo* (*Le piacevoli e ridicolose simplicità di Bertoldino*, 1608), two minor classics of Italian literature in which Giulio Cesare Croce substitutes for the name and function of Marcolf that of Bertoldo and revamps some of the same escapades. The pair was supplemented by Adriano Banchieri, under the pseudonym Camillo Scaligeri dalla Fratta, in a work entitled *Story of Cacasenno, Son of the Simpleminded Bertoldino* (*Novella di Cacasenno, figliuolo del semplice Bertoldino*, 1620). A little more than a century later, the triad was given a new lease on life by the editor Lelio Dalla Volpe, who orchestrated a versification of the materials in a book entitled *Bertoldo with Bertoldino and Cacasenno, in ottava rima* (*Bertoldo con Bertoldino e Cacasenno in ottava rima*, 1736), which was presented in such a way as to assert its indebtedness to Croce. The English of the Bertoldo section from the last-mentioned is presented, in adapted and abridged form, as chapter 10.

The Germanic fork of the supposed Germanic-Slavic branch has been accorded relatively paltry notice other than from researchers in the field of Middle High German studies. Intriguingly, the names and characters of Solomon and Marcolf are first juxtaposed in two creations of Germanic literature. *Solomon and Saturn III*, one of three Old English poems famed for these two participants, written at the latest in the tenth century and probably toward the end of the ninth, observes that the Saturn figure who is Solomon's interlocutor traveled to many destinations across the planet, including a location in the Orient he designates as "Marculf's land" (line 180b). Saturn himself is described as being connected with the Chaldeans.

What are we to make of the proper noun Marculf?[7] If parsed for its Germanic etymons, it could favor the interpretation "wolf of the marches" or "of the borderlands." Yet Marculf(us) and Marcolf(us) may be Germanizations of forms closer to Merqulis. Spelt variously in less accurate and older transliterations as Markolis or Markulis, this appears to be the Hebrew name for an idol

---

[7] For the relevant passages and context, see *S&M* Z 310–16 and 320–23. The most recent discussion with application to the Old English half line is Anlezark, *Dialogues of Solomon and Saturn*, 13–14.

that may well have been associated with the Roman deity Mercurius.[8] Sacred Scripture, the Talmud, Aethicus Ister, and Petrus Alfonsi remark upon statues and heaps of rocks in Asia Minor and the Holy Lands that may be bound up with Marcolf.[9] Merqulis is found in early medieval sources to signify a rock pile that idolaters would expand through lapidation—by tossing stones as a ritual act. In other instances, the word and the phenomenon may well be connected with the squared stone pillars in the ancient Greco-Roman sphere that are now known as herms. The monosyllable truncates the name of Hermes, the Greek equivalent to the Roman Mercury, the god who was typically represented in such boundary markers, signposts, or apotropaics. In all cases, at issue is a stone cult of some sort.

More or less simultaneously, the Old High German translation and commentary on Psalm 118 by Notker "Labeo" (meaning "big-lip") III of St. Gall (ca. 950–1022) refers in passing to Marcolf's struggle against the proverbs of Solomon. It would be a stretch to speculate that Notker fitted this reference into an exegetic context because Marcolf had become familiar through the Talmud or apocrypha. Later remarks about contentions between Solomon and Marcolf appear scattered across Latin, Old Occitan, Old French and Middle High German, with some intriguing pointers toward the eastern Mediterranean.

The foremost representative in length of the Germanic-Slavic branch is the extended Middle High German narrative poem translated in chapter 6.[10] Disconcertingly similar to the *Dialogue of Solomon and Marcolf* in the challenges that its dating raises, *Salman and Morolf* is by a good margin the longest text in any language to have come down to us from the medieval Solomon and Marcolf tradition. It survives first in manuscripts from the second half of the fifteenth century. Though the fancy that it was composed by a minstrel or that any such performer starred in it has long since been abandoned, for convenience's sake the poem is commonly qualified by the outmoded genre indicator *"Spielmannsepos"* (meaning "minstrel epic"). Even if the poem was not associated with professional entertainers, the supposition that it passed around in both oral and written forms carries conviction. Parallels and references to its constituents in other medieval French and German poetry suggest that significant elements of *Salman and Morolf* existed and spread already in the third quarter of the twelfth century.

The poem takes the dynamics between the two main figures into altogether new territory, since Morolf is not Salman's antagonist but his brother, clever

---

[8] See Kemble, *Dialogue of Solomon and Saturnus*, 8–9. For recent investigations of the cult, see Brown, "Excursus G," and Pintel-Ginsberg, "Throwing a Stone to Merculis."

[9] *S&M* Z 310–313, 314–16, 320–23.

[10] Compare *S&M* Z 339–42.

and witty, capable of being a wise counselor and valiant warrior, but by turns ruthless and cruel. The most horrifying moment comes when Morolf lures a white-haired old Jew into a tête-à-tête on the pretext of seeking out his advice, but instead seizes the occasion to stab him through the heart and skin him so that he may take on the murdered man's identity as a disguise.

Salman and Morolf is linked to the *Dialogue of Solomon and Marcolf* in many ways.[11] Nevertheless, it bears the strong imprint of other traditions. Women serve distinct functions in the poem. The German term to denote its overall structure is *Brautwerbungsschema* or "bridal-quest schema." Stories after this fashion recount the dangers that must be surmounted in the hunt to win a bride, often from a distant kingdom. According to the Vulgate Bible, Solomon secured the daughter of Pharaoh and brought her to Jerusalem, where she played a part in seducing him into idolatry. Tales about this situation were apparently rounded out on the basis of extra-biblical accounts in which the king is said to have first gained his potency from demons, particularly one named Asmodeus, and then lost it to them.[12]

The question of where the resultant narrative took shape plunges us far into the misty and murky swamp of speculation. One idea is that it surfaced in the eastern Mediterranean, absorbed elements apprehensible today only faintly in the Talmud and pseudepigraphic writings, was transported into Slavic regions, and eventually permeated Germany. The most convincing corroboration of this is in *Salman and Morolf* and in the alternative ending to the *Dialogue of Solomon and Marcolf* included in a manuscript written in Bohemia between 1453 and 1477 that now resides in the Polish city of Kraków.[13]

The *Dialogue of Solomon and Marcolf* and *Salman and Morolf* resemble each other in the peculiarities of their gestation, especially where date of origin is considered. Convincing arguments have been advanced that both came into being in the second half of the twelfth century, but neither is preserved now in any manuscript earlier than the fifteenth century.

In the fifteenth and sixteenth centuries, the *Dialogue of Solomon and Marcolf* seeped into the consciousness of readers from three distinct realms of society— namely, schools, humanists, and scholastics, especially in Germany and Austria. To ease the labors of those who may want to ground themselves in the construction and reception of the Solomon and Marcolf complexes in these later centuries and beyond, the full panoply of testimonia that Sabine Griese collected but that

---

[11] See *S&M* Z 341–42.

[12] On Asmodeus, also known as Ashmedai or Ashmadai, see *S&M* Z 20. An essential starting point for consideration of Asmodeus is Tobit 3:8. On the Talmudic story of Solomon and Ashmedai, see Kaminka, "Origin of the Ashmedai Legend," and Davis, "Solomon and Ashmedai."

[13] *S&M* Z 288–98.

was not included in appendix 2 to *S&M* Z is conveyed as appendix 1 to *SMVT* with both original-language texts and English translations. These scraps take interested parties from 1450 onward all the way to the twentieth century, but nowhere do they achieve greater critical mass than in the first hundred and fifty years of this spell. Marcolf, like Till Eulenspiegel, never found a more prominent place than in the pandemonium of the printing press and Protestantism.

Many of these extracts are hard to translate, even more so to interpret, and no claim is advanced that the work required to make full sense of them has been completed. Furthermore, more attestations of these two characters before and after that magic year undoubtedly lurk unremarked. Despite these caveats, at least now motivated readers have convenient means for grappling with all of what literary historians have accumulated since the first half of the nineteenth century. Not every step in the historical development of Solomon and Marcolf from late antiquity into the modern period will ever be certified, but the combination of *S&M* Z and *SMVT* puts the proofs, such as they are, on display as never before. Hope springs eternal that the two volumes will not merely stave off oblivion but actually enable advances in interpretation and hypothesis.

Without any doubt, more must be discovered and explored in order to reach a fuller understanding of the strange synergy between Solomon and Marcolf as it can be gleaned from the disparate tatters of textuality. No pretense is made here that this aggregation paints a comprehensive picture of all major components in the tradition, but it makes accessible at least a strong sampling. The breadth manifests itself even in the phantasmagoria of names borne by Solomon's antagonist, such as Marcolf, Marcolfus, Marcou, Marcoul, Marcous, Marcouz, Markolf, Morolf, Marcoul, and Melkólfr. The bigger story may be the altogether other personages with whom Marcolf becomes conflated or into whom he is somehow suffused, documented in this volume most saliently in the Old Russian Kitovras and the Modern Italian Bertoldo.

Solomon was a supreme authority figure, a prophet who embodied high morality in religion, while likewise a king who applied coercive power within the state. The might vested in him elicited many forms of resistance in Scripture and pseudepigrapha, starting with a woman in the Queen of Sheba and a demon in Asmodeus, still later morphing into a heathen sage in Saturn. It is unsurprising that in the Middle Ages and Reformation the great man of the Bible should elicit contradiction from a human or maybe not-so-human chameleon, truly animal-like in the bedlam of his boisterous bestiality, shading from one hue to another on a color wheel of disobedient behavior that comprehends buffoonery, cunning, foolishness, mockery, pranks, sedition, and more.

The book is long, but by necessity it suffers from omissions. One ingredient missing from the mix is art history. An expert in Middle High German literature, the late Michael Curschmann (1936–2017), helped to establish text-image correspondences as a field of study relating to medieval manuscripts and early modern incunables. Within this very broad ambit, he laid the groundwork for examining the illustration of Solomon and Marcolf narratives, as well as the correlation between images of Marcolf and the fabulist Aesop. In turn, the interchangeability of the two antiheroes in figural representation led to investigation of relations between *The Life of Aesop* (*Vita Aesopi*) and the *Dialogue of Solomon and Marcolf.*

By incorporating a full run of woodcuts that had not been reprinted since their original printing in the early sixteenth century, *S&M* Z added a modest supplement to the battery of images available for the consideration of Marcolfomaniacs. *SMVT* augments the corpus of materials accessible to would-be iconographers by supplying further cycles of illustrations. One grouping is taken from a medieval manuscript of the Middle High German *Salman and Morolf*, another from one of the Middle High German *The Book of Markolf.* Two wall paintings from medieval Sweden ca. 1500 accompany the translation of the Danish chapbook from 1805. Its frontispiece is also provided. Additionally, seven figures are reproduced from the twenty-two in the 1736 printing by Lelio Dalla Volpe of a best-selling team effort at modernizing and standardizing the story of Bertoldo, Bertoldino, and Cacasenno. Two even later images follow the appendices.

For all that, these provisions of further visual evidence are admittedly stop-gaps: the definitive treatment of Marcolf iconography awaits its author. At the early end of the spectrum, an exhaustive catalogue would have to comprehend likenesses of Marcolf in Gothic statuary as well as in manuscript illuminations. In later manifestations of the story, encyclopedic coverage of this brand would need to encompass illustrations of Marcolf in late printed sources and in folk art. Reconciling and rationalizing what can be gleaned from the imagery could aid in no small way in connecting the tantalizing dots of the far-flung literary traditions.

Come what may, the benefits of *S&M* Z as compounded now by *SMVT* will take far and fast-forward the endeavor of keeping Solomon and Marcolf alive and well for new readers living in new times and posing new questions. The trickster had the shrewdness and survival skills to elude a death sentence: may the same hold true for the cycle of stories relating to him.

1

Two Early Commentators on Solomon and Marcolf

by Jan M. Ziolkowski and Margaret Ziolkowski

John Mitchell Kemble (1807–57)

JOHN MITCHELL KEMBLE (see fig. 1)[1] died far from family and friends, in a hotel in Dublin, on March 26, 1857, just one week shy of his fiftieth birthday. Despite the brevity of his life, he left an outsized and well-documented imprint upon the study of the early medieval culture that has often been styled Anglo-Saxon. In one large branch of this research and writing, he traced the background and context to the Old English *Solomon and Saturn,* with consideration to sources and analogues for the Medieval Latin *Dialogue of Solomon and Marcolf.* Although scholarship has advanced over the past century and a half, Kemble and Aleksandr Veselovskii, a Russian who followed him in the second half of the nineteenth century, commanded substantially fuller and stronger grasps of the sprawling Marcolfian tradition in all its length and girth than have any others since their day.

The Englishman was born on April 2, 1807, into a large and celebrated dynasty of actors, the scion of the famous performer Charles Kemble (1775–1854) and his vivacious Vienna-born wife, Maria Theresa (née de Camp) Kemble (1774–1838).[2] Both his parents were themselves the children of theater person-

---

[1] For roughly a hundred years a bust of John Mitchell Kemble, bearded, was displayed in the Wren Library, Trinity College, Cambridge. Bearing the inscription "T[homas]. Woolner. Sc[ulpsit]. London, 1865," this sculpture was carved after a subscription of £250 was raised among his friends and family. In 1967 the marble was exiled in a clearing out that removed most carvings from later than the eighteenth century. For a while the Kemble has stood in the room of Simon Keynes. For this information and the photograph by James Kirwan, I am grateful to Nicolas Bell, librarian of Trinity College.

[2] See https://www.npg.org.uk/collections/search/portrait/mw03593/Maria-Theresa-Kemble. National Portrait Gallery, 1804 caricature of her in her burlesque entitled *Personation,* by Alfred Edward Chalon (1780–1860).

Figure 1. Bust of John Mitchell Kemble.
Sculpted by Thomas Woolner in 1865. Property of Trinity College, Cambridge.

alities. Among other relations, the stage pedigree of the Kemble clan included his aunt Sarah (née Kemble) Siddons (1755–1831) and uncle John Philip Kemble (1757–1823), eldest and next-eldest, respectively, among the twelve children of his paternal grandparents. John Mitchell Kemble, who was known to intimates as Jacky, received his first given name in honor of his uncle. Among his siblings the eldest sister was Frances Anne Kemble (1809–93), better known as "Fanny," actress and writer in both the United States and England, probably remembered today mostly for having been an abolitionist. The whole clan shared distinctive characteristics, not unconnected with their common profession. In the words of Anne Thackeray, daughter of the novelist William Makepeace Thackeray: "The Kembles strike one somehow as a race apart. They seem divided from the rest of us by more dominant natures, by more expressive ways and looks; one is reminded of those deities who once visited the earth in the guise of shepherds, as wanderers clad in lion skins, as muses and huntresses, not as Kembles only."[3]

In his career Fanny's brother struck out in a non-histrionic direction that differed from the rest of the family, even as he displayed traits recognizable in many of his relatives. Thanks to his high marks in school, his relations foresaw success for him in the bar or Church of England. After matriculating at Trinity College, Cambridge, in Michaelmas term of 1825, Kemble won huge favor among his fellow students. Handsome and athletic (see fig. 2),[4] quick-witted and eloquent, he achieved prominence in the Conversazione Society, a secret club better known as "The Apostles." He struck up friendships with other members, who counted future luminaries such as Alfred, Lord Tennyson. The lordly writer dedicated to this crony a sonnet that foresaw for him a future in the Church. Other associates during his years at university included William Makepeace Thackeray.

As an undergraduate Kemble spent much time on the non-academic pursuits of socializing, singing, and athletics. In another extracurricular, he excelled as a debater. He advanced from being a mere member to serving as secretary and president of the Cambridge Union, a debating society. In 1827 he won first place in the Trinity Declamations. This grounding seems to have suited his personality, since in his subsequent trajectory he more than once damaged his chances for advancement by engaging in pugilistic polemics about politics, religion, and scholarship.

Although his major focus was meant to be law, he applied himself almost exclusively to investigating its historical context, especially in medieval history. The Old English language and the history of early medieval England were not

---

[3] Ackerman, "J. M. Kemble and Sir Frederic Madden," 167–68.

[4] John Mitchell Kemble as a young man, seated at a table, from a drawing by Saville Morton, reproduced first in Johnson, *William Bodham Donne*, 27, and later in Wiley, *John Mitchell Kemble and Jakob Grimm*, xiv.

awn by poor Savile Morton.

JOHN MITCHELL KEMBLE

Figure 2. Portrait of John Mitchell Kemble.
Reproduced in Johnson, *William Bodham Donne*, 27.

established areas of study in his day, but that circumstance in no way impeded his zeal for these specializations.

Kemble stood out for his omnivorous approach to the Anglo-Saxon past. His foremost predecessor in England was Sharon Turner (1768–1847), whose initial interests in Old English and Old Icelandic literature ripened into prolific investigation of the English past, especially during the early medieval period. Kemble shared Turner's passions for belles lettres and history, but refined both through application of the latest developments in the study of Germanic languages and literatures.

Before taking his degree from Cambridge on February 25, 1830 (its award was delayed when he offended his examiners in the spring of 1828), Kemble devoted himself to philology in Germany. A sojourn in Munich in the summer of 1828 marked the start of a period in which he set out to ground himself in philological science. Within a few short years (see fig. 3),[5] Jacky completed the metamorphosis that induced his Cambridge cronies to give him the moniker "Anglo-Saxon Kemble." Understanding the need for setting texts in broad contexts, he applied himself to mastering languages and literatures necessary for situating Old English within a Germanic framework. Equally important, he ventured into allied disciplines such as archaeology, art history, diplomatics, and numismatics.[6] In pursuing such passions, he often played the role of an avid manuscript-hunter.

From 1832 to 1835, Kemble spent most of the academic years in Cambridge. In 1833, in one of forty-six surviving letters that he wrote across two decades to Jacob Grimm, he set forth, with a judiciousness that could still serve well today, what he hoped to achieve through his researches:

> I need not tell you how deeply I have at heart, the spreading among my countrymen, a wise & enlightened knowledge of, & love for these old records; without wishing them to turn back the stream of the world's great flow, and without calling upon them to become once more Anglo-Saxons, a patriot may wish them to look backward a little upon the great and good of olden time, and to emulate the virtues of their forefathers, without losing the wisdom of our own times.[7]

In the same year the rising Anglo-Saxonist, as professionals in this area were then uncontroversially known, made his reputation by publishing the first

---

[5]   John Mitchell Kemble as a clean-shaven young man, in profile, drawing, reproduced in Brookfield, *The Cambridge "Apostles,"* illustration facing p. 160. Identical to his likeness in oval medallions of Charles Kemble and his four children reproduced in Duncan-Jones, *Miss Mitford and Mr. Harness.*

[6]   Williams, "Assessing the Archaeology of John Mitchell Kemble."

[7]   Wiley, *John Mitchell Kemble and Jakob Grimm,* 34–35.

Figure 3. Portrait of John Mitchell Kemble as a young man.
Reproduced in Brookfield, *The Cambridge "Apostles,"* illustration facing p. 160.

edition of *Beowulf* in the Anglophone world that applied systematically the philological method as developed by Germans, with text and commentary that stood for two decades as the standards for the poem.[8] In 1837 he brought forth not only a second edition with glossary and notes but also a translation of it.[9] His English of the epic wore well enough to be taken as the basis of comparison with the most analyzed and acclaimed of recent versions.[10]

---

[8] Kemble, *Anglo-Saxon Poems.* For context, see Hall, "First Two Editions of *Beowulf.*"
[9] Kemble, *Translation of the Anglo-Saxon Poem of Beowulf.*
[10] Sauer, "Kemble's Beowulf and Heaney's Beowulf."

Also in 1833, Kemble happened upon the work he entitled *Dialogue of Salomon and Saturnus*. In 1834, he lectured at Cambridge on Old English language and literature. To judge by the syllabus-outline, these lectures were extraordinarily ambitious in their range. The readings included attention, at least in passing, to the *Dialogue of Salomon and Saturnus*. In 1835 he worked on a manuscript of *Solomon and Saturn,* for an edition of which he was preparing the introduction.[11] But Kemble also planted a foot on the Continent, and his project on the Old English material prompted him to establish and maintain contact with Jacob Grimm, the elder of the renowned Brothers Grimm.[12] He corresponded with the great man between 1832 and 1852. In 1834, he made his first pilgrimage to polish his command of philological science under Grimm and even lodged with him in Göttingen—and while in the city met the German daughter of a philosophy professor who in 1836 became his wife, for the decade or so that the marriage lasted. When he finally brought his researches into print in 1848,[13] he referred lightly to the fifteen-year gestation. He also described the project as arising partly out of "a desire to distract my mind and obtain some relief from severer studies."[14]

The work on the Solomon material led Kemble to renewed close engagement with Jacob Grimm and his philology. He leveled searing criticism against countrymen who clung to an older approach to the Middle Ages and contested the newer philological one associated with universities in Germany. In due course, the Germanness of his scholarship came back to bite him. The antiquarians struck back. The resultant attacks and counterattacks became known as "the Anglo-Saxon Controversy."[15] A florilegium of the anti-Kemblian vituperation was republished, together with additional material, in *The Anglo-Saxon Meteor; or Letters, in Defence of Oxford, Treating of the Wonderful Gothic Attainments of John M. Kemble, of Trinity College, Cambridge.* Among his opponents, Thomas Wright, often as perfunctory as he was prolific, proclaimed "We have no longer Anglo-Saxon but German-Saxon."[16] The dispute was one element in Kemble's subsequent inability throughout the remainder of his life to secure an appointment worthy of his intellect, erudition, imagination, and productivity.[17]

Kemble's most enduring work remains the collection of charters in his *Codex Diplomaticus Ævi Saxonici,* six volumes that appeared between 1839 and 1848. By

---

[11] Wiley, "Anglo-Saxon Kemble," 203.
[12] Wiley, *John Mitchell Kemble and Jakob Grimm,* 15.
[13] On the complex relationship between the contents of undated proofs which survive and the eventual book, see Larsen, "Kemble's *Salomon and Saturn.*"
[14] Kemble, *Dialogue of Salomon and Saturnus,* iii.
[15] On the polemics, see Ackerman, "J. M. Kemble and Sir Frederic Madden."
[16] Wright, "Saxon Scholars of England," 259.
[17] Wiley, "Anglo-Saxon Kemble," 202.

wedding shrewd discernment and vast erudition, he arrived at distinctions between authentic and spurious documents that still stand today. Out of this corpus grew his two-volume *The Saxons in England,* on which his reputation was mostly to rest for the remainder of the nineteenth century. Despite many flaws, this wide-ranging history remained a standard reference for decades after first being published in 1849, being reprinted a quarter century later in 1876.

In the early stage of his charter-collecting, Kemble retained his interest in Solomon and Saturn. In 1840 he saw into print an article on runes in which he took into account the ones found in the Old English material. In 1844 or thereabouts he brought to page proofs but set aside and left officially unpublished a study of the *Dialogue of Salomon and Saturnus.*[18] In 1848 he finally published a book on the same body of literature that omits some texts he had treated in the earlier form but that includes others.

The English polymath may not be mentioned nowadays in standard histories of comparative literature or folklore studies, but his decade and a half of engagement with the *Dialogue of Salomon and Saturnus* immersed him in both realms.[19] Before the Ælfric Society brought out his book in its final form, he had a false start with another publisher that reached the proof stage. When his monograph was finally released, he labeled it a contribution to "the development of the History of Fiction."[20] His correspondence with Jacob Grimm testifies that he framed his examination ever more broadly in terms of its linguistic and cultural reach.[21] Beyond Latin, he tracked the passage of the story into Romance languages such as Old Occitan, Old and Middle French, and medieval Italian. Within Germanic, he dealt with versions in Icelandic, Danish, German, Dutch, and of course English. In general he was modest about the monograph that emerged from his investigations, describing it as a "creditable introduction" or "work."[22] At the same time, he devoured books, boasting to Jacob Grimm: "You will see by my Marcolf that I have been pretty assiduously at work, for one book quoted, a dozen have been read."[23] Not even so deep down, he realized full well that he was onto something, seeing his book as containing "an immense mass of matter never dreamt of" by past scholars and "a lot of strange, out of the way materials, which will produce a very useful effect."[24]

[18] Larsen, "Kemble's *Salomon and Saturn,*" 445–50.
[19] "A wide-ranging study in comparative literature designed as a contribution to the history of fiction." Dickins, "Kemble and Old English Scholarship (with a Bibliography of His Writings)," 66. Quoted in Wiley, "Anglo-Saxon Kemble," 227.
[20] Kemble, *Dialogue of Salomon and Saturnus,* iv.
[21] Wiley, *John Mitchell Kemble and Jakob Grimm,* 34, 81–83, 87, 90, 100, 111, 168, 191–92.
[22] Wiley, *John Mitchell Kemble and Jakob Grimm,* 90 and 191.
[23] Wiley, *John Mitchell Kemble and Jakob Grimm,* 103.
[24] Wiley, *John Mitchell Kemble and Jakob Grimm,* 90 and 191.

In keeping with the intellectual values of the Brothers Grimm, Kemble placed the Anglo-Saxon (or what would be called now Old English) poems alongside texts in other Old and Middle Germanic languages. All of this evidence he set further within the context of as many Indo-European languages and literatures as he could explore, such as Celtic (Middle Welsh), Slavic (Polish), and modern Greek. Last but not least, he gave due attention to non-Indo-European, specifically Hebrew. He accorded pride of place to Old English for preserving the oldest evidence, all the more valuable for what he regarded as vestiges of paganism, most obviously in the second name in the title of *Solomon and Saturn*: whereas the later Latin and continental vernacular versions partner the biblical king with an antagonist named Marcolf, the Old English texts match Solomon with a prince of the Chaldeans called Saturn.

According to what Kemble reported in his eventual book, he realized early that the Solomon and Marcolf material contained elements that made it extremely attractive and relevant to the Protestants of the fifteenth century.[25] At the same time, he recognized that the biography of the tale reached back much further than the Reformation, to the early Middle Ages if not earlier. The volume, with the Old English poem of *Solomon and Saturn* as its starting point, appears fittingly under the aegis of the Ælfric Society: the first page announces the first-ever printing of the "earliest Teutonic form" of the story. The author goes on to posit that the Anglo-Saxon materials had ultimately an Eastern source, but he acknowledges that the texts to confirm this hypothesis are no longer extant if they ever were.

In Kemble's analysis, Solomon is a foreign element that probably derived in the end from the East via Jewish traditions.[26] The biblical king was paired first with the Queen of Sheba, after which he became associated with other, even more apocryphal figures. One such association was with Abdimus, whom William of Tyre connected with Marcolf. Kemble is open to the possibility that the European tradition was strongly influenced by materials brought westward by the Crusaders, but he cautions that we must not slip into thinking that the entire Solomon and Marcolf tradition arrived only then, since the testimonies are ample to confirm that it had been circulating already for centuries before.[27] As for Marcolf, Kemble regards him as a heterogeneous creature, related to

---

[25] Kemble, *Dialogue of Salomon and Saturnus*, iv.
[26] Scholarship continues to wrestle with the extraordinary range in the characterization of Solomon: see Verheyden, *The Figure of Solomon*.
[27] Kemble, *Dialogue of Salomon and Saturnus*, 13.

aliases such as Morolf, Marcoul, Marcon, and Marcolfa, as well as the remoter Morcholon, Mercurius, and Mearcwulf.[28]

Very much (and therefore in this regard excessively so) a man of the nineteenth century, Kemble thought in categories that will strike readers today as being nationalist stereotypes. Thus he identified and exaggerated the differences in the name and character of Marcolf from one language and nation to another. The French is a "jesting, japing fool," the German "rude and coarse, but very wise, and indeed far more than a match for Salomon himself."[29] The Old English he interpreted as being a hybrid:

> I assign a Northern origin to one portion of the story, while I admit the admixture of an Oriental element. I propose to show that this Northern portion is an echo from the days of German heathenism, and to restore Saturnus or Marcolfus *the God* to his place in the pagan Pantheon of our ancestors.[30]

His desire to extoll creativity as a distinguishing trait of the German national character, paired with his romantic aim of tracing remnants of Germanic heathenism, may have led him to minimize the contributions made by Eastern cultures to the literary evidence that has survived mainly in German forms.

To Kemble's way of thinking, "Saturn and Marcolf are one person."[31] The admirable values innate in his fellow countrymen caused them to shun "the ludicrous or hateful character" of the alien Marcolf and instead to embrace "the solemn and grave dignity" of Saturn.[32] Saturn was a survival from the heathen gods of pre-Christian times: "the ancient god, first became an *ent* or *eoten*, i.e. a prince of Philistia, and finally sunk into a deformed & beastly jester."[33] With the passage of time the onetime deity "dwindle[d] down into the foul, deformed but witty jester of the Germanic legend, or the profligate and dirty carper of the French."[34]

Kemble's introduction to *Dialogue of Salomon and Saturnus* has been termed "a wide-ranging study in comparative literature designed as a contribution to the history of fiction."[35] The description is fair, and its continued value is a tribute to the keen insight, wide-ranging learning, and unbounded creativity of its author.

---

[28] On "Mercurius se gygand," see Kemble, *Dialogue of Salomon and Saturnus,* 192–93, and Wiley, *John Mitchell Kemble and Jakob Grimm,* 64, 110–11.

[29] Wiley, *John Mitchell Kemble and Jakob Grimm,* 99.

[30] Kemble, *Dialogue of Salomon and Saturnus,* 6–7.

[31] Wiley, *John Mitchell Kemble and Jakob Grimm,* 134.

[32] Kemble, *Dialogue of Salomon and Saturnus,* 7.

[33] Wiley, *John Mitchell Kemble and Jakob Grimm,* 134.

[34] Kemble, *Dialogue of Salomon and Saturnus,* 7–8.

[35] Dickins, "Kemble and Old English Scholarship," 66.

Aleksandr Veselovskii

Aleksandr Veselovskii (1838–1906) was much admired by contemporary and later Russian scholars alike for his erudition and intellectual breadth. In the preface to a new edition of Veselovskii's *Historical Poetics* (*Istoricheskaia poetika*) issued in 1940 as part of the centennial celebration of his birth, the noted Soviet literary scholar Viktor Zhirmunskii praised him in characteristic terms:

> The range of interests of Veselovskii, a scholar of encyclopedic learning, was distinguished by its exceptional breadth; it embraced classical and modern European literatures, the Romano-Germanic West, the Byzantino-Slavic world, and the East, book literature, anonymous popular songs, and the poetry of culturally backward peoples. In the breadth of his scholarly interests Veselovskii had no rivals in either Russian or world scholarship. He was the first to introduce to Western European scholarship facts from Byzantine, Russian, and Slavic literatures. Veselovskii made very broad use of folkloric-ethnographic material transcribed among the numerous national minorities of tsarist Russia and Finnish, Turkic, and palaeo-Asiatic peoples. For Veselovskii privileged peoples and literatures did not exist. In this respect his research on questions of "poetics" was beneficially distinguished from the "Eurocentrism" so characteristic of bourgeois literary criticism in the West.[36]

The story of how this Russian paragon reached maturity is unusual and interesting. We are fortunate in having access to a brief intellectual autobiography that Veselovskii provided to the philologist and ethnographer Aleksandr Pypin when the latter was at work on his *The History of Russian Ethnography* (*Istoriia russkoi etnografii*, 1890–92). It supplies a wealth of detail about key moments in Veselovskii's intellectual development.[37]

Veselovskii was born in Moscow in 1838. The son of a general and a Russified German mother, who gave him great encouragement in his youthful study of several European languages, he graduated in 1858 from the historical-philological faculty at Moscow University. While at the university he worked closely with Fedor Buslaev, who at the time was one of the primary exponents of the mythological school in Russia but later shifted his allegiance to the theory of borrowing.

---

[36] Veselovskii, *Istoricheskaia poetika*, 16.
[37] Pypin, *Istoriia russkoi etnografii*, 2:423–27.

Figure 4. Portrait of Aleksandr Veselovskii.
Reproduced in Veselovskii, *Poetika*, image facing p. viii.

After graduation Veselovskii spent several years in Western Europe, first as the tutor in the family of a Russian ambassador and later as a student and independent scholar in various European cities. He traveled in Spain, France, Italy, and England, and studied in Berlin, Prague, and, for several years, Florence. His first major publication appeared in Italian and dealt with the Italian Renaissance (*Il paradiso degli Alberti,* 1867–69). Encouraged by Buslaev and others to return to Moscow, Veselovskii produced in 1870 as a master's thesis a Russian version of his Italian publication (*Villa Al'berti*). In quick succession he wrote in 1872 a dissertation on a vastly different topic, *Slavic Tales about Solomon and Kitovras and Western Legends about Morol'f and Merlin* (*Slavianskie skazaniia o Solomone i Kitovrase i zapadnye legendy o Morol'fe i Merline*).

In his autobiographical notes, Veselovskii acknowledged that the work of Theodor Benfey had a major impact on the tenor of his dissertation. He also pointed to Felix Liebrecht's 1851 German translation of John Colin Dunlop's *History of Fiction* (*Geschichte der Prosadichtungen,* 1814), and Pypin's own dissertation, "An Essay in the History of Old Russian Tales and Fairy Tales" ("Ocherk literaturnoi istorii starinnykh povestei i skazok russkikh," 1855), as important sources of influence. Veselovskii summarized his intentions in pursuing the topic of his dissertation as both specific and complex: "When the Buddhist hypothesis appeared, routes of study, and not only in the area of migratory tales, were marked for me by a perspective on historical national character [*narodnost'*] and its creative work as a complex of influences, trends, and intersections which the researcher is obliged to take into account, if he wishes to seek out behind them, in the depths, an untouched and original national character, and is not confused, since he has discovered it not at the point of departure, but as a result of the historical process."[38] This insistence on tracking down the details of the historical process became the hallmark of Veselovskii's literary scholarship.

In 1872 Veselovskii became a professor at Petersburg University, where he remained for the rest of his academic career. A prolific publisher, he continued his investigations into Renaissance Italian literature in such studies as *Dante and the Symbolic Poetry of Catholicism* (*Dante i simvolicheskaia poeziia katolichestva,* 1886) and *Boccaccio, His Milieu and Contemporaries* (*Bokkachch'o, ego sreda i sverstniki,* 1893–94); into the oeuvre of outstanding nineteenth-century Russian writers in *Pushkin—a National Poet* (*Pushkin—natsional'nyi poet,* 1899) and *V. A. Zhukovskii: The Poetry of Feeling and the 'Heart's Imagination'* (*V. A. Zhukovskii: Poeziia chuvstva i 'serdechnogo voobrazheniia,'* 1904); and, perhaps most importantly, into a general theory of the development of poetry in *Three Chapters from Historical Poetics* (*Tri glavy iz istoricheskoi poetiki,* 1899). Throughout his academic career Veselovskii remained

---

[38] Pypin, *Istoriia russkoi etnografii,* 2:427.

intellectually flexible, refusing to confine his thinking to one or another school of thought. He drew inspiration from insights of the mythological school, the theory of borrowing and the historical-comparative approach, and ethnography, anthropology, and sociology. An extraordinary polyglot and brilliant theoretician, his contributions continue to influence Russian scholarship today.[39]

Among Veselovskii's seminal ideas, his notions of *motif* and *plot* deserve special mention. Veselovskii defines *motif* as "the simplest narrative unit that figuratively responded to various spiritual needs of the primitive mind or social observation"; examples might be the conception of the sun as an eye or the topos of abduction of a wife. Veselovskii defines *plot* as "a theme in which various situation-motifs are interwoven"; examples he cites here are tales about the sun or abduction. A key principle the scholar identifies in regard to the relationship between *motif* and *plot* is the following:

> The more complicated the combinations of motifs ... the more illogical they are and the more composite motifs there are, the more difficult it is to assume, given, for example, the resemblance of two similar tales from different peoples, that they arose by means of psychological spontaneous generation on the basis of the same conceptions and social foundations. In such instances one may raise the possibility of *borrowing at a historical time* by one people of a plot that was developed by another.[40]

Such is the essence of the theoretical perspective that guided Veselovskii's research throughout his career. Zhirmunskii characterizes this approach as an attempt to infuse literary analysis with an exactitude associated with the natural sciences, as a desire "to examine motifs and their plot linkages as a kind of Mendeleevan system."[41]

It was precisely Veselovskii's unswerving and unnationalistic comparative approach to literary history that, like much creative nineteenth and early twentieth-century Russian thought, evoked the ire of the Soviet cultural establishment during the postwar campaign against Western influence, or "cosmopolitanism." At a meeting of the Union of Soviet Writers in 1947, the Union's head, Aleksandr Fadeev, identified Veselovskii as the "forefather" of a school of literary criticism guilty of servility to the West and condemned him for suggesting that specific foreign works had played a role in the composition

---

[39] On Veselovskii's intellectual legacy, see, for example, Zaborov, Muratov, and Putilov, *Nasledie Aleksandra Veselovskogo*.

[40] Zaborov, Muratov, and Putilov, *Nasledie Aleksandra Veselovskogo*, 542.

[41] Veselovskii, *Istoricheskaia poetika*, 36.

of many medieval Russian works and later Russian classics and his contemporary Soviet "parrots" and "blind apologists" for continuing to peddle such servile ideas to Soviet students.[42] A series of vitriolic studies of Veselovskii soon followed Fadeev's purported unmasking of the scholar.

It was only in the late 1950s, during the era of the Thaw, that it began to be possible to restore Veselovskii's reputation in Soviet publications. A major role in this endeavor was played by Zhirmunskii, who praised the scholar in particular for his extraordinary grasp of the significance of living oral traditions for the analysis of the epic in general.[43] A thorough and reasoned reassessment of Veselovskii's accomplishments and influence did not take place in Russia until after the collapse of the Soviet Union in 1991. This reassessment continues today.

Slavic Tales about Solomon and Kitovras and Western Legends about Morol'f and Merlin

Veselovskii's dissertation exhibits in embryonic form the scholar's decades-long preoccupation with the interrelationship of motif and plot. He begins *Slavic Tales about Solomon and Kitovras and Western Legends about Morol'f and Merlin* with a brief theoretical declaration:

> A turning point in the study of manifestations of popular European literature is taking place before our eyes. The mythological hypothesis, which has traced the diversity of tales and stories and the content of the medieval epic to a few fundamentals common to all Indo-European belief, has been forced to yield a portion of its dominance to the historical view, which relies on the disclosure of very close relationships and influences that have already occurred within the limits of history. An expression of the first tendency was the German mythology of J. Grimm; the source of the second was Benfey's well-known foreword to the *Panchatantra*. These books do not exclude one another, just as both tendencies do not exclude one another; they even necessarily complement one another and should go hand in hand, but in such a way that an attempt at mythological exegesis should begin when all accounts with history have already been settled. This is one of the general propositions that I have tried to implement in my book.[44]

---

[42] Fadeev, "Sovetskaia literatura," 1–2.

[43] Zhirmunskii, *Epicheskoe tvorchestvo slavianskikh narodov*, 3–4.

[44] Veselovskii, *Slavianskie skazaniia o Solomone i Kitovrase*, 1. Hereafter, numbers in the text enclosed in parentheses refer to pages in this edition.

Slavic Tales about Solomon and Kitovras in a sense constitutes an exhaustive and erudite attempt by Veselovskii to "settle accounts with history," an attempt that ranges from ancient India to medieval England and offers a mass of empirical evidence organized and analyzed with painstaking thoroughness. An important component of this agenda is Veselovskii's explicitly enunciated desire to apply hitherto neglected insights suggested by Slavic antiquities to the study of medieval European literature. The specific task undertaken by the scholar is the tracing of adaptations of tales about the legendary Hindu King Vikramaditya to stories about the biblical King Solomon, transmutations that Veselovskii believed ultimately resulted, in part because of apocryphal Byzantino-Slavic intermediaries, in the medieval Western European creation of the figure of Morolf and later of Merlin and the transformation of Solomon into King Arthur. In the process of outlining parallels, Veselovskii is concerned not only with establishing the possibility that borrowings took place, but with determining where possible the cultural context, both chronological and geographical, in which they took place—the who, what, when, where, and why of intellectual exchange.

The first chapter of *Slavic Tales about Solomon and Kitovras* is devoted to stories about Vikramaditya, a compilation known by the Sanskrit title *Vikramacharitra*. The major of the three redactions discussed by Veselovskii is a Mongolian reworking of Buddhist origin that appeared in German translation in 1868.[45] The frame story for this reworking and the other redactions involves an Indian ruler called Ardzhi-Bordzhi in the Mongolian version, during whose reign the throne of Vikramaditya was purportedly rediscovered in appropriately mysterious and magical circumstances. Veselovskii provides detailed, often verbatim, synopses of various narratives about Vikramaditya, focusing in particular on tales of his childhood and inspired feats of judgment; his battle with a demon who temporarily assumes the king's form, throne, and wife; and his conversations with a mysterious but wise being.

The second chapter of Veselovskii's dissertation treats Solomon's childhood as described in apocryphal Russian tales and the *Paleia*, an immensely popular medieval Slavic collection of narratives about Old Testament personages translated from the Byzantine Greek, and the king's multiple judgments as represented in a wide range of both Eastern and Western legends, including Islamic sources. Episodes from the Russian sources are generally presented verbatim in their original medieval Church Slavonic. Veselovskii concludes that both the legends about Solomon's childhood and the stories about his dozen or so acts of perspicacious judgment ultimately derive from tales about Vikramaditya, most likely

---

[45] Jülg, *Mongolische Märchen.*

transmitted through apocryphal and canonical biblical intermediaries, some of which are no longer extant.

The third chapter examines Talmudic tales about Solomon and their possible provenance. According to these tales, which center on the building of the Temple in Jerusalem, because of a prohibition in the Torah, only unhewn stones untouched by iron were supposed to be used in the construction project. What to do? Solomon is informed by rabbis that he needs to acquire the worm known as Shamir used by Moses in the setting of precious stones.[46] They suggest that demons might be of help in this enterprise. This leads to the deliberate intoxication and capture of Asmodeus, king of the demons. Asmodeus helps Solomon locate the Shamir, but then tricks the king into enabling him to take his place. Solomon is eventually able to regain his rightful place and Asmodeus flies away. At various points in the narrative Asmodeus and Solomon engage in verbal sparring, a kind of battle of wits. Veselovskii outlines the multiple plot similarities between this narrative and stories about Vikramaditya and alludes as well to other commonalities in the legendary biographies of the Hindu king and Solomon.

At this point Veselovskii makes an important programmatic statement about the significance and direction of his analysis:

> Our task is becoming more complicated; the thread of the stories that we have been telling one after another, assuming *a priori* their mutual connection, has led us precisely to the historical knot on whose resolution the complete disclosure of this connection will depend. It is not enough to propose the possibility of mutual interaction or influence in order to explain a similarity that leaps to the eyes; it is essential to prove this possibility, to disclose by what paths these influences stretched and where they crossed. (140)

Veselovskii suggests a crucial period of Iranian/Jewish contact during the sixth-century BCE "Babylonian exile" forced upon the Judeans by the Babylonian king Nebuchadnezzar. This period coincided with the flowering of Zoroastrianism, with its intensely dualistic cosmological view. Veselovskii argues that dualistic conceptions began to infiltrate Jewish religious thought and are apparent in the Talmud. The figure of Asmodeus is a logical expression of this influence. Veselovskii emphasizes on the other hand the significance of enduring Indo-Iranian contact (hence the transmission of the Vikramaditya tales to Persia).

---

[46] On Shamir, see Ginzberg, *Legends of the Jews*, 4:166, 5:53n165. The legend of a worm created on the eve of the Sabbath that could cut any stone and that was used by Solomon in constructing the First Temple in Jerusalem is related to the word *shamir* in classical Hebrew, meaning diamond/adamant (see chapter 5 below).

All of this eventually led to "the religious syncretism of the Sassanid era, in the broad contact of Jewish, Parsee, Buddhist, even Christian ideas, from which emerged the mixed teachings, the distinctive heresies whose best-known representative is Manichaeism" (154). The tale of Solomon and Asmodeus results from the fusing of accounts of the historical Solomon with folktale material originally emanating from India.

The fourth chapter of *Slavic Tales about Solomon and Kitovras* traces the dissemination within Europe of the legends about Solomon and Asmodeus and their subsequent permutations. Veselovskii is particularly concerned with the role played by medieval heresies in spreading fanciful accounts of Solomon's activities. Among the Slavs the tale of Solomon and Kitovras assumed importance, among the Germanic and Romance European peoples the story of Solomon and Morolf. These works were included in indices of prohibited books throughout the medieval period in both Eastern and Western Europe, but survived nonetheless. Veselovskii subscribes to the idea that Kitovras, both as a name and a being, represents a corruption of the Greek centaur and that a Greek original of the Solomon tale served as a source for the Slavic. He further hypothesizes that in addition to the Talmudic redaction of the Solomon story there existed in Europe another version from the East in which the king's demonic opponent did not drive him away, but instead carried off his wife (166). Veselovskii also alludes to the mythological similarities shared by the figure of the centaur and the Hindu male nature spirit called the Gandharva; the latter was noted for its weakness for the female sex. As for Morolf-Markolf, Veselovskii agrees with Jacob Grimm in perceiving a connection with the Talmudic *markolis*, an abusive or mocking nickname (170), and from there suggests a link with the Buddhist demon Mara, Vikramaditya's sometime enemy.

Veselovskii ascribes the widespread medieval enthusiasm for narratives about Solomon and Kitovras or Morolf-Markolf to the influence of Manichaeism: "no single heresy was destined to play such a significant role in the history of Christianity as Manichaeism. It promised too confidently to answer the subtle questions of dogma and eschatology on which Christian sages had dwelt with trembling" (172). From Veselovskii's perspective, the Slavic role in the transmission of dualistic thought throughout Europe was immense and underestimated. The scholar's explanation for the popularity of dualism among the common people of Europe is in part socioeconomic:

> The people always suffered most of all from the squabbling and arbitrary rule of feudal lords, from the mass of evil that rained down on them in the form of famine, crop failures, and hostile pogroms. They were accustomed to this chance and fatalism and hence inferred the

existence of some sort of special independent principle of evil in control of the world. Dualistic doctrine explained the origin of evil on earth to them in images accessible to their fantasy. (177)

As a narrative account par excellence of the conflict of equally matched good and evil, the story of Solomon and a demonic being was ripe for transmission throughout Europe by dualists of all stripes, from Bogomils to Cathars to the Templars, from itinerant priests to wandering minstrels. Veselovskii espies the workings of dualistic influence here, there, and everywhere in Europe for centuries on end, up to and including tales of King Arthur and Merlin.

The fifth and sixth chapters of Veselovskii's dissertation are devoted to Slavic tales about Solomon and Kitovras and Western European accounts of Solomon and Morolf. The Slavic tales are reproduced in the original medieval Church Slavonic. Veselovskii is particularly concerned with outlining specific similarities between Asmodeus and Kitovras, which include their demonic character, reason for and means of capture, and mysterious actions and words (249). Veselovskii views Kitovras as a relatively traditional, static creation, Morolf as a distinctly different type:

> Nothing better characterizes the comparative productivity of one or another literary milieu than the development within it of one and the same popular motifs. The legend of Kitovras ... remained archaically immobile ... all its development is limited to corruptions, as a result of the introduction of elements from the common people. The Western Morolf has an entire productive history; from the demonic opponent of Solomon ... he develops into the well-known type of the jester and clown. (279)

At the conclusion of this process of transformation Morolf emerges as Solomon's helper in regaining his wife, rather than as the abductor in older versions. Despite this softening of character, Veselovskii argues, Morolf's essential demonic quality is still expressed in his wiles and wit (281).

For Veselovskii, the multiple permutations of the Solomon saga, as evidenced in the Solomon/Kitovras and Solomon/Morolf narratives, should serve as a warning to scholars "captivated by fashionable mythological exegesis" (293). Before resorting to a mythological explanation, Veselovskii emphasizes here as earlier in his dissertation and elsewhere in his writings, it is crucial to determine whether one is really dealing with an expression of an authentic popular worldview or with a corrupted version of an originally literary source. The scholar hypothesizes that the now lost apocryphon mentioned above made its way into Western European popular culture in about the twelfth century (296), leading to the composition of a German narrative poem preserved only in fifteenth-century manuscripts (298: see chapter 7 below, *Salman and Morolf*). He further insists on the thematic links between the two parts of this poem, rejecting the widespread assumption, on the part, for example, of Jacob Grimm and John Mitchell Kemble, that there were originally two separate poems: "My opinion leads to the conclusion that the first and second Morolf were not only both of Eastern origin, but that they derived from one cycle of tales, whose historical alterations we have traced from Vikramaditya to Dzhemshid, Takhmuras, and Solomon, and from Gandharva-Gandarewa to Asmodeus, Kitovras-Centaur, and Morolf" (337–38).

The seventh chapter of *Slavic Tales about Solomon and Kitovras* focuses on the figure of Merlin. Veselovskii dismisses any attempts to construe the tale of Merlin and Arthur as Celtic in origin, viewing the wizard and the king instead as permutations of Asmodeus/Kitovras/Morolf and Solomon and adducing numerous very specific textual comparisons to support his argument. The scholar ultimately suggests that the legend of Merlin is more archaic than the German narrative poem about Solomon and Morolf and closer to the Talmudic-Slavic tales than to Morolf (370–71). So much for Celtic mystical fantasies, implies Veselovskii.

The final chapter of *Slavic Tales about Solomon and Kitovras* is a postscript of sorts about the parallels between the demonic female beings known as *dakini* who appear in some of the Buddhist narratives about Vikramaditya and the queen of Sheba who visits Solomon. Veselovskii ascribes the relative brevity of his discussion of this topic in part to an insufficiency of material at his disposal. Once again, though, the scholar adduces verbatim accounts from both Latin and medieval Church Slavonic texts to support his argument.

The relative inaccessibility of Russian sources for Western European medievalists has long meant that Veselovskii's theories and extensive textual evidence relating to *Solomon and Marcolf* have not received the attention they deserve. This situation was compounded by the peculiarities of the Soviet scholarly environment for much of the twentieth century. It is only in the past two decades that Veselovskii has been granted appropriate recognition in Russia. One hopes that this in turn will encourage more broadly based acknowledgment by medievalists worldwide that *Slavic Tales about Solomon and Kitovras and Western Legends about Morol'f and Merlin*, while admittedly dated in certain respects and marked by some characteristic late nineteeth-century ethnographic prejudices, nonetheless provides both a wealth of valuable textual data and some brilliant insights into the migratory fortunes of *Solomon and Marcolf* and its antecedents.

2

Salemon and Marcoul

(Old French)

Introduction and Translation
by Mary-Ann Stadtler-Chester

Introduction

THE VARIOUS FORMS OF THE OLD FRENCH DIALOGUE *Salemon and Marcoul* (*Salemon et Marcoul*) share with the Latin *Dialogue of Salomon and Marcolf* its two title characters and the presentation of a dialogue between them. Otherwise, what stand out are differences. The Old French texts not only lack the narrative frame in which the dialogue portion of the Latin *S&M* is embedded, but also present a different dialogue between the two characters. Both versions are heavily proverbial, but their stocks of adages are distinct. Thus the Latin cannot be viewed as a direct source of any of the French texts—or vice versa.

Salemon et Marcoul, in all but one version, shows hostility toward women, and particularly toward prostitutes. Since prostitution was often legal and familiar in medieval life, Marcoul's comments probably shocked audiences in the Middle Ages less than they do readers today. At any rate, he makes it clear that prostitutes cannot be trusted (G, stanzas 7, 18, and 21), are cunning (B, stanza 2; G, stanzas 9 and 26; I, stanza 28), and should be beaten (B, stanzas 18 and 23; G, stanzas 8, 17, 21, and 23). They are greedy (B, stanza 24; G, stanzas 11 and 32; H, stanza 16; I, stanza 23) and proud (B, stanza 11; G, stanza 28). He delights in reminding us that they are sexually insatiable (B, stanzas 15 and 28; G, stanzas 15 and 36). In the country prostitutes frequented markets and fairs (B, stanza 13, G, stanza 22); in the cities they could be found in mills, markets, and taverns (B, stanza 24).

Four sorts of prostitutes existed. "Common" or "public girls" practiced in public brothels. They could solicit freely in public, but by law they had to take clients back to brothels to exercise their profession. Married men preferred "secret girls" who entertained clients in public baths. Other prostitutes lived in small private houses owned by pimps. These often had benches in front where the women would solicit passersby (G, stanza 5). "Loose girls" worked for themselves. They would show off in public, soliciting beggars, adventurers, thieves, and assassins at the intersections of busy streets (B, stanza 19; E, stanza 13; F, stanza 15; G, stanza 27).

The Old French versions of *Salemon and Marcoul* survive in at least ten manuscripts that date between the thirteenth and fifteenth centuries. They, along with their sigla, are as follows:

A Paris, Bibliothèque nationale de France, MS fr. 837

B Bern, Burgerbibliothek, MS Cod. 354

C Cambridge, Trinity College, MS R.3.20

D Paris, Bibliothèque nationale de France, MS fr. 19152

E Épinal-Golbey, Bibliothèque intercommunale, MS 59 (217)

F Paris, Bibliothèque nationale de France, MS lat. 4641B

G Geneva, Bibliothèque de Genève, MS fr. 179bis

H Paris, Bibliothèque nationale de France, MS fr. 12483

I Paris, Bibliothèque nationale de France, MS fr. 25545

J Paris, Bibliothèque nationale de France, MS f. lat. 6707

These ten may be sorted first by comparing common errors in versification, rhyme scheme, and syntax. This comparison requires attention to variation within lines, such as the substitution of synonyms and antonyms, as well as in the order of stanzas. The manuscripts can also be dated, localized, and grouped at least approximately by scrutinizing the abbreviations and orthography used by their scribes.

The manuscripts can then be divided into four main groups on the basis of linguistic, lexical, and literary features. The first comprises A, H, and I. The second grouping encompasses five manuscripts: C, E, F, G, and J. Manuscripts B and D each forms a group of its own, and as such, both are included here in their entirety. A and G have been chosen to represent their respective groups, because they show the least number of mistakes and the fewest particularities among their peers. The English translations offered here follow the texts of these representatives. Additional verses from E, F, H, I, and J which are absent from these selected texts have been included. Since all of the verses of C are found in G, the text of C is not offered here.

The reader will notice the apocryphal verses at the beginning of H. This manuscript belonged to the convent of the Dominicans of Poissy, near Paris, and the verses of *Salemon and Marcoul* were destined to be read as a sermon before a congregation of monks or nuns. For this reason, we assume, the scribe tells us that he left out the ugly parts and wrote some himself; notably he has replaced words for whores (*putain* and *pute*) with ones for nuns (*nonnain* and *none*).

In addition to the ten manuscripts A through J listed above, there exist later manuscript copies of *Salemon and Marcoul* and some manuscript fragments in private hands. They are as follows:

Spikkestad, Schøyen Collection, MS 1275 (auctioned)

Fragments of many medieval manuscripts were cut and pasted into this album, which was compiled by Pierre-Camille Le Moine (1723–1800). The section from *Salemon and Marcoul* is purported to date from the fifteenth century.

Lyon, Bibliothèque de l'Académie, Palais des Arts, MS 28

Dating from the second half of the fifteenth century, this manuscript contains seven works. One of them, unentitled, offers an incomplete copy of proverbs from manuscripts A, C, G, and J, without indications of the interlocutors.

Paris, Bibliothèque Nationale de France, MS fr. 15111

Dating between the late seventeenth and the early eighteenth century, this manuscript includes a late copy of manuscript A.

Several previous editors have produced redactions. In 1823 Méon published for the first time the entire texts of A and C, with stanzas from B, I, G, and J.[1] In 1831 Crapelet printed the version from D in its entirety.[2] In 1836 Mone came out with the text of E.[3] In 1848 Kemble made available excerpts from A, along with excerpts from D.[4] In 2000 Hunt offered again the whole of A.[5]

---

[1] Méon, *Nouveau recueil de fabliaux et contes inédits*, 1:416–36.
[2] Crapelet, *Proverbs et dictons populaires*, 187–200.
[3] Mone, "Beitrag zum Salomon und Marcolf."
[4] Kemble, *Dialogue of Salomon and Saturnus*, 73–83.
[5] Hunt's full essay discusses three distinct Old French dialogues between Solomon and Marcolf and edits not only the text translated in the current chapter (Hunt, "Solomon and Marcolf," 213–24), but also the anonymous French verse dialogue featured in chapter 3, drawn from an entirely different manuscript (Hunt, "Solomon and Marcolf," 206–13).

All the Old French versions are anonymous, although John M. Kemble and Gaston Paris made the suggestion (since rejected) that D's text was the work of Count Pierre Mauclerc (1213–50); they were prompted to this hypothesis because the incipit refers to an unidentified "count of Brittany" as the author.[6] Besides these verse texts, a short prose account is found in Vatican, Biblioteca apostolica Vaticana, MS Reg. lat. 1716, in which Solomon's interlocutor bears the name Marchus and is not a peasant but a great philosopher. This version contains no proverbs whatsoever.[7]

One version (D) is characterized by relative decorum and literary refinement. This soberer form contrasts Solomon's sententious observations and Marcoul's more common touch. The other redactions (A, G, B) are marked by obscenity and scatology. In them Marcoul's rejoinders are all rude observations about prostitutes. The vulgarities of the Old French have been kept in the English translations. The faint of heart should beware!

Notes on this Translation

The Old French originals follow a set meter and rhyme scheme. Versions A and B generally hold to the pattern aabcddbc with two quatrains per stanza and five syllables per line. The stanzas in versions G and D are six lines long. The tercets in each stanza of version G adhere, for the most part, to the rhyme scheme aabccb. The lines are all of five syllables. The six-line stanzas in Version D adhere to the rhyme scheme aabaab. The first half of each stanza offers Salemon's observation, the second Marcoul's response. The lines differ in length; the "a" lines contain six syllables, the "b" ones only five, giving the poem a regular and pleasing 665665 rhythm. The meter and rhyme of the Old French have not been kept in the English translations here. Because the Old French manuscripts contain little punctuation, what modern conventions dictate for poetry has been added, along with stanza and line numbers.

I would like to extend sincere thanks to William D. Paden for his expertise and kindness in shedding light on intricacies of the centuries-old French language. I also much appreciate the comradery and insights into the proverbs afforded by Marguerite Mahler.

---

[6] "Ci commence de Marcoul et de Salomon que li quens de Bretaigne fist." Kemble, *Dialogue of Salomon and Saturnus*, 73.
[7] Ernest Langlois, *Nouvelles françaises inédites*, 112–13.

Translation

Salemon and Marcoul

Version A

1.
"Misery and war
are the devastation and destruction
of the earth,"
so says Salemons.
"From the whore come evil
and deadly wars
and the peril of humanity,"
Marcoul answers him.

2.
"He knows how to waste his time
who wants to build a sluice   10
to hold back the Loire,"
so says Salemons.
"Common whores
and born fools
don't deserve to be believed,"
Marcoul answers him.

3.
"He who attracts a thief
in his house,
suffers damage,"
 so says Salemons.   20
"He who favors a whore
ends up crying
when he realizes it,"
Marcoul answers him.

4.
"The little caterpillar
eats the new shoots
and the cabbage leaf,"
so says Salemons.
"The whore dresses,
provides for herself, and feeds   30

on the fool's money,"
Marcoul answers him.

5.
"When a goat is born,
you can tell for sure:
its butt is white,"
so says Salemons.
"When a scoundrel says, 'Take this,'
the whore says, 'Come,
sit on this bench,'"
Marcoul answers him.   40

6.
"He who pursues a fox
covers little ground
and often turns around and around,"
so says Salemons.
"He who pursues a whore
when she is sneaking away
takes many steps in vain,"
Marcoul answers him.

7.
"He who is sick
will be happy   50
if he escapes alive,"
so says Salemons.
"He who trusts a whore
will be left
with neither coat nor cape,"
Marcoul answers him.

8.
"Little chicks
are delicious with grease
seasoned with pepper,"
so says Salemons.   60
"If a whore has no wine,
she looks for a plan and trick
to get something to drink,"
Marcoul answers him.

9.
"The monkey is ugly
and very deformed,
and has a bald butt,"
so says Salemons.
"God has not made a cripple
who can't get his way   70
with a whore for his money,"
Marcoul answers him.

10.
"The polecat is at home
in its den in the woods
where it finds shelter,"
so says Salemons.
"A whore's sticky fingers
try to steal all she likes
and all she sees anyone possess,"
Marcoul answers him.   80

11.
"Some people chase the deer
in the woods and in the plain,
who then lose it completely,"
so says Salemons.
"Some people clothe the whore
and feed her with their bread
and another fucks her,"
Marcoul answers him.

12.
"The ripe pear
is worth more than the hard one;   90
this you know well,"
so says Salemons.
"A whore has such a disposition;
she does not take care of a scoundrel
who has nothing,"
Marcoul answers him.

13.
"A bramble sticks people

and pulls out the fleece
of ewes and sheep,"
so says Salemons.   100
"And the whore puts out,
as long as she expects
something from her scoundrel,"
Marcoul answers him.

14.
"The filthy little pig
does not seek a clean place;
rather, it looks for muck,"
so says Salemons.
"It doesn't matter to a whore
who gives her money,   110
but that he's quick to fuck,"
Marcoul answers him.

15.
"The rooster on the manure pile
scratches the straw
to find the grain,"
so says Salemons.
"A whore makes quick work
of emptying the change purse
hanging at the yokel's ass,"
Marcoul answers him.   120

16.
"A saddled horse
is quite ready
to make a journey,"
so says Salemons.
"A whore bent over
is quite ready
to fuck and to fart,"
Marcoul answers him.

17.
"If it weren't for the cat,
often the rat   130
would get to the bacon,"

so says Salemons.
"The whore with white arms
lays a trap with her cunt
to catch a rogue,"
Marcoul answers him.

18.
"The yokel's ox
yields the bread
that everyone lives on,"
so says Salemons.   140
"He wears himself out in vain
who thinks he can kill a whore
with his cock,"
Marcoul answers him.

19.
"The rested horse
is shoed for naught
if it bites and kicks,"
so says Salemons.
"He has a strong hand
who wants to make   150
a respectable woman of a whore,"
Marcoul answers him.

20.
"An unguarded pear tree
is often shaken
as long as it has fruit to pick,"
so says Salemons.
"A whore will value you
as long as she knows
that you have something to give,"
Marcoul answers him.   160

21.
"Garlic sauce is not good
if it is not crushed
and vigorously ground,"
so says Salemons.
"The whore is lost

if she is not well beaten
And often mistreated,"
Marcoul answers him.

22.
"A windswept house
is soon in flames   170
when it catches on fire,"
so says Salemons.
"The whore in make-up
is soon laid
when she sees money,"
Marcoul answers him.

23.
"Never was there so much wine
because now the mill
produces it more often,"
so says Salemons.   180
"Never would you be
so tightly held by a whore
that she will like you any better,"
Marcoul answers him.

24.
"He deserves to lose his land
who grants protection
to a traitor,"
so says Salemons.
"He who hands over
his possessions to a whore   190
deserves to go begging,"
Marcoul answers him.

25.
"You should not sow
in sand by the sea:
never will grain grow there,"
so says Salemons.
"He wastes his words
who tries by reason
to refine a whore,"

Marcoul answers him.   200

26.
"A rabbit hides
deep in the earth
so that it will not be caught,"
so says Salemons.
"With a laugh, a whore steals so much
from a scoundrel
that he is miserable,"
Marcoul answers him.

27.
"One spreads birdlime
where one has seen   210
birds return,"
so says Salemons.
"A whore looks for a fair
where she hopes to find
plenty of goods,"
Marcoul answers him.

28.
"Throw into the depths
either stick or stone,
it just gets wetter,"
so says Salemons.   220
"Give to a whore
both today and tomorrow,
she just gets prouder,"
Marcoul answers him.

29.
"Feed the hawk,
and it will be better
at hunting waterfowl,"
so says Salemons.
"Mistreat the whore,
 and keep her downtrodden: 230
she will hold you dear,"
Marcoul answers him.

30.
"The eel being fished
will never get caught,
so vigorously it wiggles,"
so says Salemons.
"The cunning whore
will never be duped;
he's a fool who tries to,"
Marcoul answers him.   240

31.
"In such large flocks
starlings fly
that not a one falls,"
so says Salemons.
"A whore keeps her word
to twenty, a hundred [scoundrels],
and still looks for more,"
Marcoul answers him.

32.
"The leopard is proud
to put on airs,   250
and the lion even more,"
so says Salemons.
"You kiss a whore;
'Be gone,' she says.
That is their way,"
Marcoul answers him.

33.
"The little child
shares a very big piece
of his bread with the dog,"
so says Salemons.   260
"A whore has such a disposition:
she does not take care of a scoundrel
who has nothing,"
Marcoul answers him.

34.
"Have you ever seen a donkey

leave fine hay
to gnaw at thistle?"
so says Salemons.
"Have you ever seen a whore
leave a good lover   270
for a wretched scoundrel?"
Marcoul answers him.

35.
"Summer is very beautiful,
as is the flower in the fields,
of which there are so many,"
so says Salemons.
"If you trust a whore,
she will take with a laugh
all that you have,"
Marcoul answers him.   280

36.
"Never will a trail appear
that a snake makes
on a dark rock,"
so says Salemons.
"The whore in make-up
will not be proven guilty
if she is not caught fucking,"
Marcoul answers him.

37.
"At the mouth of an oven
there is so much heat   290
that grass will never grow there,"
so says Salemons.
"Never will a whore's ass
by night or by day,
be without shit,"
Marcoul answers him.

38.
"He who raises a churl
and caresses him softly,   300
only makes him worse,"

so says Salemons.
"He who raises a whore
and beats her and mistreats her,
only makes her better,"
Marcoul answers him.

39.
"The scoundrel feels in his purse
and finds only bearskin;
he has no more to give,"
so says Salemons.   310
"When the whore hears this,
she closes her cunt;
no cock can enter,"
Marcoul answers him.

40.
"He who values dice
is foolish and crazy,
for soon he will be naked,"
so says Salemons.
"He who keeps a whore
suffers for it: 320
soon he will be devastated,"
Marcoul answers him,
"He who believes a whore and runs after dice
cannot die a rich man."
Here ends *Marcoul and Salemon*
which is not worth a big turd.

Version B
Here begins *Marcous and Salemons*

1.
"Misery and war
are the devastation and destruction
of the earth,"
so says Salemons.
"From the whore come evil
and cruel anguish,
and the peril of humanity,"
Marcous answers him.

2.

"A quarrel and hatred
cause faithful friends   10
to part company,"
so says Salemons.
"The cleverness of whores
makes close relatives
mortal enemies,"
Marcous answers him.

3.

"There will never be so much wine
that this mill
will turn or grind any better,"
so says Salemons.   20
"You will never be
so mistreated by a whore
that she will like you any better,"
Marcous answers him.

4.

"The whore and the servant
do everything backwards
in word and in deed,"
so says Salemons.
"They put on a good face,
but betray you in secret,   30
for it conceals their intention,"
Marcous answers him.

5.

"A servant of vile birth
and kitchen boys
do much to be feared,"
so says Salemons.
"A whore brought up in court
isn't easily able to get
into an abbey,"
Marcous answers him.   40

6.

"He who pursues the trail

of a clever fox
is on a wild goose chase,"
so says Salemons.
"He who pursues a whore
when she is sneaking away,
takes many steps in vain,"
Marcous answers him.

7.
"The pear tree will be
eyed and shaken   50
as long as it has fruit,"
so says Salemons.

....
....
....
....

8.
"The rested horse
is shoed for naught
if it does not work,"
so says Salemons.   60
"He has a strong hand,
who could make
a respectable woman of a whore,"
Marcous answers him.

9.
"You should know:
a dog has the habit
of eating rotting meat,"
so says Salemons.
"I will take care of
anyone who supports a whore: 70
never will he be without shame,"
Marcous answers him.

10.
"Eat lean meat,
for here you will never find
either grease or fat,"

so says Salemons.
"Caress a whore
and flatter her;
you will never be able to stop,"
Marcous answers him.   80

11.
"Throw into the depths
either stick or stone,
it just gets wetter,"
so says Salemons.
"Give to a whore
both today and tomorrow;
she just gets prouder,"
Marcous answers him.

12.
"An ox badly wintered
is tired in March,   90
and falls into the furrow,"
so says Salemons.
"The well-dressed whore
shows off in the street
so she will be seen,"
Marcous answers him.

13.
"One spreads birdlime
where he has seen
a bird's nest,"
so says Salemons.   100
"The whore seeks a fair
where she hopes to find
many bawdy fellows,"
Marcous answers him.

14.
"He who sees the sun
red in the morning
expects rain,"
so says Salemons.
"A whore with a pretty face

and a tavern are expensive   110
and later cause regret,"
Marcous answers him.

15.
"No usurer will ever
have as much money
as his heart would like,"
so says Salemons.
"Never in her life
will a whore be so satisfied
that she no longer lusts,"
Marcous answers him.   120

16.
"Never should you seek out a peasant
because he took an oath,
for it is good for nothing,"
so says Salemons.
"He knows her nature well
who scant believes a whore
as she takes more oaths,"
Marcous answers him.

17.
"Pack a mare
with lead or silver: 130
it doesn't care which,"
so says Salemons.
"The whore doesn't care
who mounts her ass:
all are the same to her,"
Marcous answers him.

18.
"Crazy is he who wants
to sow in the sea:
never will grain grow there,"
so says Salemons.   140
"He loses his mind
who tries to chastise a whore
with fine talk,"

Marcous answers him.

19.
"Praise the peacock,
and it shows off
its tail,"
so says Salemons.
"The well-dressed whore
shows off in the street   150
to garner praise,"
Marcous answers him.

20.
"The hawk that has molted
has a better memory
than does the young bird,"
so says Salemons.
"The more she is in the street,
the more often the pretty whore
catches prey,"
Marcous answers him.   160

21.
"The young falcon
is a little dirty
on its first day,"
so says Salemons.
"The well-guarded whore
is much desired
when she is available,"
Marcous answers him.

22.
"A wild sparrow hawk
is not very easy   170
to tame,"
so says Salemons.
"The lowly whore
attracts no one
by any act of kindness,"
Marcous answers him.

23.
"Tame the hawk,
thus it will be better
at hunting prey,"
so says Salemons.   180
"Oppress the whore
and keep her downtrodden;
she will hold you dear,"
Marcous answers him.

24.
"The dog takes off from afar
when it smells in the wind
either partridge or quail,"
so says Salemons.
"The whore notices from afar
one from whom she can   190
get a half-penny,"
Marcous answers him.

25.
"The fat little pig
does not seek a clean place;
rather, it looks for muck,"
so says Salemons.
"It doesn't matter to the whore
who gives her money,
but that he's quick to fuck,"
Marcous answers him.   200

26.
"The little child
gives a very big piece
of his bread to the dog,"
so says Salemons.
"A whore will be attentive to you
when she hears
you say, 'Take this,'"
Marcous answers him.

27.
"I think he who takes

hot coals in his hands 210
is sure to burn himself,"
so says Salemons.
"It is fair that he who puts what he has
in the hands of a whore
sleeps on straw,"
Marcous answers him.

28.
"A saddled horse
is quite ready
to make a journey,"
so says Salemons. 220
"A whore bent over
is quite ready
to fuck and to fart,"
Marcous answers him.

29.
"It is fair that he who puts the traitor
under his care
should lose his wealth,"
so says Salemons.
"If someone puts his possessions
into the hands of a whore, 230
It's right that he should beg,"
Marcous answers him.

30.
"He who attracts the thief
in his house
suffers damage,"
so says Salemons.
"He who honors a whore,
ends up crying
when he realizes it,"
Marcous answers him. 240

31.
"When the cat is handsome
and its fur is shiny,
it goes wild,"

so says Salemons.
"Caress a whore,
and you can be sure
she will abandon you,"
Marcous answers him.

Version D
Here begins the *Marcoul and Salemons* that the Count of Brittany composed

1.
"Above all other honors,
prowess is the flower,"
so says Salemons.
"I don't like such valor
by which one dies in pain,"
Marcoul answers him.

2.
"In courtliness there is suffering,
but one who practices it acts well,"
so says Salemons.
"Month and day and week,   10
work is a huge effort,"
Marcoul answers him.

3.
"By giving generously
one can rise high,"
so says Salemons.
"For practicing poverty
one is declared a fool,"
Marcoul answers him.

4.
"He who would be a learned man,
will never speak too much,"   20
so says Salemons.
"He who would never say a word,
will not make much noise,"
Marcoul answers him.

5.
"Crazy is he who takes with him
all that he owns,"
so says Salemons.
"Nothing will ever befall,
one who carries nothing,"
Marcoul answers him.   30

6.
"Drinking well and eating well
makes one feel better,"
so says Salemons.
"Fattening one's belly
makes one loosen one's belt,"
Marcoul answers him.

7.
"Why does one pursue a profession
that won't help him?"
so says Salemons.
"Such a one thinks he is getting ahead   40
who is only seeking trouble,"
Marcoul answers him.

8.
"He who cries before he laughs
does nothing crazy,"
so says Salemons.
"I know this much from experience:
he who cries, does not laugh at all,"
Marcoul answers him.

9.
"It is true that people
really desire gold and silver,"   50
so says Salemons.
"Some who have it are sorry
when forced to give it back,"
Marcoul answers him.

10.
"Why does he who knows not his way

get up in the morning?"
so says Salemons.
"A poor wretch declines,
and the day has its end,"
Marcoul answers him.   60

11.
"Many people are furious
when they are discouraged,"
so says Salemons.
"Such people would prefer death
to having wisdom calm them,"
Marcoul answers him.

12.
"A lady grants her lover
body and heart equally,"
so says Salemons.
"Unfaithful lovers have betrayed   70
many a beautiful body without amends,"
Marcoul answers him.

13.
"He who deceives his mistress
performs a dastardly deed,"
so says Salemons.
"A cheater does not seek justice
because reason would kill him,"
Marcoul answers him.

14.
"When a lady is deceived,
it is no offence,"   80
so says Salemons.
"Many a lusty lady
eats the table bare,"
Marcoul answers him.

15.
"Poor miserable men
are often covetous,"
so says Salemons.

"They are not too ashamed
to take a lot from you,"
Marcoul answers him.   90

16.
"When the innkeeper is feared,
he is a fool who lodges there,"
so says Salemons.
"By the innkeeper, you know,
much wealth is usurped,"
Marcoul answers him.

17.
"On a long pilgrimage,
armies do damage,"
so says Salemons.
"A true thief, according to custom,   100
steals, or robs, or goes mad,"
Marcoul answers him.

18.
"Never will good come from those,
who do not pay well,"
so says Salemons.
"The peasant says, 'It has been a long time
that a poor man has no friends,'"
Marcoul answers him.

19.
"In winter a fur coat,
but not when it's very hot,"   110
so says Salemons.
"He who has a dishonest neighbor
should carry a stick,"
Marcoul answers him.

20.
"The wise man prepares himself
before he comes to dire straits,"
so says Salemons.
"The fool does not believe by rights,
that there will ever be scorching heat,"

Marcoul answers him.   120

21.
"The fool throws hard stones;
the wise man doesn't care,"
so says Salemons.
"Summer does its justice
when heat takes away cold,"
Marcoul answers him.

22.
"Why is the horse
jumping high in the plains?"
so says Salemons.
"The truly foolish one by birth   130
throws stones or sticks,"
Marcoul answers him.

23.
"Moderation does not suit a fool,
nor gaiety an old man,"
so says Salemons.
"Let him seek greenery
whose own does not last,"
Marcoul answers him.

24.
"The fool is very burdened
when he has much to do,"   140
so says Salemons.
"Take a club to him
and he will be comforted,"
Marcoul answers him.

25.
"The fool is quite ready
when his desire rises,"
so says Salemons.
"A bad dog, when it is burdened,
makes the older ones rejoice,"
Marcoul answers him.   150

26.
"I don't know what to say about the fool;
our Savior forgets him,"
so says Salemons.
"Big is the brotherhood
of those who commit folly,"
Marcoul answers him.

27.
"The fool has his way:
the longer he lives, the crazier he gets,"
so says Salemons.
"Whatever he says,   160
his heart flies with joy,"
Marcoul answers him.

28.
"It is true that night and day
the fool is very happy,"
so says Salemons.
"He likes his labor better
than the wise man's tears,"
Marcoul answers him.

29.
"Whatever others say,
the fool laughs at his folly,"   170
so says Salemons.
"He makes good company
as long as he doesn't hit,"
Marcoul answers him.

30.
"I like neither poor pasture
nor unlimited work,"
so says Salemons.
"Snow in summer, and cold:
all is contrary to nature,"
Marcoul answers him.   180

31.
"I like neither the solace of children
nor giving to a beggar,"
so says Salemons.
"Nor I a sobbing woman,
nor a singing scoundrel,"
Marcoul answers him.

32.
"I like neither the cry of a mastiff,
nor getting up too early,"
so says Salemons.
"Nor I a bad cousin   190
nor water that replaces wine,"
Marcoul answers him.

33.
"He who thinks himself handsome
is full of caprices,"
so says Salemons.
"But when his skin hangs,
he thinks of new ones,"
Marcoul answers him.

34.
"He who is both handsome and good
surely must have good times,"   200
so says Salemons.
"When you really think about the world,
everything in it is too much,"
Marcoul answers him.

35.
"It is better to enjoy oneself
than to languish in great thoughts,"
so says Salemons.
"Neither enjoy oneself too much,
nor dwell in thought,"
Marcoul answers him.   210

36.
"The domination of a bad man

I would never like,"
so says Salemons.
"The kiss of a malodorous scoundrel
smells of the boards of a bedroom,"
Marcoul answers him.

37.
"More than getting up in the morning,
I like resting,"
so says Salemons.
"Through a long, bitter dispute,   220
I see little gained,"
Marcoul answers him.

38.
"The wicked one does not want
To work his body,"
so says Salemons.
"The wise man flees toil
that will not help him,"
Marcoul answers him.

39.
"He who does not want to work
should have small wages,"   230
so says Salemons.
"Neither take on too much,
nor work as much as is needed,"
Marcoul answers him.

40.
"He who is always pensive
is not at all well educated,"
so says Salemons.
"A thief is always watchful despite himself
for he thinks he will be caught at any moment,"
Marcoul answers him.   240

41.
"He shortens his life
who trusts in thoughts,"
so says Salemons.

"He causes melancholy
who forgets his own,"
Marcoul answers him.

42.
"Everyone must pray
to lengthen his life,"
so says Salemons.
"The poor wretch   250
needs to accept or deny everything,"
Marcoul answers him.

43.
"Nothing can happen
as surely as death,"
so says Salemons.
"If one cannot flee death,
then to live is to languish,"
Marcoul answers him.

44.
"For a long time God has allowed
people to live and to sin,"   260
so says Salemons.
"But who does not repent
when his guard is down and he gets caught?"
Marcoul answers him.

45.
"He who thinks himself busy,
must plan well,"
so says Salemons.
"He who steers clear of knowledge
commits a mortal sin,"
Marcoul answers him.   270

46.
"He who knows not what to do
is very ill at ease,"
so says Salemons.
"Thus it is with grave sin:
you always pay for it,"

Marcoul answers him.

47.
"From the too fickle man
spring all misfortunes,"
so says Salemons.
"He who is not afraid to sin   280
draws trouble upon himself,"
Marcoul answers him.

48.
"It is good to undertake a job
that one can finish,"
so says Salemons.
"All good things are foreign
to a frequent sinner,"
Marcoul answers him.

49.
"Thus it is with sin:
he who loves it cherishes it,"   290
so says Salemons.
"Little does he know of praise
who does not recognize his danger,"
Marcoul answers him.

50.
"From upholding sin
great harm can come,"
so says Salemons.
"When the fool gets his wish,
he thinks little of dying,"
Marcoul answers him.   300

51.
"Wicked sinning
begins with weak knowledge,"
so says Salemons.
"He who amasses and doesn't gives back
pays with his soul,"
Marcoul answers him.

52.
"All sinners want so much
they well deserve to be chastised,"
so says Salemons.
"To live comfortably in this life   310
is to be fretting and fuming in the other,"
Marcoul answers him.

53.
"He who has his wits about him
surely must want to live,"
so says Salemons.
"He who has neither common sense nor power
has the devil to pay,"
Marcoul answers him.

54.
"I consider foolish and drunk
 the old man who thinks he has lived enough,"   320
so says Salemons.
"It is evident that
he should never write,"
Marcoul answers him.

55.
"Sin is a very serious thing,
but everyone dares to do it,"
so says Salemons.
Salomon:
"However, the soul is imprisoned
where nothing rests,"
Marcoul answers him.   330

56.
"He who is overwhelmed
cannot be overjoyed,"
so says Salemons.
"Death, which has no pity,
has disheartened many,"
Marcoul answers him.

57.
"Death has noble power
over all living creatures,"
so says Salemons.
"Nothing has such great jurisdiction   340
with less courtesy,"
Marcoul answers him.

58.
"He who put it on a pedestal
gave it great power,"
so says Salemons.
"He did not forget himself,
nor will he spare another,"
Marcoul answers him.

59.
"Everyone hates death,
because no one enjoys it,"   350
so says Salemons.
"He who feels despicable and filthy
is wrong to want to live,"
Marcoul answers him.

The End

Version E

13.
Salemon: The ewe that is closely shorn
                  often moves
                  to find shade.
Marcouz: The well-dressed whore
                  often prances in the street
                  to show off her body.

15.
Salemon: One should seek and choose
                  a good doctor
                  to heal one's pains.
Marcouz: The whore prepares herself,
                  makes herself up,   10

and looks at herself carefully
to find bawdy fellows.

16.
Salomon: Virgil and Aristotle
learned much of note
through their study.
Marcouz: The whore is stupid
who makes the sage foolish
in her company.

18.
Salomon: The nettle is sharp.
Crazy is he who plants it;   20
parsley would be better.
Marcouz: He who frequents a whore
is well on the path
toward exile.

Version F

12.
Salemon: The pheasant has
very shiny plumage
and pretty eyes.
Marcoul   The whore has a pretty headscarf
answers: and soft face,
but her ass is ugly.

15.
Salemon: A worthy woman, naked,
stays in her home
to protect her body.   10
Marcoul   The well-dressed whore
answers: prances in the street
to show off her body.

Version G
The Discussion of Marcou and of Salmon

1.
Salmon: Misery and war
are the devastation and destruction

of the earth.

Marcou: From the whore come evil
and deadly wars,

....

2.

Salmon: He knows how to waste his time
who wants to build a sluice
to hold back the Loire.

Marcou: Common whores   10
and born peasants
are not to be believed at all.

3.

Salmon: He who favors a thief
in his house,
suffers damage.

Marcou: He who favors a whore,
ends up crying,
when he realizes it.

4.

Salmon: The little caterpillar
eats the new shoots   20
and the cabbage leaf.

Marcou: The whore dresses,
provides for herself and feeds
on the fool's money.

5.

Salmon: When a goat is born,
you can tell for sure:
its butt is white.

Marcou: When a man says, "Take this,"
the whore says "Come,
sit here on the bench."   30

6.

Salmon: He who chases a fox
covers little ground
and often turns around and around.

Marcou: He who pursues a whore

when she is sneaking away,
takes many steps in vain.

7.

Salmon: He who is sick
will do well
if he escapes alive.

Marcou: He who trusts a whore   40
will be left
with neither coat nor cape.

8.

Salmon: He who raises a churl
and caresses him softly,
only makes him worse.

Marcou: He who dishonors a whore
and beats her and mistreats her,
only makes her better.

9.

Salmon: The little chick
is delicious with grease   50
and roasted with pepper.

Marcou: If a whore has no wine,
she looks for a trick
to get something to drink.

10.

Salmon: Some people hunt the deer
in the woods and in the plain,
who then lose it completely.

Marcou: Some people clothe the whore
and feed her with their bread
and another fucks her.   60

11.

Salmon: An unguarded pear tree
is often shaken
as long as it has fruit to give.

Marcou: A whore will appreciate you
as long as she knows
that you have money to spend.

12.

Salmon: The ripe pear
             is worth more than the hard one:
             this you know well.

Marcou: The whore has such a
             disposition: 70
             she takes care of no one
             who has nothing.

13.

Salmon: The rabbit hides
             deep in the earth
             so it will not be caught.

Marcou: With a laugh, the whore steals so much
             from the scoundrel
             that he is miserable.

14.

Salmon: The rooster on the manure pile
             scratches the straw   80
             to find the grain.

Marcou: The whore makes quick work
             of emptying the change purse
             hanging at the yokel's ass.

15.

Salmon: A saddled horse
             is quite ready
             to make a journey.

Marcou: A whore bent over
             is quite ready
             to fuck and to fart.   90

16.

Salmon: The yokel's oxen
             make the bread
             that people live on.

Marcou: He wears himself out in vain
             who thinks he can kill a whore
             with his cock.

17.

Salmon: Garlic sauce is no good
if it is not well crushed
and vigorously ground.

Marcou: The whore is lost   100
if she is not well beaten
and often mistreated.

18.

Salmon: Summer is very beautiful,
as is the flower in the fields,
of which there are so many.

Marcou: If you trust a whore,
you will lose with a laugh
all that you have.

19.

Salmon: Never will a trail appear
that a snake makes   110
on a dark rock.

Marcou: Never is a hidden whore
proven guilty
if she is not caught in the act.

20.

Salmon: At the mouth of an oven
there is often heat;
grass will never grow there.

Marcou: You can be sure:
never will a whore's ass
be without shit.   120

21.

Salmon: You should not sow
in sand by the sea:
never will grain grow there.

Marcou: He wastes his words
who tries by reason
to scold a whore.

22.

Salmon: One spreads birdlime

	where one has seen	
	birds return.	
Marcou:	A whore looks for a fair	130
	where she hopes to find	
	plenty of goods.	

23.

Salmon:	Don't feed the hawk,
	thus it will be better
	at hunting water fowl.
Marcou:	Mistreat the whore,
	and keep her downtrodden;
	she will hold you dear.

24.

Salmon:	He who runs after dice	
	is foolish and crazy:	140
	for soon he will be naked.	
Marcou:	He who keeps a whore	
	suffers for it:	
	soon he will be devastated.	

25.

Salmon:	I think he is a fool	
	who hides hot coals	
	in his shirt.	
Marcou:	He deserves to sleep on straw	
	who gives his money	
	to an old whore.	150

26.

Salmon:	A quarrel and hatred
	cause two good friends
	to part company.
Marcou:	The cleverness of whores
	makes first cousins
	mortal enemies.

27.

Salmon:	Praise the peacock,
	then it shows off
	its tail.

Marcou: A well-dressed whore   160
         shows off in the street
         to garner praise.

28.
Salmon: Throw into the depths
         either stick or stone:
         it will get even wetter.
Marcou: Give to a whore
         both today and tomorrow:
         she will only get prouder.

29.
Salmon: He deserves to lose his land
         who grants protection   170
         to a traitor.
Marcou: He who hands over
         his possessions to a whore
         deserves to go begging.

30.
Salmon: Have you ever seen a donkey
         leave fine hay
         to eat thistle?
Marcou: Have you ever seen a whore
         leave a good lover
         for a wretched scoundrel?   180

31.
Salmon: He who wants to measure
         the drops in the sea
         is mad as can be.
Marcou: He who holds in his hand
         a whore's promise,
         gets a bad deal.

32.
Salmon: He who recognizes his crime
         is crazy if he blames it
         on someone else who's helpless.
Marcou: He who goes empty-handed   190
         to solicit a whore

commits great folly.

33.
Salmon: A servant will not be left alone
         if he doesn't get out of the way
         when someone cries, "Look out!"
Marcou: To catch a whore,
         a man can't go wrong
         with a sackcloth cloak.

34.
Salmon: He who sees the sun
         red in the morning,   200
         should expect rain.
Marcou: A beautiful whore
         hatches a plot behind the back
         of one who will go begging.

35.
Salmon: The seas are huge,
         the sun is bright,
         and the moon is white.
Marcou: He who would like to have
         a whore whenever he wants
         grabs her by the neck.   210

36.
Salmon: No usurer
         will ever have as much money
         as his heart would like.
Marcou: Never in her life
         is a whore as satisfied
         as her heart would like.

37.
Salmon: Pack a mare
         with either lead or silver,
         it doesn't care which.
Marcou: A whore doesn't care   220
         who mounts her ass:
         all are the same to her.

38.
Salmon: A house in flames
          soon burns to the ground
          when it catches fire.
Marcou: A whore in make-up
          is soon laid
          when she sees money.

39.
Salmon: Neither falcon nor hawk
          is very easy   230
          to tame.
Marcou: The lowly whore
          is not attracted
          by any act of kindness.

40.
Salmon: The fat little pig
          does not seek a clean place,
          but looks for muck.
Marcou: ....
          ....
            240

Version H

In a tricky guise
the conversation is crafted
that I want to recount to you.
Theologians,
and you, scholars,
physicians, doctors,
listen to this well.
Don't forget any of it;
it is to your benefit.
I composed part of it,
I left out the ugly parts;
I don't know who says it.

6.
"I think he's a fool
Who hides hot coals

In his shirt."
"He deserves to sleep on straw
Who gives his money
To a nun."

16.
"The mouse gnaws
the little nut so much
that he makes a hole in it."
"The loose woman takes
money from the boy
and then shows him the door."

Version I

20.
"The mule in the prairie
has a bad bed
that is made of rotten hay,"
so says Salemons.
"Under beautiful clothing,
the filthy, stinking ass
of a beautiful whore,"
Marcous answers him.

23.
"Fire in the forest
burns all around   10
whatever it touches,"
so says Salemons.
"The whore breaks her promise:
she doesn't care why,
as long as she makes a profit,"
Marcous answers him.

27.
"Foolish is he who orders the wolf
in the wooded countryside
to watch over his lambs,"
so says Salemons.   20
"And the whore often asks
the simpleton

for food and clothing,"
Marcous answers him.

28.
"The deer goes to a place
where it knows the land is cleared:
there it eats all it wants,"
so says Salemons.
"The whore knows how
to get money out of a simpleton   30
by ingenious tricks,"
Marcous answers him.

29.
"God didn't make a fish
that can live for a long time
far away from water,"
so says Salemons.
"The whore and the scoundrel
challenge each other to drink
until they are drunk,"
Marcous answers him.   40

33.
"The frog in the marsh
is in a good place
as long as the water is good,"
so says Salemons.
"The whore takes instantly:
he who gives her more
is just as disgraceful,"
Marcous answers him.

[*In the margin under column a, fol. 1, the scribe has added these 4 lines, written in red.*]

"Beside a great valley,
a great mountain,"   50
so says Salemons.
"Beside a great ass,
a great cunt,"
Marcous answers him.

Version J

43.
"From the white hunting dog,
a great leap in the heather,"
so says Salemon.
"From the fat worthless woman,
a huge, silent fart,"
Marcou answers him.

The Disputation between Marcolf and Salomon

(Old French)

Introduction and Translation
by Stephanie A. Viereck Gibbs Kamath

Introduction

T HE *DISPUTATION* SURVIVES UNIQUELY amid the miscellaneous contents of a late thirteenth- or early fourteenth-century manuscript roll.[1] The roll is English in its creation and provenance. In addition to the *Disputation*, the roll, written in multiple hands, contains formulary letters in French that name English places such as London and Hingham; a Latin *Confiteor* (a general confession of sins, to be said at the beginning of a mass), with annotations in both French and English; a seven-stanza French poem on the hours of the cross (times of the day associated with stages in Christ's Passion); and the letter of Prester John.[2] Like other French texts in the Solomon and Marcolf debate tradition, this *Disputation* has no narrative episodes. Instead, it alternates between two speakers: Salomon, whose pronouncements draw upon written authority, and Marcolf, whose responses are grounded in quotidian experience. Yet

---

[1] Formerly belonging to the Jenkins and Harries families of Crockton (Shropshire), it is now held by the Shropshire Archives in Shrewsbury, as Manuscript Roll 6000/12692. The roll comprises five membranes, and the *Disputation* appears on the back of membranes 3–5. I am grateful to archivists Helen Haynes and Sal Mager for confirming the correct reference and checking bibliography.

[2] The last item, a copy of the Insular rather than the Continental or Liège versions of the letter, signed by William (Willelmus) de Hay, has attracted the most scholarly attention, as reflected in catalogue titles for this miscellaneous roll (for example, see Ker, *Medieval Manuscripts*, 4:287–88; Hunt, "Un nouveau manuscrit"). But the *Confiteor* and the poem on the hours may be more relevant companion texts to the *Disputation*, given its unusual interest in afterlife punishments and reform, such as Marcolf's consignment of sinful knights and lawyers to hellfire and the devil Beelzebub.

certain elements differ so notably from tradition that this curious, brief poem merits attention in its own right. The obsessive concern with female sexuality for sale and the scatological language characteristic of most of the *Salemon and Marcoul* texts featured in the previous chapter are not found here; the speakers' perspectives on women do mark the breaking point of the debate, but the very presence of a breaking point, like the subsequent identification of Salomon as the contest's definitive winner, also sets this text apart. The *Disputation* is also unusual because of the perspectives distinguishing its speakers and the form and order of their speeches.

This *Disputation* offers not so much amusing pairings of utterances lofty and gross as a reflection on the difference between formulating ideals and practicing observation: Salomon speaks proscriptively of what should be, relying on books and records; Marcolf denotes what is, with grim speculation as to what will be, in this world and the next. Marcolf's responses contain undeniably parodic elements—the title "son of the devil" (24)[3] at the conclusion of his first stanza responds to Salomon's proposed "son of God" at the end of the preceding stanza (10)—yet there is never quite the same distance in register observable in other French debates between these speakers, and at moments the two voices are almost indistinguishable (see, for example, 184–86).[4] Marcolf's description of misbehaviors, particularly in his longest stanza, critiquing clerks, actually resembles that found in extremely orthodox texts such as John Mirk's *Festial*, a sermon collection probably also created in Shropshire, in the late 1380s.

Whereas most *Salemon and Marcoul* texts neatly balance in syntax equally pithy proverbial statements, the *Disputation* is divided into irregular stanzas comprising varying numbers of roughly octosyllabic lines arranged in rhymed couplets. In the first four exchanges, Salomon consistently offers ten-line stanzas to which Marcolf responds with stanzas of varying longer lengths; the biblical king runs longer in a stanza introducing the subject of clerks, however, and thereafter both speakers offer stanzas of irregular length; in fact, the only subsequent spate of ten-line stanzas in the poem is introduced by the peasant (beginning at line 157).

---

[3] Numbers in parentheses refer to lines in the *Disputation*, unless otherwise noted.

[4] Study of a fifteenth-century English compilation including French exchanges between Solomon and a foul-mouthed Marcolf (siglum C) notes that the French word *desputeyson* (disputation) internally echoes the sound of the repeated insult *pute* (whore) (Downes, "Minding Shirley's French" 292). There is less justification for attributing such wordplay to the title of this *Disputation*, as Marcolf's denigrative terms are relatively restrained ("foolish women" fairly renders the source's "femmes foles," e.g., 81, 97) and even Marcolf's concluding condemnation employs the rhetoric of inversion, declaring all women never unfaithful (to Eve's negative exemplar), rather than making more straightforward or crude accusations of sexual misconduct (213–16).

Content, rather than form or register, gives order to this piece; Salomon and then Marcolf describe, in a single stanza each, ten demographic groups: Christians, kings, bishops, priests, clerks, knights, merchants, members of religious orders, lawyers, and women. Although Marcolf declares the subject of women closed in the last line of his relatively restrained stanza of condemnation—"enough on this matter" (218)—Salomon for the first time revisits a prior subject, offering an additional stanza that contradicts Marcolf's assessment of women. The five lines that immediately follow are not assigned to either disputant, although the first unassigned line completes a couplet begun by Salomon's concluding speech. The opening of the third-person announcement of Marcolf's defeat in disputation thus echoes the last word of the last line ascribed to Salomon, the anachronistically invoked name of the Virgin Mary (225). Our appreciation of the *Disputation*'s exceptional features can thus benefit from considering how interests in social types and salvific meditations, particularly those of Marian devotion, are similarly interconnected in other medieval literatures, most notably in estates satire, which identifies the groups critiqued by their social status or 'estate.'[5]

Le livre des manières, ca. 1174–78, ascribed to Étienne de Fougères (d. 1178), chaplain to King Henry II of England's Plantagenet line, is the earliest recorded example of the estates satire tradition. Like the *Disputation*, this Francophone yet English poem survives in a single manuscript. More regular in form than the *Disputation*, the octosyllabic monorhymed quatrains of the *Livre* treat a succession of demographic groups resembling, although not exactly matching, that found in the later, briefer work: in the first half of the *Livre*, kings, clergy, and knights follow one another as subjects; the second half of the poem deals in turn with peasants, the bourgeoisie (merchants and artisans), and women. The *Livre* expounds the ideal functions and rebukes the common faults of each group without any explicit division into dialogue, although the text's editor Anthony Lodge has suggested that at least five of the six groups do divide roughly into two contrasting sections, possibly suggesting the idea of a more explicitly dialogic text.[6] In contrast to the *Livre*, the *Disputation*'s omission of peasants as a discrete subject and its additional attention to lawyers are interesting; like the *Disputation*'s introductory consideration of the generic Christian and separation of the subjects of bishop and priest from that of those in religious orders, these

---

5   On the *Disputation*'s affiliation with estates satire as a distinguishing feature, see also Schulze-Busacker, *La Didactique profane*, 120–21; Hunt, "Solomon and Marcolf," 205. Jill Mann's classic *Chaucer and Medieval Estates Satire* offers a more general introduction, listing typical ordering of estates on 203–6.

6   See Lodge, "L'œuvre et son intérêt littéraire," 23–24; Lodge, "Literary Interest," 483, 492–95 (especially 495). For modern French translation, see the *Livre* edition of Jacques T. E. Thomas.

alterations break down the *Livre*'s more strictly ordered vision of social roles, summarized between its two sections as the triad that is often called "the three orders" of prayerful clerks, protective knights, and laboring peasants.

The *Disputation* actually recalls the *Livre*'s consideration of peasants when Marcolf alludes to the sufferings of peasants in thrall to misbehaving knights (137–38). Yet these lines appear within Marcolf's stanza on knights, which concludes by threatening erring chivalric lords with hellfire; such a setting constitutes a significant departure from the *Livre*'s presentation of peasant woes in preface to an admonition that those in whom such treatment sparks rebellion are like unto Cain. The *Disputation*'s anomalous attention to lawyers may reflect a specific reading community rather than changes in social order or its perception; formulary letters are found in the same roll as this text. Similarities in the conclusion of the *Livre* and the *Disputation* may prove to be of greater interest than such textual divergences, however; both treat women as the final social category, and the *Livre*'s author then brings his poem to its end by repenting his youthful concupiscence and invoking a plethora of saints, including, prominently, the Virgin Mary, amidst grim reminders of death and threats of last judgment.

Perhaps the nature of Salomon's triumph at the conclusion of the *Disputation* and Marcolf's interest in the afterlife draw from this precedent. Certainly, the announcement of Salomon's victory through Marian devotion in the *Disputation* provides a curious counterpoint to the penultimate contest between Solomon and Marcolf within the narrative portion of the Latin *Dialogue of Solomon and Marcolf*, in which Solomon flip-flops between praise, condemnation, and then again praise of women, derailed from his initial position due to a Marcolf-orchestrated siege of his palace by angered prostitutes (*S&M* 2.15–18). Praiseworthy female characters also end a dispute with a churlish Marcolf-like figure in the allegorical *Pilgrimage of Human Life* (*Pèlerinage de la vie humaine*), a fourteenth-century French verse narrative written by the Cistercian monk Guillaume de Digulleville (or Deguileville).[7] Although markedly different in form and length, the *Pilgrimage* shares the *Disputation*'s interest in Marian devotion and clerical reformation, and only the help of the lady Reason (Raison), authorized by the lady God's Grace (Grace Dieu), enables the narrating pilgrim to pass the obstruction of the obstinate and unlettered Rude Wit (Rude Entendement).

In the earliest (ca. 1331) version of Digulleville's *Pilgrimage*, Reason frees the pilgrim with reference to Solomon and Proverbs 26:4:

---

[7]   Like the author's name, the poem and its title have variant forms; I employ the name commonly used for the earliest circulating version, drawn from its 1893 edition, with the addition of a modern French accent.

> Va, dist elle, hardiement
> Sans douter Rude Entendement,
> Rien ne li di ne ne respon,
> Quar la doctrine Salemon
> Est c'on ne respongne nul mot
> A cil c'on voit et treuve sot.[8]

"Go along boldly," she said, "without fearing Rude Wit. Say nothing to him and do not answer him, for Solomon teaches us not to answer a word to someone we find to be a fool."[9]

The pilgrim queries this instruction with reference to Proverbs 26:5, insisting that

> pres en suiant
> Salemon dit tout autrement
> Quar il dit c'on li respongne
> Pour li monstrer sa vergonge.[10]

"right after that, Solomon says something quite different. He says that one should answer him in order to put him to shame."[11]

In the revised *Pilgrimage* (ca. 1355), however, Reason assists the pilgrim without mention of Solomon.[12] Perhaps the *Disputation*'s triumphant exclamation of Salomon's superiority in debate, not found in other versions of these characters' interaction, reflects possible concern about the wisdom of such contests.

Ultimately, the *Disputation* may relate more closely to later medieval Anglophone poems within the Solomon and Marcolf tradition than to either the Latin or other Francophone texts. It is tempting to compare this Shopshire-circulated text with John Audelay's fifteenth-century use of Marcolf's voice as a vehicle for social critique,[13] while John Lydgate's possible involvement in the 1426 English verse translation of Digulleville's *Pilgrimage*[14] and the interest

---

[8] Digulleville, *Pèlerinage* (ed. Stürzinger), lines 5636–40.
[9] Digulleville, *Pilgrimage* (trans. Clasby), 76.
[10] Digulleville, *Pèlerinage* (ed. Stürzinger), lines 5641–46.
[11] Digulleville, *Pilgrimage* (trans. Clasby), 77.
[12] Compare Digulleville, *Pélerin du vie*, lines 7325–26.
[13] Green, "Marcolf the Fool."
[14] Early editors Furnivall and Locock assigned the authorship of translation to Lydgate; his authorship has been queried since then but appears likely (Green, "Lydgate and Deguileville Once More"; Kamath, *Authorship*, 141n6). Although the English verse *Pilgrimage* translates the revised version of the French *Pilgrimage* that omits reference to Solomon's advice on debating fools, the English translator slightly lengthens Rude Wit's experiential knowledge claims (*Pilgrimage*, ed.

in estates satire evident throughout Lydgate's corpus, most obviously in his English translation of the *Danse Macabre*, lend greater interest to Lydgate's references to the strife between Solomon and Marcolf in his minor poems.[15]

Notes on this Translation

This translation is based upon Tony Hunt's critical edition.[16] His assignment of stanzas to speakers as well as his notation of lacunae due to stains in the manuscript (43, 45, 49) are reproduced without comment, and I translate his conjectures of partially obscured lines (44, 50, 138, 196). An error in editorial line numbering, skipping three lines between 216 and 220, has been corrected; otherwise, line numbers correspond to Hunt's edition, but noted every ten (not eight) lines. The normalized alignment of his edition is also followed, though line 146 appears in the left-hand margin in the manuscript roll.[17] While maintaining the number of lines per stanza, I have rearranged individual lines' contents and not attempted to reproduce the rhyme.

I am grateful to William D. Paden, Géraldine Veysseyre, and Matilda Bruckner, for their excellent advice, swiftly and kindly given. Any remaining faults are entirely my own.

Furnivall and Locock, lines 10677–86; cf. *Livre du pèlerin*, ed. Edwards and Maupeu, lines 7164–66) and depicts Rude Wit ultimately rejecting the "proverbys" of Reason (*Pilgrimage*, ed. Furnivall and Locock, line 10942), whereas the French source refers only to her "paroles" (words) (*Livre du pèlerin*, ed. Edwards and Maupeu, line 7312). An independent fifteenth-century anonymous English prose translation of the earlier *Pilgrimage* version also survives, which includes the direct reference to Solomon's advice on debating fools (Digulleville, *Pilgrimage of the Lyfe of the Manhode*, lines 3053–59).

15 See Schieberle, "Proverbial Fools."

16 Hunt, "Solomon and Marcolf," 206–213. Hunt's full essay edits two different anonymous French verse dialogues, drawn from different manuscripts: "La deyputeysun," translated in the current chapter, and, as an appendix, a copy of a "Salemon and Marcoul" dialogue, translated in chapter 2. Care is necessary to avoid confusion. For example, Schieberle and Downes each use "deyputeysun" to refer to Hunt's appendix text, although Hunt employs this term only for the text translated here, probably to avoid confusion and because alternative spellings are used in the manuscript copies of the appendix text that use this term; for example, a copy beginning "Ci (com)mence de Salemon" refers on the current first folio to what follows as a "desputaison" (Paris, Bibliothèque nationale de France, MS fr. 25545).

17 Hunt, "Solomon and Marcolf," 210n31.

Translation

Here Begins the Disputation between Marcolf and Salomon

Salomon:
Whoever desires to serve God
should always do His will:
he should seek God's kingdom first,
leave all evils and do good;
he should love the holy church
and honor his father and mother;
his neighbor he should also love,
and do good to him as much as himself;
whoever lives in this manner
can be called the son of God.   10

Marcolf:
Certainly, sir, you have spoken well.
But hear me a little
and I will tell you what the people do
who love the goods of this world:
when they should go to church,
they head off to the markets to win profit;
touring their fields and their woods
delights them more in truth
than divine service,
as is apparent in the holy church,   20
and they love drinking more
than God and Saint Mary;
and whoever lives in this manner
can be called the son of the devil.

Salomon:
The king of a realm, if he lives well,
will uphold the right above all things;
he should govern well his kingdom
and maintain the peace.
he will hold fast to his word
and improve his realm;   30
he should not credit falseness
nor act as false men do;

thus should king and prince live,
as we find in our book.

Marcolf:
Certainly, sir, you speak well.
Neither king nor prince, for any cause,
should ever be false or speak ill,
but I will tell you truly, dear sir,
this rule fails everywhere.
You will hardly find, low or high,   40
one who will not lie for gain:
for now love and right fail
in all [...]s, this we see well,
those who never for any reason fear God
who maintains and formed them all
fear [...] will strongly avenge himself.

Salomon:
Bishops should often preach
and counsel the people well,
and nourish [...] clothe
the poor who are in need.   50
To their office pertain
alms, counsel, and preaching,
for they stand in the stead of our Lord;
let them keep souls from dark places
and draw the people away from evil
that they may please God.

Marcolf:
True it is, they should preach well.
But I will tell you something:
the most part of them, as you should know
are not now well educated   60
as they once were:
now they are elected by friends
and not for their learning,
and this is a sin and great folly.
And know, sir, truly,
preaching is now little loved,

pride and covetousness hold such power
that the holy church is almost forgotten.

Salomon:
A priest should love holy church
and speak plainly the service: 70
he should not be a drunkard,
a glutton, a liar, or a lecher.
For the people, I promise you,
will take an example from him
so he should be their mirror,
that they may please our Lord;
for as the good priest does,
just so should do all who live well.

Marcolf:
Of a priest who serves all people
I will tell you the truth quickly: 80
often they are among foolish women
and they are full of idle words,
and by look and appearance
he shows what he thinks;
very often the priest does so
and falls into mortal sin.
For know this: whoever makes the wolf his shepherd,
will lose some of the best
and the most tender lambs;
so does the disloyal priest   90
to those whom he should keep well;
to those, he makes great encumbrance.

Salomon:
A clerk who wishes to learn well
should pay attention at school,
and go often to church
to sing and to read willingly;
he should not hang about foolish women
nor any place as much as school;
he should not use bows or arrows,
nor love falcons or dogs too much   100

but honor God above all things,
then he can have a good office;
if he knows such commendation,
he should be loved by all people.

Marcolf:
True it is, sir, truly,
but now clerks are the people
who cling more to the folly
that is called lechery
than any other people do
except courtiers, truly.   110
A clerk who associates with foolish women
will do little good at school,
for they prefer to go wandering,
pounding the waysides with their feet.
And he will sooner go to dine
than to the church for matins.
And the clerk who has such habits
can fail of a good office
if it's known through the country
what he knows of such life.   120

Salomon:
A knight who has large lands
sufficient for his living should not only keep
from destroying his poor people,
but live loyally on what he has.
Nor should he covet great jurisdiction,
but serve God and holy Mary:
then he carries the arms of righteousness
and the devil cannot harm him.

Marcolf:
Sir, in truth, you should know
the knights are prideful   130
and take too much from their people,
for at jousts and at tournaments
they are often in great difficulties
and they lose arms and horses.
Then the people aid their lords,

for it seems to them that all is theirs;
however much their peasants have,
their chivalry is costly.
But each such knight
will be a squire in hell,   140
where Beelzebub, in truth,
is called the lord of flies.

Salomon:
A merchant who wishes to live justly
should sell his merchandise
without fraud and swearing
and take reasonable profits,
not as much as he can,
but according to what he paid.
He should take reasonable profits,
especially of poor people.   150
If he can gain more from the rich,
he is not so much to blame:
for the rich who have enough
are in no way as oppressed
as the poor mendicants.
The merchant should consider this.

Marcolf:
Sir, merchants are hasty buyers
and they often spend beyond measure,
as much, when they gain nothing,
as when they do, as you know well.   160
And whoever wishes to spend lavishly
must take from any source.
For this reason very often
they take too much profit from the people,
but this law isn't at all helpful,
since they must pay for their gluttony.

Salomon:
The people who enter religious life
have no need to misbehave,
but to serve God loyally,
they should not only keep from false oaths,   170

but be obedient
as befits their order,
and often on bended knee
utter many prayers
and intercede for their benefactors:
then are they religious.

Marcolf:
Of misdeed they have no need,
but I will tell you what they do:
they do not enter into religion
for any real devotion   180
for the most part, truly,
but rather to gain sustenance
the majority enter, you should know.
But one who for the love of God
leaves sin and serves God,
that one is religious.

Salomon:
Master lawyers and advocates
who desire the love of God
should not maintain what is false
for their friends or for money,   190
but without falseness follow the right:
this is written in their books.

Marcolf:
Master lawyers and advocates
desire no other love
except great gain on every side,
since their selling, early and late,
is done to gain wealth,
whether by falseness or by truth.
By their treacherous science,
know this: they will lose   200
eternal life,
and they will receive pain
where Beelzebub is master and lord
full of malice and of ire.

Salomon:
A married woman should love
only her husband and have no other:
for God created marriage
so woman by right
must love none but her husband,
but always avoid foolish love.   210

Marcolf:
Women by nature
are obviously evil,
for the first was contrary;
for this cause, no maid or wife,
foul or fair, ever lived
who was ever unfaithful [to her model] in any way.
Of them I know no more to say:
there is enough on this matter.

Salomon:
You say, Marcolf, that woman never
was true nor ever shall be;   220
but you misspeak and trespass:
for a woman, you know this well,
carried Jesus who redeemed us,
who never sinned all of her life:
that was the lady holy Mary.

Thus Marcolf lost his mastery.
But Salomon gathered much sense
from the folly that Marcolf spoke.
God give us thus to learn
that we may render to Him our souls.   230

4

The Sayinges or Prouerbes of King Salomon, with the Answers of Marcolphus, Translated out of French into Englysshe

Introduction by Jan M. Ziolkowski
Edition by Edward Sanger and Jan M. Ziolkowski

Introduction

THE FULL TITLE OF THIS PIECE in early Modern English is *The Sayinges or Proverbes of King Salomon, with the Answers of Marcolphus, Translated out of French into Englysshe.*[1] The translation adheres to the text of the French *Salomon and Marcoul* (see chapter 2) as redacted in early print, where it comprised 23 double stanzas (as it does here).[2] Each begins with a general observation by Solomon, to which Marcolf retorts with a three-liner that invariably describes the habits of a whore. The rhyme scheme throughout is aabccb. As the colophon confirms, the poem was printed by Richard Pynson (ca. 1449–1529/30), probably about 1527. He was likely also the translator. At this juncture he would have been in his late seventies, an impressively advanced age given the demographics of the early sixteenth century.

Born in Normandy, the native Frenchman is known to have been a student at the University of Paris in 1464.[3] By 1482 he is documented across the Channel in London, where in 1490 he is attested as a bookseller. His first dated work, a book on grammar from ca. 1199, appeared in print in 1492.[4] Though also a

---

[1] STC 22899.

[2] *Les dictz de Salomon auecques les respo[n]ces de Marcon fort ioyeuses* ([Paris]: n.p., 1530), 8 unnumbered pages.

[3] The most comprehensive resource on Pynson's biography and bibliography remains Johnston, "The Career and Literary Publications of Richard Pynson."

[4] Alexander of Villa Dei, *Doctrinale* (STC 316). Pynson's second edition is STC 317. Although this is Pynson's earliest dated product, the corpus of works he produced before it is probably includes his *Donatus Melior* (STC 7014).

bookbinder (bindings with his device are extant), Pynson retains a reputation today first and foremost as a printer. By 1402 he possessed a workshop situated within the Temple Bar. This location accorded beautifully with his specialization in legal printing. Already long since naturalized, he was appointed King's Printer in 1506 and held the title officially from 1510. Additionally, from 1517 he was Printer to the City of London.[5]

William Caxton (ca. 1422–91) rightly deserves credit for being the founding father of English printing and for having first introduced the printing press into the country. In the generation that succeeded him, Pynson occupied second place in the trade. In the early Tudor period, he counts as the most important of major printers after another non-native contemporary of his, the Alsatian-born Wynkyn de Worde (died 1534/1535).

Trilingual and far more than merely tricultural, Pynson printed Latin schoolbooks, French legal writings, and English devotional and literary texts. In the last category, he produced for the first time in about 1492 a recension of Geoffrey Chaucer's *The Canterbury Tales* that owed much to Caxton's second edition.[6] Pynson's own second edition came out in 1526. His publication of the omnibus *Chaucer's Works* in 1526 is especially noteworthy for the scope of material, both genuinely Chaucerian and not, that it comprehends.[7] He published first printed editions of literary works in translation such as John Lydgate's versions of Giovanni Boccaccio's *The Fall of Princes* (1494)[8] and of Guido delle Colonne's *History of the Destruction of Troy* (1513);[9] Alexander Barclay's version of Sebastian Brant's *Ship of Fools* (1509),[10] from the Latin; an unidentified translator's version of *Mandeville's Travels* (around 1496);[11] and John Bourchier, 2nd Baron Berners's version of Jean Froissart's *Chronicle* (1523, 1525), from the French.[12] In total he issued forty-three translations, of which seven indicate the original author and seven the translator.[13]

A few signs, not especially telling, suggest that Pynson cherished a special commitment to religion. Thus he had membership in the Corpus Christi Guild in Coventry, served as churchwarden of St. Dunstan-in-the-West (where his death knell was rung), and published reforming texts, such as Latin sermons by Savonarola (in 1509) and Colet. In 1523 he printed the first edition of Thomas

---

[5]   Hosington, "Textual Standard-Bearers," 80.
[6]   STC 4084. See Gregg, "Early Printed Editions of the *Canterbury Tales.*"
[7]   STC 5086.
[8]   STC 3175 and, for the second edition of 1527, STC 3176.
[9]   STC 5579.
[10]   STC 3545.
[11]   STC 17246.
[12]   STC 11396. Compare STC 11397.
[13]   Hosington, "Textual Standard-Bearers," 80–81.

More's *Baravellus*, an attack on Luther in which the English controversialist assumes the persona of a Spanish student named Ferdinandus Baravellus.[14] He also brought into print many unquestionably orthodox texts.

Pynson's booklet *The Sayinges or Proverbes of King Salomon* amounts to eight pages, in quarto. The title page is embellished by a woodcut. It depicts a stock figure to the left, looking nothing like any of the Aesop-like peasant Marcolfs familiar from the Continent, and Solomon to the right.[15] The wording of the title, as throughout the text, is in textura.

Publishing is always an adventure in market testing, to find out what attracts readers. By proffering *The Sayinges or Proverbes of King Salomon* to prospective bookbuyers, what qualities of the book did our printer want them to appraise? As we have seen previously, Pynson was an old hand at printing translated adaptations of French literature. Much of the contents belonged to the sanitized world of high culture, but he may have allowed himself license to stretch the canon by putting into circulation the English for texts of a humbler sort and perhaps in the process to gauge the potential appeal of such low-brow stuff.[16]

Pynson's printing of the translation should not be taken necessarily as evidence of entrenched misogamy on his part. If anything, the tenor of the version in his adopted language looks to be the exception to the rule within his oeuvre. Far more salient is the pro-matrimonial stance of *In Praise of Marriage* (*In laudem matrimonii*), published in 1518.[17] This is the title assigned to a Latin speech that Cuthbert Tunstall (1474–1559), the Bishop of London, delivered to mark the betrothal of the new-born French Dauphin to the two-year-old English princess Mary (1516–58), daughter of King Henry VIII (1491–1547). Roughly a decade earlier, Pynson published the anonymous *Solemnities and Triumphs ... at the Spousals of the King's Daughter* (ca. 1509).[18]

By the same token, the misogyny of *The Sayinges or Proverbes of King Salomon* has been labeled French, to distinguish it from the norms of the English context within which Pynson was operating.[19] If the content put out by printers should be parsed for the perspectives it provides into their personal predilections (a dubious procedure in any case), Pynson's involvement in this gamut of other productions less overtly hostile to women could dispel speculation that he

---

[14] STC2 18088.5. Compare Thomas More, *Rosseus*, ca. 1523 (STC 18089).

[15] The Marcolf belongs to a type that has been called a "slouch-hat factotum" and "an interchangeable 'debating' figure." On the first, see Hodnett, *English Woodcuts*, no. 1491. On the second, see Coldiron, *English Printing*, 74, and Coldiron, "'La Femme Replique,'" 18.

[16] Though the essay makes no specific mention of *The Sayinges or Proverbes of King Salomon*, see Boffey, "Wynkyn de Worde."

[17] STC 24320.

[18] STC 17558.

[19] Coldiron, "Translation's Challenge," 340n28.

nurtured any notable personal hostility to what he would have considered both the fair and the weaker sex. To look at the philogynist end of the spectrum, eight leaves survive from a dream vision and allegory, presumably translated from a French original, that Pynson printed, perhaps in 1528, entitled *The Knowledge of Love* (*La conusaunce d'amours*).[20]

Nothing would have stopped Pynson from promoting views favoring matrimony in high-end publications, while catering to supposedly comic anti-feminism in fiction intended for different slices of society. Here we confront the reality that numerous translations from French to English in the late fifteenth and early sixteenth century relate to women and gender relations.[21] Pynson contributed to the negative side of this literary corpus by printing not only *The Sayinges or Proverbes of King Salomon* but also about 1510 the anonymous *The Smith that Forged Him a New Dame*, a work earlier printed by de Worde about 1505.[22] This verse fabliau tells how Christ manifested himself to a blacksmith who was married to a nag and how he enabled the smith to reforge his wife.

If the misogyny of the French poem was not what motivated Pynson to print the translation, could it have been aspects of the irreverence within the colloquy, such as the wink at prurience and obscenity? Was he drawn to the original because it contained dialogue and was in a sense a debate poem, in this instance with the opposition of piety and impiety as a dominant feature? We could turn our sights reasonably to William Horman's *Dialogue of the Tongue and the Belly* (*Dialogus lingue et ventris*), a text that Pynson may have printed in 1494.[23] Did the printer gravitate to the poem out of an awareness that its proverbs and broader sententiousness would have resonated splendidly with would-be readers?[24]

Would literary history have followed a different course if Pynson had chosen to focus on another variant from within the Solomon and Marcolf complex? After his era, the theme apparently dwindled in popularity in England, even as it spread with intensified vigor in Germany, Scandinavia, Italy, and elsewhere on the Continent. The reality that the 1492 printing of the English exists in only a single exemplar may offer another metric of England's inhospitability to Marcolf. Of countless explanations for this circumstance worth entertaining, one is that Shakespeare's enormously popular Falstaff may have usurped attention that in other cultures was paid to Marcolf. But other causes could explain

---

[20] STC 5631.

[21] Coldiron, "Translation's Challenge," 321.

[22] Pynson's printing is STC2 22653.7. The only nearly complete edition is from about 1565, by William Copeland. The same text has been published in Halliwell-Philipps, *Contributions to Early English Literature*, and in W. C. Hazlitt, *Remains of Early Popular Poetry of England*, vol. 3.

[23] STC 13808.

[24] Alexandra Gillespie, "'These Proverbs Yet Do Last,'" 220, 226.

why the latter fictional character faded away in the English-speaking world faster than elsewhere in Europe.

Note on the Edition

The text constitutes a letter-for-letter transcription of the printing from ca. 1527. One change is that for ease of reading, commas here have replaced the slash marks used there. Another is that in the indications of speakers the name Marcolphus has been standardized from different abbreviations. In the space to the right of the original, glosses of obsolete words and unfamiliar usages have been provided to help readers who might otherwise stumble over English from a half millennium ago. Line numbers are also given.

Edition

The sayinges or prouerbes of king Salomon, with the answers of Marcolphus, translated out of frenche in to englysshe.

Salomon:
HE that wyll measure
Of all the sees the water
Is nat very sage.

Marcolphus:
He that holdeth in his honde
The faythe of an hore as a good bonde,   whore
He is full of rage.   rage = madness

Salomon:
Caste a stone at an ape
Or a staffe, if that he scape   escapes
The more wyll he mowe and moyle.   make faces and defile

Marcolphus:
Gyue to a hoore her askynge   10
Outher late or in the mornynge   outher = either
The more she wyll you dispoyle.

Salomon:
A house that in euery cornere
Letteth in wynde, sone burneth clere   burns brightly
Whan fyre therin taketh.   takes hold

Marcolphus:
A hoore that is gay
Is redy nowe and alway
Whan that she money seth.   seth = sees

Salomon:
Who so euer hath sycknesse
Is very ioyfull I gesse   20
Whan he with lyfe dothe scape.

Marcolph:
He that a hoore byleueth
Nothynge with hym abydeth
Nouther mantell nor cape.   nouther = neither

Salomon:
No man shall knowe or marke
A coler in the darke   coler = color
Paynted on a spoone.

Marcolphus:
Nor a preuy hoore   preuy = secret, personal
Taken shall be at any houre
In doynge, by nyght or noone.   30 in sexual intercourse

Salomon:
A conye hym selfe hydeth   conye = rabbit
And depely he ofte dyggeth
Yet at last is he take.

Marcolphus:
A hoore so moche pluketh   strips bare (by theft)
A man, and on hym laugheth
That she hym maketh leane as a take.   = as a tack

Salomon:
At a Ouen mouthe, that is hot

That thynketh yerbes shuld growe for the pot	yerbes = herbs
Of trouth he is begyled.	deceived

Marcolphus:
He that withouten fayle   40
Putteth his hande to a hores tayle
Shall haue it soone defyled.

Salomon:
Charge vpon a beest   charge = load
Money or leade in a chest
Whether, they nothyng care.   whether = whichever

Marcolphus:
A hoore taketh no kepe   has no concern
What man on her dothe leape
All is to her one fare.

Salomon:
A horse that his brydell hath on
He is redy anon   50
For to go on his waye.

Marcolphus:
A hoore clothed gayly
Is soone made redy
To begyn her ioye.

Salomon:
He that in his house as lefe   as lefe = gladly
Cheryssheth a thefe
Shall receyue great domage.

Marcolphus:
He that an hoore kepeth to honoure
At thende he shall wepe and loure   = at the end, loure = scowl
Whan he knoweth her vsage.   60 her conduct

Salomon:
A man so longe may chase
Through woddes and playne percase   = perchance
That at last he shall be wery.

Jan M. Ziolkowski and Edward Sanger

Marcolphus:
Many a hoore oft clotheth
And brede to her gyueth
That with other she is more mery.

often clothes a whore
and gives her bread

Salomon:
The oxe of the villayne
His brede dothe often gayne
Wherwith he lyueth here.

villayne = peasant

Marcolphus:
He bosteth hym selfe in vayne
That thynketh a hoore certayne
To slee with his gere.

70

= slay with his sex organs

Salomon:
He that to a dogge sayth haue
He wyll anone his tayle waue
And than he hym fawneth.

have = hail, welcome

fawneth = show fondness

Marcolphus:
He that to a hoore sayth holde
She byddeth hym be bolde
All is redy that he commaundeth.

Salomon:
Men accompte them as wyse as fooles
That the burnynge coles
In their bosomes wyll hyde.

account

80

Marcolphus:
For a foole he is tolde
That wasteth all his golde
To clothe a hoores syde.

tolde = accounted

Salomon:
Stockfysshe is of valewe none
Except it be trewly layde upon
And often tourned and beaten.

stockfysshe = cod

Marcolphus:
A rybaude she is lost

harlot

If she be nat well beate and tost   tost = tossed
And vnder fote troden.   90

Salomon:
The ape is a beest lothsom
And of a counterfayte fasshyon
It hath so shorte a tayle.

Marcolphus:
So counterfayte is none parde   parde = by God!
But by money haue shall he   he shall have his will
Of a hoore his wyll without fayle.

Salomon:
The lytell cockerell
Eateth his meate well   his food
In crowynge he nedeth no scole.

Marcolphus:
A hoore her selfe clotheth   100
And also she fedeth
With the money of a foole.

Salomon:
An asse in close kept fast   in an enclosure
Ryseth yp in haste
Whan he seeth pasture.

Marcolphus:
He that a hoore for hym selfe kepeth
She often another in his sted taketh
Whan his money no longer wyll endure.

Salomon:
The thorne in a hedge taketh   grasps
And the woll of plucketh   110 plucks the wool off
Of shepe and of mottons.   and of wethers

Marcolphus:
A hoore plucketh away
The money day by day
Of all maner companyons.

Salomon:
Mortalyte and great warre
Be exyled farre
Fro all maner of men.

Marcolphus:
For a hoore all myschefe
Mortalyte, warre and great grefe
Commeth soone agayne.   120

Salomon:
The fawcon is well loued   falcon
And of the fawconer well reclaymed   falconer
By his gentle deporte.   by his well-bred behavior

Marcolphus:
He that a hoore wyll leade
Thorough the sees, in tyme of nede
Shall neuer haue good porte.

Salomon:
He is a fole without fayle
And leseth his trauayle   wastes his efforts
That layeth a fox to slepe.

Marcolphus:
He is more foole for certayne   130
That perceyueth a hoore wolde parte fayne   would gladly part
And seketh meanes her styll to kepe.

Salomon:
The fowler there his net layeth
Where as he comonly seeth
Byrdes fede and rest.

Marcolphus:
A hoore foloweth that waye
Where as she seeth a pray   prey
Of Rybawdes a great nest.   great swarm of rascals

Finis.
Cum privilegio.

Imprinted at London in flete strete by Ry-
charde Pynson: And be for to sell at ye signe of
saynt Iohnn Euangelyst in saynt
Martyns parysshe, besyde
Charynge crosse.

The End. Printed with privilege [i.e., duly authorized] in London on
Fleet Street by Richard Pynson, and for sale at the sign of Saint John
the Evangelist in Saint Martin's parish, by Charing Cross.

The wording proves that the seller was Robert Wyer, who was active from 1530
to 1556. On the location of his shop and home, see Plomer, *Robert Wyer, Printer
and Bookseller*, 2, 11; on his sale of this book, 54.

5

The Judgments of Solomon

(Old Russian)

Introduction by Sara Kate Heukerott
and Jan M. Ziolkowski

Translation by Sara Kate Heukerott

Introduction

THE FORMULATION OLD RUSSIAN applies to the language of the Slavic family in the East as it is attested in the earliest phase of its written survival. With the passage of time, this linguistic branch ramified into modern Russian, Belorussian, and Ukrainian. Although the oldest documents in Old Russian were probably composed in the tenth century, the first extant attestation of the Solomon cycle in this tongue comes in the late fourteenth-century *Explanatory Paleia* (*Tolkovaia Paleia*). This Christian exegetic work incorporates tales from the Old Testament and apocrypha, with incidental thrusts that polemicize against Judaism and Islam.[1]

The term *paleia* is a direct borrowing from the Greek, short for *Palaia Diatheke* or "Old Testament." Beside the *Explanatory Paleia,* two other specimens of the genre exist in Old Russian, namely, the *Shortened Chronographic Paleia* (*Kratkaia khronograficheskaia Paleia*) and the *Complete Chronographic Paleia* (*Polnaia khronograficheskaia Paleia*).[2] The present chapter offers in English a section from the *Complete Chronographic Paleia* that has become conventionally entitled *The Judgments of Solomon* (*Sudy Solomona*).[3]

---

[1] Dmitriev and Likhachev, *Pamiatniki literatury drevnej Rusi*, 541. For a list of published texts of the *Tolkovaia Paleia*, see Orlov, *From Apocalypticism to Merkabah Mysticism*, 72.

[2] For a list of published texts of the *Chronographic Paleia*, see Orlov, *From Apocalypticism to Merkabah Mysticism*, 74.

[3] For brief remarks on it, see Bondar', "Slavianskie Sudy Solomona," and Bondar', "K istorii teksta povestei o Solomone v Palee."

Sara Kate Heukerott and Jan M. Ziolkowski

Despite the undisputed Greekness of the keyword *paleia,* no one can ascertain when, where, or even from what language these materials pertaining to Solomon entered into Rus' (which corresponds to Ruthenia in Latin), the region inhabited by the Eastern Slavs. For many years a scholarly consensus that rested on the thinking and writing of Aleksandr Nikolaevich Veselovskii (1838–1906) advocated that the ultimate wellspring was Greek and Byzantine, perhaps initially by way of translations produced in the South Slavic region (see chapter 1). The Russian literary historian held that the origin of the text in Byzantium makes itself manifest already in the generic label *Paleia.*[4] His theory still carries conviction, but an alternative suggestion has been advanced that the narratives may be rendered into Old Russian from Hebrew archetypes in the twelfth or thirteenth centuries.[5] In addition, oral sources, themselves of heterogeneous provenance, are likely to have played at least a contributing role.[6] Much debate has raged over the degree to which Indian, Iranian, and Semitic civilizations shaped the essence of the Solomon cycle.

On a superficial level, proof of Hebrew influence at some juncture in the cycle's history can be detected in the wording here and there in the text. For example, the untranslated word *shamir* in "The Tale of How Kitovras was Captured by Solomon" refers in classical Hebrew to a very hard substance, probably diamond/adamant. The term is employed for the substance that Solomon uses to cut through stone when building the First Temple.[7] This usage appears in the Gemara, the portion of the Talmud comprising rabbinical commentary on the Mishnah. Similarly, the designation Malkatoshka combines the Hebrew *malkat* for "queen" and the Russian feminine diminutive suffix *-oshka.* This Russianized form stands in for the Hebrew *malkat sh'va* meaning "Queen of Sheba." Solomon's dealings with this female ruler from South Arabia are mentioned twice in the Bible (3 Kings [1 Kings] 10; 2 Chronicles 9). The neologism results from misunderstanding of the Hebrew *sh'va* as an ending rather

---

[4] Veselovskii, *Slavianskie skazaniia,* 81–83. In discussing the centaur Kitovras, Dumézil takes as a given that the Old Russian Solomon cycle is a translation from a Greek original (*Le problème des Centaures,* 272–73).

[5] Meshcherskii, "K voprosu ob izuchenii perevodnoj pis'mennosti Kievskogo perioda," 217. As Lunt and Taube note ("Early East Slavic Translations," 181), the Solomon cycle is not listed as a possible translation from Hebrew in Meshcherskii, *Istochniki i sostav drevnei slaviano-russkoi perevodnoi pis'mennosti.* Though Alekseev claims in a 1987 article that the cycle can be reliably identified as a translation from Hebrew ("Perevody s drevneevreiskikh originalov," 7), Lunt and Taube rebut his assertions convincingly ("Early East Slavic Translations," 157–60).

[6] Lunt and Taube argue that, in the absence of convincing testimony to the contrary, we must assume that the Russian Solomon cycle was translated from Greek or from Latin or other European texts. They also raise the possibility that some of the tales may not be direct translations at all, but rather written down from oral tradition ("Early East Slavic Translations," 160, 183).

[7] Goldwurm, *Tractate Gittin,* 68a2–68b2.

than as a second substantive.[8] On the one hand, Alekseev sees these instances as constituting evidence that the cycle was translated into Old Russian from Hebrew. On the other, Lunt and Taube make the case that they are likelier later glosses to the Slavic text added by someone with knowledge of the Semitic language. They note that *shamir* first surfaces in fifteenth-century copies of the cycle, that is, sometime after Hebrew began to be studied in Lithuania.[9]

In this text as well as in various others, the Queen of Sheba was a magnet who attracted in equal measures curiosity and quirky folklore.[10] For instance, she is described as being as hairy as a brush. The hirsuteness may have been hereditary, related to the seven years that Nebuchadnezzar, allegedly her offspring by Solomon, spent living like an animal, with uncut hair and nails (Daniel 4:33). The Queen's most pronounced characteristic, highlighted in the Bible, was her skill in riddling. One such challenge with which she confronts Solomon is a widely documented motif in folk literature, in which the person tested must separate by gender a crowd of young males and females in identical dress.[11]

In a seminal 1872 dissertation *Slavic Tales about Solomon and Kitovras and Western Legends about Morol'f and Merlin* (*Slavianskie skazaniia o Solomone i Kitovrase i zapadnye legendy o Morol'fe i Merline*), Veselovskii maintains that texts preserved in Slavic manuscripts played a key part in the development of the Solomon and Marcolf complex (see chapter 1). In the West, the medieval era witnessed momentous political and social transformations. The birth of feudalism and the emergence of chivalry and a lively urban lifestyle gave rise to new ideals and literary genres, such as the adventure tale and the fabliau, and old legends were reshaped to incorporate and reflect these changes. In Slavdom, by contrast, the Middle Ages were far more culturally uniform, and the stories of Solomon were preserved in forms much closer to their now-lost models.[12] For these reasons, Veselovskii concludes, the Slavic heritage can shed valuable light on the probable nature of the hypothetical prototypes.[13]

---

[8] Lunt and Taube, "Early East Slavic Translations," 158.

[9] Lunt and Taube, "Early East Slavic Translations," 158–59. See also Bondar', "K voprosu o evreiskikh istochnikakh paleinoi 'Povesti o Kitovrase.'"

[10] For the most thorough coverage of traditions transmitted in Hebrew and Arabic, see Lassner, *Demonizing the Queen of Sheba*.

[11] For other tests of gender, see Thompson, *Motif-Index of Folk-Literature*, 3:517–18: "*Test of sex of girl masking as a man: ball thrown into lap.* Girls spread legs to catch it, men not."

[12] The social structures of pre-imperial Rus' stand out most prominently in the *Paleia* in the mention of boyars. These were leading warriors invested by their prince with the right to collect tribute. See Hosking, *Russia and the Russians: A History*, 34–35, 48, 67–68.

[13] Veselovskii, *Slavianskie skazaniia*, 8–10.

The present translation follows Dmitriev and Likhachev.[14] They base their text on the *Complete Chronographic Paleia*, which, beyond putting the tales in a different order from the *Explanatory Paleia*, contains a greater number of them and also more explanatory excerpts from the Old Testament.[15] In keeping with Dmitriev and Likhachev, the English here omits the biblical passages. The two departures from this policy are the judgment "Of the Two Harlots" (based on 3 Kings 3:16–28) and the tale "Of Pharaoh's Aid" (3 Kings 3:1–2).[16] These exceptions are made because, in contradistinction to the other Old Testament excerpts in the *Complete Chronographic Paleia*, both of these narratives resemble the apocryphal sections of the cycle in tone and content. The relationship of the Old Russian *The Judgments of Solomon* in the *Paleia* to any standard text of the Bible is complex. A case in point is the reference to the aristocrat Dekir, whose name may allude to Solomon's official Ben-Deker or, in English, "son of Deker" (3 Kings 4:9). Direct quotations from the Bible have been identified in square brackets.

In the *Complete Chronographic Paleia*, the report of how Solomon caught Kitovras ("The *Paleia*'s Account of Kitovras") seems very truncated. Again conforming to the recension by Dimitriev and Lickachev, a translation of "The Tale of How Kitovras was Captured by Solomon" is included for the sake of completeness of plot. Taken from the late fifteenth-century Orthodox monk and scribe Efrosin, it is placed as an addition to the section on Kitovras from the *Paleia*.[17]

Explanation of the appellation Kitovras is in order: thanks to the impact of a widely read study by the comparative mythologist and philologist Georges Dumézil (1898–1986), the form has become generally recognized as a garbling of the Greek *kentauros* for centaur.[18] In Talmudic tradition, Solomon was occasionally matched with an evil spirit called Asmodeus (or Ashmedai) whom he captured to assist him in building the Temple.[19] This demon, who materializes

---

[14] Dmitriev and Likhachev, *Pamiatniki literatury drevnei Rusi*, 66–87. See also Prokhorov, "Sudy Solomona."

[15] Saint Petersburg, Rossiiskaia natsional'naia biblioteka (Russian National Library), Rukopisnye Knigi Sobraniia M.P. Pogodina, Number 1435, Laurentian Chronicle 333–46.

[16] The first of these two tales has a strange doublet in the story "Of the Two-Headed Man and His Children."

[17] Saint Petersburg, Rossiiskaia natsional'naia biblioteka, Kirillo-Belozerskoe sobranie im. MS Saltykova-Shchedrina (M.E. Saltykov-Shchedrin State Public Library), Kirillo-Belozersky Monastery, Number 11/1088. See Lur'e, "Une légende inconnue," and Bondar', "'O Kitovrase ot Palei' i drugie siuzhety knigopistsa Efrosina."

[18] Dumézil, *Le problème des Centaures*, 272. The modern Russian for centaur is *kentavr*. See also Mazon "Le Centaure."

[19] For more on the Talmudic tradition of Solomon and Asmodeus, see Goldwurm, *Tractate Gittin*, 68a1–68b4, and Davis, "Solomon and Ashmedai." For the latest on connections between Asmodeus and Kitovras, see Konstantin V. Bondar', "Etiud ob Asmodee i Kitovrase."

in the Book of Tobit, earned a niche in the apocryphal *Testament of Solomon*.[20] Dumézil inferred that in due course Asmodeus metamorphosed into the centaur Kitovras, first in Greek and later in Russian. He explained this transformation as owing to a coincidence in timing: Solomon's dethronement took place at the New Year, the same period with which the *kentauroi* or *kallikantzaroi* are associated in Greek Christianity.[21]

Beyond the conundra that may be explicable on the basis of Hebrew and Greek, the *Paleia* contains its share of difficulties that arise from the predictable provocations of seeking to understand the Russian language and culture of more than a half millennium ago. To single out one thorny word, the magical bird that has access to the *shamir* or diamond is identified as *nogot* or *kokot*. This term may be related to the modern verb *kokat*, meaning "to crack or break." In another example, the noun *kap* denotes an old unit of weight. More familiar terminology reflective of Russia includes the class of nobleman called a boyar and the measure of distance known as a verst (roughly equivalent to a kilometer).

Translation

The Judgments of Solomon

Of the Two Harlots

And in that time, Solomon prepared a great feast for his people. Then two harlots appeared before the king, and one woman said, "I am in grave misfortune, my lord. I and this friend of mine live together in the same house, where we were both born. I bore a son, and three days after I gave birth, this woman also bore a son. And there were only the two of us together, and there were no others with us in our house. And this woman's son died that night because she lay upon him. And having gotten up in the middle of the night, she took my child from my arms and put him to sleep on her breast and placed her own infant, who had died, by me. I got up in the morning to hold my baby, and I found him dead. And I perceived that this child was not my son whom I had borne." And the other woman said, "No, this is my son who is alive, and it is your son who has died." And they quarreled before the king. And the king said to them, "You speak thus: 'This is my son who is alive, and that woman's is dead.' And you say, 'No, the live one is my son, and yours is the one which has died.'" And the king said to his servants, "Cut this child who is alive in half on the floor, and give half to this woman and half to the other woman."

---

[20] Busch, *Das Testament Salomos*.
[21] Dumézil, *Le problème des Centaures*, 186, 272–73.

And the woman whose child was alive spoke out because she had become distraught for her son, and she said, "Let me remain in misfortune, my Lord. Give her this child, and do not destroy him with death." And the other woman said, "Let him be neither mine nor that woman's. But instead cut him in two." And the king said in response, "Give the child who is alive to the woman who said, 'Give him to this woman, and do not destroy him with death.' Let him be given to that woman, for she is his mother."

When all Israel had heard of this judgment made by the king, all the people feared the king's face, for they understood that the wisdom of God was within him so that he might to pass judgment and dispense justice.

Of Pharaoh's Aid

Solomon took in marriage the daughter of Pharaoh at the time when he was building the Holy of Holies. He sent his envoy to Pharaoh, with the message, "Father-in-law! Send me aid." Pharaoh selected six hundred men, knowing from his keenness of mind that they would die in that year: he wanted to test Solomon's wisdom. When the men were led in front of Solomon, the king, having seen them from afar, ordered that shrouds be sewn for all of them. He sent his envoy to Pharaoh, with the message: "Father-in-law! If you do not have anything in which to bury your dead, here are garments for them. Bury them in your own land."

The Tale of How Kitovras Was Captured by Solomon

At the time when Solomon was building the Holy of Holies, he had need to question Kitovras. His men found out where Kitovras lived, which was in a remote wilderness. Then, in his wisdom, Solomon had an iron cable and an iron noose forged, and wrote on the latter an oath in the name of God. He sent his best boyar with men and commanded him to bring wine and honey, and they took sheep's wool with them. The men arrived at Kitovras's dwelling, at his three wells, but he was not there. Following Solomon's instructions, they poured the wine and honey into the wells and covered the mouths of the wells with sheep's wool. They poured wine into two wells and honey into the third. And they hid themselves and watched in secret to see if he would arrive to drink water at the wells. And he came at once and, having stooped towards the water, he began to drink and said, "Every man, drinking wine, does not become wiser." Then he stopped wanting water and said, "You are wine, which brings joy to the heart of man," and he drank up all three wells. Then he wanted to rest for a little while, and since the wine was weakening him, he fell fast asleep. When the boyar had arrived, he chained him firmly by the neck, arms and legs. And when he came to, he wanted to set off. And the boyar said to him, "Sir, Solomon wrote the name of the Lord with an oath on the chains now upon you." He saw them on himself and set off meekly for Jerusalem to see the king.

His disposition was of the following sort. He walked not along a crooked path but along a straight one. And when he arrived in Jerusalem, they cleared a path in front of him and tore down houses. For he would not walk crookedly. They arrived at the house of a widow. And when the widow came outside, she cried out, beseeching Kitovras: "Sir, I am a poor widow. Do not abuse me!" He went round the corner, not having left his path, and broke a rib. And he said, "A soft tongue will break a bone." When he was being led through the marketplace, they heard a man saying, "Are there no shoes which will last for seven years?" and Kitovras laughed. And he saw another man who was practicing sorcery, and he laughed for a bit. And he saw a wedding that was being performed, and he began to weep. And when he saw a man who was wandering without direction, he led him to the path. And they brought him to the king's dwelling.

On the first day, they did not bring him to Solomon. And Kitovras said, "Why does the king not summon me to him?" And they told him, "He drank too much in the evening." Picking up a stone, Kitovras placed it upon another stone. And they told Solomon of what Kitovras had made. And the king said, "He orders me to drink drink upon drink." On the next day, the king did not summon Kitovras to him. And Kitovras said, "For what reason do you not lead me to the king, and why do I not see his face?" And they said, "The king cannot, because he ate a great deal yesterday." Kitovras removed the stone from the other stone.

On the third day, they said, "The king summons you." Kitovras measured out a switch of four ells and then went in before the king and bowed. He threw down the switch before the king and then was silent. The king, in his wisdom, explained the meaning of the switch to his boyars, saying, "Power has granted you all the known world, and you are not sated: you have captured me." And Solomon said to him, "I have brought you here not for my own want, but in the question of the plans for the Holy of Holies. I brought you in accordance with the command of the Lord, since I was commanded not to cut stone with iron."

And Kitovras said, "There is a small talon of the kokot bird called Shamir. The kokot keeps its offspring safe in its nest on a stone mountain in a distant wilderness." Solomon sent his boyar with his men to the nest in accordance with the instructions of Kitovras. Kitovras gave a white glass to the boyar and instructed him to hide himself from the nest: "As the kokot flies out, cover the nest with this piece of glass." The boyar set off for the nest; there were young birds in it, and the kokot had flown off in search of food. The boyar covered the mouth of the nest with the glass. The men waited there for a little while, and the kokot returned. It wanted to enter the nest. The chicks were cheeping through the glass, but it could not go in to them. Then it brought to the nest the Shamir, which it had kept safe in a certain place, and placed it on the glass, hoping to break through it. The men cried out and the kokot let the object go. And, having taken it, the boyar brought the thing to Solomon.

Solomon asked Kitovras, "Why did you laugh at the man who was asking for shoes that would last for seven years?" "I saw upon him," said Kitovras, "that he would not be alive in seven days." The king sent to check, and it was so. And Solomon said, "Why did you laugh at the man who was practicing sorcery?" Kitovras answered, "He was telling people hidden things, but he himself did not know that in the very ground below him was a hiding place with gold." And Solomon said, "Go, check this." And they checked, and it was so. And the king said, "Why did you cry when you saw the wedding?" And he said, "I was sad that the groom would not be alive in thirty days." And the king checked, and it was so. And the king said, "Why did you direct the drunken man to the path?" Kitovras answered, "I had heard from heaven that this man was pious and that it was fitting to help him."

Kitovras remained with Solomon until the completion of the Holy of Holies.

At that time, Solomon began to say to Kitovras, "Now I have seen that your power is like human power and that your powers are no greater than our powers, and they are the same." And Kitovras said to him, "King, if you want to see my power, then take this chain off me and give me the ring from your hand, so that you may behold my power." Solomon took the chains off him and gave him the ring. Kitovras ate it and spread his wings, and he threw and struck Solomon, throwing him to the end of the Promised Land. Solomon's wise men and scribes discovered this, and they sought and found Solomon.

There was always fear of Kitovras at night. The king built a bed and ordered sixty strong men with swords to stand round it. That is why it is written in the Scriptures [Song of Songs 3:7–8], "The bed of Solomon, sixty brave men from among the Israelites and from the lands of the north."

The *Paleia's* Account of Kitovras

Kitovras is a swift beast. Wise Solomon in his cleverness captured him. Kitovras has the torso of a man and the legs of a cow. According to tales, he carried his wife in his ear. With the following bit of cleverness they seized him. His wife spoke to a young man, her lover, thus: "My husband passes through many lands in the day and at night in order to arrive at a certain place where there are two wells. He drains both wells, having become parched." Solomon ordered that one of these be filled with wine, and the other with honey. Kitovras approached both wells and drained them. There they seized him while in a drunken sleep and chained him securely. For the strength in him was great. And they brought him to King Solomon. The king asked him, "What is the most precious thing on this earth?" He said, "Better than everything is your will." Just then he jerked and broke all his fetters and galloped off according to his own will.

Of the Two-Headed Man and His Children

When Kitovras was setting off for his people, he gave Solomon a man with two heads. This man settled into life among Solomon's people. And Solomon asked him, "Of what race are you? Are you man or demon?" The man answered, "I am a man from the people who live under the earth." And the king asked him, "Do you have a sun and a moon?" The man said, "From your west towards us the sun rises, and from your east it sets. So, when you have day, then we have night. And when it is night among you, then it is day among us." And the king gave him a wife. And there were born to him two sons: one with two heads and the other with one head. And their father had much property. And their father died. Said the two-headed brother, "Let us divide the property according to heads." And said the smaller brother, "We are two; let us divide the property in halves." And they came in dispute before the king. And the one-headed man said to the king, "We are two brothers. Let us divide the property in half." The two-headed brother said to the king, "I have two heads; I want to take two lots." The king in his wisdom ordered that vinegar be brought and said, "If you are two heads different in body, let me pour vinegar onto one head: if the other head does not realize, then you will take two lots for two heads. If the other head is aware of the pouring of the vinegar, then these heads both belong to one body, and you have to take one share." Then he poured out vinegar onto one head, and the other let out a cry. And the king said, "Because you are of one body, take one share." And thus Solomon judged them.

The Riddles of Malkatoshka

There was a southern queen called Malkatoshka who belonged to a different tribe. She arrived to test Solomon with riddles. This woman was very wise. She brought him gifts: twenty kaps of gold and very many medicines, and wood that does not rot. When Solomon learned of the queen's arrival, he sat in his white glass palace on a platform, wanting to test her. She saw that the king was sitting in water, and held up a cloth of her own to shield him. He saw that her face was beautiful and her body hairy like a brush. With this hair, she was bewitching the man who was with her. Solomon said to his wise men, "Prepare a hot bath with potions and rub her body so that her hair falls off." His wise men and scribes said that he should couple with her. Having conceived of him, she went into her own land and bore a son, and this son was Nebuchadnezzar.

This was her riddle to Solomon: she gathered youths and maidens, young and dressed in the same clothing, and the queen said to the king, "In your wisdom, sort out which are youths and which are maidens." The king in his wisdom ordered that fruit be brought and scattered it before them. The youths began to gather it in their shawls and the maids in their sleeves. And Solomon said, "These are youths, and these are maids." She was amazed at his cleverness in this.

On the next day, she gathered circumcised and uncircumcised youths and said to Solomon, "Sort out which are circumcised and which are uncircumcised." The king ordered a bishop to bring him the holy crown, on which was written the word of the Lord with which Balaam had been averted from sorcery [Numbers 22–24]. The circumcised youths stood and the uncircumcised ones fell before the crown. The queen was very amazed at this.

The queen's wise men set a riddle for Solomon's wise men: "We have a well far from the city. In your wisdom, determine how we can bring it into the city." Solomon's wise men, when they understood that it could not be so, said to them, "Weave a cable of bran, and we will drag your well into the city."

And again her wise men set a riddle: "If a field should grow knives, with what could you mow it?" And they said in answer, "With the horn of an ass." And her wise men said, "But where is the horn of an ass?" To which they said, "And where is a field that grows knives?"

They set another riddle: "If salt should become rotten, with what could you salt it?" Solomon's wise men said, "Having taken the womb of a mule, we could salt it with that." And they said, "And where does a mule give birth?" Solomon's wise men answered, "Where does salt go bad?"

When the queen had seen the houses built, the plenteous food, the way of life of Solomon's men and the standing of his servants, their dress, and drink, and that which they brought as a sacrifice into the house of God, she said, "I did not have faith in the true account of your wisdom which I heard in my land, until I arrived and beheld it with my own eyes. In truth, not even half was told to me. But happy are your men who hear your wisdom."

King Solomon gave to that queen named Malkatoshka all that she asked. And she went into her land with her men.

Of the Inheritance of the Three Brothers

In the days of Solomon, there lived a man who had three sons. When he was dying, the man summoned his sons to him and said to them, "I have a hiding place in the earth. In that place," he said, "three vessels stand one on top of the other. And after my death, let the oldest of you take the topmost and the middle the middle one and the smallest the lowest." After the death of their father, his sons opened the chamber before witnesses. And the topmost vessel was full of gold, the middle full of bones, and the lowest full of earth. Then there was a quarrel among the brothers, and the two youngest declared: "Are you a son since you have taken gold, and we not sons?" And they went in dispute to Solomon. And Solomon judged them: that which was of gold was for the eldest son; and the livestock and servants were for the middle son in the understanding of bones; and the vineyards and fields and food were for the smallest. And he said to them: "Your father was a wise man, and he has divided his belongings among you."

Of the Three Travelers

There were three men going on their path who were carrying gold on their backs. Having stopped to observe the sabbath in a wilderness, they made a pledge to each other: "We will keep our gold safe together, so that if robbers should come, we will escape and our property will be preserved." They dug up a ditch and put in all the gold together. And in the middle of the night as his two friends were sleeping, one of them had evil thought, and, having gotten up, hid the gold in another place. And when, having passed the sabbath, they went to the place to take their property and did not find it there, they cried out all at once; that false one cried out very much more than both the others. And they all returned home. And they said, "Let us go to Solomon and tell him of our loss." And they arrived before Solomon and said, "We do not know, king, if it is a beast that took it, or a bird or an angel. Tell us, king." He said to them in his wisdom, "I will tell you in the morning. However, since you are travelers, I ask of you, tell me:

"There was a man who became betrothed to a beautiful maiden and gave to her a ring of faith without the knowledge of her father and mother. The man went into another land and got married there. The girl's father gave the maiden in marriage. And as the young man to whom she had been given in marriage attempted to couple with her, the maiden cried out, saying, 'In my shame I have not told my father: for I am betrothed to a certain other man. Fearing God, set off for my betrothed to ask for his command, so that I may be your wife according to his word.' The young man gathered together much property and set off with the maiden. And her betrothed ordered him: 'Let her be your wife, since you have already taken her.' The young man said to her, 'We will return again and will perform the marriage anew.' While they were on their journey back, a brigand and his men saw them and took him with the girl and the property. This robber wanted to perform violence on the maiden, and the maiden cried out and she said to the robber that she had gone for the sake of an inquiry and that she had not yet lain with the young man. The robber was amazed, and he said to her husband: 'Take your wife and go with your belongings.'"

And Solomon said, "I have told you of this maiden and of the young man. You tell me, three men, with your property lost: who is best—the young man, or the maiden, or the robber." One said in answer, "The maiden is good, since she told of her betrothal." Another said, "The young man is good, since he waited for the decision." The third said, "The robber is better than both of them, since he returned the maiden and let the man himself go. But he ought not have given back the property." Then Solomon answered, "Friend, you are one who has coveted another's property. You have taken all the gold." The man said, "Lord king, truly it is so. I will not conceal it from you."

Of the Sense of Women

After this, supremely wise Solomon, wanting to test the sense of women, summoned his boyar Dekir and said to him: "You are a very dear man to me. And I will love you even more if you will carry out my will: kill your wife, and I will give you my best daughter." He said this to him over the course of several days. And Dekir did not wish to do this. And then he said, "I will carry out your will, king." The king gave him his sword, saying, "When your wife falls asleep, cut off her head so that she will not sway you from the deed with her tongue." The man went, and he found his wife sleeping with their two children at her side. When he saw his wife and children sleeping, he said to himself, "If I should strike my spouse with this sword, then I would cause pain to my children." The king summoned him and questioned him, saying, "Have you carried out my will, that which I said to you with regard to your wife?" The man said, "I could not do it, my Lord king."

The king sent him on a mission to another city and summoned the man's wife and said to her, "You are loved by me very much among all women. If you will perform that which I order you to do, I will make you queen. Kill your husband as he sleeps in his bed, and here is a sword for you." The woman answered, "Gladly, king, as you order." Solomon understood in his wisdom that her husband did not want to kill his wife, and, thus, he gave him a sharp sword, and he also understood that the man's wife wanted to kill her husband, and, thus, he gave her a dull sword that looked like it was sharp, saying, "With this sword, stab your husband as he sleeps in your bed." She placed the sword on her husband's breast and ground it along his throat, believing that it was sharp. The man leapt up quickly, thinking that some enemies were there, and when he saw his wife holding the sword, he said, "Why, my spouse, did you think of killing me?" The woman said in answer to her husband, "The tongue of a man swayed me into killing you." He wanted to call together witnesses, and he understood Solomon's teaching.

When Solomon heard of this, he inserted the following verse into his collection, saying, "I have found one man in a thousand worthy to be called upright, but such a woman in the whole world I have not found" [Ecclesiastes 7:27–8].

Of the Servant and the Son

In the days of Solomon, there lived a rich man in Babylon who did not have any children. When he had lived half of his days, the man established his servant in the place of a son. And, having provided him with property, he sent him from Babylon to trade. The servant arrived in Jerusalem and became rich there. And there he became one of the boyars around Solomon who sat for dinner with the king.

In that time a son was born to the man at home. And when the boy was thirteen years old, his father died. And his mother said to him, "Son, I have heard about your father's servant and of how he has grown rich in Jerusalem. Go and find him." And the youth arrived in Jerusalem, and he asked about the man, that servant, by name. And the servant was very well known. They told him that he was at dinner at Solomon's palace. And the young man entered the palace of the king and said, "Who is this boyar?" And the man answered and said, "I am." Having approached, the youth struck him on the face and said, "You are my servant. You are not a boyar, sitting, but go to work and give me the property!" And the king became enraged and he was sorry for his boyar. The boy answered Solomon, saying, "If this servant of my father, o king, should not be also mine, then for the strike from my hand give me a sword to kill myself." The struck man answered, "I am the son of this gentleman, and this servant of my father's is also mine. I have witnesses in Babylon." And the king said, "I do not have the faith to seize witnesses, but let me send my envoy into Babylon, and there let him take a lower leg bone from this man's grave, and this will tell me which one is the son and which the servant. And you stay here." The king sent his faithful envoy and this man brought back a lower leg bone. In his wisdom, Solomon ordered that the bone be washed clean and seated his boyar before him, along with all of his wise men, boyars and scribes. They said to a man who knew how to let blood, "Let the blood of this boyar." And the man did so. And the king ordered that the bone be placed in the warm blood. He explained these actions to his boyars, saying, "If he is this man's son, then his blood will adhere to the bone of his father. If it does not stick, then he is a slave." And they took the bone out from the blood, and the bone was white, as before. The king ordered that the blood of the youth be let into another vessel. And, having washed the bone, they placed it in the blood of the youth. And the bone, when it was taken out, was bloody. And the king said to his boyars, "See with your own eyes how the bone communicates, 'This is my son, but that one is a slave.'" And thus the king passed judgment on them.

Of King Adarian

After this Solomon began to say to his boyars, "There once was a King Adarian, and he ordered his boyars to call him a god. And, since they did not want to do so, his boyars said, 'Our king! Do you think in your heart that there was not a god before you? If we call you the highest king among kings, then when will you take highest Jerusalem and the Holy of Holies?' The king assembled many soldiers and took Jerusalem, and when he returned, he said to his boyars: 'As a god orders and says, in the same way also he acts; in the same way I also have acted. Now call me a god.' He had three learned men. The first answered, 'If you want to be called a god, well, it is not for a boyar to be called king in the king's palace, if he will not go outside of it. In the same way also you, if you want to be called a god, then go out from all the known universe and there be called a god.'

"And another said, 'You cannot be called a god.' And the king said, 'Why?' The man answered, 'The prophet Jeremiah said, 'The gods who did not make the heavens and the earth shall perish' [Jeremiah 10:11]. If you want to perish, king, then call yourself a god.'

"And the third said, 'Lord my king! Help me in this hour quickly!' And the king said, 'What is the matter?' And the learned man spoke thus: 'My boat, three versts away, is about to sink, and all of my property in it.' And the king said, 'Do not fear. I will send people, and they will lead it to safety.' And the learned man said, 'Why trouble your people? Send a quiet wind so that it may save the boat.' The king, having considered this, fell silent with vexation and went into the palace to his queen.

"And the queen said, 'The learned men have wounded you: they said to you that you cannot be called a god.' Because she wanted to give him comfort after this disappointment, she said, 'You are a king, you are rich, you are worthy of great honor. Do,' she said, 'one thing, and then call yourself a god.' And the king said, 'What thing?' And the queen said, 'To return the divine inheritance which you have in you.' He said, 'What inheritance?' The queen said, 'To return your soul, which God gave you into your body, and then call yourself a god.' He said, 'If there is no soul in me and in my body, how will I be called a god?' The queen said to him, 'Well, if you do not possess your own soul, then you cannot be called a god.'"

Of the Captured Princess

King Solomon began to seek a princess for himself. And they did not give her to him. And King Solomon said to demons, "Go and take this queen, and bring her to me." The demons, having gone, captured her as she was going from her mother in the palace, seated her in a vessel, and whirled her away through the sea.

As they were sailing, the queen saw a man who was drinking water and from whose body water was again pouring out. She said, "Tell me what this is." They said, "He to whom we are bringing you will tell you." And they traveled far, and there was a man, lost in water, who was nonetheless asking for water, and the waves overpowered him. And the queen said, "Unkind matchmakers of mine, tell me this: why does this man, while lost in water, ask for water?" They said, "He to whom we are bringing you will tell you." And they traveled on, and they saw a man passing to mow hay and two goats, walking behind him who ate up the grass: all that he would cut, they would eat up. And the queen said, "Tell me, unkind matchmakers of mine, tell me: is he sad for these goats to eat grass not mowed into hay?" The demons said to her, "He to whom we are bringing you will tell you."

And they spirited her away up to the city. And when they had arrived, one demon told King Solomon, "We have brought your bride." And the king mounted his horse and rode out onto the shore. And the princess said to him, "I am already yours, king. But tell me what this is: a man was drinking water, and from his body water again was pouring out." He said, "But why do you wonder at this? For this is the house of a king: into here men and objects will enter and from here will depart." And the queen said, "And tell me this also, what this is: one man, lost in water, asks for water, and the waves overpower him." And Solomon said, "O bride! Why do you wonder at this, bride? For this is the steward of the king: he judges a lawsuit, and another comes, so that with it he might make a good heart for the king." "But tell me this also: a man cuts to mow hay and what he cuts, two goats walking behind him eat up. I was sorry for these goats, who had gone into the hay, to eat uncut grass." And the king said, "Bride! Why are you amazed? If a man takes another wife with another's children, that which he will produce, they will eat up. And for him himself, there is nothing left. Now go, bride, into my palace."

And thus she became his wife.

6

Salman and Morolf
(Middle High German)
Introduction and Translation
by James A. Schultz

Introduction

AS ITS TITLE SUGGESTS, the protagonists of the Middle High German *Salman and Morolf* (*Salman und Morolf*: *"Spielmannsepos"*) belong to the tradition to which this volume is devoted. Salman is the wise king of Jerusalem, Morolf an irreverent trickster. In many other ways, however, *Salman and Morolf* stands apart. Unlike the Latin and its German adaptations, *Salman and Morolf* contains neither the series of quick exchanges that make up the first part of those texts nor the group of short, relatively discrete episodes that constitute their second part. *Salman and Morolf* is instead an extended narrative. It tells how Salman's faithless wife, Salome, is abducted, with her connivance, by a pagan king and then returned to Salman, primarily through the efforts of Morolf. This happens twice. Although Morolf delights in playing tricks on Salman, he is not the grotesque rustic found in the Latin but Salman's brother and, when necessary, a valiant warrior. His principal antagonist is not Salman but the queen. Further, unlike the Latin and the other German versions, which are in prose or rhymed couplets, *Salman and Morolf* is in five-line strophes, of which there are nearly 800. This makes it by far the longest text in the medieval Solomon and Marcolf tradition.

We do not know who wrote *Salman and Morolf*, nor do we have any certain information about the date, place, or reason for its original composition. To situate the work in its medieval context we must rely on what we can learn from the manuscripts that have transmitted it, the text of the narrative itself, and relevant data from the larger world of medieval literature.

Figure 5. Marcolf, disguised as a minstrel.
Stuttgart, Landesbibliothek, Cod. HB XIII 2, fol. 333ʳ.

Salman and Morolf survives in three complete manuscripts, fragments of three more, and two printed editions.[1] We have some information about a seventh manuscript, which was destroyed by fire in 1870. One extant manuscript, dated 1479, was produced in Frankfurt am Main. The others appear to have been written between 1467 and 1484 in the regions along the Rhine between Strassburg (present-day Strasbourg) and Mainz. An "illustrated Morolf" is listed around 1450 among items available from the workshop of Diebold Lauber, which produced manuscripts about twenty miles north of Strassburg. The printed editions, nearly identical, appeared in Strassburg in 1499 and 1510. This evidence delineates a concentration of interest in this text both chronologically and geographically: during the second half of the fifteenth century, stretching into the first years of the sixteenth; from Strassburg and its environs, north to Frankfurt.

That Lauber advertised an "illustrated Morolf" is telling: all three surviving manuscripts contain, or were meant to contain, between fifteen and twenty illustrations.[2] (One has no illustrations but only the spaces intended for them.) The printed editions contain nearly fifty woodcut images.[3] The unusually fine full-page images in the Frankfurt manuscript are the work of Hans Dirmstein, a painter, sculptor, and goldsmith from a patrician family of goldsmiths in Frankfurt, who produced the manuscript for his own use. The consistency with which *Salman and Morolf* was illustrated indicates that, whatever we may think of it, it must have been held in relatively high regard by those who made and paid for the surviving manuscripts.

In two extant manuscripts *Salman and Morolf* stands alone, or did so originally. In other cases, however, the presence of additional texts gives us some idea where contemporaries placed it within their literary world. The Frankfurt manuscript opens with *Salman and Morolf* and continues, in the middle of the

[1] Unless otherwise noted, information about the manuscripts and printed editions in this and the following two paragraphs is from Griese, *Salomon und Markolf*, 86–93. Two surviving manuscripts and all fragments are online. The easiest way to access them is from www.handschriftencensus. de/werke/979. The complete (illustrated) manuscripts are in Frankfurt and Stuttgart, the fragments in Dresden, Marburg, and Hamburg. For those who know no German: click the link for the city in which the manuscript is located; from the page devoted to that manuscript, find "Abbildung" in the near left-hand column and click the link to the right.

[2] The illustrations can be viewed online as explained in note 1. In the Frankfurt manuscript, the illustrations are at 1v, 4r, 6v, 8v, 11v, 16v, 21v, 24r, 39r, 39v, 42r, 46r, 57r, 58r, 71v, 82v, and 89r. In the Stuttgart manuscript the illustrations are at 303v, 309v, 313v, 315v, 323r, 324v, 326r, 327r, 328r, 333r, 334v, and 338v. Three additional illustrations have been removed from the Stuttgart manuscript.

[3] Of the fragments, one contains rubrics indicating that the manuscript from which they come was meant to contain illustrations; the others give no indication of illustrations but are, in one case, too small to allow one to draw conclusions, and, in the other, contain parts of the text where one would not expect them. Only the lost manuscript is certain not to have been illustrated.

page where this text ends, with what the rubric separating them calls "the other Morolf"[4]—that is, *The Book of Markolf* (see chapter 7). The lost manuscript placed *Salman and Morolf* in a different environment: it was third in a collection of four narratives, the others all heroic epics associated with Dietrich von Bern, as the Ostrogothic king Theodoric the Great (454–526) became known in German legend. These manuscript combinations show two different ways in which *Salman and Morolf* was understood in the late fifteenth century: as part of a Solomon and Marcolf tradition and as part of a heroic-epic tradition. Exploring the relations of *Salman and Morolf* to each of these can help us to a historically grounded understanding of the work.

Salman and Morolf and the Larger Solomon and Marcolf Tradition

By placing *Salman and Morolf* next to the *The Book of Markolf,* a verse translation of the Latin *Dialogue of Solomon and Marcolf* (*Dialogus Salomonis et Marcolfi*), the Frankfurt manuscript links it to the larger tradition of Solomon and Marcolf. The two are connected as well by the fact that the author of each text has taken a small piece from the world of the other and incorporated it into his own. The episode in which Marcolf crawls into an oven and shows Solomon his rear end, known from the Latin and its vernacular adaptations, is inserted into *Salman and Morolf* right after Morolf has declared that Salman's wife, who appears to be dead, is only feigning death. When Salman responds angrily and banishes Morolf from court, the narrative makes a detour of six strophes for the oven escapade: suddenly Morolf, while walking, spots an oven, whereupon Salman happens to pass by and see him (137–42).[5] Then we return to the main story as abruptly as we left it. The borrowing went the other way as well. When the author of *The Book of Markolf* reaches the end of his Latin source, he continues for another 240 lines to tell the story of Salomon's faithless wife, an account that shares essentials with *Salman and Morolf,* though it is a fraction of the length and differs in numerous particulars. A similar episode provides an alternative ending to the basic text in one manuscript of the Latin *Solomon and Marcolf.*[6] In both *The Book of Markolf* and the Latin manuscript, this is the first time when Salomon's wife has been so much as mentioned, and when Markolf appears as Salomon's helper. In other words, the episode of Salomon's wife does not fit any better in *The Book of Markolf* than the one of the oven does in *Salman and Morolf.*

---

[4] Frankfurt, Stadt- und Universitätsbibliothek, MS germ. qu. 13, f. 88v, "der ander moroff [*sic*]."

[5] In this introduction, numbers in parentheses refer to strophe numbers in *Salman and Morolf.*

[6] The manuscript was produced in Bohemia in the third quarter of the fifteenth century; see Griese, *Salomon und Markolf,* 42–43. For the text of the Latin episode and an English translation, see *S&M* Z 288–98.

That these pieces have nevertheless been added to texts where they are not completely at home shows the extent to which *Salman and Morolf,* even though it stands apart in so many ways, was nevertheless felt to belong to the same tradition as the Latin *Solomon and Marcolf.*[7]

Although understood to fit within that larger tradition, *Salman and Morolf* highlights a different attribute of its biblical protagonist, not his proverbial wisdom but his inordinate love of women. It was, after all, King Solomon's "most ardent love" of his wives that, according to the biblical account, enabled them to turn "away his heart ... to follow strange gods."[8] Augustine shifts the blame more clearly onto the wives: "it was by feminine wiles that [Solomon] was compelled to commit such a sacrilege."[9] Subsequent Christian clerical writers continued in this misogynist vein, making Solomon, along with Samson and David, famous as examples of great men brought low by the malign power of women. By the second half of the twelfth century, however, these same figures began to appear in texts for courtly audiences as men who succumbed to the power of love. Here the point is not to exhort men to avoid women but to excuse them for loving so ardently.[10] If love mastered Salomon, Heinrich von Veldeke asks in one of his songs, "how can I prevent it from forcing me too to obey, since it overcame such a man, who was so wise and so mighty?"[11]

About the same time as Veldeke cited Solomon as an example of the enamored lover, probably in the 1170s, Chrétien de Troyes identified Solomon's queen as a model of the deceitful wife. In *Cligès* he tells us that Fenice drinks a potion that makes her appear dead so that she can run off with the title hero, whom she prefers to her husband. Physicians from Salerno take a look and are suspicious at once: "they remembered Solomon, whose wife so detested him that she deceived him by faking death."[12] In an attempt to confirm their suspicions, the doctors try to rouse Fenice from her sleep by subjecting her to

---

[7]   This is not to claim any direct dependence among the extant texts, only that stories concerning Marcolf and Solomon's faithless bride were in circulation and that these were then adopted into the Latin manuscript and the German *Book of Markolf.* See Curschmann, *Der Münchener Oswald,* 100; Griese, *Salomon und Markolf,* 78.

[8]   3 Kings 11:1–8.

[9]   Augustine, *The City of God against the Pagans,* 14.11.

[10]   I have adopted the distinction between the clerical "Frauensklave" and the courtly "Minnesklave" from Schnell, *Liebeskonzeption und Liebesdarstellung,* 475–505, which discusses them in detail, offering copious quotations from the primary sources.

[11]   "wie mohte ich mich erwern dan, / Si twunge ouch mich gewalteclîche, / sît si sölhen man verwan, / der sô wîse was und ouch sô rîche?" Heinrich von Veldeke (66.16–22), in Karl Lachmann, Hugo Moser, and Helmut Tervooren, eds., *Des Minnesangs Frühling,* 36th ed. (Stuttgart: Hirzel, 1977), 138.

[12]   Chrétien de Troyes, *Arthurian Romances,* 195. For the Old French, see Chrétien de Troyes, *Cligès,* vol. 2, lines 5802–4.

a series of torments, among them, pouring molten lead through her hands—much as Morolf pours molten gold through the hand of Salome. The evidence from Veldeke and Chrétien shows that, by the end of the twelfth century, two elements that distinguish *Salman and Morolf* from the other Solomon and Marcolf texts—the king overcome by love and the wife who feigns death and is tested with molten metal—were known in the literary culture at large to be part of the story of King Solomon.

In *Salman and Morolf*, Salman's love for his wife is established at the very outset. "He loved the queen," we are told in the fourth strophe, "no matter how much she did to cause him pain" (4). His love is noted twice more in the opening strophes (8, 19). At first Salman seems in every way a model king: holding court, welcoming messengers, marshalling his forces against pagan attack, and defeating King Fore in battle. But then he goes astray. Ignoring Morolf's warning, he entrusts Fore to the queen's care, refusing to believe she might be planning to escape. She does escape. Then, after she has lived with Fore for years, Salman takes her back, although Morolf tells him this is a terrible idea; Salman believes "her word that she intends to be faithful always" (538). She does not remain faithful but runs off with a second pagan king. Despite all this, Salman still "shed[s] bitter tears" (779) when Morolf finally kills the queen, an execution he has twice given Morolf permission to carry out. In no case is Salman's love of his wife given as the reason for his otherwise inexplicable failure to acknowledge her faithlessness. To be sure, Salman's behavior is criticized—by Morolf for "bringing shame and misfortune upon yourself" (87) and by the narrator, who claims Salman "never learned from experience what he would have needed to know to keep his lovely wife from deceiving him" (579). But, as the last quotation suggests, the criticism is not that Salman has been blinded by love but that he has failed, for whatever reason, to "keep [his] wife in line" (155). Perhaps the programmatic declaration at the outset that Salman loved his wife "no matter how much she did to cause him pain" is meant to explain his subsequent blindness to her faults. Surprisingly, this explanation is never offered.

The lion's share of attention at the beginning of *Salman and Morolf* is devoted not to Salman but to his wife, above all to her beauty, the description of which claims five of the first ten strophes. She is the only figure in the narrative who is described in any detail. This beauty, however, is dangerous. At table, "knights seated across from her lost their senses altogether. They felt such a need to look at her that they forgot the bread and wine in their hands" (16). Seeing her, "Salman himself didn't know how to act for joy" (18). When news of Salome's beauty (and nobility: the two qualities are understood to imply each other) reaches Fore and Princian, that is when they decide they must have her as their wife. Morolf is the only male character immune to this enchantment. Despite the narrator's warnings of trouble to come (2, 4, 20), Salome, like Salman, appears at the outset as an exemplary figure, both at court and in church. Only when Salman entrusts the captive Fore to her care, and even then, only when Fore brings pagan magic to bear, does she betray her husband. Princian too needs magic to lead her astray. Once Salome takes up betrayal, however, she stops at nothing. The "murderously vicious ... woman" (421) delivers Salman to Fore, insisting he be executed, and then, when the tables have been turned, she blames everything on Fore in a (successful) effort to regain Salman's favor. She is indefatigable in her pursuit of Morolf, once she senses that he is near her. The combination of irresistible beauty and ruthless treachery makes Salome particularly dangerous.[13]

We do not know when storytellers first enlisted the trickster Marcolf to help the foolish king regain his faithless queen. As Solomon's antagonist he was already familiar enough around the year 1000 to be cited as such by Notker III of St. Gall.[14] As Solomon's helper, however, the only evidence we have besides *Salman and Morolf* comes from the two sources mentioned above: the alternative ending in one of the manuscripts of the Latin *Solomon and Marcolf* and the epilogue to the German *Book of Markolf.* Despite suggestive differences among them, no clear relations of precedence or dependence can be established. The only certain dates we have are those of the extant manuscripts, all from the fifteenth century, mostly the last third. If stories in which Marcolf helps Solomon were told before then, we can only speculate about the form they took.[15]

In the alternative ending in the Latin manuscript (see *S&M* Z 288–98), Marcolf remains very much an antagonist. When he sees the queen lying there as if dead, he declares that she is really alive. Solomon objects, and Marcolf promises to "prove the truth of the matter."[16] When the queen fails to react to the molten lead, he promises another attempt "to prove the truth to you"—which he does in typically Marcolfian fashion, "mooing like an ungelded ox" at the queen's tomb. This episode unfolds exactly like a number of previous episodes in the Latin, in which Marcolf makes a claim and must satisfy Solomon's demand that he prove it—like the episode of the cat and the candle, which he stages to prove, as Solomon has demanded, his assertion that nature is stronger than nurture. One can imagine a writer, familiar both with the traditional Latin Marcolf and with the story of Solomon's faithless queen, thinking Marcolf would be a likely

---

[13] See Lydia Miklautsch, "Salman und Morolf," 296.

[14] See *S&M* Z 317–20.

[15] For a detailed discussion of differences among the three, see Griese, *Salomon und Markolf,* 79–82. For a plausible, hypothetical explanation of their genetic relation, see Curschmann, *Der Münchener Oswald,* 97–100.

[16] *S&M* Z 293.

candidate to perform the test with molten lead, then incorporating this episode into the Latin as another "proof" that Marcolf promises—twice—to provide. To be sure, Marcolf pursues the queen and returns her to Solomon, and to that extent he helps Solomon. But the account of his pursuit highlights his brazen disrespect for the queen and the clever stratagem by which he saves himself from execution. In other words, Marcolf acts very much like his old self. That he "helps" Solomon is the inadvertent byproduct of the fact that he wants to show once again how shameless and clever he is.

As a relatively faithful verse translation of the Latin *Solomon and Marcolf*, *The Book of Markolf* could very well have had an epilogue just like the alternative ending in the Latin manuscript. Instead, when Markolf enters the epilogue to *The Book of Markolf*, he returns to Salomon's court a new man. He is on Salomon's side without equivocation. He pours lead through the queen's hands, but not as a proof demanded by Salomon. He predicts the queen's disappearance, but does not mock the king for his gullibility. Once the queen is gone, he offers to "endure whatever hardship it takes"[17] to discover her whereabouts. Disguising himself as a merchant, he finds her and then returns to Salomon to propose a stratagem for capturing her, which they carry out in concert. The epilogue to *The Book of Markolf* (see chapter 7) suppresses any sign of tension between Markolf and the king, while highlighting the antagonism between Markolf and the queen.

Salman and Morolf is twenty times the length of the alternative ending to the Latin or the epilogue to *The Book of Markolf*, and Morolf is its principal actor. As a consequence, it offers ample opportunity to develop different aspects of his persona, yielding a figure who appears alarmingly incoherent, even by medieval standards. Morolf is introduced as Salman's "dear brother" (55) and seems at first to be a paragon of courtliness. Soon he marshals troops and invokes Christ's aid in battle. Later he shows himself to be a formidable fighter and an effective strategist. Brother of Salman, Morolf, it turns out, is also nephew to a mermaid. Although he always comes through in the end, Morolf does not hesitate to criticize the king and threatens several times to withhold his aid. Nor does he hesitate to play tricks on his brother. Returning to Jerusalem, unrecognizable after a long absence, he uses this cover to test Salman's devotion. No sooner has he revealed his true identity than he steps out briefly to don another disguise and returns to sow havoc among Salman's retainers. He just can't help himself.

Morolf's resourcefulness and prankster bravura are most evident during the two trips he makes to locate the queen, which comprise a dizzying series of risks, provocations, and disguises. As a pilgrim, Morolf challenges Salome to a game of chess, wagering his own life against the sister of the king. Once

---

[17] *The Book of Markolf* (see chapter 7 below), lines 1735–36.

recognized, he escapes, is captured, and escapes again; rather than returning home, he puts on the garments of a guard he has killed, returns to the pagan citadel, puts Salome, the king, and twelve chaplains to sleep with a potion, then tonsures all the men and replaces the king, who is in bed next to Salome, with one of the chaplains. He flees in a tiny leather boat of his own manufacture, which can be carried around like a sack; surrounded, he descends to the bottom of the sea and breathes for a fortnight through a tube. The second time he must find the queen, once he has done so, he keeps coming back in new disguises— pilgrim, minstrel, butcher, peddler—each time encountering a posse she has sent out and giving them directions to find him in his previous incarnation. As minstrel, he keeps his pursuers dancing an entire day. As butcher, he sets up a stand in Acre and actually sells meat. Morolf kills those who help him, farts when he needs to create a distraction, and sings—beautifully when he has won at chess, bravely from his little boat at sea after he has tonsured the king, in each case revealing himself to those who would take his life.

Although this hodgepodge of aptitudes, attributes, and behaviors may seem irreconcilable to us, the text suggests they derive from a single source. Morolf is called *listec* more than eighty times. The word can mean "wise" and "skillful" but also "crafty" and "cunning." Here it has been translated consistently as "clever" to indicate that it is considered a single quality. Often he is called simply "the clever man," and we know this must be Morolf. The insistence on this single quality suggests a deliberate intention to explain and unite the discrepant and often extreme behaviors of this wildly contradictory figure and give them a positive valence. Morolf's cleverness is a lot more efficacious, after all, than the "words of great wisdom" attributed to Salman in the first strophe.

Salman and Morolf and the Heroic Tradition

If the Frankfurt manuscript acknowledges the place of *Salman and Morolf* within a larger Solomon and Marcolf tradition, the manuscript that burned in 1870 locates it in a completely different context. Here *Salman and Morolf* is placed among three heroic texts: after *Wolfdietrich* and *Rosengarten*, and before *Ortnit*. These belong to a larger group of narratives devoted to the adventures of the great hero Dietrich von Bern (or, in some cases, only loosely connected to that figure) that were collected in various combinations in the so-called *Heldenbücher* from the last third of the fifteenth century and printed editions until nearly 1600. Of these, the lost manuscript is one.[18] Although *Salman and Morolf* has nothing to do with Dietrich von Bern, it nevertheless shares important attributes with its inciner-ated companions. All four are composed in strophes—as opposed to rhymed

---

[18]   On these collections, see Joachim Heinzle, "Heldenbücher."

couplets, like Arthurian romance and many other texts, including *The Book of Markolf.* Stophic form is one of the features that distinguish heroic epic (in most cases) from the rest of the Middle High German corpus. All four contain pitched battles between large armies and single combat between mighty warriors. This martial aspect is remarkable: in none of the other Solomon and Marcolf texts do the protagonists distinguish themselves as great heroes, dauntless fighters, or military commanders. While the others would be quite out of place bundled together with a group of heroic narratives, *Salman and Morolf* is not.

Salman and Morolf shares additional elements with two of the three other texts in the lost manuscript. Like *Ortnit* and *Wolfdietrich* it is set in the eastern Mediterranean and thematizes relations between Christians and Muslims. In this it differs from the Latin *Solomon and Marcolf* and the German *Book of Markolf,* in which religion is never mentioned. Even in the epilogue to *The Book of Markolf,* where those who abduct Solomon's wife are repeatedly called "pagans," the religious identity of Solomon and his allies is never specified.[19] Finally, *Salman and Morolf,* like *Ortnit* and *Wolfdietrich,* organizes its plot with the help of a widely employed narrative pattern, the *Brautwerbunsgsschema* or bridal-quest schema. Here too it differs from the other Solomon and Marcolf texts, which have no use for this narrative structure. Even in the epilogue to *The Book of Markolf,* where it might easily have played a role, it is absent. The commonalities between *Salman and Morolf* and the other texts in the lost manuscript are such that, were it not for the names of its protagonists and the fact that Morolf retains some of his familiar attributes, one would have to say that *Salman and Morolf* fits more comfortably among its heroic companions in this manuscript than next to *The Book of Markolf* in the manuscript from Frankfurt.

Traditionally, literary historians have placed *Salman and Morolf* neither with heroic narratives nor with other Solomon and Morolf texts but in a genre called "*Spielmannsepik.*" A *Spielmann* is a minstrel, and the genre designation preserves the long discredited notion that these texts were composed by minstrels. The traditional assignment of *Salman and Morolf* to this group is the reason it is frequently distinguished from other Solomon and Marcolf texts by the subtitle "*Spielmannsepos.*" Whether the five narratives conventionally grouped under this rubric have enough in common to justify considering them a single genre is a question that has been raised with increasing insistence.[20] In any case, the most important elements that *Salman and Morolf* shares with the other four, or at with least most of them, are precisely those, just mentioned, that it has in

---

[19]   Although the *women* of Jerusalem clearly identify themselves as Jews in an earlier passage: "We are of the lineage of Abraham and, like all our forebears, have kept the law of Moses" (lines 1358–1360).

[20]   Most vigorously recently by Schulz, "Morolfs Ende."

common with *Ortnit* and *Wolfdietrich* and that might account for the fact that the compiler of the lost manuscript thought it belonged among heroic narratives: the setting in the East and the reliance on the bridal-quest schema.[21]

Before turning to these topics, a detail from one of the so-called *Spielmannsepen* should be mentioned, since it provides the strongest evidence for an early dating of *Salman and Morolf*. Both *Salman and Morolf* and *König Rother* contain a sequence of events in which a royal hero enters an enemy stronghold disguised as a pilgrim; discovered and sentenced to be hanged, he chooses to be executed outside the city in front of a forest; as the execution is getting under way, he or a vassal blows a horn he has carried with him, summoning his army, which has been hiding nearby. Many scholars find these parallels too close to be coincidental. *König Rother* can be dated with some certainty to 1152–80.[22] If its author was in fact influenced by the other poem, then some version of *Salman and Morolf* must already have been in circulation in the third quarter of the twelfth century.[23]

The very first line of *Salman and Morolf* puts us in Jerusalem, Salman's city and the geographical point to which the story keeps returning. Strange to say, Jerusalem has been transported to the coast and provided with a harbor, of which the story makes heavy use. Just as startling, Salman is introduced as "lord over all the people of Christendom" (1): he is the Christian king of a Christian Jerusalem. Turning Solomon into a Christian is a bold move, but it serves a purpose: it makes the story a struggle between Christians and pagans (Muslims), thereby directing the reader's or listener's sympathy more insistently to the former and away from the latter. The relocation of Jerusalem serves the same end: it places the city at the edge of the "raging sea," across which individuals and armies repeatedly move back and forth, between Christian Jerusalem and pagan lands. The religious opposition is reproduced as a geographical separation that can be bridged only at great risk. If this situation suggests the Crusades, so does the formula "across the raging sea," which occurs more than forty times, a degree of repetition that, by itself, can "signal a crusade."[24] Crusade topoi are deliberately deployed by Morolf, who, before one of the battles, has the image of Christ embroidered onto Salman's battle standard to remind his army that they fight as Christians (71–72) and who, before another battle, invites them

---

[21] For an argument why these and other commonalities justify the category "*Spielmannsepik*," see Vollmann-Profe, *Wiederbeginn volkssprachiger Schriftlichkeit*, 215–16. For a discussion of whether some, at least, of the "*Spielmannsepen*" should be considered heroic epics, see Werner Hoffmann, *Mittelhochdeutsche Heldendichtung*, Grundlagen der Germanistik 14 (Berlin: E. Schmidt, 1974), 33–37.

[22] On the dating, see Hans Szklenar, "König Rother," 89–90.

[23] See Curschmann, "Salman und Morolf," 517–18; Griese, *Salomon und Markolf*, 77.

[24] Dobozy, "Holy War in German Literature," 341–42.

to think of the "great rewards that God will bestow" on those who risk their lives fighting on Salman's behalf (485). Beyond this, religious beliefs play no particular role in *Salman and Morolf*, although such practices as hearing mass, receiving baptism, and reading the Psalter are mentioned from time to time.

The pagans also have churches and chaplains and priests who sing mass. Their social and political structures too are very much like those of the Christians. Indeed, they often seem better at displaying Christian virtues than the Christians themselves. The pagan king Fore is willing to let Salman return home unharmed, even after he knows Salman entered his court incognito to regain Salome. The pagan king Princian gives Morolf gold and a precious ring when he turns up at the castle gate disguised as a crippled beggar. At other times, however, those "who are not baptized" (753) are reviled as "wretched pagans"—especially when leading armies against Christians or being killed in vast numbers by Christian armies. Muslims are not the only ones whose faith renders their lives expendable. In one particularly gruesome episode, Morolf kills a Jew from whom he pretended to seek advice, then flays him and puts on his skin as a disguise.[25] (Morolf's "clever trick" is cited at the beginning of a short narrative from the second half of the fourteenth century, indicating a degree of familiarity with *Salman and Morolf* at that time.[26]) To be sure, the pagans do not hesitate to kill and pillage, to abduct the wife of King Salman, or to make use of deceptions and other dishonorable means of gaining what they want. This, however, does not distinguish them from the Christians. What matters is not what they do but who they are. When Morolf takes an herb to make himself seem deathly ill, it is an example of his "great skill" (618).[27] When the pagans provide an herb that makes Salome seem dead, it is "magic" (126). Religion in *Salman and Morolf* serves to divide the world into two camps. Whatever Christians do is legitimate. Whatever pagans do, they are the enemy and their lives are expendable.

Salman and Morolf shares with *Ortnit* and *Wolfdietrich*—as well as with other heroic epics, most of the *Spielmannsepen*, and the Tristan romances—not only its setting in the East but also its use of the *Brautwerbungsschema* or bridal-quest schema. The basic elements are as follows. A king needs a wife. Often the pressure to marry comes from his vassals, who are concerned for the stability of the kingdom. The king wonders where he could find a suitable bride. Fortunately one of his entourage knows of a young woman in a distant place who, on account of

---

[25] On this episode see Poor, "Surface Reading Is Not Enough."

[26] Der arme Konrad, "Frau Metze." For the passage in question and an English translation see *S&M* Z 356–57. The dating is plausible but not conclusive. The earliest manuscript containing the text is from the 1430s. See Williams-Krapp, "Der arme Konrad," 454–55.

[27] See Dobozy, "Knowledge and Magic in *Salman und Morolf*," 29–30.

her extraordinary beauty and exalted rank, is really the only possible candidate. For one reason or another, it will be very difficult to obtain her. A messenger may be sent to make contact. Sometimes he is able to return with her. Often the king himself must set out, sometimes instead of, sometimes after the return of his messenger. Frequently the king or his messenger will meet privately with the bride and secure her cooperation. Sometimes she is won by force, sometimes by trickery, sometimes by both. In winning her, the king shows himself to be the strongest or smartest—in other words, the rightful husband for her and the rightful sovereign of his kingdom. In the ideal case, the personal desires of the king coincide with his political needs, his desires and needs complement those of his vassals, and, despite the risks, the bridal-quest ends with a consolidation of his position.

Two bridal-quest narratives establish the basic two-part structure of *Salman and Morolf*. No sooner have we been introduced to Salman and his wife than the story turns to the pagan king Fore, who announces that he needs a suitable bride. One of his retainers recommends Salome because she is "fair and beautiful [and] a noble queen" (29). Fore gathers an army, arrives in Jerusalem, and sends a messenger to Salman to demand his wife. When Salman refuses to hand over Salome, a great battle ensues, Fore loses, is taken prisoner, and is entrusted to the care of Salome. He wins her love with the help of a magic ring, she lets him escape, six months later he sends minstrels, who help her escape, and she joins him in his kingdom. Formally, this is a completely regular bridal-quest narrative. Unusually, however, the hero of the bridal-quest, Fore, is not the protagonist of *Salman and Morolf* but the *opponent* of that character. This makes it quite exceptional. Another unorthodox bridal-quest introduces the second part of *Salman and Morolf*. After Salman and Morolf kill Fore and bring Salome back to Jerusalem, "news ... reached Acre that there was no more beautiful woman than King Salman's wife" (598) and another pagan king, Princian, determines to make her his wife. He does so in a mere twelve strophes, with the help of a magic ring that he drops in a goblet of wine that Salome drinks, causing her to fall in love. "Twelve weeks later ... she snuck away and crossed the raging sea with King Princian" (609). This second bridal-quest narrative is irregular not only because, like the first, its protagonist is the enemy of our hero but also because it is so short. It serves its purpose, however, inaugurating the second series of adventures in which Morolf finds Salome and she is brought back to Jerusalem.

While the bridal-quests of Fore and Princian establish the overall structure of *Salman and Morolf*, this narrative schema shapes the text in other ways as well. The news we receive at the outset, that Salman had stolen Salome from her father and brought her back to Jerusalem to be his queen, sounds very much like the memory of a completed bridal-quest. Later, the recovery missions undertaken by Salman and Morolf are structured like bridal-quest narratives. Salman knows of a woman he wants (back) as his wife, but he knows it will be very difficult to win her. He sends out a messenger, Morolf, who makes (hostile) contact with the desired woman. Then Salman and Morolf together (the first time) or Morolf alone (the second) set out with an army to bring her home. In other words, Salome is forcibly brought to Jerusalem and Salman three times. The precondition for the final excursion is Salman's promise that Morolf can kill the queen when he brings her back.

The most surprising bridal-quest narrative is one that begins, it seems, quite by accident. On his first mission to locate Salman's errant queen, Morolf has made his way into Fore's castle and, disguised as a pilgrim, is playing chess with Salome. He wagers his head against the most beautiful maiden in Salome's chamber, who turns out to be Fore's sister. Although she resists at first, very quickly she agrees to cast her lot with him, should he win. The messenger has made contact with the (not yet) desired bride, who, against all odds, has shown some willingness to follow her suitor.[28] Fore's sister is forgotten until Salman returns with an army and, in disguise, enters the pagan castle: she is the one who greets him and offers hospitality. She suspects he is Salman and, from the start, begins to intercede on his behalf. Most notably, she gains custody of the king the night after he has been sentenced to death and before he is to be executed: she leads him to a beautiful chamber and waits on him; he plays the harp and sings for her; she offers to help him escape, but he refuses out of concern for her safety. In this traditional bridal-quest scene, suitor and bride come to an understanding when they are alone together for the first time. Once Salman has been freed and the pagans defeated, Fore's sister is brought back to Jerusalem, where, taking the name Affer, she accepts baptism—but only after Morolf promises to marry her to Salman once Salome dies. Affer disappears from sight again until the very end of the story when, having just killed Salome, Morolf keeps his promise, consoling Salman by giving him "a faithful wife without delay" (781a), that is, Affer.

As is often the case in medieval narrative, the deployment of traditional narrative patterns reveals a logic of its own, independent of the ostensible motivations of the actors or the explicit commentary of the narrator. That is certainly true of the interplay among the various forms of the bridal-quest schema in *Salman and Morolf*. The point of the schema is to get the best possible queen for an unmarried king. Salman thinks he has done this at the beginning of the story. But the bridal-quests of two pagan kings reveal that he has

---

[28] For a detailed analysis of the chess game and its significance, see Griese, *Salomon und Marcolf*, 116–20.

not found the best possible queen: susceptible to pagan magic, Salome twice shows herself lacking the most important attribute of a royal wife, faithfulness. The serendipitous bridal quest that begins when Morolf first meets Fore's sister unfolds almost by accident. Yet it manages to bring Salman the wife he needs. In contrast to Salome, Affer is a willing bride who has long since proved her devotion to Salman at great risk to herself. Affer's beauty, unlike that of Salome, does not cause men to forget themselves. Thus the elements that destabilized Salman's marriage to Salome and showed him to be a less than ideal ruler are absent from his marriage to Affer. That is Morolf's great accomplishment: at last Solomon has a faithful wife.[29]

The points implicit in the structure of *Salman and Morolf* are recognized and turned into a simplistic lesson in the continuation of the story found in the printed editions. Shifting from strophes to rhymed couplets, and thus out of the heroic mode and into a much more common prosody, the writer of the continuation presents Salman and Affer as an equally devoted, loving Christian husband and wife. They are not blinded by things of this world, but keep their sights firmly on God, praying and fasting, and withdrawing from the world when their eldest son is old enough to take his father's place on the throne. Their example is so powerful that they inspire Morolf to renounce his sinful life and beg for divine mercy. All three die on the same day and are received into heaven.

It would be a mistake, however, to reduce *Salmon and Morolf* to this simplistic teaching: kill Salome, marry Affer, and go to heaven. To be sure, the text raises questions about love, marriage, and sovereignty, but it does not give simple answers. Through the varied repetition of the traditional bridal-quest schema, it offers *multiple* perspectives on these topics, thereby opening opportunities for comparison and reflection.[30] This is true of *Salman und Morolf* in general: it presents disparate material that offers multiple perspectives on a variety of topics, but leaves it up to us to weigh the various elements against each other and reflect, if we are so inclined, on their significance. Thus, along with questions about love and marriage, we have heroic battles between Christians and pagans and an inexhaustible supply of tricks, disguises, deceptions, narrow escapes, and crude jokes. The principal actors too comprise disparate elements. Solomon is wise and foolish, heroic and cowardly. Salome is beautiful and courtly but also deceitful and unscrupulous. One should never forget that the shorthand name for these texts in the fifteenth century was not "Solomon" or "Salome" but "Morolf": Lauber offered an "illustrated Morolf." Morolf is the one who

---

[29] Michael Curschmann is the first to have read the structure of *Salmon and Morolf* as a reflection on love. See Curschmann, *Der Münchener Oswald*, 87–97.

[30] See the excellent analysis in Bachorski, "Serialität, Variation und Spiel," 7–29. For a similar but more sober conclusion see Bowden, *Bridal-Quest Epics*, 94.

gives the text its most distinctive color: his shameless provocations and virtuoso resourcefulness generate incident and excitement at the same time they make the case for a very useful "cleverness." These are some of the heterogeneous elements that give *Salman and Morolf* its interest and its vitality and that may, despite its manifest inconsistencies and irregularities, account for its popularity in the late fifteenth and early sixteenth centuries.

The Style of *Salman and Morolf* and this Translation

Theoretically the strophes in *Salman and Morolf* contain five lines of four stresses each; the first and second lines rhyme, as do the third and fifth. In practice, however, a great deal of variation is permitted. On just about any page of the modern edition one can find strophes of six lines, occasionally four, and a substantial proportion of lines that contain more, sometimes considerably more, than four stresses. Assonance, not pure rhyme, is all that is expected. While some of this variation may be attributable to those who copied the text, it does not violate the basic aesthetic, which does not aspire to perfect regularity.

The syntax of *Salman and Morolf* is relentlessly paratactic: a high percentage of strophes comprise nothing besides short independent clauses and appositional phrases. Its diction is highly formulaic: Jerusalem is nearly always "the fair city of Jerusalem," the sea almost always "the raging sea." And its vocabulary is quite limited: the author knows only a single verb for speaking, *sprechen*, which is used to introduce statements, questions, commands, replies, and every other kind of utterance. All this poses challenges to the translator, since a ruthless reproduction of the parataxis and formulaic, limited vocabulary of the original would yield an English version that would seem to have been written by a six-year-old. I have deliberately smoothed over some of the roughness in the hope of producing a translation minimally palatable to a modern reader. In doing so there is no need to worry about violating the overall feel of the original: that is so pronounced it could not be eliminated short of retelling the story in one's own words.

I have added conjunctions, coordinate and subordinate, where such relations of cause, time, and so forth seem clear, but no more than seemed necessary to make the translation bearable to modern readers. The main building blocks of the original—short independent clauses and appositional phrases—predominate in the translation as well. Similarly, I have in some circumstances employed a more varied vocabulary. The hundreds of lines that begin *Er sprach* or *Da sprach* have been rendered according to context as "replied," "asserted," "asked," and the like. Any reader who finds this an impermissible liberty is welcome to replace every verb of speaking with the only literal option, "spoke." On the other hand,

I have consistently preserved formulaic epithets: *daz wilde mer* is always "the raging sea," *des wilden maeres tran* "the waters of the raging sea"; *diu guote stat zu Jerusalem* is always "the fair city of Jerusalem." I have done so even when the formula itself is annoyingly reduplicative: *diu edele kuniginne her* is always "the noble, highborn queen," *diu schone frauwe wol getan* "the lovely, fair lady." As noted above, *listec* is consistently rendered as "clever," even when the context might suggest a more clearly positive ("skillful") or negative ("cunning") alternative, since the text seems clearly to want us to recognize Morolf's "cleverness," in all its various manifestations, as a single quality.

The translation is based on the edition of Alfred Karnein, and follows his numbering of the strophes.[31] Unlike many earlier editors of Middle High German texts, Karnein rejected the temptation to reconstruct the "original" version of his text. Always a risky undertaking, such originalism is especially problematical in this case, since so little is actually known about when or where the "original" *Salman and Morolf* might have been produced. Instead, Karnein has provided a text for which we do have historical evidence: the manuscripts of the late fifteenth century. His edition is based on the manuscript now in Stuttgart, which was probably written 1467–69. He has made changes only in cases where this manuscript, measured against its own practice, offers something that makes no sense—in other words, in cases where a fifteenth-century reader or lector would have made adjustments. In addition, he has drawn on another manuscript to fill in strophes that must have been in the Stuttgart manuscript when it was produced but that disappeared when pages were removed.[32]

---

[31] Karnein, *Salman und Morolf.*

[32] I first encountered the Solomon and Marcolf tradition in 1974, in a graduate seminar taught by the late Michael Curschmann. I am grateful that, nearly forty years later, my teacher was still willing to answer my questions and help with a number of passages in this text that caused me difficulty. Needless to say, he bears no responsibility for all those places where I should have asked for help but did not realize it.

Figure 6. Solomon and Salome play backgammon.
Frankfurt a. M., Universitätsbibliothek, Ms. germ. qu. 13, fol. 1ᵛ.

Translation

Salman and Morolf

1. A child was born in Jerusalem who was destined to be lord over all the people of Christendom. That was King Salman, who spoke words of great wisdom. 2. He took a wife from Endian, the daughter of a pagan, highborn and worthy of great praise. Yet it was an evil hour when she was born into this world, since many heroes lost their lives on her account. 3. Her father was called Crispian, from whom Salman had stolen her. He carried her across the raging sea and held her by force in the fair city of Jerusalem. 4. I'm telling you the truth: he had her baptized and taught her the Psalter for an entire year. He also taught her chess. He loved the queen, no matter how much she did to cause him pain.

5. She was the fairest woman ever born. Her throat was white as snow; her lips, fiery red like a ruby. Her eyes sparkled, as one would expect from a noble woman. 6. Her hair was like yellow silk. She was beautiful, lovely, and shapely of body. Her name was Salome, and she was marvelously fair. 7. Next to her skin she wore a shift of fine white silk, while around her head she wore a narrow band of purest gold. 8. The queen wore a cloak of exceptional quality, covered with sparkling gems. Mighty King Salman loved the handsome woman. 9. She bore a crown, radiant like the sun, into which a brilliant ruby had been set. Like the morning star, her face shone forth from among the other women.

10. It happened one year on Pentecost that the queen went to church. Two great princes escorted the proud monarch, one on each side. 11. On that day many fine minstrels preceded the lovely woman, and many proud warriors walked on her right, wearing knightly armor, attending their lady. 12. Many beautiful freeborn maidens walked on the other side, and a large number of vassals followed her, wearing knightly armor, arranged in four magnificent companies. 13. When she entered the great church, they began the high mass. A Psalter, written entirely with golden letters, was placed in her snow-white hands. 14. Hear now what offering the lady made during the reading of the Gospel: a ring of deep red gold set with precious gems, beyond compare.

15. When they had finished singing the mass, chairs were set up in the hall. King Salman sat next to his lady, who was truly enchanting. 16. Many of the knights seated across from her lost their senses altogether. They felt such a need to look at her that they forgot the bread and wine in their hands. 17. She was so beautiful and fair that she caused many knights to neglect their food. They forgot what they had in their mouths and stared at the noble queen. 18. There was a goblet of bright gold. When she brought it to her lips, her complexion glowed in the wine like a rose. Salman himself didn't know how to act for joy.

19. The song tells us that King Salman loved his lady and found the utmost joy whenever he lay in her white arms in their chamber. 20. This made the king very happy. Suffering and anguish were in store, however, since the lives of many proud knights were sacrificed on account of this wondrously beautiful woman.

21. What I am telling you is true: Salman lived undisturbed with his wife until the fourth year. Then a mighty pagan whose realm lay across the sea began to pine for the beautiful lady. 22. His father was Minnolt, a very proud pagan, and he himself was called Fore. He was an arrogant pagan who was acquainted with many lands. 23. Thirty-six dukes and fifty counts served at his court, without a doubt. Sixteen pagan kings were subject to him. 24. One Sunday he stepped into the hall before his warriors and said, "I seek counsel from all of you, my vassals, in the matter of a beautiful lady, whom I would like to have as my wife. 25. I would like to take a noble highborn queen, as you advise, appropriate to my nobility and suitable as mistress of this fair land of Wendelsea."

26. "Lord," his vassals all replied, "not one of us is able to recommend a noble highborn queen, suitable for you as mistress of the mighty land of Wendelsea."

27. When the last of them had finished speaking, the king looked down in anger. To a man, his vassals regretted that they were not able to recommend a beautiful lady to him. 28. Then one man, gray with age, spoke up: "As I have become acquainted with many lands, I know there is a Christian queen across the raging sea in the fair city of Jerusalem. 29. She is fair and beautiful, a noble queen, held by King Salman. She would suit you well as mistress of the fair land of Wendelsea."

30. When he had finished speaking, the king looked up with joy. "King Salman will not be able to keep his wife from me for long. 31. Sooner or later I will take her from him, no matter what he thinks. I will cross the sea with a mighty army and bestow lasting riches on anyone who aids me."

32. Then King Crispian spoke up: "Lord, we're talking about my beautiful, lovely daughter, whom Salman took from me against my will. I lament before you, dear lord, that my heart has never relinquished her to him. 33. Lord," King Crispian continued, "if you are going to undertake this expedition, I will send you, at my own expense, four thousand brave knights for a year. That many I can support for sure. 34. I'll send them across the raging sea to the city of Jerusalem in pursuit of my beautiful daughter. I cannot stop grieving that she has a Christian husband."

35. Then the king of Duscan spoke, "Lord, if you are going to undertake this expedition, I will bring you, at my own expense, six thousand brave knights for a year. That many I can support for sure. 36. I will bring them to you across the raging sea to the city of Jerusalem in pursuit of the noble queen. I'll never get over my grief if she remains among Christians."

37. Then King Princian spoke, "Lord, if you're going to go there, I will send you, at my own expense, six thousand brave knights for a year. That many I can support for sure. 38. At my court, thirty-six dukes and fifty counts are at my service, truly. I will send you thirty thousand men at my own expense for an entire year. 39. I'll send them to you across the raging sea to the fair city of Jerusalem. If you arrive with a mighty army, King Salman will not be able to keep his fair wife from you for very long."

40. How quickly the pagan king found a messenger! He sent him across the raging sea to mighty King Salman in the fair city of Jerusalem.

41. "Lord," said the messenger, "no matter how long it takes, my lord intends to carry off your marvelously beautiful wife, never mind what you think, using the full strength of his army, or it will cost him his life."

42. "I'm sure I can prevent that," King Salman replied. "At my court I have maintained counts as well as dukes in the greatest splendor. 43. If that arrogant man comes to me, it will cost him his life. By my body and soul, if I am able, I intend to prevent him from getting to Salome, that marvelously beautiful woman."

44. How quickly the pagan procured forty ships! He ordered clothing and provisions to be carried onto the ships, enough to last them an entire year. 45. When the ships had been made ready, that was the beginning of pain and anguish. Many pagan men sailed across the waters of the raging sea with mighty King Fore. 46. Once the ships had been loaded, they cast off from the shore without delay and crossed the raging sea. On the tenth morning they saw the fair city of Jerusalem. 47. You will want to hear what Fore said when he saw the city: "King Salman will not be able to prevent me from taking his lovely wife this very day."

48. All his vassals set their sights boldly on the same goal. But King Salman also had many proud knights and lords ready to help him defend his honor before the fair city of Jerusalem. 49. When they entered the harbor at Jerusalem, the sailors turned the ships towards the shore. The pagan fighters put on their steel armor. A duke by the name of Elian took their standard into his hand. 50. They moved onto the field towards Jerusalem, pitched their tents, and camped on the broad plain. Thus was noble King Salman besieged by a mighty army.

51. Then the pagan, Fore, said to Duke Elian, "We need a messenger, brave enough to deliver our challenge to King Salman, 52. that he must give me his beautiful wife or fight a battle with me before Jerusalem. These are the only two options: he must give me the lady or he must meet me here in battle."

53. "In that case," Duke Elian replied, "I will go up into the city of Jerusalem myself and deliver the challenge to King Salman. I will undertake this mission even if it costs me my life." 54. That same Duke Elian put on a robe of ermine interwoven with gold and set out for the city in order to challenge the king.

55. Truly, this you should know: Salman had taken his place in the palace, with the noble queen seated on one side and Morolf, his dear brother, on the other. 56. When Elian entered the palace, Salman received him very graciously, welcoming him in God's name. Morolf and the noble queen also received him courteously. 57. After Salman had welcomed him, Elian knelt down, as was fitting, and said, "Mighty King Salman, if you will grant me leave, I have a message to deliver."

58. "Say what you will," King Salman replied, "you have my leave."

Elian began, "Have you not heard the news? The King of Wendelsea has arrived here with an army. 59. You must give him your lovely wife or else meet him in battle before Jerusalem. These are the only two options: you must give him your wife or face him here in battle."

60. King Salman answered Duke Elian, "Before I surrender my beautiful wife, many a brave knight will have to lose his life."

61. Elian wanted to leave, but Morolf told him to remain where he was standing. "Elian," he said, "can you tell me, in good faith, how strong your army is?"

62. "It has a good forty thousand men," Duke Elian replied. "If I have my way," declared Morolf, the knight, "they will all lose their lives. 63. Elian, tell your lord we will be ready for battle in fourteen days."

The clever man said, "These miserable pagans will lose their lives, each and every one."

64. Elian took his leave and returned to his army. All the lords could be seen coming to meet him. King Fore asked, "What message has King Salman sent me? 65. Will he give me his lovely wife or will he meet me in battle before Jerusalem? These are the only two options: either he must give me the woman or he must meet me here in battle."

66. "Lord," Elian replied, "if it's true what I heard them both say, they have no intention of giving up without a fight. I fear that many a proud knight will have to lose his life before the beautiful woman is ours."

67. Noble King Salman dispatched swift messengers to summon many worthy knights, who were expected to stand by him loyally in the fierce battle. 68. The king of Morocco arrived and was seen riding up with a mighty army. He had come into the land of Jerusalem with many proud heroes. He showed his readiness to help. 69. The citizens of Naples came, and those of Marseilles raised a mighty troop. They came to Jerusalem along with the mighty king of Schrap, who showed his readiness to help. 70. In this way King Salman gained a great many worthy men into his service. Thirty-five thousand proud, illustrious heroes offered him loyal aid.

71. Then clever Morolf declared, "Even if the pagan has five thousand more, we are a Christian people. Christ, the mighty lord of heaven, will never abandon us." 72. Morolf ordered a banner of red silk to be made with an image [of Christ] embroidered in gold, a reminder to the noble lords that they were fighting as Christians. 73. Morolf, the clever man, took the banner in his hands, and all the noble lords readied themselves for battle. Then a challenge was delivered to the army of the miserable pagans. 74. The battle trumpets were sounded, and the highborn kings drew their armies together. Sounds of lamentation arose from the battle as many a proud knight cried out loudly in pain from his wounds.

75. The battle was vast, and one could hear many strong blows being struck. The might of the pagans turned to naught before Jerusalem, and those who managed to escape from the battle drowned as soon as they reached the sea. 76. Before the city the battle got underway, which had been provoked by the arrogance of King Fore on account of Salome, the beautiful woman. The fighting lasted until the fourth day, by which time thirty-five thousand of the wretched pagans lay dead. 77. That's how long the battle lasted, during which many men lost their lives. King Fore was defeated and, having lost many pagans, was taken prisoner.

78. Noble King Salman compelled King Fore to follow him off of the battlefield, towards Jerusalem, and up into his castle, where Salome the noble queen received him courteously. 79. Having gained victory over Fore, King Salman said, "Tell me, my men, in what way should I hold the mighty king captive?"

80. "Lord," the clever man replied, "I can give you good advice. Recall, my dear lord, the sort of loyalty with which King Fore arrived here. 81. Don't forget that the arrogant man wanted to steal your beautiful wife. No, dear lord, it should cost him his life. 82. Mighty King Salman, if you're afraid to lay hands on Fore yourself, then turn him over to me, excellent knight. I give you my word on it, I don't care a fig for my good name."

83. "That would bring me lasting shame," King Salman said, "unless he had been killed in battle. That's something I would have gotten over pretty quickly, you can take my word for it. 84. I will have him put in chains. He will lie bound, on my order, and die in captivity. And I will have Salome, that marvelously beautiful woman, watch over him."

85. "Lord," said Morolf, "I don't think that's a good idea. If you place straw near the flame, it's very likely to catch fire. That's just what you'll see happen to King Fore if you leave him near your wife."

86. Then King Salman said, "Morolf, what did she ever do to you that you hold such a low opinion of her? I give you my word, I have no worries on that score."

87. "Mighty King Salman," the clever man replied, "you are bringing shame and misfortune upon yourself. I give you my word, you'll never dare complain about it to me."

88. Salman grew angry at these words. "Morolf," he said, "you have lost my favor. Nor will you ever enjoy it again, since you can't bring yourself to trust the noble highborn queen."

89. To which the clever man replied, "Mighty King Salman, let me tell you this, if she makes a fool of you, I'll stand back and leave you to your own devices."

90. Salman ignored Morolf's threat and had the lady watch over Fore. That wasn't such a smart thing to do, since she became intimate with the pagan king.

91. After Salman ordered Fore put in chains, he had the lady watch over him. Thus he was guarded very well—just as if you turned your she-goat over to a bunch of fine billy goats. 92. Now hear, just as that she-goat was looked after, so too was the queen. King Fore was a clever man, who used powerful magic to gain the beautiful lady. 93. A pagan by the name of Elias was a master of the magic arts. King Fore was his uncle. Using powerful magic, he set a gemstone into a ring. 94. After the magic had been prepared and placed in the ring, he sent it across the raging sea to mighty King Fore, who was suffering in his chains.

95. When Fore received the ring, he placed it in the lady's hand and said, "Most noble queen, wear this ring of red gold for my sake." 96. When she looked at the ring, its magic caused her at once to delight in the gold, and she became fond beyond measure of mighty King Fore. 97. She picked up the ring and brought it to Morolf. She asked him to hold it up to the sun and look to see if there was anything in it that might diminish her good name. 98. When Morolf held it up to the sun, the gold was so bright that, for all his cleverness, he was not able to recognize the magic that lay in the ring. 99. Drawing the ring onto her finger, she very quickly felt the magic power of the gem, so that from that day forth she was devoted to King Fore.

100. Seated next to her one day, he said, "Have mercy, noble queen! Bear in mind that I sacrificed many men on your account."

101. "Don't say that, King Fore," the beautiful lady replied. "King Salman is a wise man, yet I fear his vassal Morolf much, much more."

102. "Most noble queen," the arrogant man declared, "if I knew it's what you wanted, I'm clever enough to outsmart both of them, that's for sure. 103. You realize, beautiful lady, that they should not have left you with me. You think they are smart. But I give you my word: I am smarter than three of them."

Figure 7. Salome frees King Fore.
Frankfurt a. M., Universitätsbibliothek, Ms. germ. qu. 13, fol. 16ᵛ.

104. "Don't say that, King Fore," the beautiful lady replied. "No man of any sort has ever been born who is even a tenth as clever as Morolf. 105. Indeed," said the noble queen, "just by looking at the color in my face, he can tell when I have changed my mind. I know for sure, King Fore, that this will cost us both our lives."

106. "At my court," declared Fore, "I am served by thirty-six dukes, fifty counts, and sixteen pagan kings, without exaggeration. I will make them all subject to you. 107. Your father Crispian serves me, lady, but I will release him permanently from all such obligations."

"In that case I am happy to follow you," the noble queen replied.

108. King Fore was pleased to hear these words. "Lady," the nefarious pagan continued, "I plan to give you more: you shall rule absolutely over the rich land of Wendelsea. 109. Lady," he said, "six months from today, I will send you a pagan minstrel bearing two turtledoves. You can count on it. Be sure to give him a warm welcome. 110. In his hands, lady, he will carry a German harp, which you will recognize by the fact that it sparkles with precious gems. He will also bring you a magical herb, in such a way that no one will recognize him. 111. Place it in your mouth, lady, and you will become ill and fall on the grass as if dead—although your radiant complexion will remain unchanged."

112. Then the beautiful lady declared, "Not just today but for the rest of my life I will regret that such a mighty prince should have to leave this place on foot."

113. "I have no problem with going on foot," the pagan replied. "I am lying here in great pain. Set me free, noble queen, and I'll be quite happy to go on foot."

114. She released the chains that bound the pagan and said, "Lord, now leave this land quickly and send me a messenger in good time, since I'm not happy as the wife of King Salman."

115. When the pagan had escaped and they heard the news at court, the clever man declared, "It was the noble queen who let him out, an act of great treachery."

116. "Morolf," King Salman replied, "what did she ever do to you, that you hold such a low opinion of her? A noble, young lady-in-waiting set him free, for which the queen bears no responsibility whatsoever."

117. "King," said Morolf the knight, "you should keep a close watch on her. I tell you truly, in less than six months the noble queen will have left you."

118. And the clever man continued, "Mighty King Salman, I'm only trying to tell you the truth. But even if I could prevent it, you're going to have to see it with your own eyes."

119. They didn't say another word about this matter for six months. That's when the pagan minstrel arrived bearing two turtledoves and entered the lady's service. 120. In his hands he carried a German harp, which the lady recognized without difficulty. It sparkled with precious gems. He also brought her a magical herb, in such a way that no one recognized him. 121. The queen became aware of the magic herb as she was going to church, when the pagan minstrel approached her. He recognized the beautiful lady from what he had heard said about her. 122. She took the harp from his hands. He offered the herb to her on the spot, and then she gave the harp back to him. "Hero," she said, "leave the court at once, before Morolf realizes you are here."

123. After she entered the church, they began the high mass. She didn't waste much time on the Lord's Prayer, however, since all she could think of was the magic herb. 124. Nor were her prayers really addressed to God. She could hardly wait until the blessing had been given. "Now," thought the noble queen, "I've got to find out what's up with this herb." 125. She placed it in her mouth without letting anyone see. Before long she became ill and fell to the ground as if dead, although her radiant complexion remained unchanged.

126. At court they had no choice but to spread the news that the queen had died a sudden death. At this the clever man declared, "This death of the noble queen is an effect of magic. 127. Earlier today I encountered the lady, beautiful and fair," the young knight said. "She was completely healthy, of that I have no doubt." 128. When King Salman heard the news and then saw with his own eyes what had happened, he felt such anguish of heart that he tore the hair out of his head.

129. "It is a shame," said Morolf the hero, "to see a prince take a hand to his curly, blond hair. This death of the noble queen is an effect of magic." 130. The illustrious warrior continued, "I have traveled through many lands and was, at one time, a physician's helper. If I am allowed to get to the lady, I'm quite certain she would recover."

131. "Morolf," King Salman replied, "don't talk like that. You have done too many things that brought pain to me and the noble queen. By my faith, you really should cease your mockery."

132. Morolf thought to himself, "I must test the queen further, so that I have a better idea of what has happened to her. If she escapes me here, I'll be the one who has to search for her in foreign lands."

133. Now hear what he did: he poured molten gold through her snow-white hand. She didn't feel a thing, however, on account of the powerful magic.

134. "Morolf," King Salman declared, "now you have committed a real injustice. Get out of my sight at once. What are you accusing the dead queen of having done?"

135. "Lord," the clever man replied, "I think I did exactly the right thing. She is not yet dead, since her radiant complexion has not changed. 136. Death does many things, but it does not leave people with that much color in their cheeks. Her complexion blazes like a red rose. I give you my word, her death is pure trickery."

137. These words made Salman angry. "Morolf, you have lost my favor. Get out of my way at once. By God, I never want to set eyes on you again."

138. Morolf, the peerless knight, saw an oven alongside the path. The clever man slipped into it, with the intention of mocking mighty King Salman. 139. You will enjoy hearing what Morolf had to say when the king looked into the oven. King Salman spoke first: "This is not the first time in your life that you have brought me shame."

140. Morolf replied, "You swore an oath that I had lost your favor utterly and forbade me to show my face in your presence. Now, dear lord, see what my rear end looks like."

141. Noble King Salman shook from anger. "If it wouldn't disgrace me," the wise man said, "you would lose your life for this. 142. If you really were my brother, you would have sympathy for my great suffering and put an end to your mockery. But you never were my brother. I deny you my favor now and forever."

143. Salman had a coffin made for the queen out of red gold, just as if she were an angel, and she was placed in it. 144. "It's a shame you're going to throw away all that gold," said Morolf the knight. "If anyone cared to follow my advice, she would have been carried out to a desolate bog. That's the truth." 145. Morolf went secretly to the coffin and placed a wagonload of stones on top of it. But then the pagan minstrel arrived and brought Salome home to his lord.

146. It was on the third day, according to the story, that the coffin was opened, leaving King Salman with nothing to show for his trusting devotion, 147. since the beautiful lady had stolen away with the pagan minstrel and accompanied him across the raging sea. Before Morolf got her back again, God knows, he was made miserable time and time again. 148. Five days later Salman had reason to grieve. He began to think, "It's time for me to find out if the queen is really still in the coffin."

149. Without letting anyone know, he went to the coffin, and when he saw that it had been broken open, I believe he suffered greater anguish of heart than he had ever experienced before. 150. "Alas," he cried, "now I must bear this, and I dare not tell the news at court if Morolf is present." The king saw a pretty maiden, gestured to her with his hand, and said, "Why aren't you burning incense for my wife?" 151. Having said this, he left immediately. The young lady picked up a silver censer. But when she saw that the coffin had been broken open, she brought the news to court without delay 152. and told the hero

Salman—who had, of course, actually seen it first. "The queen has run away from us," he declared. "By my faith, my brother Morolf told me this would happen."

153. Salman rushed off to find Morolf. "Morolf," he said, "my dear brother, I hope I can count on a kind reception when I tell you the terrible news that the queen has escaped."

154. "Lord," the clever man replied, "I can't believe that your wife deceived you. I give you my word, she has pulled the wool over your eyes. 155. If I were as wise as you, King Salman, and if I were as beautiful as Absalom, and if I could sing as beautifully as Horant, and if I still could not keep my wife in line, I would have a disgrace on my hands."

156. "Now let's stop this talk," King Salman said. "Find the noble queen for me and I will give you half the fair land of Jerusalem."

157. Now that the queen had escaped from Jerusalem, King Salman said, "Morolf, my dear brother, you must be my envoy to the noble queen."

158. Morolf, the clever man, replied, "Mighty King Salman, since you have declared me to be your brother, I'll do anything, lord, that you request."

159. Morolf went into the city of Jerusalem to ask advice of a Jew, who was so old that his hair was white as snow. His gray beard could be seen to fall below his belt. 160. The Jew was called Berman. The illustrious knight began, "I need your advice, Berman, since the king means to send me off in search of his beautiful wife." 161. Without a moment's hesitation, Berman took Morolf by the hand and led him into a room, planning to give him advice then and there. But Morolf drew out a long, sharp knife and thrust it through the Jew's heart, right up to his hand. 162. Morolf, Salman's favorite, removed the Jew's skin from above his waist, rubbed it with balsam, and placed it over his own body. "Now," he said, "I will never turn back until I find the amazingly beautiful woman."

163. This extremely clever man had travelled through many lands. No matter how the illustrious knight moved, the skin conformed to his movements as if it had grown on him. 164. Morolf made his way into the presence of King Salman, and said, "Illustrious, noble king, for the glory of all women, give of your wealth to make me rich."

165. King Salman replied, "If it's for the joy that I have had from the woman I wed, I won't give you very much for that! If you ask for the sake of God in heaven, however, I am ready to share my wealth with you."

166. He had him given three marks of gold on the spot. Then Morolf saw a golden ring on Salman's finger and said, "King, in the name of your greatest virtue and for the glory of all women, give me that golden ring. 167. Since it would be an appropriate gift from you, I will receive it with pleasure." The king removed the ring and offered it to him very graciously. Morolf bowed most courteously in return.

168. The fine proud knight put the ring on his finger and got out of there at once, in excellent spirits since the king had not recognized him. 169. That's how the clever man left the worthy king without being found out. Having done so, he went into a pleasant room, took off the Jew's skin, and put on garments of fine wool. 170. Then he went and stood before King Salman. "King," he said, "in the name of your greatest virtue and for the glory of all women, where is your golden ring?"

171. "I gave it to a gray-haired, old man," King Salman replied. At that Morolf began to laugh and said, "Look here, noble king, I have it on my finger."

172. The mighty king kissed him for joy and said, "My dear Morolf, your tricks are amazing. No one in all the world is really safe from them, no matter where you go."

173. Then he presented him with a wanderer's staff and a sack, that much I can tell you, both of which were richly decorated. Morolf declared, "Either I will find the dead queen, or I will remain a wanderer forever."

174. Morolf had a little ship of leather made ready. Since it was going to put to sea, it was well coated with pitch. Two windows gave him light. He made it with his own hands. 175. Winds could do him no harm on the raging sea, that much I can tell you. He carried the little ship at his side as if it were a leather sack, and it saved his life on many occasions.

176. Morolf said to Salman, "My dear lord, I entrust to your care my little child Malen."

After they had the child brought forward, Salman said, "I bestow on you all the fiefs that your father Morolf is supposed to have."

177. Then this very clever man took leave of the illustrious king and of many proud, noble knights and crossed the raging sea, suffering greatly, in search of the queen. 178. What I'm telling you is true: for a full seven years he wandered from one city to another until he came to the country of Wendelsea. Once there, he pushed his boat through the reeds and onto the sand. 179. Having left his boat where it stood, Morolf saw an old pagan walking in the street far ahead of him. Morolf called out to him, at the top of his voice, "I intend to end your life, right here."

180. "No, excellent knight," the pagan man replied, "you should let me live. Many years ago I was a gatekeeper at Wendelsea."

181. Then the clever man said, "Tell me, you old pagan, how do things stand in the city of your lord? I've been told he has an amazingly beautiful wife he loves so much, she's as dear to him as his own life."

182. "Sir," replied the pagan, "I can tell you, her complexion glows like a resplendent rose. In all my days, I have never seen a more beautiful queen."

183. Morolf, the clever man, pulled out a splendid knife, long, sharp, and a joy to behold. He stuck it through the pagan's heart, so that it went in up to his hand. 184. Then the brave, proud knight picked up the old pagan and threw him into a deep ditch. "If someone asks you what happened," he said, "you're not going to be telling anyone anything."

185. Morolf, Salman's favorite, slipped into the skin for the second time. He wrapped himself in a rough, woolen cloak, put a palm on his back, and took a crutch under his arm. 186. From there the noble hero trekked up to the strong citadel at Wendelsea. When he arrived at court, he saw King Fore and a large number of pagan men. 187. They were playing many different sorts of games. Some threw the lance. Quite a few hurled the stone. There in the presence of mighty King Fore they were playing games of many different kinds. 188. There was a linden tree in the courtyard, the story tells us, with wide spreading branches. Beneath it stood a lovely seat, but no one dared sit on it who was not of noble lineage.

189. When Morolf heard this, the clever man did not wait long: he set out across the court towards the green linden tree at an astonishing speed. 190. And when he got to the seat, the clever man sat down on it. Then, having sat down, the noble hero planted his staff in the grass and took his ease. 191. A tablet hung at court. The moment it sounded, King Fore went to church followed by many fine knights. But Morolf, the illustrious hero, was still sitting there on his seat. 192. They ordered the peerless knight to get out of their way at once. But Morolf, the worthy hero, didn't intend to yield ground to any of them, not so much as a single foot.

193. Six men, among them a chamberlain, rushed forward, all carrying sticks in their hands with which they meant to beat the worthy prince. But Morolf, the celebrated knight, stood his ground without a moment's hesitation.

194. "No, excellent knight," the clever man said. "If you deal me a single blow, I'll pay you back with my crutch so that you'll remember me till Judgment Day."

195. King Fore laughed and said, "Leave the stranger in peace. I can tell from his fine physique and see from the way he acts that he is of high lineage."

196. Then Fore, the mighty king, went to church accompanied by many worthy knights and followed by his gracious queen. That was Lady Salome, the beautiful, charming lady. 197. You will want to hear what Morolf said when he saw her approach.

"Isn't that Salome, the queen (in all my life I never saw a more beautiful woman) 198. who ran away from us in Jerusalem? Having travelled so long in foreign lands," the illustrious knight continued, "I'm delighted to see that my journey has not been in vain."

199. The queen was accompanied by three groups of beautiful maidens, all of lovely color. They walked with heads uncovered, save for narrow ribbons, by which one could tell they were maidens. 200. Morolf let counts and ladies pass by, and all the while the clever man just sat there on his seat. When the queen approached him, however, Morolf jumped up and bowed to her most courteously.

201. How quickly he sat back down on the bench! He cursed the heathen priest for taking so long to say mass. "Shameful Saracen!" he said, "what have you got to sing about today? May a thousand devils take you!"

202. When the mass was over, the pagan Fore left the church, followed by many worthy knights. Morolf, the proud, noble hero, stood up from his seat. 203. The clever man made his way to the stairs by which the queen was to leave the church and stood to one side very respectfully. 204. Seeing him, the handsome lady said, "Welcome in God's name, pilgrim. Mother's son now old and gray, what lands have you left behind you on your way into these pagan realms?"

205. "Most noble and exalted queen," he replied, "long have I travelled around the raging sea. I have come to you, noble queen, trusting in your mercy. You should give me a gift."

206. "Pilgrim," said the fair lady in response, "if you wish to remain here with me, I will gladly give you bread and wine, of which no one will deprive you save death, yours or mine."

207. "Lady," he said, "I am a sinful man and cannot remain for long in any one place. I will rest here thirteen nights. Have food given to me during that time, lovely, highborn lady."

208. Then the noble queen asked, "Pilgrim, have you ever been to Jerusalem? Did you ever see King Salman and Morolf, his brother and loyal vassal?"

209. "Mighty, noble queen," he replied, "seven years ago I was in Jerusalem, where I saw King Salman and Morolf his brother, both of them downcast. 210. Death had taken the queen from them quite suddenly. Deeply distressed, the prince and his brother Morolf lamented their misfortune. They had sealed her in a coffin beneath a rock, but then the devil came and carried her back home with him."

211. The lady started to laugh. When she turned back again, she took Morolf by the hand and asked the chamberlain to care for him and to give the pilgrim relief from all his burdens. 212. "Worthy knight," she said, "take good care of this stranger, for he is a pilgrim weary from travel. Make sure there is clear wine standing at the side of his bed tonight."

213/214. Covering his body Morolf wore fine steel armor, which a young duchess happened to see. Tables were being set up in the presence of Fore, the heathen king, befitting a mighty prince of noble birth. 215. When the tables at court had been cleared, the young duchess rose from her seat, went to the queen, and stood before her most courteously, a beautiful maiden, worthy of praise. 216. "Lady," she said, "by your leave, I would tell you something about the pilgrim: on his body I saw armor of fine steel, as a brave knight should wear."

217. The handsome queen responded, "Bring the stranger to me at once and ask him where he has come from across the sea. Perhaps he will tell me the truth." So said the noble queen.

218. The maiden left immediately and made her way across the court to where she found Morolf. "Get up, stranger," she said, "you must go to my lady's chamber as quickly as possible. 219. Tell me, where have you come from across the sea? To start with, you should tell the noble queen things she has not heard; that's what my lady likes to hear. She cannot tolerate any further delay on your part."

220. The very clever man replied, "Lovely, charming maiden, just let me rest until tomorrow morning. If my lady likes to hear unfamiliar tales, I've certainly got some I can tell her."

221. The worthy maiden insisted, "You've got to come along to the queen at once."

But Morolf, feeling a sudden terror of the murderous Salome, was afraid for his life. 222. He ignored the queen's summons, and the maiden left him sitting there. She told this to her lovely mistress, who replied, "Let the travel-weary man rest until morning."

223. Early the next morning, mighty King Fore got ready, had his hunting clothes brought to him, and rode out to hunt without delay. 224. That same morning, early, Morolf went to the queen with a plan. You will want to hear what he said to the queen when he first saw her.

225. "Lady, isn't there some game you'd like to play? Have it brought to you right away. Since I'm in need of money, I'll wager my head against your bright, red gold."

226. She said she would be happy to oblige. Thinking she was going to win great renown, the queen signaled to one of her attendants and had her fetch without delay a fine chessboard, mounted in gold. 227. It was inlaid with many precious gemstones, emeralds and hyacinths, sparkling bright as day. The noble lady made the first move with her white hand. 228. The chess set was white and red, yellow and green. Confident she'd be able to get Morolf in a tight spot, she said, "Now make your move, stranger. You're going to have a hard time keeping me from winning your head."

229. "Lady," he asked, "what are you betting against my head?"

Figure 8. Salome and Morolf play chess.
Stuttgart, Landesbibliothek, Cod. HB XIII 2, fol. 309ᵛ.

To which the noble queen replied, "Thirty gold marks I'll bet against you, and in addition I'll grant you safe conduct to travel wherever you want in this country."

230. "Lady," he said, "if you're going to bet against my head, then put up the most beautiful maiden you have in your chamber."

"Even if you do win the game," the handsome lady responded, "what would you be able to do with maidens?"

231. "Beautiful, lovely lady," this most clever man replied, "let me tell you: if I win the game, she will have to carry my pilgrim's sack."

232. Many of the ladies laughed at this and said, "He's a clever one, that graybeard."

But the queen said, "Now choose for yourself the one you like best of all, and I will bet her against you."

233. Morolf pointed to the place where King Fore's sister was seated and said, "If I can have this fair maiden, most noble queen, for her I'll wager my head."

234. The young lady burst out laughing, "You're bound to be disappointed, good pilgrim, since King Fore is my brother. Even if you win this game, you will have lost it."

235. When Morolf heard this, the clever man replied, "Lovely maiden of great beauty, unless you are set as my prize, I'll abandon the game."

236. Before he had finished speaking, he saw the young lady in front of him at the board. "Pilgrim far from home," she said, "make a move now. I trust I can protect you from the tricks of the noble queen. 237. Now make a move, noble, proud, brave knight, you are safe from any deception. You seem to be a virtuous man: if you win the game, I will cast my lot with you."

238. For many moves, the queen had the advantage. But Morolf knew how to take care of himself: his skills were so fearsome that he allowed the noble queen to gain the better position on the board. 239. "What use are all your clever moves?" she asked. "Your head is mine to dispose of. You're going to regret this game, since it will cost you your life. That's what comes from your foolishness."

240. "Lady," he said, "if you do win, you can dispose of my head as you see fit. Still, I have travelled in many lands, and in the whole world I have never found my master at this game."

241. Then he picked up a bishop and, in violation of the rules, set it down with great satisfaction in front of the queen.

"What use are all your clever tricks?" she said. "Your head belongs to me, I give you my word on it. 242. I'll have it chopped off, that's the truth. You were too quick with that move. Look," she said, "with this knight I checkmate you."

243. "Lady," he said, "if you do win, you can dispose of my head as you see fit. However, if you let me depart unharmed, I will proclaim for the rest of my days that you are a noble queen."

244. Morolf found himself in a tight spot, so he let go a loud fart right there in front of the queen. "Tell me, you old tramp," the handsome lady asked, "why did you do that?"

245. "Because I am afraid of your anger," Morolf told the queen. "I've been given to understand, beautiful lady, that if you win this game, I'll lose my head." 246.

Morolf wasn't serious when he said this. He was thinking, "I'm pretty sure my head will be safe after all. We should change places." With great cunning Morolf asked the queen to come sit at his side. 247. Now for the first time he was able to see through her hand, through the spot where he had burned a hole with the gold. When the sun shone through her glove, he was finally certain he knew who she was. Then he took another of her pieces.

248. When he crossed the sea in search of the noble highborn queen, Morolf had brought with him a ring of red gold, into which a nightingale had been beautifully worked with great artistry. 249. When he slipped the ring onto his finger, the nightingale opened its mouth and sang, filling the air with sweet sound, as it should. The queen looked intently at the ring, giving Morolf time to take a knight and two of her pawns. 250. Now he was happy to be sitting at the table. The queen stared at the nightingale for so long that she forgot about the chess pieces. And that's how Morolf won the game. As it turned out, the time he spent with the queen had passed pleasantly indeed. 251. "Lady," he said, "if you have lost the game, then the pilgrim from abroad has saved his gray head." Morolf raised his voice in song quite splendidly, thereby robbing the noble queen of a good deal of happiness. 252. He sang better than any other man, so that everyone who heard him was filled with joy. He sang a lovely melody, just as King David had taken it from three books.

253. Hearing this, the beautiful lady asked, "Pilgrim, where did you learn this delightful song? It's been many a day since I heard it sung at my father's table. Your singing reminds me of the great splendor I have had to leave behind."

254. "Most noble queen," he replied, "I was a minstrel called Stolzelin, living off the gifts of those I praised. But I gave that up to serve almighty God. 255. Noble highborn queen, for a long time I have journeyed around the raging sea, across mountains and through valleys. No country was hidden from me, no matter how great or small. 256. My travels brought me to the capital of Gilest, where the sun has its throne, next to which lies the country of Endian. That's where I learned this beautiful tune, which brings such pleasure. 257. The only place I have heard

it since then was in the fair city of Jerusalem, where it was sung in the presence of King Salman by a charming, handsome duke named Morolf."

258. "Be silent now," the lovely lady said, "and don't say another word. You are Morolf, Salman's vassal. If King Fore comes to see me, it will cost you your life."

259. "Lady," he said, "I will defend myself against the accusation you have just made. The last time I saw Morolf, truly, his beard had not yet started to grow. But look here, my hair is gray."

260. But the lovely lady insisted, "You are Morolf, Salman's vassal. You burned a hole in my hand, and that hurt me. I give you my word, you will never see Jerusalem again."

261. When Morolf heard her say that, he tore off the Jew's skin and threw it far from him. His hair was blond and quite curly. "Noble queen," he said, "behold Morolf, entire! 262. If I'm going to lose my life anyway, I'll cause you as much pain as I can beforehand, lovely, fair lady. Yes, fatally faithless woman, looking for you I have travelled a great many roads through pagan lands. 263. Let me profit from that, lady: guarantee my safety within this place until sunrise tomorrow, noble lady, and I will not ask for a longer truce."

264. "Be silent, now," the lovely lady replied, "and don't say another word about this. You are such a clever man, even if you were locked behind a thousand bolts, no one would be able to hold on to you."

265. Morolf was afraid of the wicked, murderous woman, afraid he would lose his life. The very clever man was overcome with anxiety that he would perish then and there. 266. Morolf would not let up, however, before the queen guaranteed his safety until early the next morning. He lay prostrate before the noble queen, beseeching her loudly. 267. When the sun was about to set, Morolf went and stood before the queen. "Noble highborn queen," he said, "let one of your chamberlains walk with me a short time, 268. down to the shore of the raging sea. Lovely, fair lady, a man who is not going to see midday tomorrow must enjoy whatever pleasures he can manage."

269. Then an old Saracen said, "You should not deny him that, most noble queen." The lovely queen accompanied him, bringing sixty pagan fighters along with her. 270. They went and looked out at the sea.

"Would you like to go to Jerusalem with me?" Morolf asked the queen.

"Stop right there," she said, "and don't say another word about this. At Jerusalem you caused me a great deal of intense pain. 271. Before we're done here, I plan to arrange things so that you'll never see that fair city again. I'll have you hanging from a tree, I give you my word." I do believe that she failed in this.

272. "Then," he said, "may God take my soul into his care. I was sent to find you by the peerless knight Salman, who lost you long ago. Alas, the great

anguish he will suffer, for there will never be any getting over your loss. 273. Most noble highborn queen," he said, "permit one of your chamberlains to go down to the sea with me, since I want to confess my sins to the reeds. As you are well aware, noble queen, I'm not going to find any other priest."

274. "Your clever tricks aren't going to help you," the noble queen replied. "You're going to have to leave your life here with me." She took him by the hand and led the peerless knight back in. 275. She entrusted the brave proud knight to the custody of twelve pagans. "Guard the clever man carefully," she said, "for if he runs away from you and escapes, it will cost all of you your lives." 276. They led the excellent man away to a lovely chamber. The noble queen went with him. They sat next to each other and found much to talk about.

277. One of the chamberlains said to the queen, "There's no reason why you can't get some rest, and you don't have to worry that he will run away from us. I'll wager my head on that." 278. The queen went to bed, leaving Morolf in the chamber. This excellent man sat beside his attendants and told them strange tales until they all grew drowsy.

279. Then Morolf started coughing, and the candle that had been burning there went out. "Now tell me, noble knight," one of the pagans asked, "why did you do that?"

280. "Let me assure you," he replied, "it happened quite by accident. Have another candle brought out, and we're bound to pass the time most pleasantly. 281. Now have another candle lit, since this one won't burn properly. If two or three are stationed at the door, you can all stop worrying that somebody might get away."

282. But before the candle was brought, Morolf had thought of a plan. A goblet of red gold stood next to him into which he poured a sleeping potion from a tiny cask he had with him. 283. Once the candle had been lit, he said, "Gentlemen, if you're feeling thirsty, then drink your fill of this wine. It's a very fine wine from Cyprus that was left for me by the noble queen. 284. It must be nearly daybreak. You should finish off the wine, since, as you heroes must have heard, worldly goods can't help me with the most noble queen. 285. I'm going to lose my life. Now pay attention, illustrious heroes: since worldly goods can't be of any use to me, you really should have the rest of this wine. I'll give you the goblet too."

286. He placed it in hands of the best of them. They drank heartily and fell down to the ground. Observing this, the pagan who held the goblet in his hands looked at them all 287. and said, "What has gotten into your heads that you have lain down and gone to sleep? If the Christian escapes from us, it will cost us our lives."

288. "They just did this as a joke," the clever man explained. "If you're the last one holding the wine, when you finish it off, the goblet will be yours."

289. When the pagan drank, he lost hold of the goblet and sank down onto a bench. That's when Morolf, the fine proud knight, was freed from anxiety and found himself in a very happy frame of mind. 290. He took a pair of scissors out of his sack, it's the truth, and cut the hair off all twelve of them above their ears. Then he picked up a shaving knife and, with his mighty hand, gave each of them a tonsure. 291. When Morolf had done that, he made his way to the gate and told the gatekeeper to let him out. "I must get out onto the raging sea as soon as possible," he said, "to catch some fish for the noble highborn queen."

292. "I dare not let anyone out before daybreak," the pagan replied. "The queen herself forbade me to do so, I can tell you that in truth."

293. Morolf, the great and illustrious hero, made his way into the gate-keeper's room and said, "Watchman, my dear friend, for your love of me, open the gate. 294. If you want to behold wisdom tonight," he continued "I will tell you what's going to happen to you this year. With my finger, I'll point it out to you on one of the stars."

"In that case," said the gatekeeper, "I'll be happy to unlock the gate for you."

295. When the pagan took the key in his hand and moved towards the gate, Morolf picked up a stone and struck him, breaking his heart in two 296. so that he fell to the ground, dead. His wife came running over at once and wanted to cry murder, but, the story goes, Morolf killed her with the same stone. 297. The illustrious knight took the key out of the gatekeeper's hand and opened the gate himself. He set out as quickly as possible for the waters of the raging sea, for the place where he had left his little boat. 298. He stepped in and put to sea, where he floated around until dawn.

As soon as the noble highborn queen awoke, the lady received word that the pagans had been shorn, that they were all sound asleep, 299. and that Morolf had escaped by sea. The queen went up to the battlement. When she saw him in the distance, she began to weep bitter tears. You will want to hear what she said. 300. In her misery she sank to the ground, bereft of all joy. "Lords," she said, "I would never have been able to describe this adequately to you: he is so clever he could have escaped from solid rock. 301. Listen, illustrious heroes," the beautiful lady continued, "if you bring the clever man back to me, you will have thirty marks of red gold as your reward."

302. At this, a good fifty pagans rushed into a galley. With astonishing speed, Duke Marschilian raced across the waters of the raging sea in pursuit of Morolf. 303. They had put more than four miles behind them before Morolf realized they were headed towards him. So the clever man steered his little boat out of the waters of the raging sea. 304. Having thrust under his belt a little

cask decorated with silver bands, the excellent man hastened away, saying, "The devil has made off with all the plants that are supposed to be standing at water's edge."

305. With the pagans in hot pursuit, Morolf could find no place to hide. They captured the illustrious prince and bound him so tightly that blood shot out from under his fingernails. 306. They settled down on the field, while two knights went down ahead of them, crossed the raging sea, and told the noble highborn queen what had happened. 307. As a reward for the news they brought, she gave the two of them a bright cloak of red gold. She planned to give thirty marks to the others, when they brought the peerless knight captive.

308. As night began to fall, twelve men stood guard over Morolf, who remained bound until it was time to go to sleep. You will want to hear what he said.

309. "I have gained knowledge of many lands. If you could bring yourself to undo these bonds, I would like to tell you strange tales concerning my experiences among the Jews as well as among the pagans."

310. Four of the best of them undid his shackles. As soon as they had done so, he began telling them stories, one after the other, until they all began to feel thirsty. Then the illustrious prince pulled out his little cask and placed it at his mouth. 311. He showed his cleverness by not allowing a single drop to slip down his throat. "Lords," he said, "if you're at all thirsty, drink up; you'll never taste better wine."

312. He gave it to the leader. They drank freely and sank down to the ground. Morolf took the sword of the pagan who had bound him so viciously and cut off his head. 313. "That," he said, "is your reward for the message you planned to deliver. I myself will wear your clothes in the presence of the queen." Morolf, the clever man, grabbed the eleven men who were left by the hair and dragged them away from the twelfth. 314. The fearless proud warrior dragged them from high up on the broad plain down into the valley. He tugged at them so vigorously that he pulled the hair out of their heads. 315. In truth, he took a scissors out of his sack and cut off the hair above the ears of all eleven. Then he picked up a razor, gave each of them a tonsure, and said, "Now go sing mass, gentlemen, all of you together. 316. Not even a bishop could have done this," the clever man declared. "If these brave heroes were ordained, they could easily fill a great cathedral with their singing, they have so many voices."

317. When Morolf had done this, he made his way quickly to the sea where he had left his little boat, got in and pushed off. He was the one who brought the chamberlain's clothes into the presence of the noble queen. 318. His hair was curly and blond, and his face was the same as the chamberlain's in every

regard. The very clever man steered his little boat skillfully towards the castle. 319. Morolf left the boat where it was, ran to the gate, and demanded to be let in. "I have come across the raging sea," he declared. "I want to tell the noble queen that Morolf has been captured."

320. The gate was opened, and Morolf was let into the castle. When he approached the queen, the king and the members of his court greeted him as if he were the chamberlain.

321. The king said, "Now tell me about that clever man."

"Lord," Morolf replied, "he has been captured and will never get away."

"In that case," said Fore, "I can get some sleep." King Fore, the pagan warrior, ordered beds to be made ready. 322. When the king was ready to go to bed, twelve pagan chaplains blessed him. His beautiful wife joined him.

That's when Morolf, King Salman's vassal, sprang into action. 323. Still unrecognized, the knight Morolf took a sleeping potion into his hands, knelt before the great king, and offered it to both of them to drink. They fell into a sound sleep. 324. When the chaplains wanted to leave, Morolf ordered them to stay put and pressed the same potion in their hands. All of them drank eagerly and fell down to the ground. 325. Morolf, the valiant, illustrious hero, picked up the twelve chaplains and carried them to a stone wall, where he stacked them all in a pile, one against the other. 326. Morolf, the fearless, proud knight, took one chaplain from the pile and, clever man that he was, carried him to King Fore, in bed with his lovely, fair lady. 327. He took King Fore from the bed and laid him against the wall next to a young chaplain. Then he took the habit off the oldest chaplain and put it on mighty King Fore, just as quickly as he could. 328. He took a pair of scissors from his sack, truly, and cut off the king's hair above his ears. Then he picked up a razor and gave him a tonsure. "Now," he said, "you can be bishop over all the others." 329. After he had done this, Morolf set out for the sea, where he had left his little boat. He got in, put to sea, and floated about until the next morning.

That's when mighty King Fore awoke. 330. After waking, the king lay there quietly for a bit, I can say that truly, collecting his thoughts. Eventually he decided he'd like to make love to the queen, so he reached out and grabbed the young chaplain. 331. When the chaplain realized what was going on, he made a fist and punched the king in the ear with such great strength that the king lay there for a while without moving. 332. When his ear stopped hurting from the blow, King Fore didn't fail to say, "Noble highborn queen, you have lived with me seven years, and not once have you treated me like this." 333. You will want to hear what he said when he saw he was wearing a monk's habit. "What devil has put me into this habit? Without a doubt, Morolf, Salman's vassal, has been here."

Figure 9. Marcolf tonsures King Fore and lays a chaplain next to Salome in bed. Stuttgart, Landesbibliothek, Cod. HB XIII 2, fol. 315ᵛ.

334. When the pagan Fore wanted to get into his bed, he found a naked chaplain lying there next to his wife. He grabbed the chaplain by the legs and dragged him far away. 335. "Time to get up, chaplain," he said. "Run off now and sing matins, and let me get to my lady. You had a better night than I. I had to lie on the ground, but you got to lie here next to the queen." 336. The chaplain jumped up, and King Fore went to bed, where he was happy to spend some time. However, the beautiful lady just kept sleeping, so he said, "It's really time you might think about getting up." 337. You will want to hear what she had to say when she looked him in the face.

"Mighty King Fore," she said, beside herself with anger, "what devil has shaved you?"

338. "It was done as God ordained," the king replied. "We're going to have to atone for the sins that we committed against Salman." Then the fortress was filled with a mighty sound. Out on the sea Morolf was singing so loudly that it resounded throughout the castle. 339. When Fore heard the voice, the pagan king ran up to the battlement. "Morolf," he said, "proud, noble knight, wait there for a moment until the noble queen can see you."

340. "I can't stay here any longer," the clever man replied. "What message do you want me to bring to my lord Salman? I'm headed for Jerusalem, lord, that much you should know. 341. I'm about to cross the sea, sire, but I'll send Salman and a fearsome army back to you."

Morolf wanted to get away, but mighty Fore ordered all the routes to be guarded. 342. Before Morolf realized it, he was surrounded by twenty-four galleys. Then he showed them just how clever he was: while they were all watching, he let himself sink to the bottom of the sea. 343. He was able to breathe through a tube that went into the boat, which the clever man had attached firmly with strong leather. 344. He had put a cord at the top to prevent the tube from being broken off. He hid at the bottom of the sea for a full fourteen days. 345. That was the only way he could have escaped, since the pagans demanded his life. For thirty-six days Morolf sailed upon the raging sea, until winds drove him into the harbor at Jerusalem 346. from which the clever man had departed seven years earlier.

Without wasting a moment, the noble knight set out for the fair city of Jerusalem. 347. Morolf saw King Salman standing among many worthy vassals, but no one recognized the stranger, which brought tears to the eyes of the bold knight. 348. No one recognized him since half of his hair had turned gray. When Salman was about to leave, Morolf, the proud noble knight, asked him to stay for a moment. 349. "King," he said, "I have always heard it said that you like to hear strange tales. I'm in a good position to tell you some, noble, mighty king, since

I know all the lands from the Elbe to the Termont. 350. That's the place from which, hoping for the best, I set out across the sea for Jerusalem."

Salman took him by the hand and led him graciously through the court 351. to a parapet of beautifully carved marble. Morolf told him many tales, which caused Salman to break out in lamentation. "Alas," he said, "Morolf was my loyal vassal. 352. I sent him across the raging sea in pursuit of my beautiful wife, but he has lost his life among the pagans."

Morolf replied, "King, alas, that is true. He and I were pilgrims together for a full seven years. 353. I buried him in pagan realms. He asked me to bring you a proper account."

Salman started to weep, then pulled himself together and said, "Now tell me more, pilgrim: 354. where in the lands of the pagans did you bury him? Tell me the absolute truth. His remains are so precious to me that I will not let them rest among the pagans, I give you my word. 355. I will inter him here in Jerusalem, if it costs me my life. What good are crown and kingdom now? Henceforth all the glory of the world will never mean a thing to me, 356. now that I have lost Morolf. A beloved loyal vassal, he was also my brother. I'll never get over my grief that he set out for my sake 357. to find my lovely wife. Why should I care that I am king? From this day forth I will devote myself to God. I am overcome by the utter misery I feel for my dear brother."

358. When Morolf saw that the king's grief was genuine, he said, "You should know, noble king, that I am Morolf and that I am devoted to you in complete loyalty. 359. And I've found your beautiful wife for you. If you want to get her back, however, many knights will have to risk their lives."

Both happy and sad at this news, Salman kissed the well-favored knight with woeful joy. 360. "Now that I have discovered you are alive and well," he said, "I will cease all my grieving."

Morolf left the king, slipped quickly into a room and then, with astonishing speed, showed him more of his tricks. 361. Without wasting a moment, the knight put on a fine coat of mail under his clothes. The rings were so small and white they really couldn't be seen, since he wore them close to his body. 362. Then Morolf set an iron helmet on his head, placing a gray felt hat over it. He wrapped himself in a rough, woolen cloak and put a palm frond on his back. Then he returned and stood before the emperor. 363. A chamberlain jumped forth, struck him with his hand, and said, "Take that, you ungainly beggar. How dare you stand before the mighty emperor in these miserable rags."

364. "Sir," the clever man replied, "that was a vicious thing to do. Never before have I been struck in the presence of an illustrious prince. This blow will always be counted against you as a sin; you owe me satisfaction."

365. Morolf, the clever man, made a fist and gave the chamberlain a blow of such great power that he lay at the king's feet. 366. King Salman's vassals jumped up and Morolf withdrew towards the door of the hall. "I have carried this crutch across the sea," he said. "Anyone I consecrate with it will remember me for the rest of his days."

367. Salman jumped up from his throne and signaled his heroes to withdraw. He stepped forward and looked at Morolf under the brim of his hat. That's when he realized it was Morolf, the fine, proud knight. 368. The chamberlain had to accept the blow to his teeth that the good pilgrim had given him. "This is Morolf," said the king, "showing us his tricks, with which we will win back the most noble queen."

369. "Lord," he declared, "that's just what I would say." He took off his armor and told the chamberlain to keep it.

"The devil take you," he said, "for having struck my ears so hard with your weapon."

370. "Now," said King Salman, "tell us, Morolf, excellent man, how we will win back the fair woman."

"Lord," he replied, "I can give you good advice on that score, I'll stake my life on it. 371. King," Morolf continued, "if you announce a tournament, a great many heroes will come. From among them I will choose ten thousand men so that, no matter where I carry the flag, I can never fail."

372. Salman liked this idea and proclaimed a tournament on the spot. He took Morolf by the hand and led him graciously into the presence of all the lords. 373. The clever man was received warmly by many illustrious knights who had not seen him for seven years. They all asked him the same thing, if he had found the noble queen. 374. The clever man replied, "She is across the waters at the other side of the raging sea, in the citadel at Weldelsea. We will need a mighty army to win back the noble highborn queen."

375. "Morolf," the best of them declared, "we want to join you in pursuit of the queen."

Morolf was glad to hear this and chose ten thousand men from among them all. 376. "King," he said, "now do as I instruct you. Have your treasury unlocked, and give these heroes your silver and your bright, red gold. Then they will follow me, no matter how dangerous the place into which I carry our flag."

377. Salman liked this idea. He had his chambers unlocked and his treasure brought forth, his silver and precious gems, which were given to all the lords.

378. "See there, king," the clever man observed, "that was exactly the right thing to do. Your silver and your bright, red gold will lure many fearless warriors to a grim and gruesome death."

379. At the shore the ships stood ready that were going to carry Morolf and his expedition across the sea. After the illustrious heroes had hastened onboard, he led ten thousand men across the waters of the raging sea. 380. When they had arrived at the opposite shore, Morolf ordered them to stop, then had the men and their horses disembark. Morolf, the clever man, then addressed the king with respect.

381. "King, I have long heard it said that you possess good sense. Never have you had as much need of it as now."

"Morolf," Salman replied, "I submitted to your direction back at Jerusalem. Here too, I will act as you advise. I give you my word."

382. Then Morolf took the standard in his hands and led the army down onto a narrow path, which he had often followed to reach the wondrously beautiful woman. 383. It led deep into a dark forest, where he set up camp for many highborn men.

"King," said Morolf, "I know well why you set out. I give you my word, I understand the situation completely. 384. We are already quite close to the castle. Salman, my dear brother, look: you should go up there yourself. By the faith that I owe you, I believe that's the right thing to do. 385. You're going to have to risk your life inside the castle in order to see Salome, your beautiful wife. She is fair and lovely, and a pagan is making love to her in your place. Look, king, that ought to upset you."

386. "Morolf," King Salman replied, "what have I done to you that you want put my life at risk? If I have done something to deserve your anger, peerless knight, let it go."

387. "King," said the very clever man, "now this is how it's got to be. Salome is so dear to you that, even if it costs you your head, you would not let her remain here."

388. "That love is long gone: she has chosen another love, the pagan."

"If I had known that back at Jerusalem," said Morolf, "I would never have come across the sea with you, I give you my word on it. 389. King," he said, "you should go without any fear, since I will protect you with my bright steel. And if you are discovered, then grab hold of your crutch and fight like a brave hero."

390. Without wasting a moment, the fearless knight put a fine suit of armor on Salman, under his clothes. He gave him a strong staff, which had a sword hidden inside. With this the mighty emperor had in his hands an excellent means of defense. 391. He put a good pilgrim's cloak on him inside of which a steel helmet had been hidden very skillfully. This helped the illustrious king avoid meeting his end at the hands of the pagans. 392. He put a tiny, little horn inside the edge of his rough, woolen cloak and said, "When you blow this, illustrious king, I will come to your aid with ten thousand men." 393. Morolf, the

clever man, showed the king the way out of the forest. Ahead of him he saw a castle, delightful to behold, and said, "King Fore is up there along with a large number of pagan men."

394. Salman said, "Lead me farther along the path to the castle."

Morolf hated that idea. "Have you lost your mind?" he demanded. "I was held captive up in that castle and just barely escaped the guards! 394a. If," he continued, "your heroes were to go back across the sea, there would be no one to come to our aid and we would both lose our lives."

Salman started to walk forward, but he kept looking back to see if Morolf was going to tell him to stop. 394b. "You must go into the castle alone," said Morolf, the clever man. "Once there you will know your way around. For the sake of your beautiful wife, I almost lost my life."

395. King Salman began to weep bitterly. "Morolf," he said, "excellent man, if I lose my life in the castle, then out of brotherly love, let my soul be in your care."

396. "King," said Morolf, "nothing can harm you. The pagan king will not pass judgment upon you. You must pass judgment on yourself, and that's how we shall deprive him of both life and limb. 397. Have your sentence executed at the edge of the dark forest, and I will come to your aid with ten thousand of your vassals. Your glory will be magnified, while King Fore and all of his people will have lost their lives." 398. Morolf's eyes overflowed with tears. "Salman," he said, "my dear brother, your beauty is such that you cannot hide. Do not deny who you are for any length of time, if you hold your honor dear."

399. Morolf went back into the forest, leaving Salman with much to think about. Now noble King Salman is standing there on the borad, noble plain and is very worried. 400. Salman entered the castle, where he was graciously received by the beautiful maiden who was Fore's sister.

"Welcome, pilgrim," she said. "From what country have you traveled here into pagan lands? 401. Your features are so pleasing, if you'd like to stay here with me, I'll be happy to give you bread and wine, of which no one will deprive you save death, yours or mine."

402. "Lady," he replied, "I am a sinful man and cannot remain for long in any one place. This penance has been imposed on me, and I must perform it as long as I live."

403. "Pilgrim," the admirable maiden continued, "how I would like to spare you that. It would make much more sense for you to have a beautiful wife than for you to continue mortifying such a splendid person as yourself."

404. The maiden left at once and went into the castle, where she found the queen. "Most noble queen," she said, "the most handsome pilgrim in the world has just arrived at our court. 405. He is the fairest man that any woman

ever called her own, with eyes that flash brilliantly in his head like those of a wild falcon. 406. He might very well be the king of Jerusalem, most noble queen, come for you from across the sea. His eyes have not lost their brilliance, and his eyebrows are elegantly shaped."

The queen laughed at this. 407. Then the handsome lady declared, "Woe unto you, Morolf, Salman's vassal. If you sent him across the sea, you will never again see him alive. I give you my word."

408. "He shouldn't suffer for the fact that I have betrayed him," the admirable maiden insisted. "I myself will go tell him to leave court immediately, if he values his head."

409. When the queen saw that the young lady was so distressed on his account, she said, "Tell him to stay where he is, since I myself would like to have a look at this man who has travelled so far."

410. She signaled four chaplains to come quickly and said, "Bring me the foreigner at once." You will want to hear what she said the moment she saw him approach.

411. "Welcome, Salman, my husband. It pains me that Morolf got away from us recently, that I didn't catch the knight, and—you can be absolutely certain of this—that I didn't hang him up on a gallows."

412. "That's just another example of your faithlessness," Salman replied. "Morolf cared for my good name. You must become my wife again, or, I give you my word, Morolf will kill you."

413. "I have no desire for your love," she said. "King Fore is three times as dear to me, and I intend to remain with him for the rest of my life. I am confident he will agree to take your life for my sake."

414. "Lady," said Salman, "if you let me leave here unharmed, I trust I will be able to keep Morolf from ever crossing the sea in search of you. I give you my word, believe me, noble highborn queen."

415. She said, "You'd think you'd made out pretty well if I let you leave here unharmed. I'll have you hang from a tree, I give you my word." I do believe that she failed in this.

416. "Noble highborn queen," he said, "when you were with me in Jerusalem, the country and its people were subject to you. You should let me benefit from that, noble queen."

417. Then they led the excellent man away into a lovely chamber and left him behind an exquisite hanging. The mighty emperor stood there for what seemed to him a very long time. 418. Salman remained behind the hanging until the pagan king sat down to eat. When King Fore rode into court, the noble queen was happy and sad at the same time. 419. How quickly she went towards him

and embraced him with her white arms. "Illustrious, noble prince," she said, "nothing pleases me when you are not before my eyes."

420. Salman watched this through the hanging and thought it went on much too long. "God," he said, "in your infinite perfection, what treachery and faithlessness are in this queen! 421. Dear God, help me to understand why I don't deserve more credit for my devotion. At this very moment that murderously vicious, accursed woman is going to betray me."

422. Tables, appropriate for one of his nobility, had been set up before the pagan Fore. The mighty king had the highest place, while the lovely lady sat decorously at his side.

423. While the pagan king presided at the table, the queen had not forgotten about Salman. "My dear lord," she said, "the most handsome pilgrim in the world has arrived at court. 424. He is the fairest man that any woman ever called her own. He could very well be the king of Jerusalem. Now tell me, my dear lord, how should he be treated?"

425. The pagan Fore replied, "Salman can't very well stay in this country. However, if this really is the king of Jerusalem, and if he answers me courteously, I will send him back across the sea."

426. "You don't know his tricks," the noble queen replied. "If you let him cross the sea, he will start plotting to have your head. Lord, don't miss this opportunity. 427. Now look at him standing there behind that hanging. There is no getting around it: he must come before you at once. Now treat him as you want. But remember. I have always done as you wished."

427a. Now King Salman has been betrayed by his lawful wife. If he's going to save his life, King Fore's sister must be allowed to help him.

428. The noble maiden jumped up from her seat. "Brother, what will become of you? Salman has been betrayed by his lawful wife, in pursuit of whom he crossed the sea. 429. Brother," she said, "if you want to save your life, then give Salman back his lovely wife. You should be happy to do so, since you did him great harm for no good reason."

430. Fore, the pagan king, replied, "I have not harmed him in any way. Furthermore, I intend to keep the queen for myself for as long as I live. You have my word on that."

431. The maiden gathered up her garments, crossed the court, and entered a lovely chamber. There she took a goblet filled with pure clear wine and brought it to King Salman. 432. "Drink this, noble highborn prince. Your lawful wife, in pursuit of whom you have crossed the sea, has betrayed you." When King Salman had drunk, he handed the goblet back to her courteously.

433. Then King Salman said, "Lovely maiden of rare beauty, I give you my word: if you were with me in Jerusalem, you would have to be baptized."

434. "King," the admirable maiden replied, "if it turned out I had to accompany you across the sea, I would be glad to do so. You strike me as an honorable man."

435. She continued, "Right now, however, I fear that I will do you harm, since they are watching the two of us quite closely. You should come with me and stand before my brother, then reply courteously when he speaks to you. If you do, he will send you away from here, back across the sea."

436. "How am I supposed to answer him courteously?" King Salman demanded. "After all, your brother robbed me of Salome, my exquisite wife. His head should be mine."

437. "Still," she said, "you should keep in mind that there is no one here who can save your precious life. Considering the dire circumstances, you really should reply with utmost courtesy when he speaks to you."

438. Salman, filled with the courage of a lion, stepped before King Fore and said, "Fore, you faithless man, what great anguish of heart you caused me at Jerusalem! 439. You robbed me of Salome, my beautiful wife. I should have taken your life."

The pagan king treated this as a joke. "Mighty King Salman," he replied, "may God forgive you for what you just said. 440. You know very well, King Salman, that I lost many proud heroes on account of this beautiful woman, that you captured me with your own hands, and that I spent three years in Jerusalem as your captive. 441. Then your fair wife Salome set me free. It pains me deeply that you are willing to lose your life for her sake. Alas, King Salman, what did you think you were doing, crossing the sea so wide?"

442. "Fore," King Salman replied, "what had I done to you that you led an army to fight against me in a ferocious battle for the sake of the noble queen? I should have taken your life. 443. But I wanted to give you the benefit of your high birth. Now you have treated me so faithlessly that, if I live any longer, trusting in God's grace, I will have your head."

444. Fore, the pagan king, then asked him, "Most mighty King Salman, if you held me at Jerusalem as I hold you here, tell me truly, could I depart unharmed 444a. from the city of Jerusalem and return to the rich land of Wendelsea? Tell me, King Salman, by your Christian faith, would you let me go without harm?"

445. "I'll tell you what I'd do," Salman replied. "I would have you held until early the next day. Then I would have my men prepare a gallows, strong and magnificent, 445a. between the forest and my castle. You can be quite certain that no one would be able to prevent me. I would have you hanged from it. I give you my word."

446. Then Fore, the pagan king, declared, "You have pronounced judgment on yourself. Now watch him closely, all of you who are in my service, and let him

move freely about the castle, unbound, 447. until daybreak tomorrow. Pay attention to what I am telling you. Then prepare a magnificent gallows at the edge of the dark forest, from which we will hang the mighty emperor. 448. If he loses his life here, the queen will remain mine, now and forever, and I will not have to worry that Morolf might come across the sea for her."

449. Then the beautiful lady said, "I salute you, Fore, pagan king! If you're determined to take his life, I give you my word, I will gladly remain with you."

450. "Lady," said Salman, "it is not too much to die for you.. And yet, no matter how glad I am to suffer this for your sake, noble highborn queen, as I trust in God's grace, it's not going to happen to me."

451. King Fore—I want to tell you—had them bring forth two strong chains made of iron. And then, in anger, he ordered the mighty emperor to be locked in them. 452. When the young lady saw this, she was filled with pain and sorrow. Realizing that they planned to take his life, the lovely maiden was moved to intense pity. 453. Right then she stepped before her brother and said, "We have lived happily for many days, and I have never made a request of you in a serious matter. Now I ask you to give me Salman, the mighty emperor, for this one night only, 454. so that he can move about among us here without iron chains, since his suffering affects me deeply. And if I allow him escape across the sea, oh, dear brother, then never trust me again."

455. "How do you plan to hold on to him?" the king asked. "Morolf escaped at daybreak, and then he crossed the raging sea. If Salman gets away from us, we will never get over it."

456. "As surety," she replied, "I will pledge the kingdom that is both of ours along with my own head. If I allow him to cross the sea, then have my head chopped off. Under no circumstances will I ask for pardon."

457. "I don't need any more security from you than that," he said. "But if you do let him cross the sea, I will have your head cut off, even if you were my sister a thousand times over, I give you my word on it."

458. The maiden was about to leave when King Fore asked her to stop where she was. "Sister," he said, "noble and rich, now treat him as someone of his high standing deserves, for he is an illustrious prince 459. who rules the fair city of Jerusalem. I would be sorry indeed if this admirable man should endure any injury. And if I dared in the presence of Salome, that beautiful woman, I would let him go back to his country without harming him in the least."

460. "Brother," the young queen said, "accept an entreaty to do just that." Then the maiden got up to leave. When the two iron chains were brought in, she hurled them against the wall.

461. "Get up, King Salman," she said, "I have pledged my head for you until tomorrow at dawn. I'm counting on you to help me keep it."

462. King Salman replied, "Most beautiful, lovely maiden, I give you my solemn word, I would sooner lie dead beside you than abandon you to such a terrible fate."

463. Taking Salman by the hand, the young lady led him away, across the court and into a lovely chamber, where many amazing things had been painted on the walls. There the mighty emperor spent the long night quite pleasantly. 464. She brought a handsome minstrel for him. He had picked up a German harp, and she had given him a fur coat. "Now serve the mighty emperor well," she said, "but only for this one night. 465. I myself will stay with you," said the young queen.

She sat down next to Salman and comforted him with such devotion that he forgot all his cares. 466. A drink was carried in, which the young, noble queen brought with the utmost grace to the noble prince of Jerusalem, I tell you truly. 467. Salman sat next to the young lady until he forgot his cares. She was so lovely in every regard that the mighty emperor was filled with joy. 468. He took the harp from the minstrel, placed it in his lap, and began to play with great skill. He thought of King David, his father who, before the ancient city of Troy, figured out how to play the first stringed instruments. 469. David was a noble highborn prince from the fair city of Jerusalem, from which King Salman also came. He could pluck the strings like the angels, producing a delightful sound. 470. The young lady watched intently as Salman moved his fingers with great skill. "You are an accomplished minstrel," she said, "I'll stake my word on it. I would gladly spend my life with you."

471. The maiden sat down next to him and whispered into his ear, "Mighty king Salman, by your faith, don't you want to get out of here? 472. Don't you want to cross the sea? Since the warriors at my disposal are very tired, I could tell them all to go to bed. My brother loves me so much, he won't do a thing to me, I give you my word."

473. "Young lady," he replied, "what would my life be worth to me if I were to forfeit my soul on your account? I intend to remain at your side, burdened with worry, throughout the night until daybreak, no matter what happens to me afterwards."

474. "Then I can't help you," she said. "Tomorrow morning two thousand pagans or more will come and call for your head. I am overcome with sorrow 475. that I can't help you. Mighty King Salman, they will condemn you to death. I will regret this always, since you are a peerless warrior."

476. King Salman replied, "I have great confidence that my angels in the forest will not abandon me. Now be still—your tears grieve me. If I ever get out of this danger, I will thank you for it, most noble queen."

477. As their conversation came to an end, the light of day began to shine. Then Fore the noble king awoke, and the noble prince of Jerusalem was brought to court. 478. Fore had sent for his kinsmen and his vassals, of which at least two thousand came to court on horseback or on foot. With one voice they accused the prince of Jerusalem.

479. "Fore," they said, "peerless knight, judge for us whether Salman, having come into our country, should live or die."

"That I will gladly do," the king replied at once.

480. The sentence was quickly pronounced on King Salman: the illustrious emperor was to be hanged far from the citadel at the edge of the dark forest. 481. Men and women followed mighty King Salman the whole way from the castle to the edge of the dark forest, where the mighty emperor was supposed to lose his life.

482. The young lady rode next to him and wiped away his sweat with her brightly colored cloak. "You are a praiseworthy prince," she said. "You have not turned pale but are still full of color, like a rose."

483. Morolf had not forgotten Salman. He had ridden out in front of the woods and kept watch in the direction of the city. And when he saw them coming from afar, he rode back to his men. You will want to hear what he said.

484. "Arise, illustrious heroes, and come to the aid of your lord, Salman! By my faith," said Morolf, the very clever man, "I have seen him, moving along in great distress. 485. What great rewards God will bestow on the man who risks his life today for the sake of his rightful lord! Heroes, you must not lose heart. If we ever return to Jerusalem, your reward will be great. 486. The waters are much too deep for us to ride across the sea," Morolf cried out to them all. "And don't think of your lovely wives and of your children back at home: we don't want to turn timid in battle."

487. Then the bravest among them said, "Morolf, if we meant to lose heart, we wouldn't have crossed the sea: you should know that, brave, proud knight. Now deal with him as you are able. We will not fall back from you so much as a single foot, even if we end up dying in our own blood."

488. When Morolf heard what they said, his spirits soared. The noble knight took aside two Knights Templar he had brought across the sea. 489. Giving them command of a company, he said, "Now lead these men out in front of the forest and pay close attention. If God grants me victory under the gallows and everyone starts fleeing towards the castle, make sure that not a single pagan survives. 490. Duke Friedrich," he said, "noble lord, by your virtue I ask you, illustrious, celebrated knight, to lead a company out in front of the forest for the sake of your lord."

491. Then they all rode forth. Morolf ordered them to dismount onto the grass, and said, "Now fasten your bright helmets. I tell you truly, we won't overcome them without a struggle."

492. They dismounted onto the ground and fastened their helmets at once. "Morolf," they said, "most excellent man, don't wait any longer to come to the aid of King Salman."

493. "First," the clever man replied, "let's see what fiendish things they have in mind for him. They'll have to leave them half-done. King Fore and all his men are going to lose their lives."

494. As the pagans gathered under the gallows, Salman was talking with the queen. "Lady," he said, "by all that is most excellent in you, help me to blow three times on my little horn. 495. That will be my sign to St. Michael that he should receive my soul. The angelic host will hear it, look out for my soul, and make sure it does not perish. 496. As you are well aware, beautiful lady, no prince perishes without being allowed to blow his little horn three times."

The lady was angered by this request. "Mighty King Salman," she said, "Morolf has chosen this stratagem for you. 497. If there's anyone here who lets him sound his horn, we'll all lose our lives. Order a close watch to be kept on the woods down there. One way or the other the king will get his men to come to his aid."

498. When he heard this, King Fore was incensed. "Salman," he said, "take your horn, put it to your mouth and blow it ten times—or even more, if it makes you happy. 499. But if all your men come to help you, you will be the very first to lose his life." Salman was glad to hear these words and reached inside his cloak for his little horn.

500. He placed the horn against his lips and blew it with all his strength, so that his heroes would hear it at once. He threw his pilgrim's cloak onto the grass and reached for the crutch, which he had not forgotten on his back. 501. You will want to hear what the queen said when she saw this.

"Now tell me, King Salman, what are you up to with that crutch you've got in your hands? You've got some sort of deceit in mind."

502. "Most beautiful lady," King Salman replied, "I have brought this crutch with me from across the sea. It should be hanged along with me. It will never cross the sea again."

503. Morolf had formed three companies: one was colored black; the other was white like the snow; and the third, of a pale color, was led by Morolf, the proud, noble knight.

Figure 10. Salman blows his horn.
Stuttgart, Landesbibliothek, Cod. HB XIII 2, fol. 324ᵛ.

504. The young lady kept looking down towards the forest. "Most excellent man," she said, "I see a lord in a black cloak, and when the wind gets under it and lifts it a little, you can see his armor, white as ermine." 505. She stepped directly in front of Salman and asked him to tell her what was really going on. "By your faith," she said, "tell me, King Salman, what does this Michael of yours look like? 506. You had better tell the truth, since I see a man standing there looking very capable and moving about under a black cloak. But when the wind lifts it, he is white as an ermine."

507. "Young lady," Salman replied, "if you see a black company, those are devils looking for my soul. If you see a pale company, those are our Lord's kin, who have come here out of hell. 508. If you see a white company, they are all angels looking out for my soul, for I am a sinner. You can have the pleasure of watching them fight over my soul."

509. "Salman," the young queen said, "that may very well be true. You have brought your troop of angels along with you from the fair city of Jerusalem. 510. Those are your vassals, who don't want to abandon you in your hour of need. They will come to your aid here in front of the forest. This should make you happy, Salman, brave and valiant knight. 511. But alas, mighty King Salman, do you intend to leave me alone in peril? Now strike my brother's men hard; upon my word, I am with you."

512. Salman gave her his word on that score, and said, "Stay out of the way of the horses on the field, noble highborn queen. If I am victorious, I will take you with me to Jerusalem."

513. Salman sounded his horn for the second time, and many highborn knights emerged from the forest. When Queen Salome saw this she began to shed bitter tears. You will want to hear what she said.

514. "Do you see the standard that the wind is blowing towards us? Morolf himself is carrying it, that child of the accursed devil. If he catches sight of me," she said, "by my faith, I am certain to lose my life."

515. Mighty King Fore replied, "Keep your spirits up, charming, beautiful woman; even if all his men come to help him, Salman will be the first to die."

516. When Salman heard these words, he took hold of his crutch and pulled a sharp dagger out of it. With this in his hands, the mighty emperor was able to defend himself quite well. 517. When King Fore's men saw this, they attacked the illustrious warrior. A fierce battle ensued, in which King Salman killed a great many pagans. 518. In grave danger, the celebrated warrior struck 450 dead before any of his vassals came to his aid.

519. But the fighting had tired Salman, the brave knight. The pagan saw this and, along with eleven of his heroes, attacked the emperor. 520. In grave

danger, Salman nevertheless killed the eleven pagans. Seeing this, the pagan Fore ran at King Salman with his sharp sword. 521. He gave him such a powerful blow to the head that blood shot out of both his ears, and he fell to the ground. If Morolf had not come quickly, he would have met his end then and there. 522. Morolf made things uncomfortable for Fore until he broke through the army three times. When he saw that King Salman was utterly exhausted, he came riding over immediately.

523. He dismounted and lifted Salman up by the hand. "King Salman," he said, "get up now. King Fore and all his men must lose their lives."

524. The pagan, Fore, saw this and attacked the illustrious warrior. He gave him a blow of such force that Morolf, the noble hero, lay before him on his knees. 525. But Morolf jumped back up, and his sword resounded in his hands. "Now defend yourself, pagan," he said, "for this is when it matters. Before this day is done I intend to hang you for stealing this lovely woman from Salman."

526. When the pagan heard these words, he tried to flee. But Morolf sprang after him and gave him such a powerful blow that he fell down despite himself. 527. "What now, pagan?" Morolf demanded. "I intend to pay you back for all the harm you have caused us. I will destroy you before your time, and I will have Salome, that faithless woman, hanged at your side."

528. When the queen heard this, she ran behind King Salman. "Salman," she said, "peerless knight, for the glory of all women, spare my precious life. 529. Whatever harm I did you, alas, mighty King Salman, I will never do so again. I give you my word on it. I will accompany you across the sea."

530. Morolf took Fore prisoner (he was a mighty and illustrious prince) and brought him to King Salman. Then he tore Salome, that exquisite lady, out of the king's hands 531. and said, "You're about to lose your life, faithless woman. How about that?" He grabbed her by one hand, took King Fore with the other, and brought them both underneath the gallows.

532. Then the beautiful lady said, "Why aren't you helping me, King Salman? King Fore is the guilty one here, so he's the one you should have hanged. His magic has caused me great harm."

533. But the pagan king objected, "Why don't you keep quiet, lovely lady? Yes indeed, faithless woman, if you escape with your life, you will again betray Salman, the worthy man."

534. "Salman," the lovely lady said, "I'll tell you a dream. Last night I dreamed that I was sleeping in your arms; nothing had ever brought me greater pleasure.

535. Two falcons swooped down onto my hands. I know the meaning of this dream. It foretells of an illustrious son, my lord, who will inherit your glorious kingdom."

536. Then Morolf spoke. "I'll give your dream a different meaning," said the illustrious knight. "There's a wide spreading oak tree, and in addition a lofty gallows. You can count on both of them."

537. Salman burst out laughing and said, "Morolf, you can take the pagan man, but leave me the woman, most marvelously fair. For this I will be forever in your debt, noble knight. 538. She has given me her word that she intends to be faithful always and to remain so forever. I want to take her with me across the sea and put her to the test."

539. "King," said Morolf, "this is something both of them arranged, but now only one of them is going to pay the price. If you bring her with you across the sea, I give you my word on it, she will dishonor us and harm us yet again."

540. Morolf hanged Fore, the illustrious pagan prince. He destroyed his citadel and put his country to the torch. In this way all the proud knights won a glorious victory.

541. Once King Salman had defeated Fore, he said, "Find the young queen for me and bring her here. She served me well. I want to take her with me to Jerusalem."

542. Morolf set out at once across the courtyard, where he found the young lady. "Noble queen," he said, "it's time to get going. I have been sent to fetch you by Salman, the lord of Jerusalem."

543. "Morolf," she said, "tell me by your faith, is my brother Fore still living? Will I ever see him alive again?"

"Be still," he answered graciously, "and let the matter rest. 544. I have arranged his nuptials and have hanged him from a gallows so that he can swing around in the air."

The maiden began to sob. She said, "What has the noble emperor done to me, a poor maiden! 545. I have been cast aside forever. That's what he should have done to his wife, whom he now wants to take with him across the sea. But Salome, that faithless woman, she betrayed my noble brother and cost him his life. 546. Morolf," she said, "peerless knight, you should take my brother down from the gallows and bury him in the coffin in which my father lies. In return I will show you a room which will provide you with lots of red gold."

547. Morolf took the illustrious pagan prince down from the gallows and buried him in the grave where his father lay, in the greatest splendor. That, I assure you, is the truth.

548. The young lady took Morolf by the hand, then led him across the court and over to a lovely room. When she unlocked the door and opened it wide, gold and precious gems shone forth. He was overjoyed. 549. The beautiful maiden addressed him: "Morolf, excellent man, you have led your heroes across the sea. Reward them richly, and they will never ever abandon you."

550. Morolf smiled and beckoned his heroes to come over to him. He gave them silver and rich treasure. After he had divided it up, a tournament got underway 551. on a broad meadow. Many a happy knight said to him, "God willing, Morolf, excellent man, you should keep organizing such glorious campaigns forever."

552. At the shore, the ships stood ready that were to take Morolf and his men back across the sea. The jubilant heroes hastened on board and didn't disembark until the morning of the twelfth day. Then, for the first time, they encountered serious difficulty. 553. They had come upon a castle so magnificent they wanted to plunder it. Before they were finished, however, reports reached Duscan and were soon made known 554. to the king, who was named Isolt. He offered silver and gold to those who would fight against the king of Jerusalem, gaining thereby at least thirty thousand vicious pagans. 555. His battle standard was tied on and taken up by a duke. It was red and white. A panther and two fierce dragons were painted on it, 556. indicating that it was King Isolt's. Having taken it into his hands, the duke led the vicious pagans quickly out of their country 557. into the land of Wendelsea, which had been overrun and burned to the ground. He brought thirty thousand troops or more, with which he attacked the prince of Jerusalem. 558. You will want to hear what Morolf said when he saw them in the distance.

"Most magnificent King Salman, I have just seen the banner of mighty King Isolt on the open field. 559. His father was killed outside the walls of Jerusalem. He was called Berzian, and—I want to stress this point—King Fore was his uncle. We'll be attacked ferociously, of that I haven't the slightest doubt. 560. Mighty King Salman," the clever man continued, "take four thousand brave heroes with you and show your valor today. 561. Duke Friedrich, peerless knight, because you are so capable, I ask you to take three thousand brave heroes with you and all the Knights Templar."

562. The brave knight replied, "I will cross the green meadow with my pale company. You will see me in the vanguard of the fight."

563. Morolf, the fearless knight, was the very first to ride into battle. He didn't utter a word until he had thrust the pagan standard bearer off his horse and onto the ground. 564. Once the battle standard had gone down, the pagans had no choice but to forfeit their lives and goods. Salman's fighters dealt them nothing but fear and misery. 565. Morolf possessed great strength. How ferociously he thrust and struck with his mighty hand, casting three hundred and fifty pagans to the ground! 566. Duke Friedrich also fought without restraint. With his mighty hand he struck three thousand pagans to the ground. 567. Salman too, as we are told, was ready to do his part. He and his valiant heroes forced blood to pour out of the pagans' armor.

568. Isolt was a mighty king. He held nothing back as he forced his way with all his strength towards King Salman, just as a noble prince ought to. 569. You will want to hear what he said when he saw Salman from the distance: "That is the king of Jerusalem. I trust that my God will grant me this favor, that Salman will have no choice but to give me his head. 570. My father was killed outside the walls of Jerusalem. He was called Berzian, and—I want to stress this point—King Fore was my uncle. Salman had him hanged, and for this he will never return home. 571. He'll have to hand the beautiful woman over into my custody, or I will lose my life." He took his sword in both hands and brought it down in anger on King Salman.

572. Salman, however, did not hesitate a moment but drew his sharp, broad sword and gave King Isolt such a blow that that king's head lay before his feet. 573. As soon as the pagan was killed, his troops took flight back towards Duscan. Thus illustrious King Salman gained a glorious victory. 574. They dismounted and planted their banner in the ground. When there was no one left who wanted to fight them, they set out, their hearts filled with joy, for the rushing waters of the raging sea. 575. Fifteen thousand pagans lost their lives. Salman regained his beautiful wife. He took her by the hand, while Morolf took the lovely, young lady, and they headed down to the ships.

576. They sailed across the raging sea to the fair city of Jerusalem. The queen, however, just barely survived the trip to Jerusalem, having been separated from her pagan husband. 577. Whenever she thought of him, she was no longer able to take pleasure in anything—at least until, a second time, another pagan, also relying on powerful magic, obtained her for himself. 578. That explains why every worthy man should let his wife keep watch over herself: because there has never been any vigilance as effective as that which each worthy woman exercises over herself. 579. Salman, however, never learned from experience what he would have needed to know to keep his lovely wife from deceiving him a second time. But we'll let that matter rest for the moment and turn instead to the baptism of King Fore's sister.

580. Morolf the clever man went and stood before the young lady. "Noble queen," he said, "you should have yourself baptized so that your soul will not perish."

581. The praiseworthy maiden replied, "No, Morolf, excellent man, I have just crossed the sea, overcome with anguish on account of my dear brother, Fore. 582. I will never be able to escape the sadness I feel for this tragic loss. From now on I will be a stranger to my country and my castles," the queen said, "and this will make me sad for the rest of my days."

583. Morolf, the clever man, replied, "Ah, beautiful, praiseworthy maiden, noble queen, let yourself be baptized now, and I promise to pay you back over and over."

584. "How are you going to repay me, excellent man?" the beautiful maiden asked. "By virtue of my birth I am a noble queen. I do not wish to be baptized, so don't urge me to do so any more."

585. Then the illustrious knight said, "Most beautiful, lovely maiden, if the noble queen dies, then you will rule over the rich land of Jerusalem. 586. I will make King Salman your husband," said Morolf, the peerless man.

"In that case," the lovely queen responded, "I will let myself be baptized, Morolf, excellent man."

587. Then the clever man went before King Salman and said, "Now then, noble emperor, the young lady who accompanied us across the sea will allow herself to be baptized."

588. "Morolf," the king replied, "I will leave that up to you."

She was led into the minster where they put her in a shift of fine silk. 589. The mistress of the young ladies at court had a chair brought in, and then, I'm telling you the truth, she took her onto her lap. "God," she said, "you're too heavy for me. I won't be able to hold you for the baptism."

590. Two duchesses went down to the baptism and saw the mighty emperor standing on the other side. "We can manage very well without you," they said. "We don't need you at such an affair. Who knows what's going on between the two of you?"

591. When she was lifted out of the baptismal font, she was named Affer. She was taken to the Holy Sepulcher, to which she consecrated herself, that's the truth. And there she studied the Psalter there for a full three and a half years.

592. After the baptism, Morolf went and stood before the emperor. "King," he said, "if your wife ever misbehaves again, you will have to find another envoy to cross the sea, 593. someone other than me, you can count on it, who will be ready to risk his life. I, born a free nobleman, almost lost my head on your account."

594. King Salman replied, "Morolf, excellent man, such a thought will never again cross the queen's mind, now that we have gotten her from King Fore and brought her back across the raging sea."

595. "King," the clever man declared, "you can be sure I will remind you of this."

You should know beyond any doubt that the noble queen remained in Jerusalem 596. until she had a beautiful, little son by King Salman. The noble honorable queen was steadfast in her resolve to remain there, at home, 597.

until her death. Salman escaped any serious difficulties for a full seven years. But now hear strange tidings: things began to change for him. 598. News had reached Acre that there was no woman more beautiful than King Salman's wife. King Princian said, "I will risk my life for her. 599. I will journey across the sea to the fair city of Jerusalem. If I fail to take her from him, no one will ever again see me wearing the crown at Acre."

600. Along with eleven of his vassals, noble King Princian journeyed across the raging sea and arrived on the evening of the twelfth day at the city of Jerusalem. 601. When the beautiful woman went to vespers, King Salman accompanied her. That's when the mighty emperor received the wayfarer. 602. When vespers were over, Princian went up to the castle. "Noble highborn queen," he said, "give me something to drink right now and I won't ask for anything else."

603. The noble queen had a goblet of red gold brought out, which she took into her white hands and offered to King Princian. As a consequence, she soon had to leave the country. 604. Once the pagan had drunk, he dropped a ring into the wine. Then the beautiful lady drank, and soon after she began to pine for the pagan king.

605. When Morolf saw how he pressed her hands against the golden goblet, he didn't waste a minute. "King," he said to Salman, "I have just seen something that will bring you no glory, I can tell you that. 606. These are not true pilgrims. They are trying to get the queen. Salman, your very beautiful wife intends to put her life on the line yet again."

607. King Salman replied, "Morolf, you excellent man, of what are you accusing the good queen? She intends to remain here at home; it is her unshakeable resolve."

608. "King," said the clever man, "let me remind you that you are going to be in great need of my help. Whether I will offer you that help is not clear." And with that, the brave knight left the court.

609. The beautiful lady had set a day, twelve weeks later, when she snuck away and crossed the raging sea with King Princian. 610. The beautiful, lovely lady returned to pagan lands, until Morolf got her back again with the help of a mighty army.

611. The clever man stepped up to King Salman and said, "Most noble emperor, now you're going to have to cross the sea yourself in search of the queen."

612. Salman began to weep. "Morolf," he said, "excellent man, stop reproaching me. I'm ready to go myself to look for the noble queen. 613. You can stay here in Jerusalem. The land and its castles will be in your hands. I will put my life on the line and not turn back until I find that faithless woman."

614. When Morolf saw that the king had been hurt so deeply, he said, "King, will you give me your word, that if I bring her back, I can take her life once I get here?"

615. Salman gave him his word. "Then stay put in this city, most noble emperor. If she's anywhere to be found on this earth, she will have to return to Jerusalem. 616. Now at last, for the sake of the queen, I will display my skills to their fullest," the excellent man declared. "I give you my word on that, mighty King Salman."

617. Morolf had the hair shaved off his head and stuck two rings in his ears. Now hear a greater marvel: he forced a third through his neck. Morolf suffered every day on account of the queen. 618. He placed an herb in his mouth that caused him to swell up as if he were really sick, so that he could scarcely be recognized. Then he went and stood before King Salman, who had to acknowledge his great skill.

619. Salman's eyes overflowed, and he said, "Stay here at home, my dear brother. If you put to sea when you are this sick and the wind takes hold of you, nothing in the world will be able to save you."

620. Morolf opened his cloak a bit and said, "Now look, king, what extraordinary things I have done to myself. I am doing this, sir, for your sake." He continued, "For love of your brother, take care of the maiden, whom I entrust to you. 621. If I fail to return from across the raging sea, you should make her your wife."

Out of devotion to the king, Morolf, with the help of a physician, subjected himself to excruciating torments. 622. He forced his feet against his body and bound his toes behind him, leaving Jerusalem in the manner of a cripple who moves with the help of a little stool. In addition, he turned his eyes in his head as if he were cross-eyed. 623. Then the clever man rode to the waters of the raging sea, where he found his little boat. He led his donkey on board and left the land of Jerusalem behind him.

624. He sailed the sea for thirty-six days until the winds drove him into the harbor at Acre. The very clever man sank his boat in the waters of the raging sea. 625. Then he rode to the place where he found King Princian and the queen in a hidden chamber. She had asked to be walled in there, since she believed there was no other place in the entire world where she would be safe from Morolf. 626. When Morolf heard about the king, he rode down to the gate and dismounted onto the ground. He crawled on all fours to the place where he found the gatekeeper. 627. You will want to hear what the gatekeeper said when he first saw him.

Figure 11. Morolf, disguised as a sickly old man, rides his donkey to his boat. Frankfurt a. M., Universitätsbibliothek, Ms. germ. qu. 13, fol. 71ᵛ.

"Now tell me, brave, proud warrior, how long has your body borne this great decrepitude?"

628. "I cannot say, sir," the clever man replied. "But this much is true: I have been a cripple fully twenty years."

629. "Your body is frail," the gatekeeper said. "Whatever country you have come from, you are a very sick man. Can you think of anything in my lord's castle that you'd like to eat?"

630. "I do not desire any of your food," he said, "but a drink would be very welcome. That's something I would be very glad to have from you."

"Now wait," the gatekeeper said, "I will bring it to you at the gate."

631. He went to the cellar. There he picked up a goblet, exquisitely fashioned out of gold, which he filled with a pure, noble beverage and carried to Morolf at the gate.

632. When Morolf had drunk, the gatekeeper sat down next to him on a bench. "Poor devil," he said, "let me tell you something: a German noblewoman has arrived recently from across the sea 633. with King Princian. She is beautiful and charming; her complexion is pure and bright. I give you my word on it, she will not fail to give you something."

634. "Now look where I'm pointing," he said, "at that white rock. That's where she has been shut up to keep her safe from someone called Morolf. He's a very clever man, who was never devoted to her in true loyalty."

635. "How can she enjoy herself with King Princian in that rock?" the clever man inquired. "Be so good as to explain that to me, since I find it very hard to believe."

636. "I'll tell you," the gatekeeper replied, "if you promise to treat what I say with discretion. A tunnel goes underground from my lord's chamber to the noble queen. 637. King Princian passes through it to reach the beautiful woman. When he goes to the hiding place, the tunnel is guarded by twelve counts, the best of all he has."

638. "A poor wretch should not inquire into such things," said the clever man. "Still, I entreat you by the God in whom you believe, ask the king to come to the gate just for a moment."

639. The gatekeeper went and found the king. "Lord, a poor wretch has sent me to you. He asks you, by the God in whom you believe, to meet him outside the castle for a moment."

640. The infidel went to the gate, followed by many illustrious knights. When Morolf saw him approach, he tried to fall at his feet. You will want to hear what the king said:

641. "Stop, you will hurt yourself. If you need clothes or food, I will provide you with them for the rest of my life, I give you my word, if you wish to remain here."

642. Then Morolf opened his cloak and said, "Look, king, at how strange my body is. A physician has promised to help me, if only I had something to give him."

643. "You shall have three marks of gold from me," replied King Princian. "And if you get well and need more, I'll give you another ten pounds."

644. After Morolf had received this gift, many peerless knights pushed through the gate. They all looked at the beggar and marveled greatly that anyone could be so deformed. 645. Just then, however, a chamberlain declared, "Lord, he is not suffering from a genuine debility. If you permit me, my lord, I will restore him to health this very day, that I pledge by loyalty I owe you."

646. When Morolf saw what was happening, he took an herb out of his sack and placed it in his mouth so that no one noticed. It caused him to puff up as if he were sick. 647. "You are mistaken, sir," said the clever man. "If your hands touch me anywhere, you'll know for sure that I'm sick, I give you my word."

648. The chamberlain went over to Morolf and grabbed his leg, planning to stretch it straight from his body. Skilled in trickery, Morolf began to fart copiously. 649. And that's how he defended himself against the pagan. The chamberlain jumped as far away from him as he could and said, "Beggar, you are right, you are not well, not the slightest bit. 650. Your hands, your feet, your mouth, and also the eyes in your head are all sick. Still, your eyebrows look quite elegant. All you illustrious, proud knights," he said, "you should give him what he needs."

651. Before he had finished speaking, many of them were already reaching into their purses. Of those gathered around, there was not a single one who did not give him a golden penny, even those who had scarcely a penny to give. 652. The pagan chamberlain addressed him without hesitation, "You shall have a shilling from me. Forgive me for touching you with my hand."

653. When Morolf had taken the gifts, he saw the king was wearing a red gold ring, into which an impressive relic had been worked with great skill. 654. Weeping copiously, Morolf said, "You have provided well for me, most noble, mighty, king. You should give me some sort of protection, so that if anything happens to me, I'm not robbed." 655. The king removed a breastplate of bright gold. "That's much too splendid for me to wear," Morolf said. "If I lost it, lord, I would never regain your favor. 656. I'd like to have something else from you. I give you my word that I'll bring it back."

"Beggar," said the king, "what do you want from me? By God, if you ask me, I'll be happy to give it to you."

657. Morolf pointed to the ring, and the king said, "Even if it were worth a thousand marks, it would still be yours, you can be sure of it. Now," King Princian continued, "stretch out your hand if you would like me to give it to you."

658. Morolf extended his finger, while King Princian drew the ring off his hand. Morolf bowed down to the ground before the relic and said, "Lord, you have provided well for me. Now I am relieved of all worry."

659. They brought his donkey around, and King Princian helped him mount. He took leave of the king and from the king's men and departed in excellent spirits. 660. Morolf showed them his tricks. He tickled his donkey, which started to jump up, in front and behind, so that he fell over its head, down into a deep moat. 661. Noble King Princian jumped in after him along with eleven of his men and lifted him back up onto his donkey. When the king leaned slightly against his leg, Morolf let go three big farts.

662. "Lord," said the clever man, "you have caused me such pain that I am bereft of all joy."

"Leave now," said King Princian, "and may your God watch over you."

663. Morolf took a road that led deep into pagan lands so they wouldn't think he was headed back across the mighty, raging sea. But when the sun set, he left that road and turned towards the broad sea. 664. After hiding his bridle and saddle in the rushes, he returned to the street, and his happiness knew no bounds. He took the herb out of his mouth, and look! a physician had come, and he was now a healthy man!

665. Having given some thought to what was in store, Morolf had brought with him a bright, red tunic, two shaggy beards, and a harp. These helped him out of danger. 666. Morolf got ready on the spot: he tied a shaggy beard on his head, put on a rough cloak and a palm frond on his back, and became a pilgrim. 667. He cut a staff from the rushes and started to lean on it. He said, "Now give me leave, noble pilgrim brother. I'm leaving you here in a good pasture, since I plan to travel to Jerusalem without you."

668. When King Princian was about to join his lady in bed, she said, "Noble King Princian, by your faith, what have you done with the ring? 669. My husband Salman gave it to me before I ran away from him the last time. Most noble prince, even if he knew me to be more than a thousand miles away, he would cross the raging sea to search for me."

670. "Why should I keep it?" the king replied. "A wretched beggar came up to me at court. He was a poor cripple, who asked me in the name of the god in whom I believe to give him a gift. 671. A physician had promised to help him if he had something to offer in return, so I gave him three marks of gold. After he took the gift, he asked me very courteously for protection. 672. That's when I gave him the ring. He is so sick, I don't believe he'll live until tomorrow morning."

The noble queen started questioning him at once. 673. She asked, "What were his eyes like?"

"Clear as a mirror," King Princian replied, "and his eyebrows were quite elegant."

"That's Morolf," the noble queen declared, "King Salman's vassal."

674. "Not so," said King Princian. "I saw Morolf standing in Jerusalem, wearing a sable cloak. This man is a poor beggar, believe me, noble queen."

675. "You don't know his tricks," she said. "Summon your heroes, if you ever loved me, and barricade all the landings from which ships can depart. Whoever brings me the cripple, I will give him his weight in gold."

676. That very night he summoned two thousand heroes and a mighty army. He ordered the ship landings to be completely barricaded. There Morolf encountered many pagan fighters. 677. Noble king Princian set out with many pagan men, hoping to find the cripple. He was met by Morolf himself, as you will see from this tale. 678. You will want to hear what the king said when he saw Morolf approaching.

"Now tell me, pilgrim, have you encountered a cripple, some time today or last night, riding a fine donkey?"

679. "Lord," the clever man replied, "that's something I can tell you about. Last night when the sun was about to set, I met that very cripple riding a fine donkey. 680. He said he had left King Princian and was headed to a physician who had given him help. If you continue a little farther in this direction, you will find his donkey walking very close to the street."

681. Princian gave him a golden shilling and said, "Take that as a reward for what you have told me, fine proud fellow. And if you should ever come to my home, I would free you from poverty completely."

682. All the heroes rushed off at cross purposes down to where they found the donkey walking in the street. They led it into the city of Acre, where everyone said the same thing: "Not a one of us has ever seen it."

683. "I think I have been deceived," King Princian declared, "by the pilgrim who told me about the cripple. It was Morolf himself, as I can see clearly from what has just happened. 684. Salman sent him out, and he has been gathering information here in this country. Now tell me, all my heroes, how I can keep the very beautiful queen from him."

685. "Lord," one of the pagans replied, "I can tell you what to do. Bring the donkey to the queen, and if she recognizes it, we'll know the pilgrim was Morolf."

686. When they brought the donkey to the queen, she said, "I used to see it standing in front of the temple in Jerusalem. Day after day it carried away stones. Now keep watch at the ship landings. That pilgrim was Morolf."

687. To prepare himself for what was in store, Morolf took off his rough, woolen cloak and his shaggy beard and buried his staff and sack in the rushes. Then he returned to the street, and his happiness knew no bounds. 688. Morolf put on a red silk tunic and picked up a German harp. His clothes looked suitable for court. In everything he did, he acted as if he were a minstrel.

689. A chamberlain had set out with a good fifty pagans to look for the pilgrim. He encountered Morolf himself, you can be sure of that. 690. When he saw Morolf approaching, you will want to hear what he said.

"Now tell me, proud minstrel, have you encountered a pilgrim, some time today or last night?"

691. "Lord," the clever man replied, "that's something I can tell you about. Yesterday when the sun was about to set, I saw that very pilgrim on his way to Acre to find lodging. 692. He wore a rough, woolen cloak, I tell you truly, and had a shaggy beard. I give you my word, he is well equipped for his journey."

693. "If you wait here a while," he continued, "you will see him pass by you on the street." The chamberlain dismounted and Morolf began to play his harp, producing a beautiful sound.

694. The rest of the pagans dismounted, and the chamberlain started a dance. He continued dancing throughout the day and into the evening, until he had completely forgotten his search.

695. Then the clever man said, "I can't stay here any longer, since there's a festival I've got to get to."

The pagan gave him a golden shilling, saying, "Leave then, and may your God watch over you, for you are a splendid minstrel."

696. Wisdom gained from experience prompted Morolf to leave the place. The pagans, meanwhile, returned to the city, where they delivered the news that they had not been able to find the pilgrim anywhere.

697. The beautiful lady asked, "Did you meet anybody at all on the street who told you about the pilgrim? That was Morolf himself, you can be sure of it."

698. When the pagan heard this, he said, "Lovely, fair lady, it would be strange indeed if no one could walk down the street without being taken for Morolf. 699. We did meet a splendid minstrel, whose clothes looked quite elegant on him and who carried a German harp, which he played so sweetly that the sound carried far."

700. "That was Morolf," the lovely lady declared, "Salman's vassal. Bring that minstrel to me, and as a reward you will receive thirty marks of red gold."

701. Morolf knew very well what the queen was planning. After burying his harp and his beautiful clothes, the warrior put on a gray tunic and tied two very large shoes tightly to his feet.

702. He put on an uncommonly wide belt from which hung a sharpening stone and a very sharp knife. Then he went into the city of Acre and said, "I will gladly buy cattle or sheep from anyone who offers them to me."

703. I can tell you truly, an old pagan gave him both cattle and sheep. The noble warrior slaughtered them and was in a great hurry to get them skinned. 704. With the pagans from court in hot pursuit, Morolf had no place to hide. They asked the butcher if he had seen the splendid minstrel anywhere.

705. Morolf looked down and, drawing on his cleverness, replied, "Yes, I have seen the minstrel. But I would much rather ply my trade so that my children might live." 706. Morolf, the illustrious, fine knight, cut the cattle into pieces. "Step right up," the knight said, "I'll give a good price to anyone who wants to buy meat." 707. While a great press of people gathered around Morolf, the pagans set off at once to look for the minstrel. Very soon Morolf, that clever man, had sold everything.

708. Morolf remained in the city among the pagans for three days, but did not think he would survive as a butcher, so he said, "Who will give me spindles and needles? I would like to be a merchant. 709. Who will give me belts, ribbons, and purses, suitable for a merchant who plans to put to sea, and yarn, both green and red, that looks good on ladies?" That's what helped Morolf escape danger.

710. The very clever man picked up a peddler's basket and set off down the street just as fast as he could to the place where he had left his little boat, 711. at the bottom of the raging sea. The warrior went to it at once, threw the basket of merchandise into the grass, and jumped into his little boat. He was in high spirits. 712. The clever man cast off onto the waters of the raging sea, and the illustrious knight said, "God willing, Sir Peddler's Basket, a poor man will find you."

713. Morolf had been away for half a year before he returned to Jerusalem, that's the truth. When he stepped into the presence of King Salman, the king and his court welcomed him with great affection.

714. "Once again I have found your beautiful wife," said Morolf. "But if you want to win her back, many knights will have to risk their lives. King Princian has had her walled up in a cell from which we will have to extricate her."

715. "Morolf, excellent man," King Solomon replied, "why did he have her walled up in a cell?"

"They are afraid of my clever tricks," 716. the noble knight replied. "There is a tall rock in the raging sea, my lord, on which the cell is located. An underground passageway leads to the queen. 717. King Princian passes through it to reach the lovely, fair lady. Now tell me, King Salman, how we will win her from the pagan king."

718. King Salman replied, "Morolf, excellent man, most extraordinary knight, she has paid her dues to the devil; now the devil must watch out for her. 719. If I were to cross the sea with you, I would once again have to go alone into the castle, as I did in the land of King Fore. They led me to the gallows, just as if I had put all their lands to the torch."

720. Morolf started to laugh and asked, "Does that mean you're ready to let go of your lovely, fair wife? Was it in vain that I travelled about for so long in a strange country? 721. Most mighty King Salman," the clever man continued, "you did, after all, give me your word that if I brought your wife back here, I could take her life."

722. Then King Salman said, "Morolf, excellent man, most extraordinary knight, if you bring her back here, you yourself can decide her fate."

723. Out of joy Morolf showed him the ring. "Lord," he said, "you gave this to the queen. That wasn't such a smart thing to do, and I don't think you acted very wisely. How could it be right for her to have a relic in her possession? 724. King Princian wore it on his finger. I, however, brave knight, tricked him into giving it to me, and now I will take it with me into the land of the pagans. I trust that God will show me the grace to watch over my trip. 725. You should remain here in Jerusalem. But make ready three thousand heroes at the shore of the sea for me to take into the land of the pagans. If they are willing to help me, I will bring them back to your country."

726. "Morolf," said Duke Friedrich, "for your sake I will travel into the land of the pagans, with a thousand men who will obey my command without hesitation."

727. Salman was glad to hear this. At the shore he outfitted three thousand fighters and the ships that were necessary to carry Morolf and the army across the sea. 728. Fourteen days or more they sailed across the raging sea. Then they arrived at Kastel, behind a hollow mountain, which was in the hands of a mermaid and many rough dwarves. 729. As they approached, they turned their ships towards the land and sailed up onto the beach. Their joy knew no bounds.

730. What I'm telling you is true. The mermaid said, "Listen, Madelger, my son, put on a magic cape and go out to the front of the mountain right away. 731. I smell German armor. Morolf has entered the land of the pagans." Madelger, the rough dwarf, put on a magic cape and went out to the front of the hollow mountain. 732. There he saw Morolf moving about among many worthy vassals. The moment Madelger saw him, he took off the magic cape. You will want to hear what he said:

733. "Morolf, my dear uncle, let me welcome you here in God's name." He took him by the hand and led him into the mountain, where he received a warm welcome from the mermaid and many a rough dwarf.

734. When she saw him approach, hear what she said to him: "Welcome to this country in God's name, Morolf. King Salman has sent you out after his lady."

735. "Lovely, fair lady," the clever man replied, "my dear aunt, tell me how I can win back the noble queen."

736. "Even if you had brought thirty thousand heroes into this country along with you, they would not stand you in good stead. Morolf, dear nephew, you will need my help as well."

737. "Lovely, fair lady," the clever man said, "let me profit from your noble spirit and help me to win the most noble queen."

738. The beautiful lady replied, "When night begins to fall, I will send you six rough dwarves, and they will sever the tunnel that leads down into the mountain for you. 739. Twelve of you should stand in front of the window of the cell and should capture King Princian and many miserable pagans. Let them be killed."

740. Having received this promise, Morolf took leave and departed. He brought the reassuring news to all his men. They lay down and took their rest until it began to grow light at daybreak.

741. Early the next morning, Morolf got ready and went to stand at the window of the cell. "Noble King Princian," he asked, "are you in there? 742. Then take back this ring, with which I redeem the promise I made." When the queen saw it, she began to shed bitter tears. You will want to hear what she said.

743. "That's Morolf at the window, who never showed me any loyal devotion. If he catches sight of me, on my word, I will lose my life."

744. King Princian said, "Do not despair, lovely, fair lady." He took her by the hand and wanted to leave the place. But look! the passageway had been destroyed, and he had to remain where he was.

745. With the full might of his army, Morolf destroyed the fortress and the cell. He captured King Princian and many miserable pagans, who were compelled to die. 746. When Morolf captured the king, the proud warrior did not fail to let him profit from the generosity he had shown. He took the red golden ring off his finger again. 747. He had a horse brought, and he himself helped King Princian mount. "Now flee from here, king," he said. "In return for the generosity you showed me, I will spare your life."

748. King Princian fled over the high mountains to his brother Pellian. Bowing down to his feet, he said, "Now help me, noble brother, so that my anguish might be made good. 749. My beautiful wife has been taken from me.

Figure 12. Morolf and the mermaid.
Frankfurt a. M., Universitätsbibliothek, Ms. germ. qu. 13, fol. 82^v.

Help me now, brother, for it is time. All my heroes have been killed by Morolf, Salman's vassal. I bring my grief to you and all our friends."

750. "If anything upsets a worthy man," King Pellian replied, "he should keep it in his heart. You're acting like a woman, King Princian. Morolf and all his men must lose their lives."

751. That very night, he summoned twelve thousand pagans and a mighty army and had the ship landings barricaded. Then Morolf was attacked by a large number of pagan warriors. 752. When Morolf saw what was happening, he went to his men and said, "Brave, spirited heroes, we must not step away from one another so much as a single foot. 753. The people of this country are not baptized: God will not leave us in the lurch in our pursuit of the noble queen. He will reward us for our faith and help us back across the sea."

754. Then an old Surian spoke up: "Often, before the walls of Troy, I was the one who performed the best. Nor has my sword ever failed to deliver its blows in the many fierce battles I have fought. Today too I will strike many deep wounds. 755. Tie on the battle standard for me, for I am ready to lead the army. I will lead us into a grim and gruesome death, or, you can be certain, I will help bring everyone out of danger."

756. "With my illustrious troops and my strong arm," Duke Friedrich declared, "I will attack our enemies on the broad meadow."

757. Morolf was glad to hear this and placed a banner in his hands. Then a fierce battle got underway. Many pagans were killed by Duke Friedrich. 758. Morolf and the Surian attacked fiercely and fought furiously in blood that came up past their spurs. Many pagans lost their lives at their hands. 759. Morolf was very strong: first on one side and then on the other he thrust and struck with great force. The high-spirited, noble knight brought down pagans without number.

760. Seeing that, King Pellian set out after the brave man, delivering a blow of such power that Morolf lay before him on his knees. 761. The noble knight jumped back up, and his sword resounded in his hands. He sliced through the nosepiece on Pellian's helmet with his sharp sword, which did not rebound until it reached his teeth. 762. King Pellian fell down on the field, dead. When King Princian saw that, he threw himself into the battle along with many pagan fighters. 763. Now at last a great noise rose up. Steel clashed against steel. Fear and anguish spread. The pagans turned red as they were soaked in blood. 764. The battle lasted clear through until vespers, when a ceasefire was declared. Only then did the many battle-weary fighters allow themselves to rest.

765. Early the next morning, Morolf got ready, then went and stood outside the tent of the pagans. "Noble King Princian," he asked, "are you in there? 766. We should fight one another here. If you wrest victory from me, then let my

heroes return unharmed across the sea, and I will do the same to yours. No one will take the lady from you ever again."

767. King Princian was glad to hear this. They sealed their agreement, as a result of which Christian hostages were handed over to the pagans. Then the two peerless fighters attacked one another. 768. Princian threw himself into the contest, driving Morolf all over the field until, at last, he delivered a blow of such power that Morolf, the noble knight, lay before him on his knees. 769. Morolf raised his hands on high and said, "Lord, help me out of danger. Reward me for my faith, so that I will not have to remain in a foreign land." 770. Before he had finished speaking these words, God sent Morolf such strength that he was victorious over the pagan. He jumped back up, and his fine sword resounded loudly in his hands. 771. "Now defend yourself, King Princian," he said, "or you're going to lose your life." Striking between his helmet and his coat of mail, Morolf cut off the king's head. You can trust me on that.

772. Morolf picked up the king's head, brought it to the queen, and threw it into her lap. "Look at that, noble queen," he said, "that is Princian, your beloved husband. 773. And if I bring you onto the raging sea, what more is there for me to say? If you cross the raging sea, I give you my word, nothing in the world will be able to save you."

774. The hostages were returned, Christians released from pagan captivity. Morolf didn't allow a single pagan to survive. Then he and his fighters hastened back to the ships. How could they have been any braver?

775. They had been away six months before they returned to Jerusalem, that's the truth. King Salman gave them a warm welcome, as did many noble knights and the beautiful lady. 776. "King," said Morolf, "let me tell you what I'm thinking. There's no time when it's more important to have your wife bathed than after she has made love to a stranger." Salman was glad to hear this and ordered a bath to be prepared in a beautiful marble bathtub.

777. The beautiful lady got in. Then the clever man kneeled in front of her and bled her from the vein in her arm. (I'm not making this up.) He pressed her so gently that her soul departed smiling from her mouth. She never knew what happened to her. 778. He had a goblet brought to him, placed it against her lips, and said, "Most noble queen, if you refuse to accept a drink from me, I will never offer you one again."

779. When Salman saw that, he began to shed bitter tears. "Morolf," he said, "you murderous vicious man, why did you kill that lovely, fair lady?"

780. Morolf the clever man replied, "Salman, day after day you stayed at home, while I was forced to suffer hardship on account of the noble highborn queen. I give you my word, I'm not going to do so ever again."

781. As soon as possible they carried the beautiful lady over to the minster, where they laid her in the tomb in which she had lain at first. 781a. When King Salman started to weep, Morolf the clever man said, "King, why are you making yourself miserable? I will give you a faithful wife without delay." 782. Morolf the clever man took Salman by the hand, led him across the court, and gave him the admirable maiden, King Fore's sister, as his wife. 783. She was a mighty queen in Jerusalem, it's the truth, fully thirty-three years, at which time the illustrious, noble king along with his beloved noble wife attained God's favor. 784. She was called Affer.

With this, this book reaches its end. May God help us all so that our souls will come to a good end. Amen.

Continuation in the printed edition, Strassburg, Johannes Knoblauch, 1510

The continuation begins immediately after "She was a mighty queen in Jerusalem, it's the truth, fully thirty-three years" (strophe 783). Numeration henceforth refers to the printed edition's leaves.

70b. The lovely, young queen—noble, beautiful, and praiseworthy—increased in virtue and amiability. She kept her marriage with unshakable constancy and was eager to serve God at all times. She lived without hatred and ill will and loved Salman quite beyond measure. Salman had neither quiet nor rest if he was not at her side, that you should know truly. And it was just the same for the queen: her thoughts were always with Salman. Their love for each other was great. They loved each other and lived in complete harmony, just as a loving husband and wife should. Great honor was granted to the two of them. The queen bore two beautiful sons, who grew in strength and wisdom. 71b. When the elder son turned thirty, Salman gave him power over the kingdom and confirmed that he should be emperor at Jerusalem.

Salman longed for God's grace and served God with intense devotion. To the extent he was able, the noble warrior performed long fasts, day and night. For her part, the noble highborn queen performed even greater devotions and excelled at all pious works. She withdrew from the world completely. When Morolf became aware of this he said, "Salman, mighty emperor, you and the queen are trying to deceive me. You want to commend yourselves to God and plan to let me enter hell all alone. I give my word to both of you: where you are, I want to be there as well." Wise Salman replied, "Morolf, I have grown old and gray in sin. As a result, I must do penance so that God might have mercy on me and my dear queen. If you want to be in heaven with us, then you should do penance yourself, as would be entirely appropriate in your case, since you have committed many grievous sins. Long for the grace of God. Live in the service of God. It is time. 72a. In return, God will give you eternal joy. Let us ask God to grant us all eternal life with him." Salman gave a talk filled with wisdom, but I cannot write it all down. His words were so fruitful that Morolf began to tremble violently before Salman. The exalted queen was also there. Morolf took the words to heart and was overcome with remorse. "Alas, God," he said, "what grievous sins I have committed. Alas, God, beloved creator, in your infinite mercy forgive me all my sins." Morolf fell to the ground. His remorse for his sins was so great that blood shot out of his mouth and his nose. His heart broke in two from the intensity of his lament, leaving noble Morolf lying there stretched out dead. 72b. An angel came from heaven, took Morolf's soul in its hands, and carried it to God in his heavenly kingdom. There Morolf will praise God forever.

When Salman saw this, his distress was great. He raised his hands to heaven. "Oh God, have mercy on this calamity. Alas, the great suffering that I endure! Alack and alas, I am a wretched man! Alas, Morolf, my loyal brother, how can I do penance for the sins that I unfortunately committed against you, as I would have done if you were still alive? Alas, God, what great suffering has befallen me, that I can no longer see my brother alive!" The very delicate, beautiful queen 73a. threw her crown to the ground and tore out her blond hair. She lifted up her hands. Her distress was great. Her cries rang through the air. She beat her breasts and her heart. Her lament and her pain were great. "Alas," she said, "that I was ever born! I will never be able to forget the pain of having lost Morolf, my brother and devoted servant." She lifted him up and kissed his red lips, then became so ill from her great anguish that she had to lie down in bed. 73b. Soon Salman was told that the queen was gravely ill. "Alas," said Salman, "this is painful news. My brother Morolf has just died, and now my dear wife lies in danger of death. O God, what do you have against me that you will not take pity on me?" Salman began to weep from anguish and ran quickly to the queen. When she saw the king weeping, her heart broke from the great sorrow she felt. Salman embraced her and kissed her on her dead lips. Although she was dead, he did not yet realize it. But when she didn't want to talk with him, as one would expect her to, then he looked her straight in the face and saw that she had passed away. Without gesturing in any way, he sank down to the ground. His heart broke within his body from the huge suffering and distress he endured. At once an angel came from heaven and brought the souls of both of them to the heavenly throne.

74a. Hardly ever can there have been a greater marvel, I must insist on that. Three individuals of the highest worth died on the same day. Morolf died at the hour for vespers. They prepared a grave for him in the minster, in which they planned to lay him at compline. But then Salman and the exalted queen died together just before compline. A sarcophagus was made for all three of gold weighing thirty thousand marks. Men and women wept when they were carried down to the minster. As was fitting, they were buried in the choir. A great noise arose from crying, from weeping and lamentation. No one could fully describe the terrible thing that had happened to them, 74b. that you should know for sure.

The elder son took possession of the kingdom. He was chosen by God. He was so beautiful and charming that he was just like his father, possessing virtue and great wisdom. His name was Isaac. Let me tell you of the younger son, who was called Rehoboam. He said, "Isaac, my dear brother, I too would like to be a king. You were born for an earthly crown, but God has chosen me for a spiritual one. I will receive it and accept it, as would be suitable for me from God. I intend to enter an order of monks and be ordained as a holy priest and live forever in the service of God. Dear brother, mark what I am doing: you should do the same, so that you might receive an eternal reward on earth and in heaven. Thus I bless you: may God grant you understanding and good health and, at the end of this life, eternal happiness." They kissed each other and embraced. Men and women wept from overpowering grief, as Rehoboam, a man of great nobility, left Jerusalem.

75a. He found a blessed monastery in a city named Constantinople, where he became a monk. He put on a gray cowl. He learned to say mass and to sing the liturgy and did very well at it. He never refrained from the service of God. God's grace dwelt with him. Rehoboam had been in the order for twenty years (what I am telling you is true) when God decided to take him to himself. He was beset by a great illness and died in garments of the Lord. An angel came from heaven and led him into everlasting blessedness. 75b. Thus we should pray to God in humility to grant that we acknowledge our sins and to let us live long enough to repent for them so that we may be with him in the eternal kingdom and praise him ceaselessly forever. In this may Jesus, son of God, by whom we are all blessed, help us. With this the book reaches its end. May God preserve us from all that is evil. Amen.

Figure 13. Salome, dead in the tub.
Stuttgart, Landesbibliothek, Cod. HB XIII 2, fol. 338ᵛ.

7

The Book of Markolf

(Middle High German)

Introduction and Translation
by James A. Schultz

Introduction

THE LATIN *DIALOGUE OF SOLOMON AND MARCOLF* (*Dialogus Salomonis et Marcolfi*) was translated into German a number of times. Two verse adaptations survive, of which *The Book of Markolf* (*Salomon und Markolf: "Spruchgedicht"*), offered here in English, is the older. Several different prose translations were produced in the second half of the fifteenth century, one of which, first printed in 1487, was reprinted, with variations, until the end of the sixteenth century. In the present volume, *The Book of Markolf* will represent all the German translations of the Latin original. It will be introduced first. That introduction will be followed by a brief survey of the other versions.

The Book of Markolf

The Book of Markolf begins by declaring itself to be a translation. After a few opening gestures, we hear from a monk who, while "sitting in [his] cell, ... came across a book that was in Latin" (7–8).[1] He was "requested" (1862), we learn at the very end, to turn this book into German, presumably by the "friends" (35) he mentions in another context. In the prologue, he focuses particularly on his concern that, in translating the Latin while trying to "preserve its meaning" (18), he had no choice but to use many words that do not "sound polite in the German tongue" (10–11). He asks those who read what he has written "that the courtliness they all possess might excuse" him (12–15) for the uncourtly language he was obliged to use. That a monk read a Latin book in his cell which

---

[1] Numbers in parentheses refer to line numbers in the German text.

he then translated into German for an audience defined by its "courtliness" reproduces within the text what the actual translator did in real life: he took the Latin *Dialogue of Solomon and Marcolf*, at home among clerics and schoolmen, and translated it into German for a courtly audience.[2] The ostentatious anxiety about the uncourtly words it contains serves not to disqualify the text as uncourtly but rather to define its audience as courtly. If it were not, there would be no reason to worry about the uncourtly words.

The surviving manuscripts suggest that *The Book of Markolf* did find an audience that prided itself on its courtliness.[3] One of those manuscripts was produced for his own use by Hans Dirmstein, a painter, sculptor, and goldsmith from a patrician family of goldsmiths in Frankfurt. (This illustrated manuscript also contains *Salman and Morolf.*[4]) Another was owned in the sixteenth century by Johannes Glauberg, member of another patrician family in Frankfurt. A third manuscript, destroyed in 1870 but known to have contained a single episode from *The Book of Markolf*, was written by the goldsmith Diebold von Hanowe, perhaps for his own highly respected Strassburg family. This information points not to the noble court itself but to the urban patriciate, whose members had adopted courtly forms and practices as their own, claiming them as marks of distinction.

The four surviving manuscripts all date from the fifteenth century, three of them from the second half, and two of those from the 1470s. Only the manuscript produced in Frankfurt by Hans Dirmstein can be located precisely, but the dialect in which two of the others were written places them in the same region, which extends southwest across the Rhine and northeast towards Thuringia, where, again judging on the basis of dialect markers, the fourth manuscript was produced.[5] The manuscript evidence suggests a concentration of interest in this text that overlaps considerably with the interest in *Salman and Morolf.* For *The Book of Markolf*, however, the center of gravity seems to lie farther to the northeast, in Frankfurt, and its reproduction does not extend into the sixteenth century or into print. The work of translation will have to have been done before the earliest manuscript was written, and that manuscript, which scholars date simply "fifteenth century," *might* have been written early in the century. Michael Curschmann places the composition of *The Book of Markolf* in

---

[2] Curschmann, "Marcolfus deutsch," 165. Most of what I say in the following pages was said first by Curschmann in this essay.

[3] Information on the manuscripts in this and the following paragraph is taken from Griese, *Salomon und Markolf*, 140–47.

[4] See chapter 6. The manuscript can be viewed online at http://sammlungen.ub.uni-frankfurt. de/msma/content/titleinfo/3654652. *The Book of Markolf* follows *Salman and Morolf*, beginning on folio 88v and ending on 128v. The images can be found at: 89r, 89v, 104v, 116v, 121r, and 126r.

[5] The Thuringian manuscript can also be viewed online, at http://digi.ub.uni-heidelberg.de/ diglit/cpg154. *The Book of Markolf* begins on 125r and ends on 136v.

the second half of the fourteenth century;[6] Alfred Karnein is certain it was not written until the fifteenth.[7] *The Book of Markolf* is generally known as *Salomon und Markolf: "Spruchgedicht."* Unfortunately, the first part of that title makes it difficult to distinguish this text from all the others with more or less the same name, while the second part, tacked on ostensibly to serve that function, characterizes the text in a way that is now generally regarded as misleading. Fortunately, in this case, the manuscript tradition offers an easy solution. Two of the surviving manuscripts refer, in the epilogue, to the text as "Markolfs buch" (1901). I have adopted and translated this medieval name in an effort to make it a little easier to distinguish this text from the others in the tradition.

The adaptation of the Latin *Solomon and Marcolf* for a courtly audience entailed many changes. Most obviously, Latin prose was translated into German verse. The shift from Latin to German was the precondition for intelligibility in the new environment. The verse form chosen, four-stress lines rhymed as couplets, is the lingua franca for courtly narrative: it is nearly universal in romance, in the short narrative texts that became popular in the thirteenth century, and in vernacular saints' lives. By choosing this form, the writer places his text in this tradition.

Another innovation becomes obvious as soon as one reads the first line: "I have often heard it said ...." (1) This "I" is soon revealed to be the monk who translated the text for his courtly friends. He is the narrator. The Latin source text does not have a first-person narrator. Courtly romances always do. The narrator speaks the prologue and the epilogue, thus framing the text and guiding our reception of it. Here he introduces it as "a strange tale, which no one can find displeasing" (5–6) that nevertheless contains all those questionable words. He comes back to "the uncourtliness of the words" (1877) in the epilogue. This fixation, which masquerades as embarrassment but might also seem a disingenuous strategy for piquing our interest, in fact directs our attention to what will turn out to be one of the major themes of the German adaptation. Just like romance narrators, our monk-narrator inserts himself into the narrative from time to time—expressing his own amazement: "I don't know how he did it" (1233); insisting on the veracity of his story: "you've been told the truth" (1458); and soliciting our engagement: "you will want to hear what he said" (1710). He inserts himself so actively into the description of Markolf and his wife—at one point declaring, "I wouldn't have wanted to kiss her" (94)—that he begins to resemble the unusually high-profile narrator of Wolfram von Eschenbach's *Parzival.*[8]

---

[6] Curschmann, "Salomon und Markolf ('Spruchgedicht')," 530; Curschmann, "Marcolfus deutsch," 164.

[7] Karnein, "Salomon und Markolf," 123.

[8] Curschmann, "Marcolfus deutsch," 165.

In abandoning Latin and the audience for which the Latin text was written, the translator forfeits the word play that gives the original much of its sparkle and bite. It would have been difficult in any case to reproduce in German, and the vernacular poet makes no attempt to do so. From time to time, however, he does play with words, using them ironically against the traditions from which they come. He seems to mock precisely the world that produced the Latin text when he has Salomon introduce his contest with Markolf by rhyming *disputieren* and *solvieren* (169–70), two Latinate words that, served up like this, suggest a scholar showing off his learning. He plays with a courtly tradition that prides itself on its closeness to France when, as he begins to describe how ugly Markolf's wife is, the narrator refers to her as Markolf's "worthy *amie*" (91), and when, in a scatological reply to Salomon, Markolf uses another French word, *garzun* (584), to refer to a page. He does the same with the courtly language of love, when he calls Markolf's repulsive wife "the darling of his heart" (*herzen drut*, 65) or when he has Salomon declare that "many a man suffers such distress from love" (*von minnen lidet mancher not*, 573) that it nearly kills him, only to have Markolf undercut the conventions of courtly love with his reply: the man would be restored to health the moment he sees a lovely woman waiting for him in bed.

Since the translator cannot rely on an audience for which the Latin scriptures are a constant presence, he cuts many of the passages that depend on that knowledge for their effect. When, in the Latin, Solomon denounces women, his "tirade ... is a tissue woven almost exclusively from direct quotations of Ecclesiasticus."[9] The same is true of the speech, shortly after, in which he praises women. The joke is lost on a reader who does not recognize that Solomon is contradicting himself with his own authoritative, biblical words. The translator shortens these speeches substantially and puts words in Salomon's mouth that have little to do with those in his source. Similarly, at the end of the Latin, when Marcolf looks in vain for a tree on which he would like to be hanged, the author traces his itinerary through twenty-four biblical place names, the last twelve from a list of kings in Joshua.[10] Again, the point is lost if the audience does not recognize the biblical context. The German translator omits them all. Perhaps the most telling change comes at the very beginning. The Latin text opens, "When King Solomon, full of wisdom and riches, sat upon the throne of his father, David ...."[11] Solomon is presented as a figure we will recognize, wrapped in his most famous attribute and his royal glory. In German he is not presented but introduced, as if we might not have heard of him before: "In days gone by, there was a mighty sovereign who wielded the full power of the imperial crown

---

9   *S&M* Z 233.
10   *S&M* Z 246.
11   *S&M* 1.Prologue.1.

in Israel. He was called Salomon and bore the crown during his lifetime. Many lands were subject to him" (19–24). This is the way the narrator of a courtly romance might introduce his protagonist.[12]

As these examples indicate, the changes made by the translator turn the text into something notably different from the Latin. The first part is reduced in size by about a quarter: instead of 140 exchanges, the German has 106.[13] Of those 106, fewer than half are adopted more or less intact.[14] Among the ones altered, some combine parts of what were originally different exchanges. Salomon's "Let your speech be ready with learning and wisdom" (241–42) is taken from the Latin and is found in its original place. But Markolf's answer, "When the deer is hunted, its ass turns white as snow" (243–44), is his response to an earlier statement of Salomon's, passed over in its original location but inserted here. In the earlier exchange, Salomon's opening is retained, "Often the guilty man will flee, even though no one has set out after him" (189–90), but, as he does in numerous cases, the translator has written a new response for Markolf, "A person who makes a noise shitting on himself fears everybody will smell it" (191–92). The original reply took up the theme of flight; the new one takes up the theme of fear, but in a characteristically Markolfian register. In other cases the translator will make up both parts of an exchange. The innovations, taken together, reveal several tendencies. First, they turn the contest between Solomon and Marcolf into something more like a conversation.[15] Salomon addresses Markolf directly: "Friend, tell me ..." (215). Markolf applies his response to Salomon personally: "If one were to hang all the thieves, it's unclear what would happen to you" (325–26). Salomon addresses his counterpart by name, "Markolf, when you come to court, behave so that you will be praised," introducing a series of exchanges where they really do respond to one another (423–34). Second, the translator introduces new themes or strengthens ones that were already there. He seems partial to animals and animal metaphors, which figure in many of his innovations (235–40, 268, 287–88, 295–96, 417–18, 435–36, 461–64, 467–68, 471–72, 479–80, 547–48).[16] Nearly all of these are put in the mouth of Markolf. The translator also adds lines having to do with thieves and hanging (323–26, 439–40, 511–12, 585–88). Third, precisely the theme of hanging establishes connections between this part and the next. The lines quoted just above (325–26) suggest that Markolf knows that Salomon will be led to the gallows near the end of part two. The prophecy that the king makes at the end of their disputation, that

---

12 Curschmann, "Marcolfus deutsch," 165–66.
13 Griese, *Salomon*, 154.
14 Griese, *Salomon*, 157.
15 Curschmann, "Marcolfus deutsch," 167–68.
16 Griese, *Salomon und Markolf*, 157–58.

Markolf is so committed to impudence, he "will certainly be hanged for it" (586), returns as a threat he repeats over and over in part two (742, 753–54, 808–9, 1455–56, 1559–62).

The second part is changed as well. Although most of the episodes of the Latin are retained, the story of how Solomon acquired wisdom and Marcolf cunning[17] is cut, as are parts of other episodes, mentioned above, that rely on biblical knowledge. Three episodes are added: the exemplum of the old woman, smarter than the devil, who tricks a man into killing his wife (936–1044), the episode in which Markolf climbs into a beehive and is carried off by thieves (1197–244), and the concluding episode, in which Markolf helps Salomon bring home his faithless wife (1631–874). In many ways the introduction of this material makes the text less coherent. Although the story of the old woman proves one of the claims Markolf made during the vigil he keeps with Salomon, it is not, like the other proofs, one in which the two of them are actors. It is simply a story that Markolf tells the king. The episode of the beehive, apart from being motivated by Markolf's need to hide out of fear of Salomon's anger, does not otherwise involve Salomon at all. The concluding episode, which is related to the plot of *Salman and Morolf*, is remarkable in that here "the good Markolf" (1675) is unequivocally on Salomon's side. He returns to court when the king seeks him, not once does he mock Salomon for his gullibility, and, after the queen has disappeared, he promises to "endure whatever hardship it takes" (1736–737) to find her, even if it costs him his life.

Although these new episodes undermine the coherence of *The Book of Markolf* as just mentioned, they strengthen it in others, by reinforcing certain themes that otherwise might not be so prominent. The most that can be said of the beehive episode is that it gives Markolf another opportunity to demonstrate his skill at saving his neck while causing trouble at the same time. The other two new episodes, however, elaborate the theme of Markolf's misogyny, which is central to the overall conception of the work.[18] It is sounded already during the vigil, when Markolf makes a claim "about women: if you want to keep something secret, don't entrust it to women" (786–88). To prove this, he tricks his sister Fusade into denouncing him to Salomon on the basis of false information he has given her (811–32, 858–902). The theme continues with the story of the old woman, so evil that, once she has demonstrated the extent of her wickedness, even the devil won't come near her (936–1039). At the end of the story, Salomon distances himself by distinguishing between evil women and good ones: whatever the story proves about the former, it "will not cause me

---

[17] *S&M* 2.2.
[18] Curschmann, "Marcolfus deutsch," 169–70.

to reproach good women" (1037–38). This distinction returns at the end of the episodes in which Salomon denounces and then praises women. In the Latin the point was to have the king contradict himself spectacularly by reciting his own biblical pronouncements on both sides of the issue. In the much-reduced German version, Salomon concludes: "What I said in anger should be understood to refer to bad women. No one should reproach good women. One can never repay their goodness. Certainly one should not equate them with the bad ones" (1475–80). He presents himself as the defender of good woman, against Markolf's defamation of all women. Although the dynamics are necessarily different when the woman in question is Salomon's wife (no one says a thing about good or bad women), Markolf's well-established hostility is evident in his suspicion of the queen, his readiness to pursue her, and the fact that it is he who "made sure that she died" (1872–73) in the end. The contrast between Salomon and Markolf is articulated most explicitly in the scene with which the Latin concludes, where Salomon accedes to Marcolf's request that he be allowed to choose the tree on which he will be hanged. The German adaptor has Markolf make his request "for the honor of all women" (1568). Salomon points out, rightly, that Markolf has "never had a good thing to say about women" (1574). And yet Salomon, the courtly king, cannot refuse a request made in their name.

The full significance of these changes becomes clear if we consider them in light of the changes made at the middle (the juncture between the two parts), the beginning, and the end. The first part of the Latin ends when Solomon gives up, saying "I cannot speak any more," and Marcolf insists "that you have been beaten."[19] A bit later Solomon lets Marcolf "go in peace" and Marcolf, in parting, insults him: "there is not a king, where there is not law."[20] In German the first part ends when Salomon declares, "There's nothing I can say to you that will make you cease your uncourtliness. For that reason I will not talk with you. I consign you to the fools" (601–4). Salomon gives Markolf and his wife cloaks and shoes, and, in parting, Markolf salutes him: "Have thanks king, great lord! May God increase your glory" (619–20). In Latin, the representative of official learning is defeated by the clever outsider, who gets in one last dig as he leaves. In German, the king grows tired of listening to the uncourtliness of an incorrigible fool, who doesn't much care as long as he doesn't leave empty-handed. It makes sense, then, that the German text omits the episode near the beginning of the second part of the Latin in which Markolf gives an explanation of how Solomon became wise and he became clever.[21] The issue is no longer wisdom versus cleverness. It is wisdom versus folly, which corresponds to courtliness

---

[19] S&M 1.142a–b.
[20] S&M 1.Epilogue.9–11.
[21] S&M 2.2.

versus uncourtliness. Markolf's hostility to women is the narrative realization of the verbal uncourtliness Salomon identifies at the end of part one.[22]

The Latin begins when Marcolf appears at Solomon's court and ends when those who were to hang him let him go: "thus Marcolf eluded the hands of King Solomon."[23] When he leaves there is nothing more to say. The German adaptation begins with a commonplace: "I have often heard it said that, in all ages, wise men have been found alongside fools" (1–3). That appears to be how things are left at the end. The last we hear is that Markolf has killed the queen. If, as appears to be the case, he remains at court, then indeed a wise man and a fool continue to be found alongside each other. In any case, the epilogue assures us that Markolf continued to do "many things about which I have not written" (1876). The story ends not because of any change in Markolf's nature or situation but because the narrator chooses not to write down all the uncourtly words that would be necessary to continue, of which he has already written "more than enough" (1878). That is the reason Salomon ended his contest with Markolf in part one, and that is the principal topic of both the prologue and the epilogue. The Latin contest in which cleverness gets the better of wisdom has been reframed (literally: by the prologue, by the epilogue, and at the juncture between the two parts) in German as a static opposition in which courtliness, which represents wisdom, faces uncourtliness, which is folly.

This Translation of *The Book of Markolf*

The English is based on the edition of this text by Walter Hartmann.[24] The numbers at the beginning of sentences refer to the German text, marking every tenth line. They stand at the beginning of the sentence in which the tenth line is translated, no matter where in the sentence the translation of that line falls. Numerals in the left margin in part one refer to the numbered exchanges in part one of the Latin. This system makes it possible to see what in the Latin has been translated, omitted, and changed. Sometimes it is not clear if the German is really derived from a particular Latin statement: the two may have something in common, but the connection seems tenuous. I have indicated even the uncertain cases so that readers can make their own decisions. Two ellipses are indicated, the first of a missing line at 70 and the second of a missing couplet at 520.[25]

---

22 Curschmann, "Marcolfus deutsch," 170.
23 *S&M* 2.20.10.
24 Hartmann, *Salomon und Markolf.*
25 I first encountered the Solomon and Marcolf tradition in 1974, in a graduate seminar taught by the late Michael Curschmann. I am grateful that, nearly forty years later, my teacher was still willing to answer my questions and help with a number of passages in this text that caused me

Gregor Hayden

Sometime in the last quarter of the fifteenth century, most likely around 1480, Gregor Hayden made a second German verse translation of the Latin *Solomon and Marcolf*.[26] The author tells us he undertook the task at the request of Landgraf Friedrich von Leuchtenberg, whose family had their seat north of Regensburg, between Nuremberg and what is now the border of the Czech Republic. Hayden may have been associated somehow with the court of Friedrich, although nothing certain is known about him besides his name, which he reveals in the epilogue to his work.

Hayden's translation has much in common with *The Book of Markolf*. Roughly the same length, it too is written for a courtly milieu and is rendered in the four-stress lines, rhymed as couplets, that are expected by such an audience. Like the earlier verse translator, Hayden introduces a first-person narrator, who, in a prologue, an epilogue, and a few brief interjections in the narrative, guides our understanding of the text. And, again like his predecessor, Hayden leaves out a substantial portion of the exchanges in part one (in his case nearly half) and feels free to alter what he keeps, especially Markolf's replies.

As becomes clear, however, especially in the prologue and epilogue, but also elsewhere, Hayden has his own ideas about what we should learn from Salomon and Markolf. For him these two figures represent not courtliness and uncourtliness or wisdom and folly but wisdom and cleverness (or cunning: the Middle High German could mean either). This same attribute is attached insistently to Morolf in *Salman and Morolf*. Hayden goes farther, however, and articulates a theory of the relation between the attributes that define his protagonists. Wisdom, he maintains, comes from God, while cleverness does not. But the world is such that the wise and righteous never succeed on their own. Therefore cleverness (or cunning) should be put in the service of wisdom so that wisdom will prevail.

Hayden's rebalancing of wisdom and cleverness requires an adjustment in the role of Markolf. Although he does challenge Salomon and does play tricks on him, the degree of antagonism is reduced. Markolf is not the disruptive fool he is in Latin but, unlike in all the other versions, is consistently referred to as a peasant.[27] Markolf himself articulates an awareness of the difference between king and peasant and accepts his place as that ordained by God.[28] In the first

---

difficulty. Needless to say, he bears no responsibility for all those places where I should have asked for help but did not realize it.

26 For the text, see Bobertag, *Narrenbuch*, 293–361.
27 Curschmann, "Marcolfus deutsch," 176.
28 Curschmann, "Marcolfus deutsch," 176.

part, Hayden alters some of Markolf's responses, so that, instead of parodying or mocking Salomon's statement, he extends and elaborates it.[29] In the second part, the king's difficulties with the women of Jerusalem are adjusted so that the episode can include a lesson about moderation that Markolf, of all people, gets to deliver: Salomon loved women too much. In the end the peasant joins the court as advisor and helper, thus representing narratively the way in which cunning and cleverness can be incorporated into the service of wisdom.

Hayden's verse translation survives in a single manuscript, written not long after the translation was completed, in the dialect of that region. Perhaps its failure to find any greater resonance can be explained by the fact that about the same time it was written, the first print editions of a prose translation of *Solomon and Marcolf* began to appear in nearby Nuremberg, and it was this version of the material that dominated its subsequent German reception.

Into Prose, into Print, and Beyond

In the second half of the fifteenth century at least four different prose translations of the Latin *Solomon and Marcolf* were produced. Three of them survive, each in a single manuscript.[30] The fourth, first printed in Nuremberg in 1487, is the foundation of the entire subsequent development of the German text, comprising 21 editions through 1594.[31]

With the prose versions, Solomon and Marcolf move into a new context. This is not the Latin world of the original, where scholars could delight in irreverent word games that rely on and confirm their elite status. Nor is it the courtly world of the vernacular verse translations, concerned with class-specific attributes like courtliness and cleverness and the proper relation among them. The prose versions were produced for and enthusiastically taken up by a broader, primarily urban world of educated or would-be-educated lay people. This new audience does not seem to have regarded the contest between Salomon and Markolf as problematical or transgressive. Perhaps it was the authority of King Solomon, perhaps the determination (which one sees in the contemporaneous version by Gregor Hayden) to view Markolf's cleverness in a positive light. In any case, the prose translations appear in the manuscripts along with didactic

---

29 Curschmann, "Marcolfus deutsch," 173.
30 For the most detailed description of the manuscripts see Griese, *Salomon und Markolf*, 194–206. For the most thorough analysis see Curschmann, "Marcolfus deutsch," 187–91. A fourth manuscript contains a translation of only the introductory description of Markolf and his wife. It seems to be closely related to the translation printed by Ayer (Curschmann, "Marcolfus deutsch," 189–90, 198). Three editions of two different low German translations were printed between 1487 and 1502.
31 For the clearest, most detailed list see Griese, *Salomon und Markolf*, 206–10.

texts, collections of proverbs and fables, prayers, and saints' lives. Translated into German prose at the end of the fifteenth century, the contest between Salomon and Markolf was presented to a wider lay reading public as a story that was useful and edifying.[32]

Comparing the text of the printed edition with the Latin original reveals how numerous deletions and small adjustments have changed the character of the text.[33] The disputation section is reduced by about a third. In the episodic section, the original is flattened out and reduced to the minimum necessary to keep the plot going. The regal splendor around Salomon is removed so that the conflict with Markolf begins to look like a private affair. The biblical references and allusions are reduced greatly, and when they are kept, or in some cases expanded, they do not serve as the occasion of parody. The changes reflect an orthodox piety that wants to "correct" the text and maintain the exemplary status of Salomon. At the very end, after Markolf fails to find a tree from which he wants to be hanged, he is returned to Salomon's court. Salomon declares himself vanquished by Markolf's baseness but then takes him into the court and orders him and his wife to be fed and clothed so they will not have cause to anger him in the future. Order is maintained.

The most consequential development, however, is the introduction of images. With hardly an exception, all the printed editions adopt the program of 16 woodcut illustrations first introduced by Marcus Ayrer in 1487.[34] A title image shows Markolf and his wife before Salomon, and another image concludes their disputation. The remaining images divide the second part of the work into twelve coherent episodes. This is a striking innovation: contemporary editions of the Latin, without images, divide the whole text into two or three parts. Although subsequent printers adopt Ayrer's program, his immediate successors make many adjustments in an effort to achieve the optimum relation of text and image. For instance, Ayrer's illustration for Solomon's famous judgment follows an established iconographic tradition that shows both the living and the dead child brought before the king. The text follows the Latin and mentions only one child. In later editions the second child makes its way from the image into the text. In Ayrer's edition the text of the episode in which Salomon confronts the women of Jerusalem is so long that several pages go by without a picture. Later editions shorten the text to such an extent that it becomes nearly unintelligible in order to achieve what seems to be a more important goal: at least one image on every opening. These are but a few examples of the ways the Solomon and Marcolf material was changed as it entered the new medium of print and

---

[32]   Curschmann, "Marcolfus deutsch," 190–91.
[33]   The following summarizes Curschmann, "Marcolfus deutsch," 199–203.
[34]   The following summarizes Curschmann, "Marcolfus deutsch," 203–20.

was dissemimated to new lay publics, whose interest was attracted and whose reception was shaped by carefully calculated relations between text and image.

At just the time when Ayrer first published a German prose translation of *Solomon and Marcolf*, other evidence begins to appear that this tradition was becoming more widely known in German-speaking Europe. Salomon and Markolf are the protagonists of a *Fastnachtspiel* or Shrovetide play Hans Folz wrote in Nuremberg. It exists in two versions, probably written 1487–1488. Also in Nuremberg, Hans Sachs drew on parts of the Solomon and Marcolf tradition in a comedy (1550), a *Fastnachtspiel* (1550), and two *Meisterlieder* (1538, 1550). Around the same time, Luther refers in different contexts to two different episodes involving Markolf. Markolf appears, sometimes with Salomon, sometimes with his wife, in woodcuts printed on single sheets, often accompanied by explanatory verse texts. These few examples are mentioned here to indicate the extent to which Salomon and Markolf became known in sixteenth-century Germany. The basis for this remarkable dispersal is the illustrated prose translation, first published by Ayrer in 1487.

Figure 14. A tonsured monk sits and reads.
Frankfurt a. M., Universitätsbibliothek, Ms. germ. qu. 13, fol. 89^r.

James A. Schultz

Translation

The Book of Markolf

I have often heard it said that, in all ages, wise men have been found alongside fools. If there's anyone in the mood to listen, I'll tell a strange tale, which no one can find displeasing. Sitting in my cell, I came across a book that was in Latin. 10. In that book I encountered many words that didn't sound polite in the German tongue. I ask both old and young who read what is written here that the courtliness they all possess might excuse me, since I couldn't turn the Latin into any better German and still preserve its meaning.

20. In days gone by, there was a mighty sovereign who wielded the full power of the imperial crown in Israel. He was called Salomon and bore the crown during his lifetime. Many lands were subject to him. One day it happened that the wise king saw a man and his wife coming to his court, which enjoyed great renown at that time. 30. Both of them had an exceedingly strange shape. It wasn't that they were old, just that they were misshapen. I want to give my friends an accurate description of the man's figure in words. His head was like an oil jug. The hair on top of it stood up like bristles on a pig. 40. His mouth was fixed in a grin. His forehead was broad and very wrinkled. His ears, like those of a bear, were covered with shaggy hair. If you want to hear more: his eyes were just like an ostrich's. An old nag that had molted twenty times wasn't so long in the tooth. He had short fingers and fat hands that were completely black. 50. I had almost forgotten his beard: his beard and his eyebrows were much too big. No part of him was free of hair, which could pierce like the skin of a hedgehog. I have no choice but to state this loud and clear: he had the nose of a monkey and the back of a roasted hare. The misshapen fellow had a short and flabby neck. 60. If I might have leave to say what I must: his belly, his knees, his legs, and his feet were like those of a great bear. Even an infidel would swear to that. His skin was torn.

The darling of his heart stood at his side. She could stand in for him. When she was supposed to laugh, she could only grin like an old dog. She had a crooked nose, a wide mouth, deep-set eyes, and a long head. 70. [...] that were misshapen. Her clothes, her shoes, old and in tatters, were crude, short, and narrow. A crowd gathered around the two of them, since they looked so strange. I suppose their shirts were made from old sacks. You could see their asses. 80. No matter how short his clothes, he could nevertheless be quite aggressive with the sword that he carried. It was old and quite mean: the hilt was a ram's horn, and he had lost half of the sheath. Hear about this ape: he was very good at chattering. No matter how contemptible he was in other regards, he was a talker. 90. Next to him stood his wife, his worthy *amie*, nicely decked out with a wooden crown. A brooch of lead adorned the breast of the lovely woman. I wouldn't have wanted to kiss her. She limped with each leg and her breath stank. Her ass hung down like two woolen rags. 100. The man she greeted in the morning would be filled with desire all day long. Her nose drooped into her mouth. Furthermore, on that occasion she wore two rings of black iron on her hand. What more should I say? Her hair, her forehead, her eyebrows, her nose, her mouth, her teeth, her ass, her head, her feet, her hands—all were split and black. 110. What did she look like down below, between her navel and her knees? I never saw anything like it: her vulva was all shaggy. The misshapen lump stood there and praised his female counterpart. She did the same to him.

While they were thus looking at each other, the king began to speak. "Where are you from?" he asked. 120. "Let me know that at once. Tell me your true lineage and your rightful name!"

Markolf answered, "You should go first, stating who your father was, and your grandfather, and how it has come to pass that you are feared everywhere." The king replied at once, "I will not conceal my lineage from you. 130. I am born of Judah, of whom it is written that he begot Phares and Sarah. Subsequently, Booz begot Obed. Obed begot Jesse in his time, and Jesse begot King David. David begot me with my mother Bathsheba. What more do you want? You know my lineage: I am called Salomon. 140. My friend, I have clarified this for you; now you should do the same for me!"

"I'm descended from peasants. If someone was told to polish all their swords, he wouldn't be done in a year. Now I'll tell you for sure, and I won't lie about it: the man who was my great grandfather was called Rumpolt. His son was called Ronepolt. 150. His son was a good fellow whom they called Ruprecht. That was my father's father. If you want to hear how it ends: my dear father was called Markolf, and he had me given the same name. Now you know my lineage: I am called Markolf. My wife is descended from an unblemished lineage, which is why she urinates through her beard. 160. You can judge her nobility from the jewels she's wearing, which adorn her so beautifully. She is the one I love, the one who banishes my sorrow. She is called Sludergart. Now you know us both well!"

Looking them both over quite closely, Salomon addressed the man. "You possess such a wealth of words, I think it would be a good idea for you and me to exchange words in a disputation."

4a	170. Salomon: "If you can resolve the questions I pose, I will make you rich with all manner of things."
4b, 3b	Markolf: "Many a man promises health who lacks the power to grant it. He who sings badly, let him start the song! Do that and get going."

5a   Salomon: "I came up with the judgment when two women were fighting over one child, while another lay there dead. 180. I ordered the child to be given to the mother."

5b   Markolf: "Where there are many cows, there's lots of cheese. Just the same, I say, when women get together in the street, there's lots of chatter."

6a   Salomon: "God has given me wisdom exceeding all people who are now alive."

6b   Markolf: "If you have bad neighbors, praise yourself, that's my advice."

7a   Salomon: 190. "The guilty man is likely to flee, even though no one has set out after him."
     Markolf: "A person who makes a noise shitting on himself fears everybody will smell it."

8a   Salomon: "A wife who is good and beautiful, she is her husband's crown."

8b   Markolf: "A pot full of milk, one should guard it well from cats."

9a   Salomon: "A good wife with a gentle disposition is good above all things."
     Markolf: 200. "If she starts scolding you, you won't be so eager to praise her."

9a   Salomon: "In all the countries of the earth there is no evil that can compare with an evil wife."

9b   Markolf: "If she dies, break her bones and put a big rock on top of her. Even then, you'll have to worry that she might rise up again."

10a Salomon: "The wise wife rebuilds households. The foolish one tears them down."
     Markolf: 210. "Profit was never the same on earth and in heaven."

11a Salomon: "A beautiful woman nicely dressed will bring her husband lots of joy."

11b Markolf: "A cat with beautiful fur—the heart of the fur trader longs for it."

13a Salomon: "Friend, tell me what I ask you in all seriousness: Where can one find a woman, strong and steady, who won't go astray for any price?"

13b Markolf: 220. "If a cat swore to me over and over that she wouldn't taste the milk under any circumstances, and if I believed her, the milk would be gone."

15a Salomon: "If you want to preserve your good name, turn your mind away from women who scold."

14b, 15b   Markolf: "Fat women fart a lot. Turn your nose away from their holes."

17a   Salomon: "He who sows evil reaps nothing but evil, and that's as it should be."

17b   Markolf: 230. "Where a man sows chaff, he won't reap anything but dust."

18a   Salomon: "Someone who is standing should take good care that he doesn't fall down to the ground."

18b   Markolf: "You didn't see the clump of earth in time, if your foot has already struck it."

Salomon: "Sometimes the dog is beaten for something the lion did."

Markolf: 240. "When a fart escapes a woman, she'll beat her dog for it and say, 'Get out of here, you're banished; you let loose from behind.'"

19a   Salomon: "Let your speech be ready with learning and wisdom."

7b   Markolf: "When the deer is hunted, its ass turns white as snow."

20a   Salomon: "He who praises himself doesn't really increase his renown."

20b   Markolf: "If I were to slander myself, there isn't much chance others would praise me."

21a   Salomon: "Wine leads to unchastity. 250. A person who is drunk causes suffering."

21b   Markolf: "Wine makes the poor man rich, which is why he should always be drunk."

22a   Salomon: "The man who waits patiently is likely to receive what he desires."

22b   Markolf: "The man who waits for a cat to bring forth a calf waits in vain."

23a   Salomon: "It's not good to eat a lot of honey. Turn your thoughts from it."

23b   Markolf: 260. "Anyone who can get a taste of what bees produce will lick it off his thumb as well."

24a   Salomon: "Everyone says without hesitation, 'Wisdom shuns the soul of the wicked.'"

Markolf: "He who throws gold into the salt cellar is lacking in good sense."

25a, 25b   Salomon: "It is bad to struggle against the rod. The lazy donkey should be given twice as many blows."

26a   Markolf: "The good and the evil fill the house. The mouse with nothing but a single hole is a poor mouse."

27a   Salomon: 270. "It is far better to suffer private loss than public shame."

27b   Markolf: "If someone kisses a dog on the ass, there's a good chance he'll get to smell its farts."
         Salomon: "He acts with honor and charity who treats strangers with courtesy."
         Markolf: "If you're going to abuse someone, it may well cost you your head."

29a   Salomon: "The generous act done gladly is pleasing to others and to God."

29b   Markolf: 280. "He gives little to his servants who licks his knife himself."

35a   Salomon: "Teach your son in his youth to fear God and love virtue."

35b   Markolf: "He who stops feeding his cow will never enjoy its milk."

36a   Salomon: "He who raises his servant too indulgently cheats himself."
         Markolf: "If you keep your donkey too fat while raising it, it will throw you off when you want to ride it."

37a   Salomon: 290. "I said in the past and I'll say it again now: everything acts according to its nature."

37b   Markolf: "That's true: new birch should be made into a broom."
         Salomon: "Nothing the judge says should lack justice."
         Markolf: "Sometimes a horse is confused by the idea that it can't walk right."

40a   Salomon: "A well-made black crown is a nice adornment to a white shield."

40b   Markolf: 300. "Two white thighs are an even better adornment to a hairy cunt, as you should know!"

41a   Salomon: "For the sake of knowledge one should honor the teacher, so that the young are all the more eager to learn."

41b   Markolf: "Where the donkey rolls around, it's true, that's where farts will bloom, or hair."

43a   Salomon: "Don't quarrel with a powerful man for any reason, no matter how pressing."

43b   Markolf: "It is wrong to flay a bear from its head down to its hind-quarters."

45a   Salomon: 310. "You should not lie in anything you say, nor should you deceive your friend."

45b   Markolf: "Who chats with someone who is eating, fools himself about eating."

47a   Salomon: "Friend, you should avoid all those who like to quarrel."

47b   Markolf: "If someone mixes himself up in the bran, the pigs will eat him along with their mush."

48a   Salomon: "You would never see the three tall mountains if there were no gorges between them."

Markolf: 320. "I know the saying well myself: the higher the mountain, the deeper the valley. I thought testing this would be a waste of time: that's why I shit in deep puddles."

Salomon: "It makes me sick at heart if a single thief escapes the gallows."

Markolf: "If one were to hang all the thieves, it's unclear what would happen to you."

49a   Salomon: "It seems odd to me that many live without shame."

49b   Markolf: 330. "It is quite clear to me: a dog lives like a dog."

50a   Salomon: "He forgets honor who measures out evil in exchange for good."

Markolf: "If you strike a dog that wants to shit, he will bite you."

51a   Salomon: "I wouldn't have as a friend someone who had never treated me in a friendly way."

51b   Markolf: "It doesn't take long for calf shit to stop smelling in a meadow at the edge of the forest."

52a   Salomon: 340. "A man looks for any opportunity if he doesn't want to keep his friends."

52b   Markolf: "A maiden has a scabby ass because she doesn't want to be touched."

53a   Salomon: "Surely, a king's word should never be taken back."

53b   Markolf: "Someone who means to plow with foxes will have to come back early."

54a   Salomon: "Garlic is good at a meal, but harmful in council."

54b   Markolf: 350. "He who eats garlic from time to time farts above and below."

56a   Salomon: "Listening is wasted if judgment is not engaged at the same time."

Markolf: "It's bad harping in a mill, where the donkey's foal licks its ass."

57a   Salomon: "If a man turns his ears from the cries of the poor, God will not hear his laments."

57b   Markolf: "He wastes his tears who cries out to a bad judge."

Salomon: 360. "Sand, snow, rain, and wind delight both flowers and children."

Markolf: "As long as snow and cold endure, women will get sick at the hearth."

59a Salomon: "No one should hide poverty or sickness: they should be entrusted to one's friends."

Markolf: "No one can do anything to manure so that sows won't find it attractive."

61a Salomon: "How will he ever treat another person well who never does anything for himself?"

Markolf: 370. "He who wipes his ass with chaff won't end up very clean."

69a Salomon: "He who is afraid of frost is going to get snowed on."

69b Markolf: "He who is afraid the straw will prick him shouldn't shit in the stubble."

Salomon: "He wastes his wisdom who chooses the worst for himself."

71b Markolf: "An even load breaks no one's back, unless misfortune gets piled on."

72a Salomon: 380. "I insist: one should avoid all liars assiduously."

Markolf: "He who can't get along with the truth must make his way with lies."

74a Salomon: "The friend and the physician are tested when one is afflicted by hardship."

74b Markolf: "He who locks up his cellar is rewarded for doing so with a drink."

75a Salomon: "In company, one should avoid those who like to chatter and quarrel."

75b Markolf: 390. "A leaky roof and an angry wife will shorten the life of a good man."

76a Salomon: "He who spurns a small gift should not be given a larger one."

76b Markolf: "A spurned cunt and a hungry dog will likely go to sleep sad."

77a Salomon: "Don't rebuke the mocker; otherwise, he'll hate you fiercely."

77b Markolf: "The more you spread the shit around, the worse the smell it makes."

83a Salomon: 400. "Many a man desires to live opulently who must nevertheless live in poverty."

111b Markolf: "He who has hard bread and no teeth will, it seems to me, turn it around a lot with his tongue."

140a Salomon: "You can see it written: every season has its season."

Markolf: "In the summer people like to eat cherries. In the winter they shit the pits."

Salomon: "Truly, I declare to you: lying causes great sins."

Markolf: 410. "Someone who lives by selling won't be able to tell the truth all the time."

Salomon: "If the sluggard fears the cold, he won't do much work with the plow."

Markolf: "He who wants to cut costs mustn't pay his tailors."

Salomon: "No one should suffer disgrace for the way he manages to live with honor."

Markolf: "The fox that is ashamed of raiding will be torn to pieces by hunger."

84a   Salomon: 420. "He who cannot feed himself properly shouldn't expect to take a wife."

84b   Markolf: "There was a man who often went hungry. He went and bought a dog."

Salomon: "Markolf, when you come to court, behave in such a way that you'll be praised."

Markolf: "No one can behave so well that it will seem good to everyone."

Salomon: "I'm afraid I'll suffer from the fact that I cannot teach you to behave properly."

Markolf: 430. "If you're afraid of shitting on yourself, stick a wipe into your asshole."

107a, 86b Salomon: "Gentle words put an end to anger, so that friendship can usually be preserved."

Markolf: "Anger turns hair gray. The ass farts, that's the truth."

Salomon: "Ants gather all summer so that they can get through the winter well."

Markolf: "If someone slacks off at harvest time, the lice will be happy to bite him come winter."

Salomon: 440. "When the thief sets out to steal, his wife is good at keeping it secret."

100b   Markolf: "Whatever the wolf does, the she-wolf thinks it's well done."

Salomon: "If you want to attain a happy end, you should turn all things towards that which is best."

Markolf: "If I see someone's ass is showing, how should I cover it?"

81a, 81b Salomon: "Out of respect, don't deny your wife if she complains to you of a secret need."

Markolf: 450. "It would take a long time to still her need even if there were four of me."

Salomon: "Let sleeping dogs lie. All misdeeds should be covered up."

Markolf: "What you say is true. That's just what I did: I lifted up the bed and shit into the straw."

Salomon: "Follow my teaching: You should always hope for the best."

67b   Markolf: "He who does evil but hopes for good: that strikes me as a failed calculation."

Salomon: 460. "The faithfulness of good wives always seems fresh."

Markolf: "A louse is more faithful: it won't abandon a man no matter what happens to him. It will let itself be hanged with him or drowned in a sack."

Salomon: "That man is raving mad who equates good women with bad."

Markolf: "Falcons, bats, and flies cannot be called equal—unless you're planning to lie."

85a   Salomon: 470. "With fools, one should talk foolishly."

Markolf: "The monkey thinks it possesses great wisdom, yet it has nothing to cover its ass."

87a   Salomon: "The mouth of your enemy will never speak the truth about you."

Markolf: "He who wants to lie can tell marvels; that's why donkeys have to carry sacks."

88a   Salomon: "If you want to grow old in honor, you should keep your promises."

Markolf: 480. "There's a big difference between swallows and sparrows."

92a   Salomon: "You should get a good amount of sleep. No one can reproach you for that."

Markolf: "I am often awakened by mice. Fleas and lice bite me too."

93a   Salomon: "When we are drinking and eating well, we should not forget to say grace."

93b   Markolf: "They do not sing the same tune, he who is full and he who is full of hunger."

97a   Salomon: 490. "If your poor friend gives you a small gift, take it, praising it without stinting."

Markolf: "If he brought me a turd, I would throw it in his way."

99a   Salomon: "You should avoid taking up with someone who knows how to scold."

Markolf: "If you bring a wolf back to your home, he's not going to leave without causing damage."

103a   Salomon: "A good, merciful man can attain what is best for his soul."

103b   Markolf: 500. "He will get through life with poor judgment who doesn't want to examine himself."

106a   Salomon: "No one is so perfect that he can accomplish everything that might benefit him."

106b   Markolf: "He who has nothing to ride, let him go on foot, that's my advice."

107a   Salomon: "A gentle answer breaks anger; friendship is lost through scolding."

Markolf: "When two old women scold each other, they proclaim all their misdeeds."

Salomon: 510. "The bad habits of a wicked man tend to stick with him."

Markolf: "He who finds he likes stealing likes to be among thieves."

111a   Salomon: "The man who has something should have things given to him as long as he lives."

Markolf: "The man who has little should have it snatched away and sent to the person who has lots."

Salomon: "Once the fox has been skinned, you won't find anything else of value."

Markolf: 520. "[...]"

101a   Salomon: "He who answers before he has listened acts like a fool."

Markolf: "A deaf man understands from their smell the farts one lets go."

102a   Salomon: "One can say with certainty, every man seeks his equal."

Markolf: "He whose head is bald is happy among those who are naked."

104a   Salomon: 530. "Many a man thinks he has shooed the wolf away; then the lion starts to threaten him."

Markolf: "Many a man thinks he's wiping his asshole; meanwhile, he's gotten shit on his thumb."

110a   Salomon: "It is difficult indeed to teach a child of a hundred years."

110b   Markolf: "If you force an old dog onto a lead, you'll have to watch out for your hand."

116a   Salomon: "A heart that has been affected by overindulgence often causes people to talk."

116b   Markolf: 540. "Overindulgence of the stomach often causes the ass to fart."

119a	Salomon: "I was born of the lineage of Judah and chosen to be prince over Israel."
	Markolf: "You can be certain of this: among the blind, the one-eyed man is king."
120a	Salomon: "Sometimes hardship causes the just man to sin."
	Markolf: "In bushes and fields an old donkey seldom feels any hardship."
122a	Salomon: 550. "I would be glad of the honor if God gave me possessions without number."
122b	Markolf: "Dogs aren't given all they demand when they wag their tails."
124a	Salomon: "Where a wife hates her husband, he has reason to be worried."
124b	Markolf: "Where there's a weak shepherd, the wolf will shit fleece."
125a	Salomon: "The man to whom a wicked wife is given cannot live without care."
125b	Markolf: 560. "A donkey should be beaten if it tries to avoid the right path."
126a	Salomon: "It is not suitable for the fool to speak lots of wise words."
126b	Markolf: "One would consider it strange indeed if a dog were to carry sacks."
127a	Salomon: "He who spares the rod dishonors his own child."
127b	Markolf: "He who kisses the little goat may well be the she-goat's friend."
129a	Salomon: 570. "However many small paths there are, they point to a large road nearby."
	Markolf: "You might want to try this: many eggs make a large cake."
	Salomon: "Many a man suffers such distress from love that he lies sick unto death."
	Markolf: "A woman he holds dear on the bedspread, and the sick man is restored to health in a flash."
128a	Salomon: "When the sky becomes dark, you can tell there will be rain."
128b	Markolf: 580. "When the dog wants to take a shit, you can see him hunched up."
132a	Salomon: "A fine sword looks good on a king, no matter where he goes."
132b	Markolf: "A big turd looks good beside the hedge, as do two old boots on a page."

Salomon: "You are intent on magnifying your impudence. You will certainly be hanged for it."

Markolf: "If all the thieves were to be hanged this year, gallows would become expensive."

136a Salomon: 590. "The wise son brings joy to his father; the foolish son is a danger to his mother."

136b Markolf: "The sad person and the joyous one do not sing in the same way."

138a Salomon: "If you treat the just man well, he will reward you without measure."

Markolf: "He who thrashes a wicked man has wasted his day."

Salomon: "Before the fortunate man has gotten out of bed, the unfortunate man has eaten his bread."

Markolf: 600. "Before the dog has finished shitting, God knows, the wolf has the she-goat in the bushes."

Salomon: "There's nothing I can say to you that will make you cease your uncourtliness. For that reason I will not talk with you. I consign you to the fools."

Markolf: "That can't be, as long as I live. You should admit you're beaten and pay me at once what you promised me with your own mouth."

The king's counselor responded: 610. "You peasant, as far as I'm concerned, you're too base ever to be granted what you have asked from our lord. The dust should be beaten off of you with a hard staff."

Salomon: "No one should do anything to harm him. He should be given a cloak and shoes, for him and also for his wife, cut to fit their bodies."

Markolf: "Thank you, king, great lord! 620. May God increase your glory."

Thus Markolf left court, taking his lovely wife with him.

How the king arrived at Markolf's house

Shortly thereafter the king, having hunted down the stag, came riding up with his hounds. He was told by his men, "Lord, this is where that joker of yours lives, Markolf, who is able to talk so much."

"Now ride on your way," he said. 630. "I want so see to how sad or happy he is." Then the king turned back and rode across the threshold of the house. "Where are you, my friend?" he called out. "Who is with you in your house?"

Markolf answered him from within, "One and a half men and a horse's head. Therefore leave me unharmed. 640. Furthermore, I say to you in reply, some rise, others fall."

The king asked him to tell him where his father was.

"I believe he is making two losses out of one," he replied.

"Where has your mother gone off to?"

"She is doing a good deed for her neighbor that she will never do for her again as long as the world endures."

"Tell me, where is your brother?"

650. "I'll tell you truly, he is sitting by the fence over there, committing a great many murders."

"As you love God, tell me now how things stand with your sister."

"She is sitting out there filled with remorse, weeping miserably over her joy."

"Explain this to me," said the king, "since I haven't understood you. 660. You just said, 'Some rise, others fall.' Tell me, how am I supposed to understand that?"

"I have beans on the fire: the boiling water drives some up, while others fall to the bottom."

"You have also said, 'One and a half men are here in the house along with a horse's head.' Tell me, what's that about."

"See for yourself what's meant. 670. You are half in the house. Along with me, that's one and a half men, plus your horse's head. What more do you want?"

"Continue speaking: I believe you said your father was making two losses out of one. However can that be?"

"My father planted a field with grain," Markolf replied. "People had made a path around it, which the fool blocked. 680. Now they have made two around it."

"Tell me the truth about what's happened to your mother and what she's doing to her neighbor. Tell me, what's going on here."

"Her neighbor lay dying. My mother, acting out of devotion, closed her eyes for her. She will never do that for her again."

690. "Now tell me further how your brother committed murder."

"Lice were tormenting him, so he killed them out by the fence."

"In good faith tell me more, tell how your sister was bewailing her joy."

"Last May she was so happy, the fool: no one could hear a thing because of her singing. Now my sister is bemoaning the fact that she conceived a child."

The king said, "I'm going to ride away now. 700. Tell your mother to send me soon a pot of milk, covering it nicely with a pie from the cow. You should bring it to me!"

Markolf didn't neglect to do what the king had ordered him to do. 710. "Mother, attend to this: tomorrow morning prepare milk and a pie for the king from our best cow. Use the pie to cover the pot of milk."

"I'll be glad to do that. Now get going: you're to bring it to him."

Markolf didn't wait any longer. He got ready at once, quickly picked up the milk, and set out for court with it. 720. When he came upon a meadow, he began to feel hungry, so that his stomach hurt all of a sudden. Then the miserable glutton went and ate the pie he was carrying. He threw a cow turd on top of the pot.

When the king saw him coming, he addressed him angrily, "Where is the pie from the cow?"

730. "The hunger in my stomach became too great to bear, so I ate the pie and covered the milk with this, which also came from the cow."

"Now you drink the milk: and may you get a fever and an inflammation in your throat from it! Let's put this behind us now. We will keep watch, you and I, all night long. I have considered the matter carefully, and you should know that I am not lying. 740. See that sleep does not deceive you. If you fall asleep, you are ruined: I will have you hanged in the morning!"

Markolf said, "That's fine by me." Since he had eaten, he fell asleep at once and began to snore loudly.

The king asked him what was going on and said, "Markolf, are you sleeping?"

"Not I, lord, right now I am thinking."

"Tell me what you are thinking about."

750. "I have seen more than twice as many divisions in the tail of the hare as in its entire back."

"If you don't prove that, I'll have you hanged tomorrow morning!" Then the king said nothing more. Markolf lay there and for the second time he fell asleep and snored loudly. The king asked him what was going on and said, "Markolf, are you sleeping?"

760. "Not I, lord, right now I am thinking."

"Tell me what you are thinking about."

"I'll tell you. About the magpie: you can be certain it bears an equal number of white feathers and black feathers."

"If you don't prove that, you'll have to die tomorrow morning!" Not long after, however, sleep overcame Markolf once again. He slept and snored loudly. 770. The king asked him what was going on and said, "Markolf, are you sleeping?"

"Not I, lord, right now I am thinking."

"Tell me what you are thinking about."

"I'll tell you. About the day: nothing can be as white as glorious day."

"If you don't prove that tomorrow, you're ruined." What more shall I say? 780. Markolf slept again as before. He snored loudly above and below. The king asked him what was going on and said, "Markolf, are you sleeping?"

"Not I, lord, right now I am thinking."

"Tell me what you are thinking about."

"I'll tell you. About women: if you want to keep something secret, don't entrust it to women."

790. "If you don't prove that, you'll have to die tomorrow morning."

"If you will permit me, with regard to women I will prove that a wicked woman can twist the devil around her finger with ease."

"You will prove that if you want to save your life." Not long after, sleep overcame Markolf once again. He slept and snored loudly. 800. The king asked him what was going on and said, "Markolf, are you sleeping?"

"Not I, lord, right now I am thinking."

"Tell me what you are thinking about."

"I will tell you truly: Nature drives out habit. No one can reinscribe it."

"If you don't prove that unequivocally, I will have you hanged tomorrow morning." 810. The king was tired of keeping watch, so he went to rest.

In great haste, Markolf went to his sister Fusade and pretended he was filled with anger towards his lord the king. "Sister, if you will not tell anyone, I'll entrust my secret to you."

820. "May God ruin me," she said, "if I ever report you, even if this obligation means choosing a bitter death."

"I'll tell you this in confidence: the king is threatening me. He plans to have me drowned or hanged from a gallows. But if I can get close to him without being detected, I have resolved to stab him, so that he'll lie dead in front of me. Then I'll be done with his threats."

830. "My dear little brother, I will keep your secret." He put a knife under his cloak until he returned to court.

Salomon had awakened and was sitting on his throne. Before long he recalled what they had done during the night. Now hear some amazing things. 840. Salomon had a hare brought in and counted the tail and the back: he found an equal number of pieces. A magpie was set down, and its feathers were also counted: it was determined there were an equal number of white and black. Markolf took a vessel with milk and set it down in a dark place. When the king went in, he didn't see the milk standing in front of him until he stepped in it. 850. "Wretch, what do you gain by trying to make me fall?"

"You said, milk is whiter than the day. Now the truth can be seen that the day is much whiter than either milk or snow. You wanted to convince me of the opposite.

"Now I'm going to tell you about women, as you will understand shortly. 860. Lamentably, I must lodge a complaint with you concerning my sister Fusade. She has acquired a baby, from the sort of advice that was given her. You're being told the truth. In so doing she dishonored me and saddened all her relatives. She refuses to acknowledge that this is why I will not share my father's inheritance with her. 870. For the sake of God, serve as judge for me in this matter. She should be summoned by your command." The order was quickly given. Markolf said to the king, "Lord, the filthiness of the unchaste woman who stands there has dishonored me and mine. Let her be drowned in the Rhine, since she won't deal with me. 880. Be her judge here in this affair. For the sake of God, do right by me, since I am your poor servant."

"Knave," she said, "you lie. You are deceiving my lord. You are a false murderer. I want to warn you, dear lord: he wants to avenge his anger and stab you to death."

"You lie, you filthy whore. 890. Keep silent and abandon your false ways!"

"Lord, if you would deign to do so, have him searched for the knife he has with him. It will be found at his breast. I'll stake my word on it."

The king's pages ran over and looked for the knife everywhere but did not find it. 900. Markolf then explained to the king that women should not be entrusted with anything one wants to keep secret, since they bring forth with wicked cunning things I don't even know about.

"Continue your proofs," said Salomon, "since you said earlier that nature takes precedence over habit. I would like to hear a clear explanation of this."

"For that, you should give me a little time, just until it is evening."

910. "I will gladly do so," said King Salomon.

There was a cat at court that, from habit, could do the following: When they sat at table in the evening, whether they were eating meat or fish, it held a candle between its feet until the meal was finished. Then it was allowed to go play. Markolf was familiar with the cat's ability. 920. Having thought up a plan, he brought three mice with him. He let one of them run next to the cat's legs, with which it held the candle. It just barely kept itself from seizing the mouse. He took out the second mouse and let it run by the cat. 930. The cat wavered at least twice, since it wanted to catch the mouse then and there. But it feared the king's word and held the candle firmly in place. Markolf let the third mouse jump free. What the cat had learned was no longer able to constrain it. It caught the mouse and let the candle fall.

"What more shall I show you now?" Markolf asked Salomon. "I have already proved for you what I claimed earlier."

940. "No, you also said that a wicked woman could twist the devil around her finger with ease."

"That's true, I did claim that. I had almost forgotten," Markolf said to the king. "I will tell you what happened. There was a good man and his wife who had preserved their souls and their bodies with utmost prudence. 950. This annoyed the devil a great deal, and he considered all the various tricks he knew to bring them down. They were no use at all. Then a wicked woman approached him, addressing him thus, 'Tell me, where are you coming from?'

960. "'I'll tell you what upsets me,' the devil replied. 'There's nothing I can do to destroy the harmony between the two of them.'

"'You're lacking in skill,' she declared. 'May God shame you! If you give me a reward, I'll make them live in disgrace.'

"'Yes,' he said, 'That I will do: I'll get you two new shoes.'

"Thus the two of them pursued their crime. 970. Getting down to work, the woman went to the wife and approached her with these words: 'Lady, I hope you will understand that what I am about to say is well intentioned. I have learned of an injury that has been done to you and wanted to let you know about it, as my dear friend.'

"The lady said, 'Now tell me.'

"'You have a husband,' she said, 'who treats you with great disloyalty and has taken up with other women.'

"'I don't believe it,' the woman said.

980. "'Upon my life, it is true. I can give you some help in this matter, if you don't disdain my advice.'

"In her innocence, the lady replied, 'I wouldn't do that, you can be sure.'

"'Tonight, when your husband is sitting next to you and warming himself by the fire, he will begin to sleep. Quickly you should pluck a long hair from his neck. 990. You should steal it from him, cutting it off with a knife. I will wager my life on it, the woman will become hateful to him and he will never do it again.'

"With this the wicked woman left and went to that same man, as he was walking along behind his plow. 1000. She addressed him thus: 'Perhaps you're wondering where I've come from: I'm here to help you, since you are a good person. You should know that your wife is intimate with another man.'

"'That certainly is not true.'

"'If you want to learn the truth, then hear what will happen to you,' said the wicked old woman. 'Tonight, right after dinner, you will fall asleep. 1010. Then she will reach for your throat and cut it in two. You would have been killed if I hadn't come to you. That's what I've learned. And that's why you shouldn't sleep until you see the truth of this yourself.'

"That night, after he came home, he pretended to sleep. 1020. The woman had found a knife and, thinking she was acting out of goodness, started to cut off the hair. When the man became aware of this he seized her by the throat and began to strike and beat her until she lay there dead. The wicked woman had done that which the devil was not able to do. As a result, he brought her two new shoes, which he handed over to her on a stick. 1030. He held the stick out to her and said, 'It seems to me I shouldn't risk coming any closer to you. I must acknowledge your superiority in this.'

"What more should I say? I have proved the truth of what I thought up earlier."

Salomon said, "This story will not cause me to reproach good women. You proved your point with evil tricks. 1040. Therefore I won't put up with you any longer or suffer you at my court. If you ever return, I will have the hounds bite you and tear your clothes to pieces." Thus Markolf was driven away from the king's court.

He focused his thoughts on how he might return there so that the king would take note of him. 1050. He bought a hare and set out for court at once. The servants saw him and, making a great noise, set all the hounds on him, hoping they would bite him and tear his garments to pieces. He threw the hare in front of the hounds. No one will doubt that the hounds ran after the hare. 1060. Markolf continued on his path and came where he found the king.

Salomon asked him at once, "Where did you come from? Damn you! Who let you in?"

Markolf answered without hesitating, "I'm here, whether anyone likes it or not."

Salomon said, "The entire hall has been decorated with a pleasing arrangement of carpets. 1070. Later today, when people are at court, you should silence your coughing and you shouldn't spit anywhere except where there's a bald spot on the ground, or off to the side somewhere nearby."

Markolf had to promise this. The hour arrived for people to appear at court, for many knights and ladies were coming to this event along with many noblemen. 1080. Markolf started to cough and wanted to spit. He wasn't able to hold out any longer, so he went around and around, this way and that, looking for a bald spot where he could deposit what he was carrying in his mouth. 1090. After he had looked quite a while without finding a bald spot anywhere, he saw standing right next to him, there in the middle of the hall, a knight who was bald. Markolf moved closer to him at once and, because he hadn't found anything else that was bald, spat onto his forehead, so that the top of his head and his forehead were covered with filth.

"What do you mean by this, you villain?"

1100. "Because I did not see anything else that was bald," said Markolf to the king, "I got into a bind. You yourself ordered me today to find a bald spot. That's what I've done, with the best of intentions. I fertilized his forehead. Lord, I want you to know this: if someone had done this to him over and over, he might have a long ponytail by now."

1110. This made the knight very angry. And the king was deeply pained that Markolf had behaved in such an unseemly fashion.

After this had taken place, the king sat in judgment. Two unchaste women arrived, one of whom had smothered her child and caused its death. That same night she got up and stole the living child from the other woman while she was asleep. 1120. She hid it and lay the dead child in its place. When the other woman awoke later on, she cried out and lamented loudly that the child was not hers, tearing her hair out in her profound grief. The two of them sought judgment.

1130. When this complaint was brought before him, Salomon spoke with great wisdom, "Since both of you desire judgment, bring me a sharp sword. I will soon end this quarrel between the two of you. All who are present now listen: the living child will be split through its stomach and through its back, and each of them will be given a piece."

The mother cried out loudly, "Alas, lord, do not cut the child in two. 1140. Let it be given to her before you subject it to this torture."

The other woman said, "Neither mine nor yours, the child must be divided!" The king took the little child and gave it to its mother. All who heard this stood in awe of his judgment.

Markolf was sitting not far away when the judgment was rendered. 1150. "My lord," he said, "good king, how did you recognize the mother?"

"I did so on the basis of her demeanor. And because she cried without restraint and could not bear to see the child cut in two."

"You don't understand very well what's going on. I will give you a different explanation. When a woman weeps with one eye, she laughs with the other. 1160. She'll often say things with her mouth that she does not mean from the bottom of her heart. She behaves well to you; God alone knows what she's thinking. A woman can spin, weep, and lie, and deceive many a man by the way she behaves. There is no constancy in them."

"By my faith," said Salomon, "your mother was that sort of woman, wretch, when she bore you. 1170. If she had been a good woman, she would never have produced such an evil person. Where there are women, there is much joy. A woman is a delight and a pleasure. Beautiful women brighten the day. They drive away a man's sorrow. Kings, dukes, young and old—women are able to sustain their joy. They are the source of all honor. 1180. Your tongue should be paralyzed today, this very day, if you say anything about them that sounds malicious."

Markolf asserted for the second time, "He spoke the truth who said—you can be absolutely certain of this—'whatever is in a person's heart, that same thing is always also in his mouth.' Because you lie with women, that's why they enjoy your praise. 1190. I will tell you more: no matter how much you praise them—I'll stake my life on it—a woman will still betray you."

"Get out. You lie, wretch: no one should believe you. There will be no wavering: I will have you drowned."

Having lost the king's favor, Markolf feared his anger. 1200. He wanted to keep hidden until the next morning, so he looked all around for a place where he would be safe. At last he entered a cave from which bees had flown out and crawled into a beehive. That same night two men came by who wanted to steal some bees, hoping to find the best. 1210. When one of them saw the hive in which Markolf was resting, he said to the other he was certain it was the best. "My friend," he said, "let's take this one. None of the others here is as good." They agreed then to load it quickly onto a pole between them. No doubt Markolf was thinking: 'You'll want to strike the one in front. 1220. He'll think his friend did it.' Having had this idea, he delivered a great blow, striking him from behind on his neck, so that he was completely taken aback.

"What have I ever done to you," he demanded, "that you have struck me so hard?"

"What are you accusing me of?" the other replied. "I haven't touched you all day."

1230. He said, "Now *you* should walk in front: I want to know who struck me." They did as he said. Markolf delivered another blow—I don't know how he did it—so hard that the man collapsed onto his knees. "You truly evil worthless wretch," he said, "may the devil enter your carcass! What did I do to deserve this, that you have struck me so hard? 1240. You'll pay for it, on my word, even if I'm hanged as a result." The two of them hit each other for a long time. In great fear, Markolf slipped away from the place, leaving them there.

His wickedness, however, prompted him to go to the woman who had recently gotten her child back. "Do you know what they're saying in the king's court right now?"

1250. "All I know," she replied, "is that my child was stolen and has been returned to me."

"Since then, the king has been searching for you; he wants to divide your child and bury you alive."

"Is that true?" the woman asked.

"Yes," he said, "upon my life."

"For that he will soon die, and all his descendants along with him. 1260. He is one of the falsest judges on whom the bright sun has ever shone."

"Oh, if only you knew what his council and his men have agreed on: he will issue a new ordinance according to which, from now on, each man shall have seven wives for himself in lawful marriage. And how will they get on? 1270. One woman will strike the other. If he treats one of them well, the other will not be happy about it. The most beautiful will certainly have precedence, while the other will have to stand in the corner. The result will be lots of conflict and much quarreling."

1280. "If I knew this to be true," she said, "I would run into the city and inform the good women and my other friends and relatives so that they could figure out what to do about this great crime."

"Believe me," insisted Markolf, "what I'm telling you is true."

The woman threw her cloak around her and ran with great haste until she had entered the city. 1290. She brought the women together and said, "Hear strange news: Salomon, the mighty king, along with his false counselors, has invented a new law, according to which each and every man shall have for himself seven wives in lawful matrimony. If the decree goes into effect, days of misery are in store for you. A man is burdened with one wife. How is he supposed to take care of seven, so that each will get what she wants? 1300. How will he satisfy seven when he can't provide one with that which her heart desires?" The women didn't think much of this message, which weighed down the spirits of all of them.

They gathered together very quickly and decided they would besiege the king with force and with wits. 1310. They gathered apart until there were seven hundred of them. Then they tore off the king's gates and threw them into the moat. When the king heard what they had done, he came onto a bridge nearby. They insulted him, using words he had until that moment never before heard from the mouth of a woman. 1320. He didn't really understand what was going on until he asked them, "What are you accusing me of and why are you so angry at me that you are attacking me with such hostility?"

There was one woman among them who could speak well, whom the others had asked to speak for them all. 1330. She cried out in a loud voice, "You may have your way, since you are a powerful man. Everyone brings you gold, silver, and jewels. You can give gifts or loan things to your wives and mistresses, which you have without number. If only a poor man could equal you in this! 1340. This we know for certain: if you lack anything for body or mind, you fill this need thanks to your wealth. But if it were not for your immense treasure, we would never have heard a word about your spending even one day at your ease among so many women. 1350. It's as they say: He who violates his marriage vows, and presumes to act in ways that are not appropriate, will rejoice in his heart if everyone else does the same. Thus you want to use us to cover your old misdeeds."

Salomon responded in anger, saying, "God has chosen me to be king. Shouldn't everyone obey my command?"

"Yes," they said, "that is altogether right and proper. 1360. We are of the lineage of Abraham and, like all our forebears, have kept the law of Moses. But now you want to set this law aside and teach us a new one."

He asked, "What law do you mean?"

1370. "I'll tell you right now," she replied. "We just heard that you ordered that each man should have for himself seven wives in lawful matrimony and that it will no longer be fitting for him to be satisfied with one. This has come to the attention of all of us. Where was such a thing ever heard of? Lord, mighty king, you should know this: Saul was deposed because he did not keep God's command. 1380. Your father also got into trouble for violating his marriage when he saw Bathsheba naked between her legs and her shame was visible to him. He took the woman by force, which cost Uriah his life. Everywhere in this country people say that you are not a legitimate child. If the law can't be revoked, it seems a much better idea to us for one woman to have seven husbands. She could take care of them all by herself better than one man could take care of seven wives."

1390. King Salomon laughed at this and said to those who were with him, "She certainly speaks well on behalf of her companions. Upon my life I declare, I have never seen so many women gathered together in one place as I have today."

1400. When they saw the king joking, they all cried out, "Aye, you malicious mocker, may God diminish your glory! Because you have been acting unjustly, you're now going to mock us too. In their day, Saul and David were wicked enough. Most vile filthiness, you are worse than all of them."

The king did not remain silent any longer. 1410. He turned pale from the strength of his anger and said, "How has it come to this, that I am besieged by women? No master could fully describe the baseness of bad women. A wicked woman is a weed that steals flesh and blood. It would be better to dwell among scorpions than among bad women, since all wickedness is with them. They have no constancy. 1420. From the first, the counsel of bad women has brought misfortune upon the world. Who can utter or put in verse or express in words the unworthiness of bad women?"

The members of his council said, "Lord, it pains us that you dishonor women in this way and burden their spirits."

1430. When the councilors dared to speak to him in this way, Salomon responded in anger, "You have all seen clearly how they came here in anger and attacked my good name and took revenge on me."

Markolf jumped before the king and said, "Lord, receive my thanks. You have done what I wanted. 1440. It was clear to me there was nothing I could say to you or sing about women that could stop you from praising them until now. But now you have abandoned their praise. No matter how much you were annoyed by what I said, now you have come to see that it is true."

"Just listen to this evil peasant! May your life turn sour, since you thought up the wicked plan by which you brought this to pass and brought me disgrace, because I have spoken out falsely against good women. 1450. May you be cursed! Get out! Get away from me at once! I'll tell you this, which is the absolute truth: if I ever again look you in the eyes, know for certain that I will have you drowned or hanged from a gallows."

That's how Markolf was driven away: you've been told the truth. 1460. The king's council said to him, "Lord, listen to what you should do: apologize to these lovely women with gentle words and let them return to their homes."

The king spoke courteously, "Now you all should know as the utter truth that I am deeply sorry to have upset you. What happened was caused by a wicked, worthless person, who misled me and you. 1470. He will have to wither on a gallows on account of what he did. For every good man should not have more than one wife. He should honor her and devote himself to her with joy. What I said in anger should be understood to refer to bad women. No one should reproach good women. 1480. One can never repay their goodness. Certainly one should not equate them with the bad ones. May the most exalted God of Israel by his holy dispensation bless you and preserve you, life and limb, and increase your people and your descendants."

They all said, "Amen."

Now Markolf turned this over in his mind: the king has forbidden you to let him look you in the eye. 1490. How might it come to pass that he might look me right in the asshole? He wanted to make this happen. One night snow had fallen, so it would be easy to track game in the woods. Markolf, the misshapen man, got hold of a pepper sieve. 1500. He took the sieve in one hand and tied a bear foot onto the other. His base cunning gave him the idea to turn his shoes around. In the morning, he made his way to the place where the king was supposed to ride, in time to behave foolishly. 1510. On all fours he crept from up on high down below, along many narrow paths, through bushes and through shrubs, through hedges and through herbs, on the field this way and that. At last, he saw where there was an old oven without anyone living nearby. He got into the oven and thought, this is exactly the place for you to sit.

1520. When the king came along in the morning, he gathered his retainers and said, "We're going to follow these new tracks and see what we find." They were all very glad to hear this and rode out without delay. They found the tracks right away along which Markolf had crept and where he had broken through the snow. Nothing like this had ever been seen before.

1530. "Lord," they said, "we want to get a good look at the most unusual track that has ever been seen."

When he saw it, the king paused. "This is a most remarkable spoor," he told his followers. "Let's get going. We'll pursue this animal today, to see if we can flush it out."

They followed the track back and forth, up and down the mountains, through brambles and through hedges. 1540. "I'm going to surprise this animal." The entire search was difficult until they got to the oven. As soon as Markolf heard him, he lowered his breeches and quickly turned his ass towards the mouth of the oven.

At that moment, the king said, "What sort of thing are you? You must be cursed!"

1550. "You didn't want to look me in the eyes; well, now you've looked me right in the middle of my asshole."

"Blazes!" the king then said and called all his men together. "In the presence of all of you gathered here, I make an accusation against this filthy peasant. He deceives me at every opportunity. I do not want to endure this from him any longer. 1560. Lead him away at once into the nearest forest and hang him now. Then I will be done with his deceptions." At once, they dragged him away like a shorn bat and started to lead him toward the woods.

1570. Markolf raised his hands to the king. "Noble lord, do this for the honor of all women: since I must lose my life on a tree, let me choose the one. Let me not be hanged until I have made my decision."

"You have never had a good thing to say about women and have often weighed down their spirits. Nevertheless, I won't let myself be annoyed. You will have this boon from good women: I will grant your wish." 1580. Having said this, King Salomon admonished his men upon their oath that they not harm Markolf in any way until he had selected the tree on which he was to lose his life.

Then they led him into the forest and said, "Hurry up and choose the most beautiful tree that you can imagine. That's where we'll hang you!"

"Why are you in such a hurry?" Markolf asked. "I won't be choosing a tree for a good long while. 1590. You can forget your rush. There's not a one of you, if you were going to be hanged, who wouldn't want to think it over long and hard, if the choice was up to him, since he was about to be forced to lose his life."

They led him up and down, here and there, back and forth without his ever selecting a tree, until they got tired of riding. 1600. One of them said to the other, "We've ridden all day long. We could waste many more days this way, since he clearly has no intention of choosing a tree. If we kill him, then we will disobey the command of our lord. He told us, then admonished us upon our oath not to harm Markolf in any way until he select the tree on which he will lose his life."

1610. "It's clear to me," said the other, "even if we led him about for another seven years, he wouldn't select a tree. You know what I mean. It's the plain truth: he has tricked us and our lord."

They all decided to put this proposition to him. "If you will forswear the land, you can save your life."

1620. "How am I supposed to do that? Am I supposed to walk through water? I can't survive in water, since I never learned how. I can't swim or fish."

"You can't escape from us: you must foreswear the king's court."

"If I can save my life that way, very well, I will attempt it and will go to my relatives." Markolf left them and went away free. 1630. His quick thinking helped him accomplish this.

Before the year came to an end, the king began to suffer greatly. I will explain how that came to pass, as I have come to understand it. The king's wife, dear to him above all, had turned her mind and her body and all her senses to the love of a pagan king. He sent her letters and she sent letters in return. 1640. Eventually things had progressed so far that she decided she wanted to come to him, if there was any way he could make this happen. She pretended to be sick and let the pagan know what she was thinking, that he should take strength from his goodness and send her messengers. He sent her two minstrels. 1650. They claimed they had come from the Greeks and that they were able to cure the sick with their sweet music, of which they knew a great deal. I cannot hide the fact that these same minstrels were skilled in the art of magic, according to those from whom I have this written account. 1660. As such, they were at the king's court and performed to great acclaim, until they got to the queen and heard all that she had in mind. They had brought an herb with them, which was placed in her mouth. She lay there as if she were dead. This would cause the king great misery. The next morning news rang out that the queen was dead. 1670. The king and his retainers were quite amazed that she could be dead, since her lips were so red. No one had an explanation for this.

The king said, "Upon my oath, if the good Markolf were still alive he would surely have some advice about what to do."

"Indeed," one of them said, "he is in hiding, because he is very afraid. 1680. He has sworn to avoid your court and fears he would lose his life if anyone were to see him here. I believe it will be hard to find him."

"You must not give up," said the king. "Run from street to street and cry out: 'Let it be known to all that my pot lies broken on the ground at my feet. 1690. Is there anyone who can fix it?' No matter where Markolf is hiding, he will answer you right away."

As the page ran through the streets calling out these words over and over, chance ordained that he came to the place where Markolf was. 1700. The moment

Markolf heard clearly what was being said, he came forward and declared, "If there is anyone, man or woman, so quick they can take the pot from me, I will pay for it with my life." That's how they found Markolf. The king sent for him at once, swore to forgive him, and gave him a pledge. 1710. When Markolf came back to court and heard the news that the queen lay there dead, you will want to hear what he said. "There's magic involved here. Bring me molten lead, and I will pour it through her hand. If she is alive she will twitch at once."

But when he poured the lead as he proposed, she didn't twitch so much as a mite. Then they all said, "She is dead." The king ordered her laid to rest.

1720. "Now keep close watch on the lady," Markolf admonished. "I will forfeit my head if you don't lose her tonight." But no one gave any weight to what he said. During the following night the two minstrels brought the queen away with them. In the morning the lady was lost; they all would have sworn an oath on it.

1730. When the king learned this he went secretly to Markolf. "You're the one who has most often told me the truth. By your faith, advise me. I will provide everything you request so that you can find out what has happened to the lady."

1740. Markolf replied, "I will endure whatever hardship it takes to discover what country the woman has gone to, or I will die in the attempt. Provide me with very costly merchandise, as I will instruct you. I will hasten throughout the land in every direction to see if I find her anywhere." That's what happened. 1750. He was in fact given, as he had asked, expensive merchandise, gloves, and clothes for sale, with which he travelled around the country. Markolf disguised himself marvelously with his clothes. I'll tell you the truth: at that time, he acquired a cap with beautiful hair. His hair, his eyebrows, and his beard were died red. 1760. When he had been outfitted with clothes and garments, he left the country and journeyed through many foreign lands, but he failed to find the lady. At last, he came to a castle where he got word of her. And there, beneath a linden tree, is where he began to unpack his wares. 1770. It wasn't easy for anyone to understand his language or his speech, since his cunning nature had inspired him to distort what he said. No one who saw him there would ever have claimed, on the basis of his words or actions, that this was Markolf. When he had set out his wares, the women of the city hurried over boisterously to see everything he had to sell. The queen came too. 1780. Markolf paid close attention to her when she went to look at the gloves. That's when Markolf got a glimpse of the hole that the lead had burned through her hand. The merchandise, for which he had been asking a price people thought outrageous, he now offered at a great bargain until he hurried away from that place. 1790. Markolf returned to Salomon and told him with all due respect that he had found his wife.

Salomon replied, "What am I to do now? You must advise me again."

"Put on a coarse woolen cloak," Markolf told him, "as if you were an old fool. When I show you the castle, go and ask them to give you food. 1800. Furthermore, you should add that you have come from the sea. Leave your men in the woods. Direct them to come at once when they hear the sound of the horn; otherwise you will lose your life."

Salomon headed for the castle, as Markolf had instructed him, in the manner of a pilgrim, and asked to be given food. 1810. As soon as the lady saw him, she said to the pagan king, "My Lord, this is Salomon. Consider carefully what you want to do with him."

The pagan was very glad to hear this. "Now tell me dear sir, if this had happened to me, so that you had me in your chains (which the gods do not desire!), what sort of death would you want to give me as punishment?"

"If only God might grant that's the way things stood! 1820. I would take you into the nearest woods and let you select a tree, from which I would then have you hanged."

The pagan declared, "That's what's going to happen. You can count on it. Let's get going, men and women, anyone who can carry a staff! We're going to hang the mightiest king of whom you have ever heard tell."

1830. When they entered the woods, they took Salomon at once and told him to choose the tree on which he would lose his life. "I'll choose soon. However, it would only be proper for you to let me sound the horn three times, since I am of the lineage of kings."

"Fine," said the pagan, "sound the horn at once and come away!"

1840. The queen said to the pagan, "Lord, the day has progressed quite far. It would be a bad idea to wait any longer. I greatly fear the plans of Markolf, since he is very ingenious. Therefore, make an end of this!"

"You can carry on as much as you want," he said, "but be still and let him blow: I am in my own country and am quite safe from his men."

1850. Salomon sounded the horn as the pagan had ordered, once and then again. The third time, Salomon's attendants and his men burst forth with a host of fighters and captured everyone who was there. I heard it said truly that not a single one escaped them. 1860. They hanged the pagan on the spot, and killed everyone who was there so that none survived save the queen alone. Filled with hatred, they led her away. When she saw Markolf, she cried out loudly and said, "Markolf, you didn't look like this when I paid you for the glove. Alas, that miserable hour! I have learned the truth of that." Then they brought her back home. 1870. There a most shameful act was committed. She was left in a bath, in which Markolf made sure that she died. She received the reward that she had earned.

Subsequently Markolf did many things about which I have not written, on account of the uncourtliness of the words, of which there are already more than enough in this account. 1880. Markolf's skill is well known: I will leave him as I found him. This tale was written in Latin, and I have turned it into German as I was asked so that those who do not understand Latin might understand it. 1890. My most fervent request now is this: that whoever intends to read this book, in which I have written many uncourtly words, excuse me as much as possible, whether you are a lady or a man, since I am not so skillful that I could turn the German any other way than as the Latin instructed me. Let them not reproach me who hear this. 1900. I have shortened the account considerably on account of the impropriety of the German, of which more than enough remains. This is the end of Markolf's book. May God direct us to that which is best.

Figure 15. Marcolf and his wife.
Frankfurt a. M., Universitätsbibliothek, Ms. germ. qu. 13, fol. 89ᵛ.

8

The Saga of Melkólfr and King Salomon

(Old Icelandic)

Introduction by Jan M. Ziolkowski
Translation by Jess H. Jackson†

Introduction

*T*HE SAGA OF MELKÓLFR AND KING SALOMON (*Melkólfs saga ok Salomons konungs*) is an imposing name that modern scholarship has attached to one short fragment of Old Icelandic.[1] Although anonymous, this prose piece may be connected with the circle of Jón Halldórsson (d. 1339), the Norwegian bishop of Skálholt, Iceland.[2] Nothing apart from its two opening episodes is preserved. It is extant on the first of only two leaves (both damaged from rubbing along a fold) in Copenhagen, Arnamagnæan Collection, MS AM 696 4to III. As the final Roman numeral signifies, this pair of folios is the third item within a collection of fragments, what could be called a fragmentarium. The single hand in which the recto and verso of the first leaf in this unique manuscript are written has been dated to ca. 1400. The second leaf transmits part of an abridged *Saga of Plácítus* (*Plácítus saga*), which tells the story of the Roman warrior named Placidus who converted and became St. Eustace after encountering a crucifix-bearing stag.[3]

Likely composed in the first half of the fourteenth century, the saga relating to Salomon (as Solomon is spelled here) and Melkólfr (as Marcolf's name is Icelandified in this case) opens with the theme of wisdom. First it relates how Salomon acquired wisdom and built the temple. Then it tells how Melkólfr, a

---

[1] The manuscript is Copenhagen, Arnamagnaean Manuscript Collection, MS 696 III 4° 1ʳ–1ᵛ (ca. 1390). The text has seen two editions, the better of which is the more recent: Tucker, "*Melkólfs saga ok Salomons konungs*" (with photographs of the folio sides between diplomatic transcription on pp. 210–11). On the title, see his first sentence and footnote. On the dating, see the end of his first paragraph.

[2] On the ascription to Jón Halldórsson, see Einarsson, *History of Icelandic Literature*, 164.

[3] For essential information, see Tucker, "*Plácítus saga.*"

farmer's son, possessed such wisdom that his parents kept him locked up for fear that Salomon would abduct him. Both Salomon and Melkólfr are connected explicitly with Jerusalem in the sentences that introduce them, a circumstance that is likely a nod to the Eastern roots often ascribed to the Solomon and Marcolf complex of traditions. The first editor concluded that it drew upon folk traditions from the East. More specifically, he hypothesized that the saga might have Byzantine origins.[4]

Most of the fragment comprises two episodes. In the first, Salomon makes a detour from a hunting expedition to Melkólfr's house to test his cleverness. At the time Melkólfr is identified as having been twelve years old, which has the effect of associating the text with others in which sages such as King Solomon are put in dialogue with youthful interlocutors. There are at least two strong oppositions here: Salomon as king stands at the pinnacle of societal power, whereas Melkólfr as the child of peasants squats at the bottom, and Salomon is older, Melkólfr younger.

Having put out one of his horse's and one of his hawk's eyes, the king asks the peasant boy for a tally of eyes. Melkólfr responds that he counts six—Salomon's two, his horse's one, his hawk's one, and his own two. The scene brings to mind loosely 1 Kings 10:1–13, in which the Queen of Sheba poses "hard questions" while visiting Solomon. Melkólfr declines Salomon's attempt to take him away, but eventually visits the court and makes a good impression there.

In the second episode, Salomon, who is to be absent from home, deputizes Melkólfr to judge in his stead. A case arises involving a rich, cunning, and treacherous man and a poor, kind, and respected one. The fragment breaks off long before the episode has been recounted in its entirety, but the contents suggest that the tale if completed would relate to the "pound of flesh" motif in *The Merchant of Venice*. If so, Melkólfr as judge would serve a function similar to Portia's in Shakespeare.

Too little of *The Saga of Melkólfr and King Salomon* survives for any definitive determination to be reached about its nature and origins. The challenges are heightened by the uncertainties surrounding the gestation and date of the Latin *Dialogue of Solomon and Marcolf*. All components available for consideration are moving targets. That said, the first episode of the Icelandic text resembles—like a reflection in a distorting mirror—the corresponding one in the second part of *S&M* 2.1, which offers twenty chapters of episodic narrative. In this chapter King Solomon while hunting learns that he happens to be in the vicinity of Marcolf

---

[4] Jackson, "*Melkólfs saga ok Salomons Konungs*," 117. Jackson's English, which immediately followed the Old Icelandic in the *editio princeps*, is reproduced in this volume, with slight changes: for the text, see 107–8; for the translation, 108–11. Both Wolf, "Some Comments," 2 and Tucker, "*Melkólfs saga ok Salomons konungs*," 209, echo the speculation about oriental origins.

the fool's home. Accordingly, he makes a side trip to pay a visit. Whereas in the first part of the Latin Marcolf is a married adult, in the second he is a youth living with his parents and sister. Solomon, mounted on horseback, bows his head under the lintel of the front door and asks who is inside, to which Marcolf answers "a man, and half a man, and the head of a horse."

The similarities between the saga and the first tale in the second part of *S&M* are intriguing. Melkólfr and Marcolf are both unmarried youths living at home with their families. Solomon is a king out hunting who visits the home, sets a conversation in motion with a question, receives a riddling reply that refers to the king and his horse, and has the young man later come to the court.[5]

The Latin *Dialogue of Solomon and Marcolf* reached Scandinavia in chapbook form first by way of Denmark, perhaps at the beginning of the fifteenth century.[6] From there the text radiated into Swedish and Icelandic. So much is clear. Utterly mystifying is the place of *The Saga of Melkólfr and King Salomon* in the genealogy of the Solomon and Marcolf complex. It could offer evidence that the narrative, the second part of the *Dialogue of Solomon and Marcolf,* circulated separately and maybe orally before becoming concretized in a text similar to what we know now.[7]

Translation

Saga of Melkólfr and King Salomon

In the time when Solomon son of King David ruled over Jerusalem and had become king, next after David his father, God revealed to him that he would grant him any boon which he should ask him. And he asked God for wisdom and sagacity; and God granted him that he was wiser than all other men in the world have been. To the honor of God he built that temple like which there has not been another in the world in size and beauty. Within, it was all adorned with gold, and of gold were made all things that were for use there.

Solomon had also with him many remarkable men and wise. That man grew up there in Jerusalem who was named Melkolf. He was a farmer's son. His father and mother were not of importance and not rich. They loved their son much. It was said that the man did not grow up who, at the same age, was wiser than this boy; and they feared that, if the King became aware of his wisdom, he would

---

[5] Wolf, "Some Comments," 6, takes a more nuanced view of the relationship between the two texts than does Finnur Jónsson, who dissociates them completely (*Den oldnorske og oldislandske litteraturs historie,* 3:112).

[6] Seelow, *Die isländischen Übersetzungen der deutschen Volksbücher,* 163–74, and Wolf, "Some Comments," 4–5.

[7] This is my restatement of the thrust in Wolf, "Some Comments," 6.

take him away from them. And they loved him so much that they could not do without him. If there was a day when his father and mother had to work away from home, they locked him in a loft that was boarded up all round, with no window and no hole. He was then twelve years old.

One day King Solomon went to the forest with his men to amuse himself by hunting with his hawks. The King was stationed quite alone during the day, and he rode to the house that Melkolf's father had, because he had heard about the wisdom of this boy, and he wants to try him. And when the king came to the house with the loft up over it and the boy inside, he stabs out one eye of the horse that he rode and also one out of the hawk, and rides in and under the house, and asks whether there was anybody there.

"Yes, there is somebody here," said Melkolf.

The King asks how many eyes there are here.

"Six," says the boy.

"Why six?" says the King.

The boy says, "You have two eyes, your horse has one eye, and your hawk has one eye, and I have two eyes."

"You are a keen boy," says the King, "and I want you to go home with me."

The boy says, "I am grateful for this offer, although I cannot at the present go with you."

"What is the reason for that?" says the King.

"Because my father and my mother love me so much that they will go out of their wits if I have disappeared, and they will suppose that I have been killed upon seeing blood here. But we will come to you all together a little later."

And they came to the King and were well received. And Melkolf was with the King and thought much of and was the greatest sage.

One time when the King went away from home, he set Melkolf to steer the men and to give judgment in all suits. And it is said that two of the men bore grudges against each other. One of them was rich and cunnning and false, and the other was frank and more kindly and blessed with friends, and had the greater honor from the King. But the other one envies that and wished to destroy him.

One evening they sat drinking, and the less wise one drank deep and got very tight and little knew what he said. Then said the wiser one, "I wish that all were well between us, and I repent that I have not been friendly with you."

"Yes; I wish all were well," said the less wise one.

" — And let this be for a token: if you will sell me some butcher's meat, I will buy it from you and pay you for it later."

"Surely, I will do that," said the rich one, "but how much meat do you want?"

"Just a little," said the poorer one. "I will take a side from you, and you shall have a side of me later."

And now agrees the other one to this, and he delivers to him the butcher's meat. A little later, he demands his debt, and the debtor said he would get him a side of meat.

"I will certainly," said the creditor, "have a side of you as was fixed between us."

Then finds the other [...]

9

A Merry Conversation
between King Salomon and Marcolfus

(Modern Danish)
Introduction and Translation
by Stephen Mitchell and Pernille Hermann

Introduction

BY FAR THE EARLIEST NORDIC EVIDENCE of Solomon and Marcolf is
preserved in the Old Icelandic *Saga of Melkólfr and King Salomon* (*Melkólfs saga
ok Salomons konungs*), an anonymous prose fragment from the first half of the
fourteenth century (see chapter 8). The popularity of the Solomon and Marcolf
tradition in late medieval and early modern literature in Iceland is also attested
in some twenty manuscripts that include two cycles of the epic stanzas known as
rímur.[1] The broad currency of Solomon and Marcolf in late medieval Scandinavia
can be inferred from the wall paintings of Marcolf and his wife in Husby-Sjutolft
Church (ca. 1500)), 25 miles from Uppsala.[2] These works of art were produced by
Albertus Pictor or "Albert the Painter," the most famous painter in late medieval
Sweden.

An extensive investigation into the Swedish Marcolf tradition and its
analogues has located the natural home for the original Latin dialogue's
moralizing and pedagogical tendencies in "the learned culture of the cloister."

---

[1] On the Icelandic manuscripts, including the *rímur*, see Seelow, *Die isländischen Übersetzungen*,
163–74, who believes most of them are ultimately based on a Latin text. For the opposing argument, see Finnur Jónsson, *Den oldnorske og oldislandske Litteraturs Historie*, 1:112, who, titles aside,
dismisses the medieval Icelandic materials as unrelated to the Solomon and Marcolf tradition.
On the possibility of a link between the Icelandic text and the Latin *Dialogue of Salomon and
Marcolf*, see Wolf, "Comments on *Melkólfs saga ok Salómons konungs*," and Wolf, "*Melkólfs saga ok
Salómons konungs*."

[2] On these paintings, see Ridder, *Der schwedische Markolf*, 169–88.

The story, the argument goes, was not simple entertainment but instead a rhetorical handbook. As time passed, the Latin entered court culture. In the process it acquired parallels to the literary genre known as mirrors of princes.[3] Paradoxically, this sort of grotesque proto-chapbook has been interpreted as appealing to very different audiences by challenging the authority of the established elite.[4] Citing Martin Luther's engagement with the Marcolfus tradition,[5] others have suggested that beyond having entertainment value, the text might have played a role in the religious debates of the sixteenth century.[6]

The Danish text, entitled *A Merry Conversation between King Salomon and Marcolfus* (*En Lystig Samtale imellem Kong Salomon og Marcolfus*), does not follow slavishly its model, which came from among the German prose translations produced in the second half of the fifteenth century. The one first printed in 1487 was reprinted until the end of the sixteenth century (see introduction to chapter 7 above). In contrast to the German forms, the Danish shows greater variation in its replies, plays more with the grotesque style (leading to an especially striking description of Marcolfus and his wife), and contains more invective.[7] Marcolfus's responses in the Danish tradition are not drawn from biblical or classical sources but more likely reflect medieval proverbial utterances.[8] Particularly relevant in this context is Peder Låle's famous fourteenth-century collection of over one thousand Latin and Danish proverbs, *Parabolae*, later published in Copenhagen in 1506.[9] A connection has occasionally been asserted between the Marcolf tradition and the widespread Nordic ballad variously known as *King David and Sun-Fair* (*Kong David og Solfager*), *Sun-Fair and the Snake-King* (*Solfager og ormekongen*), and so on, in evidence already in the seventeenth century.[10]

---

3 Ridder, *Der schwedische Markolf*, 215–24.
4 Gradenwitz, "Marcolfus og Uglspil."
5 See appendix 1, items G27, G32–G34, G40–G42, G44–G45, G48–G51, G53–G55, and G57–G61.
6 Jacobson, *Marcolfus*, LXXIX–LXXXI.
7 Jacobsen, *Marcolfus*, LXXXIV.
8 Horstbøll, *Menigmands medie*, 242–43.
9 The collection was published in a modern edition, together with Old Swedish analogues, in Kock and Petersens, *Östnordiska och latinska medeltidsordspråk*.
10 Jonsson, Solheim, and Danielson, *Medieval Scandinavian Ballad*, no. D 392. Schück argues that the two traditions spring from the same source, but hastens to add that they now bear no similarity to one another ("Markolfsagan i Sverige," 111), a view quietly accepted for *King David and Sun-Fair* by Grundtvig et al., *Danmarks gamle Folkeviser*, 8:15. The Swedish multiform of the ballad is *David och Solfager* (Jonsson, Jersild, and Bertil, *Sveriges medeltida ballader*, no. 174). The Norwegian is *Solfager og ormekongen* (Heggstad and Grüner-Nielsen, *Utsyn*, no. 128; Landstad, *Norske folkeviser*, no. 56; the database *Norske ballader* contains six variant versions at https://www.dokpro.uio.no/ballader/lister/alfatitler.html). Bugge argues that this "Sleeping Beauty"-themed ballad came to Scandinavia in oral form from the Byzantine world, first through south Slavic ("Serbian-Bulgarian"), then through Russian ("Kong David og Solfager," 27–31). In this argument he is

The first printed version of the Marcolfus story in Scandinavia was the 1486 Latin version from Schleswig (Slesvig), attached until the late nineteenth century to the Danish crown. Printed Danish editions of the Marcolf story are recorded in 1540, 1554, and 1599.[11] The Danish folk-books, including "Marcolfus," were famous enough to have been mentioned by the so-called father of Swedish poetry, Georg Stiernhielm (1598–1672), in his *Hercules* (1658).[12] Swedish editions are known from as early as 1630;[13] the earliest extant Danish edition of Solomon and Marcolf is from 1699, a text very close to the present one from 1805. The printing of these folk-books continued well into the nineteenth century. Through "domestication and civilizing," these bawdy stories were turned into acceptable reading for polite bourgeois society.[14]

A note on the translation: chapter headings and divisions in the translation follow those in the original "folk-book." For ease of reading, dialogue, which runs continuously in the original, is here presented with breaks to indicate changes in speaker between Salomon and Marcolfus. Another change from the original is that the words *ass, piss, shit,* and *turd,* which were bowdlerized to abbreviated forms in the Danish, have been expanded to their foul fullness here. Marcolf would be happy.

The translation holds close to the Danish, but occasionally rewording has been required to make the English understandable to twenty-first-century readers. For example, the word "unnecessariness" has been replaced by "luxury." The term monk-socks denotes a sort of slipper-sock.

---

followed by W. P. Ker, "On the Danish Ballads," 390, and Liestøl and Moe, *Norske folkevisor,* 244–45. This ballad formed part of Edvard Grieg's musical encomium to his country's native traditions as no. 12 in his *25 Norwegian Folk Songs and Dances* (*25 norske folkeviser og danser*), Op. 17 (ca. 1869).

[11] For a discussion of the tradition in Denmark, a list of the known Danish chapbooks (including those no longer extant), and the text of the oldest extant version, see Jacobsen, *Marcolfus,* iii–lxxxvi, 4–94. This information, including a transcription of the 1699 text, is also available at http://www.skramstad.no/folkebok/homemarcolfus.htm.

[12] Nordström, *Samlade,* 13 (line 135).

[13] For a transcription of the Swedish original, as well as a German translation, see Ridder, *Der schwedische Markolf,* 61–76, 235–50. A dozen Swedish printings from 1646 to 1846 are listed in Bäckström, *Öfversigt af svensk folkläsning,* 63–65.

[14] The process of *Domestikation und Zivilisierung* is carefully examined, with a focus on the Nordic *King Salomon and Marcolfus* tradition, in Glauser, "Eulenspiegels Sünden, Markolfs anderes Gesicht."

Figure 16. Painting of Marcolf by Albertus Pictor (ca. 1440–1509) on the north side of Husby-Sjutolft Church, Sweden, with the Latin text, "I am Marcolf" (*marculfus ego sum*). On the opposite side of the nave is the painting of Marcolf's wife, Politana. Photograph by Stephen Mitchell.

Figure 17. Painting of Marcolf's wife, Politana, by Albertus Pictor (c. 1440–1509) on the south side of Husby-Sjutolft Church, Sweden, on the wall opposite the image of her husband, Marcolf. Photograph by Stephen Mitchell.

Figure 18. Title page of *En lystig samtale imellem Kong Salomon og Marcolfus: Meget fornøjelig at læse til Tidsfordriv i de lange Winter aftener.Trykt 1805.*

Translation

A
Merry Conversation
between
King Salomon and Marcolfus,
Very Pleasurable to Read
as
Amusement during the Long Winter Evenings

Prologue

Once when King Salomon, who was very wise, stood in his power and glory in the hall of his father, King David, and looked about, he saw someone standing before him who was named Marcolfus, and he was very deformed, yet he was artful and cunning in speech; he also had a wife with him who was very ugly and clumsy; both of them came from the East. King Salomon ordered them to come before him, and it happened right away, and Marcolfus and his wife both stood before the king, and they did not greet him, but they looked at each other; and as they stood and looked at each other, their form and figure were described as follows: Marcolfus was short and fat, he had a big head and a broad forehead or face, filled with red wrinkles; his ears were hairy and hung down by his cheeks; he had large, broad eyes and they were sly; under his lips was a sort of horse muzzle; he had a hideous and smelly beard, like a billy goat; he had wide and chubby hands, stubby and plump fingers, pudgy and chubby feet, a long, pointed and crooked nose with a bump, and big, thick lips; he had a long face, like a donkey; his hair stood on head like a hedgehog brush, and was black, white, red and gray; he had sagging cheekbones and a big, forked chin; he was completely without a neck, and with a big hump on his back; his tunic was rather short, and came down no further than to his buttocks; his hose were large, bunched up and much botched; he had large peasant-like shoes in which there were two gray monk-socks, and an ancient sword on his belt with a split scabbard: his belt buckle was a woman's broach, the hasp of which was like a short bell clapper; he had a haircloth cape, set with deer antlers.

His wife was very young, and had large breasts, each like a flask with four flagons of beer in it, and each nipple like a bucket; her hair was like a thorn bush, she had eyebrows like bristles on a hog back, and a beard like a billy goat's; her ears were long like donkey ears; she was also cross-eyed; her complexion was full of wrinkles; she had a cross of lead that was as broad as a bolster and hung down on her bosom; her fingers were short and pudgy, and adorned with many iron rings; she had nostrils the size of a big man's knotted fist and thick legs each like a beer firkin, and they were shaggy as a bear's paw; her clothes were quite ragged, so that they hung in tatters.

Here you have something of Marcolfus's and his wife's form and figure, and they resembled each other. And when the true story comes from Jerusalem, then you shall get to hear more of their subtlety.

King Salomon's Ancestry and Marcolfus's and His Wife's and Family's Ancestry

When King Salomon saw them standing before him, and gazing at each other, then he spoke to them, and said, "What sort of people are you, and who were your forefathers?"

Marcolfus answered, "Name first your parents and from whom you are descended, then I will tell you of our family."

Salomon said, "I am descended from twelve patriarchs; Juda begat Phares, Phares begat Esron, Esron begat Aram, Aram begat Aminadab, Aminadab begat Salma, Salma begat Boas, Boas begat Obed, Obed begat Isai, Isai begat King David, David begat Salomon, and I am Salomon."

Then Marcolfus answered the king, and said, "I am one of the twelve families. Rusticorum begat Rusticum, Rusticum begat Rustibaldum, Rustibaldum begat Rustihardum, Rustihardum begat Rusticellum, Rusticellum begat Tariam, Tariam begat Tarcol, Tarcol begat Forsum, Forsum begat Marcol, Marcol begat Marcolfus, and I am Marcolfus. And my wife is of the twelve families Lupitanarum, Lupitana begat Lupitan, Lupitan begat Boledrok, Boledrok begat Plendrut, Plendrut begat Lordon, Lordon begat Luriellan, Luriellan begat Polinam, Polinam begat Polimara, who stands here and is my wife."

Many Remarkable Questions between King Salomon and Marcolfus

Salomon said, "I hear that you are cunning and loquacious, even if you are chubby and cruel. I have some questions for you; if you can answer them, then you will become a renowned man throughout all my kingdom."

Marcolfus answered, "The doctor promised health and soundness for the sake of the kingdom, even if he had little power."

To that Salomon said, "I have wisely and well judged between two women who had killed a child."

Marcolfus said, "It is blissful where there are eagles, and where women are, there is chatter and gossip."

Salomon said, "God has given me manifold wisdom in speech, such that no one is my equal throughout the world."

Marcolfus: "He shall praise himself who has evil neighbors."

Salomon: "He who is vanquished and a tyrant, he is always saved, yet no one pursues him."

Marcolfus: "When the goat runs, her tail hinders her."

Salomon: "A good and delightful woman is always a great adornment to her husband."

Marcolfus: "A bucket with sweet milk must be well hidden from the cats."

Salomon: "A wise woman improves her house, but a bad woman destroys and perverts the building."

Marcolfus: "A clay pot which is well fired lasts long."

Salomon: "A pious and righteous woman should be praised and honored."

Marcolfus: "A cat with a fine pelt should be flayed."

Salomon: "A modest woman should be loved."

Marcolfus: "The poor man's life should be fed with white food."

Salomon: "Where does one find a strong and steady woman?"

Marcolfus: "Where does one find faithful cats near sweet milk?"

Salomon: "Nowhere."

Marcolfus: "One likewise seldom finds a faithful woman."

Salomon: "A delightful and modest woman is to be desired above all desirable things.

Marcolfus: "A large, fat woman is a good housewife."

Salomon: "Protect yourself from a outspoken woman."

Marcolfus: "Protect your nose from a filthy ass."

Salomon: "A white headscarf looks fine on an honest woman's head."

Marcolfus: "It is written that sleeves are not like a leather tunic, and often under a white headscarf there will be much rash."

Salomon: "He who sows injustice reaps evil."

Marcolfus: "Whoever sows chaff reaps misery."

Salomon: "Good people always need wisdom."

Marcolfus: "Where a donkey eats, there it is fed, and for every plant it spares, it then eats sixty; where it shits is dunged, where it pisses is watered, and where it tramples about, clods are broken asunder."

Salomon: "He who stands takes care that he does not fall."

Marcolfus: "He who crashes against a stone willingly goes around it."

Salomon: "Let someone else, and not yourself, make promises to you."

Marcolfus: "If I blame myself, then no man pleases me."

Salomon: "In a house are both evil and good."

Marcolfus: "A privy is always filled with droppings and ass wipers."

Salomon: "Secret harm is much better than blatant disgrace."

Marcolfus: "He who desires to drink waste must kiss a dog's ass."

Salomon: "The one who gives in good faith is dear to God."

Marcolfus: "The one who licks his knife gives his servant little."

Salomon: "Twelve earldoms make a duchy."

Marcolfus: "Twelve tailors make a shit."

Salomon: "Twelve duchies make a kingdom."

Marcolfus: "Twelve shits make a turd."

Salomon: "Twelve kingdoms make an empire."

Marcolfus: "Twelve turds make a full barrow."

Salomon: "You should nurture a child from childhood, and afterwards you must hold him to good wisdom."

Marcolfus: "He who feeds his cow well will get good milk."

Salomon: "The servant one indulges too much, he will oppose his master often."

Marcolfus: "A mendacious servant's honor always smells."

Salomon: "The four elements hold the world by force."

Marcolfus: "Four posts support a privy."

Salomon: "A dark color looks fine on a white shield."

Marcolfus: "A black ass looks fine on a white lap."

Salomon: "One should honor the master who nurtures his disciples."

Marcolfus: "Whoever butters the judge's cheekbone, he feeds his gaunt horses."

Salomon: "A judge ought to judge justly and truthfully."

Marcolfus: "A tithing bishop is good for a porter."

Salomon: "Against a powerful man and a rushing stream you should not struggle."

Marcolfus: "He who flays a buzzard gets a thin roast."

Salomon: "Abandon your ridicule, so our quarrel will end."

Marcolfus: "Quit shitting, so your crap will end and cease to smell."

Salomon: "Have no intercourse with the wanton."

Marcolfus: "He who hides under the mash, swine eat him."

Salomon: "Let us regret from the heart what we have ill done."

Marcolfus: "When you stroke your ass, then you certainly have something to take care of."

Salomon: "Many do evil for good."

Marcolfus: "He who gives his dog bread, no one ought reward him for it."

Salomon: "He is not a friend, who cannot maintain a friendship."

Marcolfus: "A calf turd doesn't steam for long."

Salomon: "He who wants to escape will find a way."

Marcolfus: "The woman who will not allow herself to be used, says of herself that she has a mangy ass."

Salomon: "A king's word ought not be disdained."

Marcolfus: "One never plows well with a wolf."

Salomon: "Winter radish is good for a banquet."

Marcolfus: "He who eats winter radish can cough with both mouth and ass."

Salomon: "He who shuts his ears to the poor, that one God will not hear."

Marcolfus: "He weeps in vain who weeps before a judge."

Salomon: "My stomach gives me pain."

Marcolfus: "So go quickly to the latrine."

Salomon: "You cannot profitably hide death and destitution in hiddenness."

Marcolfus: "He who keeps his turd does not grow it longer and larger."

Salomon: "He who makes a scoundrel of himself is content with no one."

Marcolfus: "He who can tolerate garbage may become a tramp."

Salomon: "When you sit at a rich man's table, then scrutinize with care what is placed before you."

Marcolfus: "It all concerns the stomach."

Salomon: "A man in difficulties seeks a good friend and an artful doctor."

Marcolfus: "Support harms no one; he who is dear to a storeroom's steward always drinks."

Salomon: "A man should eject the depraved and wanton from his company."

Marcolfus: "An angry woman and broken pot are dangerous in a house."

Salomon: "He who denies little seldom gets rich."

Marcolfus: "An old dog goes pitifully to its lair."

Salomon: "You shall punish the taunter, so that you are not taunted by him."

Marcolfus: "The more one disturbs a turd, the more it smells."

Salomon: "You shall not single out anyone whom you wish to do good."

Marcolfus: "One greases a fat sow's rump in vain."

Salomon: "One shall love all for God's sake."

Marcolfus: "If you love the one who loves you, then you lose your work."

Salomon: "You shall not mention to a friend tomorrow that you have given him something today."

Marcolfus: "I want to give you instead that which I cannot now give."

Salomon: "You shall not denigrate your wife's bed."

Marcolfus: "When your wife asks something of you, then you shall not deny it to her."

Salomon: "A drunk does not respect his words."

Marcolfus: "An empty ass has a master over it."

Salomon: "There are many who desire riches and yet live in destitution."

Marcolfus: "Eat what you have, and see then what is left over."

Salomon: "A fool speaks fool's words."

Marcolfus: "What did the stones hear, when no one spoke?"

Salomon: "When we are satisfied, then we ought to thank God for his goodness."

Marcolfus: "The full and the hungry do not sing alike."

Salomon: "Whatever we eat or drink, we are all deadly."

Marcolfus: "The hungry die like the full."

Salomon: "When one plays on the harp, then he cannot debate."

Marcolfus: "When the dog howls, he cannot bark."

Salomon: "You shall not have dealings with the quarrelsome, so that you shall not be in danger with them."

Marcolfus: "A dead bee makes no honey."

Salomon: "Be careful that no one does you harm."

Marcolfus: "One should not have faith in running water and a servant."

Salomon: "A person cannot know everything."

Marcolfus: "It is written that he who does not have a horse must walk."

Salomon: "That person is said to be cursed who cannot become wise in his old age."

Marcolfus: "It is difficult to accustom old dogs to being chained."

Salomon: "Woe to the person who has a double heart, and to those who go on two paths."

Marcolfus: "The one who walks on two paths shall split either his rump or his trousers."

Salomon: "A person's mouth speaks from the heart."

Marcolfus: "From the stomach's fullness, a person's ass speaks gladly."

Salomon: "Luxury makes a person sin."

Marcolfus: "A wolf, when he is placed in a sheep shed, will either bite or do something else."

Salomon: "A modest honor is enough for me, even if God had subjected the whole world to me."

Marcolfus: "The dog does not get something as often as he raises his tail."

Salomon: "All paths will often lead to the main road."

Marcolfus: "All veins run to a fat intestine."

Salomon: "A good man will readily have a good woman."

Marcolfus: "From a fat feast a large turd comes easily."

Salomon: "A lovely woman is loved by her husband."

Marcolfus: "A good jug of wine fits well by whoever next to me is thirsty."

[Salomon: ...]

Marcolfus: "A big pile of thorns passes for my fence."

Salomon: "The more you are elevated, the more you must be humbled to everyone."

Marcolfus: "He rides well, who rides with his equal."

Salomon: "I am tired of your weavings."
Marcolfus: "I will therefore not abandon my chatter."
Salomon: "I care for it not at all."
Marcolfus: "Then give me what you have promised me."

The King's Treasurers Spoke to Marcolfus, and Marcolfus Answered Them

The king's treasurers, Bonaya, Sabus, and Atanius, said to Marcolfus, "Do you mean, you misshapen wretch, that you should be third in the kingdom? Before that your nasty eyes shall be ripped out of your misshapen head. You would be better off held among our master's bears, than held in honor and glory."

Marcolfus answered, "What's next to the butt other than the asshole? Why has the king let this slip out?"

Marcolfus with the King and His Twelve Chosen Good Men

At that the king's twelve chosen good men said, "He who mocks our good king, beat him so much that the stick is worn out and let him flee."

To that King Salomon answered and said, "That shall in no way happen, but rather he shall have food and drink, and then he shall go in peace."

Then Marcolfus answered, "I am pleased to see that it comes to pass as you have said, but I say this for a truth: that where there is no king, there is neither law nor justice."

King Salomon Rode Out on a Hunt, and Found Marcolfus's House, and They Spoke Together

Some time later, King Salomon rode out with his retinue on a hunt, and those who rode with him saw Marcolfus's house. Then the king turned his horse around and rode to the door, and looked into the house, and said, "Who is inside?"

Marcolfus, who sat by the fire and cooked a pot of beans, answered and said, "In here are one and a half men, and a horse head, and as fast as they go up, they go down."

Salomon said, "I want to know what you are saying."

Marcolfus answered, "I am the entire person who sits inside, and you are the half who sits on a horse, half inside and half out, and the horse head belongs to the one you are sitting on."

Salomon asked, "Who runs up and down?"

Marcolfus: "Those are the beans seething on the fire."

Salomon: "Where are your father, mother, sister, and brother?"

Marcolfus: "My father is in the field and makes two harms of one, my mother is with the woman next door, and doing for her what she never wants to do for my mother, my brother is sitting outside the house and slays everyone he sees and overcomes, and my sister sits in her room and weeps about that which she laughed about last year."

Salomon said, "What does what you have said mean?"

Marcolfus answered, "My father is in his field and is blocking a gate with thorns, so that when people approach it, they make two paths of one, and thus he has made two harms of one."

Salomon: "Where is your mother?"

Marcolfus answered, "My mother is with the woman next door, and if she closes her eyes, she will die. And she does to her what she never does to my mother."

Then King Salomon laughed, and said, "Where is your brother?"

Marcolfus answered, "My brother sits outside the house and lifts his clothes, and everything he finds he kills."

Salomon asked, "Why does your sister weep because she laughed last year?"

Marcolfus answered, "My sister loved a young man last year, who hugged and kissed and patted her so often that she grew ill and gave birth to his child, and thus she weeps because she laughed last year."

Salomon asked, "From whom have you acquired such depravity?"

Marcolfus said, "It happened once, at the time of your birth in King David's time, that his doctor was to make medicine from a griffin, and your mother, Bathsheba, took the griffin's heart and laid it on a bread crust, and she grilled the same heart and gave it to you to eat, but she cast the same crust on which the heart had laid to me, and I ate it, for I was in my father's kitchen, and as you got from the griffin's heart which you ate the great wisdom you have, so I likewise got from the crust I ate my bit of depravity."

Salomon said, "So help me God, my wisdom is from no one but God, the Almighty."

Marcolfus: "He is held to be wisest who holds himself for a fool."

Salomon: "Have you not heard of what great wisdom and riches God has given me?"

Marcolfus: "I heard, saw, and know that where and when God wants it, it rains."

Salomon laughed and said, "My people are outside waiting for me. Therefore I cannot stay any longer with you, but tell your mother that she should give me a pail of milk from the best cow she has, and covered by the same cow."

Marcolfus said, "Lord, I will do that." And the king rode home to Jerusalem. Thereafter Marcolfus's mother came home, and Marcolfus relayed to her the king's order. She immediately took an egg cake which was topped with milk, and laid it over the same pail of milk, and gave it to Marcolfus, that he should present it to King Salomon.

Marcolfus Bore the Pail of Milk to King Salomon

As Marcolfus walked along the road with the pail—and he was very hungry—he became aware of a dry cow turd lying on the road, and he took the egg cake, which lay on the milk, and ate it, and laid in its place the cow turd, which he took to the king. When he became aware of the cow turd, King Salomon said to Marcolfus, "Why is the milk pail thus covered?

Marcolfus answered, "Have you not commanded that it should be covered with a piece of the same cow?"

Salomon said, "I did not command it thus."

Marcolfus answered, "Thus I understood your words."

Salomon said, "What I meant was that there should be an egg cake baked with milk."

Marcolfus: "That was also done, but my hunger led to a swap."

Salomon asked, "How did that occur?"

Marcolfus: "I was hungry, and knew that you had not the great need for the cake that I, who was hungry, had. Therefore I laid the cow turd over the milk, so that your orders should be fulfilled."

Salomon said, "Let us forget your chatter; if you cannot stay up with me tonight, but instead sleep, so that I must call you, then it will cost you your neck."

Marcolfus: "I'll cease my talking now."

King Salomon and Marcolfus Stayed Up Together

When night fell, King Salomon and Marcolfus sat and stayed up together. When Marcolfus began to snore, and acted as though he slept, Salomon said, "Are you sleeping?"

Marcolfus said, "No, I am not sleeping, but I am thinking."

Salomon said, "What are you thinking?"

Marcolfus said, "I am thinking that a hare has as many body parts on its scut as it does on its back."

Salomon said, "You'll have to demonstrate that or it will cost you your neck." A little later King Salomon fell quiet. When Marcolfus began to bray again, Salomon said, "You're sleeping."

Marcolfus: "I am not sleeping, rather I am thinking."

Salomon: "What are you thinking?"

Marcolfus: "I am thinking that a magpie has as many white feathers as black."

Salomon said, "You'll need to demonstrate that or it will cost you your neck." A little after that, Marcolfus began to bray again. Then King Salomon said, "Now I can tell that you are sleeping, Marcolfus. What are you pondering?"

Marcolfus: "I am pondering that nothing is whiter than a clear day."

Salomon: "Isn't milk whiter than the day?"

Marcolfus: "That we'll have to find out."

Thereafter King Salomon sat and grew quiet, when Marcolfus began to bray and blow. Salomon said, "Now you're sleeping."

Marcolfus: "Not at all; rather, I am thinking."

Salomon said, "What are you thinking about?"

Marcolfus said, "One should not say to a woman anything one doesn't want to hear again."

Salomon said, "You'll need to demonstrate that, or else you'll have both sorrow and anguish." King Salomon fell silent again, and Marcolfus acted as though he slept. The king said, "You're sleeping."

Marcolfus said, "No, I'm not sleeping, rather, I am thinking about marvelous things!"

Salomon: "Whatever it is, tell me right away."

Marcolfus said, "Nature is much more powerful and stronger than rearing and upbringing."

Salomon: "You'll also need to demonstrate that, or tomorrow you'll lose your head."

Thereafter King Salomon became sleepy, and went to bed. Then Marcolfus hurried home to his sister, Fudasa, who was sickly, and Marcolfus admitted to her that he was sorrowful, and said, "Dear sister, the king has become quite angry, and wants to drive me out. If you won't betray me, then I will tell you what I am going to do to him. I will take a knife under my gown, and secretly stab him to death with it, but I ask that you not betray me, dear sister, or tell my brother Bufrido or any others, as that would cost me my life."

To which his sister answered, "Dear brother, have no doubts about me in any way, for I would lose my life before I would betray you." Then Marcolfus went secretly to the king's courtyard, and the sun was newly risen, and the courtyard was full of people.

Marcolfus Proved All His Thoughts to King Salomon

King Salomon got up from his bed, and sat in his royal seat, and had brought to him a hare, and Marcolfus proved his first thoughts to the king, and counted as many joints on the hare's scut as on its back. Next he proved the second thought for the king and said, "Lord, here is a magpie that has as many white feathers as black," and it was proved. Then Marcolfus secretly took a pail of milk, and went into the king's residence and closed all the windows and doors and placed the pail with milk before the door, where the king would enter, and Marcolfus called hastily to the king, and when he went into his residence, he stepped in the pail with milk, such that he had to catch himself with both hands; otherwise, he would have fallen. Then the king grew angry, and said, "Oh you miserable wretch, what have you done?"

Then Marcolfus said, "You must not be angry with me for this act, for you have said that milk is clearer than the day, so why did you not see through the milk as through the day? I have not sinned against you, if you would be just."

Then the king said, "May God forsake you! My clothes are covered with milk, and I have nearly fallen on my face, and you say that you have not sinned against me."

Marcolfus said, "Look more carefully next time, and sit down to pronounce judgment over him who would be unjust toward me."

King Salomon sat down. Marcolfus began his complaint by saying, "I have a sister named Fudasa. She's a whore, and has a child by which she has shamed all my family, and yet she would share equally with me our inheritance, even though the law forbids it."

Salomon said, "Have your sister come here, that I may hear her words before I judge her."

Marcolfus Accuses His Sister

When Marcolfus's sister, Fudasa, stood before King Salomon, the king laughed at her and said, "Truly this is Marcolfus's sister, for there is no difference between them in any way, other than that she is sickly and he is not." Then the king said to Marcolfus, "What accusation do you have against your sister?"

Marcolfus said, "O merciful King, my sister is obviously a whore, and with her life she has shamed all my twelve finest and coarsest peasant families, or 'Rusticums,' and, against the law and justice, would have an equal inheritance with me. Lord King, forbid her, following the law and justice, to share the inheritance with me!"

When Fudasa heard this trick of her brother's, she grew quite angry, and said, "Oh you poisonous wretch, why should I not inherit just like you? Florentina was just as much my mother as yours."

Marcolfus answered, "In no way should you inherit with me, for you have forfeited it by your nasty, whorish life."

Fudasa answered, "My life has not cost me my inheritance. If I have sinned, then I will improve myself, but if you are not satisfied and will not leave me in peace, then I will tell my lord king that for which he will have you hanged."

Marcolfus said, "You powerless whore, what would you say about me for which I should be hanged? I know of nothing that I have committed against anyone in any way."

Fudasa grew angry, and revealed the secret that Marcolfus had told her from his depravity and said, "Oh, you poisonous wretch, you revealed that you intended to murder our merciful lord and king with your knife, when you could approach him stealthily, and as proof and evidence, that knife which you intend to use in your treachery is without doubt under your tunic." Then Marcolfus was immediately searched, and what Fudasa had said about him was found to be a lie.

When she was discovered in this lie, Marcolfus said, "Merciful lord King, have I not told the truth, that one should not reveal to a woman anything other than what one wants to hear again, when one doesn't want to conform to them?"

Salomon laughed heartily, and said, "Oh, Marcolfus, is it in your cunning nature always to engage in such antics?"

Marcolfus answered, "No, my sister, Fudasa, did it from her perverse nature, because she could not keep quiet about what I told her in secret, even though it was not the truth.

Salomon said, "Why have you said that nature is stronger than upbringing? You must prove that."

Marcolfus answered, "Dear Lord, wait a moment; I will prove it before you go to bed."

Marcolfus Has Three Mice Run from his Sleeve for King Salomon, and Thereby Proved One of His Thoughts

When the day was past and evening had come, and King Salomon wanted to go to his table, Marcolfus secretly put three mice up his sleeve, and seated himself at a distance from the king. Salomon had a cat who had been trained to hold a lighted candle between its front legs every evening for the king when he dined, and Marcolfus had a mouse run out of his sleeve in front of the cat. The cat saw the mouse and would have eagerly dropped the candle if the king had not spoken to it. A short time thereafter, Marcolfus had a second mouse run in front of the cat, and the third one soon thereafter. When the cat saw that so many were running by him, he dropped the candle and ran after the mice, so that he caught one of them. Then Marcolfus said to the king, "See how I have proved that nature is stronger than rearing or habit?"

Then King Salomon grew angry, and said to his men, "Remove this hopeless wretch from my presence, and when he comes here to the courtyard again, set all the dogs on him, so that they can take revenge for me on him."

Marcolfus said, "I know clearly that this is an evil court where no justice exists." When Marcolfus was driven from the king's court, he thought, "What counsel can I now find, so that I can come into the king's court without the dogs biting me?"

Marcolfus Snuck into the King's Court with a Hare

A day or two later, Marcolfus bought a live hare. He bore it under his tunic, and went into the king's court, where one of the men became aware of him, and immediately sent the dogs after him, and when they came running against him, Marcolfus released the hare towards the dogs, and called just as quickly as the men were used to doing on the hunt, and the dogs ran after the hare, and Marcolfus went in to King Salomon. When the king caught sight of Marcolfus, he said to him, "After whom did they send the dogs?"

Marcolfus answered, "The one that ran before them."

Salomon asked, "What was it that ran before them?"

Marcolfus answered, "That which they chased after."

The king said to Marcolfus, "Be careful not to spit in here, but only where there is bare earth." And that he did.

Marcolfus Spat on the Head of a Bald Man

Shortly thereafter Marcolfus was seized by a strong cough, and he did not know where he dared spit; and when he had a mouth full of spittle, he looked about himself in every direction to see if he could find a place where the earth was bare. At that point he became aware of a bald person standing not too close to the king. As he stood among the others, he spat on the man's bald head, on account of which the man became rather shamefaced and red. He held his tongue, wiped the globule from his pate, and fell on his knee before the king, complaining strenuously about Marcolfus. The king said to him, "Why have you spat on this man's head?"

Marcolfus answered, "I haven't spat on his forehead; rather, I fertilized him, for where there is acid soil, one usually fertilizes it so that it can better bear fruit and yield more produce."

Salomon said, "What does this have to do with this bald man?" Marcolfus said, "Did you not forbid me from spitting on any place in here, and only on bare earth? Now I saw that his head was bald and without hair, therefore I understood that to be bare earth, and that if it were well fertilized every day, soon hair would grow there again."

Salomon said, "May all the Franciscans in hell spit on you! To be bald is no shame, rather it is blissful and honorable."

Marcolfus said, "A bald pate is a marvel to flies, and they eagerly gather there."

Salomon said, "I do not see that flies gather more on his pate than elsewhere."

Marcolfus answered, "Because it is not constantly greased; if it were always greased as it is by me, or with something fattier, then the flies would be on him."

To which the bald man answered, "How is it allowed that this scoundrel deride us before the king?"

Marcolfus said, "Be at peace; I will be silent."

King Salomon Judged Fairly between Two Women

Thereafter two promiscuous women came before King Salomon with two children; one was alive, and the other dead. Then one woman said, "O just King! Pass judgment regarding this living child; we were together in a house, and each of us successfully had her child, and she laid her child down for the night with her and crushed it to death, and when she perceived that I slept, she stood up, and took my child, who was alive, from the cradle, and laid down the dead child instead which was hers."

But the other woman answered, "It is your vice to lie, for my child lives, and yours is dead."

When King Salomon heard these words and speeches, he said to one of his men, "Take a sword, and separate the living child into two parts, and give each of the women her part."

Then the one who rightly claimed the living child said, "O merciful king, by no means allow the child to be killed; rather, she may keep it if it may live, and I will relinquish it."

Then the other said, "You shall by no means have it, for it will be cut in two parts, so that you won't get any more than I do."

To which the king answered, "Let the woman have the baby who does not want it to be killed, for I see from her countenance that she is the mother of the living child."

Marcolfus stood up and said, "How can you know that she is the mother of the child rather than the other?"

Salomon said, "I can see that from the great desire she had that the child should live."

When Marcolfus heard this from King Salomon, he said, "You do not understand it correctly, for when a woman weeps with one eye, then she smiles with the other, and when she shows sorrow in her face, she has happiness in her heart; what she says with her mouth is from the lung; and when she changes color, then she thinks about and plans falsehood and fraud."

King Salomon said, "So many connivances and amusements as a woman has, so many pieties she has as well."

Marcolfus answered, "No, you should not say piety, but rather testiness and falseness."

King Salomon said, "Truthfully, was that woman a whore who bore such a son?"

Marcolfus said, "Why do you say so, Lord?"

The king said, "For you always speak ill of women. A modest and good woman desires God, and she is honorable and beloved."

Marcolfus answered, "You should say she is weak and loose."

Salomon said, "She is weak, like everyone, but her being susceptible comes from her voluptuousness. She is formed from the rib of man to be a help to man, a lust, and a joy; she is called *mulier* in Latin, which is in our language a soft thing."

Marcolfus said, "She may well be said to be a soft delusion."

Salomon said, "You lie like a poisonous wretch, for you interpret everything about women nastily, and yet we all come from women, and it is certainly a wretch who speaks ill of women, and he ought to be punished."

Marcolfus says, "Lord and King, you hold many women dear, as is obvious. And so you agree so much with them. But you shall accuse them before you go to bed."

Salomon said, "You lie like a scoundrel; I have always loved and will always love good women; go away from me and speak no more ill of women in my sight."

Marcolfus Came to the Woman to Whom Salomon Gave the Living Child

Marcolfus went down from the king's palace, and ran to the woman who was given the living child, and said, "Do you not know what is happening at the king's court?"

She answered, "Nothing other than that I kept my dear son alive again."

Marcolfus said, "The king has commanded that tomorrow you should be brought before the court again, so that your child can be cut in two parts."

When the woman heard that, she said, "Oh, what a tyrannical king he is in all his judgments!"

Marcolfus said to her, "I will tell you a terrible thing, which has never before been heard since the world began, which the king and his council have decided: a man shall have seven wives; and if it should come to pass, then it will go badly for the women, and there will be no peace or concord among them. For the one the man is most fond of will always be beside him, and that one will be well-clothed, but the others will be naked. The dearest one will have gold, silver, and costly gems. And she will have the key to all the riches in the house, and she will be called a lady by the others. And when one shall be loved, what will the other six say? If there are two, what will the other five say? If there are three, what will the other four say? If there are four, what will the other three say? If there are five, what will the other two say? And if there are six, what will the one say to the fact that the others will be embraced, and kissed, and patted, and always with the man? Of this will come great strife, quarrels, and jealousy, and, in few words, an eternal hatred and persecution among them, so that the one will slay the other. And I offer in friendship to you and yours this advice, that you gather all throughout Jerusalem, and deny to the king and his council such tyrannical laws." When Marcolfus had told this woman his trick, he went secretly back to the king's palace, and hid in a corner.

When the woman heard this, she ran up one street and down another in Jerusalem, and with flowing tears shouted the alarm until seven thousand women gathered. Then she wrung her hands and beat her breast, and told the others what Marcolfus had said, and they all began to complain, saying that they would not disperse before they got revenge on the king and his council.

The Seven Thousand Women Came In before King Salomon, and Delivered Their Complaint

Note now how angry and impetuous many women are as soon as they hear a loose word, and until they have their revenge and have vented their anger. Thereafter the seven thousand women attacked the king's palace, and quickly smashed both doors and windows, and derided King Salomon and his council, each more than the next. And they shouted in each other's faces, but one among them spoke for them all, saying to King Salomon, "O merciful king, who are so rich in gold, silver, and costly previous jewels, and, in few words, rich in all things, you do everything according to your will, against which you do not want anyone to speak. You have so many queens, and innumerable concubines, you can harm whom you want, and likewise do good to whom you please. Not everyone can have or give such pleasing gifts."

Salomon said, "God has made me king over the people of Israel, not so that I might work my will, but His."

Then the woman answered, "Do your will with your own, and leave us in peace, we who are noble and free-born of Abraham's family, and have Mosaic law to live by, which you would simply destroy, but you will not be permitted to do so. It would be better for you to strengthen and promote justice which you clearly pervert and eradicate."

When King Salomon heard the woman speak so remarkably, he said, "O perverse and promiscuous woman, what wrong or injustice have I done to you or yours?"

The woman said, "You have done a great injustice, in that you want every man to have seven wives, but that shall in no way come to pass; for no prince, duke, or count, no noble or commoner can with all his riches or power block a woman's desire; what would he do if he had seven? If that were to happen, it would be better for a woman to have seven husbands."

Then King Salomon laughed heartily, and said to his council and good men, "This woman speaks well for herself and the others, but I cannot believe that a person could assemble such a large gathering in so little time as this woman has done."

Then all of Jerusalem's women who were there shouted with loud voice and said, "In truth, you are a blasphemer and an unjust king in all your judgments. We can clearly see that what was said is true, and on top of that, you mock us openly. Lord God, things were bad when King Saul ruled, things were yet worse in your father King David's time, but worst of all are things in your time and rule."

When King Salomon heard that, he grew angry and said, "As there is no more poisonous head than the viper's, so is there no anger greater than a woman's anger, and it is better to be with lions and dragons than with poisonous women, for a woman's evil is superior to all other evils, and a wanton woman is a scandal and a shame. A perverse woman is an incompetent heart, and a sorrowful mien, and the torment of death. An evil woman is the beginning of all promiscuity and whoredom; in addition to all shame and scandal, she is a daily heart's sorrow; and, in few words, she is all sin, the beginning by which we all would be lost."

When that was said, the prophet Nathan stood up, and said to the king, "Why do you humiliate all of Jerusalem's women so much?"

Salomon answered, "Have you not heard what a great scandal they have visited on me without cause or offense?" Nathan said, "He who is at peace with his subjects must often be blind, dumb, and daft at the same time."

Salomon said, "A fool ought occasionally to have answers to his speech."

Now Marcolfus sprang from his corner, and said, "You have spoken my words well."

King Salomon answered, "How so?"

Marcolfus answered, "For yesterday you praised women in the extreme, and today you have much dishonored them, and that was what I wanted, that in my words would be the truth."

Salomon said to Marcolfus, "What is this you say, thief, have you not created this uproar?"

Marcolfus answered, "No, not me, rather your wavering and laxity; and one should not believe everything one hears."

Then King Salomon grew exceedingly angry at Marcolfus and said to him, "Depart from me, you poisonous wretch, and come no more before my face, for I never again want to look you in the eyes."

Then Marcolfus was driven out of the king's palace. And they who stood before the king said, "The king must give the women an answer, so that each can go home."

Then the king turned around, and spoke to the women, and said, "You should know that I am altogether blameless in this case, which you have forced on me; that poisonous wretch, whom you have seen here, has done it. And I say to you, each man should be content with his wife, and keep her in honor and glory, as she deserves, for what I have just said about women, you should understand to be about evil and perverse women, for no one should speak evil about the good ones. Because possessions and riches can be given by parents, but a modest and good woman is given by God alone. As is said, that man is blessed to whom God awards a good and virtuous woman. May God with his right hand protect you all and give you much fruitfulness here on earth, then eternal life for eternity."

To which they all answered, "Amen."

Marcolfus Crept on Hands and Feet, and Had a Sieve in one Hand and a Bear's Paw in the Other

Thereafter Marcolfus grew angry, because he should not see the king's face, and he began to consider what counsel and methods he could discover. And it began that same night to snow, and Marcolfus took a sieve in one hand and a bear's paw in the other. Next, he took off his shoes and turned them around backwards, and crept on his hands and feet until he had left Jerusalem, where he found a baking oven. Marcolfus crept into it and lay down.

The King's Men Find the Remarkable Tracks Marcolfus Had Made

Early in the morning some of the king's servants went out and found the tracks Marcolfus had made in the snow, which they thought very strange, and went back and told the king about these tracks. When the king heard it, he became very happy and said that they had discovered curious animal tracks, and he immediately had his hunters called for with all their dogs, and they followed these same tracks to the oven in which Marcolfus lay. And then the king and his good men began to deliberate about who should examine what was in there, and it was concluded that the king should himself go in and examine things. King Salomon got off his horse, and went to the oven with his good men. When they got there, Marcolfus had bent over and had pulled his pants down to his knees, and had laid his ass in the oven's mouth, so that his hidden thing hung in clear view; when the king saw that, he said, "Who lies here?"

Marcolfus answered, "It is I, Lord."

King Salomon said, "Why do you lie in such a fashion?"

Marcolfus answered, "Have you not forbidden that I ever look you in the face, and you in my eyes? Because you do not want to look me in the eyes, you must therefore look at me in the ass." Then the king was very humiliated, and gave the order that they should hang Marcolfus from a tree. Then Marcolfus said, "Merciful Lord, because you have judged me to be executed, permit me to be hanged from whatever tree pleases me."

Salomon said, "That is happily granted to you."

Marcolfus Sought a Tree in Which He Should be Hanged

Then the king's men bound Marcolfus and led him first through Josapha's dale, and then over the Mount of Olives, until they came to Jericho, and they could not find a tree from which Marcolfus wanted to be hanged. Next they accompanied him throughout Jordan, and the Arab lands, but no tree could be found from which Marcolfus agreed to be hanged. And at last they accompanied him over the Carmel mountains, and in the Compestri desert, to the Red Sea, but there was no tree so lovely that Marcolfus wanted to be hanged from it.

They Led Marcolfus Home Again to King Salomon

They accompanied Marcolfus back home again to King Salomon, and said to him, "We cannot find a tree where Marcolfus wants to be hanged."

Then King Salomon said, "Whether I want to or not, I must leave you in peace. And I will take you and your wife as my servants, and give you food and clothing for as long as you live."

10

Bertoldo

(Modern Italian)

Introduction by Jan M. Ziolkowski
Translation by Palmer Di Giuliot

Introduction

IN THE CLOSING THREE DECADES of the sixteenth century and opening few years of the seventeenth, Giulio Cesare Croce (1550–1609) composed prolifically in both standard Italian based on the Florentine type of Tuscan and the Bolognese variant of the Emilian-Romagnol regional dialect, to say nothing of hybrids of the two. This writer and performer devoured language omnivorously and regurgitated it just as plentifully, spitting out his own recombinations of everything he heard and read without conforming to any constrictive codes or rigid registers.

Of his vast literary output, Croce's comic *Bertoldo and Bertoldino* (*Bertoldo e Bertoldino*) is his best remembered work. It laid the cornerstone for what in 1736 Lelio Dalla Volpe (1685–1749) of Bologna transmuted into a book by "divers hands" entitled *Bertoldo with Bertoldino and Cacasenno, in ottava rima* (*Bertoldo con Bertoldino e Cacasenno in ottava rima*). The translation in this chapter relies upon a twentieth-century prose refashioning of the adaptation into verse by twenty-three poets that Dalla Volpe oversaw. To those who wish to think genealogically, the English offered here qualifies as a grandson of Croce's text and a greatgrandson of the *Dialogue of Solomon and Marcolf*—but let us not get ahead of ourselves. The story must be told slowly, step by step.

The son of one blacksmith and nephew of another who raised him after he was orphaned, Croce supported himself by engaging in the family trade until he turned twenty-five. Meanwhile, he earned extra as a street singer or, to state the case more colorfully, a piazza poet. Later his early sideline of versifying became his main employment, although intermittently he returned to the hammer and anvil to supplement his income.

GIVLIO CESARE CROCI
DETTO DALLA LIRA
BOLOGNESE

Figure 19. Portrait of Croce. *Bertoldo con Bertoldino e Cacasenno,*
fol. a7ʳ.

Born and bred in the Bolognese countryside, he relocated into the city proper—moving, in Italian terms, from *contado* to *comune*. True to the designation of *cantastorie* or "story-singer," Giulio picked up the byname "dalla Lira" for singing to the accompaniment of a traditional fiddle (the "lyre" in his nickname) that he played: people dubbed him "Giulio with the string instrument."[1] Despite improvising as traditional performers have always done, he was as indebted to literary as to oral traditions. Because the uncle who took him in after his father died arranged for him to have a formal education, it would be a mistaken fancy to think of Croce as an illiterate bard out of place in a capital known for its learning: one of Bologna's nicknames is "the learned" (*La Dotta*), in deference to its university. To the contrary, the turn of phrase *poeta campestre* sums up the situation nicely, labeling him a "rustic poet" while applying an Italian adjective that stands a cut above equivalent words for boor, hick, redneck, yokel, or other such disparagements in American English.

Croce lived in an era of extraordinary changes, when performances presented on the piazzas of Bologna made passages through printing presses to please publics of readers who would have been hopelessly out of reach a century earlier—readerships inconceivable for any of the authors who had a hand in the manuscript transmission of either the dialogues or the narratives that eventually fused to become the Latin *Dialogue of Solomon and Marcolf*.[2] The beneficiary of fortunate timing as well as authorial talent, Croce's writing, preserved in more than four hundred different chapbooks, is embedded in Italian culture even today. He can be considered popular in a twofold sense, for being widely read as well as for drawing heavily on materials associated with the common folk.[3] Croce, who came into existence during the revelry and masquerade that precede Lent (or at least so he claimed), understood from personal experience the topsy-turviness of feast and famine alongside the opposition of piazza and palace.[4] Knowing his place even if not liking it, he portrayed a world upside down, but so as to delight the entire hierarchy without favoring and destabilizing either end of it. He was not simply pro-peasant and contra-courtly.

His most famous work was and remains *The Sharpest Strategems of Bertoldo* (*Le sottilissime astutie di Bertoldo*), first printed in Milan in 1606.[5] The sequel he wrote,

---

[1]   On the complexity of his identity as a professional poet, see Tetel, "Giulio Cesare Croce." On the relationship between the music and the storytelling, see Wilson, "*Cantastorie/Canterino/ Cantimbanco* as Musician."

[2]   Bellettini, Campioni, and Zanardi, *Una città in piazza*.

[3]   Franco Croce, "Giulio Cesare Croce."

[4]   On the first topic, see Camporesi, *La maschera di Bertoldo*, and Casali and Capaci, *La Festa del mondo rovesciato*; on the second, Camporesi, *Il Palazzo e il cantimbanco*.

[5]   This first edition that is known to have survived into the early twentieth century to be consulted by a scholar disappeared in 1943, but was rediscovered and published in 1993: Giulio Cesare

generally agreed not to be on a par with its predecessor, is called *The Amusing and Ridiculous Simplemindedness of Bertoldino, Son of the Late and Cunning Bertoldo* (*Le piacevoli e ridicolose semplicità di Bertoldino, figlio del già astuto Bertoldo*). It came out in Bologna in 1608, shortly before the writer's death in the same city in January 1609. In turn, Croce's two texts had their continuation in *Story of Cacasenno, Son of the Simpleminded Bertoldino* (*Novella di Cacasenno, figliuolo del semplice Bertoldino*). The protagonist's name means literally that he defecates sense—simultaneously a shitwit and a nitwit. This third composition was produced by a monk and musician-composer from an Olivetan Benedictine monastery in Bologna, Abbot Adriano Banchieri (who published under the pseudonym Camillo Scaligeri dalla Fratta, 1568–1634). If the continuation of *Bertoldo* in *Bertoldino* fell short of the original, *Cacasenno* was even worse. But apparently strength can be found in numbers. The trilogy as a totality is designated as *Bertoldo, Bertoldino e Cacasenno*. Entitled after its principal characters, the tripartite text deals with a grand-father, son, and grandson of the same lineage. The initial printing as a threesome occurred in 1620.

In 1736 an editor and man of letters in Bologna named Lelio Dalla Volpe had the stroke of genius of converting the poems in the Bolognese dialect into more standard Italian.[6] His title page, leaving authorship indeterminate, announces the contents of the book to be *Bertoldo with Bertoldino and Cacasenno, in ottava rima* (*Bertoldo con Bertoldino e Cacasenno in ottava rima*). He divided the content into twenty cantos of the metrical form given titular status. Ottava rima consists of stanzas of eight lines, each of eleven syllables, with the rhyme scheme abababcc.

Dalla Volpe arranged the work to be one of collaborative fiction by recruiting a total of twenty-three different poets.[7] The poem proper started with a sonnet, by the first on his team, that faced an author portrait depicting Giulio Cesare Croce with violin and bow in hand. Each canto of verse paraphrase began with first an argument and then an allegory. These other components of the project were all composed by two other versifiers, one responsible for all the arguments and the other for all the allegories. The poetry was embellished by twenty etchings made by Lodovico Mattioli on the basis of earlier ones by Giuseppe Maria Crespi (1665–1747).[8] Dalla Volpe's composite product became a bestseller of its day.

Croce, *Le sottilissime astuzie di Bertoldo*. The only other that survives from Croce's lifetime is dated 1609, but Camporesi, 73–77, hypothesizes that the actual first edition, no longer extant, was printed in early 1605 in Bologna.

6   See Rondinini, "Lelio dalla Volpe."

7   For an edition and study of the first, see Bernasconi, "Giampietro Riva e il primo canto del 'Bertoldo' in rima."

8   Varignana, "La fortuna editor. del Bertoldo crespiano."

Figure 20. Bertoldo's family. *Bertoldo con Bertoldino e Cacasenno,* frontispiece.

Ultimately a reworking of the medieval *Dialogue of Solomon and Marcolf,* the section *Bertoldo* by Croce tells the story of the main character, after whom it is entitled.[9] Bertoldo is married to the ingenuous Marcolfa, both of them rooted in a small village. The peasant *paterfamilias,* as cunning as he is ugly, a prankster who plies proverbs and practices practical jokes with abandon, wins an invitation to the court at Verona from King Alboino (often rendered as Alboin in English), here a distant legendary relative of the historical personage who ruled the Lombards from about 560 until 572. While his wife remains at home, Bertoldo worms his way into the affections of the Germanic monarch through his exceptional wit, even as he reaps the queen's hostility through his unchecked candor.

Apart from shifting the denomination of the leading man to the spouse, Croce retains much of the original story along with the essential antiheroic and trickster-like nature of Marcolf in the person of the disrespectful and foul-mouthed Bertoldo, of his interlocutor and antagonist Solomon in the powerful, po-faced, and pompously learned Alboino. Bertoldo is a demon of double entendre who exploits the ambiguity of language in speaking turds to power. To look at the relationship from the opposite direction, the king speaks truth to bowels. At the same time, the sixteenth-century author allowed himself a free hand in cutting, appending, and modifying irreverent witticisms, homespun wisdom, minor motifs, and specific quips. While reducing the misogyny of the Latin text, he introduced an out-and-out villainess in the queen.

As Bertoldo's quick-wittedness and world-savviness elicit recognition from the king, the country cousin clambers up the courtly career ladder to assume a role as a much-esteemed and well-rewarded royal counselor. In making this ascent, he oversteps the mark. In the end Bertoldo meets his doom as a direct result of his social displacement from countryside and rusticity to city and urbanity. He dies when Alboino compels him to forgo the simple fare of turnips and beans to which his natural physical constitution had accustomed him for the overrefined food of the courtiers. Thus whereas the Marcolf of the Latin text escaped execution by betaking himself cleverly to the Orient, Bertoldo is unable to outsmart the lethal outcome of the incongruity that arose from being a contadino at court.

The ambivalence of the ending stamps the whole of the Italian text. The complicated views of society that filter through are not unqualifiedly favorable either to the poor and powerless stratum from which Croce arose or to the rich and powerful one from which he sought patronage. It's complicated. So too was his own life, by many measures successful but still a recurrent struggle to stay

---

[9]   On the sources of *Bertoldo,* see Pagani, "Il *Bertoldo* di Giulio Cesare Croce"; Biagioni, "Marcolf und Bertoldo und ihre Beziehungen"; and Marini, *Bertoldo, Bertoldino, Marcolfo,* 54–87.

a step ahead of hand-to-mouth desperation. A widower with seven children, he married a second wife and had seven more children by her: that double or nothing of offspring made many mouths to feed, even when famine was not a factor.

The adage-intensive *Bertoldo* and its leading man occupy their own distinctive, even if dwindling, niche in Italy, not so well known as the mainstays of the *commedia dell'arte* but all the same still a familiar figure on the broader cultural landscape. A complete enumeration of reworkings across media would require a monograph. Let us pick up the highlights of its trajectory after Dalla Volpe's multimedial tour de force of 1736. In 1749, the playwright Carlo Goldoni (1707–93) shaped a libretto from the interlocking stories. His countryman Vincenzo Legrenzio Ciampi (1719–62), a composer, set the drama to music. The resultant comic opera *Bertoldo, Bertoldino e Cacasenno* probably premiered in Venice in late 1748. Also known under the alternative title *Bertoldo in corte*, it debuted to great acclaim in Paris in 1753. The piece was revised in a French-language parody as *Bertholde à la ville* and reworked by Charles-Simon Favart (1710–92) as a *pasticcio* in 1755 in *Le caprice amoureux, ou Ninette à la cour*.[10]

In the second half of the twentieth century the trilogy of Bertoldo, Bertoldino, and Cacasenno more than held its own. Already a film in 1936, it was put twice more into cinematic guise.[11] Croce's text was reprinted over and over again, often as a paperback.[12] It even became an illustrated children's book.[13] Concurrently, it became a darling of literary and cultural critics during the long spell in which the preoccupations of Marxism held sway. The story of Bertoldo in particular allows insurgents to relish class warfare in which the underdog comes out on top through sheer wit, while conservative members of privileged elites may laugh at the scatology and crudity of the boorish lower orders. In the end, the flexible multivalence of the work makes perfect sense: Croce was a poet and not a politician.

Mikhail Bakhtin makes no mention of Giulio Cesare Croce in *Rabelais and His World*, but he dwells long enough on Marcolf to have intensified interest among

---

[10] Sonneck, "Ciampi's *Bertoldo, Bertoldino e Cacasenno*."

[11] In 1936 by Giorgio Simonelli, in 1954 by Mario Amendola and Ruggero Maccari, and in 1984 by Mario Monicello.

[12] *Bertoldo e Bertoldino*, ed. Luigi Emery (Florence: Le Monnier, 1951); *Bertoldo e Bertoldino*, ed. Gian Antonio Cibotto (Rome: Canesi, 1960); *Bertoldo e Bertoldino*, ed. Giampaolo Dossena (Milan: Feltrinelli, 1965; 2nd ed., 1981); *Bertoldo e Bertoldino (col Cacasenno di Adriano Banchieri)*, ed. Giampolo Dossena (Milan: Rizzoli, 1973; 2nd ed., 1984); *Le sottilissime astuzie di Bertoldo: Le piacevoli e ridicolose semplicità di Bertoldino*, ed. Piero Camporesi, Piccola biblioteca Einaudi 336 (Turin: Einaudi, 1978); *Le astuzie di Bertoldo e le semplicità di Bertoldino*, ed. Piero Camporesi (Milan: Garzanti, 1993).

[13] Giulio Cesare Croce, *Bertoldo e Bertoldino*.

Italians in that character's peninsular cousin. The Italian literary historian Piero Camporesi (1926–97) stands out for his indefatigability in tying Bertoldo to folklore, particularly the carnival spirit that the Russian critic traced from the *Dialogue of Solomon and Marcolf* down all the way to its culmination in the later French literature of Rabelais.[14]

This Translation

Palmer Di Giulio (1898–1959) was Italian by birth, brought as a small child to America, taken back while still a youth to his native land, and returned once again at the age of thirteen to the United States. While subsisting first as a manual laborer but later holding positions in the penal and judicial system, he acquired his high school and college degrees. A long-term employee of the U.S. Postal Service, he eventually passed the bar examination to become an attorney with nationally recognized expertise in immigration and naturalization law. A devotee of Italian culture, he participated actively in the Order of the Sons of Italy in America.

Di Giulio's early jobs as a steelworker and blacksmith, it may readily be imagined, could have made the author of *Bertoldo* especially interesting to him, since Croce too had been a smith. The Italian-American's fascination with his native language and literature would have added attraction to the challenge of giving a mid-century modern American audience access to so complexly folksy and seemingly traditional a literary creation from the sixteenth century.

Only a year before Di Giulio's death his slim book, not even a hundred leaves in length, achieved print through publication by a kind of vanity press.[15] Nothing near a complete translation of either Croce's or Dalla Volpe's texts, his version offers a sampling of six episodes that he reshaped from an account of Bertoldo's escapades at the Veronese court of King Alboino of the Lombards. Di Giulio took as the basis for his translation into prose not any early expression of Croce's work but rather an abridged adaptation into Italian prose made centuries later from Dalla Volpe's twenty cantos. Thus Di Giulio's English stands in a very indirect relationship to any hypothetical original by the celebrated Bolognese author of the late sixteenth and early seventeenth century. Di Giulio does not provide full bibliography on the text on which he depended. Without signaling date, place, editor, or illustrator, he reveals that it was an Italian prose adaptation, printed in large type, illustrated, and published by Casa Editrice Salami. Those details suggest that he may have used Giulio Cesare Croce and

---

[14] For an attempt to move interpretation in a new direction while building on both Bakhtin and Camporesi, see Catalfamo, *Giulio Cesare Croce*.

[15] Di Giulio, *Bertoldo*.

Giuseppe Moroni, *Astuzie sottilissime di Bertoldo* [...]: *con l'aggiunta del suo testamento e altri detti sentenziosi: operetta piena di moralità e di spasso* (Florence: Salami, 1929). Croce's renowned text richly deserves translation in full, and perhaps the selection furnished here will inspire someone with command of Italian and the gift of leisure to put into English the entirety of the earliest version.

In this extremely light recasting of Di Giulio's translation, his chapter divisions have been retained, but the morals of the tales have been transferred from the bottom to the top, to sit immediately below the statements of their themes. This modification brings the format back into alignment with what is found in Dalla Volpe's 1736 edition and its many reprintings. Where Di Giulio italianized classical names and toponyms with consequences that would be unrecognizable to many readers, the corresponding English ones have been substituted. To take just one example, Isicratea has been rendered into Hypsicratea, wife of King Mithridates VI of Pontus.

The Italian followed by Di Giulio and therefore the English produced by him contain occasional ambiguities and obscurities that can be clarified here. More than thirty times he uses the word *villain*, in most instances to mean a peasant. In chapter 1 (to employ the internal designations within his translation), Farfarello is a goblin-like demon in Dante's *Inferno*, Agramante a Saracen king in Boiardo and Ariosto; Chiaramonti is the family of Agramante's opponent, Rinaldo. In chapter 2, the mention of a Longbeard refers to the Lombards. Fagotto is a word for a "fool." In chapter 3, the text refers to the name of a knight as being easily mistakable for "blind," because in Italian *bornio* means "one-eyed." In chapter 4, Morea was how people once designated the Peloponnese peninsula, a Sorian (or Syrian) cat is what English styles a tabby cat, Zucca denotes a pumpkin, Buonasperanza means "good hope." In chapter 5, an arquebus was a portable gun supported on a fork or tripod. In chapter 6, the siege of Oran of 1556 was made unsuccessfully by Ottomans against the Spanish garrison in this Algerian city; the name Cerfoglio is the common noun meaning "chervil," the aromatic herb. Shortly afterward, Farinaccio signifies "wheat middlings." The name Membrot may derive from the word for "member." Pasquino likely pertains to a tradition connected with the statue by this name in Rome: supposedly it was named after a clever local tailor. Fittingly, *fichetto* can denote a young troublemaker.

Figure 21. Bertoldo riding a jenny-ass. *Bertoldo con Bertoldino e Cacasenno,*
illustration facing p. 3.

Translation

Bertoldo

Chapter 1

THEME

While Alboino, King of the Lombards, is seated upon his throne in the royal palace of Verona, Bertoldo unexpectedly appears before him, and stops a few paces away to attentively gaze upon him. The ugly chin of the villain, and his actions, clothes, and manners, at first move the king to laughter; but as the undismayed villain keeps gazing at him, the king becomes angry and orders his immediate departure. Bertoldo is not discouraged; he simply answers that he will go, but return again. In fact, he says that it is his intention to become as annoying as a fly. The king dares him to return, and Bertoldo departs from the royal palace, promising that within a short time he will have news for him. Later on, Bertoldo returns riding a jenny-ass. During the interview with the king, Bertoldo knows how to answer questions so well that the monarch cannot get offended with him.

THE MORAL OF THE TALE

Virtue, even though it abides in a body that is crude and malformed, and in a person who, at first sight, seems uncultured and austere, finally receives its reward. And if at times the great threaten to overshadow it, sure of itself, it fears nothing, for it is always easy for the wise man to find a way to avoid dangers.

He who wishes to banish the shadow of gloom and of worry; he who, annoyed by disappointment in love or wounded by jealousy, seeks to find relief from his troubles, and he who, above all, wants to be entertained and laugh heartily, need do nothing more than read the story of the villain Bertoldo and of his descendants. This story we herewith undertake to tell in its most unusual and intimate particulars.

In this story the reader is in no danger of running into bloody brawls, of finding rose water turn to a nauseous odor. Moreover, the story will not include any of those eccentric oddities intended to accelerate the beat of the heart that so many poets have called to their aid to fill their books. No, our story will not include those things, but it will deal with keen wit, liveliness, and peculiar events (all in good taste) that will improve the blood of those who read them.

We shall begin with Bertoldo. In a few words, Bertoldo can compare with any other hero whose legend has been transmitted to us by historical tradition. We will tell of his astuteness, of his tricks; and then we will proceed to Bertoldino, his son, and will end with his grandson, Cacasenno.

All three of these peasants, for their jests, jokes, and pranks, were held in high esteem by a great king, no other than Alboino, King of the Lombards, whose lordship lasted a long time in our Italy.

Let Virgil keep silent, and let Homer hang up his lyre; the heroes of Greece and Rome are insignificant in comparison with Bertoldo; Aeneas and Ulysses were idlers compared to our rascal; and their descendants, so glorified in Greece and Italy, are really a pusillanimous progeny. Let the cruel and bloody scenes of which the two great poets make us spectators be forgotten; we want to laugh and be entertained.

So let us say no more and come to our story. Let us go to where Alboino, King of the Lombards, is expecting us.

After having suppressed Narses and conquered all of northern Italy, after having besieged and taken Pavia by storm, and after having conquered almost all the cities of Tuscany and Emilia, Alboino proclaimed himself King of Italy. Tired now of war, he consigned to the devil all bellicose ideas and established himself at Verona, intent only upon seeking solace and entertainment.

Let us leave, for the moment, what belongs to history. He who wants factual information can find it in books written five hundred and seventy years ago.

Immediately, then, we come to Verona.

Verona is a city that has few equals. It has great arsenals, triumphal arches, a coliseum, and many magnificent and ancient monuments. A large river passes through it, and on one side of the city, beyond the walls, there is an interminable plain; on the other side, not far from the city, rises a mountain, upon the peak of which one may breathe the gentle, friendly, genial, and vivifying air.

In this rich and beautiful city Alboino had settled, as we have said, and there he had stored the immense amount of booty he had captured during many years of war and plunder, and there he maintained a most splendid imperial court.

Dukes, marquises, clowns, and lords surrounded Alboino's throne in large numbers, particularly when there were no priests from Rome or doctors from Bologna. All these persons passed their days in feasting and merriment, as though they were trying to make up for the time they had spent fighting for their lord.

Now it came to pass that, while a big feast was going on in the royal palace, and Alboino was seated upon his throne there, surrounded by all his barons, those present noticed a strange man pushing through the crowd of courtiers, who were stunned by such audacity. The stranger boldly sat down upon a stool next to the king. He did this without saying a word, just as he had entered the palace, passed the soldiers on guard, entered the door despite the presence of doormen, and crossed the reception hall without anyone blocking his way or opposing his entrance.

After having seated himself upon the stool a short distance from the throne, this queer, strange man gazed curiously upon the king, but he still remained silent.

Let it also be noted that, before he sat down, he had not even removed the soiled old cap that covered his head.

Who was this audacious man that in such a manner dared to face the power and anger of Alboino? Who but our hero, Bertoldo?

Bertoldo was so ugly that be resembled an ogre, a monster. He had red, shortsighted eyes; he walked sideways; he was hunchbacked, deformed, and almost like a dwarf in stature. On his chin were a few bristles of auburn-colored hair. For an overgarment he wore a jacket that was tattered and torn, spotted and soiled, and had long since lost both color and shape. Surely he must have worn that jacket since the day of his marriage. He wore his collar in reverse, like the hermit who had been a gardener in a Bolognese garden plot, and everyone chided and laughed at him.

In one word, Bertoldo was horrible. He was almost fearsome! All his attributes and characteristics were diametrically opposed to those that betoken Narcissuses and Adonises.

Imagine the resentment of the courtiers who watched that figure, that ugly-faced man, seated undismayed at the side of the king!

What business had this baboon among gentle and charming persons? What did he want? What was the significance of his audacity and his impudent behavior?

After the first few moments of wonder and astonishment, the courtiers were about to seize Bertoldo and do with him what is usually done to a madman. But Alboino, who in reality was a good Christian, with a gesture of his hand bade his barons to stop. The king first wanted to know with whom he had to deal. Turning affably toward Bertoldo, he asked: "Good man, who are you?"

The king may have thought that he had before him an individual with a strange brain; possibly through his mind there ran thoughts of the creatures of Aesop or of Farfarello, the fire demon, of whom, notwithstanding his barbarous ignorance, he had heard some mention.

Nevertheless, King Alboino knew that nature quite often delights in hiding great geniuses in ugly and monstrous bodies, where they develop without geometric or architectural order, like a delicious fruit whose outer surface is a repulsive bark. And such, in fact, was Bertoldo. Without any exaggeration he could be compared to Seneca, the great Roman philosopher.

Since Bertoldo did not belong to that flock of merry men who are nurtured in soft feathers, he possessed only such virtues as fit in with natural simplicity and frugal living. He condemned and despised all things that were considered a luxury, and for that reason lived near the peak of a solitary, barren mountain, far away, segregated from all human contacts. His home was a small, solitary cottage upon Mount Bertagnano, some five hundred paces from the hamlet nearby; and the cottage itself, so badly cracked were its walls, looked like an owl's nest. Furthermore, that solitary cottage was surrounded by leafy trees and terrible cliffs, which made access to it very difficult, in fact, almost impossible. It was less like a home than the hut of a religious penitent, but Bertoldo was quite happy in it, because there he found all that was necessary for his frugal existence. And there the shrewd rogue eked out a living for himself and his modest family. On a small garden patch, next to the cottage, he raised beans, beets, and a few common herbs.

He had little thought for the future, convinced, like the good Christian be was, that the eternal Father would never completely forsake His creatures; and when at night he lay next to his wife, Bertoldo slept peacefully and soundly, for his sleep was never disturbed by unpleasant and terrifying dreams.

(Oh, you, who in this corrupt age live in softness and luxury, immersed to your neck in dreadful vice, continually pursuing mean and perverted phantasms, turn back from the ugly path on which you are traveling and follow the example of the good Bertoldo, who certainly can teach you the course to follow to attain peace of mind and perfect virtue.

And in thinking about this, it is a matter of wonder that no printed legend exists of Bertoldo, while so much labor is spent to extol vain and idiotic men!

What we shall say of Bertoldo is but a small part of what he taught but at any rate we hope his life will be a spur, so that every effort can be made to correct the corrupt customs of our own day.)

But let us return to the keen-witted peasant we left seated upon the stool next to King Alboino. There the throng of courtiers continued their sinister mutterings, and the king had to use his full authority to restrain them from violently assaulting Bertoldo, for, as we have said, Alboino seemed to have become strangely interested in Bertoldo.

As soon as order was restored in the large hall, the king began to question Bertoldo. "Now tell me who you are, where you live, and also whence you have come. Who are your parents, your relatives? At least, give me enough information so that I may know what country you are from and what language you speak."

And Bertoldo replied: "If you want to know my name and who my relatives are, I shall be glad to please you. I am a native of Bertagnana, and my name is Bertoldo. My father, now dead, was named Bertolazzo. He was very well known in his native hamlet, and, when he died, he left considerable fame behind him. As to my grandparents, one was named Bertino, another Bertuccio, and a third, Bertolino. Of my other predecessors, to tell you the truth, I have no recollection, for they did nothing worthy of note to be transmitted to posterity."

Asked the king: "But why did you come to Verona? And for what reason have you sneaked into my royal palace? Speak quite frankly, my good man. What do you wish? Remember that you have to do with good people, not with Saracens or Jews. I have already had occasion to do much good, and to uplift from nothing many individuals, among them some who now are in your presence. I have created counts and barons, and I will deny you nothing of what you seek from me, if your requests are honest and discreet."

To the king, Bertoldo replied thus: "I will at once tell you, and with much good reason, the purpose of my visit to Verona, and why I came to the royal palace. Note, therefore, that I came here only because of the compelling desire to see you and to admire your power. Somehow, I believed, like the rude peasant that I am, that your person stood above all other men, exactly as a church steeple towers above the surrounding dwellings, or as pine trees rise above willows.

"But even though you differ in fortune and circumstances, I now see that you are no different from other men. This fact confirms my opinion that almighty God made us all equal, all alike, of flesh and bone. Apparently we all eat, drink, sleep, and wear clothes, even though these, according to taste, can be gray, green, or red. We all live under the same sun, which illuminates and warms all of us without distinguishing one from the other. We all experience the same ills and are subject to the same miseries. Similarly the years weigh heavy upon the shoulders of us all. Death has respect for no one; it inexorably swings its terrible scythe, and woe to those whom it touches, for all collapse like a bundle of hay. If things remain as they are, why, I ask, do we worry about gaining position or rank in this world? Why crave wealth, which today we accumulate, tomorrow we lose?

"What I pursue is happiness. Aside from happiness, I cherish no other objective. But despite all of my exertions and my persistence, I am unable to find the road that leads me to it. And neither can you, despite the greatness of your state, of which you are so proud; nor despite the power of empire that you now hold can you give me that happiness of which you are deprived. For this very reason I ask nothing from you."

The king, surprised and at the same time irked, exclaimed: "How is that? Am I not happy? Is it not apparent to you that I have reached the greatest happiness, sitting high upon this throne, so rich with gold and gems? Look at the number of barons, knights, and great personages who, humble and reverent, crown me. I dominate them all; above them I lord; and my glory shines almost as brilliantly and as vividly upon them as does the brilliant light of the sun upon the stars of the firmament. I feel sorry for you because, accustomed to live like a mole among the dark shadows of the forest, you have been blighted, blinded by so much glory and such living splendor."

But the wise Bertoldo was quick to reply: "You must not forget, O Sire, that he who sits highest runs the risk of falling, and falling cannot be dangerous to him who sits below. The wheel of fortune turns on forever and without interruption, and, the worst of it is, turns blindly, with regard to no one. And because fortune is fickle, today it may favor you, tomorrow turn against you. Remember also that it is impossible to hold the wind in a net; as impossible as it is to put all the water of the Po into one bucket. And do you know how those who surround you appear to me? They are like so many vultures and so many crows, ready to pounce upon your carrion and devour it. Worse yet, they give me the impression that they are wasps buzzing around a tree loaded with ripe apples about to drop to the ground. And what one does they all do, since avarice in the courts is like a pestilence, like a boundless sea, like an abyss without bottom, like Etna or Vesuvius, incapable of being filled, impossible to satiate. Furthermore, in the courts there is another vice, another disease—I mean most contemptible adulation. Adulation can be compared to the treachery of a cat that purrs when you watch it, but scratches you pitilessly when you turn away. And you may be sure that adulation, like the greedy and thirsty rook that never leaves its hiding place to go to a dry spring, or like the small bird that cannot be caught without a snare and a call, would not be lavished upon you unless there was some gain to the adulator."

It is impossible to describe the pleasure of the king as he listened to the frank yet subtle remarks of Bertoldo. He was so pleased that he interrupted him to say: "Good, very, very good! From this moment I proclaim you one of the greatest of men, and, if you wish, I will take you into my service in my court."

"He who has the good fortune to be born free," replied Bertoldo, "does not easily barter his liberty. Liberty is the greatest of good; compared to it, all other fortunes amount to naught, and can be cast aside. He who, being born, is destined to feed himself with turnips and beets must not try to fill his stomach with delicacies or dainties, because the body cannot very well tolerate them, and he will run the risk of indigestion. Likewise, he who is accustomed to handle the spade and the hoe should not try to wield the lance and the sword in war.

I am not accustomed to jest or to say foolish things. I maintain that he who is in good health does a foolish thing if he risks being attacked by the itch. I also maintain that it is a very difficult thing for a wild bird to get used to life in a cage."

For a long time, in this same vein, the dialogue between Bertoldo and King Alboino continued.

Some historians claim that on that day Bertoldo spoke much better than the great philosopher Plato. Unfortunately his words were not transcribed and thus transmitted to us; otherwise, they might be taught today in every school. If the maxims of Bertoldo were now known, the learned as well as the unlearned might confine themselves to them, and there would be no need to consult other books.

However, from one legend that is prevalent among the people, we gathered that at one point Bertoldo called the king foolish. On account of this, Alboino became very angry, although we feel that he should have done nothing but laugh. But, according to the legend, the king of the Lombards wanted Bertoldo thrown out of the palace, swearing that at a proper time and place, and with the severity he customarily visited upon those who paid him no respect, he would have him treated with the noose or the ax.

How easily and swiftly does the wheel of fortune change!

The king, who shortly before had shown himself to Bertoldo as liberal, magnanimous, and refined, now displayed an ugly countenance. He shook, be snorted, he beat his brains. Never before had he shown himself so enraged, not even when, the bridle, the saddle, and the back of his horse being broken, he plunged to the ground while rushing full speed to put to the sword, to fire, and to sack the beaten but intrepid Pavia.

He who wishes to know exactly how the matter ended may read what historians wrote about it. According to them, the outcome was like this: it seems that the king laughed. Bertoldo, irked, suddenly exclaimed: "Sire, laughter abounds in the mouths of fools."

To tell the truth, Bertoldo should never have said such words, particularly since they were aimed at a powerful sovereign.

We know that all take pleasure in laughter, rather than in tears; and it was for this reason that King Alboino laughed.

I have heard someone speak of an ancient philosopher who, when he laughed, made as much noise as ten men. However this may be, the insolent words of Bertoldo did not please the king; the taste was so bitter that he could not swallow it.

Bertoldo, although so sly and so sharp that he could give counsel to a fox, did not become disconcerted by the rebuff; he felt that he had said nothing wrong. Such was Bertoldo's nature. He never said anything without reason. He knew how to distinguish right from wrong, and was accustomed to call things by their true names; for instance, bread, bread, and wine, wine.

Hence his calm answer to the king: "Note that if you now force me to go away and hide I shall return like flies return—the more you drive them away, the more they come back to bite and annoy you."

And the king replied: "Try it, and we shall see if you can make me touch with my hand what you have said about flies."

Bertoldo accepted the challenge and hurried away to hide, but without disclosing his hiding place.

Alboino decided to wait for him, just to see if Bertoldo would keep his word.

Upon leaving the royal palace, Bertoldo returned to his native mountain, where, grazing in the pasture, was a jenny-ass, the like of which had never been seen. The poor beast was scrawny and hairless, and had so many sores on its back and sides one could almost see what the beast's insides looked like.

Bertoldo's jenny-ass was a real monster; and in some ways more like carrion or a deformed carcass than a live animal. The beast could be compared only to malaria, to a specter, to the effigy of starvation, to the Lenten season, to misfortune itself. Aristotle, the philosopher who always made a thorough examination of things, would have probably called such a beast an accident, a demon, or a phantasm.

The unhappy beast had seen several jubilees. It had begun its life work at birth, and had fasted so many times that the number of its fast days would almost cover the calendar. Its body resembled a geographical map, its hide showing formations like islands, and from valleys there exhaled such a stench that one drew back in dismay. Yet, still patient and unruffled, even though lame, the beast continued to haul bundles of wood, and it was said that throughout the whole province of Verona hardly another beast as faithful could be found.

The peasant took the beast by the halter, and mounted without either saddling or bridling it. Balancing himself as best he could, since he had no stirrups, he directed the beast toward the city at a trot.

No spurs were necessary, for the poor beast was driven forward by a swarm of files and gnats that literally covered it all over. It proceeded as though it were lured more by the confused buzzing that encircled its ears like a sweet and delightful harmony than by anything else.

Circe did not draw so many people, when, casting a bridge over the Hellespont, she set out to conquer Greece in that cruel war that widowed so many women in her kingdom, nor did so many people follow Agramante, when he invaded France and undertook that war from which the glory of the

Chiaramonti was to spring, as now gathered around the knight of Bertagnana as he entered the city of Verona, riding astride his jenny-ass.

All the children and all the women came out of their homes; and even barking dogs pounced at the poor beast.

Some cried out as though they were mad: "Beat it! Beat it!"

Others kept repeating: "Look! Look!"

The villain was forced to make way for himself by pretending to strike at people around him with a club, although he had no weapons but his hands.

Finally, tired, perspiring, and snorting, Bertoldo reached the royal palace of Alboino.

When the king saw him riding upon the back of the jenny-ass, now all covered with flies, he exclaimed: "Did I not tell you that if you returned followed by flies I would turn you over to the executioner? Now, tell me, why did you choose to come before me in such an unbecoming way? Don't you have any fear? Don't you tremble before my royal rage?"

Bertoldo, feeling no fear whatever, answered thus: "Did I not tell you that flies swarm upon cadavers? Now does it not seem to you that, without need of any more proof, I can resemble a fly? Am I not upon a carcass? Can't you see that the hide of this animal is eaten by flies? I ask anyone to judge whether I have kept my word. To me it seems that I have undoubtedly kept it. Do you not think the same?"

At these words of wisdom the king could not restrain his admiration, and started to laugh. Bertoldo's escapade appeared highly amusing. In fact, he thought it was so marvelous that he doubted whether anyone else could have duplicated it.

Thereupon the king, in a tone of real benevolence, said: "I will be generous with you. Now that I know how great your wisdom is, I want to take care of you. I shall never permit you to lack anything. From now on you shall be my counselor. And if now you have nothing else to tell me, you may go in peace and be happy. I see two women coming toward me, and I cannot avoid giving them an immediate audience."

And Bertoldo, quite readily, remarked: "Be careful, Sire. Be careful not to make a mistake. Make sure that your decision is in accordance with justice."

In what way King Alboino was to decide the question that the two women were about to submit to him, the reader will learn in the following chapter.

Chapter 2

THEME

Two women appear before King Alboino and create such a commotion that he is unable to get them to agree. Finally he says some words in praise of the female sex, but Bertoldo, with ingenious arguments, makes the king retract his words. Then the king, to put Bertoldo to trial, orders him to depart, but to return in such a manner that he can be seen yet not seen. The villain goes away undaunted, taking with him the stable, the flour mill, and the garden, and thus again is able to please King Alboino.

THE MORAL OF THE TALE

Even though to listen carefully to the views of all his subjects is the office of a good prince, he should never undertake to decide the quarrels of the common people nor of women. In some cases, the king should see and not see, neglect certain things and care for others. The sharp courtier does not lack the art of understanding the orders of his lord, even though such orders are not clearly explained, nor does he lack the prudence to execute them.

NOW I want all chatterers who, full of vanity and pride, sit around tables in coffeehouses or hang around the corridors of the tribunals and waiting rooms of the great, where they speak ill of everyone and everything that unfortunately comes to their attention, not even sparing the reputation of their lords, to listen to the golden words spoken by Bertoldo, the poor peasant, in the hall where King Alboino usually dispensed justice.

Let us now consider the situation that confronted Alboino, as he sat thoughtfully in his seat of judgment.

I do not really know whether, after having heard the question submitted to him (a question as ridiculous as it is intricate), he will be able to decide it quickly with the sagacity of a Longbeard, obtain general approval with high praise, or a cordial laugh; or whether in the end he will deem it advisable to keep silent and bite his tongue.

However, I do know that, while the king was meditating, two women, with downcast eyes, quietly approached him, and made such awkward bows that they moved even that most austere sovereign to laughter.

The two women were notable for their ugliness of face, their distorted bodies, their manner of dress, their ruffled hair, their threatening gestures, and their loud speech. In fact, they looked like two furies right out of Satan's shop and ready to serve any fiend whatever.

One was named Elisa, the other Emilia; the first was hunchbacked, the second, lame; one's body twisted to the left when she walked, progressing like a not-too-well-rounded ball, while the other dragged in the rear like the stern of a ship whose bow was forced down by a violent headwind. Both had faces the color of saffron.

While the two women were bowing, there was an interval when they were not trying to snatch from each other a contraption of which each held an end. The contraption, then called an infant-guard but now known as a girdle, was a very curious thing, then much in style. It was made of several loops, like a cage, and created, though I am not sure, either in Spain or in France, unless the devil himself invented it. In fact, it seemed as if the devil himself had whipped up the mutual rage of the two women, who screamed like damned souls, or like lawyers when they wrangle with judges.

At this point it becomes necessary to say that Elisa had stolen the girdle from Emilia and did not want to return it. Elisa even affirmed that it had always belonged to her. For this reason they had come, for judgment before the king. But even in the royal palace they continued to quarrel.

The king, stunned by the racket, finally managed to impose silence upon the two furies, and had them explain the cause of their dispute. He also wanted to know what kind of a contraption it was that each was trying to snatch from the other's grasp. He could see that it was shaped like a funnel, formed by several steel loops, upon which was stretched a colored cloth. On one end, the loops narrowed; on the other, they spread out into the shape of a pair of wings. The narrow side was supposed to come in contact with the body in such a way that when a woman wore it it seemed as though she were walking within a funnel. In a word, as the king soon learned, it was ancient and well-known feminine implement called, as we have said, an infant-guard, an implement so ingenious and refined that it could give a woman's hips any shape she liked. If the body was portly, it could make it appear thin; if the abdomen was too prominent, it could almost hide it completely; in short, it was so cunningly made that even a pregnant woman would appear to be a slender spinster, when wearing it.

Possession of this infant-guard was the cause that had driven the two women to insult and scratch each other, and eventually to come before the king, and there continue to exchange most ungracious epithets.

Each woman claimed to be in the right; each reciprocally accused the other, with interspersed epithets of "thief" and "rogue"; and each comported herself in such an unbecoming way as to make the king appear to be an idiot.

As it was, the Lord God, who surrounds thrones with superhuman virtue, came to the aid of King Alboino, and an idea sprang up in his mind that suggested a way of resolving the dispute and making the snake come out of the hole, as it were. The king thereupon rendered this strange and unusual decision: the infant-guard should be divided in two parts, in such a way that two loops would be given to Elisa and two to Emilia.

Elisa, who had stolen the infant-guard from her friend, was satisfied with the king's decision. She bowed to the ground. But Emilia was infuriated. She turned to King Alboino. "Then," she cried, "must this be my destiny? Is this what is to happen to the infant-guard that came from England? What good is it to be of steel, so rare, so strong, so pliable, so light? What good is it that this, which has served me so well for four long years, must in such a manner be forsaken? No, no, I do not want to be pointed out by scornful fingers while wearing only half of you. Let it all be her own; I give it to her."

But in speaking those words Emilia felt as though her heart was being rent, and grief took such violent possession of her spirit that, her face a grotesque mask, crying and sobbing, she fell prone to the ground.

Those present hastened to assist her, but neither the Cologne water, the salts that were placed under her nose, nor the unlacing of her bodice were sufficient to bring her back to her senses. And that great grief is easily explained: she no longer had the beloved infant-guard, which was fitted to hide the ugly deformity that made her twist to one side; she no longer could make use of those springs that, running lengthwise, brought equilibrium to her person.

But King Alboino was moved. Her tears, her altered face, the swoon, the unselfish interest to let Elisa take the whole infant-guard rather than have it divided, induced the king to order that the whole girdle be restored to her. And thus he stopped the quarrel in the best way possible.

Today, however, no one would have the heart to imitate the example of King Alboino; and there would be, even for causes of minor account, many court hearings.

(Anyway, that is the story. It can be found, it is said, in ancient script in a very famous library. Not being fully convinced, I wrote to a learned friend, a man of vast and profound erudition, and he confirmed in every detail what is in the manuscript. Whether the story is true or false, I neither can nor care to affirm. On the other hand, another book attributes the dispute to a mirror and says nothing of the infant-guard. But we must rely, of course, upon the most ancient writers.)

When silence was restored in the hall of the royal palace, Alboino turned to Bertoldo, who had witnessed the scene with mounting astonishment.

"What are you doing, you cunning rogue?" asked the king. "Speak! What are you seeking with those burning eyes of yours?"

"I am looking for a penny," answered the sly villain, "so that your decision may at least have an adequate reward. But good, O King Alboino! What a surprising decision you have rendered! I can assure you that it is worthy of being perpetuated by the erection of a large marble column or a triumphal arch, or at least printed upon the dress of every woman, or painted upon the leather of a pair of boots. Let thanks be given to the eternal Father that He did not make you a woman at birth, otherwise (what would it avail to deny it?) you would have reached the point of forgiving a man who let his concubine lead him by the nose. But don't you really know that in every woman there is a certain amount of imposture? Don't you know that, as dogs have their weapons in the mouth, oxen in the forehead, and mules in the rear, women have them in their eyes and in their ever-ready tears? Women are gay or sad as they find it convenient; they change color with the ease of a chameleon; and they feign with their hearts as they do with their faces, covering them with a little embellishment. Above all, they are liars when they speak, liars!"

"By Bacchus, Bertoldo, this is too much!" interrupted Alboino.

At this display of displeasure, Bertoldo became quiet, even though Alboino did not appear to be very angry, since he was a man of mild and gentle spirit. For a moment, the king confined himself, in a rather severe tone, to calling him insolent and impudent. Then, keeping his eyes fixed on Bertoldo's face and with his hands upon his hips, with a grave voice the king spoke. "Now tell me, from whom is man born? Who nurses him? With whom does he unite in the greatest pleasure? Who makes him the father of a fair and numerous offspring? Who keeps the home in order? Who goes to milk the cows? Who gets dinner ready?"

To each of these questions Bertoldo hastily replied: "My wife."

"Very well," resumed the king. "Why, then, you rogue, do you treat women worse than you do old slippers? Women," continued Alboino with enthusiasm, "were and are now the pride and the glory of all countries, of all ages, of all times. Without woman life becomes annoying. A city where there were no women would be deserted and inhospitable. Furthermore, it would be deserted unless it cherished the memory of some matron who was illustrious either for sagacity or beauty. In fact, one would die of boredom and run away at breakneck speed from any place where there were no women. Woman, in every circumstance of life, knows how to demonstrate great acumen and the maximum of prudence. She is always able to give us good counsel. She is a rare example of patience and wisdom in nourishing and rearing children. She is respectful toward her husband, polite to and considerate of the servants. She is the joy of the young as well as of the old. Woman, in fact, is a combination of every virtue."

Hearing the king talk in this vein caused Bertoldo to burst out laughing.

"It readily can be seen," said Bertoldo, "that you are very tenderhearted, when with such gentle phrases you honor a sex that is exceedingly loathsome and revolting. Very well, I promise you, Sire—and keep it well in mind—that no later than tomorrow you will retract all that you have said in favor of women. If I do not succeed in this, I am willing that you should have me devoured by dogs."

It was now beginning to get dark, and bats could be seen flying about, for which reason the king retired to his chamber.

Bertoldo, meanwhile, went down to the stable to lie down with two small donkeys and an old horse. While resting, he wondered how he could make the king retract his words. He turned over in his mind many, many thoughts and many plans, none of which was better than any other, and during the whole night he did not close an eye. He could not think of any plan by which he could make Alboino appear to be a fool.

When daylight came and the sun rose above the horizon, Bertoldo arose more ugly in countenance than usual. He left the stable, where he had spent the night, and headed for the home of Emilia. "Oh, strumpet, it seems that you do not mind your own business. What are you doing here? Don't you know what King Alboino has decided to do?"

Said Emilia, "But no! I swear I really know nothing."

"Very well," resumed Bertoldo, "the king has ordered that the infant-guard be divided into two parts because, being ignorant though scrupulous, he fears that he made a mistake in rendering his decision."

"Oh, that rascal of a king!" shouted the infuriated Emilia, "That swindler of a king! Oh, that unfortunate man! But no, no, it cannot be! You are trying to play a trick upon me, Bertoldo. Go away! I don't believe you."

So Bertoldo added: "But I heard it from the very lips of the king! And there is something worse! I can assure you that the king has issued a decree that will infuriate all the women of the kingdom. Do you know what the decree provides? Well, it says that from now on each man must have not only one wife, but seven. Imagine the confusion! No less than seven owls together in the same cage!"

"Look here," said Emilia. "Divide a single morsel among so many mouths. That's frugality!"

Bertoldo wanted to hear no more, so he left for the royal court. There, undismayed, he awaited the results of his stratagem.

On her part, the sad Emilia, who believed what Bertoldo had told her, left home and began to spread the news throughout the city. All the women who heard it were upset, and soon more than a thousand women met together, to discuss a remedy for the calamity that was about to fall on them.

No one gave any thought to the infant-guard; they had something else upon their minds; another misfortune oppressed their hearts. They ran through the streets as though they were mad; some going one way, some another.

For fear of having their husbands taken away, they continued to denounce the infamous decree, and to curse it a thousand times. But from some remarks that were overheard, some women were of the opinion that, instead of one man having seven wives, it would be much better for one woman to have seven husbands.

Then all the frantic and infuriated women set out for the royal palace, like so many furies. In their present mood they would have scared the most valiant man, so inflamed were their looks, so altered their features. Some of the women were determined to speak out frankly to Alboino, and not try to disguise the anger that inflamed them. Others hoped to induce the king, with weeping, sighs, and prayers, to withdraw the ill-fated decree.

But as soon as they reached the court, they began to make a diabolic uproar. Some sighed, wailed, and shrieked, while others cursed the infamous, horrible, and unbearable edict. The clamor was so great that it reached the ears of Alboino, who, having lowered his trousers for certain needs, ran toward the women, breeches in hand, hastily trying to lace himself as best he could.

In a rage he began to roar: "Are you mad? Have you devils in you? What whirls in your heads? What brings you here to make all this stench? What a horde! How many are you? Oh, may cancer come upon your bones! Now then, silence! If you have something to say, speak, but stop that noise! Why have you come here? What do you want? Speak, ugly ones fit only to be shackled!"

When Alboino had finished, one woman, who felt that she was a fair speaker, came forward with set purpose, and, fixing a squinting look upon the king, in the name of all the other women, spoke thus: "If the rumors circulating among the people are true, that is, that you have issued a decree making it your expressed will that every male subject should have seven wives instead of one, then, Sire, you are a great idiot. Tell me," continued the woman, "does this seem to you to be of small import? Don't you know that in this way you take the bread from our mouths? And do you believe that we will consent to give this one or that the best morsel? Do you think we have too much? Oh! I understand. You would like to immortalize your name by having this edict written in some hall or gallery of your palace. Very well, then. Under that edict, and in big letters, you should affix your signature thus: That Stupid King Alboino.

"Oh, ugly strumpet!" roared the infuriated king. "How dare you! I never thought of doing what you say! What brazenness! But fear not. I will think of some way to punish you. What? Are you not ashamed to show yourself enraged over having one husband all of your own? Do you not blush at being such a chatterbox and so insolent? You women are all alike! You are all strumpets! Get away from here! You can all go hang!"

In this brusque way King Alboino drove the infuriated women from his presence. As they went out, they continued to denounce him, and even to curse the one who had brought him into the world and nursed him.

For his part, Alboino could not figure out how the whole scrimmage had come about. He continued to rave at the women. In fact, it almost seemed that he had memorized some of the phrases he recited. Finally out of his wits through anger, Alboino threw himself upon a chair.

Then Bertoldo, who had been standing meekly aside witnessing the scene that was the fruit of his sly roguery, came forward, determined to gloat over the affair at the expense, naturally, of the royal dignity.

Planting himself before the king, Bertoldo said smilingly: "Pardon me, if I present myself before your royal person. It is only because I came to tell you that whenever I make a promise I always keep my word. I promised you," Bertoldo continued, "that today you would have changed your mind about all those good things you said about women yesterday. Now listen to me with attention."

And he related to the king in detail how the thing had come about. Alboino was very much surprised. He then started to laugh. "You really have great ingenuity, by God! You are worthy, in preference to other men, to rule a great empire. From now on I want you to share my power and my throne with me."

"Oh, Sire," answered Bertoldo, "it is impossible for two persons to sit in the same chair."

But the king insisted. "We will order another chair made; it does not matter whether we have one or two."

"No," said the shrewd villain, "that would be folly. In love and in government there cannot be two."

This obstinate refusal made a profound impression upon the spirit of the king, whose love for Bertoldo by this time had grown out of bounds. He said that such a gesture was not that of a villain, but of a man worthy of the greatest consideration.

Bertoldo thanked the king for the consideration shown him for his act, which, in his opinion, did not deserve so much praise, and concluded: "If you wish it, we can divide the love that you show me. With this division I shall be satisfied."

At that moment the queen's messenger came to the king to say that her majesty wanted to see Bertoldo in her chamber at once. The purpose of this call was to have him beaten, a thing that the poor man was not expecting.

The queen had learned about the trick Bertoldo had played on the women, and she yearned to avenge them by having him punished.

The king told Bertoldo that the queen wished to see him, and bade him go to her at once. But Bertoldo, distrustful of women and aware of his guilt, hesitated for a moment, figuring what to do. He finally decided to go, confident of being able to find a way to survive the threatening storm, which, in fact, he did.

Bertoldo therefore directed himself toward the queen's chamber, saying to himself: "We shall see if her scabs are harder than my nails that scratch them."

The queen had ordered her damsels to give Bertoldo a good beating. To have it properly administered the queen picked the boldest and toughest from among the women who made up her retinue. She ordered them to give Bertoldo a good clubbing.

When Bertoldo came into the presence of the queen, she said to him: "You are very welcome, Bertoldo." But after this greeting, in rage, she said: "Right now I shall make you see, you ugly baboon, whether this is the way to treat women."

And Bertoldo, bowing clumsily, replied: "Queen, to tell you the truth, I believe you are crazy."

"Oh, you unmitigated scoundrel!" exclaimed the queen. And so saying she took off her slipper and threw it in Bertoldo's face. But he was quick to avoid the blow. Then he began to laugh and to poke fun at the raging queen.

One can very easily see how this kind of behavior would infuriate the wife of King Alboino.

But the clever villain did not wait for the storm to break out; he ran off. Whether by accident or chance, he ran right into the damsels who were waiting to give him a clubbing, as they had been ordered to do by the queen. The women were enjoined to give Bertoldo such a beating that afterward he would have nothing else to wish for.

As soon as they found him in their midst, they immediately raised their clubs to rain blows upon him and flatten him to the floor.

But the villain sensed the danger and shouted: "Listen! First listen to my reasons! I have not told them to you yet. And then, with the help of God, from whom we hope to have our sins forgiven, I want to tell you something. I want you to know that I have kept a secret for a long time, a secret that can be useful to you also."

The queen's damsels, curious to know what the villain had to say, kept still and listened.

"Note, my daughters," Bertoldo began, "that four years ago I had my horoscope read, that is, I had my fortune told. The astrologer told me that some day I would be beaten by some fair damsels. And to tell you the truth, I could not wait for the moment when the beating would be administered, because chastisement by fair and graceful young women can neither hurt you, nor be anything but delicious and pleasant. At this point it is necessary to tell you that this astrologer was very skilled in his art. Moreover, he was even familiar with necromancy. According to him, he was taught this latter science by the greatest wizard of the king of Tartarus. He also told me that, in company with that wizard, he had descended into hell several times to transact business directly and amicably with the devil. After the astrologer had revealed to me the secret I have just told you, that is, that some day I would be beaten by five, six, or seven fair damsels, exactly like you, he told me not to worry about the matter, because, shortly after, the justice of God would completely avenge me. And the punishment for those who beat me would be this: no matter how much they might desire it, those damsels would never be able to find a husband."

After they had heard Bertoldo's words, the damsels of the queen quite naturally thought no longer of beating Bertoldo. In fact, they threw away the clubs with which they were armed.

Beat Bertoldo with clubs? No! They wouldn't run the risk of remaining spinsters all through life. This kind of punishment was too severe; they could not reconcile themselves to it.

However, although Bertoldo insisted—and even begged—to be beaten, none of them dared to lift a club against him.

And in this way the astute villain succeeded in dodging the effects of the terrible storm that the queen had contrived for him. When the queen was informed of what had happened, she became so enraged that she bit her tongue. She could not find peace for having suffered such a terrible humiliation.

When the story reached the king's ears, noticing that the villain was never short of expedients, he thought to himself: "I want to put him to trial. We shall see how he absolves himself."

The king immediately sent a messenger to say he rejoiced that Bertoldo had so happily evaded the clubbing, and was now safe and sound, away from the snare contrived by feminine malevolence. If Bertoldo had not had boldness and presence of mind, he might have found himself in a serious predicament. Furthermore, the messenger was instructed to tell Bertoldo that on the following morning he should appear at the royal court, but in a very unusual way, which the messenger explained to him.

Here is how Bertoldo was to appear: the king was to see yet not see him. In addition, he was to take with him the stable, the garden, and the flour mill.

In such a manner was Bertoldo to appear at the royal palace the next morning.

Upon receiving the message Bertoldo began to think seriously, not knowing just then what to do. For some time, with his head bowed on his chest, he walked up and down. Finally he exclaimed: "Yes, yes, I found it! I will do it! The king will be satisfied!"

He then had a cake made. This cake was to be made out of beets, cottage cheese, cheese, and butter. While the cake was being made, being somewhat of a glutton, he repeatedly tasted it and pronounced it excellent. He then took a sieve, placed it in front of his face, and set out for the royal palace of Alboino.

You will soon know why Bertoldo, after he had made careful preparations and performed many tests, went to the royal palace bringing that sieve and that cake with him.

At first, not even the king understood the meaning of this strange appearance, and as soon as he saw Bertoldo, he immediately asked him to explain why he had appeared in such an unusual way. The king urged him to speak clearly and without hesitation.

Bertoldo, fixing a reassuring look upon the king, replied thus: "Here I have presented myself precisely in the manner in which you ordered me to appear before you. Maybe it does not seem so to you. Very well. I will explain, and you will be convinced. I well know," continued Bertoldo, "that because of the sieve that covers my face you see me and don't see me; therefore you must confess that if in this world there is a crafty man, I am such a man. Now look at this cake that I have placed at your feet. In this cake there is the garden, the stable, and the flour mill that you ordered me to bring. This cake is composed of various things. Oh! I guarantee that it is very good. Taste it and very shortly you will be convinced. The principal part of the composition of this cake is the beet, which represents the garden where it grows, and the beet seems to be created on purpose by nature to make cakes appetizing. The cottage cheese, the butter, and the layer of cheese—what else can you hope to get from the stable? I believe you cannot hope for anything else. Finally, does it not seem to you that the flour mill is indicated by the flour, which forms the outer part of the cake and contains within it such delicious food? Here, therefore, your wish is satisfied, and as long as I have life I always hope to do likewise."

The king embraced and kissed him, and lovingly spoke to him thus: "Good Bertoldo! Go, for you really are a prodigious man!"

At that very moment, a certain Fagotto, who was a musician and also a clown, came into the hall where the king was. Thinking that Bertoldo was a dullard, the clown began to make fun of him in a thousand ways, though Bertoldo had done nothing to provoke the assault.

Fagotto believed that he could trifle with Bertoldo as it pleased him, but as he kept up his taunts, and Bertoldo lost his patience, the clown soon learned that he had found bread too hard for his teeth. Thus the villain and the clown began to exchange such stinging words and phrases that it was a real pleasure to listen to them.

As the exchange continued, it appeared that one was as insolent as the other, and each could use his tongue in a marvelous way. Gradually the controversy became embittered, and finally the two contenders pounced upon each other with fists, bites, and kicks.

Figure 22. Bertoldo, "seen and yet not seen." *Bertoldo con Bertoldino e Cacasenno,* illustration facing p. 17.

In the struggle, though, Fagotto got the worst of it. Bertoldo cut and bruised the clown's face so much that he was bleeding all over.

When the king saw that the contest was becoming quite serious, he ordered the two opponents separated, and commanded that they be immediately reconciled. So the two contenders embraced and kissed each other. The clown wanted to say something else, but Bertoldo prudently kept still.

The king beckoned the clown to leave, and accordingly he went, but not without first throwing a contemptible look at Bertoldo, who looked back at him, undismayed. The king said: "Depart, clown!"

The sky was gradually darkening, and night was about to fall. King Alboino took leave of those present and retired to his chamber, but before going he turned to Bertoldo and commanded that on the following day the rogue appear in the royal palace neither dressed nor naked.

Chapter 3

THEME

In order to appear at the royal court neither dressed nor naked, Bertoldo undresses himself and wraps himself in a net. Meanwhile, among the Veronese women springs the desire to sit in the senate like the men: but the clever villain, by means of a bird that he bought in the public square, puts them in an unfavorable light. Then, with a rabbit that he carries under his garment, he succeeds in foiling the queen's plot and in eluding a pack of furious dogs that rush upon him.

THE MORAL OF THE TALE

To the eyes of the court, the courtier should appear to be neither too rich nor too poor; neither too learned nor too ignorant. He should never expose himself to either envy or disgrace. He who does not know how to keep a secret is not fit to handle state affairs, and such a man is more of a weakling than a woman. Only a man of skill can save others from the anger of the powerful, against whom nothing but his own cleverness is of any avail.

Oh, thief and witless vanity! Yours is the blame if the greatest of men run toward their own ruin. From morning till night you are the only thing thought of, as though there was nothing better to talk about.

Oh, how many go without food, and deprive themselves of the most essential things, to dress and wear clothes that the current style calls for. Men in general are almost all victims of this fatal disease. What then can be said of women?

As soon as she marries, a woman likes to have a lacy dress and a gown with a long train, just as if she were the daughter of the Great Sultan. And woe, if the lace is not from Flanders and the cloth from France or Germany, she becomes more roiled and more terrible than a fury!

And if perchance the husband is a good man who is not disposed to face ruin, she puts the home in turmoil, worse than if the devil dwelled in her body.

Do you know how people should dress? Precisely in the same way that Bertoldo appeared before King Alboino. And this custom would not only adapt itself to the rich, but also to the poor.

In the previous chapter, you have already read about the command King Alboino gave to Bertoldo, that he appear before him at the royal palace neither dressed nor naked.

The king hoped the villain would not be able to solve the riddle, and, as a consequence, Alboino would have a hearty laugh at his expense. But the clever Bertoldo, who was never at loss to find an expedient, soon devised a way to overcome the difficulty.

Lest I be in error, I had better not try to name the exact day or the month in which the occurrence took place, for I have not been able, for certain, to learn this. Despite numerous researches, I have found no hint regarding it. Apparently all writers, because of laziness, have neglected the episode.

Oh, if similar things would only occur today! How many writers would consider it a duty to note the most minute details! I do know, however, that the weather was particularly bad, that particular day, and that the sky was as black as the mantel of a fireplace.

The sun, hidden behind clouds, resembled a poor man who, heavily in debt, wraps himself in a mantle for fear of being recognized by officers who have orders to arrest him.

Oh, debts! Judges! Officers! Oh, misfortune! I know only too well what you all mean, and how much fear you instill in us!

The sun at least has this to rejoice about: even should it have debts, it can hide behind the clouds and go about its own business.

Therefore, to return to Bertoldo, I shall say that on that memorable day he appeared before King Alboino as naked as he was at birth, wrapped only in a thin fisherman's net.

What impression he made in that costume, I leave to your imagination. Really, I would not know how to describe him, or to whom to compare him. But try to imagine him as very ugly, hunchbacked, of the color of smoked ham, and, moreover, shaggy as a bear.

Since I already have given you a portrait of Bertoldo, and you already know what a lovely-looking person he was, imagine what he seemed like naked and covered only by that net.

I can assure you that, to see him, no one would mind spending more than a cent. If a similar monster allowed himself to be viewed as an exhibit enclosed in a cage in the public square, public attendance would be immense, and money could be made by the shovelful.

As soon as King Alboino saw this strange and unusual figure appear before him, he broke out in a loud laugh, and laughed so much that afterwards he complained of kidney pains. However, since he did not want to debase his royal dignity, he restrained himself, and turning to the villain said this to him: "Are you mad, Bertoldo? Does it seem proper to you to appear before the king in such a manner?"

The good but shrewd villain, without bowing and with his usual boldness, quickly replied: "My lord, you ask me questions as though you really were out of your mind! If you do not remember what you commanded, I will remind you myself. Last night, you gave me an unusual order: to appear before you neither dressed nor naked. Very well. I am fitted precisely in the manner you imposed upon me. And, in fact, if you wish to see me naked, no doubt you can, and you may even count the parts of my body. I believe I am before you in the costume of Father Adam, and exactly as we came at birth. On the other hand, with your permission, I am covered from head to foot by this net, however transparent it may be. From all of this you can draw the conclusion that the consequence of an attempt to fool Bertoldo always reacts against the one who thinks he can dupe him."

As soon as the villain had finished speaking these words, a page came to the hall where King Alboino was seated, and having paid the customary homage to him said: "Sire, in the anteroom there is a knight of Her Majesty the Queen, who seeks an audience."

"He may enter if he wishes to talk to me," affably replied the king.

Just then, Bertoldo hid himself in a corner.

The messenger of the queen entered and the king went to meet him, embracing him as he came close.

The name of the knight was Bornio, a name that could easily be mistaken for the word 'blind,' and he was the secretary of the queen.

This messenger had a habit of always appearing haughty and surly; moreover, while talking, he would use carefully chosen words and studied phrases, not then customarily used.

After having paid the usual and customary respects to the king, he spoke thus: "Sire, even though I am perfectly aware of the high honor the queen has conferred upon me, nevertheless, finding myself in the presence of so great a king, I am so moved, so upset, that I am afraid of becoming confused, and forgetting how to express myself. It seems as though I were in a ship at the mercy of the storm. Sire, your august wife sends me here to make known to you one of her wishes. She, through my lips, warmly recommends that you cause the female to be respected as she should be. Generally speaking, how valuable women are you know as well as she. Therefore it behooves you to take care of them and give a sparkling example of your love for them. Consider, Sire, that it was a woman who carried you in her womb for nine long months and then gave you birth; consider that it was a woman who nursed you, raised you, appeased, with loving care, all your little humors, satisfied all your wishes, cultivated all your good qualities. To a woman, finally, you owe the circumstance that you have grown so fair, so kind, so well-bred. Have I, perhaps, made you what you are? No, it was a woman. Woe, if I had made you! You would resemble a boot! That magnificent royal mantle that descends from your shoulders—who has woven that, if not a woman? Consider that the shirt you wear, the drawers you have on, and the clothes that cover your body are all the work of a woman. Sire, the woman combines all virtues in herself; therefore you should elevate her, not permit her to be degraded. Remember, God did not give us woman only to sweep our toilets and empty our urinals."

And possibly Bornio would have continued in this vein for a long time, telling the king what the queen wanted, had not an outburst of coughing interrupted the words in his throat.

Actually, Bornio had memorized his speech. But when he reached the best part of it he forgot the rest. At this point, he made an attempt to save time and to say what he could. Finally, becoming dumbfounded, he drew a paper from his pocket.

Thereupon he reached for a pair of large glasses, took another bow, and placed them upon his nose.

Bertoldo, who was hidden a few steps away, did not lose sight of him for a single instant. Observing Bornio as he put on his glasses and began to read from the paper, he began to snort to suppress his laughter. The noise he made resembled the gurgle of grape juice when it ferments in a vat. Finally, no longer able to restrain himself, Bertoldo broke out into a roaring and irrepressible guffaw.

At that sudden and unexpected outburst, Bornio was seized by such a great tremor that his glasses dropped from his nose to the ground and broke in a thousand pieces.

At that sight, you can imagine Bertoldo, his hilarity knew no restraint. The poor secretary, his face as pale as a cadaver, tried to read the paper, but despite his attempts he was unable.

Alboino, anxious to know what was written on the paper, snatched it from the messenger's hand, and after some effort succeeded it reading it through.

Then turning to the unhappy Bornio, who in his confusion could not lift his eyes from the ground, the king affably and mildly said: "You may go and tell my wife that you have made known to me her wish. Now I know her most passionate desire. You must add, however, that I cannot, upon my two feet, immediately reply to what she asks, since her question is of such importance that it requires long and serious thought. I shall let her know as soon as I shall see her. You may now go and greet her in my stead."

The king had no sooner pronounced these words than the unhappy ambassador disappeared.

The king then turned to Bertoldo and said: "My dear Bertoldo, I consider you my most trusted comrade and my best friend. I pray you, give me a suggestion, since truly I have never before found myself in such dilemma. You know what the humor of the queen is! Now I tell you what she would like to have. She wants women to wear trousers instead of skirts. She wants them to sit in my council like the men, give their opinions, boldly support them, furiously discuss them, and spit out sentences according to their own whims. To gain their objective, all the women of the city have banded together and are ready to stir up a diabolic row. They are pestering my wife, who, in turn, is plaguing me. This mess cannot end well. If I deign to satisfy the wishes of my wife, certainly I will commit a great folly, and take the chance of having the whole world laugh at my expense. If, on the contrary, I tell her: 'My dear wife, I cannot please you,' I am sure she will become angry, and whenever she has the opportunity she will make me pay for it. Now what would you do in my place, my dear Bertoldo? Speak, I beg you! Find a way for me to settle the matter. I should like to have you find a way to deny their request and at the same time not infuriate my wife."

For a while, Bertoldo stood immersed in thought, scratching his head with both hands. Finally, indulging his inclination to draw a moral from every situation, he answered thus: "It necessarily would have to be said that he who now has the ability to be serious-minded is indeed mad; it is up to the shepherd to guide his flock, not up to the flock to guide the shepherd; rather, it is in the natural order of things, so established by God. The night is feminine, and light belongs to the day, which is masculine and is illuminated by the sun. The rooster is the one that crows, not the hen."

And Bertoldo would have continued to spit out sentences of the same tenor for at least another hour, to prove that women should be subordinate to men, but the king interrupted him. "Be quiet! May calamity strike you!" shouted the king. "This is no time for idle words. I need you to help me solve this difficulty. I really don't know to which saint to turn! Therefore words are of no avail. Try to think of something new. You always have a bag full of tricks. Try to find some plan; and I beg you to rush your effort."

Bertoldo then exclaimed: "Very well, illustrious and mighty king. I swear that I will do whatever I can to please you. Until I am completely exhausted I will continue to search for a good idea, so that you may be pleased with me, because I have a great yearning to see these blessed women fall into a trap."

Having said this, Bertoldo left the royal hall and went to dress himself in his usual clothes. After this, at breakneck speed, he ran to the public square.

After he had wandered about for a time and had seen a quantity of birds, he finally decided to buy one, spending four or five cents for it. Note well that Bertoldo had four or five cents, while to me it often happens that I have not even one.

Having bought the bird, Bertoldo placed it in a small case, and in all haste returned to the royal palace. There, turning to the king, he told him this: "Sire, you should immediately send this case to the queen. At the same time you should have someone tell her to immediately give this little box to the women, and to bring it back to you as soon as you get out of bed tomorrow morning, promising to grant their request as soon as you have made certain they did not open the case."

After this, Bertoldo told the king what he had placed in the case and what he expected from his stratagem.

Alboino took the case and gave it to one of his trusted knights, ordering him, exactly as the good Bertoldo had counseled, to take it to the queen, and tell her that she should, in turn, give it to the women, who, in their turn, were to return it intact to the king the following morning. The knight did not wait to have the order repeated. He hastily ran to the queen's apartment.

As the king had ordered, the small case was turned over to the women, and they were so tickled that more than ten of them got on their knees to thank God.

However, since the female of the species is so constituted that, at any cost, be it good or bad, proper or improper, she is fond of wanting to know other people's affairs, many of the women wanted to open the case to see what was in it. Other women, however, were opposed to the idea.

One of them said: "Since our sovereign so ordered, we should not and must not open this box."

Another remarked: "Good, but if we do open it, who is there among us that will go and tell him about it?"

Several shouted: "Let's open it! Let's open it!"

They made such a row, shrieking so shrilly, that they sounded like a flock of sparrows disputing over a worm.

The agitation lasted all day. Many of the women were on the verge of pulling each other's hair and scratching each other's face. Undoubtedly, the turmoil would have ended with bodily damage to someone if the majority had not ultimately decided to open the box to see what was in it.

As the case was opened, all the women focused their eyes upon it, but before they could do anything to prevent it, the enclosed bird took flight and disappeared.

At this, some of the women became ashen pale, and several exclaimed: "Oh, god Bacchus!"

Astonished, they stood still as if made of stone. Then they sighed and looked through the small window through which the bird had flown. The bird had flown away so fast that not even an arrow shot from a bow could have overtaken it. The women were left like the dull villain who, going to drink his broth, found that it already had been gulped by the stable dog, which still showed its bloated belly.

Finally one and then another began to cry out: "Oh, the bird! Oh, my, it flew away. We cannot get another like it, for we did not see it very well, and we do not know its kind."

Some said it was a wood thrush, some a chaffinch, and others a figpecker. They ranted and raved so much that one of them rashly seized her own slipper and chewed on it.

One said: "How can we excuse ourselves for having done such a great wrong?"

Another said: "If the king wanted to do us so much honor, he should suggest it himself."

A third said: "Let's hang ourselves!"

"No," responded another, "whoever hangs herself will die; and death is certainly far worse than losing a bird!"

So they talked among themselves, unable to decide whether or not to appear before king Alboino. All were conscience-stricken and in despair, and in the apartment of the queen, where they had reunited, only weeping and wailing could be heard. But the queen, who was still hopeful, commanded: "Quick! Bring me my gowns and my gloves!"

After one of her damsels had brought what she wanted, she determinedly added: "And now let us go to the king. Yes; let's go to implore his clemency, his mercy. Actually, it was not a very great crime that we opened the box. I know he is good, and he will not be adamant when confronted by so much distress and despair."

So saying, the queen walked forth, followed by the multitude of wailing and sobbing women. Except the queen, all the women trembled, for they feared that some great calamity would strike them. In fact, they believed that they had committed a terrible crime, for which they could hope to receive no mercy. They felt that the king would be both grieved and enraged, and could be comforted by no other bird but the one that had flown away. Therefore, the poor women were panic-stricken with fear.

The queen walked slowly, for she was very portly. At either side strode two damsels, hands at her elbows, to enable her to walk more rapidly.

Her circumference at the hips was no less than five feet and four inches. From this, with due regard for proportion, one can easily imagine the rest, exactly as did the man who, from the sight of the claw, surmised the lion.

The queen's name was Hypsicratea, and she was a descendant of a princely family, whose coat of arms bore the figure of an eel emerging from a pot.

Hypsicratea, the queen of the Lombards, had nothing to do aside from gossiping and laughing with her pussy cat, and from time to time mend the shirts that her royal husband was accustomed to wear at night.

Do not wonder, dear reader, that the queen should occupy herself with such ignoble things. If you have studied a little history and have some erudition, you must know that Homer sang of a similar queen, just as he described certain gods who engaged in fistfights among themselves.

The women therefore, with the queen as their leader, descended on the king like a flock of cranes. When the queen came into his presence she made a very graceful bow and began to expound her reasons for being there and those of the women who followed her. "Sire, you know very well that our sex is a little obstinate and has always committed small sins because of extreme curiosity. You should forgive them if sometime they overstep their proper bounds. Perhaps you have not understood what I aim to avoid but I want you to know—"

"I think I know enough," the king said, interrupting her, "and I wish you would tarry here no longer wasting my time. I know, and it is not necessary for me to resort to the fire devil, that you have come here because of the case with the bird enclosed in it."

As soon as he pronounced these words, the feminine mob began to scream: "Mercy! Have mercy on us! Blessed be you, and blessed be the breasts on which you nursed when an infant! If we have done wrong, it was because nature has instilled a weakness in us. Certainly not out of malice, nor because of a bad spirit. You must believe our statements, for our weakness in being curious is generally known. And since we know you to be so generous of heart, in unison we implore your forgiveness."

Thereupon the king answered: "I will gladly pardon you if you dispel the mad desire that has arisen in your minds to take part in the council of my state, and promise that you no longer will think of certain things."

"Yes, Your Majesty," they replied in chorus.

Now the women, feeling that they had been dealt with leniently, suddenly became gay and happy, and their faces brightened until they looked as beautiful and fresh as brides.

But the next day, when they thought it over, they realized they had lost the right to participate in the council of the crown, and their resentment welled up within them. They became aroused and yelled: "Oh, beaked villain! Cuckold! Infamous Bertoldo! Dog! Scoundrel!" And thus, making a devilish clamor, they returned to the queen, shouting at the top of their voices: "Vengeance! Vengeance!"

Right then and there they wanted to see Bertoldo and rend him to pieces. Queen Hypsicratea, who hated villains, promised to do all that the women asked for, and even more!

At the royal palace the queen had two fierce, ferocious mastiffs, and she swore to feed that rogue Bertoldo to the dogs. In fact, when evening came, she summoned Bertoldo to come to her the next day, saying that she had something important to tell him, and that under no circumstances must he fail.

When Bertoldo received this message, he became perplexed and did not know what to do. For a while, he was undecided whether he should go. He knew the queen was apt to play some unpleasant trick upon him, and his conscience in regard to her was not clear. All night the poor devil brooded over the problem, but he sustained his courage.

As soon as dawn came, unbeknown to the queen, her cook, the one whose only job was to prepare meat loaf for their majesties, went to see Bertoldo.

He told Bertoldo about the ugly intentions of the women and warned him that, if he went to see Queen Hypsicratea, she would have him torn to pieces by the two mastiffs.

Upon hearing this, Bertoldo became enraged and exclaimed: "So, Queen, it seems that you really are of good lineage!"

After thanking the cook for the warning, Bertoldo began to think about how to get out of his predicament. Suddenly a marvelous idea came to his mind. He decided to go to the queen, despite the warning, but to assure his own safety he provided himself with a rabbit with which to fool the dogs.

Happily now he waited for day to come, and when the proper hour arrived he set out for the royal palace, heading directly for the queen's apartment, undismayed. No sooner had he reached the threshold of the door than the two mastiffs, furious and as mad as demons, rushed upon him, ready to tear him to pieces.

Figure 23. Bertoldo with a rabbit. *Bertoldo con Bertoldino e Cacasenno,* illustration facing p. 35.

As the mad beasts dashed for him, Bertoldo dropped the rabbit, which he had been concealing under his cloak. The two mastiffs, diverted by the little beast, took after him as he bounded away. He ran with the swiftness of a streak of lightning, and in time both the dogs and the rabbit were out of sight. Thereupon Bertoldo, in high spirits, proceeded to the queen's apartment.

Bowing before the queen, he asked her what she wanted of him, but angry because she had been outwitted she shouted: "Ah! So you are here, you ugly, murderous rogue! How impudent you are! You are like one of those apes that are only good to make children laugh!"

Bertoldo, however, knowing that there was nothing now that the queen could do to him, became quite insolent, and started to poke fun at the queen. "Look now who speaks! Gaze upon the beautiful Helen!" he cried, and continued in that tone, blurting offensive phrases. Finally he called the queen a harlot.

At that the queen's rage knew no bounds. She jumped to her feet and screamed at the top of her voice: "Die, you villain." She repeated this over and over with unabated fury, and finally added: "Will no one call the hangman and have this infamous rogue hanged and quartered? Oh, you impious scoundrel!"

Hearing her screams, her servants came running from every side to see what was happening. Some carried clubs, some brooms, and one carried a spear.

Bertoldo, figuring that the whole matter might take a turn for the worse, deemed it advisable to leave, so he ran off like the wind.

Chapter 4

THEME

To make Bertoldo bow before him, King Alboino had the top of the doorway that led to the throne room lowered. Bertoldo, however, to avoid bowing entered the room backward. A little later, the queen sends for Bertoldo. At first he was inclined to ignore the summons, but the king pleaded with him and he finally went. Thus again he found himself trapped by the wily queen.

THE MORAL OF THE TALE

Either from self-love or by force, the great wish to be adulated and worshipped by their subordinates. Often, however, even a peasant can humble the pride of the one who is haughty. Women are very vehement in anger, particularly when they are offended in their most delicate passions—vanity and pride.

The wise man never tells a secret to a woman. Women are too eager to chatter, too loquacious, and neither reason nor threats can hush them up.

In fact, if women were born mute, and unable to give vent to their feelings through speech, they would doubtless spout through some other part of their body, and some quite unbecoming discourses might be spurted out from under their skirts. If they could not refrain from opening the case that enclosed the bird sent to them at the instance of Bertoldo by the king, it is impossible to believe that they have brains enough to perform the duties incumbent upon magistrates.

Let a thousand benedictions rain upon the good Bertoldo, who saved his contemporaries as well as us from a great danger like the one described in the preceding tale.

We left our hero making ready to run, with the speed of an arrow shot from a bow, from the furious group of servants and of court damsels who were threatening him. As he emerged below, the queen, who had rushed to the window, hurled a chamber pot at his head. Bertoldo saw it coming, however, and threw himself to one side, dodging the missile. Then, with his rear turned in the queen's direction, he lifted one leg and let go a thunderous roar, which was quite unbecoming.

Queen Hypsicratea became furious with anger. "May a horn sprout on you!" she shouted. And all her retinue repeated: "A horn! A horn!"

Then the queen retired to her chambers to quietly ponder some way to have Bertoldo executed. During that whole day she fumed with rage, and there were some who feared it might impair her health. In fact, when King Alboino heard about it he sent her a gift of a couple of eggs.

I have read about all this in the municipal archives of Verona, in which city there is a museum that exhibits the mattress upon which Bertoldo died. I have also seen there a marble tablet upon which is inscribed, word for word, his last will and testament.

At first, I doubted whether all the curious things told about Bertoldo were true; but what I have seen makes it impossible for me to remain in doubt. Still preserved in Verona are Bertoldo's shoes, his belt, a black glove that belonged to his wife, who was named Marcolfa, and finally the drawers he wore when he was at the royal court of King Alboino.

How prudent were our forefathers! What fine habits, what laudable thoughts they had! Truly virtuous men were then held in high esteem. Those times were not like today, when ignorance and arrogance prevail. Then only the really great ones rose to fame; and even the garments of such learned men were religiously preserved.

But let us return to Bertoldo, who had begun to wonder whether it might not be wise to leave the royal court for good. He knew that sooner or later the women would find some way of striking back at him. Guessing his possible intention, King Alboino, who, after all, had a kind nature, gave orders to his major-domo to fetch the rogue, and induce him, with promises and flattery, to remain at the royal court.

The major-domo, to comply with the wishes of his lord, set out in search of the rogue and found him in the public square. He took Bertoldo aside and added his own entreaties to those of the king. He knew quite well what to say in order to convince Bertoldo, and, sure enough, that evening, the rogue returned to the royal palace.

When the king received news of Bertoldo's return, he immediately rose from his throne and went to see him. He embraced him affectionately, tenderly grasping him by the hand, and led him to the throne and made him sit at his side. Afterward, to give him even more proof of his friendship and good will, the king asked him: "Why, my dear Bertoldo, did you want to leave without even bidding me good-bye?"

The shrewd rascal, glib-tongued as always, replied with a very serious air: "My lord, the royal court not only burns the palate, but also spoils the taste. One who lives at it must always be in fear of sudden death, or at least landing in the hospital. The proverb says: 'Shadow of a courtier, hat of a lunatic,' which means unfortunate is he who confides in the great. He who goes to a dance and knows not how to dance will find himself in the way."

The king persisted: "You must stay with me. I want you at the royal court, and I want you to be my counselor in ruling my people. You should not have to fear the rifts at court; you have enough sense and foresight. You can be a strong pillar in upholding my throne, and I will protect you with paternal love. In you, my brother, I expect nothing except a little less rudeness, and manners a little more becoming. Education, which has honor as its companion and guide, makes man superior and different from brute animals. Without education reason cannot prevail. Without education every act of our lives would have much less meaning. Education is the most essential thing in this world, because it helps to do good."

"Oh, my king," replied Bertoldo, "forgive me, but I believe and will always believe that we should live on friendly terms with men. We are all made of the same mixture; we all come from the same bosom. And from what I have heard doctors say, we all alike are born between dung and urine. I do not believe that one can rise above the rank to which Providence has destined him, since all men, both nobles and plebeians, and all women, both great dames and charwomen, are made of dust and dung. Where do you think the great philosopher Plato and the poet Homer now are? Do you think I don't know? Both have returned to dust, and perhaps from the earth that contains their ashes some poor potter has already made a chamber pot. Who knows but that at this very moment some Greek may be hastily using it for his private purposes. Certainly ill-bred and uneducated is he who, full of vanity, envies the good of others; certainly misinformed and stupid is he who, ignorant and haughty, refuses to satisfy his creditors. Truly, glory, culture, and honor consist of performing good deeds. Furthermore, even though some are forced to nourish themselves with onions while others dine on partridge and quail, the same flesh covers the bones of us all."

The king replied: "This philosophy of yours is founded on sound principles, but it is a little antiquated. Today, the world demands that certain duties be performed and certain distinctions be observed among lord, friend, and servant. He who wants to be a noble knight and live up to the code of chivalry must realize that the wealthier is more elevated than he who begs for alms. And it is for this reason that, at the same time, he is the greatest and the most esteemed. Personally, however, I have a different viewpoint. I do not approve of these customs. The more elevated a man is, the greater should be his temperance and civility. I only say to you that when with me you should be a little better mannered; and I don't believe that I am too far wrong, for, after all, I am your lord. And for that reason, tomorrow, I will arrange things so that, to spite you, you shall bow before me."

Having said this, the king bade good night to the rogue, went to supper, and afterward retired. He tossed and turned in bed, however, and could scarcely sleep, so impatient was he for the next day to come so he could have more fun with the sharp Bertoldo. In fact, daylight had barely dawned when Alboino rose from bed with a new plan. He went to the throne room and took the door off its hinges. Then, by means of a crosspiece, boards, and nails, he made the entrance so low that even a man of the shortest stature could not pass through the opening without bowing his head. Alboino spent more than an hour performing the task.

Shortly afterward, Bertoldo reached court, and as soon as he saw the change in the doorway, he surmised the reason that had induced the king to make the alteration.

Bertoldo suddenly stopped and, for a minute, stood still, figuring what to do. Then, turning, he backed in, showing those within the throne room his rear instead of his face.

Upon seeing him come in backward, Alboino burst out into a boisterous laugh. Then he pretended to be vexed and shouted: "Oh, you monstrous rogue! Who taught you such manners?"

But Bertoldo at once replied: "They were taught to me by lobsters and crabs, when they were in the service of the mice, for the latter depended upon them and fought for them. If you wish to know the whole story, I will gladly tell it to you, since I remember it very well."

King Alboino, despite his long study of philosophy, had never heard this story told, asked Bertoldo to relate it to him, for he would gladly hear it.

And Bertoldo, after rubbing his nose with his fingers, began his narration, which he finished without interruption from the king; and, if I well remember, these were the words that Bertoldo used to tell the story: "In the days when beasts were exactly like men, and conducted themselves like men in doing their chores, that is, when animals spoke like us, and oxen and jackasses could be seen hanging around tribunals in starched collars and wrapped in rich togas, the king of the weasels, whose dominions extended beyond Morea, was the fortunate father of a very fair and most gentle daughter.

"The daughter of the king of the weasels was so beautiful that it could be said that Mother Nature never created an animal of greater comeliness than she. She had brilliant, soft, very fine hair; her eyes were round and of the color of chickpeas; her mouth was quite wide; her feet short and pleasing; and her tail bushy and black as pitch. She had two magnificent long mustaches. Some even claimed she was an hermaphrodite.

"Moreover, the daughter of the king of weasels had rare ingenuity. She was very erudite, and correctly wrote both prose and poetry. As an instructor she had had a donkey who had published a commentary on Demosthenes, and who spoke Latin, Arabic, and French. The chronicles, referring to the pupil of this learned donkey, mention a great scholarly work that possibly is still preserved in Egypt.

"The father loved his daughter very tenderly, and catered to all of her wishes. In his mind, he already had destined her for marriage with the king of the marmots, whose vast dominion extended eastward from his own kingdom. And in this proposed marriage, he was also spurred by the political expediency of having a successor for the throne of Morea, where the bold and restless weasels were manifesting republican and subversive ideas.

"Now, while negotiations for the marriage were being conducted, or, rather, after the accord had reached a stage where no obstacle could intervene, two greyhounds wearing boots hurriedly arrived at the royal palace. Led into the presence of the king and his court, the greyhounds stated that they had come in advance of the ambassador of the squirrels, who was coming to ask for an audience in connection with a matter of great urgency and importance.

"The king of the weasels climbed upon the throne, and in a stately manner wrapped himself in a mantle made of spider webs. Afterward, he had chestnuts and apples presented to the ambassador as a gift, and he commanded an attendant to ask if he cared for some turnip soup. Having done all this, and after having sprinkled the ambassador with salt and urine, the king of the weasels gave a signal and a tune began. At the end of it the squirrel snarled, showed his teeth three or four times, and began to speak thus: 'The august emperor of the squirrels, whose name is Myrmidon Buzzimelecco, lord of many kingdoms in Kolkata, builder of the Colosseum of Rome, by virtue of whose great skill and insuperable valor the infamous race of the horsefly was overwhelmed and terrified, through me, his great ambassador, asks your loyal friendship and faithful allegiance. When he passed through your kingdom to go to Holland, he had occasion to see your most beautiful daughter. Now, therefore, he is asking you to give this very daughter to him in marriage, feeling sure that you will do so most willingly. Should you refuse to lend a willing ear to this most fair request, pardon me, my dear king, but I have heard that he will come here and seize your fair daughter by force of arms.'

"The king of the weasels, in a tone that bespoke his full anger and scorn, answered the ambassador thus: 'I have destined my daughter for another suitor, and she shall ascend into a different bridal bed. Accustomed to scrupulously keeping my word, I am not in the habit of unsaying what I have promised. Let Myrmidon do what he pleases and likes. I am prepared for everything, and if he wants war, I will gladly fight.'

"So saying, and to give the ambassador further proof of his munificence, the king ordered that new gifts be brought to him. Immediately, as gifts to his excellency the ambassador, were presented two green scorpions, a white cockroach, seventy-six lice from Valencia, two small Indian pigs and a wild lizard. Note that in those days these beasts were the equivalent of such gifts today as lions, bears, tigers, panthers, and the like.

"After the ambassador returned to Kolkata, he reported the reply of the king of the weasels to his own sovereign. Imagine the anger of Myrmidon! He immediately ordered that all weasels in his kingdom, if there were any, be banished. Having declared war, he stated that he would have all the enemy's cities razed to the ground, particularly the capital of the weasels, which then was named Sparta, now Mystra, against which he wanted unforgettable vengeance. And without losing a minute of time, he sent couriers to the nearby sovereigns, who hastened to send large sums of money in gold and silver, provisions, arms, munitions, and soldiers. In Kolkata animals were armed in every respect, and often in strange and unusual ways.

"In a very short time more than six hundred thousand soldiers were under arms, without taking into account the battalions of cats, dogs, and rats. The knights of this immense army were the bucks, under whose orders were large numbers of other armed combatants. From flies, gnats, wasps, horseflies, and bees were formed various squadrons of flyers for the purpose of reconnoitering.

The outposts then, which were to begin the fight, were organized with a large number of lice, fleas, and other like and despised little animals.

"Still Myrmidon was not satisfied with all these preparations. Therefore, to devastate the cultivated fields of the weasels, from far-off Libya and from deserted Arabia he summoned about sixty thousand grasshoppers. For open field combat, where the need of skill to handle spear and sword is greatest, he selected monkeys, for these had already been exposed and were accustomed to the hardships of war. Even from far away Barbary he called the moles, which were very skilled in manipulating the bow, and born and created for the very purpose of boring tunnels.

"The generalissimo of this immense army, who in a previous war had lost a leg and one ear and had not taken a minute of rest, reviewed, company by company, the whole army, and decided to take the field. At his side was a large black rat who wore an old patched-up insignia, upon which was painted a nightingale with its beak up the rear part of its young.

"Near Sparta, the peak of a very high mountain rises. It is known by the name of Stymphalus. From one side springs a very thin jet of water, which plunges from ledge to ledge, glistening when hit by the rays of the sun. This jet of water is the source of the Alpheus River, which flows west of the cities of Tripoli and of Olympia, and eventually empties into the great River Eurotas.

"Leaving Kolkata after a month of forced marches, the army of the allies finally reached Stymphalus. Thereupon the general was immediately informed that the weasels, having entered the country, were planning to ambush him.

"Actually, all the bridges had been destroyed and the roads were well guarded and defended, so that it was impossible to penetrate into the enemy's territory. But the general of the squirrels was not discouraged, and, to explore the territory, sent two squadrons of flies to the opposite side of the river.

"With surprising speed and agility, these flies threw themselves against the spot where they had been ordered to attack and the place to which their own audacity led them; but they soon ran into nets that the spiders had built as a defense against them, so that the flies became snagged, and fell into the snare headlong.

"The weasels, armed to the teeth, rushed over with lightning speed and made a great slaughter of them. The poor flies attempted to defend themselves with the ferocity of despair, but their courage and audacity were of no avail, and the boldest ones, after being captured, were impaled in the Turkish manner.

"Out of seven thousand that participated in the attack, only one hundred were able to flee; at least, that is what the historians of the war affirm. And of those that did not perish, the weasels clipped their wings and led them into slavery.

"After this, to terrify the enemy still more, on the following day, within full view of the whole army of squirrels, the weasels devoured their prisoners alive, and about a thousand heads were raised high on the points of the weasels' spears.

"The few squadrons of flies that survived brought back to their own camp the alarming news of the great slaughter. To this information they added that the enemy continued to make great preparations for defense, that their troops were most innumerable, and that wolves, foxes, marmots, and other large beasts, whose infinite numbers joined with the weasels, had dug ditches everywhere, constructed causeways, and prepared every kind of attack.

"The general, who was an old soldier, did not lose heart as he heard the unhappy news, but remained fearless and undaunted in his place. He stood under a fig tree and swore to destroy even the name of the weasel race.

"After retiring under his tent, the general meditated upon the best way to successfully attack the enemy, and, what was more important, ways and means of crossing to the opposite side of the river. But to make sure not to commit errors, he called his staff together to discuss the plan of attack.

"Thus the great captains of the army met under the royal pavilion. They presented a stupendous spectacle, and it certainly was delightful to hear their discourses, follow their discussions, and admire their gestures, then ceremonies, and their ways.

"The great variety of arms and dress presented another magnificent spectacle. It seemed as though one were viewing a green pasture sprinkled with bowers of every form and color.

"For helmets some wore eggshells; some held branches of fennel to be used for spears; some were armored with the rind of a walnut. One was armed from head to foot; another only had his chest covered; a third had no other armor but his own head.

"Among so many, though, the one that appeared best of all was a louse. He had the stripes of a corporal and was armed with a boar spear and round shield. On his head he had a heavily powdered wig.

"As to garments, one wore a Roman costume, another a French, still another a Polish one. In one corner sat a mole, a native of Ancona; in another corner one could hear the cry of a Modenese grasshopper. A rat, born and raised in Bologna, gravely sat upon a mold of Parmigiano cheese, and so it went.

"All talked, all wanted to express their views; and because they could not agree, and all spoke at the same time, they made an infernal row.

"Now, while the army captains were gathered in council under the royal pavilion, discussing the plan for the great field battle, all at once outside of the tent came a roar, a devilish turmoil, cries of joy and cheers.

"What had happened? A very simple thing. A group of rabbits, having gone out to explore enemy positions, raided the outskirts of the enemy's camp and captured some prisoners, and they were coming to the generalissimo's tent.

"As a leader, the group had a pregnant pussy cat, famed for its bloody and valorous battles. The rabbit group led two heavily bound prisoners.

"These two prisoners were of a species entirely unknown in the camp; they had been surprised in the river and captured while they were winking at the daughter of a Tuscan frog.

"Suddenly the captains who sat in council under the pavilion, to which the two prisoners were being conducted, rose to their feet and surrounded them. They viewed them curiously, acting like a swarm of ants encircling a grain field at harvest time.

"Some thought the two prisoners were plebeians, some thought them knights; others, because of their faces and bearing, suspected them to be spies. The general of the squirrels, without losing any time, turned to them and rudely asked: 'I will have you skinned immediately unless you tell me who you are, where you came from, and where you are going.'

"'I am named Lobster,' replied the boldest of the two prisoners, 'and my companion is named Crab. Both of us were born in a swamp that reaches the ditch that surrounds the territory of Castelfranco. Both of us were in the business of selling spider webs, but, tired of such a trade, we decided to wear the black mantle, and, like others, become errant knights. We have been at Melfi, Thule, Tierra del Fuego, New Zealand. We passed through all of the cities of inner Asia, and everywhere we left traces of our unsurpassable valor. You, my lord, certainly remember the great war that was fought in Gothland between the grasshoppers and the gnats. Well, I am the one who, in a single night, slew more than a thousand gnats in a fish pond.'

"So saying, Lobster reached into the pocket of his trousers and pulled out a large number of documents, patents, and lists of addresses. From among these, he chose a document of very ancient date, written by the very hand of the king of the winds, Aeolus, and which greatly exalted Lobster.

"The general of the squirrels, having read the document over several times, became ceremonious and complimentary, exactly in the manner that courtiers usually do when they purchase something for which they have to pay nothing. Then he told Lobster and Crab: 'Lords, if you wish to remain with us and be assured of our love and gratitude, I will give you command of two battalions of grasshoppers who are most skilled in the handling of arms and well trained in the labors of war. In this way, in addition to the great favor you will render to our king, you are certain to see your talent rewarded, since, if we have the good fortune to gain victory over our enemies, the credit shall be all yours, the glory all your own.'

"Crab replied: 'We are ready to risk our lives for your king, and to shed our blood for him. The insults you have received from the weasels are well known to us, and we are aware of your longing for vengeance. We know this has caused you to take up arms. Furthermore, for us to go to the enemy camp, it will not be necessary to span the river with bridges because we know a shortcut that is more convenient, so much so that both of us will undertake to cross the river at midnight, unnoticed by the enemy. After we have reached the enemy's camp, we will spy on the flies, attempt to learn the number of forces at their disposal, and upon our return we will become your leaders in battle and in victory. Meanwhile, from the ford that you see down there, and which I am now indicating to you, we will freely and safely cross the river underwater. The only suggestion we give you is to keep yourselves in readiness to attack the enemy at our slightest signal. We will thus surprise the unsuspecting enemy.'

"And, in fact, as soon as the sun went down and nightfall came and great calm prevailed in the camp, the two warriors, without armor and without helmets, set forth for the river and went to the exact spot where they had decided to cross.

"When they reached midway, they stopped in the home of a lady frog who usually gave a free supper to her guests; then about midnight, following the course of the river and going along with the current, they reached the opposite bank.

"There they found deep ditches, high embankments, strong palisades, and war implements of all kinds. They also found a huge number of animals armed to the teeth. When they reached the enemy camp, no sentry moved, for the sentries were all asleep.

"Crab was by nature very shrewd, for he begged Lobster time and again to proceed with caution and to keep a good lookout; but Lobster was so stupid that, unaware, he proceeded directly to the pavilion of the weasels' generalissimo.

"The generalissimo was a large weasel, a native of Armenia, and a famous destroyer of pistachio nuts. More than once he had held back the Polish owls. When Lobster entered, he was seated upon the bare ground playing chess with a Sorian cat, while thirty-two blackbirds, six parrots, and twelve quails guarded his person.

"A Lombard quail, noticing Lobster entering the general's pavilion with so much ease, believed him to be a soldier, who, after getting drunk in a tavern, had come to commit an impertinence. So seizing a large pole, he let such a heavy blow fall upon the head of the unfortunate Lobster that the latter was stunned and after several kicks in the rear he threw him out of the pavilion and sent him tumbling into a ditch.

"Crab, who wisely kept hidden at a safe distance, witnessed the unhappy scene, and viewed with terror the heavy blow that had fallen upon the cranium of his ill-fated comrade. He ran to the ditch where his friend lay, and making then and there an albumen mixture from the whites of ants' eggs, he applied it to his back. And because he had some familiarity with medicine, he made an herb plaster to draw the pain from his head, and gave him an enema.

"When poor Lobster regained his senses, he began to think about his own affairs, and turning to his comrade said: 'My friend, if we return to the squirrels' camp, what will become of us after the promise we have given? On the other hand, if we stay here and are discovered, will they not hang us on some tree? Therefore, to avoid shame and even death, there is nothing for us to do but return to Bologna. Our greatest difficulty is that we must return home through unfamiliar and unknown places, so that we may travel in safety and without fear of being pursued.'

"The suggestion was agreeable to Crab, and they immediately took to the road and eventually had the good fortune to save themselves.

"From then on, to commemorate the fortunate escape, Lobster and Crab always walked backward. In fact, before they died they made a will, drawn by Mr. Zucca, the notary, under the dispositions of which their descendants were enjoined to walk backward, and even today they walk in that manner, that is, backward.

"The little story I have related to you, my king," concluded Bertoldo, "was written by Mr. Buonasperanza. From it you undoubtedly recognize the reason that impelled me to enter this hall by turning my back to you. When I saw the entrance altered, different from its usual and normal size, and afraid that a tempest of blows might fall upon me, to save my head I preferred to expose my rear."

With that, Bertoldo fell silent. Alboino appeared to be well pleased by the foolish story the rogue had told him, for Bertoldo probably related it better than I have done. So the king said to Bertoldo: "Bertoldo, please do me a favor. Finish the story, for I am curious to know the turn of events, and also what was the result of the war between the weasels and the squirrels."

As Bertoldo was about to comply with the king's wish and tell him the outcome of the war between the weasels and the squirrels, a kitchen servant came in haste, bringing a letter that Queen Hypsicratea had written with her own hand for her husband.

Alboino took the letter and rapidly glanced over it. Then turning to Bertoldo he said: "My dear Bertoldo, I am sorry to have to give you an unpleasant message, but there is nothing I can do! The queen has sent for you. You should feel at ease and go there, for apparently she is disposed to forgive and overlook the wrongs you have done to her. If you present yourself to her in a submissive and meek manner, you will find her to be considerate and kind. Last night, I discussed your case with her and took up your defense. She seemed to be persuaded of the reasonableness of your conduct. And then you should remember that the anger of women is not only quickly aroused, but it is also quickly spent at the slightest blast of the wind."

The rogue, somewhat disconcerted, replied: "A woman is a very unreasonable little animal with honey on her lips and a razor ready in hand. At the same time that she offers you bread, she lifts a stick to strike you. The queen does not want me for something small; she wants to see me dead, or at least thrown in prison. Listen, my king, he who is born of a cat or a wolf always thinks and dreams of a mouse or of a lamb grazing in the pasture. The anger of women never has respite; it is never extinguished. When you least expect it, it vents itself and strikes you. The very smile, the very pleasantries are feigned. He who takes the chance of walking with his eyes shut trips and falls. Furthermore, he who has a wolf as a godfather must always have a good mastiff at his side to follow him. But since you command it of me, I hasten to go to see Queen Hypsicratea."

After he had said this, Bertoldo left the hall. As he entered the room where the queen was, he observed her sprawled upon a divan embroidering a pair of taffeta trousers for her husband, Alboino.

As soon as the queen saw Bertoldo, she shouted: "Ah, ruffian, you have finally come into my grasp! Here he is, the great man destined by heaven to disgrace the female sex! Here is the one who enjoys making fun of me! Here is the sage mender of my advices to the sovereign! I don't know what holds me back, for with my own hands I would like to tear the heart right out of you! But from the example of the punishment I am going to mete out to you, others may learn how they should act toward me. Even the old fox falls into the noose, and the higher the place one falls from, the more his bones will be broken. Sometimes it happens that when a villain attempts to fell an old and knotty oak, he strikes his feet with the axe. The mariner who is unprovided with compass and charts faces the terrible might of the liquid element to his sorrow; and he who handles thorns or vermin gets pricked or infected. How much better it would have been for you to stay in the mountains to milk goats and deal with no one but beasts; they would have tolerated your bad manners, abuses, and offenses. But since you have had the audacity to come to this royal court, and to tangle with me, the Queen of the Lombards, I shall make you see what my indignation is capable of doing, so that you may learn, at your own expense, a great truth that you have forgotten, which is not to slur the great, my equals."

Bertoldo, even though actually quite impertinent and by no means tongue-tied, was unable to reply to the queen's diatribe. At first his face became as red as a boiled lobster, then, unable to contain himself, he bowed his head and motioned that he wished to say something. He purposely made the gesture so meek and acted so reverently that the queen felt obliged to give him permission to explain why he had acted as he had.

"Madam," said he, "it is very true that I am your humble servant, but you cannot deny that I am also the servant of King Alboino. I do not relish adulation, and I prefer always to tell the truth—that is, as it appears to me—so much so that, if the king willingly listens to me, it is precisely because I bow only to truth and to what is right. I am not a follower of that ancient proverb that says: 'Tie the ass where the owner wants.' I was in the royal court when the Veronese women made the foolish request to be allowed to take part in the king's council. My lord the king asked for my views, enjoining me to speak at once. I quickly replied that women have neither the ability nor the head to govern, since they must occupy themselves with the distaff, reel, and spindle, and try to cheer man's existence. I frankly admit that I was the one who gave him the case in which the bird was enclosed, so that he could send it to the women. I confess that it was this stratagem that thwarted their hopes; but you too, my queen, should grant me that if women were to take part in public life, dictate our laws, and at the same time do their domestic chores, indescribable confusion would result."

At this point the queen, interrupting Bertoldo, exclaimed: "You speak of the affronts you have done to me and do not realize who I am. And with such insolence, do you think you can receive forgiveness from my goodness? But doubt not. Shortly you will become aware of everything! I resign you to your unhappy fate, and, to make certain that I shall not see you again, I will have you put into a sack and thrown into the river."

As soon as the queen had pronounced these words, the whole court personnel, full of rage and fury, like dogs goaded by the hunter after a fox or a rabbit, set upon the unfortunate rogue.

Poor Bertoldo tried to defend himself, but the group was more powerful than he, so the poor devil was placed in the sack; and to make sure that he would not run away, the queen ordered a constable to guard him during the night.

She intended to have him drowned the next morning.

Chapter 5

THEME

Finding himself enclosed in a sack, Bertoldo wonders how he can extricate himself. In fact, he forms a scheme, and knows so well what to do and what to say that the constable assigned by the queen to guard him falls into the snare and agrees to take his place. Bertoldo then runs away from the royal palace of Alboino. The next morning, when the queen does not find Bertoldo in the sack, she orders the witless constable who had taken his place to be beaten and then thrown into the river.

Figure 24. Bertoldo in a sack. *Bertoldo con Bertoldino e Cacasenno,*
illustration facing p. 51.

THE MORAL OF THE TALE

The wise man who finds himself in danger either meets it with courage or escapes it by craft. It is an old custom at royal courts for one to save himself at the expense of others. Interest and impious love corrupt the prudence of men and expose them to very serious dangers.

Man tends quite naturally to act foolishly; he concerns himself only with the present and cares very little for the future. Usually he sails the high and stormy sea, while believing himself peacefully slumbering in the calm waters of a port. Only when danger is imminent, or, rather, to say it better, when he has actually fallen into a ditch, does he try to avoid his difficulties and begin to look for a way to safety, but he does not always find such a road.

This was the precise situation of Bertoldo, who, finding himself in the sack, began to think of a way by which he could save himself from imminent danger. But what was he to do? What clever plan, what scheme, could he devise to find his way out of that strange prison? How could he elude the vigilance of the mercenary guard, who carefully watched him? How was he to induce him to untie the cords that closed the sack? How could he persuade the guard to open the sack and permit him to go about his business?

A thousand ideas whirled through his head, but he did not know which to select, since all entailed great danger and innumerable risks.

By force of circumstances the hapless rogue was compelled to remain bagged in the sack. In this predicament and bemoaning the unwelcome fate which awaited him, he went so far as to envy the lot of little birds, who, though caged and deprived of their freedom, could at least stick their beaks through the openings of their place of confinement; while he, because of the solid burlap of the sack in which he was confined, could not even stick out the tip of his finger.

Usually constables are very shrewd, and perhaps the one that guarded him was more so than others, so that the unhappy Bertoldo felt he had reason to fear that an attempted flight would end with a noose around his neck. Despite all these dangers, however, it could succeed with a masterstroke, which he was then contemplating, for he was almost certain he could achieve his purpose. After some hesitation, he finally decided to take a chance.

Having made his decision, he began to wail aloud, as though he were talking to himself: "Oh, unjust and pilfering destiny! Look a bit on poor me! In what miserable state do I find myself! Why did I have the bad fortune of being born a knavish villain!" He slopped a moment and then continued: "Who would have ever dreamed that because I possess too much property the queen would have me put in this accursed sack! And for what reason? Why should I find myself in this condition, not even able to move as I would like? Because I am rich! And that is not enough, no, not enough! Against my will, and to spite me, they want to force me to take a wife! I who wanted to enjoy my fortune alone—a happy bachelor—to please the queen must keep a fair woman by my side! I take a wife—I who am uglier than Aesop! I take a beautiful wife—I that am crippled and deformed! Oh, no, it shall never be! I shall never commit such a folly! I shall never sign such a contract! I should do like a rat—gnaw the remains of others! Never! To do such a thing I would have to be mad! Oh, when the queen returns here, I shall know what to tell her. I do not feel like getting married—no, under no condition will I consent to become a cuckold with a lot of horns!"

The guard was listening to Bertoldo like a curious woman might when she overhears someone tattle about other people's affairs. And feigning pity for the painful anguish of which Bertoldo was wailing so much, the guard asked the unhappy rogue to tell him the cause of his predicament.

Thereupon the constable begged Bertoldo to tell him who he was, to disclose the incidents that had led to his imprisonment or the transgression he was expiating, and that had reduced him to such a miserable condition.

Bertoldo replied by saying that he was rich, that he received rents amounting to five or six thousand dollars per year, and that this was his only blemish.

"They wish," he continued, "that I take a wife, and I, on the other hand, do not want to marry. I will not be forced to get married. That is why I am now in this sack in your custody. The marriage they are trying to force me to enter into would be a blessing for another, but for me it suits my blood in no way whatever. My dear brother, I would willingly describe to you the one they are trying to give me in marriage, but for pity's sake let me out of this blessed sack for a moment! Truly, to be so curled up and crammed in a sack has cracked all my bones! But what does it matter to you if I am more or less in discomfort? Therefore do me this favor and I will tell you all—I will tell you exactly how things stand."

The constable longed to hear Bertoldo's story, and also to get a look at him. He replied: "Very well, I will open the sack and you may come out, but you must solemnly promise that as soon as you have finished your woeful and mournful story without being urged, you will re-enter the sack of your own accord, and will let me tie you inside, exactly as you are now."

"I promise all this to you," replied Bertoldo at once.

So the guard quickly untied the sack, opened it, took Bertoldo by the hand and helped him out. Then, with the aid of a small oil lamp, which the guard was accustomed to carry with him, he began to observe Bertoldo with great curiosity.

On seeing that horrible snout, that chest, that back, that face, it seemed as though the constable was then gazing upon a large ape that is shown to children in the Orient to frighten them.

"Might of the world!" exclaimed the stunned guard. "I did not believe I would ever see such a horrible snout! Has your fiancée seen you? Have you been to see her?"

"But it is for that very reason," answered Bertoldo, "that they have placed me in the sack! They intend to have us married while I am in this sack, before she has a chance to see me! They want her to take me blindly and know me only after our marriage. Then the poor girl will have to keep me exactly as I am, since it then would be too late to remedy the situation. And upon our marriage, by special grace of the queen, I will be given two thousand unclipped coins, a sum that she has promised the future husband of the girl. But I very well know that when the bride is pretty and the husband is ugly like me great risks are taken, and for this reason I want nothing to do with the large fortune that will rain upon me from heaven. I have made up my mind not to yield to the will of the queen, and no matter what happens I will keep my resolve."

"Look, look, what a beautiful youth would be embraced and kissed by a fair and delicate damsel!" the guard exclaimed: "And to such a poor girl should be given a snout so ugly? Poor women, to what a miserable condition you have come! You unhappy women are constrained to suffocate the throbs of your heart, to smother your taste and your desires, to follow in everything the will of your barbarous parents! Because he is rich, it does not matter whether he is fair or ugly, whether he pleases the one who must be his companion for life. What would it matter even if he were demented? The girl must marry him regardless—exactly as he is. As to myself, whenever I go for a walk, everyone avoids me as though I were a mad dog because I am poor. Just the same, I am in good health and I believe I am not too ugly! But no! Fortune favors him who has twisted and deformed arms and legs."

Bertoldo interrupted the guard to say: "If you wish, in one moment I can make you rich."

The other asked: "How can you do that? I don't see how you could do it."

"It would be enough." Bertoldo said, "that I give you my place, and that you get into the sack in my stead. I don't want to marry the girl, because I know only too well that I would run into many difficulties. In all this I am very determined, as I have already told you."

"But you, my dear, are mad," countered the guard. "Is this not true? Tomorrow morning the queen undoubtedly will come here, and, finding me in your place, the least she will do is to have me put in the pillory and whipped in the public square. No, my brother, I wish to take no such risk. I do not want to get myself in trouble of my own accord. All this would have serious consequences for me."

"Listen," added Bertoldo, becoming alarmed by the terrible fear that had seized him, "you can trust me and not get alarmed. After you have married the girl and she has seen you to be so fair, she will be more than glad to keep you, the plump dowry will be given to you, and you will then be rich. Your wealth will increase when death takes her father, because he is full of infirmities and not expected to live long. Therefore imagine that you will be related to a knight, which makes it unnecessary for you to continue to be a constable."

"No, no," insisted the guard. "You, my friend, get back into the sack. The matter is not as plain and as simple as you think."

"Think, boy," chided Bertoldo. "Follow a better counsel. You think, perhaps, that after the marriage has been celebrated the father will deny you his daughter? And do you believe that the queen, after the marriage is performed, will become indignant and refuse to make the payment? You may feel reassured that she will disburse the dowry, counting the two thousand coins one upon the other. By nature the queen is quite generous, and she will not fail to keep her word. As to the prospective bride, who in reality is a good girl, she will be most happy when she learns about the exchange of bridegrooms. Fortune, my friend, passes, but it does not abide. If you do not catch it by the hair while you have a chance, it flies away never to return. And then I, at the risk of renouncing the crown of Lombardy, if it were offered to me, would never want to beguile you and to tell you a lie. You will go to happily stay in the home of the bride, where, if you wish, they will address you as 'your excellency.' Today, such a title is very common, nor do you need much to acquire it. It is enough that one be rich, or at least have the appearance of being wealthy. Your life will run along happily and smoothly. Therefore decide once and for all—have no fear of anything! Put yourself in the sack, and even before tomorrow you will know whether I counseled you wrong, or if I have spoken with sincerity and for your own good."

The constable, after having reflected a little, resumed: "You have explained things so well to me and have shown the matter to be so simple that I have almost decided to take a chance. Who knows but that a great fortune may be in store for me—a poor man! He who wishes to eat chestnuts must take the trouble of removing the shell, and he who does not risk cannot munch."

Bertoldo, happy of heart, noticed that the mouse was about to be caught in the trap. And to reassure the guard, he pretended no longer to be interested in the proposal he had made.

"He who knows how to take advantage of the opportunity that presents itself," murmured the sharp rogue, "must pull his own hair and say: 'It was my own fault!' I have no desire to babble unnecessarily. Open the sack and put me back into it. I want to get back to my place again."

"Wait a minute," said the guard. "There is still time. Why all this haste?"

And Bertoldo in return said: "I no longer want to stay out. He who has time must not wait for time. Why should it be necessary to wait for hours to make a decision of this kind? The more I go through life, the more I am forced to realize the truth of that proverb that says: 'He who washes the donkey's head, wastes labor, water, and soap.'"

"Wait, wait, my brother," replied the guard. "I am determined to enter the sack at once. I am convinced that you are really fond of me."

"Ah! I am no longer the man I was before!" Bertoldo interrupted. "In vain you now ask me for what I no longer wish to give you. Begone, for I no longer want to listen to you.

"Ah, for pity's sake!" exclaimed the guard. "I ask it of you as a favor. Permit me to get into the sack and be closed into it in your stead!"

Bertoldo leaped for joy, but still pretending indifference he added: "Oh, I have too soft a heart and I like you very much. If to all this you add the horror that the marriage inspires in me, you undoubtedly will understand why I am still disposed to favor you. Now be quick and try to make no noise. I will hold the sack and you can get into it very quietly. It seems to me that this is no time for unnecessary idle talk. So pull this other arm inside and bend your head."

"Oh, my!" the guard cried. "You want me to ruin my face! You will make a monster out of me!"

"Be brave, be brave," repeated Bertoldo. "There is no other way, for your height keeps me from tying the sack properly. You are much taller than I am, and for this reason you should curl a little more than I would have to do." So saying, Bertoldo worked hard and lost no time to securely tie the sack, and to prevent it from opening through internal strain he unlaced his stocking and removed a strong hempen cord. With this cord he again carefully tied the sack and made four or five knots, one over the other, to really make certain it would not become untied.

Furthermore, the sly Bertoldo had the foresight to remove the dagger from the guard, which the latter carried in a scabbard hung on his belt, for in those days guards carried no arquebus, as they were not yet in use, and anyway under severe penalties, a royal decree forbade the use of arms to guards.

Bertoldo therefore hid the dagger in a certain place and later used it for a purpose, as we shall shortly see, that the guard could have never imagined.

When Bertoldo had made sure that the guard could not move, and was in helpless position, he asked him: "Well, are you comfortable?"

"So, so," replied the hapless guard. "But to stand this way without being able to lean on something is very uncomfortable. Bring me close to the wall so that I may more comfortably wait for the bride's coming."

C. 5 Quadri f.

Figure 25. Bertoldo puts the constable in a sack. *Bertoldo con Bertoldino e Cacasenno*, illustration facing p. 73.

Thereupon Bertoldo lifted him and, to amuse himself, carried him around the room for a while. Then he set the sack down against the wall. "Now keep still," he said. "Do not even breathe. The bride will soon come."

Said the guard: "Leave it to me. I want the bride and with her the dowry."

"I must leave," said Bertoldo. "Here they usually rise early. I would like to go out before someone awakens." And bidding the guard good night, he put out the oil lamp and got ready to leave the palace.

Let us for a moment leave the guard in the sack, dreaming about his future, and follow Bertoldo, faced by the necessity of getting out of the royal palace, and see how he managed it.

Bertoldo knew the passage in the apartment where he stood, and also the habits of those who occupied the various rooms. Furthermore, he knew that the queen slept in a nearby chamber. Therefore he quietly walked to the door, put his ear against the keyhole, and listened to make sure that the queen slept.

Hearing no noise, he opened the door and on tiptoe entered the room. He moved about so lightly that not even the dust under his feet left a trace of his being there. In fact, he walked so lightly that it seemed as if he were stepping on eggs and was afraid to crush them.

He would take a couple of steps and then stop, to make sure nothing had stirred. He would then quietly advance, making no noise whatever. He was even afraid that his bones might crack.

He kept his ears wide open for fear that the queen might stir. Gradually he became convinced that she slept soundly, and it was improbable that she would awaken, for she snored like a dormouse.

On the opposite side of the room, in the darkest corner, was a very magnificent alcove, in which was a luxurious bed upon which slumbered Queen Hypsicratea. Rich and graceful curtains kept the sunrays from penetrating the room. A gorgeous crimson velvet canopy, splendid for its gold ornamentation, decorated the bed. Under that canopy rested Her Majesty Queen Hypsicratea.

Assured that the queen slept soundly, the depraved Bertoldo conceived the idea of taking the silk gown that she was accustomed to wear. This gown, the use of which went back to remote times, had been discarded for a time and then brought back in vogue in France and thence transmitted to our own days. It was very roomy, since its ample folds were designed to submerge the deformities of the body.

Bertoldo, with his arms projecting forward, very quietly felt his way toward the bed. He put aside the curtain and then attempted to reach for the gown. After a few trials, he finally touched it with his fingers. Thereupon he managed to grab it, and carefully and slowly pulled it toward him. After some anxiety, he finally succeeded in removing it from the queen.

After this, he withdrew from the alcove and dressed himself in the gown.

In the room next to the queen's chamber slept an old hag, with thin hair, bearded chin, pale cheeks, and bleary eyes. Irritable, mean, and suspicious, this old woman did nothing but rave continually from morning to night, and she was so unpleasant that not even the other servants could tolerate her, though she was held in high esteem by the queen and occupied a position of trust.

This horrible old hag had charge of the keys of the royal apartment, and at night she was accustomed to hang these on a nail near the head of her bed. She also had charge of closing all the doors at night; and in addition she had another task, most common among women of her own age who, no longer able to indulge in the pleasures of love, found pleasure in arousing the passions of young women.

After he left the queen's chamber and entered the old woman's room, Bertoldo went straight to the head of the bed and took the bunch of keys, which gave him the means of opening all the other doors and thus escape.

While in the old hag's room be went around leisurely and without taking many precautions, because he knew the old woman was as deaf as a haddock. He also knew that she hated him to death and would not let any opportunity pass to do him harm. So he conceived the idea of avenging himself and playing a trick upon her.

Taking the dagger he had removed from the witless guard, be grabbed her chamber pot from under her bed and punched a hole in the bottom of it, in a way that, when used for its proper purpose, the liquid would run out and wet her mattress.

As he was about to cross the threshold, the old hag, apparently in a dream, said, "Eight." At first Bertoldo thought she was dreaming about playing some game, but then, hearing her utter two other numbers, twenty-eight and seven, he understood what it meant. He knew the old woman was in the habit of playing the lottery, and in the evening, before retiring, she would place a list of numbers under her pillow, as lottery players often do.

What was that sly and spiteful rogue up to?

He reached for a piece of charcoal in the bed-warming pan, and, going over to the wall, wrote the figure four, which resembled the snout of a hog.

If something similar should happen today, and a woman awakened to find a number written on the wall without knowing who had placed it there, she, according to present-day custom, would first consult a dream book. Then, I can assure you, a woman would even pledge her own bed to raise the money to play such a number.

Meanwhile, Bertoldo, wearing the queen's robe, left the old woman's room and walked through the royal apartment with no interference from anyone, and finally left the royal palace.

It was just before daybreak, and it was very cold. During the night snow had fallen and the ground was white. At first, Bertoldo paid attention to nothing, so intent was he in fleeing from the royal palace of Alboino. But he had not gone far before he had to admit to himself that he was in an embarrassing situation.

He said to himself: "And now what am I to do! On the snow they will see the imprint of my feet. Ah! Now I have it! I will put on my shoes backward, so the impression will look as if I passed going to the royal palace, not away from it." And by this trick he solved his difficulty.

In the meantime, while Bertoldo was on his way from the royal palace, dawn had begun to spread its pale wings, or, rather, its face was suffused with the blush of shame, for it felt compelled to confess that it had remained a little too long in bed, enveloped in the arms of its lover. The sun was already high above the horizon, when Queen Hypsicratea left the soft, sweet comfort of her bed to put on her robe.

That was a happy age. It was the custom to make night out of night and day out of day. Nor did the people believe that their reputations would suffer if at night they went to bed to sleep and during the day did their public and private chores.

But search here and search there, frisk in one place and frisk in another, the queen could not find her robe. She could not remember where she had left it. She asked her damsels, but none of them knew anything about it.

Who could have stolen it? There was no doubt. The thief could be no one but the guard, who, in the next room, supposedly was standing watch over the sacked Bertoldo.

Actually it was a rash suspicion, but women reflect very little!

The queen put on another dress, and went to the room, where the previous evening, she had left the guard outside and Bertoldo inside the sack. Not finding the guard she became more convinced than ever that he had stolen the robe, and she began to rage with indignation, making great oaths, and swearing upon the crest of her husband's helmet, the powerful King of the Lombards, that she would avenge herself.

Actually she got so mad that she bit her fingers. Then approaching the sack and figuring that she was talking to Bertoldo she said: "Very well, gallant. Do you have any more ravings in your bead?"

"No, madam," answered the guard. "I will maintain a behavior that is becoming, and I will never refuse to take what may be profitable to me."

"Take? Take what?" exclaimed the amazed queen. "Do you want to take some kind of a physic? Wait a second. I will give you the medicine!"

"I shall be very glad to take it," answered the unsuspecting guard. "Have it brought to me and I shall be very grateful to you."

Said the queen: "You can enjoy it very peacefully, for right now I will have you taken where it can be given to you."

"How is this?" exclaimed the guard. "Is it not here that she should come? Here the marriage is to be celebrated, and here, as a consequence, they are to disburse the dowry."

The queen was most surprised and amazed. She kept still for a moment, then continued: "I want to know what's new here and what all this means. Take this beast out of the sack, that I might see him."

The queen was promptly obeyed. The sack was emptied, and the prank was discovered. Thereupon the queen shouted: "That accursed villain has done it to me!"

And at this last outrage she could not suppress an outburst of terrible rage.

When a woman is infuriated she has no self-control; her fury runs amok. Seeing herself so humiliated, Queen Hypsicratea's determination to be revenged had no limits.

Her blood once more boiled so hotly that she suffered a rupture in her side, making it necessary for her to have a special brace made.

"'Right now," she finally cried, "take this miserable dupe and club him well; then put him back in the sack and immediately throw him into the river. I want him to die, do you understand? This is my irrevocable decision, and no one will dare, I hope, to contradict me!"

And the command of the queen was carried out; the constable was clubbed, sacked, and thrown into the Adige River.

Poor guard, to have the misfortune of falling into the hands of an enraged woman when he least expected it, instead of enjoying the smiles a pretty bride should shower upon him, and then to come to his death.

Should one therefore trust in the promises of a depraved rogue? Who is not unfamiliar with the old proverb: "Should you trust a villain to the same extent that you trust a mortal enemy?"

Upon my honor, in those days Bertoldo could not have escaped alive. Today, constables are different. Now they are cautious, shrewd, impertinent, haughty, deceitful, and inclined to be overbearing and oppressive in every way.

But in the days when Alboino reigned in Italy and when the event I have just related came to pass, conditions were different, and Bertoldo was able to profit at the expense of the witless guard.

The infuriated Queen Hypsicratea scurried about the royal palace like one possessed by a demon.

The greatest part of that day was used in a vain search for Bertoldo. Bertoldo had disappeared, and no one was able to guess where he could have taken refuge.

Chapter 6

THEME

King Alboino, having at last found Bertoldo secreted in an oven, commands that he be immediately hanged; but yielding to the rogue's entreaties, the king grants him the privilege of picking his own tree to hang from. Afterward, Bertoldo states that he likes no tree, and the king, admiring his wit, forgives him. Thereupon the king chooses him as one of his most trusted counselors. But before long, he contracts a serious illness and poor Bertoldo dies. However, before he dies Bertoldo makes his will. After his death he is given a decent and honorable burial.

THE MORAL OF THE TALE

While it is within our power to forestall misfortune, foolish indeed is he who blindly runs headlong into it. Though we have much to choose from, passion often leads us into pitfalls that will invariably torment our soul and punish our body. He who dies after birth indeed dies a glorious death. A good Christian and a wise man is usually prepared for the final call. A sage man should strive to make himself useful to his fellow man through good examples and teachings he leaves behind.

When a skilled artist wants to paint a picture of death, he portrays a scene of wretchedness, full of anguish and grief. In such a scene he usually tries to convey the idea of a throng of frantic and excited people struck by the gloomy idea of imminent death. He wishes to reproduce something somber, frightful, gloomy, unreal, or even ghoulish. To accomplish his purpose, he may paint the figure of a sordid and mean old hag in her most natural and realistic aspect.

And truly, so far as I can think of it, in the whole world there is no uglier figure than that of an old woman. In fact, it appears to me that one should be more frightened of an old hag than by a cannon or a streak of lightning.

If an old woman is able to learn something about others she immediately runs to bear the tale, whether others wish to know it or not. Quite often such gossip brings more harm to a lover than a storm brings to a small and fragile vessel.

C. 6   *Quadri f.*

Figure 26. Bertoldo, wearing the queen's robe, hides in an oven.
Bertoldo con Bertoldino e Cacasenno, illustration facing p. 89.

Through the evildoing of these accursed old hags, Bertoldo was on the verge of being hanged, and, if he should escape the terrible fate that attended him, it would be due to a special grace that not everyone could have received.

In the last tale you read how a witless guard, by order of Queen Hypsicratea, was cast into the river. That poor devil, imprisoned in the sack, could in no way save himself and he perished.

The guard certainly had no desire to drown. Equally certain was the fact that he had done nothing to deserve to be put to death. But whether he wished it or not, whether he was at fault or not, meant nothing, for he had to resign himself to his fate and be drowned in the waters of the Adige.

Without describing it, you can easily imagine the uproar, the chatter, and the foolish clamor that arose in the royal palace when the theft of the robe was discovered. It is enough to say that the queen had only that one robe and that day, being a holiday, she was to wear it.

At first, the queen, as we have said, suspected the guard; but she soon surmised who the real thief was. Certainly it could be no one but Bertoldo, so she unleashed about a hundred guards to track him down and to bring him back in any condition—alive or dead.

The guards sought him everywhere, took great pains, and spent the whole day on their assignment. Their efforts were in vain, however. Bertoldo had secreted himself in an oven, where he lay low until the search was abandoned.

One can imagine the queen's rage during that day! She was so frantic that she plucked out her hair and bit her fingers. She shrieked and shouted, so impatient was she to have Bertoldo in her power. Snorting like a bull and gritting her teeth, she fumed. "Never again shall I be called queen, and may my whole progeny be accursed, if I don't have him hanged by the neck!"

Throughout the entire city people talked of nothing but the disappearance of Bertoldo and of the mean joke he had played on Queen Hypsicratea. The gist of the talk went like this: "Let him be as clever as he can be, this time Bertoldo will not escape. This time he has figured wrong and will pay dear for it. True, Bertoldo is clever and very shrewd, but there have been others just as clever and just as shrewd who ended by falling into a trap and paying for all their sins at one time."

Bertoldo, in the oven, had his ears perked. He heard these words repeated by people walking on the street near where he lay, and he was forced to admit to himself that their remarks were correct. Furthermore, he realized that some terrible doom was being prepared for him. And it is not difficult to imagine how terrified the poor devil was. It did not suit his blood to be hanged. He was as much of an enemy to the gallows as any other good Christian.

However, he was determined not to move out of the oven, even though he might starve to death. He preferred that kind of a death rather than one on the gallows. The hangman inspired in him too much aversion and too much horror. And if one considers that Bertoldo had such a good stomach that, for lack of other food, he even could have digested stones, his determination was really heroic, so much so as to overshadow the heroism of any ancient Roman.

But the poor rogue had made his calculations without those ugly and horrid old hags of whom we have spoken above, and one old wench, noticing the hem of the robe projecting out of the oven door, and spurred by the curiosity innate in all women of her ilk, quietly came closer to inspect it. When she recognized the color of the drapery, she began to shout at the top of her voice: "Oh, my! The queen is in here!"

In an instant a throng of women gathered in front of the oven. All those strumpets also looked at the protruding hem of the robe, and like the first wench they kept repeating in low voices: "Yes, it's the queen. It can be no one but her!"

Meanwhile Bertoldo kept silent and motionless, like an abbess at dinner, but his mind was actively considering what the women would do to him if they discovered him. But no matter how he racked his brain, he could figure no solution for his predicament, aside from realizing that he would be sent to the gallows, and from this terrible fate there seemed to be no escape.

Finally the news of the discovery reached the ears of King Alboino, who became very shocked when he heard that the queen had been found in such a strange hiding place. The poor king was sad and worried, and shook from head to foot, but as he began to recover from the shock he exclaimed: "That scoundrel has now committed too many rogueries! And if he is really responsible for this knavery, I swear to God that it shall be his last. Woe, woe unto him!"

Before doing any other thing, and without taking any resolve, he first went into the queen's apartment to learn whether she had left the royal palace. There be found her in her private room in the act of satisfying one of her bodily needs.

"I am truly happy to find you," said Alboino, "but I do not wish that my royal presence be embarrassing to you. Proceed with your purposes, or, rather, pretend you are alone and I am not here."

Queen Hypsicratea, blushing and with her head bowed, replied: "Since you permit it, my lord, I will continue to relieve myself of the discomfort."

So saying, and while she became red of face because of the severe griping she was forced to register, an irritating and thunderous sound was heard.

"What now!" cried the sad Alboino. "This really grieves me. Now I realize you must have great pains, for I just heard you do something I have never heard from you before! Be at ease, my dear," he continued, "otherwise you may die."

Said the queen: "Oh, how great, my lord, is your generosity! If you only knew how enraged I am with that rascal and wicked Bertoldo! He has committed a very great offense—very great. Certainly he could not have done me a greater wrong. That infamous villain has taken my silk robe, the one you gave me as a gift on our marriage day. You know how beautiful it is, how rich, how fine a texture, how splendid and gorgeous its colors. When I became aware that I'd been robbed, I got so angry and excited that I became sick. I have such acute pains in the abdomen that I am forced to sit here, as you see. If I was compelled to do an unbecoming thing, what can I do? Am I to blame? You should punish the horrid rascal as he deserves. You should make an example of him. If necessary, do not hesitate to put him to death."

The king quickly replied: "My angel, feel at ease. I shall think about it! Leave it to me. Now I understand what has happened. But I will make him pay a price for his temerity, and he shall pay through the hand of the hangman. Let him escape, let him hide. I will know how to get him out of his den, even if he has hidden himself below the equinox, or has already reached the moon. Regardless of what he may do, I assure you he shall not escape my indignation and the avenging sword of justice."

Having said these things, the king left Queen Hypsicratea's apartment and ordered that a large number of troops, or, as some claim, several groups of guards be assembled. Truly, Alboino's soldiers preferred to have their bellies for figs rather than face the dangers and risks of war; but the king gave them encouragement and aroused their enthusiasm with these words: "Come, come. Do not tremble, rabble! We are not going to the siege of Oran, but to assault an oven to capture a man."

King Alboino, armed in every respect, walked at the head of his army. He led his men directly to the oven, where he thought Bertoldo had taken refuge. Nor was he wrong, for it can truly be said that his inspiration came from heaven. The trembling throng of soldiers followed him, for they did not know as yet what fate awaited them.

After a march of several hours, Alboino and his men finally reached the oven in which the terrified villain was hidden. "Here, we have arrived!" shouted the proud king. "Here is the oven!"

A guard, bolder than the rest, rushed forward and the others followed him. The oven was opened, and Bertoldo appeared to their view. He stood crouched deep in the oven, wrapped in the queen's robe.

The poor man made no movement of any kind. He was as still as an owl cuddled in its own feathers, a bird he resembled in many ways.

All of a sudden the throng of guards precipitated themselves upon Bertoldo and forcibly pulled him out of the oven. Some dragged him by the feet, some by the arms.

Even King Alboino took part in the hunt, roaring and swaggering like the rest.

The king shouted with all his might: "Now, courage, sons! But be very careful not to tear and damage the robe, for I would like to bring it back intact to my wife! I don't care if it is dirty and soiled; but I do not want to see it torn. You understand me, do you not?"

Then turning to Bertoldo, in an infuriated voice he said: "So, rogue! Finally you have fallen into my hands, you thievish villain. Had I not decided to send you to the gallows, this would be the very last moment of your life, for I would slay you with my own hands! There is no excuse for the offense you have committed, and it cannot be forgiven. In vain you will seek mercy. I will be deaf to your prayers. Very shortly you shall see what King Alboino is capable of doing."

Thereupon he ordered that the queen's robe be removed from him.

As soon as his order was carried out, Alboino continued: "Now let's finish it! There, my knights, hurry. Take and bind him as securely as possible. This accursed baboon has already committed too many wrongs. He is a blot upon the honor of myself and of my august spouse. He would make the most docile man lose his patience. After you have bound him well, turn him over to the hangman, and tell him for me to hang him immediately."

"Go slow!" cried Bertoldo. "Go slow, my lord. It seems that you are too much in a hurry. Does it seem right to you to hang a poor Christian on the spur of the moment, while he is still standing on his two feet? It would not be so bad if they were to cut off my hands, a foot, a leg, or an arm. Perhaps that I could understand. But to have me hanged so quickly—does it seem right to you? I would really be a madman fit for the madhouse if I permitted you to do it. I think I have explained myself clearly enough."

"Listen! Listen to this rogue!" roared the angry king. "It seems that he still likes to dupe me. Ah, my dear, this time you will have little to say, but much to do—nothing will avail to save your life." Thereupon Bertoldo, as a clever man who is aware of his own power, showed himself to be hurt and started to cry. He began to make nasty faces and to recite bad verses, in imitation of a sibyl. While so acting, the rogue appeared uglier than usual.

When Alboino saw him in such a miserable state, he took pity on him. Actually he had the queer notion to laugh, but he contained himself to not appear foolish to those around him.

Finally, being unable to restrain himself any longer, the king decided to leave. Before departing, however, he ordered one of his barons to keep a close watch over the rogue and not to let him escape.

"I want to show I am merciful," the king stated. "It is finished. I believe they will hang him tomorrow morning."

Meanwhile, Bertoldo was thrown in prison. He was treated none too gently. He passed a very uncomfortable night, unable to close his eyes even for a single instant.

The poor man was in despair. It was worse than if he were dying of thirst or hunger. Actually it was really a miracle that he did not lose his head or dash it against the prison walls.

"Yes, it is quite true," he kept saying to himself. "One must stay away from royal palaces, because you can expect from them nothing but trouble of all kinds."

And because he was to be hanged the next day, one can easily imagine why during the night he could not sleep. However, as the hour of his doom approached, Bertoldo's wits grew sharper, so that his head felt like a whirlpool. Yet he still could figure out no way to escape from his predicament.

The next morning, meek and full of tears, he turned to a knight of Alboino's court, and with joined hands and as a favor asked him to arrange a talk with the king. He urged the knight to hurry, for time was running out and hangmen do not wait. This hangman was in the habit of doing his work expeditiously. And Bertoldo realized that after they had hanged him he would have no further need of the king, nor of his reply.

Poor Bertoldo! The time has really come now to show whether you studied philosophy to good purpose, particularly the kind that is known as moral philosophy!

This world is certainly like a latrine, the stench of which compels us poor mortals to block our nostrils to keep from being overpowered by the unwholesome odor. Yet even though Bertoldo knew these things, he could not reconcile himself to leave the world, since he who is born in filth rolls in it quite freely, and in so doing feels no degradation whatever.

(Up, comrade! Be cheerful! Have courage! Cities, kingdoms fall. Cows, horses, asses, pigs die! And you, don't you want to die? Come, let them hang you like a good man. Don't get angry over this! Let them kill you—do it as a favor to me! For how can you escape your doom? Come, convince yourself. It is only a matter of a minute. You will be glad when it's all over!)

Meanwhile, the knight whom Bertoldo had sent to King Alboino, having performed his errand, returned. To Bertoldo's questions the knight replied that he had rushed to the royal palace, and Alboino, upon receiving the message, had ordered that the rogue be brought to him at once. The king was waiting in the kitchen. Bertoldo immediately put on his trousers, washed his face, combed his hair, and attempted to make himself presentable. Then panting, groaning, and crying, he rushed to the palace, where he found Alboino sitting among his scullions.

Bertoldo threw himself on his knees before the monarch and implored: "Sire, I am a traitor. If you have me hanged you have every reason in this world. But I am convinced that I am receiving too great an honor. I did not expect such great distinction. Do not believe that I now want to preach to you and gain forgiveness for my misdoings. No! I know I must die, and I have resigned myself to my fate. Sire, it is in other ways that I want to put your clemency to a test. Oh, my lord, I have offended Your Majesty so much that I am sorry, as you can well imagine! I am not afraid to die; I regret only to lose my honor. As you know, when honor is lost it is never regained. Actually what grieves me most is a thing that I do not well understand. What concerns me is the type of death to which you condemn me. Now I believe that a man who is about to die shall not be denied his last request before death. Often I have seen poor hanged men swinging from the limbs of certain nasty, deformed, leafless trees, which the wind rattles like canes, and to myself I have said: 'Poor devils!' I felt sorry for those unfortunate persons. To me it seemed an honor to be hanged from a large, well-formed, lovely leafy tree. Sire, I am more than glad, in fact, very glad to die this very day by the hand of the executioner, but, I repeat, I cannot be denied a last favor as a condemned man. I have shown you I have no fear of dying, rather, I wish to die to atone for the guilt of my innumerable misdoings. But, by God, if it has finally been determined that I must go to the other world, I believe I have the right to go there in a way that pleases me. In one word, I ask you to let me pick out my own tree. If I am given this privilege, I offer no resistance. I will not even breathe. Let them concern themselves with performing their duty, since, if the noose breaks, I will quickly die like a lamb."

The king replied: "Let it be! I want to satisfy this caprice of yours. You shall have the privilege of picking the tree you choose to be hanged from. After that I hope you will have no occasion to again complain of my way of dispensing justice. Believe me, Bertoldo, I am sorry, but this time you must have patience and resign yourself to your doom."

Bertoldo was one of those old foxes that know how to break into every chicken coop; and the king, who believed Bertoldo and granted him the favor he asked, was really a dolt. And even though it displeases me to speak thus of a king, yet I am forced to defend the assertion against everything and everyone.

Meanwhile the guards got ready to hang Bertoldo. The rogue was therefore bound and led away; but by this time he entertained no fear whatever.

The guards had no idea of the trick he had in mind. For this reason, Bertoldo pretended to be sad and disturbed, and mumbled prayers.

From time to time he lifted his eyes to the sky and exclaimed: "Yes, it's quite true. I have committed great sins, but I believe the Lord will forgive not my body, which is good only to enrich the soil so that watermelons may grow, but my soul, which is destined to go to heaven and fears neither prison, noose, iron, ax, nor executioner, for the soul cannot be hanged."

By this time the guards leading Bertoldo had reached a very dense forest, full of charming trees which, spreading their leafy branches above the ground, kept the sun's rays from penetrating the paths below, where in the summer one could enjoy heavenly coolness. While there, Bertoldo said: "My friends, quite well I realize that you would like to hang me here. I too confess that this is a very delightful place. The atmosphere is good, temperate, and very cool, but if a little obstacle were not in the way the idea would be good. To speak frankly, I see no tree here that I like. Do not think I am so dull as to keep you waiting. God forbid! If I hesitate to pick the tree, it is only because I do not want people to laugh at me. For whoever would pass along this path and see me hanging from one of these trees certainly might say: 'Look at that lazy rogue who had himself hanged like a fool, or like the last dirty rascal!'"

The guards were forced to lead him still farther into the forest, but while wandering here and wandering there, Bertoldo kept repeating the same thing—no tree suited him.

Finally the guards began to lose patience. Meanwhile Bertoldo comforted and consoled them, saying: "Please be not angry, my friends, for I have already promised to die today. Find a tree that pleases me and then hang me, for this will relieve you of your trouble."

After they had tramped through the forest for a long time, the guards realized they had something difficult to deal with, and became convinced that the rogue was not only duping them, but he was also fooling the king, who by this time had given proof of being an idiot, while Bertoldo revealed that he possessed the keenness and shrewdness of a superior genius.

Therefore the hangman and the guards decided to go back to the royal palace to inform the king of what had happened. They felt that if the king persisted in allowing Bertoldo to pick his own tree, he could at least order them to return to their own homes, for they realized that Bertoldo wanted no part of the hanging.

And the guards did exactly what they had decided to do; they informed the king of the occurrence in all its minute particulars. Alboino became confused and found it difficult to conceal his embarrassment.

Under the circumstances and to avoid humiliation, the king was forced to seize upon the only expedient left to him, and forgive and pardon Bertoldo. To accomplish this, he ordered Bertoldo to be brought to him at once. And this was done.

The next day, Bertoldo, shackled and bound with strong cords, reached the court. The king had him quickly unbound, and then cried: "Hurrah, hurrah, my dear Bertoldo! May you be blessed! You have shown yourself to be a genius. Your intellect is greater than that of any other man. Even Aristotle, had he found himself in your situation, would have been unable to save himself from the predicament and escape from the talons of the executioner. And to show that I have taken no offense at the joke you were able to play on me, and make an idiot out of me, I not only pardon you, but also wish you to remain at court among my most intimate servants. You shall have bread, wine, oil, salt, and whatever you may need. It is my intention, in short, to have you treated as you deserve, that is, as a great lord. I believe this offer, since it is not made as a ceremonial gesture but as something which comes straight from the heart, you should consider."

Bertoldo, thanking the king, declined the offer, however, because he was tired of court life. Furthermore, he was aware that had he not been really clever, he would have perished by this time.

He told the king that he wanted to see his whiskered wife and return to till the soil, but Alboino made so many promises and lured him so much that the rogue yielded to his entreaties and consented to remain at the court.

Shortly thereafter Bertoldo was named counselor to the king and took his place among the barons and his dearest friends.

But his health soon began to fail and the poor man was seized by convulsions. He who was accustomed to feed on onions and roots now ruined his stomach by eating capon and quail. The more they cared for him, the more ill he became.

Within a short time Bertoldo was bedridden. Numerous court doctors came to see him. Alboino was so devoid of sense that he believed their tales, and kept them around the court. The doctors, as usual, did everything contrary to what they should have done, for not long afterward Bertoldo became a pitiful figure.

"Please bring me a bowl of beans," he pleaded, "and I will soon get well! Yes, I want beans," repeated the poor devil, "and besides beans I would like to have turnips and onions. Only in this way can I recover and return to life. Only these foods can refresh my blood and make it flow again. Of what avail is to bring a villain like me a little juice from small bottles? Why do they give me syrups instead of broth? All of this will bring the end of me."

The unhappy Bertoldo said these things because he knew which medicine he needed to get well; but all his lamentations came to naught, since his doctors were only interested in observing, examining, and studying his excrement.

For which reason, aware that he was gradually getting worse and noticing that death was approaching with rapid steps, one day he intimated that he wanted to make a will, and for this purpose he asked that a notary be called.

Bertoldo thus made his will, received the last rites of the Church, and prepared to close his eyes forever. In fact, it was not very long before death came, and heaven called unto itself its elected soul, which quietly and calmly ascended to the Creator.

On the day Bertoldo died there was great mourning at the court. When the news reached Queen Hypsicratea, who apparently had begun to love him, she became grief-stricken and it took a great deal of effort and patience to calm her.

On that fatal day all the church bells tolled mourning peals. Even at court they pealed the large solemnity bell.

Very great was the grief manifested by the Veronese people. Dames of the highest and lowest rank wept; men, women, and children of all ages, whether married or single, cried. Most likely there was less talk about the death of Caesar than there was about the death of Bertoldo.

The king ordered that the body of Bertoldo be buried with all possible pomp and magnificence. But before the funeral honors began, he commanded that Bertoldo's will be read, so that his last wishes should be known. Meanwhile, the notary who had drawn the instrument was summoned. He rushed to the royal palace and humbly bowed before King Alboino.

The name of the notary was Cerfoglio, and he was a horrible scribbler. Upon being invited by the king, he read as follows:

"I Bertoldo am the son of the once renowned Bertolazzo, who was the only son of Bertuccio, who lived in the days of Farinaccio and descended from Bertino and from a series of great men, of whom it is here impossible to relate their glorious achievements. I have heard say that the first progenitor of our family was one who sold paper, pen, ink, and inkwells to priests.

"Therefore, since I wish to make my will, I start by saying that upon this earth we are all subject to die; that indubitably we are all bladders full of wind, and that our bodies are nothing more than a sink full of troubles and pains. And because today I hear my heart telling me: 'Bertoldo, make sure you put your boots on well, for you must ride the horse of death, and it is necessary for you to go straight to the next world,' I have here written my last wishes.

"To Marcolfa, my wife, and to my son Bertoldino, I leave my belongings, provided she preserves intact the white lily of chastity, and he does not make of herbs a single bundle, because he would run the chance of being quartered.

"It is ten years since I saw my wife and my son, and they have never known where I stayed during that time.

"To the cobbler I leave my old shoes, which up to now he has fixed many times. I leave to the cook, the good Membrot, so many eggs that he may make an omelet. To Pasquino I leave, with a good night, my patched trousers; and I leave to the washerwoman Pandora my straw bed.

"To Fichetto, a very unruly boy with me, I direct that he be given a blow in the rear with the whip.

"I leave to the king my advice that he do as he pleases, but I remind him always to love justice, to make words correspond to facts, and not to be an example of wrongdoing. With the queen let him act without malice or restraint so that he, at a proper time, may have a worthy heir—a big royal child.

"To all men I leave my best wishes, urging them to be honest and of good will."

Here the notary stopped reading. The king was moved and wept. At sunset of that same day Bertoldo was buried. At the request of the king, a famous contemporary poet wrote the following epitaph:

> *In this dark, somber and noble tomb*
> *A villain lies of such deformed aspect*
> *That like bear more than a man appeared,*
> *But of such noble, keen, and lofty intellect*
> *That amazed were Nature and the world.*
> *While he lived, Bertoldo he was called.*
> *Pleasing to the king; he died of acute pains*
> *Not being able to eat turnips and beans.*

Pompous and solemn was the funeral; the whole court followed the hearse.

The king made no attempt to repress his copious tears, and even Queen Hypsicratea had tears in her eyes.

Appendix 1

Testimonia

Introduction by Jan M. Ziolkowski

Translation by Edward Sanger, Michael B. Sullivan, and Jan M. Ziolkowski, with Amiri Ayanna and Steven Rozenski

AS A TECHNICAL TERM IN THE PRESENT CONTEXT, testimonium signifies an entire text or extract from one that provides evidence for the knowledge and reception of an earlier work or tradition. The 2008 book that this volume flanks contains four appendices. Of the four, the second comprises thirty-four consecutively numbered entries that offer headnotes and in most cases the modern English of the items under discussion. The materials assembled consist of sources, analogues, and testimonia through 1450 that pertain to the Solomon and Marcolf cycle. In most cases the translation is preceded by the passages in the original languages. The linguistic spectrum encompasses Latin, Old and Middle English, Old and Middle High German, Old Occitan, and Old French.

The present appendix complements its predecessor by furnishing brief headnotes, texts and translations, and essential bibliography for the invaluable testimonia collected in Sabine Griese's 1999 book *Salomon und Markolf: Ein literarischer Komplex im Mittelalter und in der frühen Neuzeit* that were excluded from *S&M Z*. The entries in this new resource, to differentiate them from the thirty-four items already offered in 2008 while easing consultation of Griese, are identified by the letter G preceding the number that she allotted to them.

Some of the early modern texts have been made more readable by modernizing punctuation, particularly by replacing slash marks with commas or periods. More substantively, Griese occasionally included mistaken listings whose contents refer not to the literary and legendary figure Marcolf who was often paired with the biblical King Solomon, but instead to the real-life monkish author who compiled a formulary in the early eighth century. These references to this or that Marcolf unrelated to Solomon's nemesis by the same name have not been excised, but they have been flagged clearly. Small errors, such as mistranscriptions or typos, have been corrected silently.

Without doubt, many additions can and will be made eventually to the corpus of attestations. The hope is to facilitate such advances in knowledge by equipping researchers with a convenient context for what has already been discovered and by putting the passages into English, since translation can deliver the most elementary form of commentary and interpretation.

G21. From the *Kolmarer Liederhandschrift*, "Another about the Penny" ("Ein anders von dem pfenning"), strophe 2. Munich, Bayerische Staatsbibliothek, Cgm 4997, fols. 306^v–307^r. 1459–62.

The Colmar song manuscript, encompassing nearly 950 pieces of poetry with slightly more than one hundred melodies, is the largest extant collection of lyrics associated with the guilds of German lyric poets that held sway from the twelfth to the seventeenth century. Its dating of around 1460 rests on the watermarks of its paper. The codex, now in Munich, takes its first epithet from the Alsatian city where it was preserved from the sixteenth until the eighteenth century. It was produced in the Middle Rhine region, perhaps in Mainz or Speyer.

The passage that follows unfolds a dense roll call of personages from the Bible, classical tradition, and medieval literature. Solomon's wisdom, flagged early in this extract, became proverbial thanks to his depiction in Scripture, deuterocanonical books, and apocryphal texts. Samson's blinding is recounted in Judges 16:15–21. Absalom's handsomeness is mentioned in 2 Kings [2 Samuel] 14:25. In medieval legend Virgil, here indicated by the potentially misleading spelling of Filius, was credited with vast knowledge that led to his portrayal as a sage and magician. In the Book of Judith (an important constituent of the deuterocanon), Holofernes was an Assyrian general whom Nebuchadnezzar directed to destroy cities which had not supported him. The mention of him here differs from his frequent portrayal as an example of pride: see for instance Dante, *Purgatorio* 12.58–60. The liberal arts, which the Middle Ages often standardized as seven, have long been associated with Aristotle. Saint Christopher, whose name means "Christ-bearer" in Greek, is routinely portrayed in medieval art and literature as a very tall and imposing man who carries Jesus across a river. In 2 Kings [2 Samuel] 2:18, Asahel is described as "a most swift runner, like one of the roes that abide in the woods" (Douay-Rheims). Lorengel is the title hero of an anonymous fifteenth-century version of the Lohengrin story.

Pfenninc, wol im der dich mit êrn gewinnen kann,
und wære ein man als wîs als künic Salomôn,

und wære als starke als der blinde Samesôn,
wær er als schoene als Absolôn und künd daz Filius wiste.
Wær nu ein man als liep als was Holifernes
und künd die siben künste als Aristotiles
und het die groeze und lenge als sant Cristoffeles,
wær er als snel als Asahel und het Môrolfes liste,
Und wære er aller kempfen ein rehter kerne
und het die starken risen mit der hant betwungn
und wær zwelf schuoch vor den Lôrengel hin gesprungn
und het al meister mit sînr künste übersungn,
hât er die leng niht gelt ze geben, sô siht man in niht gerne.

O penny, happy is he who can come by you honestly.
And were a man as wise as King Solomon
and as strong as blind Samson,
as lovely as Absalom and with the knowledge of Virgil,
were there ever a man as dear as Holofernes,
who knew the seven arts like Aristotle,
and had the size and height of Saint Christopher,
and if he were as swift as Asahel and had Marcolf's cunning,
and if he were the very heart of every battle,
and had conquered strong giants by his own hand,
and jumped up twelve feet to face Lorengel,
even if he had surpassed all the masters with his singing—
if he had, in the end, no money to spare—
even then no one would be happy to see him.

Bibliography

Frieder Schanze, *Meisterliche Liedkunst zwischen Heinrich von Mügeln und Hans Sachs*, vol. 2, *Verzeichnisse*, Münchener Texte und Untersuchungen zur deutschen Literatur des Mittelalters 83 (Munich: Artemis, 1984), 58–83, esp. at 60.

Michael Baldzuhn, *Vom Sangspruch zum Meisterlied: Untersuchungen zu einem literarischen Traditionszusammenhang auf der Grundlage der Kolmarer Liederhandschrift*, Münchener Texte und Untersuchungen zur deutschen Literatur des Mittelalters 120 (Tübingen: Niemeyer, 2002), 265–68.

G22. From *Bollstatters Proverb Collection* (*Bollstatters Spruchsammlung*). London, British Library, MS Additional 16581, fols. 168ᵛ, 173ᵛ. 1468/69.

Konrad Bollstatter (born in the 1420s and died 1482/83), likely a native of Augsburg, was a professional scribe and writer of impressive erudition. His German adages comprise two compilations, which together make up the most consequential assembly of such didactic material from the fifteenth century. The sayings are ascribed to many disparate figures. In each case the identification of the individual leads into verse, in the first collection a four-line stanza, or in the second (as here, on fol. 168ᵛ) a couplet.

Morollf, as in this instance the name is spelled in the codex, is mentioned between the Libyan Sibyl, a prophetic priestess who presided over the oracle of the Greco-Egyptian deity Zeus-Ammon at Siwa Oasis in the Libyan desert, and Orpheus (or Orphanus, as his name is spelled in the manuscript) the Songmaster, a musician and poet of ancient Greek mythology, son of the god Apollo and the muse Calliope.

> Morolff spricht
> Göttlich vorcht vnd wiltlich schamm
> zyeret wohl ainen yeglichen man.

> Morollf says,
> "Fear of the Lord and worldly shame
> well adorn each and every man."

On a later folio (fol. 173ᵛ), a different hand has written under the caption "On the Lives of Princes" ("Von der fürsten leben") another ditty in couplets that juxtaposes key figures from the Bible, personages from antiquity, and protagonists of sagas. In each case, a pair of individuals with opposing traits is cited.

Famed from Homer and Virgil among many others, Hector was the greatest fighter for Troy until being killed by the Greek warrior Achilles, while Attila the Hun was legendary and in many circles infamous as the ruler of a vast but short-lived tribal empire that collapsed after his death in 453.

The giant Sigenot gave his name to an anonymous Middle High German poem, which was printed until the seventeenth century. According to the story recounted in it, the hero Dietrich von Bern (as legend designated King Theodoric the Great of the Ostrogoths, who lived from 454 to 526) was captured by this antagonist but eventually was liberated. The dwarf King Laurin occupied a central place within the cycle of Dietrich von Bern thanks to his role in an anonymous Middle High German poem entitled *Laurin* or *The Little Rose Garden* (*Der kleine Rosengarten*).

The monk Elsân (the name is rendered variously as Ilsân, Ilsâm, Ilsung, and Ilsing) is a leading figure in *The Great Rose Garden* (*Der grosse Rosengarten*). Also known as *The Rose Garden at Worms* (*Der Rosengarten zu Worms*), this anonymous thirteenth-century poem forms part of the cycle of Dietrich von Bern. Elsân is characterized as being strong and high-born, not unexpected since he is Hildebrand's brother.

Codrus was a semi-mythical king of Athens who ruled ca. 1089–1068 BCE. Out of devotion to the Athenians, he disguised himself as a peasant, provoked Dorian soldiers to combat, and was slain. His death motivated the enemy to retreat, since a prophecy had been made that their attack would fail if the king was harmed. The Trojan Aeneas, star of Virgil's *Aeneid* and in one sense the founder of Rome, is characterized as faithless after he abandons his lover Queen Dido of Carthage.

Freidank, a Middle High German poet of the early thirteenth century, is renowned for his authorship of a proverb collection entitled *Bescheidenheit* (meaning "wisdom").

Caesar Augustus, the first Roman emperor, commanded a substantial fraction of the Roman empire's economy, and is plausibly entitled to be deemed the wealthiest man of antiquity. Nebuchadnezzar may be presented as the poorest of men owing to the seven years of madness he spent eating grass like an ox (Daniel 4).

> Hector von troy der lenost
> Künig eczel der zegost
> Riß signott der gröst
> lorey der klenost
> lorengel der subteilost
> münch jlsung der grebost
> Zoderus der getrewest
> Eneas der ungetrewest
> Friderancus der warhafftest
> Marolt der lugenhaftest
> Kaysser augustus der reichost
> Nabuchodonosor der armost.

> Hector of Troy the most gentle,
> King Attila the most barbaric,
> the giant Sigenot most tall,
> [the dwarf] Laurin most small,
> Lorengel the most refined,
> Ilsung the Monk the coarsest,
> Codrus the most faithful,
> Aeneas the most unfaithful,
> Freidank the most truthful,

Marcolf the fullest of lies,
Caesar Augustus the richest,
Nebuchadnezzar the poorest.

Bibliography

Robert Priebsch, *Deutsche Handschriften in England*, vol. 2, *Das Britische Museum: Mit einem Anhang über die Guildhall-Bibliothek* (Erlangen: Junge, 1901), 147–58.

Ulrich Seelbach, *Späthöfische Literatur und ihre Rezeption im späten Mittelalter: Studien zum Publikum des "Helmbrecht" von Wernher dem Gartenaere*, Philologische Studien und Quellen 115 (Berlin: Schmidt, 1987), 154.

G23. Ulrich Füetrer, *Lannzilet*, strophe 5985. From *The Book of Adventures* (*Das Buch der Abenteuer*). Ca. 1473–84.

The poet and artist Ulrich Füetrer (born before 1450, died between 1493 and 1502) came from the Bavarian town of Landshut, in southeastern Germany. *The Book of Adventures*, his important digest of Arthurian Grail legends, relates primarily to Merlin, Perceval, and Gawain. Containing over 11,500 Titurel-strophes, it was compiled under the patronage of Albrecht IV (1447–1508), Duke of Bavaria.

The third book of Füetrer's poem, *Lannzilet* (On Lancelot), alludes to the story narrated in *Salman and Morolf* and mentions the fates of King Fore, King Princian, and Queen Salome. The three last-mentioned characters die in strophes 540, 771, and 777, respectively, of that Middle High German *Spielmannsepos* (see chapter 6). Mamelon does not appear in *Salman and Morolf*. Parsed etymologically, Wendelsea means "Vandal Sea," a designation for the Mediterranean that reaches back to Old English.

Kvngk Phar von Wenndlsee
Was pschach dem durch euch, Wellt?
Ewrs lones was nitt me,
Dann das ain strang des was sein widergellt;
Moroldes grossen lyst das kunden werben:
So pschach dem künig Pryncian,
Der durch her Salomones weyb müst sterben
[...]
Malmelon vnd Salme verzawbert waren.

King Fore from the Wendelsea,
what befell him thanks to you, World?

Your reward was no more
than the hangman's rope that was your recompense;
Morolf's great cunning found a customer:
so it happened to King Princian
on whose account Solomon's wife had to die
[...]
Mamelon and Salome were bewitched.

Bibliography

Ulrich Füeter, *Lannzilet, aus dem "Buch der Abenteuer,"* Str. *1123-6009*, ed. Rudolf Voß (Paderborn: Schöningh, 1996), 393.

Friedrich Vogt, ed., *Die deutschen Dichtungen von Salomon und Markolf,* vol. 1, *Salman und Morolf* (Halle an der Saale: Max Niemeyer, 1880), CXVI–CXVII.

G24. From the *Large (Tirolian) Neidhart Play* (*Großes [Tiroler] Neidhartspiel*), lines 343-52. Wolfenbüttel, Herzog August Bibliothek, Cod. Guelf. 18.12 Aug. 4°, fols. 280ʳ-280ᵛ. Late fifteenth century, perhaps ca. 1492/93.

Five distinct texts have acquired the title *Neidhart Play* or a closely related one, all of them with an initial modifier to indicate a place and some of them with another parenthetic adjective as well. This one, extant in a single codex, is the *Large (Tirolian) Neidhart Play*. It is the longest comic play in German to survive from the Middle Ages, with 2624 lines, 70 different roles, 13 dances, and 8 songs.

In the verses here the anonymous poet, in the character of Engelmayr, singles out eleven individuals whom he urges to celebrate their inner beast or wild ways—perhaps "celebrate that beast within, the wildness of the wolf." Ten comically rustic names come to a crescendo in the identification of Marcolf.

Engelmayr spricht,
So will ich auff an den rayen
Last vns tantzen umb den mayen
Wol auff vnd wol her
Lat uns aber rayen mer
Runtzolt puntzolt gundlwein
Gumpp vnd epp vnd peterlein
Jr sült all an den Rayen gan
Gumpolt gumprecht entzlman
Humel und marcolff
Wol an ir vngestrafften wolff.

Engelmayr says,
I want to join the round dance:
Let us dance around the maypole,
now here and now there,
and let us line up again!
Hey, Runtzolt, Puntzolt, Gundlwein,
Gumpp, Epp, and Peterling,
you should all get up and do a round dance!
Gumpolt, Gumprecht, Entzlman,
Humel and Marcolf,
celebrate your inner, untamed wolf!

Bibliography

John Margetts, ed., *Neidhartspiele*, Wiener Neudrucke 7 (Graz: Akademische Druck- u. Verlagsanstalt, 1982), 27.

John Margetts, ed., *Die mittelalterlichen Neidhart-Spiele: In Abbildungen der Handschriften*, Litterae: Göppinger Beitrage zur Textgeschichte 73 (Göppingen: Kümmerle, 1986), 10–11. (Facsimile of the manuscript.)

G25. From *Reynard the Fox* (*Reynke de Vos*), lines 12–15. Wolfenbüttel, Herzog August Bibliothek, 32.14 Poet., fol. 7ʳ. 1498.

This anonymous Middle Low German beast epic on the adventures of Reynard the Fox, written in four books that total 7791 rhyming verses with prose commentary, survives in complete form only in a single exemplar printed in Lübeck. Its immediate source was a Middle Dutch poem that has not been preserved but that was closely related to the verse preserved in fragments from the 1497 incunabula of the Middle Dutch *Reinke de Vos* by Hinrek van Alkmaar. Marquart the Jay, arguably connected with Marcolf and not evident in any extant Dutch poetry that preceded the Middle Low German poet, was apparently his invention.

Dar quemen vele heren myt grotem schal,
Ok quemen to houe vele stolter ghesellen,
De men nicht alle konde tellen:
Lütke de kron vnde Marquart de hegger.

There came many lords with a great clatter,
and there came rushing into the court many proud peers,
that one could not name everyone who was there:
Lutke the Crane, and Marquart the Jay.

Bibliography

Albert Leitzmann, ed., *Reinke de Vos: Nach der Ausgabe von Friedrich Prien*, Altdeutsche Textbibliothek 8, 3rd ed. (Halle an der Saale: Max Niemeyer, 1960), 7.

Timothy Sodmann, ed., *Reinke de Vos, Lübeck 1498* (Hamburg: D. u. K. Kötz, 1976). (Facsimile of the incunable.)

G26. From Thomas Murner, *Fool's Meadow* (*Die Gäuchmatt*), lines 3720–23. Composed 1515, published 1519.

Murner (1475–1537), a Franciscan friar from the region of Alsace, had a reputation for his satires as well as for his opposition to Luther. This tale of folly caused by love became controversial for both its pervasive misogyny and disparaging remarks about Maximilian I (1459–1519), the Holy Roman Emperor. In it, a female fool insults an unwanted suitor by calling him Marcolf as a term of harsh abuse (with reference to his ugliness and awkwardness).

> So wer mir worlich wol geholffen,
> Das ich trüg ein solchen marckolffen,
> Dich vnflat trüg in mynem hertzen;
> Das müst mir ewig bringen schmertzen!

> So it would have truly helped me well,
> that I should endure such a Marcolf,
> should endure you, a brute, in my heart;
> that would have had to bring me pain forever!

Bibliography

Thomas Murner, *Die Gäuchmatt (Basel 1519)*, ed. Wilhelm Uhl (Leipzig: Teubner, 1896), 139, 229–30.

G27. From Martin Luther, "Fifteen Theses Treating the Question of whether the Books of the Philosophers are Useful or not for Theology" ("Conclusiones quindecim tractantes, An libri philosophorum sint utiles aut inutiles ad theologiam"). 1517.

Luther (1483–1546) writes here that grammar, but not Aristotle, merits study. In building his case, he contends that if terminology from the Greek philosopher were a worthwhile concern, then the language of Marcolf and rustics would be too.

2. Inter omnis scientias humanitus inventas praecipue est ad propagandam theologiam utilis grammatica.
3. Non ideo in Aristotele et eius philosophia studendum est, quia terminis eisdem quandoque sancti doctores utuntur.
4. Aut eadem sequentia studendum est in Marcolpho vel in tabernis rusticorum.
5. Immo sequeretur, quod in omnium omnibus (id est in nullis) sermonibus esset studendum, quia omnium aliquibus utuntur verbis.

2. Among all forms of knowledge discovered by human beings, grammar is especially useful for promulgating theology.
3. One does not need to study Aristotle and his philosophy just because the Church Fathers from time to time make use of the same terms.
4. Or, by the same token, one needs to study Marcolf, or in the taverns of country bumpkins.
5. Indeed it would follow that one needs to study every manner of speech (which is to say, none) of all people just because they [the Church Fathers] make use of some words from everyone.

Bibliography

Martin Luther, "Conclusiones quindecim tractantes, An libri philosophorum sint utiles aut inutiles ad theologiam," ed. Karl Kraake, in *D. Martin Luthers Werke: Kritische Gesamtausgabe* (Weimar: Hermann Böhlau, 1888), 6:28–29.

G28. From Thomas Murner, "Christian and Fraternal Admonishment to the Learned Doctor Martin Luther" ("Ein christliche vnd brüderliche ermanung zů dem hochgelerten doctor Martino Luter"). 1521.

Murner throws the Reformer's reference back at him by referring to the ruse that Marcolf employed to avoid being executed. The wily peasant, sentenced to death, asks as his last wish to be granted the right to choose the tree from which he would be hanged. The text ends as he moves ever farther eastward, finding no tree to his liking. The episode of the tree for Marcolf's hanging in *S&M* 2.20 was beloved during the Reformation, by both supporters of the Church and Reformers (see G39, G42, G48, G79, G83, and G88).

So [...] du allenthalben richterlich zů erscheinen besorgest, vnd dir kein geistlich recht, kein Concilium es sei dan deines gefallens, kein heiliger lerer zů halten sein will, der vff dein meinung geschriben hab, als auch marcolffus nie kein baum finden kundt doran er begeret zů hangen.

So you take pains everywhere to look like a judge, and in your eyes there may be then no spiritual authority, no council to your liking, no holy teacher to be supported, who has written in accordance with your opinion: just as Marcolf too could never find any tree from which he wished to be hanged.

Bibliography

Thomas Murner, "Ein christliche vnd brüderliche ermanung zů dem hochge-lerten doctor Martino Luter" (Strasbourg: Johann Grüninger, 1520), fol. Bii^v.

G29. From Erasmus of Rotterdam, *Colloquies* (*Colloquia familiaria*). 1522.

In this dialogue by Erasmus (1466–1536), the interlocutor Gaspar begins a conversation with an allusion to the *Disputation* tradition.

Gaspar: Age, nos auspicabimur. Victo succedet Marcolphus.

Gaspar: Come, we will begin. Marcolf will take the loser's place.

Bibliography

Erasmus of Rotterdam, *Opera omnia* (Amsterdam: North-Holland, 1972), vol. 1, pt. 3, 168.

G30. From Erasmus of Rotterdam, *On the Writing of Letters* (*De conscribendis epistolis*). 1522.

In this treatise, Erasmus deals with the nature and style of the letter as a genre. Its most recent editor says with good reason that the personage at issue was not the legendary Marcolf associated with King Solomon but rather an early medieval monk from the region around Paris who wrote what has come to be known as the *Formulae Marculfi*. The text in question is a formulary, comprising Merovingian juridical acts composed between the second half of the seventh century and the beginning of the eighth, when this Marculf completed his work. For practical purposes, this testimonium should be excluded from the corpus relating to Solomon and Marcolf.

[S]i numerus mutatus honorem habet, cur non eadem opera videtur honorificum, plures singulari numero compellare? Cur non idem fit in tertiis personis? Honorificum est, si quis Marcolpho dicat: "gratulor vobis." Qui minus honorificum est, "saluta eos," cum unum jubeas salu-tari, sed honorabilem?

If a change of number shows respect, then why does it not for the same reason seem respectful to address multiple people in the singular? Why is it not the same in the third person? If someone should say to Marcolf, "I congratulate thee," it shows respect. Why is it less respectful to say "Greet them" when commanding that one person—but deserving respect—be greeted?

Bibliography

Alf Uddholm, ed. and trans., *Marculfi formularum libri duo*, Collectio scriptorum veterum Upsaliensis (Uppsala: Eranos' Förlag, 1962).

Alice Rio, trans., *The Formularies of Angers and Marculf: Two Merovingian Legal Handbooks*, Translated Texts for Historians 46 (Liverpool: Liverpool University Press, 2008).

Erasmus of Rotterdam, *Opera omnia* (Amsterdam: North-Holland, 1971), vol. 1, pt. 2, 269.

Erasmus of Rotterdam, "On the Writing of Letters / *De conscribendis epistolis*," trans. Charles Fantazzi, in *Collected Works of Erasmus*, volume 25, Literary and Educational Writings, volume 3 "De conscribendis epistolis formula. De civilitate," ed. J. Kelley Sowards (Toronto: University of Toronto Press, 1985), 45.

G31. Erasmus of Rotterdam, "The Funeral" ("Funus"), in *Colloquies*. 1526.

In this portion of the *Colloquies*, Erasmus explores the issue of dying well. In the late Middle Ages precepts on this topic became codified in a genre designated the *ars moriendi*. Here the interlocutors, who discuss the deaths of two men, are called respectively Marcolphus (Marcolf) and Phaedrus. The reason for which the name was chosen is not discussed explicitly nor is the literary work mentioned outright in the dialogue.

Bibliography

Erasmus of Rotterdam, *Colloquies,* trans. Craig R. Thompson, in *Collected Works of Erasmus,* vols. 39–40, at 40: 763–95.

Erasmus of Rotterdam, *Opera omnia* (Amsterdam: North-Holland, 1972), vol. 3, pt. 1, 537–51.

Erasmus of Rotterdam, *Vertraute Gespräche (Colloquia familiaria)*, trans. Hubert Schiel (Cologne: B. Pick, 1947), 152–75.

G32. From Martin Luther, *In Esaiam Prophetam.* 1527–30.

In this snippet from "Lectures about Isaiah," the Reformer begins by quoting from Isaiah 1:20 (*"because the mouth of the Lord* hath spoken it"). Afterward he lists Marcolf somewhat incongruously before the highly esteemed Greek orator Demosthenes (384–322 BCE) and Roman poet Virgil (70–19 BCE).

> "Quia os domini." Sic certe procedet nec aliter. Ad terrendum illos hoc addit, non enim loquutus est Marcolphus, non Demosthenes, non Virgilius, sed quoniam frustra docet, promittit, comminatur, ideo ad se redit et rursus incipit conqueri, quemadmodum et nos nullum profectum verbi videntes clamamus: Nonne plaga est tantam lucem sic contemni?

> "Because the mouth of the Lord." It shall undoubtedly proceed thus and not otherwise. He adds this to strike fear into them, not because Marcolf or Demosthenes or Virgil said it, but because he instructs, promises, and threatens in vain, and therefore he returns to himself and again begins to complain, just as we too, when seeing nothing of the Word accomplished, cry out, "Is it not a blow that so great a light be disdained in such fashion?"

Marcolf is mentioned again later in the same work, in a passage that begins with a lightly altered quotation from Isaiah 42:7 ("That thou mightest open the eyes of the blind, and bring forth the prisoner out of prison").

> "Ut aperias oculos caecorum et educas de carcere vinctum." [...] Sed nostro tempore a tot monasteriis et scolis vilipenditur, ut stupendum sit, negligimus illum et legimus monstra quaedam Aristotelis. *Sie syndt nicht werdt, das sy Marcolvum leszen. Untrew wyrdt sy treffen.*

> "So that you may open the eyes of the blind and lead forth the prisoner out of prison." [...] But in our time he is held in so little esteem in so many monasteries and schools that one is dumbfounded. We neglect him and read instead some of Aristotle's monstrosities. *They are not worthy to read Marcolf. Falsehood will strike them.*

Bibliography

Martin Luther, *In Esaiam Prophetam D. Doc. Martini Lutheri Enarraciones,* ed. Georg Buchwald and Oskar Brenner (Weimar: Hermann Böhlaus Nachfolger, 1914), vol. 31, pt. 2, pp. 15, 314–315.

Jan M. Ziolkowski, Edward Sanger, Michael B. Sullivan

G33. From Martin Luther, "Confession Concerning Christ's Supper" ("Vom Abendmahl Christi, Bekenntnis"). 1528.

Luther wonders sarcastically why the Catholic zeal for relics does not extend to memorabilia of such literary protagonists as Marcolf or Dietrich of Bern. Incidentally, he quotes from 1 Corinthians 11:24.

> Widerrumb hie, da er nicht stehet, da glotzen sie, sperren maul und nasen auff und suchen solchen text, gerade als müste S. Paulus an allen örtern und ynn allen riegen kein ander wort setzen denn diese: "Das ist mein leib" etc., auff das sie es sehen künden. Weil aber all yhr vleis ist, diesen text "Das ist mein leib" etc. anderswo, da er nicht stehet, zu suchen, Warumb suchen sie yhn nicht auch ym Marcolpho odder ym Dietrich von bern, da weren sie doch gewis, das sie yhn nicht funden?

> Again here, where it does not exist, they gawk, unclench their jaws, and sniff about, seeking out such a text, just as Saint Paul must have done, in all passages and in all lines, to set down no other word than these: "This is my body," etc., so that they could see it. Because however all their effort is to seek out this text "This is my body," etc. elsewhere, where it does not exist, why do they not also seek it out in Marcolf or in Dietrich of Bern, where they would nevertheless be sure not to find it?

Bibliography

Martin Luther, *Vom Abendmahl Christi, Bekenntnis*, ed. Ernst Thiele and Oskar Brenner, in *D. Martin Luthers Werke: Kritische Gesamtausgabe* (Weimar: Hermann Böhlaus Nachfolger, 1909), 26:480.

G34. From Martin Luther, "Weekly Sermons on John 16–20" ("Wochenpredigten über Joh. 16–20"). 1528–29.

To communicate visually the twofold nature of this bilingual sermon, the German phrases are italicized here in both the original text and English translation. In this passage, Luther discusses Mary Magdalene's visit to Jesus's tomb (John 20:1–13: compare Mark 16:1–8, Matthew 28:1–10, and Luke 24:1–8). Thereafter he shares platitudes about the desirability of training trees while they are still young. He quotes two German sayings. The first of them often reads in full "Alte Hunde sind nicht bändig zu machen" (meaning that old dogs are not easily accustomed to collars and chains), the second "Alte Schälke mag man nicht fromm machen" (one may not make old rogues pious). The homely proverbiality may put Luther in mind of Marcolf's responses to Solomon. In any case, soon thereafter he uses the expression "to preach of Marcolf" to signify sermonizing about something that has nothing to do with Christianity.

Cum illum non habet, nihil habet; eo habito omnia. Dic Christianum, qui sic adfectus, ut Euangelio habito etc. Paulus iactat se talem. Si deberem antiquis praedicare, cessassem ante 3 annos. Sed praedicandum propter iuventutem [...] *Alte hunde sind nicht, etc., alte schelck mag man nicht gesund machen.* Nos indigni, ut audiamus talia exempla. *Man sol uns predigen de Marcolfo.* Innocentia corda suscipiunt.

When [Mary Magdalene] does not have him [Christ], she has nothing; when she has him, she has everything. Call a Christian someone who is so minded, that when he has the Gospel, etc. Paul boasts that he is such a man. If I had to preach to the old people, I would have stopped three years ago. But I must preach for the sake of the young. [...] *Old dogs are not, etc. One can't make old servants healthy.* We are unworthy to hear such exempla. *One might as well preach to us about Marcolf.* Innocent hearts receive them.

Bibliography

Martin Luther, *Wochenpredigten über Joh. 16–20*, ed. Otto von Albrecht and Gustav Koffmane, in *D. Martin Luthers Werke: Kritische Gesamtausgabe* (Weimar: Hermann Böhlaus Nachfolger, 1903), 28:454.

G35. From Johannes Agricola, *Seven Hundred and Fifty German Proverbs* (*Sybenhundert und fünfftzig Teütscher Sprichwörter*). 1529/1534.

In this treasury of proverbs, Agricola (1494–1566) makes note of what he designates simply as Marcolf among the authors, protagonists, and titles of other similar narratives in circulation. Whether he intends the name to denote the supposed personage who uttered many sayings or to serve as a short title for a specific literary work, he probably has in mind the German prose *Schwankroman* or anecdotal novel and its derivatives (stemming from part 2 of *S&M*: see chapter 7 above).

Agricola's catalogue begins with Freidank, a Middle High German poet of the early thirteenth century who produced a collection of proverbs. The next item, *The Knight of Thurn* (*Der Ritter vom Thurn*), first printed in 1493, is a translation into German, made in 1485 by Marquard vom Stein (d. 1559), of the *Book for the Instruction of His Daughters* (*Livre pour l'enseignement de ses filles*) by the Chevalier de la Tour de Landry; the name of the French author served double duty as the title, which means "The Knight of the Tower." *The Seven Sages* (*Die sieben Meister*) was the designation affixed to a narrative cycle that was very popular in the Middle Ages. *Centinovella*, a slight garbling of the Italian *cento novelle* "one hundred stories," was a title under which German versions of Giovanni Boccaccio's *Decameron* (completed by 1353) were published. *The Parson of Kalenberg* (in German, *Pfarrer von Kalenberg*, of which the initial element could also be rendered as *The Priest*) was the protagonist of humorous tales. Eulenspiegel, for which a literal translation into English would be "Owl-Mirror," was a prankster famous in chapbooks who became a German folk-hero. *Theuerdank* is a German poem by Maximilian I (1486–1519), the Holy Roman Emperor, that relates in romanticized form his journey to marry Mary of Burgundy, Duchess of Cleves, (1457–1482) in 1477. Its title refers to the name of the poet's fictional alter ego, whose *nom parlant* certifies him as a knight of "adventurous thinking" (approximating the final two syllables of the Modern German *Abenteuer* and the key element of the verb *denken*). The poetic work was first printed in 1517.

> Es ist gerhumet Freidanck, *Ritter vom Thurn*, Marcolphus, *Die sieben Meister*, und was bey unserm gedencken ist new worden: *Centinovella, Das Narrenschiff* Sebastian Brands, *Der Pfaff vom Kalenberg*, Ulenspiegel, und *Thewerdanck*.

> Freidank, *The Knight of Thurn*, Marcolf, and *The Seven Sages* are famed— and what, to our way of thinking, has become new: the *Centinovella, The Ship of Fools* by Sebastian Brant, *The Parson of Kalenberg*, Till Eulenspiegel, and *Theuerdank*.

Agricola later relates his Proverb 131, "Nature will not depart from its kind, the cat does not leave off its mousing" ("Art lest von art nicht, die Katze leßt yhres mausens nicht"), to Marcolf's correction of Solomon by way of the cat and the candle trick (*S&M* 2.8).

> Salomon sagt, Wenn du den narren in eynem moerser zustiessest mit eynem stempffel wie grütz, so lest doch sein torheyt nicht von yhm. Man sagt, Daß Marcolfus mit dem weisen Salomon disputiert habe, und gefragt, Ob art und einpflantzte naturliche neygung mehr sey denn gewonheyt, die durch fleiß der menschen uber die natur eingefueret wirt, und da Salomon schloß, Wes einer auffs newe gewonet, das hange yhm gleich so hart an, als daß er von natur empfangen hatt. Nun ließ konig Salomon Marcolfus diß nicht gut sein, sonder wolte, wie es auch war ist, art gieng fur gewonheyt. Unnd die weil Salomon eyne Katzen hette, die yhm nach gewonheyt das liecht hielte bey nacht, brachte Marcolfus etliche meuse zu wegen, und kam des abends zu Salomon, unnd ließ erstlich eyn mauß lauffen, unnd als bald die katz der mause

gewar ward, tapt sie eyn wenig mit der pfoten, und ließ doch das liecht nicht fallen. Do aber die ander unnd dritte maus furüber lieffen, ließ sie das liecht fallen und lieff den meusen nach. Darauß hernach Marcolfus beweisete, Art gieng fur alle gewonheyt. Eyn jung reiß, wenn es krump wechset, so lest sichs nit biegen, man understurtze es wie man wolle, so wechset es doch krump. Der katzen art ist, daß sie nicht mauset auß hunger, sonder auß lust, also daß, Ja mehr man der katzen zu essen gibt, ja mehr sie mauset. Also auch, was einem menschen angeboren ist, und wozu er von natur geneigt ist, das thut er, unnd lest sich hieran nichts hyndern, und wen man eynen solchen gleich briete, kochete, fresse, doch konde er nicht davon lassen, so er widerumb lebendig wurde.

Freydanck sagt.
Schluffe eyn schalck inn Zobels balck
Dennoch wer er drynn eyn schalck.

Solomon says, if you grind up a fool like groats in a mortar with a pestle, even then his foolishness does not leave him. It is said that Marcolf argued with the wise Solomon, and that he asked whether nature and ingrained natural proclivity count for more than habit imposed upon nature by human diligence. Then Solomon concluded that what a person newly makes a habit, stays just as deeply with him as what he has received from nature. Now Marcolf did not allow this to stand as good and well for King Solomon, but instead wished also to show how it is also true that nature took precedence over habit. Seeing that Solomon had a cat that had been trained to hold a candle for him at night, Marcolf arranged to bring some mice to prove his point and came in the evening to Solomon, and he at first let [just] one mouse run loose. As soon as the cat noticed the mouse, it swatted a bit with its paw and yet did not let the candle fall. But then, when the second and third mice ran past, the cat let the candle fall and ran after the mice. Marcolf thereby proved definitively that nature took precedence over all habit. When a young branch grows crookedly, and does not permit itself to be bent no matter how one tries to prop it, it will still grow crooked. It is in the cat's nature that it hunts not out of hunger but for pleasure. It is likewise the cat's nature that the more a person gives the cat to eat, the more it hunts mice. It is just so with man. Whatever is innate in him and whatever he is inclined by nature to do, he does that, and he will let nothing impede him from it. If one were right away to fry, cook, and gobble up such a man, still he could not leave his nature behind any more than he could come back to life.

Freidank says:
Dress a scoundrel up in sable fur,
even so he would be a scoundrel within.

Bibliography

Johann Agricola, *Die Sprichwörtersammlungen*, ed. Sander L. Gilman (Berlin: de
Gruyter, 1971), 1:4, 1:94–95.

G36. Ludwig von Passavant, *Response: The shameful and blasphemous writing of the
man named Johannes Agricola* [...] (*Verantwortung: der schmach und lesterschrift so
Johannes Agricola Eyßleben genant* [...]). 1529.

The author, a nobleman in the service of Duke Ulrich of Württemberg (1487–
1550) who was active ca. 1530, wrote a letter of complaint against Johannes
Agricola and his anthology of common sayings. Agricola was a Protestant
Reformer, a friend and follower of Martin Luther whose native town was the
same German city in Saxony-Anhalt where Luther was born and baptized. In
the missive, Passavant sought to show that "the name of God and the Holy
Scriptures [were] misused by this slanderer," that Agricola's work mocked and
disgraced the German nation, and that he was a false poet and a spreader of lies.

> [...] dem er mit scherpff und sinn der kunst, in seinem spruchbüchlin
> ser nachvolget, mit namen dem hochachtbarn Magistro Marcolpho,
> wiewol der nun kein Teütscher lerer noch geschicht schryber, sunder
> des als lobwirdige historien und ergangen thatten außwysen, bey künig
> Salomons gezeitten, ein Hebreisch man geweßt. Aber die weil sein
> gschrifft so lang zeit bey den Tütschen in grosser achtung gehalten,
> so zelt er in billich zü den Tütschen geschicht schrybern, oder villeicht
> hatt er in von nüwem auß dem Hebreischen transferiert.

> ... the man whom the author in his little book of proverbs closely
> emulates in his art with wit and taste, the respectable Master Marcolf
> by name. Although now no German teacher or historian other than
> that writer has provided praiseworthy accounts and documents of
> deeds done in the times of King Solomon, a Jewish man for sure, but
> since his writings have for so long a time been so highly esteemed by
> the Germans, he belongs properly to German historians, or perhaps he
> translated these stories afresh from the Hebrew.

Passavant characterizes Marcolf as a Jew who lived in the time of Solomon and
composed a highly esteemed book originally in Hebrew. The sixteenth-century

polemicist purports that this alleged author of biblical oldentimes exercised a constant influence on Agricola. For this reason, he suggests that the Reformer's text be reentitled *The New Works of Marcolf* instead of *German Proverbs*. Passavant is adamant that Agricola vitiates whatever is serviceable in the Marcolfian underpinning to his proverb collection.

> Marcolfus zů leßen vil nutzlicher und gründiger sey, auch vil besser sprüch wort hab, dan dieser im selbst hochberümpter lerer. Bey Marcolphus gedicht, weyßt man die narheit, und das gedicht offentlich zü erkennen, ob er gleich narr, so schadet er doch nit. Bey disen schalckspossen, sind aber vil schmach unterm schein der warheit eingezogen.

> Reading Marcolf is more useful and profound, it also has much better proverbs than this teacher, very famous to himself. In Marcolf's poem, the reader knows to recognize openly foolishness and the poem. Even if himself a fool, he causes no harm. But in this rogue, there is much shame inserted under the guise of truth.

Marcolf is much more useful to read than Agricola because from the writings of the first, one may learn to discern what is fiction. Passavant compares Agricola's accusations against Duke Ulrich with Marcolf's behavior toward King Solomon.

> wen du aber sagest, Marcolphus hatt des bey künig Salomon auch macht gehapt, das were schier die best antwort, schalcksnarren, haben zů zeitten etwas im schimpff macht, sy werden aber auch warlich offt wüst darumb uffs maul geklopfft.

> If you were to say that Marcolf also had a power over King Solomon, that would be practically the best retort for a mischievous fool to have at times when something causes him affront. And thus, knowing this, the fool might also often have real reason to swagger and brag.

Bibliography

Friedrich Latendorf, ed., "L. v. Passavant gegen Agricola's Sprichwörter," *Jahresbericht des Gymnasium Fridericianum* (1873): 3–34.

Johann Agricola, *Die Sprichwörtersammlungen*, ed. Sander L. Gilman (Berlin: de Gruyter, 1971), 2:281, 2:283, 2:295.

Michael Curschmann, "Marcolfus deutsch," 234–35.

G37. From Daniel Hopfer von Kaufbeuren, *Marcolf and Bolikana* (*Marcolfus und Bolikana*). Ca. 1530.

This broadsheet, which circulated independently, features an ugly, grotesquely dandified and garishly adorned couple of dancing farmers. The wordplay at the end between *Mahl* ("meal") and *Mal* ("times") brings home the point that if Marcolf and his wife Bolikana had not forgotten virtue, they would have been spared the worst consequences of death:

> Der Tugend Lieb vnd Thorheit übung macht,
> Das offt noch spatt an manchen wird gedacht,
> Der seinen Lauff schon längsten hat volbracht.
> Marcolphus den die würmer längst gefressen,
> Sambt seinen Weib wer Tausend mahl vergessen,
> hätt ihr gehirn die Thorheit nicht besessen.

> Who holds virtue dear but also practices folly,
> that often only too late becomes a consideration to many a one
> who has already completed the longest part of his life's course.
> Marcolf, whom worms long ago ate,
> would have been forgotten together with his wife a thousand times,
> if folly had not possessed their minds.

Bibliography

Eduard Eyssen, "Daniel Hopfer von Kaufbeuren: Meister zu Augsburg 1493 bis 1536" (PhD Diss., Heidelberg University), 62.

Michael Curschmann, "Markolf tanzt," 971.

G38. From Hans Sachs, *Zwey Newr schöner Lieder ins Schillers hoff thon vnd ins Saxen kurtzen thon.* 1530.

This octavo was printed in Nuremberg in 1530 by the book dealer and printer Hans Guldenmund (d. 1560). This second of three strophes lists exemplary personages of the Bible and other traditions. Marcolf, named Marckart in this passage, is granted admittance into such illustrious company for his cleverness, as Solomon is for his wisdom.

The mention of the chamber of glass refers to a legendary episode in which Alexander the Great had himself lowered to the bottom of the sea in a sort of bathysphere *avant la lettre*, so that he could experience the world of the deep. Virgil is here called Filius, a name applied sometimes to him in his legendary role as a magician.

Es ist ein dor,
der wenden will der frawen dinst,
ja meint er dz man jn allein
lieb hab für alle manne.
Ich sprich fürwar,
vnd steund jhm alle welt zů zinst,
so möcht er woll ein herre sein,
des ganzen reichs ein krone.
Wer er als weis als Salomo(n)
Vn(d) se die wunder durch ein glaß,
die Alexander wiste,
wer er als schön als Absolon,
vn(d) wer als stark als Samson was,
vn(d) het des Marckartz liste,
vn(d) kundt als vil als filius [Virgilius]
mit seiner zauberey,
yedoch wolt ich dem schönen Fraylein wonen bey,
mit seiner zauberey so wert er mir nit ser,
ich sing der aller liebsten heint,
sing ich jr hy in dinst zů eer.

He is a fool
who intends to turn to the service of ladies:
yes, he thinks that he may be held most dear
before all other men.
I speak truly,
and the entire world stands in tribute to him,
as he would probably like to be a lord,
one crown for the whole kingdom.
Were he as wise as Solomon
and through a glass saw the wonders
that Alexander had seen,
and were he as beautiful as Absolom,
and were he as strong as Samson was,
and had he Marcolf's tricks,
and if he knew as much as Virgil
with his magic,
still I would rather live with the beautiful damsel.
With his magic he would not be much to me:
I sing for the loveliest one tonight,
I sing to her here in service to honor her.

Bibliography

Arthur Kopp, *Bremberger-Gedichte: Ein Beitrag zur Bremberger-Sage*, Quellen und Forschungen zur deutschen Volkskunde 2 (Vienna: Dr. Rud. Ludwig, 1908), 58–59. (For edition.)

F. Schanze, *Meisterliche Liedkunst zwischen Heinrich von Mügeln und Hans Sachs* (Munich: Artemis, 1984), 2:263, no. 19.

Horst Brunner and Burghart Wachinger, *Repertorium der Sangsprüche und Meisterlieder des 12. bis 18. Jahrhunderts* (Tübingen: Niemeyer, 1991), 5:221.

G39. From "Lazarus Spengler's Work against the Papists through Canon Law" ("Laz. Spenglers Schrift wider die Päbstler ex iure canonico"). Nürnberg Stadtbibliothek, Cent. V, App. 34k, Nr. 12, fol. 3^r. 1530.

A fervent Lutheran, Lazarus Spengler (1479–1534) wrote religious tracts and poetry. The following extract comes from an unpublished work of his which survives in an autograph. The title was supplied by a later hand. The treatise outlines a response to criticism that Johann Cochläus (1479–1552) had lodged against his writings on canonical law. In general, Cochläus defended Roman Catholicism staunchly against Lutheranism.

> Dann sie meinen vielleicht, derselb Auctor wird sich von diesen roten Pirreten, hochsinnigen Theologen und so ansehlichen Leuten dermaßen entsetzen, daß er sich in ein Winkel verkriechen und seinen Namen vor ihnen nit offenbaren dörf, darumb sie ihrs Achtens gut machen und keinen Widerstand gegen ihnen haben und finden werden. In mittler Zeit wollen sie so lang schreiben, geifern und hohlhippen, daß man ihr vergessen oder aber die ausgangen Canones der Fabeln Marolfi gleich achten soll. So haben sie dann aber ein ritterlichen Kampf gegen dem armen, verachten lutherischen Haufen erstanden.

> Then perhaps they think that the same author will be so disgusted by these red caps, high-minded theologians, and such respectable people that he would crawl into a corner and not dare to reveal his name before them because he might repay them for their attention and have no means of resistance against them and be found. In the meantime they will want to write so long, slaverers and vituperators, that a person should forget about them or else respect superseded canons equally with Marcolf's fables. In this way they mounted then a chivalrous battle against the poor, despised crowds of Lutherans.

In a letter from November 11, 1520, Spengler commented "Dr. Eck finds no offer sufficient, so little as Marcolf's one tree" ("Dr. Eck findet kein genugsam Erbieten, so wenig als Marcolfs einen Baum"). This terse simile relates to the inability of Solomon's nemesis to identify a tree to his liking in *S&M* 2.20, when he is supposed to choose one to serve as an arboreal gallows for his own hanging (see G28). Spengler also says, in a letter from 1530 written under the pseudonym Hieronymus von Berchnishausen, "people try to bypass the resolutions of old councils with disparaging speeches, as if they were Marcolf's fables" ("über die alten Konzilsbeschlüsse sucht man mit geringschätzigen Reden hinwegzukommen, als wären es des Markolfus Fabeln").

Bibliography

Friedrich Braun, "Lazarus Spengler und Hieronymus von Berchnishausen," *Beiträge zur bayerischen Kirchengeschichte* 22 (1916): 26, 65.

Lazarus Spengler, *Lazarus Spengler Schriften*, ed. Berndt Hamm, Felix Breitling, Gudrun Litz, and Andreas Zecherle, vol. 3, *Schriften der Jahre Mai 1529 bis März 1530* (Gütersloh: Gütersloher Verlagshaus, 2010), 107n119.

Paul Kalkoff, *Die Reformation in der Reichstadt Nürnberg nach den Flugschriften ihres Ratsschreibers Lazarus Spengler* (Halle an der Saale: Buchhandlung des Weisenhauses, 1926), 113n2.

G40. From Martin Luther, *Table Talk* (*Tischreden*), no. 1089. 1530–35.

Luther's *Table Talk* collects sayings that he uttered on diverse occasions in various places, but particularly in his home around the dinner table, as the title suggests. The immense aggregation of utterances and anecdotes was compiled between 1531 and 1544 by his students. In this section, Luther approves the *ars iocandi* (art of joking) as an effective remedy for religious melancholy, or lapses of faith. He extolls the cheerful, spirit-raising, gloom-banishing arts of jesters and storytellers, and advises those plagued by doubt or despondency to distract themselves with tales of Schlaraffenland (the land of plenty often called Cockaigne in English) or, when in need, to let themselves be helped by Till Eulenspiegel and Marcolf.

> Des Teufels fürnehmeste Anfechtung. "Der Satan plaget die Gewissen allermeist mit dem Gesetz und hält ihnen Christum fur als einen strengen Richter. Denn also sagt er: 'Gott ist den Sündern feind; weil er gerecht ist [...]' Die beste Arznei wider die Anfechtung ist, daß du deine Gedanken davon abwendest, das ist, redest von andern Dingen,

von Markolfo, Eulenspiegel und dergleichen lächerlichen Possen, so sich gar nichts zu solchen Händeln weder reimen noch dienen, damit du jener schweren Gedanken vergessest oder haltest dich stracks ans Gebet und einfältig an den Text des Euangelii."

The devil's noblest charge. "Satan plagues the conscience most of all with the law and holds up Christ to them as a strict judge. For so he says, 'God is hostile to sinners, because he is just. [...]' The best medicine against this charge is to turn your thoughts away from this, that is to say, talk about other things, about Marcolf, Eulenspiegel, and laughable pranks of the sort, so that they neither accord at all with such matters nor serve them, so that you can forget those weighty thoughts or keep yourself firmly in prayer and singlemindedly on the text of the Gospel."

Bibliography

Martin Luther, "Veit Dietrichs und Nik. Medlers Sammlung," ed. Ernst Kroker, in *D. Martin Luthers Werke: Kritische Gesamtausgabe*; *Tischreden* (Weimar: Hermann Böhlaus Nachfolger, 1912), 1:547–48, no. 1089.

G41. From Martin Luther, *Table Talk* (*Tischreden*), no. 2242. 1531.

The personage labeled Ritesel here has been identified with Johannes Riedesel zu Neumark, an official in the court of Saxony who was an associate of Martin Luther. The identification has been disputed, and the suggestion made that a man called Johann Reiling, although not born a Riedesel, acquired that honorific from having served the family. The prosopography is examined in a privately printed study: Hans Gutekunst, *Johannes Riedesel zu Neumark: Kurfürstlich-sächsischer Kämmerer 1528-1532 und Gevatter Martin Luthers* (Norderstedt: Books on Demand, 2019).

Marcolphus vere delineat in unaquaque aula esse oportere unum insigniter rebellem et stultum, qui principi non oboediat, sed sua quaerentem, velut in nostra curia est Ritesel. Etiam significat sapientiam mundi non esse tantam, quae ludi vel rideri non possit vel hallucinari. Est autem poema eius vere Teutonum, quia Germani poetantes perpetuo habent stercora in ore et anum.

Marcolf rightly demonstrates that in every palace there ought to be some notable agitator and fool who does not obey the ruler, but pursues his own purposes, as Ritesel does at our court. He also shows that the wisdom of the world is not so great, that it cannot be mocked or laughed at or idly discussed. But his poem is truly Teutonic, since Germans who poeticize continually have shit in their mouth and their asshole.

Bibliography

Martin Luther, "Die Sammlung von Konrad Cordatus," ed. Ernst Kroker, in *D. Martin Luthers Werke: Kritische Gesamtausgabe; Tischreden* (Weimar: Hermann Böhlaus Nachfolger, 1912), 2:374, no. 2242.

Michael Curschmann, "Marcolfus deutsch," 232.

G42. From Martin Luther, Letter to Nikolaus von Amsdorf. March 11, 1534.

The Reformer wrote this letter from Wittenberg. The addressee, Nikolaus von Amsdorf (1483–1565), was a German Lutheran theologian and a Protestant reformer.

> Haec est Satanae malitia [...]. Sic posset diabolus ad Christum ipsum dicere: Etiam si vera dicas, tamen quia non dicis talibus verbis, qualibus ego velim, nihil dicis, velim autem nullis verbis dici, sicut Marcolfus suspendi voluit ab arbore a se electa, nullam tamen voluit eligere.

> This is the wickedness of Satan [...]. Thus the devil could say to Christ himself: Even if you should say the truth, yet because you do not say it in such words as I would wish, you say nothing; I would however like for it to be said in no words, just as Marcolf agreed to be hanged from a tree chosen by him, yet was not willing to choose one.

Bibliography

Martin Luther to Nikolaus von Amsdof, March 11, 1534, in *D. Martin Luthers Werke: Kritische Gesamtausgabe; Briefwechsel* (Weimar: Hermann Böhlaus Nachfolger, 1937), 7:35.

G43. From Rabelais, *Gargantua and Pantagruel* (*Gargantua et Pantagruel*). 1534.

The last king of Assyria was Ashur-uballit II (612–ca. 605 BCE), but the Greek historian Ctesias (fifth century BCE) awarded that dubious distinction to Sardanapalus. In Rabelais, the character Spadassin mentions this other Mesopotamian ruler. Immediately afterward he cites proverbial wisdom from Solomon, to which his interlocutor Echephron responds by quoting a comeback from Malcon (one alias for Marcolf in the French tradition).

O (dist Spadassin) par Dieu, voicy un bon resveux! Mais allons nous cacher au coing de la cheminée, et là passons avec les dames nostre vie et nostre temps à enfiller des perles, ou à filler comme Sardanapalus. Qui ne se adventure, n'a cheval ny mule, ce dist Salomon. Qui trop (dist Echephron) se adventure, perd cheval et mulle, respondit Malcon.

"O," said Spadassin, "By God, here is a fine dotard! But let's go hide ourselves in the chimney corner, and there spend our life and our time with the ladies, in stringing pearls or spinning like Sardanapalus. Who ventures nothing has neither horse nor mule: Solomon says this." "Who ventures too much," says Echephron, "loses horse and mule: Malcon replies."

Bibliography

Francois Rabelais, *Œuvres complètes*, ed. Pierre Jourda (Paris: Garnier Frères, 1962), 1:130.

G44. From Martin Luther, *Table Talk* (*Tischreden*), no. 3673. February 1536.

In his words here, Luther refers to S&M 2.19. This famous episode, often called "the bum in the oven," has as its defining moment when Marcolf, who has been forbidden ever to set eyes upon Solomon again, arranges for the king to be mooned by him. It is frequently made a point of departure for what might be called posterior analytics.

Deus agnoscitur a posteriori. Mirabilis est Deus, mirabiliter a suis agnoscitur, ut Paulus ait: Quia Dei sapientiam mundus non cognovit per sapientiam, placuit Deo per stultitiam salvos facere credentes. Nam cum Deum [ex] creatione et misericordia non vellet mundus, *hatt er sich in infirmitate crucifixi Christi offenbaret, daß sie sich zu tod an im ergere. Vnd geschicht ir eben recht! Weil sie Gott von angesicht* in gloria *nicht sehen will, mus sie in ignominia erkennen vnd in hindern sehen, wie Salomon mit dem Marcolfo geschehen ist,* et Mosi, qui dorsum Dei in caverna videbat. Exodi 33: Ubi posteriora Dei videbat; faciem Dei videre non poterat. Also mussen wir Gott a posteriori erkennen itzunder.

God is recognized *a posteriori*. Wondrous is God, and wondrously he is recognized by his own people, as Paul says [1 Corinthians 1:21]: "Because the world did not recognize the wisdom of God through wisdom, it pleased God to save those who believe through foolishness." Since the world would not recognize God through his creation and mercy, *he revealed himself* in the weakness of the crucified Christ, *that they might take offense with him even to death. And so it happened, indeed justly so! Because they do not want to see God in his glory face to face, they must know him in ignominy and see him from behind, as it happened to Solomon with Marcolf,* and to Moses, who saw the back of God in a cave. Exodus 33: "There you may see the back [posterior] of God, but the face of God you may not see." So too must we now know God *a posteriori.*

Bibliography

Martin Luther, "Tischreden aus dem 1. Abschnitt der Handschrift Math. L.," ed. Ernst Kroker, in *D. Martin Luthers Werke: Kritische Gesamtausgabe; Tischreden* (Weimar: Hermann Böhlaus Nachfolger, 1914), 3:513, no. 3673.

G45. From Martin Luther, *Table Talk* (*Tischreden*), nos. 5541, 6059, 7004. February 1536.

This passage in Luther reprises G44, except in German rather than Latin with a mere sprinkling of the vernacular. The same general context applies here.

Gott wird a posteriori erkennet. "Gott ist wunderbar, und wunderlich wird er auch von den Seinen erkennet, wie Sanct Paulus auch 1. Cor. 1 davon saget: 'Quia Dei sapientiam mundus non cognovit per sapientiam, placuit Deo per stultitiam salvos facere credentes.' Die Welt will Gott *ex creatione et misericordia* nicht erkennen, so hat er sich *in infirmitate filii crucifixi* offenbaret, auf daß sie sich zu Tode an ihm ärgere. Und geschicht ihr aber recht. Weil sie Gott von Angesicht zu Angesicht, *in gloria* nicht sehen will, so muß sie ihn in ignominia erkennen, und ihm sehen in den Rücken. Gleichwie dem Könige Salomo auch mit dem Marcolfo geschehen ist. Und Mosi auch geschahe, Exodi am 33., der in einer Höhlen oder Steinklippen steckte, und Gottes Rücken sahe, da seine Herrlichkeit mit Donner, Blitz, und großem Winde und Wetter furüber war, da sahe er Gottes Hintern, denn sein Angesicht konnte er nicht sehen. Also mussen wir noch unsern Herr Gott a posteriori erkennen, und an Christo hangen bleiben, und von ihm durch Aergerniß und Ungeduld nicht abfallen."

God will be known *a posteriori.* "God is wondrous, and wondrously he will also be recognized by His own people, as Saint Paul also says in 1 Corinthians 1 [verse 21]: 'Because the world did not recognize the wisdom of God through wisdom, it pleased God to save those who believe through foolishness.' The world does not want to recognize God from creation and mercy, thus he has revealed himself in the weakness of the crucified Son, that they might take offense with him even to death. And it happened justly. Because they do not want to see God face to face, *in glory*, they must recognize him in ignominy, and see him from behind. Just as it happened with King Solomon and Marcolf. And just as it happened in Exodus 33 to Moses, who hid himself in a cave or behind a rock cliff and saw God's back—when his glory with thunder, lightning, and great wind and storms went overhead, he saw God's behind, for he could not see his face. So must we still know our Lord God *a posteriori*, and remain fixed on Christ, and through offenses and impatience not fall away from him."

See also *Table Talk*, no. 5541 (1542–43).

Liber Proverbiorum. Ist ein schon buch. Regenten soltens lesen. Da siehet man, wie es in der welt zugehet; da stehet nichts dan furcht Gottes und bethe. [...] So spricht er denn: Ey, lieber, nim mich doch nicht gefangen! Nein, nein! Vnd vber 3 jar lest dich dan in das arsloch sehen.

Book of Proverbs. It is a lovely book. Rulers should read it. In this book one may see the direction the world takes; in this book are found nothing but fear of God and prayer. [...] Then he speaks in this way: Oh, dear, please do not take me prisoner! No, no! And for more than three years, he has you look in the asshole [...].

See also *Table Talk,* no. 6059, in which one sees that the trope of "'looking Marcolf in the asshole' had, at least in this circle, already become a common expression, if not one of downright proverbial character."[1]

Bibliography

Martin Luther, "Kaspar Heydenreichs Nachschriften aus den Jahren 1542 und 1543," ed. Ernst Kroker, in *D. Martin Luthers Werke: Kritische Gesamtausgabe; Tischreden* (Weimar: Hermann Böhlaus Nachfolger, 1919), 5:226, no. 5541.

Martin Luther, "Tischreden aus Anton Lauterbachs Sammlung B," ed. Ernst Kroker, in *D. Martin Luthers Werke: Kritische Gesamtausgabe; Tischreden* (Weimar: Hermann Böhlaus Nachfolger, 1919), 5:467, no. 6059.

Martin Luther, "Tischreden Doct. Mart. Luthers von Aposteln oder Jüngern Christi," ed. Ernst Kroker, in *D. Martin Luthers Werke: Kritische Gesamtaus-*

---

[1] Curschmann, "Marcolfus deutsch," 224.

gabe; Tischreden (Weimar: Hermann Böhlaus Nachfolger, 1921), 6:319, no. 7004.

G46. From Sebastian Franck, *Chronicle, History, and Historiated Bible continued from the beginning until the present year 1536* [...] (*Chronica Zeitbůch vnnd Geschichtbibell von anbegyn biß in diss gegenwertig MDXXXVI iar verlengt* [...]) 1536.

Franck (1499–1543) was a German Protestant Reformer. His *Chronicle, History, and Historiated Bible* contains a short section on "Aesop the Poet of Fables and his Life" in which Franck brings up Solomon. This reference to the biblical king leads him in turn to mention an unidentified book that is obviously *Solomon and Marcolf*.

Esopus, aus der statt Phrygie Ammorio genant, seines glücks ein eygen knecht, aber eins freien künstreichen gemüts, doch weyt von aller leybs schöne [...] wie paürisch, vngestalt er von leib war, so höflich, adelich von gemüt, tugent vnnd sitten.

Aesop, from the Phrygian city named Ammorius, a slave to his fortune, but one of an unrestrained and cunning disposition, yet far from having any beauty of body [...] how he was deformed like a boor in body, yet was so courteous and noble-minded in character, virtue, and customs.

Franck's mention of Aesop leads him in turn to Marcolf, with whom the cunning Greek slave was closely associated by many in the Reformation (fol. cxxiiij^r).

Sein [Esopi] fabeln sein noch vor handen, Griechisch, Teütsch, vnd Latein. Ein solcher kunstreicher abenteürer sol auch Markolphus sein gewesen, zur zeit Salomonis, von dem auch ein büchlin nit gar vnge-saltzen vmbfleügt.

His [Aesop's] fables are available now in Greek, German, and Latin. Marcolf too is supposed to have been such a cunning adventurer, during the time of Solomon, about whom also circulates a little book, not wholly without wit.

Bibliography

Michael Curschmann, "Marcolfus deutsch," 238.

Sebastian Franck, *Chronica Zeitbůch vnnd Geschichtbibell* [...] (Ulm: 1536; repr., Darmstadt: Wissenschaftliche Buchgesellschaft, 1969), fols. cxxiij^r–cxxiiij^r.

G47. From Hans Sachs, "The Slurping Stork" ("Der schlürchet storch"). February 21, 1538.

Sachs (1494–1576) was both a professional shoemaker and a prolific writer. Among his many poems was a *Spruchgedicht* entitled "The Slurping Stork." Three verses (40–42) in this "proverb poem" identify Marcolf as the narrator of a story that resembles an Aesopic fable. The tale tells of a stork that flies over a pond where it drops a satchel of gold. After pecking in vain in search of the sack, the bird swears everlasting enmity against the frog, which it holds responsible for the loss.

> Düet Marcolfüs peschreiben,
> Istoriographüs,
> Der roczig rüsticüs.

> Marcolfus did write,
> that historiographer,
> that raucous peasant.

Bibliography

Hans Sachs, *Sämtliche Fabeln und Schwänke*, ed. Edmund Goetze and Carl Drescher (Halle an der Salle: Niemeyer, 1900), 3:198.

Horst Brunner and Burghart Wachinger, *Repertorium der Sangsprüche und Meisterlieder des 12. bis 18. Jahrhunderts* (Tübingen: Niemeyer, 1986), 9:285.

G48. From Martin Luther, preface to "Recommendation of a Committee of Several Cardinals, Written and Entrusted to Pope Paul III on his Command." ("Ratschlag eines Ausschusses etlicher Kardinäle, Papst Paulo III. auf seinen Befehl geschrieben und überantwortet"). 1538.

In this invective against Pope Paul III (1468–1549), Luther makes reference to *S&M* 2.20, in which the clever peasant secures permission to choose the tree on which he is to be hanged but cannot find any to his liking. Compare G28, in which the same trope is used in an attack against Luther.

> Es schleppet sich der Bapst mit dem armen Concilio, wie die Katze mit jren jungen [...] Ich acht, er will ein Markolfus werden, der nirgend einen Baum finden kund, daran er gern hengen wolt. Also kan der Bapst keinen ort finden, da er gern ein Concilium hette.

The Pope trudges around with his poor council, like a cat with her kittens [...] I suppose he wants to be a Marcolf, who could find nowhere a tree on which he would like to be hanged. Just so, the Pope can find no place where he would like to hold a council.

Bibliography

Martin Luther, preface to "Ratschlag eines Ausschusses etlicher Kardinäle, Papst Paulo III. auf seinen Befehl geschrieben und überantwortet," ed. Otto Clemen and Oskar Brenner, in *D. Martin Luthers Werke: Kritische Gesamtausgabe* (Weimar: Hermann Böhlaus Nachfolger, 1914), 50:288.

Michael Curschmann, "Marcolfus deutsch," 224.

G49. From Martin Luther, "Preface to the First Volume of the Wittenberg Edition of Luther's German Works" ("Vorrede zum 1. Bande der Wittenberger Ausgabe der deutschen Schriften"). 1539.

Luther makes a passing remark about the similarity and interchangeability of Marcolf and Aesop. Whereas images of the two characters are sometimes equated and transferred from one to the other out of a belief that they had more or less the same physical aspect, the analogy here is driven by the worldly wisdom and outsider status that they share in their respective worlds.

> Denn da werden Rottengeister aus, die sich lassen duncken, die Schrifft sey jnen unterworffen und leichtlich mit jrer Vernunfft zu erlangen, als were es Marcolfus oder Esopus Fabeln, da sie keins heiligen Geists noch betens zu durffen.

> Then the rabble-rousers go out, who let themselves think that the Scripture was subject to those and that it could be easily obtained by their own reason, just as though it were Marcolf's tales or Aesop's fables—for these men truly had no need of the Holy Spirit nor of prayer.

In regard to the interchangeability of Marcolf and Aesop in the fifteenth and sixteenth century, reference should be made also to a Tegernsee manuscript (Munich, Bayerische Staatsbibliothek, Clm 19870, fol. 1^v, upper left) into which a copper engraving by the German engraver Martin Schongauer (d. 1491) entitled "Peasant on the Way to the Market" has been pasted. Above this paste-down is written in a sixteenth-century hand: "Marcolfus vel ezopus." The comment means either that the writer did not know which figure was portrayed, or that it could represent either Marcolf or Aesop, since at this time they were represented similarly.

Jan M. Ziolkowski, Edward Sanger, Michael B. Sullivan

Bibliography

Martin Luther, "Vorrede zum 1. Bande der Wittenberger Ausgabe der deutschen Schriften," ed. Otto Clemen and Oskar Brenner, in *D. Martin Luthers Werke: Kritische Gesamtausgabe* (Weimar: Hermann Böhlaus Nachfolger, 1914), 50:659.

Michael Curschmann, "Marcolfus deutsch," 237–38.

G50. From Martin Luther, *Table Talk* (*Tischreden*), no. 5096. June 1540.

Philip (1504–67), Landgrave of Hesse, an important figure in the Reformation, never found his first wife to his taste, and covertly took a second in 1540. Because he failed to keep his bigamy under wraps, and the legal penalty for it was death, he soon set about appeasing Charles V (1500–58), the Holy Roman Emperor. This turn of events was bad news politically for Luther, made worse because he learned at the same time that Philip Melanchthon (1497–1560), another Reformation bigwig, had fallen ill. Luther's response to the situation, which references twice how Marcolf shows Solomon his posterior (*S&M* 2.19), was recorded by his student Johannes Mathesius (1504–65). In the passage, Philip refers to the given name of Melanchthon, and Macedo to the Landgrave of Hesse. In the penultimate sentence, the term *Scheflimini*, here designating Christ seated by the right hand of God, transliterates Hebrew words in Psalm 109 (110):1: "sit at my right hand" (*shëv liymiyniy*).

> De Macedonio negotio. Cum redderentur Doctori literae a Pontano, lectis eis dixit: Philippus maerore paene contabescit et incidit in febrim tertianam. Quare tamen is bonus sic se macerat propter hanc causam? Non potest suis curis mederi huic rei. *Ich wolt, das ich bey im were!* Ego novi ingenii teneritatem. Valde dolet viro hoc scandalum. Ego occallui, sum rusticus et durus Saxo ad eiusmodi [...]. Ego credo me vocari ad Philippum.
>
> Tum quidam: Domine Doctor, inquit, fortasse sic impedietur colloquium? — Tum Doctor: *Sie mussen vnser wol warten.*
>
> Non ita longe post reddebantur Doctori literae a principe. Quas cum serio vultu perlegeret, tandem inquit: Macedo plane insanit; iam caesarem orat, ut utranque habere possit!
>
> Et serenissimo vultu rediens ad nos dixit: *Es ist fein, wenn wir ettwas zu schaffen haben, so kriegen wir gedancken; sonst sauffen vnd fressen wir nur.* Quam clamitabunt papistae nostri! Sed clament, sane in ipsorum perniciem! Nostra tamen causa bona est et nostra vita inculpabilis, eorum tamen, qui serio agunt. Si Macedo peccavit, peccatum est et scandalum.

Nos saepe optima responsa dedimus et sancta; innocentiam nostram viderunt, sed noluerunt eam videre. *Drumb sehen sie nuhn dem Hessen in den ars.* Ipsi debent scandalis perire, quoniam noluerunt sanam doctrinam audire, *vnd Gott wirdt vns vnd sein wortt drumb nicht lassen vnd irer schonen, ob wir woll* peccata *haben, den er will das bapstumb sturtzen.* Hoc plane decrevit, ut est in Daniele sub finem eius, qui nunc instat: "Nemo ei opitulabitur." Superiori saeculo nulla potentia potuit evertere papam; hoc saeculo nulla potentia salvabit papam, quia Antichristus revelatus est. Si nos habemus scandala, et Christus habuit. [...] *Gott will die leutt vexiren, vnd kumpts an mich, wie will ich inen die bösesten wort darzu geben vnd sie heissen Marcolfo in ars sehen, weil sie im nicht wollen vnter die augen sehen. Ich weiß mich nichts vmb die sachen zu kummern. Ich befelchs vnserm Gott. Feldt Macedo von vnß, so stehe Christus bei vnß, der liebe Scheflimini! Er hat vnß woll aus grössern nöthen geholffen.*

On the matter of Macedo. When the Doctor received a letter from Pontanus [Gregor Brück (1483–1557)], he said upon reading it: "Philip is consumed by grief and has fallen into a tertian fever. Why is that noble man tormenting himself over this matter? He cannot mend it with his concern. How I wish that I were with him! I know how gentle his nature is. This scandal pains him immensely. I'm hardened, I'm a rustic Saxon insensible to such [s***]. I feel myself called to Philip."

Someone then said, "Lord Doctor, perhaps this will impede the conference [at Hagenau]?" — The Doctor said, "They will have to wait for us."

A short while later, the Doctor received a letter from the prince. He read through it with a serious expression, then said at last: "Clearly Macedo has gone mad! He's now entreating the emperor to allow him to have both wives."

Turning back to us he said with a completely tranquil expression: "It's good when we have have something to do. That's how we find ideas. Otherwise we'd just drink and eat all day. How our papists will clamor! But let them clamor straight to their own demise. Our cause is good, and our life blameless—at least for those of us who live seriously. If Macedo has sinned, that is a sin and a scandal. We have often made ideal responses, and holy ones; they have seen our innocence, but did not wish to see it. This is why they now look the Hessian in the asshole. They ought to be destroyed by scandals, because they refused to hear sensible doctrine. And therefore God will not abandon us or his word, nor will he spare their words, even if we also have sins, for he wants the papacy to collapse. He has decreed this clearly. As it says in Daniel [11:45] of the oppressor's end: 'Nobody will aid him.' In the last century, no power was able to overturn the pope; in this century, no power will be able to save him, for the Antichrist has been unveiled. If we have had scandals, so did Christ. [...] God wishes to vex people, and the burden falls to me to present them at the same time the foulest words and bid them look Marcolf in the ass, because they do not want to look him in the eye. I myself do not know how to handle the matter. I commit this matter to God. Macedo is lost to us, thus let Christ be with us, our dear *Scheflimini* [Christ seated by the right hand of God]! He's certainly helped us out of worse situations.

Johannes Aurifaber (1519–75), another of Luther's students, records a supposed instance in which the Reformer recounts in detail how Marcolf, forbidden by Solomon from looking him in the eye (*S&M* 2.17.14), mooned the king.

Doctor Martini Luthers Antwort auf einen fürgeworfenen ärgerlichen Fall. Doctor Martinus Luther ist ein Mal zu Leipzig Anno 1545 in einem Convivio gewesen, da hatte man ihm fürgeworfen einer hohen Person Fall und Aergerniß, und ihn darmit sehr vexiret und geplagt; da hat er zur Antwort gegeben: "Ihr lieben Junkern von Leipzig! Ich, Philippus und Andere wir haben viel schöner nützlicher Bücher geschrieben und Euch lange gnung das rothe Mündlein gewiesen, da habt Ihrs nicht gewollt; nun läßt Euch der N. in Ars sehen. Ihr habt das Gute nicht wollen annehmen, so möget Ihr nun in das Böse sehen!"

Und erzählete drauf die Fabel mit Marcolfo und König Salomon, und sprach: "Es kam ein Mal Marcolfus bey König Salomo in Ungnade also, daß er ihm seinen Hof verboten hatte und sollte dem Könige nicht mehr für die Augen kommen. Nun ging Marcolfus in ein Holz oder Wald, und als es geschneiet hatte und ein tiefer Schnee lag, da nahm er ein Fuß von einem wilden Thier in eine Hand, und in die ander Hand ein Sieb, und kroch also mit beiden Füßen, auch mit dem Sieb und Fuß gleich als ein wild Thier im Schnee umher, bis er zu einer Hölen kam; darein verkroch er sich. Als nun König Salomons Jäger im Schnee Wildpret ausspürete, kam er auf die Spur, und sahe, daß so ein wünderlich Thier in dieselbige Hölen gekrochen war. Derhalben eilete er an den Hof, und zeiget solches dem Könige an. Da war Salomo eilends auf und mit seinen Jagdhunden für die Höle, und wollt sehen, was für ein Wild drinnen wäre. Da stak Marcolfus im Loche. Als ihn nun der König hieß heraus kriechen, da deckt er den Ars auf, und kroch also rücklings heraus. Da wurde das ganze Hofgesinde zornig auf Marcolfum, und sprach der König zu ihm: 'Du Schalk, warum hast Du mir diese Shalkheit gethan?' Da antwortet Marcolfus: 'Ihr wolltet mir nicht mehr unter Augen sehen, so mußt ihr nu in den Hintern sehen.'"

Und sagt der Herr Doctor drauf: "Also gehts allhier auch zu. Was an uns zu tadeln ist, das klaubet Ihr heraus; aber was wir Gutes thun, das wollet Ihr nicht haben."

Doctor Martin Luther's response to an irritating incident raised as a reproach. Doctor Martin Luther once was at a banquet in Leipzig in the year 1545 where someone reproached him for the fall and irritation of a high-born person, which vexed and distressed him; and he answered thus: "My dear noblemen of Leipzig! I, Philip, and others have written many beautiful, useful books and we have now for a long enough time revealed to you our red dainty little mouth. Since you didn't want that, now look in the ass. You didn't want to accept the Good, so now you may look upon the Bad!"

And after that he told the story of Marcolf and King Solomon, and said: "One time Marcolf fell so far out of favor with King Solomon that he forbade Marcolf to come to his court and said that he should no longer come before the king's eyes. Marcolf then went into the woods or a forest. As it had snowed and a deep snow lay, he took a wild animal's foot in one hand and a sieve in the other, and so crept around with both feet as well as with the sieve and the foot, just like a wild animal in the snow, until he came to a cave; he crept inside. Then, as one of King Solomon's hunters was tracking game in the snow, he found his tracks and saw that a strange animal was hidden in the same cave. Therefore he hurried to court and reported this to the king. Then Solomon rose in a hurry and went with his hunting hounds to the cave and wanted to see what kind of a wild animal was inside. But Marcolf was hidden in the hole. When the king called for Marcolf to crawl out, he uncovered his ass, and crawled backwards out of the cave. The whole court retinue was furious with Marcolf, and the king said to him: "You rogue! Why have you committed this roguery against me?" Then Marcolf answered, "Since you never again wanted to look me in the eyes, now you must look me in the backside."

And after that Doctor Luther says: "It is happening just the same here too. Whatever there is in us to rebuke, you pluck out; but what good we do, you wish not to have."

Jan M. Ziolkowski, Edward Sanger, Michael B. Sullivan

Bibliography

Burghart Wachinger, "*Convivium fabulosum:* Erzählen bei Tisch im 15. und 16. Jahrhundert, besonders in der 'Mensa philosophica' und bei Erasmus und Luther," in *Kleinere Erzählformen des 15. und 16. Jahrhunderts,* ed. Walter Haug and Burghart Wachinger (Tübingen: Niemeyer, 1993), 256–86.

Martin Luther, "Nachschriften von Johannes Mathesins," ed. Ernst Kroker, in *D. Martin Luthers Werke: Kritische Gesamtausgabe; Tischreden* (Weimar: Hermann Böhlaus Nachfolger, 1916), 4:655–60, no. 5096.

G51. From Martin Luther, "Report on the Case of M. Johannis Eissleben" ("Bericht auff die Klage M. Johannis Eissleben"). 1540.

The name Magister Johannes Eisleben refers to the German Reformer, Humanist, and close acquaintance of Luther's better known as Johannes Agricola, who was born in Eisleben. Luther uses the character of Eulenspiegel, the famous German prankster, to defame his opponents, and mocks Agricola with ironic neologisms designed to debunk him.

> Das er einen kockismum oder Grekismum geschrieben, auch viel anders, da zu auch gepredigt, hab ich wohl gewust (wolt wol, er hette es gelassen oder dafür Marcolfum oder Eulenspiegel gepredigt).

> I knew quite well that he had written "kakismus" and "greckismus," and also much more, besides also preaching (I would have preferred that he had left it aside or instead preached Marcolf or Eulenspiegel).

Compare G34, in which Luther also talks about "preaching about Marcolf."

Bibliography

Martin Luther, "Bericht auff die Klage M. Johannis Eissleben," ed. Otto Clemen and Oskar Brenner, in *D. Martin Luthers Werke: Kritische Gesamtausgabe* (Weimar: Hermann Böhlaus Nachfolger, 1914), 51:429–43, at 434–35.

Reinhard Tenberg, *Die deutsche Till Eulenspiegel-Rezeption bis zum Ende des 16. Jahrhunderts,* Epistemata 161 (Würzburg: Königshausen & Neumannm, 1996), 110–11.

G52. From Sebastian Franck, *Sayings, Beautiful Words, Wise Words, Wonderfully Clever Turns of Phrase, and Courtly Proverbs* [...] (*Sprichwörter, Schöne, Weise, Herrliche Clugreden, und Hoffsprüch* [...]), part two. 1541.

The first passage begins with three words in the learned language (italicized) that Franck himself made famous. In the third sentence, he repeats in Latin a saying taken from Horace, *Epistles* 1.10.24 (again in italics). For his application of this famous tag (quoted likewise in G66, G74, and G80) about the nature of nature itself, the German writer is probably indebted to his countryman Agricola. A few sentences later, he cites in Latin (once again italicized) a Greek proverb about salt that gained wide dissemination through its inclusion in Erasmus. At the end of the first passage (fols. 6ʳ–6ᵛ), Franck likely relies upon Agricola again for the episode of the cat and the candle (also referenced in G60 and G66) which is narrated in *S&M* 2.8.

> *Consuetudinem superat natura.* Natur geht für. *Naturam expellas furca, tamen usque recurret.* Art laßt von art nit. Katz laßt irs mausen nit. Das vnkraut wil von dem garten nit. *Sal unde uenerat, redit.* Was wasser gewest ist das kompt wasser wider. Saltz eiß schnee kompt von wasser vnd artet sich immerzů vnd hat kein růw bißwider zu wasser würt. Also artet sich Adam in vns wo er wonet vnd Christus spiegelt sich auch in sein gleubigen ob gleich vil zwerchs lere dargegen kompt so hafftet es doch nit. Die natur geht für. Hieher dient der schwanck Marcolffi von der katzen so das licht hůb den meusen.

> *Nature overcomes nurture.* Nature takes precedence. *You may drive nature out with a pitchfork, but it will continue to come back.* One's nature does not simply go away. Cats do not release their mice. The weed does not want to go from the garden. *Salt returns where it came from.* What was once water becomes water again. Salt, ice, and snow come from water and change form all the time, but have no respite until they become water again. Therefore Adam maintains his nature in us, where he dwells, and Christ mirrors himself in his faithful. Though teaching opposes much in opposition, it does not stick. Nature takes precedence. In this particular Marcolf's tale serves well, about the cat who held up a candle for the mice.

The second passage comes on fol. 47ʳ.

> Camelus saltat. Ein dapinsmůß, ein flegelhůt. Es steht im an als dem bern das tantzen. [...] Wann einer tauben hat vnnd im sein ding vbel ansteht sagen wir: Er hat mucken Die fliehen stechen jn Die alt geyß hüpfft auch Marcolfus tantzet Esopus ist im spil Vnderbunden wie ein garb Er ist ein narr wann got sein vatter were [...] Der Esel spilt auff der leiren Der Beer tantzet Die Saw ist ein Apotecker worden [...] Also magstu die red varieren wann du wilt sagen eim stehe ein ding vbel an [...]

The camel dances. [Two Swiss dialect insults for peasants.] It suits him just as much as it suits bears to dance. [...] If a man has doves and ... If his circumstances suits him ill, we say: he has midges, the fleas bite him, the old she-goat hops and Marcolf dances too. In playing Aesop has been bound like a bundle of wheat. He's a fool even if God were his father [...] The donkey played the lyre, the bear dances, the sow had become the druggist [..] And thus you may change the topic of conversation if ever you might wish to tell him that something doesn't well suit him.

The third comes on fols. 68^v–69^r.

Es geht eben so vil liebs ghenn kirchen als schöns. Mein bůl die schönest. Man findt kein scheußlich bůlschafft. Quis filius non formosus matri? Einn ieden dunckt sein eul ein falck sein. [...] Nun aber setzt venus den jren solche brillen auff daß ye ein Bintzger baur einen eyd schwüre es wer kein schöner bild auff erden dann ein Bintzger beurin mit eim grossen kropff solt sie den nit haben er meynt sie were ein genßkrag und hette jre glider nit alle. Also bleibt Marcolfo sein viereckichts weib die schön Helena vnnd gehet eben so vil liebs als schöns ghen kirchen [...].

Just as many sweet as beautiful people go to church. My lover is the most beautiful. No hideous pair of lovers is to be found. What son is not handsome to his mother? Everyone thinks their owl to be a falcon. [...] But now Venus puts such glasses on them, then every peasant would swear an oath that there was no more beautiful image on earth than a peasant wife with a big goiter. Should she not have it, he thinks her to be goosenecked and not to have all her limbs. Thus to Marcolf his four-square wife remains beautiful Helen of Troy, and similarly just as many sweet as beautiful people go to church.

Bibliography

Michael Curschmann, "Markolf tanzt," 967.

Sebastian Franck, *Sprichwörter, Schöne, Weise, Herrliche Clugreden, und Hoffsprüch*, with a foreword by Wolfgang Mieder (Hildesheim: George Olms, 1987), pt. 2, fols. 6^r–6^v, 47^r, 68^v–69^r.

G53. From Martin Luther, Letter to Hieronymus Weller. July 25, 1542.

The Reformer wrote this letter from Wittenberg. One small portion of it confirms that, thanks to the so-called oven-tale in *S&M* 2.19, "looking Marcolf in the ass" becomes a common turn of phrase that may be applied "in practically any suitable (or unsuitable) occasion" (Curschmann, "Marcolfus deutsch," 224). Compare G45 and G50 as well.

> vnd iücket sie die haut [= "wollen sie Schläge herausfordern"], vnd wollen Marcolfus ins arßloch kucken, so heißt sie von mir den brief foddern.

> and their skin itches [to receive blows], and they want to look Marcolf in the asshole—so it's said they demand the letter from me.

Bibliography

Martin Luther to Hieronymus Weller, July 25, 1542, ed. Otto Clemen, in *D. Martin Luthers Werke: Kritische Gesamtausgabe; Briefwechsel* (Weimar: Hermann Böhlaus Nachfolger, 1947), 10:113.

Michael Curschmann, "Marcolfus deutsch," 224n105.

G54. From Martin Luther, "Of the Jews and their Lies" ("Von den Juden und ihren Lügen"). 1543.

In this anti-Judaic and anti-Semitic treatise, Luther refers three times in passing to Marcolf. In the first instance he seems to imply that in his view even Marcolf's tales are too sacred for Jews, whom he regards as depraved.

> Das man gnugsam verstehet, Wie die Jüden nicht jrren noch verfüret sind, Sondern böslich und mutwilliglich, wider jr gewissen, die erkandte warheit leugnen und lestern. Einen solchen Menschen sol niemand werd achten, das er ein einiges wort mit jm reden wolt, Wens auch were vom Marcolfo, schweige von solchen hohen Göttlichen worten und wercken.

> A person should understand sufficiently how the Jews neither err nor are misled, but rather maliciously and wantonly, against their own consciences, deny and blaspheme the known truth. No one should think such a man worthy, that he would speak a single word with him, even if it were of Marcolf, to say nothing of such high godly words and works.

In the second snippet he develops a metaphor of smokiness to which he resorts also in G60. He argues that in matters of doctrine people lay claim to knowledge that is never truly supported by textual authority. Such support is not to be found in the haze of such smoky places as ecclesiastic councils (compare G60).

> Nu sage mir: wo stehet solchs geschrieben? Im Rauchloch. Wer hats gesagt? Marcolfus. Wer künds sonst sagen oder schreiben?

> Now tell me, where is such a thing written? In a hall of smoke and mirrors. And who has said such a thing? Marcolf. Who else would say or write it?

In the final passage, Luther groups Marcolf with Agrippa and Thersites as personages who are elevated as Messiahs instead of the true one. Agrippa I, called Herod Agrippa in Acts 12:1, ruled as King of Judea from 41 to 44 CE. Acts 12:23 describes how Agrippa was struck down by an angel of the Lord, eaten by worms, and died. The choice of Thersites as a peer for Marcolf is particularly apt, since the character from Book 2 of the *Iliad* became in later tradition a stock figure for physical deformity and verbal scurrilousness, both features associated powerfully with Marcolf.

> Messia ist der König Agrippa, der ist getödtet und hat nach seinem tod nichts mehr gehabt, und kein König ist nach jm komen. [...] Ja ich acht, sie nehmen ehe Marcolfum oder Thersitam fur Messia, ehe sie den rechten Messia lidden.

> The Messiah is King Agrippa, who was killed and had nothing at all after his death, and no king succeeded him [...] Yes, I notice, they prefer to have Marcolf or Thersites as Messiah, rather than proclaiming the true Messiah.

Bibliography

Martin Luther, "Von den Juden und ihren Lügen," ed. Ferdinand Cohrs and Oskar Brenner, in *D. Martin Luthers Werke: Kritische Gesamtausgabe* (Weimar: Hermann Böhlaus Nachfolger, 1920), 53:456, 53:505, 53:508.

G55. From Martin Luther, "The Word Was Made Flesh, that is, God Was Made Man" ("Verbum caro factum est, hoc est, Deus homo factus est"). Ca. 1544.

The Reformer had a soft spot for the fourth book of the New Testament, which he ranked high above the three synoptic Gospels. In this sermon on John 1:14 Luther emphasizes the miraculousness of the doctrine that God should become man. In turn he opines that a reader uninterested in such a miracle might as well read about Marcolf and his ilk.

Solch wunderlich vnd vberwunderlich ding, das Gott ist Mensch worden, leret dis gantz vnd einig Buch (die Bibel), dauon kein ander Buch nichts weis. Denn wo du nicht suchest in diesem Buch das *Verbum caro factum est*, So were dir besser, einen Marcolfus oder Ulenspiegel gelesen.

Such a wonderful and miraculous thing, that God became man, this one book alone (the Bible) teaches; no other book knows anything about this. For if you do not seek in this book to learn how the Word became flesh, it would be better then for you to have read a tale of Marcolf or Eulenspiegel.

Bibliography

Martin Luther, "Verbum caro factum est, hoc est, Deus homo factus est," ed. Otto von Albrecht, in *D. Martin Luthers Werke: Kritische Gesamtausgabe* (Weimar: Hermann Böhlaus Nachfolger, 1927), 48:130.

Reinhard Tenberg, *Die deutsche Till Eulenspiegel-Rezeption bis zum Ende des 16. Jahrhunderts*, Epistemata 161 (Würzburg: Königshausen & Neumann, 1996), 123–24.

G56. From Kaspar Goltwurm, *Rhetorical Devices, in German* (*Schemata rhetorica, Teutsch*). Marburg, 1545, fols. Pij^r–Pij^v. 1545.

Kaspar (also known as Caspar) Goltwurm (1524–59) was a theologian and reformer. The first of his writings was this text, a rhetorical manual for preachers. In it he emphasizes to his readers the utility of the classics and of contemporary humanistic authors. Incidentally, he warns against incorporating into serious speeches proverbial sayings from handbooks of popular anecdotes.

dar zu muß hierinn auch fleiß fürgewendet werden, das inn ernstlichen hochwichtigen sachen nit nerrische, vnnütze, oder vndichtige sprüch auß dem Eulenspiegel, Marcolfo, oder andern leichtfertigen gedict geholt, sonder gewaltige, ernstliche, nützliche, weißliche, so von weisen, verstendigen leuthen geredt, genommen, vnd inn die Oration geflochten werden.

In addition, effort must be applied in this matter, so that in serious and weighty matters no foolish, needless, or unpoetic sayings should be taken from Eulenspiegel, Marcolf, or another slapdash poem, but rather monumental, serious, useful, and sage ones, as pronounced by wise and insightful people, and woven into the speech.

Bibliography

Heinz-Günter Schmitz, "Sophist, Narr und Melancholievertreiber: Zum Eulenspiegelbild im 16. und 17. Jahrhundert," in Herbert Blume and Eberhard Rohse, eds., *Hermann Bote: Städtisch-hansischer Autor in Braunschweig, 1488-1988; Beiträge zum Braunschweiger Bote-Kolloquium 1988* (Tübingen: Niemeyer, 1991), 217.

Reinhard Tenberg, *Die deutsche Till Eulenspiegel-Rezeption bis zum Ende des 16. Jahrhunderts*, Epistemata 161 (Würzburg: Königshausen & Neumann, 1996), 117–18.

G57. From Martin Luther, "Against the Papacy in Rome Established by the Devil" ("Wider das Papsttum zu Rom, vom Teuffel gestiftet"). 1545.

Pope Paul III wrote two epistles to Emperor Charles V to assert that only the bishop of Rome may convoke a council. In his treatise "Against the Papacy in Rome Established by the Devil," Luther compares this pair of letters to degenerate literature, including romance-like novels associated with Marcolf, Dietrich of Bern, and Eulenspiegel.

Wer sind sie denn, die da Christen sein mügen? Sinds die, so Marcolfum oder Diedrich von Bern oder Ulenspiegel lesen? oder, das gleich viel und noch erger ist, die des Bapsts dreck und stanck lesen?

So who are they then, those who wish to be Christians? Are they the ones who read Marcolf, Dietrich von Bern, or Eulenspiegel? Or, what is much more aggravating still, those who read the noxious filth of the Pope?

Bibliography

Martin Luther, "Wider das Papsttum zu Rom, vom Teufel gestiftet," ed. Otto Clemmen, in *D. Martin Luthers Werke: Kritische Gesamtausgabe* (Weimar: Hermann Böhlaus Nachfolger, 1928), 54:288.

Michael Curschmann, "Marcolfus deutsch," 232n118.

Reinhard Tenberg, *Die deutsche Till Eulenspiegel-Rezeption bis zum Ende des 16. Jahrhunderts*, Epistemata 161 (Würzburg: Königshausen & Neumann, 1996), 116–17.

G58. From Martin Luther, "Sermon Given on the Occasion of the Wedding of Sigmund of Lindenau in Merseburg" ("Predigt bei der Hochzeit Sigmunds von Lindenau in Merseburg"). August 4, 1545.

This is the second sermon that Luther delivered on the text of Hebrews 13, "Marriage should be honorably preserved by all and the marriage bed should remain pure." Sigmund (died 1544) was deacon of the chapter of Merseburg. Luther refers here to Marcolf's mirror, which he discusses more fully in the following testimonium, G59.

The reflective device may have become associated with Solomon's antagonist partly owing to the mirror element in the name of Eulenspiegel (which could be translated literally as Owl-Mirror or Owlglass), with whom Marcolf was linked. Both serve as looking glasses in which society could see itself reflected and judge itself. Both Solomon and the owl symbolized wisdom, which in characters like Eulenspiegel and Marcolf were distorted as in a funhouse mirror.

So sie mich nicht wollen sehen noch hören, so sehen sie jnns Teuffels namen dem Marcolffo jnn sein spiegel.

As they wish neither to see nor hear me, so they see in the devil's name Marcolf in his mirror.

Bibliography

Martin Luther, "Predigt bei der Hochzeit Sigmunds von Lindenau in Merseburg," ed. Georg Buchwald, in *D. Martin Luthers Werke: Kritische Gesamtausgabe* (Weimar: Hermann Böhlaus Nachfolger, 1913), 49:800.

G59. From Martin Luther, "Against the Thirty-Two Articles of the Louvain Theologists" ("Contra XXXII articulos Lovaniensium theologistarum"). 1545.

In the first passage quoted from this treatise, Luther mentions Marcolf's mirror, which reflects a world turned upside down—what could be styled in Latin a *mundus inversus* and what has been described in recent times as upended. The image may also allude to Eulenspiegel, whose very name has a looking-glass embedded in it as its second element.

Ea, quae art. XXI cum sequentibus octo dicunt, sunt perfecte Marcolfica nec nisi in speculo Marcolfi visibilia, simul tamen blasphema et Idolatrica.

What the twenty-first article along with the following eight teach is entirely Marcolfian, and not perceptible except in Marcolf's mirror, yet at the same time blasphemous and idolatrous.

There is a German version of the passage, also written by Luther.

> Alles, was sie im XXI. Artikel sampt den folgenden achten leren, das ist aus der massen gantz fein Marcolfisch. Welches man auch sonst nirgent finden noch lesen kann denn im Marcolffs spiegel, Doch gantz lesterlich vnd abgöttisch.

> Everything that they teach in the twenty-first article, along with the following eight, is beyond measure, through and through, purely Marcolfian. One can otherwise neither read nor find anything elsewhere than in Marcolf's mirror, yet through and through vicious and idolatrous.

In the second passage (no. 63), Luther presents the theologians of Louvain (or Leuven, to use the Flemish form) as foolish and heretical for their preference of Latin over the vernacular, their pretentious regalia (a liripipe is the long tail of the hood worn by academics), and their predilection for the tales of Marcolf.

> Aber weil sie nicht auff Löuanisch und der Rangen weise Lyrrapippa zu tragen geweiht sind noch der Röllinge Marcolfum gelernt, sind sie von der Hiemelischen Vakuldet zu Löuen noch hinfurt als Ketzer zu verdamnen.

> But since they have not been consecrated in the dialect of Louvain and to wear the liripipe in ranks, nor have they learned the rutting ones' Marcolf, they have been led off by the divinity faculty to Louvain to be damned as heretics.

The marginal note *in Marcolfo* (on Marcolf) is used in the sense "in the fantasy" in the twelfth article in this treatise, which reads: "The sacraments of confirmation and extreme unction have been established by Christ, but are not necessary for salvation as the two preceding ones are; yet to omit them out of contempt is a mortal sin."

Bibliography

Martin Luther, "Contra XXXII articulos Lovaniensium theologistarum," ed. Otto Clemen, in *D. Martin Luthers Werke: Kritische Gesamtausgabe* (Weimar: Hermann Böhlaus Nachfolger, 1928), 54:428 (Latin), 54:439 (German), 54:441 (for no. 63), 54:419 (for the marginal note).

G60. From Martin Luther, "Sermon given in Leipzig" ("Predigt in Leipzig gehalten"). August 12, 1545.

This sermon takes as its principal theme discovery and deception (or, to give the concepts a slightly unconventional twist, fabrication and lie). In one passage from it, Luther juxtaposes the murkiness of a papal conclave and the obscurity of the monkish tales about Marcolf. In the second passage, the author makes another reference to the episode of the cat and the candle in *S&M* 2.8.

> Denn wo ist das geschrieben denn in des Bapsts Rauchloch und der Münche Marcolfo, ein new fündlin von jnen selbs erdacht.

> For where is it written, then? In the Pope's smoke-filled chamber and in the monks' Marcolf, a new little discovery devised by them themselves.

One's nature does not simply go away. Cats do not let their mice run by. At this point the manuscript version of the same sermon reads.

> Wo sthet das geschryeben? ym Marcolfus buch, neyn, sunder das yst der alt glaub, das Christus sagt [...].

> Where is that written? In the book of Marcolf, no, rather it is the old belief that Christ said [...].

Bibliography

Martin Luther, "Predigt in Leipzig gehalten, " ed. Georg Buchwald, in *D. Martin Luthers Werke: Kritische Gesamtausgabe* (Weimar: Hermann Böhlaus Nachfolger, 1914), 51:29.

Michael Curschmann, "Marcolfus deutsch," 232.

G61. From Martin Luther, "Sermon on Christmas Day" ("Predigt am Weihnachtstage"). December 25, 1544.

Luther mentions Marcolf in a Christmas sermon while discussing Luke 2.

> Las mirs predigen, malen, singen, gehe aber darvon, als hett Ich ein Merlein gehoret aus Marckolf.

> Let me preach it, paint it, sing it, and go on about it, as though I have heard a little tale from Marcolf!

Bibliography

Martin Luther, "Preidgt am Weihnachtstage," ed. G. Buchwald, in D. *Martin Luthers Werke: Kritische Gesamtausgabe* (Weimar: Hermann Böhlaus Nachfolger, 1913), 49:634.

G62. From Joachim II, Elector of Brandenburg, Letter to Antonius von Schonberg. 1546.

The young prince Joachim (1535–71), a member of the House of Hohenzollern, was to be educated in, alongside other subjects, the use of his native German tongue. The theologian Doctor Jakob Schenk (ca. 1508–after 1546) was hired for the purpose at the recommendation of the counselor Antonius von Schonberg, but did not meet expectations. The prince ultimately cast him out from Brandenburg in 1546 because of his unamenability. Joachim then received an apologetic letter from Schonberg, to whom he replied as follows.

> Lieber besonder. Wir haben ewr schreiben Doctor Jacob Schencken belangend lesend vernommen [...]. Was uns aber zu solcher verurlaubung und seiner verlassung, domit wir jne doch gern, Sonderlich Gottes wort zu ehren und seins Ampts halber verschonet hetten, [...] und wurd nit weniger ein Seltzam und lecherlich histori oder legend daraus werden dan von Eulenspigel und Marcolfe, oder dem Pfaffen von kalenberge [...].

> My dear friend,
> We have examined your letter concerning Doctor Schenk [...]. As for the matter of his departure and dismissal, we are in agreement, though we hold him dear, and would have preferred to spare his position, especially to do honor to the word of God [...] and he made no less a peculiar and ridiculous story or tale of it than did Eulenspiegel, Marcolf, or the Priest of Kalenberg [...].

Bibliography

Georg Schuster and Friedrich Wagner, *Die Jugend und Erziehung der Kurfürsten von Brandenburg und Könige von Preussen*, ed. Georg Schuster and Friedrich Wagner, Monumenta Germaniae Paedagogica 34 (Berlin: A. Hofmann, 1906), 1:369.

Reinhard Tenberg, *Die deutsche Till Eulenspiegel-Rezeption bis zum Ende des 16. Jahrhunderts*, Epistemata 161 (Würzburg: Königshausen & Neumann, 1996), 118–19.

G63. This item in Griese's testimonia has been stricken here, since it duplicated exactly **G55.**

G64. From Hans Sachs, "The Twenty-Seven Plays of Schmidlein" ("Die 27 spil des schmidlein"). 1551.

Hans Sachs's *Meistergesang* of March 6, 1551 describes the roles played by a mastersinger named Schmidlein in performing twenty-seven plays, mainly by this same playwright. In the general index to this work, twenty-seven discrete theatrical parts are listed, all of which this single singer took on. One of the roles is that of Marcolf in the episode of Solomon and the rebellious women (*S&M* 2.11–17). The scene alludes in verses 41–43 to Sachs' comedy "The Judgment of Solomon" ("Juditium Salomonis"), which was first performed on March 6, 1550.

> Nach dem wart ich Marcolfus pey kung Salomon,
> Die weiber ich pald auf den kunig hezet on,
> Erzelt ir duegent in manigen dingen.

> Afterward I, Marcolf, was with King Solomon,
> and I soon set loose the wild women upon the king,
> told them about virtue in many things.

Bibliography

Victor Michels, "Zur Geschichte des Nürnberger Theaters im 16. Jahrhundert," *Vierteljahresschrift für Litteraturgeschichte* 3 (1890): 44.

Horst Brunner and Burghart Wachinger, *Repertorium der Sangsprüche und Meisterlieder des 12. bis 18. Jahrhunderts* (Tübingen: Niemeyer, 1986), 11:36.

G65. From Caspar Scheidt, *Grobianus.* 1551.

Scheidt (ca. 1520–65) was a schoolmaster in Worms. His *Grobianus,* a bestseller of sorts, translates into German rhyming verse the Latin satire of the same name (1549) by Friedrich Dedekind (1525–98). The noun that gives the work its title, which remained in use into the eighteenth century, is a playful humanist Latinization of the fifteenth-century German equivalent Grobian. Both terms refer to a crude and ill-mannered person. They derive from the adjective *grob,* which remains in use to this day in German to describe rough manners and discourteous behavior. Accordingly, it makes good sense that Scheidt (*nomen est omen!*) subtitled his poem "On Rough Manner and Discourteous Behavior," which replaces Dedekind's "or two books on moral simplicity."

The poet makes mention of Marcolf four times. The first three come in verses 51–58, 81–82, and 110–114. The third instance may shade away from the Marcolf known from folklore and literature into a similarly named wine, the correlation of which with the character is sometimes hard to sort out.

> Auch Satyros bring mit ein par,
> Vnd der Waldgött ein grosse schar,
> Den Pfaffen auch vom Kalenbergk,
> Der trib sein tag vil narrenwerck.
> Vergiß mir auch Marcolphum nit,
> Vnd bring den Vlenspiegel mit,
> Vnd was sonst sind für grobe gsellen
> Die mir zur arbeit helffen wöllen.
> [...]
> Wo bleibt Marcolphus, ist er hie?
> Kein schönern gast gesah ich nie.
> [...]
> Man spricht, was wüst ist, macht auch feist.
> Da laß mich thůn ein gůten suff,
> Marcolffe sich, der gilt dir druff.
> Hehem, das heißt ein gůter tranck,
> Jetz bin ich gesundt, vor war ich kranck.

> And bring along a pair of satyrs
> and a large company of forest gods,
> and also the Priest of Kalenberg
> who spent his days on much foolish activity.
> In addition, do not forget Marcolf for me,
> and bring along Eulenspiegel,
> and whatever remains in the way of coarse fellows
> who wish to help me in my activity.
> [...]
> Where is Marcolf staying? Is he here?
> A handsomer guest I've never seen.
> [...]
> People say that what is indecent makes one fat.
> Well, let me take a good long swig,
> Marcolf himself, that applies to you.
> My, oh my, that is a most fine drink.
> Before I was sick, but now I'm well.

The fourth and final mention comes thousands of verses later in the poem (3165–69, 3175–78). Here, the spelling "Morolf" is used, possibly through assimilation of an unaccustomed Latin-Romance form for "mulberry" to a more familiar version of Marcolf's name.

> Jeder des besten weins ein maß,
> Den er die gest versuchen laß,
> Da will jeder der förderst sein,
> Der bringt ein gůten Rheinschen wein,
> Der ist auß Elsaß her gesandt,
> [...]
> On die man sonst erst hat erdact,
> Die man mit zůsatz hat gemacht:
> Morolff, Zitwen, vnd Alantwein,
> Vnd da man thůt rot beren ein.

> Everyone a cup of the best wine,
> that he lets the guests try,
> since each will want to be the foremost,
> who brings a good Rhineland wine,
> which is sent here from Alsace.
> [...]
> which one otherwise just made up,
> which one made with additives:
> Morolf, white turmeric, and elecampane wine,
> and then one puts in red berries.

Bibliography

Caspar Scheidt, *Grobianus: Von groben sitten vnd vnhöflichen geberden*, ed. Rolf D. Fay (Stuttgart: Helfant, 1985), 12–14 and 102.

Reinhard Tenberg, *Die deutsche Till Eulenspiegel-Rezeption bis zum Ende des 16. Jahrhunderts*, Epistemata 161 (Würzburg: Königshausen & Neumann, 1996), 132–33.

G66. From Anonymous *Proverbs: Beautiful, Wise, and Clever Sayings* [...] (*Sprichwörter, Schöne, Weise Klügredenn* [...]). 1552.

This book was published at Frankfurt by Christian Egenolff (1502–55), the first major printer to operate in Frankfurt am Main. The anonymously compiled anthology agglomerates proverbs extracted from the works of Sebastian Franck and Johannes Agricola. Translating its extensive title may be the most efficient introduction to its contents: "Proverbs: Beautiful, Wise, and Clever Sayings. This book contains courtesy, ornament, and highest reason and intelligence, in German and other languages, which in the service of both contemporary and eternal wisdom, virtue, art, and character are here noted and explained. How old and new proverbs are used is described. A few thousand are brought together here."

The two extracts quoted here refer to the famous story of the cat and the candle that is related in S&M 2.8 (see G52). In the first passage (fol. 11ʳ), Agricola quotes Horace, *Epistles* 1.10.24, a famous tag about the nature of nature itself (see G52).

> Natur geht für lehre. *Naturam expellas furca, tamen usque recurret.* Art laßt von art nit. Katz laßt jrs mausens nit. Das vnkraut will vom garten nit. *Sal unde uenerat, redit.*
>
> Was wasser gwesen ist, wirt wider zu wasser. Saltz, eiß, schnee, kommen von wasser, vnd artet sich immerzu, hat kein růhe, biß wider zu wasser wirt. Also artet sich Adam in vns wo er wonet, Vnnd Christus spiegelt sich auch in seinen gläubigen, ob gleich vil zwerchs lere dargegen kompt, so hafftet es doch nit. Die natur geht für. Hieher dienet der schwanck Marcolffi, von der katzen so das liecht hübe, und meusen.

> Nature takes precedence over teaching. *You may drive nature out with a pitchfork, but it will continue to come back.* "As the call, so the echo." A cat does not give up its mousing. Weeds won't leave gardens. *Salt returns where it came from.*
>
> What was once water will return to being water. Salt, ice, and snow come from water, and they keep on and never rest until they return to being water. And Adam returns in us, where he abides, and Christ too is mirrored in those who believe in him; although many oppose false teaching, yet it does not stick. Nature takes precedence over teaching. Here Marcolf's tale is serviceable, about the cat who held up a candle and the mice.

The second passage appears on fols. 80ᵛ–81ʳ. Compare also G35.

> Art laßt von art nicht, die Katz laßt jhres mausens vnnd die Atzel jhres hupffens nicht.
>
> Salomon sagt: Wann du den narren in einem mörser zerstiessest mit einem stempffel wie grütz, so laßt doch sein thorheyt nit von jm. Mann sagt, daß Marcolfus mit dem weisen Salomon disputiert hab, vnd

gesagt, Natur geht für lehr. So wolt Salomon daß gewonheyt vnd lere so hart anhange, als die natur. Vnd dieweil Salomon ein Katzen hette, die jm nach gewonheyt das liecht hielte bei nacht, brachte Marcolfus etlich meuß zu wegen, vnd kam des abends zu Salomon vnnd ließ erstlich ein mauß lauffen, Vnnd als bald die Katz der mauß gewar warde, tapt sie ein wenig mit der pfoten, vnd ließ doch das liecht nicht fallen. Da aber die ander vnd dritte mauß fürüber lieffen, liesse sie das liecht fallen, vnd lieff den meusen nach. Darauß hernach Marcolfus beweisete, Art gieng für alle gewonheyt. Ein jung reiß wann es krumm wechst, so laßt sichs nit biegen, mann vnderstütze es wie mann wöl, so wachset es doch krumm. Der Katzen art ist, daß sie nit mauset auß hunger, sonder auß lust, also daß, ie mehr mann der Katzen zu essen gibt, ie mehr sie mauset. Also auch, was einem menschen angeboren, vnnd warzu er von natur geneygt ist, das thût er, vnd laßt sich hieran nichts hindern.

One's true nature is not ever really abandoned. The cat doesn't give up its mousing and the magpie does not just stop hopping.

Solomon says: If you grind up a fool with a mortar and pestle like grain, even then his foolish ways do not leave him. They say that Marcolf argued with the wise Solomon, and said to him that nature takes precedence over teaching. And Solomon held that training and teaching can take hold just as firmly as nature. At that time, Solomon had a cat that he had trained to hold a candle for him at night. One evening, Marcolf brought some mice, and he came to Solomon and at first let just one mouse run free. As soon as the cat noticed the mouse, the cat tapped just a bit with its paws, and yet did not let the light fall. But then when the second and third mouse ran past, the cat let the candle fall and ran after the mice. On this basis Marcolf proved as a consequence that nature took precedence over all habit. A young branch that grows crookedly will not be unbent, and no matter how one may try to support it as it grows, it will still grow crookedly. It is a cat's nature not to hunt mice out of hunger, but for pleasure, and the more one feeds a cat, the more that it will hunt mice. And so it is when a person is born disposed toward to certain tendencies, he pursues them according to his nature; that is what he does, and nothing will prevent him from doing so.

Bibliography

Christian Egenolff, *Sprichwörter, Schöne, Weise Klügredenn* [...] (Frankfurt: 1552; facsimile of the first edition, with an afterword by Hanns Henning, Munich-Pullach: Verlag Dokumentation, 1968), fols. 11^r, 80^v–81^r.

G67. From Johannes Mathesius, Letter 60, to Paul Eber. June 6, 1559.

Mathesius (1504–65) was a reformer and one of the compilers of Luther's *Table Talk*. The addressee of his letter, Eber (1511–69), was likewise a follower of Luther, a German theologian and hymnwriter. In a passing mention of Marcolf, the Lutheran groups him with Zoilus (a Greek rhetorician of the fourth century BCE who came to embody petty and spiteful criticism) and Thersites (a warrior on the Greek side during the Trojan War who slandered the chiefs above him).

> S. D. Reuerende vir et amice carissime. Praeclare meriti sunt de posteritate qui conscripsere bonam historiam superiorum annorum. Ego qui absens semper meos oculos in vestros vtiles labores direxi, ago bonis viris gratias, qui sancte inseruierunt in hunc vsque diem veritati et ecclesiae et propono mihi imitandam ipsorum moderationem cum constantia coniunctam. Reliquos Zoilos, Thersites et Marcolphos vt fanaticos odi. Et certus sum ipsos portaturos esse suum iudicium, quia conturbarunt ecclesiam dei viuentis et contristauerunt spiritum sanctum in piorum cordibus.

> Reverend man and dearest friend, [Johannes Mathesius] sends greetings. The authors of good histories of bygone years deserve from posterity renown with distinction. I, who have always focused my eyes from a distance on your useful toils, give thanks to good men, who have served the sacred truth and church down to this day, and I intend to imitate their restraint, joined together with their steadiness. I hate for their extremism the other Zoiluses, Thersitai, and Marcolfs. And I am sure that they are going to bear his judgment, because they have disrupted the Church of the living God and have distressed the Holy Spirit in the hearts of the pious.

Bibliography

Johannes Mathesius, *Ausgewählte Werke*, ed. Georg Loesche, Bibliothek deutscher Schriftsteller aus Böhmen 14 (Prague: J. G. Calvesche k. u. k. Hof- u. Universitäts-Buchhandlung, 1904), 4:572.

G68. From Hans Sachs, "Aesop, the Teller of Fables" ("Esopus, der Fabeldichter"). 1560.

The language in this treatise is filled with challenges. In the short comic tales known in German as *Schwänke* the term *stal* may have a specialized meaning with a double entendre: this is the case in Pauli's *Schimpf und Ernst*. A greater conundrum is *Schuesselkorb:* after attempting to define the term, Sebastian Brant admits defeat. The *Deutsches Wörterbuch* by Jacob Grimm and Wilhelm Grimm achieves more success in its entry.

In these verses (77–83) a merchant, speaking to Aesop at the market, compares the ugliness of the fabulist with that of Marcolf. He says that Aesop "has a big mouth, a swollen back, a big swollen belly, with bow-legged thighs, fat and short." In this context, Marcolfian means ugly.

[Mercator spricht:]
Das verpaffelt pfenbert thuet mir nit liebn.
Solt ich dich kauffen an dem ent,
Ein sewmarck grempler man mich nent.
Dw pist vnsawber vnd vngstalt,
Eben wie man Marcoluüm malt,
Wie ein sewstal gelidmasirt
Vnd ein schuessel korp proporzenirt.

[The Merchant says:]
The degraded penny's worth doesn't please me.
Should I sell you at the end,
they would call me a fishmonger.
You are unclean and unattractive,
just as a person paints Marcolf,
heavy-set like a fish-shop stall
and with a body proportioned like a basket of fish.

Bibliography

Hans Sachs, *Sämmtliche Fastnachtspiele*, ed. Edmund Goetze (Halle an der Salle: Niemeyer 1887), 145.

Michael Curschmann, "Marcolfus deutsch," 235.

Sebastian Brant, *Narrenschiff,* Commentary on Chapter 4.11, ed. Friedrich Zarncke (Leipzig: Georg Wigands Verlag, 1854), 308.

G69. From Hieronmyous Rauscher, *One-Hundred* [...] *Selected Papist Lies* (*Hundert auserwelte* [...] *Papistische Lügen* [...]). 1562.

The complete translated title of this work is "One-Hundred Selected Huge, Brazen, Thick, Well-fatted, Stinking Papist Lies, Which Far Outstrip the Lies of All Fools (such as those of Eulenspiegel, Marcolf, the Priest of Kalenberg, Fortunatus, Rollwagen, etc.) with Which the Papists Defend the Most Noble

Articles of Their Teaching, but Which Blind Christians and Ensnare Them in the Abyss of Hell. Compiled from Their own Writings, and with Special Commentary Appended to Each by B. Hieronymus Rauscher, the Count-Palatinate High Preacher at Newburg on the Danube."

A Lutheran theologian, Rauscher died in 1569 while serving as court preacher at Amberg. In the very title of his work, he mentions Eulenspiegel, the Priest of Kalenberg, and Marcolf either as titles of fictions about comic tricksters or as examples of their protagonists. After naming them, he refers to Fortunatus, the legendary hero of a German chapbook (1509), and *Rollwagen,* short for *Das Rollwagenbüchlin* (*The little trolley book,* 1555), a collection of tales by the prolific author Georg or Jörg Wickram.

The fourteenth of Rauscher's "papist lies" concerns various heretics who kept the sacrament in a box. The author theorizes that the account is likelier to have been written by Marcolf or the Priest of Kalenberg than by any of the evangelists (fols. Diiij^r–Ei^r).

Etliche ketzer sind auffgestanden, welche jr Lehr auch mit Wunderwecken bezeugt, haben auff dem Wasser gewandelt, vnd nicht vntergangen. Da solchs ein Catholischer Priester gesehen, welcher wol gewust das die rechten Warzeichen bey der falschen Lehre nicht sein können, hat er das Sacrament in einer Büchsen mit sich getragen, an das Wasser getretten, an welchem die Ketzer jre zeichen für dem volck theten vnd vor jederman gesagt, Ich beschwere dich Teuffel bey dem, so ich in meiner hand trage, das du nicht mehr solche fantasey in diesem Wasser treibest, zu verderben dieses Volck. Da er solchs geredt, sind sie auff dem Wasser daher gesprungen, das hat dem Priester also wehe gethan, das er zorniglich den Herrgott mit der Büchssen ins Wasser geworffen, alsbald hat sich die macht Christi sehen lassen. Denn so bald das Element das Sacrament angerürt, ist die Fantasey gewichen, vnd sind die verfürischen Lehrer, so zuuor auff dem Wasser gangen, so schwer als Bley worden, vnd vntergangen, die Engel aber haben die Büchssen mit dem Sacrament hinweg gefüret, da der Priester das Wunderwerck gesehen, ist er sehr erfrewt. Aber es ist jm leid vmb seinen Herrgott gewest, wo er nun hinkomen sey, hat derhalben dieselbige gantze nacht geweinet vnd geheulet. Da er aber zu morgens früe in die Kirchen gehet, hat er die Büchssen vnd Sacrament auf dem Altar gefunden.

Erinnerung.

Dieses ist ein kûne that, das dieser Pfaff seinen Herrgot also grimmiglich ins Wasser wirfft, vnd dar nach die gantze nacht vmb jn weinet, weis nicht wo er hinkommen, ob er lebendig oder tod sey. Gleichwohl hat er dem Pfaffen seinen willen ausrichten müssen, die Ketzer ertrencken, vnd gehorsamlich sich widerumb als ein verstricker in sein Gefengnis stellen, man hette jm sonst nicht mehr vertrawet, vnd so bald nicht wider ausgetragen. Von dieser Papistischen wirckung des Sacraments haben die heiligen Euangelisten vnd Paulus nichts geschrieben. Es wird vielleicht Marcolffus oder Pfaff vom Kalenberg erdicht haben. Der Ketzer jrthum wird mit diesem eingesperten Brod niht widerlegt, es gehört Gottes wort, vnd die gaben des heiligen Geistes darzu.

Numbers of heretics have risen up, who have proven their teaching with miraculous deeds; they have walked upon the water and not sunk. A Catholic priest saw such as this, and knowing full well that the true signs could not appear where there is false teaching, he brought the host in a box with him and stepped up to the water at which the heretics made their signs for the people. Before everyone he said: "I exorcise you, devil, by what I carry in my hand, that you no longer carry on with such a fantastic illusion on this water, to lead these people into error." When he spoke this, they all jumped upon the water and that so pained the priest that he angrily threw the host with the box into the water. Immediately the power of Christ revealed itself, for as soon as the water touched the sacrament the illusion was weakened, and the misleading teachers who had earlier stepped out upon the water became as heavy as lead, and they sunk down. But the angels carried away the box with the sacrament. When the priest saw the miraculous deed, he was overjoyed. But it did pain him that his host was in a place where it had now disappeared, and for this reason he cried and howled the whole night long. But then when he went into the church early in the morning, he found the sacrament upon the altar.

Rauscher's Commentary:
It is a daring deed that this cleric so furiously threw his host into the water and then proceeded afterward to cry the entire night long because of it. I do not know what is become of it, whether it is living or dead. Either way, it had to fulfill the cleric's intention, to drown the heretics and obediently put itself in its prison again as an accomplice. Otherwise one could no longer have trusted it nor so soon have taken it out again. The holy evangelists and Paul have written nothing about this papal effect of the sacrament. Perhaps Marcolf or the Priest of Kalenberg concocted it. The error of heretics is not refuted by this locked-up bread: the Word of God and the gifts of the Holy Spirit belong to it.

Rauscher's thirty-eighth "papist lie" is the story of "How Saint James was Miraculously Freed from a Tower" (fols. Hiij^r–Hiij^v). The commentary opens with mention of a proverb that remains current in German today, namely, "to lie, so that the beams bend."

> Es ist ein Kauffman von einem Tyrannen beraubt, gefangen, vnd in einen tieffen Thurn gelegt, derselbig hat S. Jacob trewlich angeruffen, das er jm in solcher grosser not zu hülff keme. Sanct Jacob aber hat jn nicht vmb sonst bitten lassen, sondern ist jhm erschienen im Thurn, da die Wechter, so jn bewaret, noch gewacht haben, vnd hat diesen Gefangenen zu öberst auff den Thurn hinauff gefüret, da hat sich der Thurn auff die Erden geneiget, das er dem Erdboden gleich ist gewesen, da ist der gefangen zum Fenster hinaus gestiegen, vnd dauon gangen. Da das seine Hüter vnd Wechter gesehen, sind sie jm fluchs nachgelauffen, haben jn wider fangen wollen, aber jre Augen sind verblendet worden, das sie jn nicht sehen haben können.
>
> [*Marginal comment:* Allhie haben die Papisten etwas nötiges ausgelassen, das sie nit auch darzu gesetzt haben, Ob sich der thuren darnach wider auffgericht hab, oder also ligen blieben sey.]
>
> Erinnerung.
> Es ist ein Sprichwort, wenn einer gar ein vnglaubige Lügen thut, das man spricht, Dieser hat gelogen das sich die Balcken biegen. So hat dieser, so diese Lügen geschrieben, gelogen, das sich die hohen Thürn biegen, vnd der Erden gleich werden, auff das der gefangene, vnd die Wechter oben zum Fenster heraus lauffen können. Wie gedunckt dich aber vmb diese Bepstische Lügen, damit man darzu die anruffung der verstorbenen Heiligen bestettigen wil, Marcolffus, Eulenspiegel, der Pfaff vom Kalenberg, haben so grob nicht liegen können, als diese heilige geistliche Leut, das ist, jr Bibel damit sie jre Lehre bestetigen.

Once, a merchant was robbed by a tyrant, captured, and put in a high tower. This man faithfully called upon Saint James that he come to aid him in his time of great need. Saint James did not let his request be in vain but appeared to him in the tower. The guards, in order to keep watch over the prisoner, were still awake, and brought him up higher into the tower. Then the tower leaned toward the ground so that it was even with the ground level. Then the prisoner climbed out the window and left. Then the lookouts and guards, having seen this, ran after him immediately, trying to capture him again. But their eyes were blinded so that they were unable to see him.

[*Marginal comment:* Right here the papists have left out something important that they have not put about it, namely, whether the tower righted itself again afterward or whether it remained lying down.]

Rauscher's commentary:
When somebody tells a very unbelievable lie, an expression that one says is, "This one has lied so much that the beams bend." The one who has written such lies has lied that the high towers bent and became level with the ground to the point where the prisoner and guards above could run to the window and out. How does it strike you then regarding these papist lies, that a person will confirm the invocation of dead saints? Will be affirmed as true if one calls upon the dead saints and asks them to do so? Marcolf, Eulenspiegel, the Priest of Kalenberg could not lie so crudely as these holy and spiritual people, that is, who use the Bible to make their teaching valid.

Rauscher's eighty-third "papist lie" is "How the Fish in the Water Hear the Preaching of Saint Anthony" (fol. Oj^v). This chapter takes as its point of departure a famous miracle in which the Franciscan friar St. Anthony of Padua (1195–1231) is supposed to have preached to an attentive school of fish at the mouth of the Marecchia river near Rimini.

Sanct Anthonius prediget am Meer, da kamen die Fisch hergeschwummen, vnd höreten jm zu, die grossen Fisch hielten sich in der tieffe, guckten mit den heuptern heraus, vnd die mittel messigen hielten nicht fern vom vffer, die kleinsten aber, da es am aller seichsten war. Vnd da die Predigt aus war nickten sie mit den köpffen vnd fiengen an zu schreien, da hiesse sie Bruder Anthonius wider hin ziehen, sie waren frölich, vnd theten grosse sprünge in dem Wasser, vnd furen dahin.

[*Marginal comment:* Es ist ein wunder das sie nit auch begert haben, Mönch zu werden.]

Erinnerung.
Dieses weren wir wol zu frieden, wenn diese Gottlose Mönch nur den Fischen vnd wilden Thieren predigten, die köndten sie nicht verfüren. Aber Eulenspiegel vnd Marcolphus hetten sich solcher offentlicher feisten vnd wolgemesten lügen geschempt, vnd nicht von sich sagen dürffen, das die Fisch jnen zugehöret hetten. Aber dieses Teufels geschmeis schemet sich solcher lügen gar nicht.

Saint Anthony was preaching at the sea when the fish came swimming up and listened to him. The big fish stayed deep below and peered with their heads out of the water and the medium-sized fish stayed close to the shore. But the smallest ones were in the shallowest water of all. When the sermon was over, they nodded their heads and began to call out to Brother Anthony, since they wanted him to come back to the water. And they were happy and made great leaps in the water and went there.

[*Marginal comment:* It is a miracle that the fish did not also desire to become monks.]

Rauscher's Commentary:
We would be most satisfied if these godless monks preached only to the fish and wild animals, because they could not lead these astray. But Eulenspiegel and Marcolf would have been ashamed of such clearly crass and well-fatted lies, and they would not have allowed to be said of them that the fish had listened to them. But even this devil's vermin is not in the least ashamed of such lies.

Rauscher's ninety-sixth "papist lie" is the story of "How the Wounds on a Painted Francis were Scratched Open" (fols. Pijʳ–Pijᵛ). The author's terminology reflects the fraternal orders of his day: he refers to Dominicans as preachers, to Franciscans as barefoot monks. Congregations of religious who go barefoot, a custom introduced into the West by St. Francis of Assisi, are known technically as discalced. The five wounds in question are the stigmata, marks or actual wounds that appeared on the body of Francis in the same places as the wounds of the crucified Christ (two on his palms, two on his feet, and the fifth on his side).

In einem Prediger Kloster war Franciscus mit seinen fünff wunden gemalt, darein kam ein Mönch, vnd als er Franciscum sahe, verdros es jn, eins mals da die Brüder schlieffen stieg er zu dem gemel, vnd machet jn schwartz mit kolen, des morgens war Franciscus schöner dan zuuor, welches den Prediger Mönch vbel verdros, die ander nacht schabt er an der wunden Francisci, aber des morgens waren sie viel schöner, da war der Mönch gar toll auff Franciscum vnd in der dritten Nacht gedacht er jhn gar auszutilgen. Als er nu mit dem kratzen kam, bis an die Wunden der lincken seiten sihe da sprützet das blut heraus, das der Mönch hinter sich fiel, als hette jn der Donner geschlagen, vnd die Wunden blutet dieselben gantze nacht. Des morgens wird man des grossen schadens gewar, die Mönch finden das Gemach voll blutes, wie ein See flos das blut, vnd lag der arm bruder darin halb tod, da stopfften sie die Wunden zu, aber es wolt kein stopffen helffen, das blut sprang heraus, wie aus einem springenden Brunnen, Sie giengen zusammen, hielten rath darüber, vnd beschlossen, nach der Barfussern Mönnichen zuschicken, das sie bald kemen, vnd gaben den rath, Gott vnd Franciscum anzuruffen, das sich die wunden Francisci stillet, vnd der arme blutige Bruder wider zu jm selbs keme, das geschach also, vnd der Bruder gewan darnach Franciscum lieb. Das Bilde wolt man wider lassen malen, aber es hat sich selbst gemalet, vnd feiner gewest dan zuuor.

Erinnerung.
Dieses ist vber des Eulenspiegels vnd Marcolphi kunst, sie hetten nicht so meisterlich liegen können. Vnd dieses were schier das geringste, sie wollen damit auch die gemalten Bilder erheben, das man sie ehren vnd anbeten sol. Thut man aber dem Bapsthumb vnrecht, wenn man sagt, wie D. Martinus Luther seliger gethan, es sey vom Teufel gestifft, denn die furnempsten Artickel jhrer lere, sind grobe, stinckende, greiffliche lügen, wie diese auch ist.

In a Dominican monastery Francis was painted with his five wounds. A monk came in and, when he saw Francis, it annoyed him. One time when the brothers were sleeping, he climbed up to the painting and made it black with coal. But in the morning Francis was more beautiful than before, which deeply annoyed the Dominican monk. The second night he scraped off Francis's wounds, but in the morning they were far more beautiful. Then the monk was truly furious with Francis and during the third night he thought that he would utterly efface the painting. When in the scraping he got to the wounds on the left side, then suddenly blood spurted out and the monk fell backwards as if he had been struck by a thunderclap. And the wounds bled like this the whole night. In the morning people became aware of this great injury, and the monks found the chamber full of blood: the blood flowed like a sea. And the poor brother lay half-dead in the chamber. So they plugged the wounds, but no plugging would stop it: the blood spurted out as out of a spurting spring. They went together and discussed the matter, and decided to send for the barefoot monks, who came quickly and advised that they call upon God and Francis to stop Francis's wounds. And they did just that and the poor bloody Brother came to his senses. And after this the Brother dearly prized Francis. People wanted to have the image painted again, but it painted itself and became even finer than it had been before.

Rauscher's Commentary:
This is far beyond the craft of Eulenspiegel and Marcolf: they could not have lied so masterfully. And this might be nearly the worst: they want to elevate the painted image so that one should honor and pray to it. A person does the papacy an injustice, however, if one says, as blessed Doctor Martin Luther did, that it is founded by the devil, for the most refined articles of their teaching are crude, stinking, biting lies, as this one is too.

Bibliography

Hieronymus Rauscher, *Hundert außerwelte, grosse, unverschempte, feiste, wolgemeste, erstunckene, Papistische Lügen* [...] (Regensburg: Geißler, 1562), fols Diiij^r–Ei^r, Hiij^r–Hiij^v, Oj^v, Pij^r–Pij^v.

G70. From Johann Albrecht, *A Refutation of the Unchristian Creed Which They Call the Servant of the Evangelist in the Church at Regensburg, Taken from Articles of Disputation Found there* (*Widerlegung der Vnchristlichen bekandtnuß, deren die sich nennen diener des Euangelij, in der Kirchen zů Regenspurg, von gegewertigen streytartickeln*). 1563.

Vanishingly little is known about Albrecht beyond the fact that he was a Franciscan and that he dedicated his treatise to Abbot Blasius Baumgartner of St. Emmeram, the Benedictine monastery in Regensburg. In his *Refutation* he takes to task Rauscher, whom he calls by the German equivalent of Friar Rush (see G73), for having pronounced lies and for being more familiar with folk-books associated with title characters such as Eulenspiegel, Marcolf, and Fortunatus (the list goes on) than with the Bible and patristic writings. *Katzipori*, one of two such digests by Michael Lindener (ca. 1520–62), brings together coarsely comic tales. Its author was a kind of German François Villon, a wandering scholar (and schoolmaster) whose life ended when he was executed for murder.

Also haben der Apostel nachkümling, vnsere Vätter bey leben vnd nach jrem tod, jren berüff, glauben vnd lehr, auch mit grossen vnd vnerhörten miraculn bestetigt. Doch nit mit sollichen miraculn vnd zeichen, von denen brůder Rausch in seinem lugen bůch meldung thůt, sonder mit sollichen wunderzeychen die allwegen von allgemeyner Catholischen kirchen, für rechte, ware, offentliche vnd gewisse wunderzeychen seind erkendt vnd gehalten worden. [...] Dieweil Brůder Rausch, baß vnd besser, wie in seinem lugenbůch zů vernemen, imm Eulenspiegel, Marcolpho, Pfaffen vomm Kalenberg, von Fortunatus seckel, Rollwagen, Narrenschiff, Kazibori, Schimpff vnnd Ernst, Centonouella ist belesen vnd erfaren, dann in der Bibel, vnd der Vätter schreiben. Er künde auch wanns von nöten, dieweil er so wol mit außerwölten, grossen, vnuerschämpten, faisten, wolgemesten vnd erstuncknen lugen verfasset einen Holhipper, Lottersbüben, Freyartsharten, Schalcksnarren vnd was dergleichen mehr, außbündig vnd gût geben.

Thus the successors of the apostles, our fathers, during life and after their death, affirmed their vocation, beliefs, and teaching with great and unheard of miracles. Yet not with such miracles and signs as the ones made known by Friar Rush in his book of lies, but instead with such miraculous signs, which have always been recognized and held to be right, true, public, and certain miraculous signs by the universal Catholic Church. [...] Meanwhile, Friar Rush, better and better, as is to be perceived in his book of lies, in Eulenspiegel, Marcolf, the Priest of Kalenberg, Fortunatus and his purse, *Rollwagen, The Ship of Fools, Katzipori, Schimpf und Ernst*, and the *Centinovella*, is more often read and better known than the Bible and the writings of the Church Fathers. He could also compose, if necessary, just as he did so well with carefully selected, great, shameless, leering, well-fatted, and stinking lies, a reviler, a mountebank, a ..., a pseudo-fool, or something else of this sort even more exemplary and good.

Bibliography

Johann Albrecht, *Widerlegung der Vnchristlichen bekandtnuß, deren die sich nennen diener des Euangelij, in der Kirchen zu Regenspurg, von gegenwertigen streytartickeln* (Ingolstatt: Weyssenhorn, 1563), fols. 21ᵛ–22ʳ.

Reinhard Tenberg, *Die deutsche Till Eulenspiegel-Rezeption bis zum Ende des 16. Jahrhunderts*, Epistemata 161 (Würzburg: Königshausen & Neumann, 1996), 162–63.

G71. From Hans von Francolin, *Tournament Book: A True, Actual, and Brief Description of all Amusement and Tourneying* [...] (*Thurnierbuch: Warhaffte, eigentliche vnd kurze Beschreibung aller Kurtzweil vnd Ritterspiel* [...]). 1579.

A Burgundian, Hans von Francolin (known also as Jean de Francolin, 1522–86) had direct personal experience of chivalric life. Among other things, he served as the first noble-born herald to the Holy Roman Emperor. He became an expert in heraldry. In 1566 he published a tournament book. As the title suggests, the treatise describes rules for tournaments. One entertaining episode (p. XVIII) within Francolin's text achieves comic incongruity by portraying the fool

Marcolf on an unsaddled donkey as if he were a knight on a stallion. To heighten the atmosphere of unknightliness, our antihero is mounted wrong way round and faces backwards. This posture was associated with humiliation. To make matters worse, he must maintain his balance by gripping the donkey's *Schwanz,* which in German can mean both "tail" and "penis."

> Wie ein gar kurtzweiler Marcolfus auff einem vngesattletem Esel erschienen ist.

In dem aber da dises alles geschach, ist dieser dieweil kommen auff einem vngesattleten Esel, welcher Esel hat grosse lange zottete Hosen, auff Landtsknechtliche weiß angehabt an allen vieren, von gelb vnd blaw farben vnd auff dem Kopff ein schönen grossen Federbusch, von Hanenfedern gemacht. Der aber so auff jm gesessen ist, war diser theurer Marcolfus, welcher auch nicht weniger gestaffiert gewesen als sein gewaltiger Hengst etc. Dann sein kleidung war allenthalben grün vnd rot, mit Wollen oder Rosszhar außgefüllt, damit wann er gefallen jhm kein schad möcht widerfahren, zu vorauß auff der Brust, an Armen, vnd auff dem Rukken. Vnnd hette auff dem Kopff ein rot Paret auff Schweitzerisch art, ist also auff dem Esel hinderwertz gesessen, vnd den schwantz in die Hend gefaßt, hin vnd her geritten in der Schrancken, vnd vnder dem Volck platz gemacht, auß diesen vrsachen, wann er den Esel anstach, da fieng er dann an gumpen vnd springen, vnd wurff jn ab. Trieb in summa vil Gaucklerey, daß sein sehr gut zu lachen was, trieb es auch so lang für vnd für biß zu end deß Thurniers.

> How a very ridiculous Marcolf appeared upon a donkey with no saddle:

But as then this all happened, this one appeared in the meantime on a donkey with no saddle. This donkey had on all four of its legs large and long, tattered pants, blue and yellow, like a peasant, and on its head a beautiful large plume made of rooster feathers. But the person sitting on the donkey was this dear Marcolf, who was no less decked out than his mighty steed, since his clothes were everywhere green and red, and, so that if he fell no injury might befall him, stuffed with wool or horsehair in front on his chest, on his arms, and on his back. He had upon his head a red cap in the Swiss style, and he sat upon the donkey backwards, held the donkey's tail in his hand, rode back and forth in the lists, and made way among the people. For this reason when he goaded the donkey, it began then to buck and jump, and it tossed Marcolf off. That caused in the end much joking, that it was good to laugh. It continued, on and on, until the end of the tournament.

Bibliography

Francolin, Hans von, *Thurnierbuch: Warhaffte, eigentliche vnd kurze Beschreibung aller Kurtzweil vnd Ritterspiel* [...] (Frankfurt am Main, 1579), XVIII.

Ruth Mellinkoff, "Riding Backwards: Theme of Humiliation and Symbol of Evil," *Viator* 4 (1973): 153–76.

G72. From Johannes Nas, *Friar Johannes Nas of Ingolstadt's Ape-play: The Entire Kingdom of Apes, Including the Land of the Cunning Apes; Good Night, Pope* (*Affenspiel F. Johan Nasen zu Ingelstad: Sampt dem gantzen Affenreich in Schlauraffen Land; Gute Nacht Bapst*). 1571.

The Franciscan Nas (1534–90) preached the Counterreformation, wrote theology, and served as bishop from 1580 on. His name evokes both the German *Nase* and Latin *nasus* for "nose," which sets the stage for mention of that organ as well as of related words such as *Schnudel* "snot."

The wordplay is not limited to Nas's name. The very title of his work is challenging for the translator: the first word *Affenspiel* would correspond most closely to the English "monkey business," while the usual translation of *Schlauraffenland* [*sic*] as Land of Cockaigne misses out on the "ape" element and awakens misleading associations with the drug *cocaine* (which has an altogether unconnected etymology). In one passage the author names a whole band of popular fools and "folk-books" associated with them.

As often elsewhere, Marcolf is paired with Eulenspiegel and mentioned in proximity to the Priest of Kalenberg. Other authors and texts are enumerated. The designation Neidhart refers to a legendary trickster named Neidhart Fuchs (meaning "fox"). The latter was based on a famous real-life minnesinger called Neidhart von Reuental (1190–1237), who plied his trade in southern Germany and Vienna. The trickster had entitled in his honor an anonymous verse collection, which was composed in the late fourteenth or early fifteenth century and was printed in the late fifteenth and early sixteenth. Jakob Frey (ca. 1500–ca. 1562) wrote *The Garden Company* (*Die Gartengesellschaft*, 1536), a treasury of *Schwänke* or comic tales. The name Tristrant most likely refers to *Tristrant und Isalde*, a Middle High German verse romance by the twelfth-century poet Eilhart von Oberge, which enjoyed considerable popularity in both manuscript copies and printed versions. *Schapler* and *Galmy* are frequently coupled. The former is *Hug Schapler*, a "folk-book" printed in 1500. The latter is designated more fully *Knight Galmy from Scotland* (*Ritter Galmy aus Schottland*), a romance-like fiction by Georg or Jörg Wickram (ca. 1500–before 1562). The form Eurialum could refer to the love story of Nisus and Euryalus as told in Virgil's *Aeneid*. More probably it refers to the bestselling novel on Lucretia and Euryalus written by Aeneas Sylvius Piccolomini, who later became Pope Pius II. Duke Luppolt is a character from the Middle High German epic poem *King Rother* (*König Rother*), composed in the mid-twelfth century.

> Wenn man die Lügen nem heraus
> Da er sein Bücher spickt mit aus,
> Darnach die Schmachwort vngereumbt,
> Da er manchen Man mit verleumbt,
> Darzu auch alle Narnfratzen,
> Vnd Schalcksbossen thet auskratzen,
> Die ander kunst werde so klein,
> Man brecht sie auff ein Zettelein.
> Drumb sag ich aus seim eigen Maul,
> Wer gern lachte der sey nicht faul,
> Er les sein Schnudel Bücher all,
> Das Affenspiel jm wol gefal.
> Aulnspiegel wird da vbermand,
> Marcolphus auch von jm geschand,
> Der Pfaff vom Kalnberg gilt nicht mehr,
> Nasus beraubt jn seiner Ehr,
> Den Neydhard, sampt dem Jacob frey,
> Tristrant, Schapler, vnd den Galmy,
> Eurialum, Hertzog Luppolt,
> Vnd all was kurtzweilig sein wolt,
> Sampt den andern Centonouel,
> Vberschreit all dieser Esel.
> Der Rolwage ist ausgethan,
> Man mus Nasum an des stat han.
> Schimpff vnd Ernst ist worden nun alt,
> Bilch das man sich an die Nas halt.
> Da find mans all auff einem hauff,
> Ist on not das man weiter lauff.
> Du fints kaum bas in einer sum,
> *In libro conformitatum.*

> If one were to take out the lies
> with which he has larded his books,
> and afterward cleaned out the shameful words,
> since he has slandered many men,

and furthermore also acted to scratch out
all the faces a fool pulls and
japes a juggler makes,
the rest of the artistry would be so small,
that a person could reduce it to a tiny scrap of paper.
Therefore I say, whoever loves to laugh
from his own mouth is not lazy—
he must have read all his snotty books [to find something laughable].
The Ape-play well pleased him.
Eulenspiegel will thus be overpowered,
Marcolf too will be put to shame by him.
The Priest of Kalenberg no longer carries weight,
for Nas strips him of his honor.
Neidhart, together with Jakob Frey,
Tristrant, *Schapler* and *Galmy*,
Euralium, Duke Luppolt,
all those who wish to entertain,
together with the other *Centinovella*—
this donkey surpasses all.
The *Rollwagen* is outdone,
a person must have Nas in its place.
Schimpf und Ernst [by Pauli] has now grown old.
Fitting it is, that one keeps on reading Nas,
for there one can find everything in just one pile.
One need not run any farther.
You will hardly find a better in a summa,
in a book of similar forms.

Bibliography

Johannes Nas, *Affenspiel F. Johan Nasen zu Ingelstad: Sampt dem gantzen Affenreich in Schlauraffen Land; Gute Nacht Bapst* (1571), fols. H2ʳ–H2ᵛ.

Reinhard Tenberg, *Die deutsche Till Eulenspiegel-Rezeption bis zum Ende des 16. Jahrhunderts*, Epistemata 161 (Würzburg: Königshausen & Neumann, 1996), 180–82.

G73. From Bruno Seidel, *Proverbial Commonplaces about Customs, Written in Ancient Meters, with a German Translation, Now for the First Time Selected and Published* (*Loci communes proverbiales de moribus, carminibus antiquis conscripti: Cum interpretatione Germanica, nunc primum selecti et editi*), Basel, 1572.

Seidel's foreword, written in Latin hexameters while he was at Basel, sets Marcolf alongside various figures and tales: Gryllus, who earned fame through a dialogue in Plutarch's *Moralia* in which he argued his side while transformed into a pig by Circe; tales of the Priest of Kalenberg, Pfaff Amis or Affis (told by the thirteenth-century poet known by the pseudonym Der Stricker or "the Knitter"); Neidhart, the dwarf king who is the title character of the early thirteenth-century poem *König Laurins Rosengarten*; Horn-Siegfried; and Eulenspiegel. Friar Rush is a kind of elf-trickster, similar to Robin Goodfellow, whose story, a satire against monks, was first printed at the latest in 1620.

The name Smosmannus (Smausmann?) remains a conundrum. Suarmus was the point of departure for Theodor Georg von Karajan, *Ein Kurtzweilige Fasznacht-Predig vom Doctor Schwarmen zu Hummelshagen auff Grillenberg und Lappeneck: Ist lustig zu gebrauchen bey dem Deponiren, Hoblen und Hänßlen,* printed with the initial heading *Svarmus spvrca loqvens* preceding the title page (Vienna, 1851).

> Sunt tamen ipsi illi, qui amant dicteria Grylli,
> Et qui Smosmannum cupiunt audire per annum
> Turpia dicentem, uel Suarmum spurca loquentem,
> Quique legunt Pfaffi Calebergi facta, uel affi.
> His placet insanus Neidhart, Larin quoque nanus,
> Corneus Seufridus bonus est nonas per et idus,
> Marcolf laudatur, Eulenspiegelus amatur:
> Et quis non legit, quae frater Rauschius egit?

> Yet there are those very people who love the witticisms of Gryllus
> and who wish to hear of Smosmann yearlong
> saying vulgarities, or Swarmus talking dirty,
> and who read the deeds of the Priest of Kalenberg or of Pfaff Amis.
> They like mad Neidhart, the dwarf Laurin too.
> Horn-Siegfried is good for the nones and ides.
> Marcolf is praised, Eulenspiegel is beloved:
> and who has not read what Friar Rush did?

This passage (Frankfurt, 1589: fol. B 3), or one closely related to it, was later put into internally rhymed hexameters within a Latin poem that prefaces Seidel's *Ethical Proverbs* (*Paraemiae ethicae*).

> Quis non legit quid Frater Rauschius egit?
> Et qui Smosmannum cupiunt audire per annum
> Turpia dicentem, vel Suarmum spurca loquentem?
> Quique legunt Pfaffi Calenbergi facta vel Affi?

Who has not read what Friar Rush did?
And who wish to hear of Smosmann yearlong
saying vulgarities, or Swarmus talking dirty?
And who read the deeds of the Priest of Kalenberg or of Pfaff Amis?

Bibliography

Bruno Seidel, *Loci communes proverbiales de moribus, carminibus antiquis conscripti:*
    Cum interpretatione Germanica, nunc primum selecti et editi (Basel, 1572),
    fol. a4^r.

G74. From Bartholomäus Krüger, *Hans Clauerts werklichen Historien*. 1587.

Bartholomäus Krüger (ca. 1540–after 1597) was a German writer. His folk-book
about Hans Clauert is based on a real-life cattle dealer by that name (ca. 1506–
66) whose fictitious counterpart has been called "the Eulenspiegel of Mark
Brandenburg" ("der märkische Eulenspiegel") or "the Eulenspiegel of Berlin"
("der Berliner Eulenspiegel").

In this narrative the author relates the story of the cat that is told in *S&M*
2.8. The first story in the book tells "How Hans Clawert Was Forced Into Manual
Labor, and How his Master Came to Share his Fate." In offering the moral to it
(which relies heavily on Horace, *Epistles* 1.10.24; see G52), Krüger writes (p. 8):

Naturam expellas furca, tamen vsque recurret.
Hie wirdt das alte sprichwort war:
Der Hane kreht durchs ganze Jar.
Auch lest die Katz das mausen nicht,
Wie man dann beym Marcolpho sicht.

You may drive out Nature with a pitchfork; she will all the same always return.
Here the old saying is revealed as true.
The rooster crows the whole year long.
And likewise the cat doesn't let the mice run free,
As one can observe from Marcolph.

Bibliography

Bartholomäus Krüger, *Hans Clauerts werklichen Historien: Abdruck der ersten
    Ausgabe (1587)*, ed. Theodore Raehse (Halle an der Saale: Niemeyer
    1882), 8.

G75. From Johann Fischart, *Affentheurlich Naupengeheurliche Geschichtsklitterung.* 1590.

Fischart (1546–90) wrote fierce satires in both prose and poetry. The most famous work by this ardent Lutheran and opponent of the Counterreformation is his free adaptation of Rabelais's *Gargantua et Pantagruel* (see G43), which was published first in 1575 under an extended "(and untranslatable) title but which has been designated since the second edition in 1582 as *Geschichtsklitterung.* The last word, alive today in the sense "deliberately biased account of history," gives exuberant evidence of the author's punningly creative approach to language.

In the prefatory section entitled "The Entrance and First Ride, or the Readying and Preparatory Blow, in the Chronicle of Grandgousier, Gargantua, and Pantagruel," Fischart makes the first of several references to Marcolf in the book (p. 25). He concludes the passage by citing a proverb that was entrenched within most European languages. The most common Latin form is "Cucullus non facit monachum," while English has "The cowl [or habit, or hood] does not make the monk."

> Ein Scheißhauß ist ein Scheißhauß, wann man es schon wie ein altar bauet, unnd ein Schatzkammer pleibt ein Schatzkammer, wann man sie schon unter die Erd welbet: Es kan sich im Marcolfischen Esopo auch ein Salomon verbergen: Ihr pfleget doch selber zusagen, das Kleid mach kein Mönch [...].

> A shithouse is a shithouse even when it is built like an altar, and a treasure chamber remains a treasure chamber even when people vault it under ground. A Solomon can also hide in the Marcolfian Aesop. Yet you yourself make a habit of saying that clothes do not make a monk.

In the foreword, Fischart mentions Marcolf again, this time in close proximity to the ancient figure Bacchus and the fictitious newcomer Grobian (see G65), supposed patron saint of vulgar people according to Sebastian Brant in *The Ship of Fools* (*Narrenschiff*). Fischart starts out by referencing Chapters 22–23 of Tacitus's *De Germania*, on the drinking habits of Germans.

> Es gibt doch unter dem Wein die besten keuff, ja die besten rhatschläg, als Tacit von den Teutschen meld [...], wie der fromm C. Scheit im Grobiano zu dem Bacho spricht, Ich muß mich vor eyn wenig kröpffen, Daß ich ein guten Trunck mög schöpffen: Hör Bache mit dem grossen Bauch, Lang mir dorther den vollen schlauch, Eyn gute Pratwurst auß dem sack, Daß mir ein küler trunck darauff schmack, Da laß mich thun

eyn guten suff, Marcolfe sich, der gilt dir drauff, Hehem, das heist eyn guter tranck, Jetz bin ich gsund, vor war ich kranck.

But amid wine there are the best purchases, truly the best pieces of advice, as Tacitus reported of the Germans [...] as pious Caspar Scheidt in *Grobianus* says to Bacchus, "I must first graze a little, so that I might be sure to draw a good draught. Listen to Bacchus with the big belly, pass me from there the full flask, a nice bratwurst from the sack, so that a cool drink tastes so good to me with that, then let me take a good long swig, Marcolf himself, that applies to you [compare G65]. Marcolf swears by it, too. Ahem, now that is what I call a good drink. Now I am healthy, I was sick before."

This excerpt (p. 32) comes from chapter 1, "On the Long-Forgotten Arrival of Gargantua of Gurgelstroslingen, and How Curiously the Same Antiquity was Invented and Preserved to the Present Day." It relates to the genealogy of the Rustici—the family of peasants from which Marcolf descends—that can be traced back to *S&M* 1.2b.

O wie köstlich gut wer es, daß jederman sein geburtsregister von staffel zu staffel und stigenweiß so gewiß auß dem Schiff Noe schöpffen, Bronnenseylen, auffkranen, dänen und ziehen könnte, wie wir [...]: O wie würd der Flegelbeschiltete Marcolfus so stoltz mit seim Rustinco Rustibaldo werden?

O how delightfully good it would be, if everybody could trace their pedigree so certainly step by step and in ascending fashion from Noah's ship, lift it up with a crane on well ropes, draw it out, and pull it, as we [...] O how proud should Marcolf be, with a flail as his blazon, of his [ancestor] Rusticus Rustibaldus?

Chapter 4 is entitled "On Grandgousier's Well-Stocked Kitchen, Pantry, and Cellar: What Belongs either in the Glass or on the Plate." The eleven wines listed here (p. 81) contain a few names that are otherwise unattested and difficult to translate. One is called "Brother Morolf" (see G65). The noun, documented elsewhere (see Jacob Grimm and Wilhelm Grimm, *Deutsches Wörterbuch*, vol. 12, col. 2590, s.v. "Morolf"), may have been a transformation through folk etymology (to associate it with the more familiar name Morolf) of a foreign term from French or Latin for a mulberry wine, which was eventually extended to cover other types of wine made with various ingredients.

> Da war Ehrwein, wie man ihn möcht dem Schultheiß ins Ampt schen-
> cken, war Landwein, Brachwein, Traberwein, Fuhrwein, Fuderwein,
> Rappis, Kirschwein, Bastard, Bruder Morolff, Weichseln Wein,
> Trupffwein [...].

> There was noble wine, of the sort a person might present to the mayor
> in office, there was local wine, brake wine, grape wine, barrel wine,
> wine by the wagonload, wine made from chaff, cherry wine, bastard
> wine, Brother Morolf, fruit wine, wine that has dripped out [...].

Chapter 10 relates "The Circumstances under Which Gargantua Was Given
His Name: And How He Spent his Life with Grape Must and Berry Wine." Kunz
is a nickname for Konrad, apparently used to call swine, much as the term *sooey*
is employed in colloquial American English. The passage proceeds to discuss
Marcolf and Morolf as onomastically distinct entities, a fact accentuated by the
intervening mention of Margret (p. 155).

> Wolst darumb nicht Kuntz heissen, weil man inn Sachssen den
> Schweinen also locket [...] Noch Marckhulff von wegen des
> Salomonischen Marcolphi (welcher Nam demselben Marcolffdichter
> auch Grell in den Ohren gethan), noch Margret von wegen Murrgret,
> noch Morolff vonwegen Bruder Morolffs des Holtzvogels, aber von
> wegen des guten Weins [...].

> For this reason you do not wish to be named Kunz, because in Saxony
> they lure pigs that way [...] Nor [do you want to be known as] Marckhulff,
> after Solomon's Marcolf (a name that, to that same Marcolf poet, also
> grated upon the ears), nor Margret after Murrgret, nor Morolf after
> Brother Morolf the Golden Oriole but instead after the good wine [...].

This passage (p. 180) from chapter 13, "What Is Signified by Blue and White,
According to the Ways of Nature," relates to *S&M* 2.6.

> Hingegen erfreut nicht die klarheit, der Tag und das Liecht die gantz
> Welt? Ist aber der Tag nit weiß, so muß Marcolfi rechenung mit der
> Milch fälen, darüber Salomon ful. In summa es ist weisser als kein ding.

> On the contrary, don't brightness, day, and light please the whole
> world? But is the day also not white? So then Marcolf's reckoning
> about the milk over which Solomon tripped must be wrong. In conclu-
> sion, the day is whiter than anything.

This passage (pp. 332 and 334) from Chapter 36, "How a Bit of Advice and Servants of King Picrocholi of Grollenkoderingen Brought Them to Ultimate Destruction and Injury with the Help of Some Sudden and Unexpected Secret Guidance," assumes that Marcolf is a singer and poet (see G36).

Als er nun eins morgens frü im Bett lag, und dichtet wie Marcolfus, bauet Schlösser in Spanien unnd Stätt in die lufft, da sah er sein liebes Honigkrüglin über ihm zu haupten hangen, lacht es an, und redet mit ihm selber.

[...] den Meidlein die Agen schütteln, die Rocken anstecken, oder, wie Sardanapal, Gold spinnen und tapffer schupffen: Was? sagt nit Salomon, wer sich nicht darff wagen, bekompt weder Pferd noch Wagen: Hingegen sagt nicht Malcon, wer sich, sprach Hattmut, zu viel waget, Wagen und Roß verwaget.

As he lay in bed early one morning, crafted songs like Marcolf, and built castles in Spain and cities in the air, he saw then his dear little honeypot hanging above his head, and he smiled at her and spoke with her himself.

[...] to shake the stalks for the girls and to set their skirts on fire, or like Sardanapalus, to spin gold and thrust gallantly. What? Does Solomon not say, "Who does not allow himself to take risk, obtains neither horse nor wagon." In return, does Marcolf not say, "Who risks too much, said Hattmut, loses wagon and mount."

Bibliography

Johann Fischart, *Geschichtsklitterung (Gargantua): Text der Ausgabe letzter Hand von 1590*, ed. Ute Nyssen (Düsseldorf: Karl Rauch, 1963), 25 and 28 (preface), 32 (Chapter 1), 81 (Chapter 4), 155 (Chapter 10), 180 (Chapter 13), 332 and 334 (Chapter 36).

Michael Curschmann, "Marcolfus deutsch," 233n122 (on Chapter 13), 238 (on the onomastics in Chapter 10), 239n140 (on the genealogy of the Rustici).

John Mitchell Kemble, *Dialogue of Salomon and Saturnus*, 69 (on Chapter 10, 13, 36).

G76. From Anonymous, "The Racecourse of the Rabbits with the Bird-Catchers, Or: The Racecourse to be Run Strongly in Argumentation" ("Rennplatz der Haasen mit der Leimstangen, vel Stadivm, Disputando percvrrendvm fortiter"). 1594.

The three passages in which mention is made of Marcolf are found on fols. Ciij^v (left margin), Eiiij^v, and Fij^v (left column), respectively. They contain so many hapax legomena and such strained usage that translation seems futile, when instead they could benefit from close study and commentary beyond the scope of this appendix.

> Ausgeschweisste, Vielerleyweise Gebogene, Gecirculirte, Gepolsterte, Marcolfische, Leimstenglerische, Krausen, ruhende Halstrat.

> Kue Martini, Hans von Behna, Parum loquentes, raro ridentes, superciliosi, Grobiani Agrestes, inconditi, non saliti Kaalfinckij, Dockmeuseri Videntes [...] Inconcinne granuientes, rancidi, putidi, Marcolfiani, ore hiante, quasi de uoratori caeteros ...

> Aus hoher leut Schrifft vnd Werck Mit fleis dis obseruir vnd merck Wirstu erlangen mit verstandt, kunst, sitt, Doctrinam aller handt. Darzu dir hilfft ohn vnterlaß Grobiani Civilitas. Darneben auch, vnd vber diß, Cum obscuris Epistolis. Herr Eulenspiegel weisen thut De Moribus: viel lehren gut. [...]
> Magister Noster Schimpff et Ernst,
> Der gibt ein guten Schein von fernst.
> Auch laß alhie Den Reinken fuß Passiren,
> Nam est classicus. Marcolfi facta Regia
> Sunto vobis egregia.
> Belangende das leben teuwr
> Gefahr vnd thaten vngeheuwr.

Bibliography

Reinhard Tenberg, *Die deutsche Till Eulenspiegel-Rezeption bis zum Ende des 16. Jahrhunderts*, Epistemata 161 (Würzburg: Königshausen & Neumann, 1996), 199–200.

G77. From Anonymous, "A Very Useful Marcolf Tale, In Which the Capacity for Free Will, Before, During, and After a Person's Conversion is Depicted in a Very Funny Scene" ("Eine gar nützliche Marcolfische Historia: Inn welcher durch ein fast lustig Bildt angezeigt wird, Was der Freye Wille, vor, in und nach der Bekehrung des Menschen vermag"). 1598.

An exemplar of this anonymous booklet exists in Berlin, Staatsbibliothek, Preussischer Kulturbesitz, Yh 3597. It narrates in 150 rhyming couplets of iambic tetrameter the cat episode from the *Dialogue of Solomon and Marcolf* (2.9). Marcolf demonstrates "that nature does not allow cessation from nature" ("Art nicht lassen thut von Art," fol. A2^r), which prepares the ground for further observations on nature versus nurture (fol. A3^r).

> Was angeborn vnd geschaffen ist
> Steht fest vnd bleibt zu aller frist.
> Kunst vnd Gewonheit gilt für sich
> Doch gegen art nicht helt den stich.

> What is inborn and already formed
> Stays fast and remains for all time.
> Art and custom have value in themselves
> but against nature have no validity.

This example gives the anonymous composer the occasion, in the second part of the tale, to laud the virtues of Christian faith and to make a plea for true Christianity.

> Drumb wer ein rechter Christ will sein
> Der geb sich nur gedültig drein
> Bekenn sein schuldt vnd böse art
> Das sie nichts gelt nichts helff noch rhat.

> For this reason, whoever wishes to be a proper Christian
> devotes himself with nothing but patience
> to confessing his faults and evil ways
> that they have no worth, no help nor counsel.

Bibliography
Biagioni, "Marcolf und Bertoldo," 9.

G78. From Theobald Hock/Höck[h], *A Beautiful Meadow of Flowers, in Its at Present Generally Very Sad State, but Particularly Courtiers and All Others Well-Placed and Even Very Well-Placed in Their Jobs and Way of Life (Schönes Blumenfeldt, auff jetzigen Allgemeinen gantz betrübten Standt, fürnemmlich aber den Hoff-Practicanten und sonsten menigklichen in seinem Beruff und Wesen zu gutten und besten gestellet).* 1601.

Hock (1573–1622/1624) was a German lyric poet—and an activist in the politics of his day. The first part of this passage presents a half dozen titles of popular literary works, all in the same folksy genre. *Schimpf und Ernst* (1522) is a "folk book" that collected 232 comic and satiric tales, written in an unelaborate style.

As the title suggests, the book was motivated by a desire to entertain and edify. The author was Johannes Pauli (ca. 1455–after 1530), a Franciscan from Alsace who wrote in the German language. *The Little Trolley Book* (*Das Rollwagenbüchlin*, 1555) is a similar collection of tales, by the prolific author Georg or Jörg Wickram. *The Garden Company* (*Die Gartengesellschaft*, 1536) is a title that applies to two aggregations of *Schwänke* or comic tales, in the first instance by Jakob Frey and later its continuation (or "mate") in *The Other Part of the Garden Company* (*Das Ander Theyl der Gartengesellschaft*, ca. 1559), by Martin Montanus (born ca. 1537). *The Little Nighttime Book* (*Das Nachtbüchlein*, 1558) is yet another summa of *Schwänke*, in this case by Valentin Schumann (ca. 1520–after 1559). *Turn Away Displeasure* (*Wendunmuth*) is an even more massive assemblage of such tales, a jestbook brought into print in seven volumes between 1563 and 1603 by Hans Wilhelm Kirchhof(f) (ca. 1523–ca. 1603).

After listing titles, Hock reels off the names of a half dozen well known fictitious protagonists: Fortunatus; Faust, the equally legendary but less forgotten protagonist of a story about a pact with the devil that was popular in early modern Germany; the Priest of Kalenberg; Horned (or horn-skinned) Siegfried and the dwarf Eugel who helps him; Marcolf; and Eulenspiegel. This extract ends by mentioning the little bells, customarily attached to the fringes of clothing, that belonged to the standard trappings of fools in the late Middle Ages and early modern period.

> So billich du das lisest,
> Wenst müssig bist, vnd dir ein zeit erküsest,
> Als andere lähre Fabeln,
> Darinn du vmb sonst die kunst willst ergrabeln,
> Hierauß du viel mehr lernste,
> Alß auß dem Schimpff vnd Ernste,
>
> Darffst du den Rollwagen lesen,
> Die Gartengsellschafft vnd ihr wesen,
> Das Nachbüchlein voll Posen,
> Vnd dem Wendt vmb mut, wirst drob nit verdrossen,
> Den Fortunatum eben,
> Den Faustum auch darneben.
>
> Den Pfaffen am Kalnberge,
> Der Hirnen Seyfrid mit seim kleinen Zwerge,
> Den Marcolphum alte,
> Den Eulenspiegel auch in solcher gstalte,
> Vnd die Centonouellen,

Das Narrenschiff mit Schellen.

So you read it rightly,
if you are idle, and choose for yourself a time,
when others teach fables,
in which in vain you wish to grasp the artistry.
From these you learn much more
than from *Schimpf und Ernst*,

May you read the *Rollwagen*,
Die Gartengesellschaft and its essence,
Das Nachtbüchlein filled with buffoonery,
And *Wendunmuth*—you will not become glum because of it!—
Fortunatus, to be precise,
Faust alongside it too,

The Priest of Kalenberg,
Horned Siegfried with his little dwarf,
Old Marcolf,
Eulenspiegel, too, in such form,
and the *Centinovella*,
The Ship of Fools with bells.

Bibliography

Thomas Hock, *Schoenes Blumenfeld: Abdruck der Ausgabe von 1601*, ed. Max Koch (Halle an der Saale: Niemeyer, 1899), 10–12 (text).

Wilhelm Grimm, *Die deutsche Heldensage*, 4th ed. (Darmstadt: Hermann Gentner, 1957), 715.

G79. Hans Wilhelm Kirchhof, *Wendunmuth*, Book 4, no. 264, "A Thief Requests to to Choose Where He is to be Hanged" ("Ein dieb erlangt zu hencken, wo er wil"). June 4, 1601.

The lifelong Lutheran Kirchhof (1525–1605) was born in Kassel, in the German region of Hesse. *Wendunmuth,* his principal work, is a characteristically sixteenth-century collection of comic tales. Its title means more or less "Turn away displeasure." A poem in seven books, it owes heavily to his vast reading in popular culture. The first book, which came out in 1563, comprises two parts with a total of 550 stories. The second through seventh books appeared in 1602 and 1603. The whole composition comprehends 2083 pieces. Books 4–5 reveal many parallels to Luther's *Table Talk*.

Die lügenden von Marcolfo sagen, nachdem er den könig schwerlich hette erzürnet, daß er befelch thete, in an ein baum den nechsten zu hencken, sprach der arm Marcolfus: So ich denn ie sterben sol, bit ich zum letzten nit mehr, denn die barmhertzigkeit, daß mir erlaubet und ich erhangen werde an einem baum, der mir auch gefalle. Diß ließ ihm der könig zu, da namen die diener, denen solche execution befohlen, und führeten Marcolfum umbher, durch berg und thal deren provintzen und grentzen, dem könig zugehörig, etliche viel tage lang, und wolte sich doch kein baum erzeigen, der ihm gefiele, daran gehencket zu werden. Letztlich kereten sie wider zum könige, denselbigen irer vergeben reise, müh und arbeit berichtende. Also denn, sagt der könig, ich wöll oder wöll nit, so muß ich dich doch nehren; darumb so laßet ihn los, ich wil ihn und sein haußfraw in ewigem dienst behalten und ernehren.

Hett noch ein dieb Marcolfus wahl,
Setzt ers ziel gewiß auch nicht zu schmal;
Selten geschichts nun einem, der stal.

The lying legends of Marcolf tell that after he had so deeply angered the king that the latter ordered Marcolf to be hanged from a tree the next day, poor Marcolf said, "Since I am to die, I make only one final request: that mercy might permit me to be hanged from a tree that pleases me." The king granted him this wish, and so the servants who were ordered to execute Marcolf led him all around for quite a few days, through the mountains and valleys of the provinces and marchlands that belonged to the king, and yet he did not want to point out a tree anywhere that suited him well enough on which to be hanged. Eventually they returned to the king and reported to him about their wasted journey, efforts, and toil. "So then," the king said, "whether I like it or not, you are another mouth I must feed. For that reason let him loose. I will keep him and his wife in service for perpetuity and keep them fed."

If another thief has Marcolf's choice,
let him certainly make his target likewise not too limited;
It rarely befalls a person, who stole.

The last episode is also found in the German prose piece, "Solomon's and Marcolf's Question and Answer" ("Frag vnd antwort Salomonis vnd marcolf") under the heading "A Thief Asks to be Hanged Where He Chooses" ("Ein dieb erlangt zu hencken, wo er wil"). In addition, see Johannes Pauli, *Schimpf und Ernst*, no. 283. The episode is cited, but Marcolf is not named.

> Doch solt man im die wal geben, an welchem baum in glust zů hangen, daran solt man in hencken. Man fůrt in in ein wald vnd zögt im alle bäum, einen nach dem andern, aber in glust an keinem baum zůhangen.

Then they were supposed to give him the choice of which tree it pleased him to be hanged from. They lead him into a forest and show him every tree, one after the other, and he did not wish to be hanged from any of them.

Bibliography

Hans Wilhelm Kirchhof, *Wendunmuth*, ed. Hermann Österley, Bibliothek des litterarischen Vereins in Stuttgart 97 (Tübingen: Laupp, 1869), 3:239.

Johannes Pauli, *Schimpf und Ernst*, ed. Johannes Bolte (Berlin: Stubenrauch 1924), 179.

G80. From Eucharius Eyring, *Another Part of the Plentiful Proverbs, in Which Several Hundred [...]* (*Ander theil copiae proverbiorum: Darinnen ethliche viel Hundert [...]*). 1602.

The cleric Eyring (ca. 1520–97) published three volumes of Latin and German proverbs, arranged alphabetically, many with accompanying short narratives. For his material he relied heavily upon Johannes Agricola.

One proverb illustrates, with reference to apes, the principle that people cannot change their basic nature. After quoting Horace, *Epistles* 1.10.24 (see also G52, G66, and G74), Eyring mentions (pp. 11–12) the episode of the cat and the candle in *S&M* 2.8.

> Ein Aff bleibt ein Aff ob er gleich, vff einem güldenen stul seß,
> Symia est Symia, etiamsi aurea gestet insignia.

> Diß sprichwort trifft nur in der Sum,
> Des Menschen art, ingenium,
> Wie das weder durch glück noch zierd,
> Zu keiner zeit geendert wird,
> [...]
> *Naturam expellas furca tamen vsque recurret*
> Wie solchs Marcolffus gantz geflissen,
> Mit Meuß vnd Katzen hat bewiesen,

Vnd gleich mit diesem sprichwort traff,
Ein Aff bleibt für vnd für ein Aff.

An ape remains an ape, even if it should sit upon a golden seat.
An ape is an ape, even if it should wear golden tokens of rank.

This proverb relates only in sum
to human nature, disposition,
how it will never be changed
through either good fortune nor adornment.
[...]
You may drive out Nature with a pitchfork; she will all the same always return.
How Marcolf proved this quite zealously
with cat and mouse,
and right away hit the target with this proverb:
An ape remains forever an ape.

Later (p. 116) the rhymester relates another string of proverbs to bring home how love distorts a person's judgment. The expression in the first line resembles a proverbial saying in the third passage in G52.

Ein jeden dünckt sein Jldnis Balck,
Sey ein Sperber vnnd schöner Falck,
Si quis amat ceruam, ceruam putat esse Mineruam.
Si quis amat ranam, ranam putat esse Dianam.
Sequitur captiuus amantem.
Suum cuique pulchrum.

To everyone his owl seems a falcon,
a sparrowhawk and handsome falcon.
If someone loves a hind, he thinks the hind to be Minerva.
If someone loves a toad, he think the toad to be Diana.
A captive follows a lover.
To each his own is beautiful.

In the following passage (pp. 116, 119-20), the English "silly Billies" translates the German *Heintzen*, a name commonly attached to peasants, servants, or commoners.

Diß sprichwort trifft Fraw Venus knecht,
Die albern Heintzen freyer schlecht,
Die aus der Weiber Narren zunfft,

So jn hinnimpt all jr vernunfft,
Sie blend, das sie in lieb ersauffen,
Der Narr der Nerrin nach thut lauffen,
Als sey kein schönner in der Welt,
Dann die so er (ohn bdacht) erwehlt,
[...]
Nun ist es auch offt nütz vnd gut,
Das Venus jr Kind blenden thut,
Dann wer wolt sonsten Ehelich werdn,
Wann er vor seh alle beschwerdn,
Die sich im Ehestand thun begeben,
Das gans Müselig Ehlich leben,
Wo wollten hin die vngestalten,
Vnd auch die sonsten ziemlich alten,
Die scheelen hinckenden vnd knappen,
Die einfeltigen vnd diltappen,
Els schwertze mit jrm gelen leib
Auch Marcolffi vierecket Weib.

This proverb applies to Lady Venus's vassal,
the freeborn silly Billies,
the fools-because-of-women guild:
thus all her reasoning takes him in,
she blinds so that they drown in love.
The foolish man rushes after the foolish woman,
as though none in the world were more beautiful,
than she whom he has chosen so heedlessly
[...]
Now it is often right and good,
that Venus blinds her own child,
for otherwise who would want to marry?
If he could foresee all the troubles
that happen in married life,
that being married is very arduous,
then where would the misshapen go,
and also otherwise the very elderly,
the hunched, lame, hobbling,
the simpleminded and dimwitted,
than blacken with their randy body
even Marcolf's ungainly wife.

417

The section on prayer also leads to mention of Marcolf (p. 503).

Ein Merlin man ehe lernen thut,
Dann ein Gebet, löblich vnd gut,
Marcolffum vnd Eulnspiegel schnöd,
Lernt man ehe, dann des Herrn gebot,
Das Narn Schiff, Schimpff und Ernst verstehen
Bhelt man ehe, dann den Salomon,
Die Bulers Lieder wir ehe fassen,
Dann geistlich Psalmen die wir hassen.

A person does well to learn a little tale
before a prayer, commendable and good.
A person learns Marcolf and vile Eulenspiegel
before the Lord's Prayer.
A person should understand *The Ship of Fools*
and *Schimpf und Ernst*, before Solomon.
We should grasp the Song of Songs
before the spiritual Psalms, that we hate.

Bibliography

Eucharius Eyring, *Copiae Proverbiorum: Darinnen Etliche viel hundert/lateinischer vnd deutscher schöner und lieblicher sprichwörter* [...], 3 vols. (Eissleben: Typis Grosianis, 1602), 2:11–12 (for the ape), 2:116–20 (for love), 2:503 (for prayer).

Michael Curschmann, "Markolf tanzt," 968n5.

Wolfgang Viemond, *Eulenspiegel und seine Interpreten* (Berlin: Serene, 1981), 90.

G81. From Anonymous, *The Jester* (*Grillenvertreiber*). 1603.

In 1597 a "folk-book" entitled *Das Lalebuch* (*The Lale Book*) was published, filled with amusing short tales about the inhabitants of a supposed town named Laleburg. In 1598 it was republished under the title *Die Schildbürger* (*The Citizens of Schilda*), to record the doings of the townspeople in the fictitious town of Schilda. Another version was printed in 1603, this time called *The Jester* (*Der Grillenvertreiber*). The final title refers to a person who drives away boredom with bawdy stories.

The author initiates the prologue by sketching the nature and causes of foolishness. To his way of thinking, people who lay claim to omniscience are fools. Aesop, introduced as the main case in point, is described from the outset as being Marcolfian—presumably, like Marcolf in his shrewd and witty character. When two other men are sold into slavery with him and pretend to know everything, Aesop has the sense to deny having any knowledge and thus to avoid much extra toil.

Also werden viel Leut betrogen durch den Unverstandt, daß sie nicht wissen, warinnen die rechte Weißheit bestehe, vnnd demnach in dem sie sich selbst bedüncken, vnd in ihrem Hertzen bereden, sie seyen so witzig, daß sie das Gras wachsen, die Fliegen an der Wand husten hören, [...] so versteigen sie sich gar hoch in der Witz, vnd betriegen sich selber, köndten auch billicher vnter die Narrenzunfft, als anders wohin immatriculiert werden. Solches hat gnugsam verstanden der Marcolphische Esopus, dan als er als ein Leibeygener, sampt zweyen andern auff dem Marck feyl gebotten vnd verkaufft werden sollte, auch jhrer jeder von der Käuffern gefraget wurde, wie zu geschehen pflegt. Als nun die andern zween auff die Frag, was sie kondten antworten, sie köndten alles.

Many people are so tricked by foolishness that they do not know what actual wisdom consists in, and then, by fancying themselves and telling themselves in their hearts that they are so clever that they make the plants grow and that they can hear the flies on the wall clearing their throats [...] they think themselves to be so advanced in wit that they fool themselves and could be initiated more rightly into a guild of fools, just as men are elsewhere. Marcolfian Aesop understood as much sufficiently, when he was wrongly auctioned and sold at the market along with two other men, who when asked by their buyers for what sort of work they were suited, answered that they could do everything.

Bibliography

Karl von Bahder, ed., *Das Lalebuch (1579), mit den abweichungen und erweiterungen der Schiltbürger (1598) und des Grillenvertreibers (1603)*, Neudrucke deutscher litteraturwerke des XVI. u. XVII. Jahrhunderts 236–39 (Halle an der Saale: Niemeyer, 1914), 154–155.

Curschmann, "Marcolfus deutsch," 238.

John Mitchell Kemble, *Dialogue of Salomon and Saturnus*, 69.

G82. From Moses Pflacher, *Instructive, Christian Explanations of the First Book of Samuel* [...] (*Christliche vnd Lehrhaffte Erklerung des ersten Buchs Samuelis* [...]). 1604.

Jan M. Ziolkowski, Edward Sanger, Michael B. Sullivan

Pflacher (ca. 1545–d. 1589) was a parish priest and theologian. This treatise by him contains his admonishments against books such as *Markolf, Eulenspiegel,* and the *Rollwagen,* which he looks on as blasphemous and deceptive. It is difficult to pinpoint which particular moment in the letters of St. Paul Pflacher has in mind at the end of this passage, perhaps 2 Corinthians 11:19.

Vppiche schertz, leichtfertige schwenck, lame zotten, vnnd faule bossen, so die Schalcksnarren vnnd Lotterbuben treiben, den Leuten damit kurtzweil vnnd frisch Blut zu machen. Denn solche vnartige bossen bessern niemand, sondern ergern nur beides junge vnnd alte. Vmb dieser Vrsasch willen werden auch hiemit nicht gebilliget die Fabeln vnd erdichte Mehrlin, so das Weibervolck treibet bey spinnen vnd in den Rockenstuben. Item die böse Nerrische Historien vom Marcolpho, Eilenspiegel, Rollwagen, vnnd dergleichen, welche alle Paulus nennet Narrenteiding, die keinen Christen geziemen oder anstehen.

Idle kidding, smutty jesting, dirty jokes, and risqué humor—thus fools and slovenly slackers try to entertain and to stir up the people. For such shoddy humor edifies no one, but instead only annoys both young and old. For this reason such fables and fanciful fairy tales as womenfolk tell while spinning or in the nursery are not permitted. Likewise, the foul and foolish tales of *Markolf, Eulenspiegel,* the *Rollwagen,* and their like, all of which Paul calls fool's blather, are neither seemly nor decent for any Christian.

Bibliography

Moses Pflacher, *Christliche und Lehrhaffte Erklerung des ersten Buch Samuelis* (Leipzig: Jacob Apels, 1604).

Heinz-Günter Schmitz, "Sophist, Narr und Melancholievertreiber: Zum Eulenspiegelbild im 16. und 17. Jahrhundert," in Herbert Blume and Eberhard Rohse, eds., *Hermann Bote: Städtisch-hansischer Autor in Braunschweig, 1488-1988: Beiträge zum Braunschweiger Bote-Kolloquium 1988,* 212–29 (Tübingen: Niemeyer, 1991): 217.

Reinhard Tenberg, *Die deutsche Till Eulenspiegel-Rezeption bis zum Ende des 16. Jahrhunderts,* Epistemata 161 (Würzburg: Königshausen & Neumann, 1996), 194–95.

G83. From Friedrich Peters, *Wisdom of the Germans, that is: Select Short, Clever, Instructive, and Mannerly Sayings and Proverbs* [...] (*Der Teutschen Weisheit, Das ist: Außerlesen kurze, sinnreiche, lehrhaffte und sittige Sprüche vnd Sprichwörter* [...]). 1605.

Peters (1549–1617), also known as Petri, was a Lutheran theologian as well as a civic authority in Braunschweig. In addition he made himself known by assembling the most extensive casebook of German proverbs that exists from the sixteenth and seventeenth centuries. Entitled *Wisdom of the Germans* (*Der Teutschen Weissheit*), it comprises upward of 21,000 entries gleaned from older dossiers, poems, and oral tradition. The contents are divided into three sections. The first is on God, belief, and heresy; the second on sins, virtue, and the perils of life; and the third offers cynical observations. It includes mention of Marcolf's inability or unwillingness to select a tree from which to be hanged (see G28).

Marcolphus kont keinen Bawm finden, daran jhn gelüst zu hangen.

Marcolf could find no tree from which he wished to be hanged.

Bibliography

Friedrich Peters, *Der Teutschen Weissheit: Faksimiledruck der Auflage von 1604/05,* ed. Wolfgang Mieder (Bern: Lang, 1983), 621.

Karl Friedrich Wilhelm Wander, *Deutsches Sprichwörter-Lexikon: Ein Hausschatz für das Deutsche Volk,* 5 vols. (Darmstadt: Wissenschaftliche Buchgesellschaft, 1964), vol. 3, col. 463.

G84. From Georg Rollenhagen, *The Frog-Mouser* (*Froschmeuseler*). 1608.

Rollenhagen (1542–1609) was an educator, progressively a schoolmaster, private tutor, and headmaster. A Lutheran who served on one stage as a pastor, he wrote plays for school performance on biblical topics. But his most famous work is the *Froschmeuseler* (1595), a free adaptation of the Pseudo-Homeric *Battle of Frogs and Mice* (*Batrachomyomachia*). The German writer had been acquainted with the originally Greek poem since his student days.

At one point (1.2423–26) Rollenhagen refers to the episode of the cat and the candle in *S&M* 2.8.

Wie auch Salomons Katz nicht wolt
Das liecht mehr halten wie sie solt
Sondern der Mauß nach sprang zuletzt
Die Markolff aus dem Ermel setzt.

Just as Solomon's cat did not want
To hold the lamp up as it ought
but instead with intent to harm leapt after the mouse
that Marcolf set down from his sleeve.

Jan M. Ziolkowski, Edward Sanger, Michael B. Sullivan

In a section entitled "The jay promises the peacock," Rollhagen involves Marcolf a second time. During the election of their king, the birds chose the peacock to rule. A critic stepped forward, enumerated the weaknesses of the peacock, and argued in support of the eagle. Marcolf, the jay, acted as advisor and, more specifically, as a mocker (2.469–72).

Biß endlich ein spöttischer Mann
Markolff der Häger dazu kam
Besahe an Pfawen Schnabel vnd füß
Ob er auch beissen kund die Nüß [...].

until at length, a mocking man, Marcolf the jay, came by, and he had a look at the peacock's beak and feet, whether he too could bite the nut [...].

Bibliography

Georg Rollenhagen, *Froschmeuseler*, ed. Dietmar Peil (Frankfurt am Main: Deutscher Klassiker Verlag, 1989), 121 (cat and candle), 276 (Marcolf the jay)

John Mitchell Kemble, *Dialogue of Salomon and Saturnus*, 71 (cat and candle).

Curschmann, "Marcolfus deutsch," 234n123 (cat and candle).

Erika Schönbrunn-Kölb, "Markolf in den mittelalterlichen Salomondichtungen und in deutscher Wortgeographie," *Zeitschrift für deutsche Mundartforschung* 25 (1957): 122 (Marcolf the jay).

G85. From Robert Burton, *The Anatomy of Melancholy*. 1621.

At first blush Robert Burton's (1577–1640) book looks to be a medical treatise, but it turns out to present a gentle satire on the futility of human learning and ambition. In a discussion (Part 3, 2.5.3) of the differences between the charm of human beings while alive and their repugnance when dead, it refers to Marcolf's ugliness. The other mythological, legendary, or biblical characters touched upon include Nireus (king of Syme, an Achaean leader in the Trojan war, and the handsomest of the Greeks after Achilles, according to Homer), Thersites (more or less the opposite of Nireus in his ugliness and vulgarity, according to Homer), and Solomon.

As a posy she smells sweet, is most fresh and fair one day, but dried up, withered, and stinks another. Beautiful Nireus, by that Homer so much admired, once dead, is more deformed than Thersites, and Solomon deceased as ugly as Marcolphus: thy lovely mistress was erst *caris carior ocellis,* dearer to thee than thine eyes, once sick or departed, is *vili vilior aestimata caeno,* worse than any dirt or dunghill.

Bibliography

Robert Burton, *The Anatomy of Melancholy,* ed. Holbrook Jackson (Totowa, NJ: Rowman and Limited, 1975; repr., 1978), 208.

G86. From Adolph Rosen von Creutzheim, *Donkey-King: A Wonderfully Curious Story of How the Monarchy and Government over Four-legged Animals Changed [...]* (*EselKönig: Eine wunderseltzame Erzehlung, wie nämlich die Monarchei vnnd Gubernament vber die vierfüssige Thier geändert [...]*). 1625.

Creutzheim was a pseudonym for Wolfhart Spangenberg (1567–after 1636), a translator from the Latin as well as a poet who wrote beast fables and school dramas. In the "Prologue to the Well-Disposed Reader" ("Vorrede an den Günstigen Leser"), he includes Marcolf among comic romances worthy of condemnation (fols. Aiiij^r–Aiiij^v).

Bevorab weil es zu keines einigen Menschen Hohes oder Niderstandes Personen verkleinerung und nachtheil gemeinet: sondern allein vmb einiger ergetzung unnd Kurtzweil willen viel nützlicher zulesen als die ärgerlichen schandbare unnd schädliche Bücher vom Eulenspiegel Marcolpho Katzibori Pfaffen vom Kalenberg und dergleichen wie auch Schand und Schmachkarten: welche mehr zu zerrittung dann zu ergetzlichkeit dienen.

Especially because it is not intended to the belittlement or detriment of anyone of either high or low standing: rather it is much more useful to read on its own for the sake of some pleasure and enjoyment than galling, scandalous, and harmful books such as Eulenspiegel, Marcolf, Katzipori, the Priest of Kahlenberg and the like, as well as little defamatory and libelous tracts, which serve better to aggravate than to provide amusement.

Bibliography

Gerhard Dünnhaupt, *Personalbibliographien zu den Drucken des Barock,* 6 vols. (Stuttgart: Hersemann, 1991), 5:3924.

John Mitchell Kemble, *Dialogue of Salomon and Saturnus,* 68.

Wolfhart Spangenberg, *EselKönig: Eine wunderseltzame Erzehlung, wie nämlich die Monarchei vnnd Gubernament vber die vierfüssige Thier geändert, das Königreich vmbgefallen, vnd die Krone auff einen Esel gerathen* [...] (Ballenstet: Papyricus Schönschrifft, 1625), fols. Aiiijʳ-Aiiijᵛ.

Wolfhart Spangenberg, *Sämtliche Werke*, ed. András Vizkelety, Ausgaben Deutscher Literatur des 15. bis 18. Jahrhunderts 79 (Berlin: de Gruyter, 1978), vol. 3, pt. 2, 6.

G87. From Heinrich Kornman, *The Lineage of Love (Linea amoris)*. 1629.

Already in the sixteenth century, the educated elite reacted negatively to the old German novels or *Schwankbücher*. Consistent with this reaction, Heinrich Kornmann (d. ca. 1640), a jurist from Kirchain in Hessen, voiced disapproval of the books associated with Marcolf, Grobianus, and the like, since they contain such dirty language. Yet at the same time he recommended these novels as furnishing good content for enthusiastic readers. He referred for example to the *Witticisms* (*Facetiae*, 1508–12) of Heinrich Bebel (1472–1518), the *Letters of Obscure Men* (*Epistulae obscurorum virorum*, 1515–19), *Grobianus*, *Marcolphus*, and the *Garden of Venus* (*Hortus Veneris* an unidentified text that Kornman cites on pp. 37 and 106).

Kornmann wrote of such publications in his book *Linea amoris* (1629), the title of which refers to a medieval commonplace of the five stages or lines of love (sight, conversation, touch, kiss, and coitus): see Ernst Robert Curtius, *European Literature and the Latin Middle Ages*, 512. The passage quoted (p. 37) concludes with words from Matthew 12:34.

> Obscena ibidem verba, quibus hodie nonnulli expresso student, ex libris istis obscaenis et prohibitis ut sunt: Ioci Bebelli, Epistulae Obscurorum virorum, Grobiannus, Marcolphus, Hortus Veneris, et si quae sunt alia: obscaenum iudicant animum, hominem arguunt obscaenum, qualibus enim quis vtitur verbis reipsa censetur. Ex abundantia cordis os loquitur.

> In the same place is found obscene language, for which some people today are clearly eager, drawn from those obscene and forbidden books, such as the *Facetiae* of Bebel, the *Letters of Obscure Men*, *Grobianus*, *Marcolfus*, the *Garden of Venus*, and any other such works. They judge the mind dirty, they blame the person as obscene. The one who employs such words is convicted by that very fact. Out of the abundance of the heart the mouth speaks.

Bibliography

Heinrich, Kornman, *Linea amoris, sive Commentarius in versiculum glossae, visus, colloquium, convictus, oscula, factum: in l. 23. ff. ad l. Juliam de adulteriis* (Frankfurt, 1610), 37.

Hildegard Beyer, "Die deutschen Volksbücher und ihr Lesepublikum" (Diss., Goethe University Frankfurt, 1962), 75.

G88. From Christoph Lehmann, Florilegium Politicum: *A Flower Garden of Politics* (Florilegium Politicum: *Politischer Blumen Garten*). 1639.

Lehmann (1588–1638) was a teacher, statesman, and chronicler of the German city Speyer (1604–28). By the seventeenth century Marcolf's fruitless search for a hanging-tree had become a common saying that characterized any man who simply cannot be satisfied. Marcolf appeared in seventeenth-century collections of sayings in this sense, here under the keyword *Lust* (Curschmann, "Marcolfus deutsch," 225).

> Es ist manchem wie Markolpho der kunde keinen Baum finden, daran er hencken wolt.

> There are some men like Marcolf, who could not find any tree from which he wanted to be hanged.

Bibliography

Christoph Lehmann, Florilegium Politicum: *Politischer Blumen Garten* (Lübeck: Jung, 1639; facsimile of the 1639 edition, ed. Wolfgang Mieder, Bern: Peter Lang, 1986), 492.

Karl Friedrich Wilhelm Wander, *Deutsches Sprichwörter-Lexikon: Ein Hausschatz für das Deutsche Volk*, 5 vols. (Darmstadt: Wissenschaftliche Buchgesell-schaft, 1964), vol. 3, col. 463.

G89. From Anonymous, *An Explanation of the Wondrously Unique Map of UTOPIA, the Newly Discovered Land of Cockaigne, Where Each and Every Vice in Cockaigne is Described as a Particular Kingdom, Sovereignty, or Region* [...] (*Erklärung der wunder-seltzamen Land-Charten Utopiae, so da ist, das neu-entdeckte Schlarraffenland, worinnen all und jede Laster der schalk-hafftigen Welt, als besondere Königreiche, Herrschafften und Gebiete*). 1694.

in 1694 a Utopian literary map by Johann Baptist Homann was printed together with an explanatory guide, both in the German language. Authorship of the book has been credited to the military officer Johann Andreas Schnebelin (d. 1706). Chapter 12 of this companion volume is entitled "Concerning the Kingdom of Marcolf, or the So-Called Peasant's Paradise" ("Von dem Königreich Marcolfi, oder dem so genannten Bauren-Paradeis"). The assumption is that the cunning fool who is Solomon's interlocutor in *The Dialogue of Solomon and Marcolf* rules as king over a region in the West, a so-called paradise of peasants. Crass and lecherous, his subjects suffer from the physical and spiritual degradation associated with their social class.

Bibliography

Johann Andreas Schnebelin, *Erklärung der wunder-seltzamen Land-Charten Utopiae* [...] ([Nuremberg?]: ca. 1650), 231–38.

Dieter Richter, *Schlaraffenland. Geschichte einer populären Phantasie* (Cologne: E. Diederichs, 1984), 209–214.

Michael Kuper, *Zur Semiotik der Inversion: Verkehrte Welt und Lachkultur im 16. Jahrhundert* (Berlin: Verlag für Wissenschaft und Bildung, 1993), 140.

G90. Christian Rehebold, *Salomon & Marcolphus.* 1678.

Rehebold (born ca. 1625) was an expert in law who earned his doctorate in 1662. He published a few volumes, this one under the initials D. X. A., in the third quarter of the seventeenth century. The book, comprising 933 keywords in alphabetical order from *Abbatissa* to *Zoili frater*, catalogues cleverness and foolishness in deeds and events. It contains much German-Latin material, with points of interest taken from juridical life. The pairing of the names Solomon and Marcolf in the title conveys the range of the contents. *Salomon & Marcolphus* was put on the index by the Catholic Church.

Bibliography

Christian Rehebold, *Salomon & Marcolphus Iustiniano-Gregoriani; hoc est Sapida, ac insipida, Sana, atque insana, Nimirum Theologica; Iuridica, tam publica, quam privata* [...] *aliaque plura, Vel ad Observationem, vel Cautelam, vel Delectationem, omnia vero ad Usum, facientia* (Frankfurt: Christian Bergen, 1678).

John Mitchell Kemble, *Dialogue of Solomon and Saturnus*, 71.

Munich, Bayerische Staatsbliothek, Diss. 36, supplement 12.

G91. Christian Weise, *The Comedy of King Solomon* (*Comödie vom König Salomo*). 1685.

Weise (1642–1708), a schoolmaster's son who himself became a teacher and headmaster in grammar schools, wrote didactic poems, novels, and plays. In a late twentieth-century edition his collected works total a daunting twenty volumes.

This play, extant in two manuscripts in the Christian-Weise-Bibliothek in Zittau (MS B 48 and MS B 50d), comprises five acts, with pre- and postlude. It was performed on October 23, 1685, at Theater Zittau under the title "The Incomparable King Solomon." The piece deals with the prophet's turn from heathenism and conversion: the Judgment of Solomon, the attempt of his heathen wives to lure him into heathenism, the dedication of the Temple, the contest of wisdom with the Queen of Sheba, the Queen of the Ethiops, the luring of Solomon into idolatry, and his turning away from God.

Marcolf comes on stage as a fool who, like his wise opponent, steps forth with sententious sayings—but they are characterized primarily by their humorous misogyny, or they conceal wild nonsense in seemingly profound language. The main episode in which Marcolf takes part reenacts the Judgment of Solomon. Arpa and Chasbi are the names the playwright assigns to the two women in the scene. In the short dialogue, no fewer than four of Marcolf's short utterances begin ponderously with the Latin *Nota bene.*

> Marcolphus: *Nota bene* die will ihr Kind behalten. Aber warům wolt ihr eůers nicht behalten?
>
> Casbi: Eÿ von Hertzen gerne, deßwegen kömmt der Streit her, daß ich mir mein Kind nicht will nehmen laßen.
>
> Marcolphus: *Nota bene* Die Fraů will ihr Kind aůch behalten. Was gehts denn nůn den König an, ob ihr eůre Kinder behalten oder wegwerfen wolt.
>
> Arpa: Der Herr můß weiter fragen, die hat mir das Kind gestohlen das ich behalten will.
>
> Marcolphus: *Nota bene* Die hat sich ihr Kind stehlen laßen. Aber seyd ihr deßen geständig?
>
> Casbi: Nein ich habe nichts gestohlen, ich habe das Meinige und wills behalten.
>
> Marcolphus: *Nota bene* Gegentheil spricht es ist nicht wahr. Nůn wer hat es gesehen, daß ihr es nicht gestohlen habt?

> Marcolphus: *Nota bene,* she wishes to keep her child. But why do you not want to keep yours?
>
> Chasbi: Ah, from the heart, I want gladly to do so. The source of the conflict is that I will not allow my child to be taken from me.
>
> Marcolphus: *Nota bene,* the woman also wishes to keep her child. How does it then involve the king now, whether you would keep your children or discard them?

Arpa: The Lord must question further. She has stolen from me the child that I want to keep.

Marcolphus: *Nota bene,* she has allowed her child to be stolen from her. But have you then confessed to it?

Chasbi: No, I have stolen nothing. I have what is mine and will keep it.

Marcolphus: *Nota bene,* the opposing party says it is not true. Now who has seen that you did not steal it?

Bibliography

Christan Weise, *Comödie vom König Salomo,* ed. Imelda Rohrbacher and Michaela Neidl, Zeitsprünge: Forschungen zur Frühen Neuzeit (Frankfurt: Vittorio Klostermann, 2019), 254.

Ludwig Fulda, ed., *Die Gegner der zweiten schlesischen Schule,* Deutsche National-Literatur 39 (Berlin: Spemann, 1884), vol. 2, XXXVII–XXXVIII.

Karl Friedrich Flögel, *Geschichte des Grotesk-Komischen,* ed. Max Bauer (Munich: Müller, 1914), 1:286.

G92. From Johann Christoph Ettner von Eiteritz, *The Loyal Eckhart's Dishonorable Doctor* [...] (*Dess getreuen Eckharts Unwürdiger Doctor* [...]). 1697.

Ettner (1654–1724) was a German doctor and novelist of the Baroque period. In this treatise, the author styles himself "The Loyal Eckhart" (meaning "trusty friend"). In one passage (p. 112) he categorizes the text *Marcolfus* with four others as *Volksbücher.* Such "folk-books" were popular literature in the form of prose narratives. Many of them derive ultimately from verse romances of the thirteenth and fourteenth centuries. Although their heyday fell in the sixteenth century, they continued to be printed through the eighteenth century and in some regions even into the nineteenth. Paracelsus was a theologian and alchemist.

Die Autoritäten, die er [Paracelsus] mit dem Venus-Berge, Dannheuser, und dergleichen alter Weiber-Mährlein vorbringt, sind Alphanzereyen, von welchen man in der Schweitz, woher er gebürtig, im Reich und anliegenden Oertern unzehlig vil hören wird, und von müßigen Leuten hernach Bauer-Romanen als Marcolphus, Ritter Wigelaieis, Peter mit dem silbernen Schlüssel, der gehörnete Seyfried, Melusina, unter welchen der unvergleichliche Grillen- und Brembsenfänger der Amadis mit zu rechnen, geschriben, und von den Meistersingern Comœdien und Lieder verfertiget worden; mit solchen und dergleichen Narren-Possen trug sich die Welt damals herumb, und lag unter disen Sachen ein solches Gifft verborgen, welches vil tausend Menschen auch der Seelen nach schädlich gewesen [...].

The authorities that [Paracelsus] brings forth, with the Venusberg, Tannhäuser, and other old wive's tales of the sort, are wickednesses of which a person will hear countless times throughout Switzerland, no matter where one is a native, in the kingdom and nearby places. And after that these peasant novels such as *Marcolfus, Knight Wigoleis, Peter with the Silver Key, Horned Siegfried,* and *Melusine,* among which we can include in the reckoning the incomparable eccentric and rabble-rouser of *Amadis,* are written down by idle people and are firmed up as comedies and songs by master singers. Then the world carried on with such foolish pranks and their like, and beneath these things such a poison lay hidden, which was harmful to many thousands of men, even spiritually [...].

Bibliography

Gerhard Dünnhaupt, *Personalbibliographien zu den Drucken des Barock,* 6 vols. (Stuttgart: Hersemann, 1990), 2:1432.

Helmuth Huemer, "Untersuchungen zur Volksbuchliteratur Oberösterreichs in neunzehnten Jahrhundert" (Diss., University of Vienna, 1950), 46–47.

Hildegard Beyer, "Die deutschen Volksbücher und ihr Lesepublikum" (Diss., Goethe University Frankfurt, 1962), 88.

Johann Christoph Ettner von Eiteritz, *Dess getreuen Eckharts Unwürdiger Doctor: in welchem wie ein Medicus, der rechtschaffen handeln will, beschaffen seyn soll ... dann sonderliche philosophische, politische, chymische, am meisten aber medicinische Observationes* (Augsburg: L. Kroniger und C. Göbels, 1697), 112.

John L. Flood, "The Survival of German 'Volksbücher': Three Studies in Bibliography," 2 vols. (Diss., University of London, 1980), 1:114.

G93. From August Schumann, *Solomon the Wise and His Fool Marcolf, according to an Old German Manuscript* (*Salomo der Weise, und sein Narr Markolph: Nach einer altdeutschen Handschrift*). 1797.

In addition to being a bookseller and publisher, August Schumann (1773–1826) edited numerous works and composed various others. He published this novel anonymously in 1797. The book gave the place of publication as Jerusalem, when in fact it was the municipality of Ronneburg in the German state of Hesse.

The author derived the idea for the story from "an Old German folk-poem entitled *King Solomon and Marcolf*" (p. III). This citation refers to *Salman and Morolf,* the Middle High German literary work that belongs within the subgenre of "minstrel epics" concerned with a bridal quest (see Chapter 5 above). He consulted the poem in a codex that the literary historian Johann Joachim Eschenberg (1743–1820) purchased at auction in 1792. This now-separate fascicle is the 1479 Dirmstein manuscript of *Salman and Morolf* (Frankfurt am Main, Stadt- und Universitätsbibliothek, MS germ. qu. 13). Thus Schumann describes Princian as having 60,000 men at his disposal (p. V), a detail mentioned only in this manuscript (see p. 13 and Karnein, *Salman und Morolf,* line 37). To take another example, his depiction of Marcolf's ugliness (p. 10) corresponds to a section of *The Book of Marcolf* (lines 34–61), which in the Frankfurt manuscript follows the bridal quest and is entitled "The Other Morolf" (fol. 88v).

Schumann offers entertaining narratives that relate to Solomon's twilight years, "nothing more than a brief contribution to the secret history of the human heart" (p. XIV). In telling the story of the biblical ruler's relationship with Marcolf, the late eighteenth-century author appears to be interested mainly in the wise king's desire to become close to the fool. Among other noteworthy incidentals, the novelist indicates that Marcolf was an Egyptian: the copper-plate engraving by Friedrich Rossmässler that serves as frontispiece before the title-page, bearing an image of Marcolf wearing antlers, has below it the legend "I am an Egyptian, my name is Marcolf" ("Ich bin ein Aegiptier, mein Name ist Markolph") [see Figure 27].

Bibliography

August Schumann, *Salomo der Weise, und sein Narr Markolph: Nach einer altdeutschen Handschrift* (Ronneburg [but according to the book, Jerusalem], 1797).

Hermann Schulze and G. Semper, eds., *Allgemeine Deutsche Biographie,* 56 vols. (Leipzig: Duncker und Humblot, 1891), 33:40.

Biagioni, "Marcolf und Bertoldo," 10.

G94. Anonymous, *Marcolf, the Figure of Terror, or the Blood-Wedding of the Black Brothers: Fragments from the Times of Our Ancestors* (*Markulf der Schauermann, oder, die Bluthochzeit der schwarzen Brüder: Bruchstücke aus den Zeiten der Väter*). 1821.

This thriller, in 13 chapters and 266 pages, belongs to the earliest stage of the literary form known in English literature as the Gothic novel. The genre reflects the predilection of the Romantic era for the Middle Ages. In this fiction Marcolf is the son of the count of Klingenberg. As a result of baseless slander, the youth has had to give up the place in the world to which his noble upbringing and nearly royal rank destined him. As the longtime leader of a band of supposedly good robbers, he is described as having a terrifying demeanor that belies his true nature. Despite appearances, he is actually a "benevolent, kindly, young man" (p. 11) with blond curls and a helmet adorned with black feathers. Marcolf's story comes to a happy ending, and he reattains his unjustly lost status, when he marries the daughter of a count.

The book warrants further examination to determine if the name of its protagonist signals a genuine connection with the Solomon and Marcolf cycle or is instead mere happenstance.

Bibliography

Markulf der Schauermann, oder, die Bluthochzeit der schwarzen Brüder: Bruchstücke aus den Zeiten der Väter (Leipzig: Rein'sche Buchhandlung, 1821).

G95. From Alfons Paquet, *Marcolf, or King Solomon and the Peasant: An Enjoyable Play* (*Marcolph oder König Salomo und der Bauer: Ein heiteres Spiel*). 1924. [See Figure 28.]

Paquet (1881–1944) was a German writer and journalist. In the 1920s he shifted most of his energies from journalism, travel writing, and storywriting to theater. The play about Solomon and Marcolf belongs to this phase. It was performed in Frankfurt at the Marionette Theater in June 1922, in Saarbrücken on February 20, 1927, in Altona on April 11, 1929, and in Koblenz in 1929. In addition, it was aired in Stuttgart as a radio-play under the title "Marcolph: An Enjoyable Play" on March 15, 1927.

Bibliography

Alfons Paquet, *Marcolph oder König Salomo und der Bauer: Ein heiteres Spiel* (Frankfurt am Main: Verlag des Bühnenvolksbundes, 1924).

Figure 27. Marcolf, wearing antlers, says "I am an Egyptian, my name is Marcolf" ("Ich bin ein Aegiptier, mein Name ist Markolph"). Frontispiece from August Schumann, *Salomo der Weise, und sein Narr Markolph*. Göttingen, Niedersächsische Staats- und Universitätsbibliothek, 8 FAB VI, 7157.

Figure 28. Front cover of Alfons Paquet, *Marcolph oder König Salomo und der Bauer: Ein heiteres Spiel* (1924).

Appendix 2
Addenda and Corrigenda to *S&M*
By Jan M. Ziolkowski

THESE INDICATIONS of additions and corrections to be made to *S&M* Z are keyed to page numbers in that volume. The compilation draws primarily upon reviews of *S&M* Z that appeared between 2009 and 2014, such as Bayless (2010), Classen (2009), Colker (2009), Donnini (2011), Hays (2010), Kauntze (2010), Meckler (2011), Nissan (2012 and 2014), Rigg (2010), and Stanzak (2009). Additionally, it takes into account notes on the Latin in the Italian translation printed by Macchi in 2011. In contrast, no attempt has been made to integrate information from the facing-language edition with the Latin and Middle English published by Bradbury and Bradbury in 2012, where the commentary (though useful) relates primarily to the English.

p. 53   In 1a consider replacing the opening phrase "in fact" with "but" or "however" (Rigg, 484).

p. 55   In 2a change "Obed begot Isaiah, Isaiah begot King David" to "Obed begot Jesse, Jesse begot King David" (Meckler, 307).

p. 61   In 44b recast "there is nothing for you to do" as "what you are doing is nothing" (Rigg, 485). Rigg comments "if you just sit there anally constricted and unable to move ... you are achieving nothing." Hear, hear!

p. 65   In 81b the English may stand (if the infinitive of the deponent carries a passive meaning), but it is worth pondering the suggestion to translate "when your wife wants to use herself" with the implication of autoeroticism (Rigg, 485).

p. 69   In 109a revise "disaster" "to "punishment" (Rigg, 485).

p. 77   In 2.1.13 consider replacing "moreover" with "but" (Rigg, 484).

p. 79   Compare p. 53. In 2.3.5 think of rewording "in fact" as "but" or "however" (Rigg, 484).

p. 99   Compare pp. 53 and 79. In 2.19.1 think of replacing "in fact" with "but" or "however" (Rigg, 484).

p. 112   In the note on *tunica usque ad nates* (only to the buttocks), add at the bottom (appropriately!): "In 2 Kings 10:4, Hanun, to humiliate ambassadors sent by David, *praecidit vestes eorum medias usque ad nates* (cut away half of their garments even to the buttocks)" (Swift Edgar, personal communication, 14 May 2009).

p. 116   In 2a delete "—but note Isaiah, where Jesse would be expected as the father of King David."

p. 122   At end of 4a, add: "*in regno meo* (in my realm): Macchi puts into the mix *omnibus diebus tuis*, a reading not in Benary's text but attested in two manuscripts, and translates 'for all your days.' See G. C. Macchi, trans., *Il dialogo di Salomone e Marcolfo* (N.p.: Lulu, 2011), 13n22."

p. 123   In 6a add at the end of the first paragraph: "See also Ecclesiastes 1:16" (Macchi, *Dialogo*, 13n24).

p. 126   In 10b add at end of first full paragraph: "Compare Walther 2:650, no. 132007: *Jure bibit merdam, qui fonte suo caccat illam* (rightly he drinks shit, who craps it in his fountain). See also Macchi, *Dialogo*, 13n26."

p. 156   At the end of the comment on 65a, add "*auffert* (takes away):" If not a typographical error, Benary's Latin presents a spelling variant for *aufert*" (Rigg, 485).

p. 158   At end of 69b, add: "One manuscript offers instead of *caccat* (shits) the verb *sedeat* (may sit) (Macchi, *Dialogo*, 19n49)."

p. 166   At end of 85b, add: "A few manuscripts have the reading *mons* (mountain) instead of *petra* (stone)."

p. 172   On line 18, replace "101a" with "100a" (Rigg, 485).

p. 177   At end of 113a, add: "This is another passage in which a reader has to wonder if the original sequence of lines has been disrupted over time, because 111b and 113a both begin with *Ve* and end with *dentes* and *incedenti*, respectively."

p. 182   At end of 124a, add: "Rigg proposes ingeniously that Solomon's observation is explained by *Distichs of Cato* 3.20, 'Fear a woman's tears rather than her anger.'"

p. 184   At end of 127b, supply a new paragraph: "Macchi (*Dialogo*, 25n75) invokes a proverbial saying in Petronius, which he interprets to mean that after 'taking up' or 'bearing' a calf, it is more possible to 'take up' or 'bear' a bull. See Otto, 341, no. 1744, *taurus* 1, and compare Adams, *Latin Sexual Vocabulary*, 167."

p. 201   In line 10, read "Solomon had at least two brothers" and not "David" (Hays, 1176).

p. 202   At 2.2.7 a more apt parallel than "When it rains, it pours" would be "The wind blows where it lists" (Hays, 1176).

p. 221   Correct 2.6.1 to 2.6.2 (Nissan, "Wily Peasant," 118).

p. 230   At 2.13.4 change "This redundant phrase" to "This phrase, a wordy synonym for *cras*" (Hays, 1176).

p. 236   At 11, Macchi (*Dialogo*, 42n95) takes issue with the translation, which is drawn verbatim from the Douay-Rheims English version for the Vulgate Bible quoted here.

p. 239   On the question of whether Marcolf in 2.19 wears his shoes crosswise or back to front, take into account the lore of the people known as the Antipodes, whose heels are in front and whose toes are turned backwards (Nissan, Review of *Solomon and Marcolf*, 169; Nissan, "Wily Peasant," 143–5).

p. 244   Carmel refers not to the village that was in the Maon district of Judah but to the forest on Mount Carmel on the coast of Palestine (Nissan, Review of *Solomon and Marcolf*, 168; Nissan, "Wily Peasant," 141). The citation of 4 Kings 19:23 is not an error (*pace* Nissan), since the numbering of the Books of Kings follows the conventions of the Latin Vulgate Bible rather than the Hebrew.

p. 245   Cades et Barne (Kadesh and Barne): Both the Vulgate and the Vetus Latina transmit the name as Cadesbarne, without breaking the elements or adding the conjunction *et* between them (Nissan, Review of *Solomon and Marcolf*, 168; Nissan, "Wily Peasant," 142).

p. 292   At 29 *ille rex* (that king) is not Solomon but the pagan king.

p. 314   In SAT 8, line 5, read *quam* instead of *quae* (Rigg, 485).

p. 318   Revise "[Mishnah]" to "[Aggadah]" (Nissan, Review of *Solomon and Marcolf*, 167; Nissan, "Wily Peasant," 139–40).

p. 321   In translating *quidem* and *vero* in SAT 11, lines 1 and 3, give thought to revising the English in lines 7 and 10 to "they go to Mars [*quidem*] when the sun enters the first degree of Aries ... but to Saturn [*vero*] when the sun enters the first degree of Libra" (Rigg, 484).

p. 321   In SAT 11, line 5, the antecedent of *quę* is unclear. Perhaps assume *quae festa* or *quae ydola* (Rigg, 485).

pp. 328–32 Rigg comments (485): "There is much that is puzzling here. The tone of the poem, an attack on one Robert who has written a *Marculfica vita,* is that of the poetry contest exemplified by Henry of Avranches and Michael of Cornwall, in which one contestant abuses his opponent for immorality and incompetent versification." He goes on to suggest translating lines 15–16 as "I call to witnesss the right of law and other gods of the countryside: these [verses] offer pormise of blots [i.e., more solecisms]" and lines 17–18 "What you seek in verse you deserve to have pleased in verse, but you will always be Vergil if you never versify" (which he equates to *si tacuisses, philosophus fuisses,* with reference to Boethius, *Consolation of Philosophy* 2 pr. 7 fin. and Proverbs 17:28).

p. 335 Change "in prison" (lines 2–3 from bottom) to "a youth" (Rigg, 485).

p. 336 Change "would pay a certain sum of money as a forfeit" (line 5 from top) to "would pay money to the one solving them" (Rigg, 485).

p. 338 In last line of Latin, correct "proparavit" to "properavit" (Rigg, 485).

p. 343 In line 14 of the Latin, rectify *precius* to *precium;* in line 18, *nose* to *nosse.* In line 22, consider removing the comma after *veste.* In line 8 of the English, change "plows fields with great hope" to "plows many fields in hope" (Rigg, 485).

p. 344 In line 22 of the English, think of translating as "If you take care of Thais with food, she will suffer less in her clothing" in tandem with the above punctuation change to the Latin (Rigg, 485).

p. 350 correct *in* to *is*: "if the identity of the names in indeed deliberate" (Nissan, "Wily Peasant," 118).

Appendix 3

Texts of Old French *Salemon and Marcoul*

By Mary-Ann Stadtler-Chester

Version A

1.
Mortalitez, <> guerre
est escil de terre
et destruiemenz,
ce dist Salemons.
De putain sourt maus
et guerre mortaus,
et peril de gent,
Marcoul li respont.

2.
Molt sot de la muse
qui vout fere escluse   10
por retenir Loire,
ce dist Salemons.
Pute communaus
et fols naturaus
ne font pas a croire,
Marcoul li respont.

3.
Qui en sa meson
atret le larron,
domage i reçoit,
ce dist Salemons.   20
Qui putain honeure,
en la fin pleure,

quant il s'aperçoit,
Marcoul li respont.

4.
Et la chenillete
menjüe l'erbete,
la fueille du chol,
ce dist Salemons.
La pute se vest
Et conroie et pest   30
De l'avoir au fol,
Marcoul li respont.

5.
Quant chevrel est nez,
de voir le savez;
il a le col blanc,
ce dist Salemons.
Quant gars dist: "Tenez,"
pute dist: "Venez
seoir en cest banc,"
Marcoul li respont.   40

6.
Molt fet menu orne
et sovent se torne
qui porsuit gorpille,
ce dist Salemons.
Maint pas fet en vain
qui trace putain,
quant ele gondille,
Marcoul li respont.

7.
Qui langor avra,
molt liez en sera   50
se vis en eschape,
ce dist Salemons.
Qui putain croira,
ne li remaindra
ne cote, ne chape,
Marcoul li respont.

8.
Li petit poucin
sont bon au saïn
atorné au poivre,
ce dist Salemons.   60
Quant pute n'a vin,
art quiert et engin
comment ait a boivre,
Marcoul li respont.

9.
Li singes est lais
et molt contrefais,
s'a le cul pelé,
ce dist Salemons.
Diex ne fist contrait
qui por argent n'ait   70
de putain son gré,
Marcoul li respont.

10.
Bien set li putois
son recet ou bois
ou il doit garir,
ce dist Salemons.
Pute a les dois crois;
tout veut prendre a chois,
quanques voit tenir,
Marcoul li respont.   80

11.
Tels chace le dain
par bois et par plain
qui puis le pert tout,
ce dist Salemons.
Tels vest la putain
et pest de son pain
c'uns autres la fout,
Marcoul li respont.

12.
La pore meüre

441

vaut miex que la dure,   90
ce savez vous bien,
ce dist Salemons.
Pute a tel nature:
de garçon n'a cure
puis que il n'a rien,
Marcoul li respont.

13.
Roinsce acroche gent
et poile souvent
brebis et mouton,
ce dist Salemons.   100
Et la pute tent,
tant comme ele atent
riens en son garçon,
Marcoul li respont.

14.
Le cras pourcelet
ne quiert pas le net,
ainz quiert le palu,
ce dist Salemons.
A putain ne chaut
qui argent li baut,   110
mes tost ait foutu,
Marcoul li respont.

15.
Le coc ou fumier
grate le paillier
por trover le grain,
ce dist Salemons.
Pute a bon mestier
de borse vuidier
a cul de vilain,
Marcoul li respont.   120

16.
Chevaus enselez
est bien aprestez
de fere son oirre,

ce dist Salemons.
Pute bien corbee
est bien aprestee
de foutre et de poirre,
Marcoul li respont.

17.
Se n'estoit li chas
molt iroit li ras   130
souvent au bacon,
ce dist Salemons.
Pute o ses blans bras
de son con fet las
por prendre bricon,
Marcoul li respont.

18.
Li bués au vilain
gaaingne le pain
dont li mondes vit,
ce dist Salemons.   140
bien se lasse en vain
qui cuide putain
tuer a son vit,
Marcoul li respont.

19.
Chevaus sejornez
a paine est ferrez
qu'i mort et repane,
ce dist Salemons.
Molt a bone main
qui veut de putain   150
fere preude fame,
Marcoul li respont.

20.
Periers mal gardez
est sovent crollez
tant qu'il a que prendre,
ce dist Salemons.
Tant vous prisera

pute que savra
que avrez que tendre,
Marcoul li respont.   160

21.
Riens ne vaut aillïe,
s'ele n'est bro<ïe>
et fort pestelee,
ce dist Salemons.
La pute est perdue
s'ele n'est bien batue
et souvent foulee,
Marcoul li respont.

22.
Meson esventee
est tost alumee   170
quant li feu s'i prent,
ce dist Salemons.
La pute paree
est tost enversee
quantz el voit l'argent,
Marcoul li respont.

23.
Ja n'ert tant de vin,
que ja li molin
plus sovent en mueille,
ce dist Salemons.   180
Ja tant ne serois
por putain destrois,
que miex vous en vueille,
Marcoul li respont.

24.
A droit pert s'onor
qui a trahitor
otroie baillie,
ce dist Salemons.
Qui done a putain
son bien en sa main   190

a bon droit mendie,
Marcoul li respont.

25.
Ne vous chaut semer
en sablon de mer:
ja n'i croistra grain,
ce dist Salemons.
Bien pert son sermon
qui veut par reson
chastoier putain,
Marcoul li respont.   200

26.
Connins se repont
en terre parfont
que il ne soit pris,
ce dist Salemons.
Pute poile tant
garçon en riant
que il est chetis,
Marcoul li respont.

27.
L'en tent a le glu
ou l'en a veü   210
reperier oisiaus,
ce dist Salemons.
Pute cerche foire
la ou ele espoire
plenté de troussiaus,
Marcoul li respont.

28.
Getez au plonjon
ou pierre ou baston,
et il plus se moille,
ce dist Salemons.   220
Donez a putain
et hui et demain,
et el plus s'orgueille,
Marcoul li respont.

29.
Norrissiez l'ostor,
si l'avrez meillor
por bien rivoier,
ce dist Salemons.
La putain foulez
et sous pié tenez,   230
dont vous avra chier,
Marcoul li respont.

30.
Anguille peschie
n'ert ja empoingnie,
tant fort se demaine,
ce dist Salemons.
[La] pute vez<ie>
n'ert ja engingnie;
fols est qui s'en paine,
Marcoul li respont.   240

31.
A molt granz tropiaus
vont les estorniaus
que uns seus n'en chiet,
ce dist Salemons.
Pute tient convent
a [vint] ou a cent,
e[ncor]e en aqui<er>t,
Marcoul li respont.

32.
Li liepars est fiers
a prendre maniers,   250
et li lyons plus,
ce dist Salemons.
Putain embraciez:
ele dist: "Fuiez!"
ainsi l'ont en us,
Marcoul li respont.

33.
Li petis poupars

fet molt bones pars
de son pain au chien,
ce dist Salemons.   260
Pute a tel nature:
de garçon n'a cure
puis que il n'a rien,
Marcoul li respont.

34.
Asne avez veü
lessier fain menu
por rungier chardon?
ce dist Salemons.
Pute avez veü
lessier son bon dru   270
por mauvés garçon?
Marcoul li respont.

35.
Molt est biaus estez
et la flor es prez
dont il i a tant,
ce dist Salemons.
Se putain creez,
quanques vous avez
prendra en riant,
Marcoul li respont.   280

36.
Ja ne parra trace
que culuevre face
desus pierre bise,
ce dist Salemons.
La pute pa<r>ee
n'ert prise provee
s'en foutant n'est prise,
Marcoul li respont.

37.
A bouche de four
a si grant chalor,   290
ja n'i croistra herbe,

ce dist Salemons.
Ja cul de putain,
au soir ne au main,
ne sera sanz merde,
Marcoul li respont.

38.
Qui vilain norrist
et souef blandist,   300
adonc l'a pior,
ce dist Salemons.
Qui putain norrist
et bat et laidist,
adonc l'a meillor,
Marcoul li respont.

39.
Gars taste a sa borse
s'i trueve piau d'orse:
n'a mes que doner,
ce dit Salemon.   310
Quant la pute l'ot,
son con li reclot:
vit n'i puet entrer,
Marcoul li respont.

40.
Qui prise les dez,
fols est et dervez,
quar tost en est nus,
ce dist Salemons.
Qui putain maintient,
toz maus l'en avient: 320
tost est confondus,
Marcoul li respont.

Qui putain croit et dez quarrez
ne puet morir sanz povretez.

Explicit Marcoul et Salemon qui
ne vaut pas un grant estron.

Version B
Ci commance de Marcou et de Salemon

1.
Mortalitez, <> guerre
est essil de terre
et destruisemens,
ce dit Salemons.
De putain sort max
et ires mortax,
et peril de gent,
Marcous li respont.

2.
Tençons et envie
depart compaignie   10
de feax amis,
ce dit Salemons.
Engins de putains
font parens prochains
mortiex anemis,
Marcous li respont.

3.
Ja tant n'en ier<t> vins,
que por ce molins
mialz en tort ne muelle,
ce dit Salemons.   20
Ja tant ne serez
por putain grevez,
que miax vos en<vueille>,
Marcous li respont.

4.
La pute et li sers
font tot entravers
en dit et en oevre,
ce dit Salemons.
Or font bele chiere,
traïssent derriere,   30
lor corage cuevre,
Marcous li respont.

5.
Sers de pute orine
coistrons de cuisine,
font molt a doter,
ce dit Salemons.
Pute en cort norie
n'est en abaïe
legiere a entrer,
Marcous li respont.   40

6.
Molt fait fole chace
cil qui porsuit trace
de cointe gorpille,
ce dit Salemons.
Maint pas va en vain
qui porsuit putain,
quant ele grandille,
Marcous li respont.

7.
Tant iert regardez
periers et croslez,   50
con il a que rendre,
ce dit Salemons.
....
....
....
....

8.
Cheval sejornez
a poinne est ferrez,
se en travaille n'entre,
<ce dit Salemons.>   60
Molt a bone main
qui porroit putain
fere preude feme,
Marcous li respont.

9.
Ce sachiez vos bien:

coustume est a chien
de mengier charoigne,
ce dit Salemons.
Je preig bien en main
qui maintient putain: 70
ja n'iert sanz vergoigne,
Marcous li respont.

10.
Maigre char prenez,
ja n'i troverez
graisse ne saïn,
ce dit Salemons.
Putain blandissiez
et la chierrisiez;
ja n'i metre<z> fin,
Marcous li respont.   80

11.
Gitiez au plunjon
o pierre o baston,
et il plus se moille,
ce dit Salemons.
Donez a putain
et hui et demain,
ele plus s'orgoille,
Marcous li respont.

12.
Bués mal ivernez
en mars est lassez;   90
si chiet en la roie,
ce dit Salemons.
Pute bien vestue
se demostre en rue,
por ce qu'en la voie,
Marcous li respont.

13.
La tent en la glu
o l'en a veü
repaire d'oisiax

ce dit Salemons.   100
Pute cerche foire
quant ele i espoire
plenté de bordiax,
Marcous li respont.

14.
Qui voit lo solel
au matin vermel,
si atent la pluie,
ce dit Salemons.
Pute a bele chiere
e taverne est chiere,   110
puis apres anuie,
Marcous li respont.

15.
Ja nus useriers
n'avra tant deniers
con ses cuers voudroit,
ce dit Salemons.
Ja pute en sa vie
n'iert tant replenie
que plus ne covoit,
Marcoul li respont.   120

16.
Ja por sairement,
com n'i <sert> noient,
mar querrez vilain,
ce dit Salemons.
Bien set sa nature
con ele plus jure
qui mains croit putain,
Marcous li respont.

17.
Chargiez au jument
ou plunc o argent,   130
lui ne chaut lo quel,
ce dit Salemons.
Pute ne tient conte

qui son con cul monte:
tuit li sont iguel,
Marcous li respont.

18.
Fox est qui semer
viaut enz en la mer:
ja n'i quiaudra grain,
ce dit Salemons.   140
Bien pert sa raison
qui vialt par sermon
chastoier putain,
Marcoul li respont.

19.
Loëz le poon,
si fait a bandon
sa queue pa<r>oir,
ce dit Salemons.
Pute bien vestue
se demostre en rue,   150
por loenge avoir,
Marcous li respont.

20.
Li ostors muiers
est plus soveniers
que nen est li sors,
ce dit Salemons.
Con plus est en voie,
plus sovent prent proie
pute o lou gent cors,
Marcous li respont.   160

21.
Li faucons sorsis
est auques ordis
au premerain jor,
ce dit Salemons.
Molt est desirree
pute bien gardee
quant ele a loisor,

Marcous li respont.

22.
Sauvage espervier
n'est mie legier   170
a fere privé,
ce dit Salemons.
Pute de mal aire
ne fait nul atrere
a nule bonté,
Marcous li respont.

23.
Abaissiez l'ostor,
si l'avroiez mellor
a miauz <as>proier,
ce dit Salemons.   180
Putain destraingniez
et metez soz piez;
si vos avra chier,
Marcous li respont.

24.
De loing cort au vent
li chiens quant il sent
o perdriz ou caille,
ce dit Salemons.
De loing aperçoit
pute, de cui doit   190
traire la maaille,
Marcous li respont.

25.
Li gras porcelet
ne quiert pas lou net,
ainz quiert la palu,
ce dit Salemons.
A putain ne chaut
qui argent li baut,
mes tost ait foutu,
Marcous li respont.   200

26.
Li petiz pouparz
fait molt larges parz
de son pain au chien,
ce dit Salemons.
Bien vos entendra
pute, quant orra
que vos diroiz: "Tien,"
Marcous li respont.

27.
Bien s'art, ce m'est vis,
qui les charbons vis   210
reçoit en sa main,
ce dit Salemons.
A droit gist en paille
qui son avoir baille
en main de putain,
Marcous li respont.

28.
Chevax enselez
est bien aprestez
de faire son oirre,
Ce dit Salemons.   220
pute bien corbee
est bien aprestee
de foutre et de poirre,
Marcous li respont.

29.
A droit pert s'anor
qui lou traïtor
met en sa baillie,
ce dit Salemons.
Qui met a putain
ses biens entre main   230
a bon droit mendie,
Marcous li respont.

30.
Qui en sa meson

atret lou larron,
domage i reçoit,
ce dit Salemons.
Qui putain anore,
en la fin plore,
quant il s'aperçoit,
Marcous li respont.   240

31.
Quant lo chat est bel
et luisant la pel,
lors asauvagist,
ce dit Salemons.
Chierisiez putain,
donc soiez certain
qu'ele vos guerpist,
Marcoul li respont.

Version D
Ci coumence de Marcoul et de Salemon que li quens de Bretagne fist

1.
Seur tote l'autre hennor
est proesce la flor,
ce dit Salemons.
Ge n'aim pas la valour
dont l'en muert a doulor,
Marcoul li respont.

2.
En cortoisie a paine,
mais bien fait qui la meine,
ce dit Salemons.
Mois et jor et semaine,   10
travail est dure paine,
Marcoul li respont.

3.
Por largement doner,
puet l'en enpres monter,
ce dit Salemons.
De povreté user,

se fait l'en fol clamer,
Marcol li respont.

4.
Qui saiges hom sera,
ja trop ne parlera,   20
ce dit Salemons.
Qui ja mot ne dira,
grant noise ne fera,
Marcol li respont.

5.
Fox est cil qui menra
o soi quanque il a,
ce dit Salemons.
Qui riens ne portera,
ja riens ne li cherra,
Marcol li respont.   30

6.
Bien boivre et bien mengier
fait home assoagier,
ce dit Salemons.
Et ventre angroissier
fait çainture alaschier,
Marcol li respont.

7.
Porquoi maine mestier
qui ne s'en set aidier?
ce dit Salemons.
Tel se cuide avancier   40
qui quiert son encombrier,
Marcoul li respont.

8.
Qui pleure ainçois qu'il rie,
donc ne fait il folie,
ce dit Salemons.
Taint sai ge de maistrie:
qui pleure, il ne rit mie,
Marcol li respont.

9.
Voirs est qu'or et argent
desirrent molt la gent,   50
ce dit Salemons.
Tex a qui s'en repent,
quant a force, le rent,
Marcol li respont.

10.
Porquoi lieve matin
qui ne set son chemin?
ce dit Salemons.
Malostruz a declin,
et li jors a sa fin,
Marcol li respont.   60

11.
Mainte gent sont irié
quant il sont deshetié,
ce dit Salemons.
Morz mielz qu'asoagie
vorroient tex saigie,
Marcol li respont.

12.
Dame otroie a ami
cors et cuer autresi,
ce dit Salemons.
Fax amanz sanz merci   70
ont meint beax cors trahi,
Marcol li respont.

13.
Qui sa d[r]ue deçoit,
trop fait vilain esploit,
ce dit Salemons.
Trichierres ne quiert droit
quar raison l'ociroit,
Marcol li respont.

14.
Quant dame est decëue,

c'est sanz desconnëue,   80
ce dit Salemons.
Il <ara> mainte drue
qui bien font table nue,
Marcol li respont.

15.
Povre home soffroiteus
sont sovent covoiteus,
ce dit Salemons.
No sont pas trop hontox:
il prannent bien de vos,
Marcol li respont.   90

16.
Quant ostes est doutez,
fox s'i est ostelez,
ce dit Salemons.
Par oste, ce savez,
est mainz avoirs ostez,
Marcol li respont.

17.
En grant pelerinaige
font li oste domaige,
ce dit Salemons.
Droiz lerres, par usaige,   100
robe ou enble ou s'enraige,
Marcol li respont.

18.
Ja d'els bien ne sera,
qui bien nes paiera,
ce dit Salemons.
Le vilains dist: "Pieça
que povres amis n'a,"
Marcol li respont.

19.
En yver, peliçon,
mais par le grant chaut, non,   110
ce dit Salemons.

Bien doit porter baston
qui a voisin felon,
Marcol li respont.

20.
Li saiges se porvoit
ainz qu'il vigne a l'estroit,
ce dit Salemons.
Fox ne cuide par droit
que jamais granz chauz soit,
Marcol li respont.   120

21.
<Li> fox giet pierre dure;
de ce n'a saiges cure,
ce dit Salemons.
Estez fait sa droiture
quant chauz oste froidure,
Marcol li respont.

22.
Porquoi fait li chevax
parmi les plains granz sauz?
ce dit Salemons.
Li droiz fox naturax   130
giete pierre ou pax,
Marcol li respont.

23.
A fol ne siet mesure,
n'a viel envoiseüre,
ce dit Salemons.
Mais bien quiere verdure
qui la soe ne dure,
Marcol li respont.

24.
Molt est fox encombrez
quant afaire a assez,   140
ce dit Salemons.
Maçue li portez,
si ert reconfortez,

Marcol li respont.

25.
Toz est fox aprestez
quant talent est montez,
ce dit Salemons.
Mauvais chiens encombrez
envoise les ainz nez,
Marcol li respont.   150

26.
De fol ne sai que die,
nostre Sire l'oublie,
ce dit Salemons.
Granz est la confrarie
de ceus qui font folie,
Marcol li respont.

27.
Fox est a tel escole:
c'on plus vit, plus afole,
ce dit Salemons.
Quel que soit la parole,   160
ses cuers de joie vole,
Marcol li respont.

28.
Voirs est que nuit et jor
est li fox en baudor,
ce dit Salemons.
Mielz prise son labor
que du saige le plor,
Marcol li respont.

29.
Que qu'autre gent en die,
fox rit de sa folie,   170
ce dit Salemons.
Bone est sa compaignie,
mais qu'il ne fiere mie,
Marcol li respont.

30.
Ge n'aim povre pasture,
ne travail sanz mesure,
ce dit Salemons.
Noif en esté, froidure,
tout est contre nature,
Marcol li respont.   180

31.
Ge n'aim soulaz d'enfant,
ne doner a truant,
ce dit Salemons.
Ne ge feme plorant,
ne de felon le chant,
Marcol li respont.

32.
Ge n'aim cri de mastin,
ne lever trop matin,
ce dit Salemons.
Ne ge mauvais cousin   190
ne eve qui tolt vin,
Marcol li respont.

33.
Cil qui cuide estre beax
est bien en ses aviax,
ce dit Salemons.
Mais quant li pent la peax,
lors li croist dels noveax,
Marcol li respont.

34.
Qui est et beax et boens
bient doit avoir bon tens,   200
ce dit Salemons.
Quant bien au siecle pens,
toz est fors qui est enz,
Marcol li respont.

35.
Mielz se vient esbaudir

qu'en grant penser languir,
ce dit Salemons.
Ne soi trop esjoïr,
ne pensé maintenir,
Marcol li respont.   210

36.
Le dangier de mauvais
n'amerai ge jamais,
ce dit Salemons.
Le baiser de punés
set de chanbre les es,
Marcol li respont.

37.
Plus que matin lever,
me plaist a sejorner,
ce dit Salemons.
Por grant <con>teste amer,   220
voi ge poi conquester,
Marcol li respont.

38.
Mauvais n'a desirrer
de son cors travailler,
ce dit Salemons.
Saiges fuit au mestier
dont ne se puet aidier,
Marcol li respont.

39.
Qui ne velt travailler,
si ait petit loier,   230
ce dit Salemons.
Ne soi ainz agreger,
n'au besoig travailler,
Marcol li respont.

40.
Qui toz tans est pensis
n'est mie bien apris,
ce dit Salemons.

Lierre regarde enviz,
adés cuide estre pris,
Marcol li respont.   240

41.
Cil acorte sa vie
qui en penser se fie,
ce dit Salemons.
Ce fait melencolie
qui les siens n'i oublie,
Marcol li respont.

42.
Chascun doit bien proier
de sa vie aloignier,
ce dit Salemons.
Chetif a tot mestier,   250
de tout prenre ou noier,
Marcol li respont.

43.
Riens ne puet avenir,
si bien com au morir,
ce dit Salemons.
S'en ne puet mort foïr,
donc est vivre languir,
Marcol li respont.

44.
Diex sueffre longuement
vivre et pechier la gent,   260
ce dit Salemons.
Mais qui ne se repent
quant ne garde s'i prant?
Marcol li respont.

45.
Qui cuide afere avoir,
bien se doit porvëoir,
ce dit Salemons.
Il i a pechié noir
qui destorne savoir,

Marcol li respont.   270

46.
Molt est mesaiesiez
qui est desconseilliez,
ce dit Salemons.
Ainsint a grant pechiez;
tozjorz les sienz paiez,
Marcol li respont.

47.
De l'ome trop legier
sont tuit mal prinsautier,
ce dit Salemons.
Cil s'atret ancombrier   280
qui ne doute a pechier,
Marcol li respont.

48.
Bon est d'enprenre afaire
dont l'en puet a chief traire,
ce dit Salemons.
Qui pechié charge gaire,
tuit bien li sont contraire,
Marcol li respont.

49.
Ainsi vait de pechier:
qui l'aime si l'a chier,   290
ce dit Salemons.
Poi set de losangier
qui ne croit son dangier,
Marcol li respont.

50.
De pechié maintenir
puet grant mal avenir,
ce dit Salemons.
Quant fox a son desire,
petit pense a morir,
Marcol li respont.   300

51.
Pechier vilainement
muet de foible escïent,
ce dit Salemons.
Qui acroit et ne rent,
l'ame fait paiement,
Marcol li respont.

52.
Tant vuelent tuit pechier,
fort sont a chastïer,
ce dit Salemons.
En cest siecle aesier,   310
est en l'aultre enraigier,
Marcol li respont.

53.
Vivre doit bien voloir
qui est en son savoir,
ce dit Salemons.
Qui n'a sens ne pooir
vit par deable noir,
Marcol li respont.

54.
Vielz qui cuide assez vivre,
tieg a fol et a ivre,   320
ce dit Salemons.
Ce pert bien a delivre,
ja nel covient escrivre,
Marcol li respont.

55.
Pechiez est molt fort chose,
mais chascun faire l'ose,
ce dit Salemons.
Salomon:
Por tant est l'ame enclose
la ou riens ne repose,
Marcol li respont.   330

56.
Qui molt est deshetiez
ne puet estre envoisiez,
ce dit Salemons.
Molt en a deshetiez
mort en cui faut pitiez,
Marcol li respont.

57.
Mort a la seignorie
sor tote riens en vie,
ce dit Salemons.
Riens n'a si grant baillie   340
a meins de cortoisie,
Marcol li respont.

58.
Qui si haut la poia,
grant pooir li dona,
ce dit Salemons.
Cil ne s'i oblia,
n'autre n'espargnera,
Marcol li respont.

59.
Por ce het chascun mort,
que nus n'i a deport,   350
ce dit Salemons.
Qui se sent vil et ort
de voloir vivre a tort,
Marcol li respont.

Explicit

Version E

13.
Salomon: Berbis prez tondue
                souvent se remue
                pour l'ombrel trouver.
Marcouz: Putain bien vestue
                souvent sault en rue,
                pour son corps monstrer.

15.

Salomon: On doit le bon meire
          querir et eslire,
          pour garir sez mauls.

Marcouz: La putain s'atire   10
          et farde et remire,
          pour trouver ribauls.

16.

Salomon: Virgile, Aristote
          sceurent molt de note
          par lor estudie.

Marcouz: La putain est sote,
          que le saige assote
          de sa compaingnie.

18.

Salomon: L'ortie est poingnante,
          fouls est qui la plante, 20
          mieulz vault le persil.

Marcouz: Qui la putain hante,
          bien est en la sente
          d'aler en exil.

Version F

12.

Salemon: Mout a le faisant
          les plumes luisant
          et les yeulx bien fais.

Marcoul   Pute a belle guinple
respont: et la chiere simple
          mais le cul est lais.

15.

Salemon: Preude femme nue
          se tient en sa mue
          pour son corps garder. 10

Marcoul   Putain bien vestue
respont: sault emmy la rue
          pour son corps monstrer.

Version G
La disputacion de Marcoux et de Salmon

1.

Salmon:	Mortalité, <>guerre sont exil de terre et destruisemens.
Marcoux:	De putain sourt maulx et guerres mortaulx,

....

2.

Salmon:	Moult scet de la muse qui veult faire escluse pour retenir L<o>ire.
Marcou:	Putains communaux 10 ne <s>erfs naturaulx ne sont mie a croire.

3.

Salmon:	Qui en sa maison avance larron, dommage y reçoit.
Marcou:	Qui putain honneure, en la fin en pleure, quant il s'apperçoit.

4.

Salmon:	Et la cheneiette mengüe l'erbette, 20 la fueille du choul.
Marcou:	La putain se vest et conroye et pest de l'avoir au fol.

5.

Salmon:	Quant chevreaux est nez, de voir le savez, qu'il a le cul blanc.
Marcou:	Quant homs dit: "Tenez," putain dit: "Venez, si seez ou <banc>." 30

6.

Salmon:	Moult fait menue ourne
	et souvent se tourne
	qui chace gouppille.
Marcou:	Maint pas fait en vain
	qui trace putain,
	quant elle gandille.

7.

Salmon:	Qui langour ara,
	bien esploittera
	se vif en eschappe.
Marcou:	Qui putain croira,	40
	ne lui demourra
	ne seurcot ne chappe.

8.

Salmon:	Qui villain nourrist
	et souef blandist,
	adonc l'<a> piour.
Marcou:	Qui putain honnist
	et bat et laidist,
	adonc l'a meillour.

9.

Salmon:	Le petit poucin
	est tres bon au sain	50
	et rosti au poivre.
Marcou:	Se putain n'a vin,
	elle quiert engin
	comment ait a boire.

10.

Salmon:	Tel chasse le dain
	par boys et par plain
	qui puis le pert tout.
Marcou:	Tel vest la putain
	et pest de son pain
	q'un aultre la fout.	60

11.

Salmon: Perier mal gardez
est souvent croulez
tant qu'il a que rendre.

Marcou: Tant vous prisera
putain que sara
qu'arez a despendre.

12.

Salmon: La poire meüre
vault mielx que la dure,
ce savez vous bien.

Marcou: Pute <a> tel nature: 70
de nul luy n'a cure
puis que il n'a rien.

13.

Salmon: Connil se respont
en terre parfont
que il ne soit pris.

Marcou: Putain pille tant
garçon en riant
que il est chetifs.

14.

Salmon: Le coq au fumier
grate le paillier   80
pour trouver le grain.

Marcou: Pute a bon mestier
de bourse vuidier
a cul de villain.

15.

Salmon: Chevaux ensellés
est bien aprestez
de faire son aire.

Marcou: Putain bien courbee
est bien aprestee
de foutre et de poirre.   90

16.

Salmon: Les beufs au villain
si gaingnent le pain
dont le siecle vit.

Marcou: Bien se lasse en vain
qui cuide putain
tuer a son vit.

17.

Salmon: Ren ne vault aillïe
s'<el> n'est bien broÿe
et fort pestellee.

Marcou: Putain est perdue   100
s'el n'est bien batue
et souvent foulee.

18.

Salmon: Moult est beaux estez
et la fleur es prez
dont il y a tant.

Marcou: Se putain creez,
quanque vous arez
perdrez en riant.

19.

Salmon: Ja ne perra trace
que culeuvre face   110
dessus pierre bise.

Marcou: Ja pute celee
n'est prise prouvee
s'an forfait n'est prise.

20.

Salmon: A bouche de four
a souvent chalour;
ja n'y croistra herbe.

Marcou: Bien soiez certain:
ja cul de putain
ne sera sans merde.   120

21.

Salmon: Ne vous chault semer

en sablon de mer:
ja n'y croistra grain.

Marcou: Bien pert son sermon
qui veult par raison
chastïer putain.

22.

Salmon: L'en tent a la glu
la ou en a veu
reparier oyseaux.

Marcou: Putain cerche foire   130
la ou elle espoire
<p>lenté de trousseaux.

23.

Salmon: Maigrissiez l'ostour,
dont l'arez meillour
pour bien rivoier.

Marcou: La putain foul<ez>,
soubz piez la tenez,
lors vous ara chier.

24.

Salmon: Qui poursuit les dez,
fol est et desvez,   140
car tost en est nus.

Marcou: Qui putain maintient,
tout mal lui en vient:
tost est confondus.

25.

Salmon: Fol est, ce m'est vis,
qui les charbons vifs
escont en son sain.

Marcou: De droit gist en paille
qui son argent baille
a vielle putain.   150

26.

Salmon: Tençons et envie
depart compaignie
de deux bons amis.

Marcou: Engins de putains
fait cousins germains
mortaulx ennemis.

27.
Salmon: <Loëz> le paon,
lors fait a bandon
sa roe apparoir
Marcou: Putain bien vestue   160
se demonstre en rue,
pour louenge avoir.

28.
Salmon: Gectez au plungon
ou pierre ou baston,
tant plus se remo<i>lle.
Marcou: Donnez a putain
et huy et demain,
et plus s'en orgu[ei]lle.

29.
Salmon: A droit pert s'onneur
qui a traïttour   170
ottrie baillie.
Marcou: Qui livre a putain
son bien en sa main
de bon droit mendie.

30.
Salmon: A asne avez veu
lessier fain menu
pour mengier chardon?
Marcou: Putain avez veu
lessier son bon dru
pour mauvais garçon?   180

31.
Salmon: Qui veult mesurer
les gouttes de mer,
moult est plain de rage.
Marcou: Qui tient en sa main
la foy de putain,

moult a mauvais gaige.

32.
Salmon: Qui sent son forfait,
folz est s'il en plait
aultre sans aïe.
Marcou: Qui va vuide main   190
deprier putain,
il fait grant folie.

33.
Salmon: Gars <n'est> a delivre
quant ne se delivre
quant on dit: "Eschac!"
Marcou: A putain tenir
ne peut nul faillir
a manteau de sac.

34.
Salmon: Qui voit le souleil
au matin vermeil,   200
s'atende la pluye.
Marcou: Pute en belle chiere
engigne derriere
tel qui puis mendie.

35.
Salmon: Moult sont grans les mers
et li solel <clers>,
et la lune est blanche.
Marcou: Qui bien veult avoir
pute a son vouloir
le col lui <enmanche>.   210

36.
Salmon: Ja nul usuriers
n'ara tant deniers
con son cuer voudroit.
Marcou: Ja pute en sa vie
n'est tant replenie
con son cuer vouldroit.

37.

Salmon: Chargiez a jument
ou plomb ou argent,
ne lui chault le quel.

Marcou: Put<e> ne fait compte   220
qui sur son cul monte:
tous lui sont ysvel.

38.

Salmon: Maison embrasee
est tost affinee
quant le feu y prent.

Marcou: Putain bien paree
est tost renversee
quant el voit argent.

39.

Salmon: Gerfoux n'esperviers
n'est mie legiers   230
a faire prive.

Marcou: Putain de mal aire
ne se scet atraire
a nulle bonte.

40.

Salmon: Le gras pourcelet
ne quiert pas le net,
mais quiert le palu.

Marcou: ....
....
....   240

Version H

Par desguisee guise,
faite est la devise
que je vous vueil dire.
Theologïen
et vous arcïen,
phisicïen, mire,

entendés i bien,
n'en oubliez rien,

c'est vostre pourfist.
Partie en ay fait,
j'ay lessié le lait;
ne sai qui le dit.

6.
Folz est, ce m'est viz,
qui les cherbons viz
repont en son sain.
A droit gist en paille
qui son argent baille
a une nonnain.

16.
La souris menjüe
tant la nois menue
qu'el i fait pertuis.
La fole si prent
du garçon l'argent,
puis le met a l'uis.

Version I

20.
Li mules ou pré
a mavais soustré
qu'est de porri fain,
ce dist Salemons.
Souz bel vestement
or cul et puent
de bele putain,
Marcous li respont.

23.
Feus en brueroy
art environ soy   10
kenques il ataint,
ce dist Salemons.
Pute ment sa foy,
ne li chaut por coy,
mais qu'ele gaaint,
Marcoz li respont.

27.
Fox est qui conmande
au louf en la lande
garder ses aingniax,
ce dist Salemlons.   20
Pute si demande
au musart vïande
sovant et drapiax,
Marcous li respont.

28.
Cers va cele part
ou il set l'essart:
si paist volentiers,
ce dist Salemons.
Pute de mal art
set bien de musart   30
traire les denniers,
Marcous li respont.

29.
Dex ne fit poisson
qu'est de l'iaue loing
que longues puit vivre,
ce dist Salemons.
Putain et garçon
boivent a tençon
tant que il sont yvre,
Marcous li respont.   40

33.
Grenoulle en marois
est en son defois
tant com l'eve est bonne,
ce dist Salemons.
Pute prent manois:
de tant est sordois
cilz qui plus li donne,
Marcous li respont.

[*In the margin under column a, fol. 1, the scribe has added these 4 lines, written in red.*]

De lez grant val,
grant mont,   50
ce dist Salemons.
De lez grant cul,
grant con,
Marcous li respont.

Version J

43.

Salemon:	De blanche levriere
	grant sault en bruyere,
	ce dit Salemon.
Marcou:	De grosse lodiere
	grant vesse pleniere,
	respont luy Marcou.

Version in Unidentified MS Edited by Méon

The following two stanzas, each comprising eight five-syllable lines, were printed in Méon, *Nouveau recueil de fabliaux et contes inédits*, 1: 435. His text has been left unmodified, except that the punctuation has been supplemented to clarify what is direct speech. Since the stanzas do not figure in any of the ten known versions (sigla A-J), they were likely contained in a manuscript that has been lost since 1823, when Méon's volumes came into print.

"Li chien aime bien
Cil qui li dist, 'Tien,'
Et non autrement,"
Ce dist Salemons.
"Quant on dit, 'Tenez,'
Putain dit, 'Venez,'
Tout à vos commant,"
Marcoul li respont.

"La truie enserrée
Est tantost levée
Si lui vient pasture,"
Ce dist Salemons.
"La putain qu'on fout
I prent autre gout
Se l'argent ne dure,"
Marcoul li respont.

Bibliography

Ackermann, Gretchen P. "J. M. Kemble and Sir Frederic Madden: 'Conceit and Too Much Germanism'?" In *Anglo-Saxon Scholarship: The First Three Centuries,* edited by Carl T. Berkhout and Milton McCormick Gatch, 167–81. Boston: Hall, 1982.

Alekseev, Anatolii Alekseevich. "Perevody s drevneevreiskikh originalov v drevnei Rusi" [Translations from Old Hebrew originals in Old Russia]. *Russian Linguistics* 11, no. 1 (1987): 1–20.

Anlezark, David, ed. and trans. *The Old English Dialogues of Solomon and Saturn.* Anglo-Saxon Texts 7. Cambridge: D. S. Brewer, 2009.

Audelay, John the Blind. *Poems and Carols (Oxford, Bodleian Library MS Douce 302).* Edited by Susanna Fein. Kalamazoo, MI: Medieval Institute Publications, 2009.

Augustine. *The City of God against the Pagans.* Translated by R. W. Dyson. Cambridge: Cambridge University Press, 1998.

Bachorski, Hans-Jürgen. "Serialität, Variation und Spiel: Narrative Experimente in *Salmon and Morolf.*" In *Heldensage, Heldenlied, Heldenepos: Ergebnisse der II. Jahrestagung der Reineke-Gesellschaft, Gotha, 16.–21. Mai 1991,* edited by Danielle Buschinger and Wolfgang Spiewok, 7–29. Wodan 12. Greifswald: Reineke, 1992.

Bäckström, Per Olaf. *Öfversigt af svensk folkläsning från äldre till närvarande tid.* Stockholm: A. Bolin, 1848.

Bąkowska, Nadzieja. "Komizm obsceniczny w trzech odsłonach. Relacje między przekładami *Dialogus Salomonis et Marcolfi* na języki polski, włoski i angielski." *PL.IT / rassegna italiana di argomenti polacchi* 6 (2015): 57–71.

Batkin, Michael. *Rabelais and His World.* Cambridge, MA: M.I.T. Press, 1968.

Bayless, Martha. Review of *Solomon and Marcolf,* by Jan M. Ziolkowski. *Journal of English and Germanic Philology* 109, no. 4 (2010): 526–27.

Bellettini, Pierangelo, Rosaria Campioni, and Zita Zanardi, eds. *Una città in piazza: Comunicazione e vita quotidiana a Bologna tra cinque e seicento.* Bologna: Compositori, 2000.

Bernasconi, Fiorenzo. "Giampietro Riva e il primo canto del 'Bertoldo' in rima. Introduzione, elenco dei testimoni, criteri di edizione, testo critico, apparato delle varianti redazionali e commento." *Pagine Storiche Luganesi* 3 (1987): 97–146.

Biagioni, Giovanni Luigi. "Marcolf und Bertoldo und ihre Beziehungen: Ein Beitrag zur germanischen und romanischen Marcolf-Literatur." PhD Diss., Universität Köln, 1930.

Biblia sacra iuxta Vulgatam versionem. Edited by Robertus Weber and Roger Gryson. 5th ed. Stuttgart: Deutsche Bibelgesellschaft, 2007.

Bobertag, Felix, ed. *Narrenbuch: Kalenberger, Peter Leu, Neithart Fuchs, Markolf, Bruder Rausch.* Deutsche National-Litteratur 11. Berlin: W. Spemann [1884].

Boffey, Julia. "Wynkyn de Worde, Richard Pynson, and the English Printing of Texts Translated from French." In *Vernacular Literature and Current Affairs in the Early Sixteenth Century: France, England and Scotland,* edited by Jennifer Britnell and Richard Britnell, 171–83. Studies in European Cultural Transition 6. Aldershot, UK: Ashgate, 2000.

Bondar, Konstantin V. "Etiud ob Asmodee i Kitovrase" [Study regarding Asmodeus and Kitovras]. *Tirosh: Trudy po iudaike* 8 (2007): 111–14.

———. "K istorii teksta povestei o Solomone v Palee" [Toward the history of the text of stories of Solomon in the Paleia]. *Naukovi zapysky Kharkivs'koho national'noho pedahohichnoho universitetu im. H. S. Skovorody, Seriia: Literaturoznavstvo,* 64, no. 4 (2010): 3–8.

———. "K voprosu o evreiskikh istochnikakh paleinoi 'Povesti o Kitovrase'" [To the question of Hebrew sources of "The Story about Kitovras" in the Paleia]. In *Materialy vos'moi ezhegodnoi mezhdunarodnoi mezhdistsiplinarnoi konferentsii po iudaike,* 2:136–44. Moscow: 2001.

———. "'O Kitovrase ot Palei' i drugie siuzhety knigopistsa Efrosina" ["On Kitovras from the Paleia" and other stories of the scribe Efrosin]. In *Materialy sed'moi ezhegodnoi mezhdunarodnoi mezhdistsiplinarnoi konferentsii po iudaike,* 2:123–29. Moscow: 2000.

———. "Slavianskie Sudy Solomona: istochniki, sostav, tekstologiia" [The Slavonic *Judgments of Solomon*: Sources, composition, textual criticism]. In *Materialy dvenadtsatoi ezhegodnoi mezhdunarodnoi mezhdistsiplinarnoi konferentsii po iudaike,* 1:352–56. Moscow: 2005.

Boeye, Kerry Paul. "Mutable Authority: Reimagining King Solomon in Medieval Psalm Illustration." PhD Diss., University of Chicago, 2010.

Bowden, Sarah. *Bridal-Quest Epics in Medieval Germany: A Revisionary Approach.* MHRA Texts and Dissertations 85. London: Modern Humanities Research Association, 2012.

Bradbury, Nancy Mason. "The Proverb as Embedded Microgenre in Chaucer and *The Dialogue of Solomon and Marcolf.*" *Exemplaria* 27, no. 1/2 (2015): 55–72.

———. "Representations of Peasant Speech: Some Literary and Social Contexts for *The Taill of Rauf Coilyear.*" In *Medieval Romance, Medieval Contexts*, edited by Rhiannon Purdie and Michael Cichon, 19–33. Studies in Medieval Romance 14. Cambridge: Brewer, 2011.

———. "Rival Wisdom in the Latin *Dialogue of Solomon and Marcolf.*" *Speculum: A Journal of Medieval Studies* 83, no. 2 (2008): 331–65.

Bradbury, Nancy Mason, and Scott Bradbury. *The Dialogue of Solomon and Marcolf: A Dual-Language Edition from Latin and Middle English Printed Editions.* TEAMS Middle English Text Series. Kalamazoo, MI: Medieval Institute Publications, 2012.

Brandt, Rüdiger and Henning Wuth. "Markolf." In *Verführer, Schurken, Magier*, edited by Ulrich Müller and Werner Wunderlich, 595–612. Vol. 3 of *Mittelalter-Mythen.* St. Gallen: UVK, 2001.

Brookfield, Frances M. *The Cambridge "Apostles."* New York: Charles Scribner's Sons, 1906.

Brown, John Pairman. "Excursus G: The Cairn and the Pillar." In *Sacred Institutions with Roman Counterparts*, 130–34. Vol. 2 of *Israel and Hellas.* Berlin: de Gruyter, 2000.

Bugge, Sophus. "Kong David og Solfager." *Danske Studier* (1908): 1–34.

Busch, Peter. *Das Testament Salomos: Die älteste christliche Dämonologie, kommentiert und in deutscher Erstübersetzung.* Texte und Untersuchungen zur Geschichte der altchristlichen Literatur 153. Berlin: de Gruyter, 2006.

Camporesi, Piero. *La maschera di Bertoldo: Giulio Cesare Croce e la letteratura carnevalesca.* 2nd ed. Milan: Garzanti, 1993.

———. *Il palazzo e il cantimbanco: Giulio Cesare Croce.* Milan: Garzanti, 1994.

Casali, Elide, and Bruno Capaci, eds. *La Festa del mondo rovesciato: Giulio Cesare Croce e il carnevalesco.* Bologna: Il Mulino, 2002.

Catalfamo, Antonio. *Giulio Cesare Croce: Bertoldo e il mondo popolare; nuogve soluzioni critiche.* Chieti: Solfanelli, 2016.

Chastel, André. "La légende de la Reine de Saba." Pt. 3. *Revue de l'histoire des religions* 120 (1939): 160–74.

Chrétien de Troyes. *Arthurian Romances.* Translated by William W. Kibler. Harmondsworth: Penguin, 1991.

———. *Les romans de Chrétien de Troyes, édités d'après la copie de Guiot (Bibl. nat. fr. 794).* Vol. 2, *Cligès.* Edited by Alexandre Micha. Les classiques français du moyen age 84. Paris: H. Champion, 1975.

Classen, Albrecht. Review of *Solomon and Marcolf*, by Jan M. Ziolkowski. *The Medieval Review* (2009).

Coldiron, Anne E. B. *English Printing, Verse Translation, and the Battle of the Sexes, 1476–1557*. Farnham, UK: Ashgate, 2009.

———. "'La Femme Replique': English Paratexts, Genre Cues, and Versification in a Translated French Gender Debate." In *French Connections in the English Renaissance*, edited by Catherine Gimelli Martin and Hassan Melehy, 15–26. London: Routledge, 2013.

———. "Translation's Challenge to Critical Categories: Verses from French in the Early English Renaissance." *The Yale Journal of Criticism* 16, no. 2 (2003): 315–44.

Colker, Marvin L. Review of *Solomon and Marcolf*, by Jan M. Ziolkowski. *Medievalia et humanistica: Studies in Medieval and Renaissance Culture* 35 (2009): 155–57.

Crapelet, Georges Adrien. *Proverbes et dictons populaires, avec les dits du mercier et des marchands, et les Crieries de Paris, aux XIIIᵉ et XIVᵉ siècles, publiés d'après les manuscrits de la Bibliothèque du Roi*. Paris: Crapelet, 1831.

Croce, Franco. "Giulio Cesare Croce e la realtà popolare." *La rassegna della letteratura italiana* 73, no. 2/3 (1969): 181–205.

Croce, Giulio Cesare. *Bertoldo con Bertoldino e Cacasenno in ottava rima: Con argomenti, allegorie, annotazioni, e figure in rame; Ultima delle tre impressioni fatte in Bologna nell' anno MDCCXXXVI*. Bologna, 1736.

———. *Bertoldo e Bertoldino*. Edited by Gian Carlo Testoni. Illustrated by Carlo Galleni. Milan: Fratelli Frabbri, 1975.

———. *Le sottilissime astuzie di Bertoldo*. Biblioteca dell'Utopia 4. Milan: Silvio Berluschoni Editore, 1993.

Curschmann, Michael. "Marcolfus deutsch: Mit einem Faksimile des Prosa-Drucks von M. Ayrer (1487)." In *Kleinere Erzählformen des 15. und 16. Jahrhunderts*, edited by Walter Haug and Burghart Wachinger, 151–255. Fortuna vitrea 8. Tübingen: Niemeyer, 1993.

———. "Markolf tanzt." In *Festschrift für Walter Haug und Burghart Wachinger*, edited by Johannes Janota et al., 2 vols., 2:967–94. Tübingen: Niemeyer, 1992.

———. *Der Münchener Oswald und die deutsche spielmännische Epik: Mit einem Exkurs zur Kultgeschichte und Dichtungstradition*. Münchener Texte und Untersuchungen 6. Munich: Beck, 1964.

———. "Salman und Morolf." In *Die deutsche Literatur des Mittelalters: Verfasserlexikon*, edited by Kurt Ruh, Burghart Wachinger, et al., 8:515–23. 2nd ed. 14 vols. Berlin: de Gruyter, 1978–2008.

———. "Salomon und Markolf ('Spruchgedicht')." In *Die deutsche Literatur des Mittelalters: Verfasserlexikon*, edited by Kurt Ruh, Burghart Wachinger, et al., 8:530–35. 2nd ed. 14 vols. Berlin: de Gruyter, 1978–2008.

Davis, Joseph M. "Solomon and Ashmedai (bGittin 68a–b), King Hiram, and Procopius: Exegesis and Folklore." *Jewish Quarterly Review* 106, no. 4 (2016): 577–85.

Dendle, Peter. "The Demonological Landscape of the 'Solomon and Saturn' Cycle." *English Studies* 80, no. 4 (1999): 281–92.

Dickins, Bruce. "John Mitchell Kemble and Old English Scholarship (with a Bibliography of His Writings)." *Proceedings of the British Academy* 25 (1939): 51–84.

Les Dictz de Salomon auecques les respo[n]ces de Marcon fort ioyeuses. [Paris]: n.p., 1530. 8 unnumbered pages.

Di Giulio, Palmer, trans. *Bertoldo.* By Giulio Cesare Croce. New York: Vantage Press, 1958.

Digulleville, Guillaume de. *Le Livre du pèlerin de vie humaine (1355).* Edited and translated by Graham Robert Edwards and Phillipe Maupeu. Paris: Librairie Générale Française, 2015.

———. *Le Pèlerinage de Vie Humaine de Guillaume de Deguileville.* Edited by J. J. Stürzinger. Roxburghe Club Publications 124. London: Roxburghe Club, 1893.

———. *The Pilgrimage of Human Life.* Translated by Eugene Clasby. Garland Library of Medieval Literature, Series B, 76. New York: Garland, 1992.

———. *The Pilgrimage of the Lyfe of the Manhode: A Critical Edition of the Middle English Prose Translation of Guillaume de Deguileville's 'Le Pèlerinage de la Vie Humaine.'* Edited by Avril Henry. Early English Text Society, o.s., 288, 292 (Oxford: Oxford University Press, 1985, 1988).

Dmitriev, Lev Aleksandrovich, and Dmitrii Sergeevich Likhachev, eds., *Pamiatniki literatury drevnei Rusi XIV-seredina XV veka* [Texts from the literature of Old Rus' from the fourteenth to the mid-fifteenth century]. Moscow: Khudozhestvennaia literatura, 1981.

Dobozy, Maria. "The Function of Knowledge and Magic in *Salman und Morolf.*" In *The Dark Figure in Medieval German and Germanic Literature,* edited by Edward R. Haymes and Stephanie Cain Van D'Elden, 27–41. Göppingen: Kümmerle, 1986.

———. "The Theme of the Holy War in German Literature, 1152–1190: Symptom of Controversy between Empire and Papacy?" *Euphorion* 80 (1986): 341–62.

Donnini, Mauro. Review of *Solomon and Marcolf,* by Jan M. Ziolkowski. *Studi Medievali* 52 (2011): 1018–21.

Downes, Stephanie. "Minding Shirley's French." *Studies in the Age of Chaucer* 38 (2016): 287–97.

Dumézil, Georges. *Le problème des Centaures: Étude de mythologie comparée indo-européene.* Paris: Librairie Orientaliste Paul Guthner, 1929.

Duncan-Jones, Caroline M. *Miss Mitford and Mr. Harness.* London: Society for Promoting Christian Knowledge, 1955.

Einarsson, Stefán. *A History of Icelandic Literature.* New York: Johns Hopkins University Press, 1957.

Fadeev, Aleksandr. "Sovetskaia literatura posle postanovleniia TsK VKP(b) ot 14 avgusta 1946 goda o zhurnalakh 'Zvezda' i 'Leningrad'" ["Soviet literature after decree TsK VKP(b) of 14 August 1946 about the journals *Zvezda* and *Leningrad*]. *Literaturnaia gazeta,* June 29, 1947.

Fougères, Étienne de. *Le livre des manières.* Edited by R. Anthony Lodge. Textes littéraires français 275. Geneva: Droz, 1979.

———. *Le livre des manières.* Edited by Jacques T. E. Thomas. Ktémata 20. Paris: Peeters, 2013.

Geonget, Stéphan. "Du couple *magister-discipulus* au couple Salomon-Marcoul: De la certitude pour l'autre à la certitude pour soi." In *Certitude et incertitude à la Renaissance,* edited by Margaret Jones-Davies and Florence Malhomme, 153–66. Turnhout: Brepols, 2013.

Gillespie, Alexandra. "'These Proverbes Yet Do Last': Lydgate, the Fifth Earl of Northumberland, and Tudor Miscellanies from Print to Manuscript." *The Yearbook of English Studies* 33 (2003): 215–32.

Ginzberg, Louis. *The Legends of the Jews.* 7 vols. Baltimore, MD: Johns Hopkins University Press, 1998.

Glauser, Jürg. "Eulenspiegels Sünden, Markolfs anderes Gesicht: Ausgrenzungs- und Diszplinierungsprozesse in der skandinavischen Populärliteratur." *Ethnologia Europaea: Journal of European Ethnology* 23 (1993): 27–40.

Goldwurm, Hersh, ed. *Tractate Gittin.* Vol. 35, pt. 2, of *Talmud Bavli.* 72 vols. Brooklyn: Mesorah Publications, 1990.

Gradenwitz, Michael. "Marcolfus og Uglspil—to groteske folkebøger." *Folk og kultur* 90, no. 1 (1990): 5–20.

Green, Richard Firth. "Langland and Audelay." In *My Wyl and My Wrytyng: Essays on John the Blind Audelay,* edited by Susanna Fein, 153–69. Research in Medieval and Early Modern Culture 9. Kalamazoo, MI: Medieval Institute Publications, 2009.

———. "Lydgate and Deguileville Once More." *Notes & Queries* 223 (1978): 105–6.

———. "Marcolf the Fool and Blind John Audelay." In *Speaking Images: Essays in Honor of V. A. Kolve,* edited by R. F. Yeager and Charlotte C. Morse, 559–76. Asheville, NC: Pegasus Press, 2001.

Gregg, W. W. "The Early Printed Editions of the *Canterbury Tales.*" *Publications of the Modern Language Association of America* 39 (1924): 737–61.

Griese, Sabine. *Salomon und Markolf: Ein literarischer Komplex im Mittelalter und in der frühen Neuzeit; Studien zu Überlieferung und Interpretation.* Hermaea, n.s., 81. Tübingen: Niemeyer, 1999.

Gruenler, Curtis. "How to Read Like a Fool: Riddle Contests and the Banquet of Conscience in Piers Plowman." *Speculum: A Journal of Medieval Studies* 85, no. 3 (2010): 592–630.

Grundtvig, Svend, Axel Olrik, et al., eds. *Danmarks gamle Folkeviser.* 12 vols. Copenhagen: Universitets-Jubilæets Danske Samfund, 1966–76.

Hall, James R. "The First Two Editions of *Beowulf:* Thorkelin's (1815) and Kemble's (1833)." In *The Editing of Old English: Papers from the 1990 Manchester Conference,* edited by D. G. Scragg and Paul E. Szarmach, 239–50. Cambridge: D.S. Brewer, 1994.

Halliwell-Philipps, James O., ed. *Contributions to Early English Literature: Derived Chiefly from Rare Books and Ancient Inedited Manuscripts, from the Fifteenth to the Seventeenth Century.* London, 1849.

Hartmann, Walter, ed. *Salomon und Markolf: Das Spruchgedicht.* Vol. 2 of *Die deutschen Dichtungen von Salomon und Markolf.* Halle an der Saale: Niemeyer, 1934.

Hattaway, Michael. "Paradoxes of Solomon: Learning in the English Renaissance." *Journal of the History of Ideas* 29, no. 4 (1968): 499–530.

Hays, Gregory. Review of *Solomon and Marcolf,* by Jan M. Ziolkowski. *The Sixteenth Century Journal: The Journal of Early Modern Studies* 41 (2010): 1175–76.

Hazlitt, W. C. *Remains of Early Popular Poetry of England.* 4 vols. London: Smith, 1864–66.

Heggstad, Leiv, and Hakon Grüner-Nielsen, eds. *Utsyn yver gamall norsk folkevise-diktning.* Christiania: Olaf Norlis forlag, 1912.

Heinzle, Joachim. "Heldenbücher." In *Die deutsche Literatur des Mittelalters: Verfasserlexikon,* edited by Kurt Ruh, Burghart Wachinger, et al., 3:947–56. 2nd ed. 14 vols. Berlin: de Gruyter, 1978–2008.

Hill-Zenk, Anja. "Woodcuts and Popular Literature: The English Salomon and Marcolf in the Fifteenth and Sixteenth Centuries." In *Vir ingenio mirandus: Studies Presented to John L. Flood,* edited by William Jervis Jones, W. A. Kelly, and Frank Shaw, 2:559–77. Göppinger Arbeiten zur Germanistik 710. Göppingen: Kümmerle, 2003.

Hodnett, Edward. *English Woodcuts 1480–1535.* 2nd ed. Oxford: Oxford University Press, 1973.

Hoffmann, Werner. *Mittelhochdeutsche Heldendichtung.* Grundlagen der Germanistik 14. Berlin: Schmidt, 1974.

The Holy Bible: Douay-Rheims Version. Baltimore, MD: John Murphy Company, 1899.

Horstbøll, Henrik. *Menigmands medie: Det folkelige bogtryk i Danmark 1500–1840*. Danish Humanist Texts and Studies 19. Copenhagen: Museum Tusculanums Forlag, 1999.

Hosington, Brenda M. "Textual Standard-Bearers: Translated Titles and Early Modern English Print." In *Thresholds of Translation: Paratexts, Print, and Cultural Exchange in Early Modern Britain (1473–1660)*, edited by Marie-Alice Belle and Brenda M. Hosington, 75–100. Cham, Switzerland: Palgrave Macmillan, 2018.

Hosking, Geoffrey. *Russia and the Russians: A History*. 2nd ed. Cambridge, MA: Belknap Press of Harvard University Press, 2011.

Hunt, Tony. "Un nouveau manuscrit de la Lettre du Prêtre Jean." In *Miscellanea Mediaevalia: Mélanges offerts à Philippe Ménard*, edited by J. Claude Faucon, Alain Labbé, and Danielle Quéruel, 1:691–702. Paris: Champion, 1998.

———. "Solomon and Marcolf." In *"Por le soie amisté": Essays in Honor of Norris J. Lacy*, edited by Keith Busby and Catherine M. Jones, 199–224. Amsterdam: Rodopi, 2000.

Iafrate, Allegra. "Weather Lore and the Throne of Solomon." In *The Wandering Throne of Solomon*, 281–87. Mediterranean Art Histories 2. Leiden: Brill, 2016.

Jackson, Jess H., ed. and trans. "*Melkólfs saga ok Salómons Konungs*." In *Studies in Honor of Albert Morey Sturtevant*, edited by Levi Robert Lind, 107–18. Humanistic Studies 29. Lawrence: University of Kansas Press, 1952.

Jacobsen, Jacob Peter, ed. *Marcolfus*. Vol. 13 of *Danske folkebøger fra 16. og 17 århundrede*, edited by Jacob Peter Jacobsen, Richard Jakob Paulli, and Jørgen Olrik. 14 vols. Copenhagen: Gyldendal, 1936.

Johnson, Catherine Bodham. *William Bodham Donne and His Friends*. London: Methuen, 1905.

Johnston, Stanley Howard. "A Study of the Career and Literary Publications of Richard Pynson." PhD Diss., University of Western Ontario, 1977.

Jonsson, Bengt R., Svale Solheim, and Eva Danielson, eds. *The Types of the Medieval Scandinavian Ballad: A Descriptive Catalogue*. Skrifter utgivna av Svenskt visarkiv 5. Stockholm: Svenskt Visarkiv, 1978.

Jónsson, Finnur. *Den oldnorske og oldislandske Litteraturs Historie*. 2nd ed. 3 vols. Copenhagen: G. E. C. Gad, 1920–24.

Jülg, Bernhard, trans. *Mongolische Märchen: Die neun Nachtrags-Erzählungen des Siddhi-Kür und die Geschichte des Arschi-Bordschi Chan; Eine Fortsetzung zu den "Kalmükischen Märchen."* Innsbruck: Wagner, 1868.

Kamath, Stephanie A. Viereck Gibbs. *Authorship and First-Person Allegory in Late Medieval France and England*. Gallica 26. Woodbridge: D. S. Brewer, 2012.

Kaminka, Armand. "The Origin of the Ashmedai Legend in the Babylonian Talmud." *Jewish Quarterly Review* 13, no. 2 (1922): 221–24.

Karnein, Alfred, ed. *Salman und Morolf.* Altdeutsche Textbibliothek 85. Tübingen: Niemeyer, 1979.

———. "Salomon und Markolf." In *Literaturlexikon: Autoren und Werke deutscher Sprache,* edited by Walther Killy, 10:123. 15 vols. Gütersloh: Bertelsmann, 1988–93.

Kauntze, Mark. Review of *Solomon and Marcolf,* by Jan M. Ziolkowski. *The Modern Language Review* 105, no. 1 (2010): 193–94.

Kemble, John M, ed. *The Anglo-Saxon Poems of "Beowulf," "The Traveller's Song," and "The Battle of Finnesburh."* London: William Pickering, 1833.

———, ed. *The Dialogue of Salomon and Saturnus with an Historical Introduction.* London: Ælfric Society, 1848.

———, ed. and trans. *A Translation of the Anglo-Saxon Poem of "Beowulf" with a Copious Glossary, Preface, and Philological Notes.* London: William Pickering, 1837.

Ker, Neil Ripley. *Medieval Manuscripts in British Libraries.* 4 vols. Oxford: Clarendon Press, 1969–92.

Ker, William Paton. "On the Danish Ballads." *The Scottish Historical Review* 5, no. 20 (1908): 385–401.

Knudson, Karen R. "The Power of the Medieval Solomon-*Magus* and Solomon-*Auctor* Revealed through the *Canterbury Tales, Sir Gawain and the Green Knight,* and the *Tale of the Sankgreal.*" PhD Diss., Purdue University, 2016.

Kock, Axel, and Carl Justus Fredrik af Petersens, eds. *Östnordiska och latinska medeltidsordspråk: Peder Låle ordspråk och en motsvarande svensk samling.* Samfund til Udgivelse af gammel nordisk Litteratur 20. Copenhagen: Berlingska boktryckeriet, 1889–94.

Lachmann, Karl, Hugo Moser, and Helmut Tervooren, eds. *Des Minnesangs Frühling.* 36th ed. 3 vols. Stuttgart: Hirzel, 1977.

Landstad, Magnus B., ed. *Norske folkeviser.* Christiania: C. Tønsberg, 1853.

Langlois, Ernest. *Nouvelles françaises inédites du quinzième siècle.* Bibliothèque du XVᵉ siècle 6. Paris: H. Champion, 1908.

Larsen, Henning. "Kemble's Salomon and Saturn." *Modern Philology* 26, no. 4 (1929): 445–50.

Lassner, Jacob. *Demonizing the Queen of Sheba: Boundaries of Gender and Culture in Postbiblical Judaism and Medieval Islam.* Chicago: University of Chicago Press, 1993.

Liestøl, Knut, and Moltke Moe, eds. *Norske folkevisor: Folkeutgåve.* Christiania: J. Dybwad, 1920.

Lodge, R. Anthony. "The Literary Interest of the '*Livre des Manières*' of Etienne de Fougères." *Romania* 93 (1972): 479–97.

―――. "L'œuvre et son intérêt littéraire." In *Le livre des manières*, by Étienne de Fougères, edited by R. Anthony Lodge, 23–36. Textes littéraires français 275. Geneva: Droz, 1979.

Lunt, Horace G., and Moshe Taube. "Early East Slavic Translations from Hebrew?" *Russian Linguistics* 12, no. 2 (1988): 147–87.

Lur'e, Ja. S. "Une légende inconnue de Salomon et Kitovras dans un manuscrit du XVe siècle." *Revue des études slaves* 43, no. 1/4 (1964): 7–11.

Lydgate, John. *The Minor Poems of John Lydgate*. Vol. 2, *Secular Poems*. Edited by Henry Nobel McCracken. Early English Text Society, o.s., 192. London: Oxford University Press, 1934.

―――, trans. *The Pilgrimage of the Life of Man*. By Guillaume de Digulleville. Edited by F. J. Furnivall and Katharine B. Locock. 3 vols. Early English Text Society, e.s., 77, 83, 92. London: Kegan Paul, Trench, Trübner, 1899–1904.

Macchi, Gian Carlo, trans. *Il dialogo di Salomone e Marcolfo, con testo latino*. N.p.: Lulu, 2011.

Machulak, Erica. "Langland's Sages: Reading Aristotle and Solomon in their Medieval Context." *The Yearbook of Langland Studies* 31 (2017): 87–118.

Major, Tristan. "Saturn's First Riddle in *Solomon and Saturn II:* An Orientalist Conflation." *Neophilologus* 96, no. 2 (2012): 301–13.

Mann, Jill. *Chaucer and Medieval Estates Satire: The Literature of Social Classes and the General Prologue to the Canterbury Tales*. Cambridge: Cambridge University Press, 1973.

Marini, Quinto. *Bertoldo, Bertoldino, Marcolfo*. Casale Monferrato: Marietti, 1986.

Mazon, André. "Le Centaure de la légende vieux-russe de Salomon et Kitovras." *Revue des études slaves* 7, nos. 1/2 (1927): 42–62.

Meckler, Michael. Review of *Solomon and Marcolf*, by Jan M. Ziolkowski. *The Journal of Medieval Latin* 21 (2011): 305–7.

Méon, Dominique-Martin, ed. *Nouveau recueil de fabliaux et contes inédits des poètes français des XIIe, XIIIe, XIVe et XVe siècles*. 2 vols. Paris: Chasseriau, 1823.

Meshcherskij, Nikita Aleksandrovich. "K voprosu ob izuchenii perevodnoj pis'mennosti Kievskogo perioda" [On the question of the study of translated texts from the Kievan period]. *Uchennye zapiski Karelo-Finskogo pedagogicheskogo instituta* 2 (1956): 198–219.

―――. *Istochniki i sostav drevnei slaviano-russkoi perevodnoi pis'mennosti IX–XV vekov* [Sources and composition of translated Slavonic-Russian literature of the IX–XV centuries]. Leningrad: Izd-vo Leningr. un-ta, 1978.

Miklautsch, Lydia. "Salman und Morolf: Thema und Variation." In *Ir sult sprechen willekomen: Grenzenlose Mediävistik; Festschrift für Helmut Birkhan zum 60.*

Geburtstag, edited by Christa Tuczay, Ulrike Hirhager, and Karin Lichtblau, 284–306. Bern: Lang, 1998.

Mone, Franz Joseph. "Beitrag zum Salomon und Markolf." *Anzeiger für Kunde der deutschen Vorzeit* 5 (1836): cols. 58–63.

Nissan, Ephraim. "The Importance of Being Hairy: A Few Remarks on the Queen of Sheba, Esau, and the Andromeda Myth." *La Ricerca Folklorica* 70 (2015): 273–83.

———. "On Nebuchadnezzar in Pseudo-Sirach." *Journal for the Study of the Pseudepigrapha* 19, no. 1 (2009): 45–76.

———. Review of *Solomon and Marcolf*, by Jan M. Ziolkowski. *Fabula* 53, no. 1/2 (2012): 165–69.

———. "A Wily Peasant (Marcolf, Bertoldo), a Child Prodigy (Ben Sira), a Centaur (Kitovras), a Wiseman (Sidrach), or the Chaldaean Prince Saturn? Considerations about Marcolf and the Marcolfian Tradition, with Hypotheses about the Genesis of the Character Kitovras." Review of *Solomon and Marcolf*, by Jan M. Ziolkowski. *International Studies in Humour* 3, no. 1 (2014): 108–50.

Nordström, Johan, ed. *Samlade skrifter av Georg Stiernhielm*. Svenska författare 8. Stockholm: Bonnier, 1929.

Orlov, Andrei A. *From Apocalypticism to Merkabah Mysticism: Studies in the Slavonic Pseudepigrapha*. Supplements to the Journal for the Study of Judaism 114. Leiden: Brill, 2007.

Pagani, Gina Cortese. "Il *Bertoldo* di Giulio Cesare Croce ed i suoi fonti." *Studi medievali* 3 (1911): 533–602.

Pearsall, Derek. "Audelay's Marcolf and Solomon and the Langlandian Tradition." In *My Wyl and My Wrytyng: Essays on John the Blind Audelay*, edited by Susanna Fein, 138–52. Research in Medieval and Early Modern Culture 9. Kalamazoo, MI: Medieval Institute Publications, 2009.

Pintel-Ginsberg, Idit. "Throwing a Stone to Merculis: Symbolizing the 'Other' in a Jewish Cultural Context." In *Gershom Scholem (1878-1982): In Memoriam*, edited by Joseph Dan. 2 vols. Jerusalem Studies in Jewish Thought 21 (Jerusalem: Mandel Institute for Jewish Studies, 2007). 2:455–68.

Plomer, Henry R. *Robert Wyer, Printer and Bookseller: A Paper Read before the Bibliographical Society, January 21st, 1895*. London: Bibliographical Society, 1897.

Poor, Sara S. "Why Surface Reading Is Not Enough: Morolf, the Skin of the Jew, and German Medieval Studies." *Exemplaria* 26, nos. 2/3 (2014): 148–62.

Prokhorov, G. M. *Istoriia russkoi etnografii*. [History of Russian Ethnography]. 4 vols. Saint Petersburg: M. M. Stasulievicha, 1890–92.

———. "Sudy Solomona" [The Judgments of Solomon]. In *Biblioteka literatury Drevnej Rusi* [Library of Old Russian Literature], edited by Dmitrij S. Likhachev, 3:172–90. 20 vols. Saint Petersburg: Nauka, 1999.

Ridder, Iris. *Der schwedische Markolf: Studien zu Tradition und Funktion der frühen schwedischen Markolfüberlieferung.* Beiträge zur Nordischen Philologie 35. Tübingen: Francke, 2002.

Rigg, Arthur George. Review of *Solomon and Marcolf,* by Jan M. Ziolkowski. *Speculum: A Journal of Medieval Studies* 85 (2010): 483–86.

Rondinini, Ada. "Lelio dalla Volpe e l'edizione del 'Bertoldo.'" *L'Archiginnasio* 23 (1928): 191–207.

Sauer, Hans. "Kemble's *Beowulf* and Heaney's *Beowulf.*" *Ljuboslovie* 18 (2018): 26–51.

Schieberle, Misty. "Proverbial Fools and Rival Wisdom: Lydgate's Order of Fools and Marcolf." *The Chaucer Review* 49, no. 2 (2014): 204–27.

Schnell, Rüdiger. Causa amoris: *Liebeskonzeption und Liebesdarstellung in der mittelalterlichen Literatur.* Bibliotheca Germanica 27. Bern: Francke, 1985.

Schück, Henrik. "Markolfsagan i Sverige." In *Ur gamla papper: Populära kulturhistoriska uppsatser,* 1:111–27. 8 vols. Stockholm: A. Bonnier, 1892.

Schulz, Armin. "Morolfs Ende: Zur Dekonstruktion des feudalen Brautwerbungsschemas in der sogenannten 'Spielmannsepik.'" *Beiträge zur Geschichte der deutschen Sprache und Literatur* 124, no. 2 (2002): 233–49.

Schulze-Busacker, Elisabeth. *La Didactique profane au Moyen Âge.* Recherches littéraires médiévales 11. Paris: Classiques Garnier, 2012.

Schumacher, Meinolf. "Der Mönch als Held oder: Von Ilsâns Kämpfen und Küssen in den *Rosengarten*-Dichtungen." *Jahrbuch der Oswald von Wolkenstein-Gesellschaft* 14 (2004): 91–104.

Seelow, Hubert. *Die isländischen Übersetzungen der deutschen Volksbücher.* Reykjavík: Stofnun Árna Magnússonar, 1989.

Shalev-Eyni, Sarit. "Solomon, his Demons and Jongleurs: The Meeting of Islamic, Judaic and Christian Culture." *Al-Masaq* 18, no. 2 (2006): 145–60.

Simpson, James. "Saving Satire after Arundel's *Constitutions:* John Audelay's 'Marcol and Solomon.'" In *Text and Controversy from Wyclif to Bale: Essays in Honour of Anne Hudson,* edited by Helen Barr and Ann M. Hutchinson, 387–404. Turnhout: Brepols, 2005.

Sonneck, George Oscar. "Ciampi's *Bertoldo, Bertoldino e Cacasenno* and Favart's *Ninette à la cour:* A Contribution to the History of *Pasticcio.*" *Sammelbände der Internationalen Musikgesellschaft* 12 (1910–11): 525–64.

Stanzak, Steve. Review of *Solomon and Marcolf,* by Jan M. Ziolkowski. *Journal of Folklore Research Reviews* (2009). http://jfr.sitehost.iu.edu/review.php?id=853.

Szklenar, Hans. "König Rother." In *Die deutsche Literatur des Mittelalters: Verfasserlexikon*, edited by Kurt Ruh, Burghart Wachinger, et al., 5:82–94. 2nd ed. 14 vols. Berlin: de Gruyter, 1978–2008.

Taylor, Barry. "Medieval Proverb Collections: The West European Tradition." *Journal of the Warburg and Courtauld Institutes* 55 (1992): 19–35.

Tetel, Marcel. "Giulio Cesare Croce: *Cantastorie* or Literary Artist." *Forum Italicum* 4, no. 1 (1970): 32–38.

Thompson, Stith. *Motif-Index of Folk Literature: A Classification of Narrative Elements in Folktales, Ballads, Myths, Fables, Mediaeval Romances, Exempla, Fabliaux, Jest-Books, and Local Legends.* Rev. ed. 6 vols. Bloomington, IN: Indiana University Press, 1955–58.

Tucker, John, ed. "*Melkólfs saga ok Salomons konungs.*" *Opuscula* 10 [= Bibliotheca Arnamagnaeana 40] (1996): 208–11.

———. "*Plácítus saga.*" In *Medieval Scandinavia: An Encyclopedia*, edited by P. Pulsiano, K. Wolf, P. Acker, and D. K. Fry, 504–5. New York: Garland Publishing, 1993.

Varignana, Franca. "La fortuna editoriale del Bertoldo crespiano." In *Le collezioni d'arte della Cassa di Risparmio in Bologna: I disegni*, edited by Andrea Emiliani, 1:421–30. Bologna: Edizioni Alfa, 1973.

Vayntrub, Jacqueline. "Before Authorship: Solomon and Prov. 1:1." *Biblical Interpretation* 26, no. 2 (2018): 182–206.

Verheyden, Joseph. *The Figure of Solomon in Jewish, Christian and Islamic Tradition: King, Sage and Architect.* Leiden: Brill, 2013.

Veselovskii, Aleksandr Nikolaevich. *Istoricheskaia poetika.* [Historical Poetics]. Edited by Viktor Maksimovich Zhirmunskii. Leningrad: Khudozhestvennaia literatura, 1940.

———. *Poetika.* Vol. 1 of *Sobranie sochinenii Aleksandra Nikolaevicha Veselovskogo.* Saint Petersburg: Tipografiia Imperatorskoi Akademii nauk, 1913.

———. *Slavianskie skazaniia o Solomone i Kitovrase i zapadnye legendy o Morol'fe i Merline.* [Slavic Tales about Solomon and Kitovras and Western Legends about Morol'f and Merlin]. Vol. 8, pt. 1, of *Sobranie sochinenii Aleksandra Nikolaevicha Veselovskogo.* Petrograd: Dvenadtsataia gosudarstvennaia tipografiia, 1921.

Vollmann-Profe, Gisela. *Von den Anfängen bis zum hohen Mittelalter: Wiederbeginn volksprachlicher Schriftlichkeit im hohen Mittelalter (1050/60–1160/70).* Vol. 1, pt. 2, of *Geschichte der deutschen Literatur von den Anfängen bis zum Beginn der Neuzeit*, edited by Joachim Heinzle. Königstein in Taunus: Athenäum, 1986.

Wiley, Raymond A. "Anglo-Saxon Kemble: The Life and Works of John Mitchell Kemble, 1807–57; Philologist, Historian, Archaeologist." *Anglo-Saxon Studies in Archaeology and History* 1 (1979): 165–273.

———, ed. *John Mitchell Kemble and Jakob Grimm: A Correspondence 1832–1852.* Leiden: Brill, 1971.

Williams, Howard. "Heathen Graves and Victorian Anglo-Saxonism: Assessing the Archaeology of John Mitchell Kemble." In *Anglo-Saxon Studies in Archaeology and History 13,* edited by Sarah Semple, 1–18. Oxford: Oxford University School of Archaeology, 2006.

Williams-Krapp, Werner. "Der arme Konrad." In *Die deutsche Literatur des Mittelalters: Verfasserlexikon,* edited by Kurt Ruh, Burghart Wachinger, et al., 1:454–55. 2nd ed. 14 vols. Berlin: de Gruyter, 1978–2008.

Wilson, Blake. "The *Cantastorie/Canterino/Cantimbanco* as Musician." *Italian Studies* 71, no. 2 (2016): 154–70.

Wolf, Kirsten. "*Melkólfs saga ok Salómons konungs.*" In *Medieval Scandinavia: An Encyclopedia,* edited by Phillip Pulsiano, Kirsten Wolf, Paul Acker, and Donald K. Fry, 412. New York: Garland Publishing, 1993.

———. "Some Comments on *Melkólfs saga ok Salómons konungs.*" *Maal og Minne* (1990): 1–9.

Wright, Thomas. "The Saxon Scholars of England." *Gentleman's Magazine,* n.s., 2 (July–December 1834): 259–60.

Zaborov, Petr Romanovich, Askol'd Borisovich Muratov, and Boris Nikolaevich Putilov, eds. *Nasledie Aleksandra Veselovskogo: Issledovaniia i materialy.* [The Legacy of Alexander Veselovskii: Research and materials]. Saint Petersburg: Nauka, 1992.

Zhirmunskii, Viktor Maksimovich. *Epicheskoe tvorchestvo slavianskikh narodov i problemy sravnitel'nogo izucheniia eposa* [Epic Works of the Slavic Peoples and Problems in the Comparative Study of the Epic]. Moscow: Izdatel'stvo Akademii nauk SSSR, 1958.

Contributors

Amiri Ayanna received her Ph.D. in History from Brown in 2019, with a dissertation entitled *"The Ethics of Everyday Life: Vernacular Devotional Literature by Women in Germany's Long Fifteenth Century."* Her research has been supported by scholarships from the Fulbright scholarship program and the American Council of Learned Societies, among others.

Palmer Di Giulio (1898–1959) was a native Italian and naturalized U.S. citizen. He spent most of his career as an employee of the U.S. Postal Service. Not too long before his death, he published, as an independent scholar and Italianophile, a translation and adaptation of six episodes involving a figure named Bertoldo. This antihero, still a bit character in Italian literary culture, became the basis for a substantial narrative cycle that drew heavily on Solomon and Marcolf material.

Pernille Hermann is Associate Professor of Scandinavian literature in the School of Communication and Culture, Scandinavian Studies, Aarhus University, and Adjunct Professor at the University of Iceland. Her research interests are primarily within Old Norse literature and Comparative Literature, and most recently she has published on medieval memory cultures, mnemonics, genre, and human geography.

Sara Kate Heukerott received her A.B. in Slavic Languages & Literatures with a secondary field in Mathematics *summa cum laude* from Harvard in 2008. She then spent two years at Oxford University as an Oxford University Press Clarendon Fund Scholar, completing her M.Phil. in Slavonic Studies with distinction in 2010. Since then, she has worked in academic book and journal publishing. She is currently an Executive Editor in Physics and Materials Science at Springer Nature in New York.

Jess H. Jackson (1888–1957), after receiving his PhD in English from Harvard University in 1926, studied Scandinavian languages and literatures at the University of Copenhagen. In 1929 he became an English professor at the College of William and Mary, where he remained until his death. His scholarly specialization was Old Norse literature, in particular sagas.

Stephanie A. Viereck Gibbs Kamath is an independent scholar in Northern Virginia, who has taught medieval literature at the University of Massachusetts, Boston; King's College, London; and the University of Pennsylvania. Her research interests lie in allegory, first-person narration, translation studies, and the history of the material text. Past publications include *Authorship and First-Person Allegory in Late Medieval France and England*; *The Pèlerinage Allegories of Guillaume de Deguileville*, co-edited with Marco Nievergelt; and the English translation of *Le livre du cuer d'amours espris*, co-authored with Kathryn Karczewska and Per Nykrog.

Stephen Mitchell teaches courses in the fields of Scandinavian and folklore at Harvard University, and is the author of *Heroic Sagas and Ballads* (Cornell Univeristy Press) and *Witchcraft and Magic in the Nordic Middle Ages* (University of Pennsylvania Press). Collaboration with some 80 scholars culminated in 2018 in *The Handbook of Pre-Modern Nordic Memory Studies: Interdisciplinary Approaches* (De Gruyter), co-edited with Jürg Glauser and Pernille Hermann. Together with Louise Nyholm Kallestrup, he is currently a series co-editor of the forthcoming 6-volume *A Cultural History of Magic* (Bloomsbury).

Steven Rozenski earned a Ph.D. in English from Harvard University in 2012. An Alexander von Humboldt Postdoctoral Research Fellow at the Seminar for English Philology, University of Göttingen, from 2014 to 2015 and a Fulbright Scholar at Queen Mary University of London from 2018 to 2019, he is now an Assistant Professor of Medieval English at the University of Rochester (New York). He is the author of the forthcoming *Wisdom's Journey: Continental Mysticism and Popular Devotion in England, 1350-1650*.

Edward Sanger graduated from Harvard in 2019 with an A.B. in Classical Languages and Literatures. He is now a Postgraduate Fellow in Medieval Literature at Dumbarton Oaks, where he works on academic publications.

James A. Schultz retired recently from UCLA, where he was Professor of German and Gender Studies and founding chair of the LGBTQ Studies Program. His research focuses on German literature of the Middle Ages and the history of sexuality, interests he brings together in his final book, *Courtly Love, the Love of Courtliness, and the History of Sexuality* (2006).

Mary-Ann Stadtler-Chester is Professor Emerita at Framingham State University in Massachusetts. She has also taught French at Harvard, Simmons, and Emmanuel Colleges. While preparing her MA at the University of Chicago, she fell in love with Old French. She earned her Doctorate in Romance Philology from the Sorbonne in Paris where she studied paleography. She had originally planned to produce a critical edition of a saint's life for her dissertation, but when she discovered the dialogue between *Salemon and Marcoul*, she found it more enticing. She is delighted to contribute to bring the Salemon et Marcoul tradition to light.

Michael B. Sullivan is Managing Editor of the Loeb Classical Library (Harvard University Press), Assistant Editor of *The Virgil Encyclopedia* (Wiley-Blackwell, 2014), and author of various articles on Hellenistic and Augustan poetry. His work on the present volume was completed during his tenure as Research Associate at Dumbarton Oaks Research Library and Collection (2011–14).

Jan M. Ziolkowski, Arthur Kingsley Porter Professor of Medieval Latin at Harvard University, directed Dumbarton Oaks (2007–2020). Ziolkowski's books combine critical editions and translations with literary history, such as *Talking Animals: Medieval Latin Beast Poetry* and *Fairy Tales from Before Fairy Tales: The Medieval Latin Past of Wonderful Lies*. He co-edited *The Medieval Craft of Memory* (with Mary Carruthers), *The Virgilian Tradition: The First Fifteen Hundred Years* (with Michael C. J. Putnam), and *The Virgil Encyclopedia* (with Richard Thomas). He edited *Dante and Islam* and *Dante and the Greeks* and published *The Juggler of Notre Dame and the Medievalizing of Modernity*.

Margaret Ziolkowski is professor of Russian at Miami University (Ohio). She has worked on topics in Russian literature ranging from the medieval to the contemporary. Recent and forthcoming books include *Alien Visions: The Chechens and the Navajos in Russian and American Literature* (University of Delaware Press, 2005), *Soviet Heroic Poetry in Context: Folklore or Fakelore* (University of Delaware Press, 2013), and *Rivers in Russian Literature* (University of Delaware Press, forthcoming).

Index of Subjects

This book was composed by Ivy Livingston
(Department of the Classics, Harvard University)
and manufactured by Sheridan Books, Ann Arbor, MI.

The cover was designed by Joni Godlove (big*bang creative).